The CARIBBEAN Community

Beyond Survival

The
CARIBBEAN
Community

Edited by

Kenneth O. Hall

Ian Randle Publishers
Kingston

First published in Jamaica 2001 by
Ian Randle Publishers
11 Cunningham Avenue, Box 686
Kingston 6

ISBN 976-637-047-8 paperback
ISBN 976-637-046-x hardcover

A catalogue record for this book is available from
The National Library of Jamaica

Set in Plantin light 9.5/13 x 26
Cover and book design by Robert Harris

Printed and bound in the United States of America

[Contents]

PART IV: DIPLOMACY FOR SURVIVAL

PART V: BEYOND SURVIVAL

[Preface]

This book begins with the predictions of CARICOM's failure by academics and newspaper editors and writers, and ends with an affirmation of its importance and its ability and capacity to successfully face the challenges of the new millennium. Such optimism is premised on the capacity of the region to ensure that the international environment is rendered propitious to its development. This, combined with improved negotiating skills, judicious alliances, and the effective utilisation of human resources, can ensure that the Community is 'not devoid of policy options in the twenty-first century.'

But the region had to traverse major obstacles and challenges to arrive at this position of optimism and hope. For as the articles in Part 1 of the book so vividly demonstrate, there was a general feeling that the Community would not survive. This pessimism resulted from the belief that the Community would not surmount the crisis generated by the dislocation in the world economy in the 1970s and 1980s. Indeed, as recorded here, one intellectual was not above predicting the failure of the Community.

The Community's demise, however, like the reported death of Mark Twain on one occasion, was grossly exaggerated. What was not recognised is that the intellectual tradition of the English-speaking Caribbean is a powerful and effective weapon in any crisis. This tradition is embodied in the personality of that Caribbean polymath, William Demas. Those who have known him and understood his particular genius have done the region a service in recording the many aspects of his character. In Part II Alister McIntyre has sketched a touching human portrait of William Demas, his foibles, his absolute dedication to the cause of regionalism and his ability to 'walk with kings and not lose the common touch.' Lloyd Best has described in lucid prose Demas' knowledge of Sparrow's calypsos as well as his understanding of the intricacies of the thought of Maynard Keynes. Marius St La Rose and Laurence Clarke have detailed the essence of Demas' economic philosophy and thinking.

Demas' faith in the Community's ability to overcome the consequences of its shortcomings and the difficulties of the seventies and the eighties, is also reflected in the declarations, decisions, studies and commissions established by the Heads of Government Conference of the Caribbean Community. These decisions and declarations are far-reaching in their scope and consequences. For collectively they represent a revolution in the conception and design of the Community. The decisions of the Heads have ensured that the Community no longer represents an entity in pursuit of self-sufficiency, but one that now contemplates not only the liberalisation of the movement of goods within the Caribbean region, but the movement of capital, services, and human resources.

The change in the conception of the Community is not merely economic; it is also profoundly institutional. Part III of the book focuses on the changes made to the institutional framework of the Community in order to accommodate the consequences of the Community's economic decisions. Notably, there is the article by the former Prime Minister of Barbados, Erskine Sandiford, on the Assembly of Caribbean Community Parliamentarians and that by P.I. Gomes on the new modes of governance in the region. The Caribbean Court of Appeal, a key institution in the long-term development and survival of the Community, is treated with expertise and insight by Duke Pollard.

Another vital institution created by the Caribbean Community is the Regional Negotiation Machinery (RNM). The RNM is intended to bring coherence and unity to the external economic relations of the Community. It is an important creation. For it seems certain that the twenty-first century will be a century of negotiations. Having completed the important post-Lomé negotiations, the Community must now face the prospect of undertaking major negotiations within the councils of the World Trade Organisation (WTO), those leading to the Free Trade Association of the Americas (FTAA), and other negotiations which will evolve from the on-going process of globalisation and liberalisation. Both Shridath Ramphal, the Community's Chief Negotiator, and Alister McIntyre, Technical Adviser to the RNM, in the articles entitled 'The Challenge in the Negotiating Process' and 'The Importance of Negotiation Preparedness' respectively, emphasise the importance of current negotiations to the Caribbean region. As Ramphal has said 'the negotiations will involve . . . challenges we have not faced before.'

The importance of key institutions of the Community which have played an undeniable role in its evolution, stability and success, such as the Caribbean Development Bank (CDB) and the Caribbean Examinations Council (CXC), is explored in articles by Neville Nicholls, Compton Bourne, Havelock Ross-Brewster and Lucy Steward. Alister McIntrye and Rex Nettleford elegantly describe the work and success of the University of the West Indies.

The major theme struck in Part IV is the requirements for CARICOM's survival in the new economic dispensation. There is a wealth of high-level thinking, expertise and insight. The Caribbean is challenged to mobilise its resources and bring them up to the standard required to enable the region to participate successfully in the twenty-first century. The vulnerability of small states, trends in international and economic relations and a description of the new liberal trade order are handled with the expected expertise in the commentaries by Henry Gill, Duke Pollard, Anthony Bryan, DeLisle Worrell, Anthony Gonzales, Clive Thomas, Joseph Farrier and Lloyd Searwar, to name a few.

Part V of this book is aptly titled 'Beyond Survival', for it deals with the prospects for the Community's progress and survival. In particular, Rex Nettleford expresses confidence that the Community's creative energies will guarantee its survival. The Prime Minister of Barbados, Owen Arthur feels sure that the Community will survive the challenges of the twenty-first century, even though the difficulties and obstacles to progress will be many. What this book has demonstrated is that the Caribbean Community has the ability, capacity, and intellectual power not only to overcome the problems and difficulties inseparable from the process of its evolution, but also the will to go on to the heights of prosperity and progress. In his address to the Caribbean Media Conference on May 5, in Guyana, which is reproduced here, Owen Arthur quotes the Socrates of the Caribbean, C.L.R. James, to this effect: 'Nobody knows what the Caribbean population is capable of. Nobody has ever attempted to find out . . .'

This was written before the Caribbean Community, in a series of unparalleled decisions, proclaimed to the world that it does not only intend to survive but to prosper and progress. In a sense, the Community has found out that it has the mettle to compete and stay the course in proceeding to its destiny.

[Acknowledgements]

This publication provides a golden opportunity for extensive inquiry into the reasons for the survival of the Caribbean Community and for rigorous analysis of the many factors which enabled the integration movement to surmount the crises of the 1970s and 1980s and to equip itself to face the challenges of the twenty-first century. It is a major initiative undertaken under the UWI-CARICOM Project which began in February 2000, as a result of the Memorandum of Understanding for Institutional Co-operation, signed between the University of the West Indies and The Caribbean Community Secretariat on December 9, 1999.

The publication owes its existence to the commitment, dedication and professionalism of the members of the Project team; in particular its Project Manager, Mrs Myrtle Chuck-A-Sang whose relentless pursuit of excellence ensured that the deadlines set for the finalisation of the various sections of the book were not exceeded and that the draft contributions to the preparation of the manuscript were at all times consistent with the quality guidelines established.

I wish also to thank the University Research Fellowship Grant, Mona, which funded the work of a researcher to the Project and in so doing enhanced the drafting capacity of the UWI-CARICOM Project.

The staff of the Caribbean Community Secretariat, the University of the West Indies, Mona, particularly those of their libraries and documentation centres must be thanked for the valuable assistance they rendered to all those involved in the preparation and completion of the Project. Pulling together all the critical ingredients to make this research project a reality deserves a high level of praise.

Kenneth O. Hall
University of the West Indies,
Mona campus
September 2000

[Foreword]

The Caribbean Community: Beyond Survival is a timely addition to the growing literature on the integration process. This publication not only describes and analyses the particular problems of the Caribbean Community, but deals in a comprehensive way with prospects for its future survival. No one can study the progress and survival of the integration process, as detailed here, and not recognise that they are important and vital lessons for the leaders of the Community, its member states, the peoples of the region and those involved in the technical formulation and implementation of its various functional programmes.

We tend to forget that the Caribbean Community is a unique phenomenon in what is described as the 'third world'. It is unique because it has survived. Other attempts at integration movements and economic groupings in Asia and Africa have not been characterised by their longevity. The integration process in the English-speaking Caribbean is a monument to the determination of its peoples and governments to overcome its early perils and trials.

As is demonstrated in the present volume, the Community, by dint of the intellectual endeavours of its leaders and those associated with the integration movement, has been able to overcome the threats posed to its existence and create the conditions for continued progress. There is a point here that must be emphasised. The body of ideas on which the survival of the Community is based was formulated for the region and by the region. They are completely endogamous. And these ideas have led to the transformation in the ethos of the Community: from an inward- looking organisation, it bids fair to become one that is likely to be characterised by the movement of production, labour and capital.

As the Community moves into the new millennium, it will encounter many difficulties and challenges. Many contributors to this volume argue that as a participant in the new scheme of things, CARICOM will demonstrate strengths of its own. Our region is known for its remarkable intellectual prowess; in a global economy that is knowledge-based, it is more than an assumption that it will have in its own hands the very instruments for its survival, progress and prosperity.

It is appropriate for me to congratulate Professor Kenneth Hall, Pro-Vice Chancellor and Principal, University of the West Indies, Mona campus and the Project Manager and staff of UWI-CARICOM Project for making available to the public this volume, which has many insightful presentations on the early period of the Community, its evolution to this particular point in its history, and the challenges and possibilities that confront it in the period of globalisation.

Edwin Carrington
Secretary-General,
CARICOM
29 September 2000

[Acronyms]

AAMA	American Apparel Manufacturers' Association
ACP	African, Caribbean and Pacific States
ACS	Association of Caribbean States
ASEAN	Association of South East Asian Nations
BIT	Bilateral Investment Treaty
BLADEF	Latin American Bank for Export Finance
BMCs	Borrowing Member Countries
BNHI	Business Network for Hemispheric Integration
BWIA	British West Indian Airways
CACM	Central American Common Market
CANA	Caribbean News Agency
CAP	Common Agricultural Programme
CAPE	Caribbean Advanced Proficiency Examinations
CARDI	Caribbean Agricultural and Research Development Institute
CARICOM	Caribbean Community
CARIFORUM	Caribbean Forum of ACP States
CARIFTA	Caribbean Free Trade Area
CAST	College of Arts, Science and Technology
CBD	Caribbean Development Bank
CBU	Caribbean Broadcasting Union
CCC	Caribbean Council of Churches
CCJ	Caribbean Court of Justice
CCMSC	Caribbean Common Market Standards Council
CDERA	Caribbean Disaster Emergency Response Agency
CEDA	Caribbean Export Development Agency
CEDP	CARICOM Export Development Project
CEHI	Caribbean Environment Health Institute
CEMLA	Centre for Latin American Monetary Studies
CER	CARICOM Enterprises Regime
CET	Common External tariff

CFC	Caribbean Food Corporation
CIDA	Canadian International Development Agency
CIEF	Conference on International Economic Cooperation
CIF	Caribbean Investment Fund
CIPS	Caribbean Industrial Programming Scheme
CCL	Caribbean Labour Congress
CLE	Council of Legal Education
CMO	Caribbean Meteorological Organisation
COFAP	Council for Finance and Planning
COMECON	Council for Economic Mutual Assistance
COTED	Council for Trade and Economic Development
CRDTL	Caribbean Regional Drug Testing Laboratory
CSME	CARICOM Single Market and Economy
CTFC	Commonwealth Fund For Technical Cooperation
CTUSAB	Congress of Trade Unions and Staff Associations of Barbados
CXC	Caribbean Examinations Council
DSB	Dispute Settlement Body
EAC	East African Community
EAI	Enterprise of the Americas Initiative
ECCM	Eastern Caribbean Common Market
ECEDA	Eastern Caribbean Export Development Agency
ECIPS	Eastern Caribbean Investment Promotion Service
ECLAC	Economic Council for Latin America and the Caribbean
ECM	European Common Market
ECOWAS	Economic Community of West African States
EEC	European Economic Community
FTAA	Free Trade Area of the Americas
GATS	General Agreement on Trade in Services
GATT	General Agreement on Tariffs and Trade
GDP	Gross Domestic Product
GSP	Generalised Systems of Preferences
HDI	Human Development Index
ICJ	International Court of Justice
IDB	Inter-American Development Bank
IGC	Inter Governmental Committee
IMF	International Monetary Fund
ISER	Institute of Social and Economic Research
ITC	International Trade Commission
ITP	Interim Trade Programme

LAFTA	Latin American Free Trade Area
LDCs	Less Developed Countries
LIAT	Leeward Island Air Transport
MDCs	More Developed Countries
MERCOSUR	South American Common Market
MFA	Multifibres Agreement
NAFTA	North American Free Trade Area
NGO	Non Governmental Organisation
NIEO	New International Economic Order
NIHE	National Institute of Higher Education
NTBs	Non-Tariff Barriers
OECS	Organisation of Eastern Caribbean States
OMAs	Organised Market Arrangements
OTEC	Ocean Thermal Energy Conversion
PAHO/WHO	Pan American Health Organisation/World Health Organisation
PNC	People's National Congress
PNM	People's National Movement
QPSII	Qualified Possession Source Investment Income
RDC	Regional Cooperation for Development
REPA	Regional Economic Partnerships Agreement
REPAHA	Regional Education Programme for Animal Health Assistants
RNM	Regional Negotiating Machinery
SAFTA	South American Free Trade Area
SBA	School-Based Assessment
SCEC	Caribbean Secondary Education Certificate
SCME	Standing Committee of Ministers for Education
SEC	School Examinations Committee
SELA	Latin American Economic System
SIRG	Summit Implementation Review Group
TASU	Technical Action Services Unit
TIEA	Tax Information Exchange Agreement
TPLs	Tariff Reference Levels
TPRM	Trade Policy Review Mechanism
TRIMs	Trade Related Investment Measures
TRIPs	Trade in Intellectual Property Rights
UCWI	University College of the West Indies
UNDCP	United Nations International Drug Control Programme
UNDP	United Nations Development Programme

USAID	United States Agency for International Development
UWI	University of the West Indies
VERs	Voluntary Export Restraints
WIC	West Indian Commission
WINBAN	Windward Island Banana Association
WIPO	World Intellectual Property Rights Organisation
WISA	West Indies Associated States
WISCO	West Indies Shipping Corporation
WTO	World Trade Organisation

[Introduction]

The Caribbean Community
Beyond Survival[1]

Twenty-seven years after its creation, the Caribbean Community, consisting of fifteen states stretching from the Bahamas in the north to Suriname in South America, presents a picture of a relatively mature and stable regional organisation characterised by successful programmes of functional cooperation, important formal links with the major global powers, trade and other partnerships with the principal states of the Caribbean Basin, and a demonstrated capacity to withstand the vicissitudes of its evolution. And even though it has been criticised for a number of deficiencies, as have the European Union and other economic groupings, the fact remains that it has survived and can be said to have made significant contributions in regional and international affairs.

Yet at one crucial moment it was not expected to survive. Overwhelmed by the world economic crisis of the 1970s, unsettled by ideological divisions, weakened by internal differences, the Caribbean Community seemed destined for failure. That it did resolve these problems is not only testimony to the power of the integration idea among the peoples and the Governments of the region, but also to its ability to fashion its own instruments for survival and success. This survival and success must also be attributed to a body of ideas and analyses which have emerged out of the various heads of government conferences in the 1980s and the studies and commissions authorised and brought into being by them. There is a distinct ideology of survival encapsulated in the ideas which have emerged from these studies and declarations.

Having overcome the crisis of the 1970s and the challenges of the 1980s, CARICOM is in a position, indeed has the capacity, to re-position itself to face the challenges of the new century and take advantage of the opportunities it will offer. The changing nature of the integration movement will make this a distinct possibility. The Caribbean Community has been transformed from an economic grouping concerned with the promotion of economic self-reliance in relation to the rest of the world, to one in which the movement of labour and capital will be a notable feature. Measures to enhance its negotiating capacity and its capacity to harness the benefits of globalisation have also been taken.

The Caribbean has every right to face the future with confidence. For this region of only six million people has demonstrated its ability to compete at the level of ideas in global society. Small as it is, it has produced two Nobel Prize-winners, outstanding thinkers, writers and creative artists, and the anthem of the millennium was composed by one of its sons. These are significant achievements. These historical, spiritual and cultural strengths will ensure that the success of the movement towards unity is assured. The Caribbean Community also has a lesson to teach the world as far as cultural dynamism and racial harmony are concerned. This has been noted by Gordon Lewis in his seminal work, *Main Currents in Caribbean Thought:*

. . . it (the Caribbean) possesses features that might well make it the envy of so-called more advanced societies. Its various groups, whether identified in racial, ethnic, or religious definitional terms, live, if not in complete harmony, at least in a peaceful coexistence that other Third World areas ravaged by communalism and tribalism might envy. Its peoples and cultures, indeed, being so much a rich mixture of America, Europe, Africa, and Asia, have shaped out of their experience some of the leading ideas of the modern world especially relevant to Third World problems: negritude, black power, black nationalism, Creole Marxism, Cuban socialism, and the rest. Indeed, relative to its size, the region has produced a disproportionate number of artists, thinkers, and scholar-politicians, many of them with an international fame . . . and many of them, in addition, combining political leadership and intellectual culture in a way that has almost disappeared in the political life of countries like Britain and the United States. All of these things . . . are the elements of the promise of Caribbean life. The future of the Caribbean lies within the capacity and the willingness of those elements to fulfil and indeed enlarge that promise.[2]

More than fifty years ago in September 1947, a generation of West Indian leaders met in Montego Bay to chart a future for this region in the postwar era. They met under the banner 'The Closer Association of the British West Indian Colonies', a clear indication that it was recognised that Caribbean unity was essential to the progress of the region. The meeting was the culmination of a relatively long process in the search for integration. It laid the foundation for the creation of the West Indies Federation and was the result of the recognition that a politically and economically unified Caribbean would not only foster and promote economic development but, more importantly, would be a barrier to the twin evils of particularism and fragmentation. Important spiritual as well as political milestones were laid on the road to Montego Bay.

But the impetus towards West Indian Federation had manifested itself long before, in the ideologies and activities of a number of individuals, associations and organisations which helped to raise the consciousness of the people of the region. The precursors of the Montego Bay conference included the Dominica Conference of 1932 and the Caribbean Labour Congress (CLC), which as early as 1926 had declared its interest in a federal union. Various professional associations organised on a regional basis: the Caribbean Union of Teachers which after 1935 sought support for uniform education standards; the Caribbean Bar Association which after 1916 had as an objective the codification of the separate Island Laws; and the Civil Service Federation which after 1944 wanted the unification of the Regional Civil Service – all in their various ways supported the idea of the Caribbean integration movement. The work of men such as T. A. Marryshow, Uriah Butler and Albert Gomes also contributed to the process.

But even from as early as the mid-nineteenth century, individuals and organisations with different motives have sought to achieve Caribbean unity. The historical and cultural consanguinity of Caribbean peoples has been remarked on by persons as removed from each other in history, time and space as Père Labat, a Jesuit priest who was in the Caribbean in the eighteenth century, and Norman Manley, Premier of Jamaica in the 1950s and early 1960s. Labat made note of the cultural affinity of the region:

I have travelled everywhere in your sea of the Caribbean . . . from Haiti to Barbados, to Martinique and Guadeloupe, and I know what I am speaking about . . . You are all together, in the same boat, sailing on the same uncertain sea . . . citizenship and race unimportant, feeble little labels compared to the message that my spirit brings to me: that of the position and predicament which History has imposed upon you.

. . . I saw it first with the dance . . . the merengue in Haiti, the beguine in Martinique, and today I hear, de mon orielle morte, the echo of calypso from Trinidad, St Lucia, Antigua, Dominica and the legendary Guiana . . . it is no accident that the sea makes no difference to the rhythm of your body.[3]

Norman Manley also remarked on the historical and spiritual bonds which unite the West Indian people. Addressing the Caribbean Labour Congress in 1947 in Jamaica he observed:

Above all I am impressed by the fact that wherever there is an Assembly of West Indians in the Caribbean area, there, immediately and obviously and without the slightest difficulty, you feel at home and as one. You are conscious of being with your own people . . . the sense of unity in the West Indies . . . is so powerful and so rapidly growing today that the minor historical differences are irrelevant in the face of [our]e innumerable common ties . . .

The question might well be asked if there is buried in the psyche of the Caribbean peoples such a compelling and powerful urge towards integration that it can survive the temporary setbacks and mistakes which have dogged the integration process. It is a salient question, for there has never been a movement or programme in the English-speaking Caribbean which has challenged or sought to reverse the move towards integration.

Gordon Lewis[4] has pointed out that the Montego Bay Conference arose out of the conjuncture of two factors: the need for West Indian unity and the reluctance of a weakened Britain, depleted and ravaged by the Second World War, to sustain the Caribbean, which had become a burden on the Exchequer. Decisions taken in Britain, then, were a prelude to the establishment of the West Indies Federation, and it was Britain that laid down the bases of the Federation experiment. The Federation, externally inspired, was of brief duration. The late Eric Williams, Prime Minister of Trinidad and Tobago, described its end in these terms: 'The infant nation was presented to the world in the swaddling clothes made in the United States of America and out of the made-in-Britain shroud of colonialism.'[5]

The failure of the West Indies Federation has had a powerful impact on the imagination of the Caribbean peoples and their Governments. This is not surprising: Federation was the great divide in the integration process. The problems leading to its dissolution have served as a lesson to the architects of the Caribbean Community. It may therefore be worthwhile to look briefly at some of the factors which hastened that dissolution.

The salient fact about the Federation's birth as an external imposition is that it could not attract the support of the peoples and institutions of the region. But there were other factors at work, which might have undermined the federal idea propounded by the British Government. One of the most compelling of these was the creation of a structure which was so repugnant to the Caribbean people's sense of their history and their sense of independence, that one wonders how it could have been considered in the first place, even allowing for the prevailing political ethos of the time. Most of the main positions of the Federal structure were staffed by expatriates and the Federal Prime Minister, to all intents and purposes, was the clerk of the expatriate Governor General. The latter was all-powerful:

> The Governor-General, in brief, had at his disposal powers normally accepted in Dominion Constitutional practice as belonging to the Prime Minister – the power to dissolve Parliament, the power to set up a 'packed' Upper House, even the power to argue his case in Cabinet as the recognised Master of certain of its members.[6]

The differences among the major states on the issue of the West Indies Federation had a negative impact on the smaller Leeward and Windward Islands. At several points along the way when Trinidad, Barbados and Jamaica could not harmonise their positions in such a way as to protect their interests, these smaller islands understandably felt abandoned. But despite the resulting bitterness, a centralised federation under the leadership of Trinidad and Tobago seemed a distinct and hopeful possibility after Jamaica departed from the Federation. This did not materialise, as Trinidad and Tobago too saw the necessity to 'go it alone'. The financial costs of leading the Federation were a prime consideration in this regard. The experiences of the smaller states with the Federation were to colour their attitude to the integration process and impel them to greater unity among themselves. But this sequence of events remains to be told.

Apart from the weakness inherent in its exogenous nature, the Federation was also undermined by insularity, suspicion, different conceptions as to how it should function, and the seductive attraction of national independence. But although the Federation perished, the idea of unity endured, as was reflected in developments in the mid-1960s.

In 1963, Prime Minister of Trinidad and Tobago Eric Williams, concerned about Britain's imminent entry into the European Economic Community, appreciative of the significance of the formation of economic groupings in different parts of the world, and convinced that the Caribbean must be part of this trend, initiated a number of meetings of the Heads of Government of the Commonwealth Caribbean. These conferences provided the Heads of Government with a forum to discuss plans and programmes to advance the cause of Caribbean integration.

The Prime Minister of British Guiana, Forbes Burnham, believed that Dr Williams was 'courageous' to re-start the integration process so soon after the collapse of the Federation. For it was the worst of times. Leaders shouted at each other across the Caribbean Sea. There was no dialogue or understanding. The unity of the region seemed to be in tatters. But Williams' statesmanship was shrewd. He knew that whatever hostilities might be expressed in the meeting, the act of meeting in itself could serve to put an end to the impasse in the integration process. Williams introduced a measure of coherence, stability and progress by initiating the meetings of the Heads of Government of the Commonwealth Caribbean.

In 1965, others who had inherited the mantle of Marryshow, Butler, Gomes and other visionaries of Caribbean integration met at Dickenson Bay to discuss the advancement of the integration process. And this has been the trend: the quest for identity remains at the centre of the thoughts, plans and actions of successive leaders of the region. It points to a compelling recognition that West Indian regionalism is a sustaining force and that the journey to the rendezvous of unity, though interrupted at points in our historical circumstances, must be continued. The contributions of these early West Indian politicians and statesmen have been of immense and lasting value because they were founded upon a common historical inheritance and an abiding faith in the common destiny of this region.

As founding fathers of the integration movement, Errol Barrow, Prime Minister of Barbados; Vere Bird, Prime Minister of Antigua; and Forbes Burnham, Prime Minister of Guyana, understood that there had been times in the West Indian past when faith and commitment to regionalism could be sustained only by taking a 'higher view' of history. Burnham in particular recognised the urgency of the moment and the necessity for action. At the 1967 Conference of Heads of Government of Commonwealth Caribbean countries, Burnham, then Prime Minister of a newly independent Guyana, urged that the imperative for integration must supersede any problems real or imagined:

We cannot start off with some ideal or perfect arrangement. Neither can we hope to be so prescient of the future as to be able to determine all the consequences and difficulties of integration. We can, and must, of course, try to analyse and anticipate as best as we can from available data, what the effects of integration may and can be made to be, but it would be folly *par excellence* to wait for perfect foresight. A perfect solution to, or institution for, integration cannot be hoped for. Let us to our own selves be true. These are the facts. This is the naked truth, either we integrate, or we perish, unwept, unhonoured.

The new arrangements for Caribbean integration were substantially different from those which had characterised the Federation. The Federation as an imposition had ignored the intellectual leaders of the region and taken no account of public opinion. The new Caribbean leaders eschewed any idea of a supra-national authority and sought to advance the economic development of the region. Their efforts led to the creation of the Caribbean Free Trade

Area (CARIFTA) of 1968 and the Caribbean Community and Common Market (CARICOM) in 1973. A Free Trade Area of three became a full-fledged Community of twelve. A Secretariat and a Regional Development Bank were established.

The signing of the Treaty of Chaguaramas on July 4, 1973, provided Williams, Burnham, Barrow and then Prime Minister of Jamaica Michael Manley an opportunity to offer their vision of the Caribbean Community.

Williams reflected on the significance of the creation of the Community:

> The Treaty is a landmark on the long road the Commonwealth-Caribbean has travelled since the dissolution of the West Indies Federation eleven years ago. We have experienced difficulties, friction, misunderstandings and tension. More than once we have faltered on the way, we have learned the hard way . . . the lessons of economic growth . . .

Burnham spoke in these terms:

> I hope, I pray, I dream that the Caribbean will be able to teach the world a lesson, a lesson of how people who numbered their populations in terms of a few million can mobilise their resources for the benefit of their nation, the benefit of their region and ensure social justice, ban unemployment . . . some of us feel this as a matter of conviction, I hope that others of us will accept it as a matter of good sense and survival.

Manley made the following declaration:

> We, in Jamaica, have regarded this occasion as implied in our mandate from the people of Jamaica last year. We have debated it in our Parliament, we have had full and fruitful discussions with our institutional leaders about the aspects of the Common Market which we now enter upon and the Community which we are now joining, and we have explained calmly, but I hope clearly, that it is inevitable when countries from the separate posture of their sovereignty seek to create new and meaningful relationships that there must be compromise and that compromise is justified by the size of the goals we pursue.

Barrow on this occasion contented himself with a description of how the Dickenson Bay Agreement led to the Treaty of Chaguaramas. But he had shared his vision in other addresses to meetings of the Caribbean Community. He believed that the Community should be people-centred, and argued that integration had taken place at the level of the peoples of the region but the political leadership had failed to institutionalise this development. At the Seventh Meeting of the Conference of CARICOM Heads of Government held in Georgetown, Guyana, in 1986, Barrow criticised the Community for inappropriate communication practices and for what he saw as its reduction of the regional integration movement to matters exclusively related to trade.

The politicians and statesmen did not monopolise the decision-making process. Another important feature of the renewed quest for Caribbean integration was the direct involvement in the process of leading of well-known Caribbean intellectuals. This is in contrast to the establishment of the West Indies Federation in which neither intellectuals nor people were involved. It is an imposition from top to bottom. But it was a different story when the process resumed in the post-Federation period and the Caribbean leaders made a great determination to ensure that the intellectuals and the people were to be involved in building a common Caribbean home. It was in this context that in the early days of the Caribbean Community, intellectuals were asked, before the 1967 Commonwealth Caribbean Conference, to participate in charting a course for the region. One outcome was the pioneering study done by Clive Thomas and Havelock Ross-Brewster entitled *The Dynamics of West Indian Integration*. What became clear was that the sense of commitment generated by the idea of Caribbean unity was not confined to the leaders, but was present in the intellectual community and the people themselves.

The signing of the Treaty of Chaguaramas represents a high point in the integration movement. It is appropriate to recall some of its main features. The Treaty stipulated that the Caribbean Community was to promote the unity of the region. It agreed that functional cooperation would be fostered in all relevant areas. In that context, the organs of the Community (the Conference of the Heads of Government and the Common Market Council of Ministers) were enshrined as its 'supreme policy-making bodies' (Article 9). Coordination of external economic relations and economic integration were to be facilitated through the Caribbean Common Market. The Common Market Council was created to ensure the smooth functioning and development of the Common Market.

A number of other institutions came into being with the signing of the Treaty. These, created under Article 10 (a-j) of the Treaty, were the permanent Standing Committees of Ministers, each mandated by Article 12 of the Treaty to 'formulate such policies and perform such functions as were necessary for the achievement of the objectives of the Community within (its) respective spheres of competence.' Nine Standing Committees were instituted:

(a) The Conference of Ministers responsible for Health;
(b) The Standing Committee of Ministers responsible for Education;
(c) The Standing Committee of Ministers responsible for Labour;
(d) The Standing Committee of Ministers responsible for Foreign Affairs;
(e) The Standing Committee of Ministers responsible for Finance;

(f) The Standing Committee of Ministers responsible for Agriculture;

(g) The Standing Committee of Ministers responsible for Industry;

(h) The Standing Committee of Ministers responsible for Transportation; and

(i) Any other institutions that may be established and designated as such by the Conference in accordance with Article 8.

In July 1983, the Heads of Government brought to an end the Standing Committee of Ministers responsible for Mines and created a Standing Committee of Ministers responsible for Energy, Mines and Natural Resources; and a Standing Committee of Ministers responsible for Science and Technology.

Article 14 of the Treaty of Chaguaramas determined that the associate institutions of the Community should be designated as separate regional bodies with their own charters and legal autonomy. These institutions are:

(a) The Caribbean Development Bank (CDB);

(b) The Caribbean Examination Council (CXC);

(c) The Council of Legal Education (CLE);

(d) The University of Guyana (UG);

(e) The University of the West Indies (UWI);

(f) The Caribbean Meteorological Organisation (CMO);

(g) The West Indies Shipping Corporation (WISCO).

The Treaty did not prescribe the relationship between the Community and the associate institutions. Under Article 14(2) it was left to the Community to 'seek to establish such relationships with its Associate Institutions as will promote the achievements of its objectives.' The Community's organs and institutions, along with the Secretariat, comprised the major part of the central institutional framework of the integration movement.

Perhaps also conscious of the sensitive nature of the Community's relationship with the Less Developed Countries (LDCs), its founders sought to ensure that the small states would benefit from its activities. A special regime was inaugurated which was intended to protect the interests of the LDCs.

Economic and Social Crisis

Despite efforts to ensure the success of the integration movement after the signing of the Treaty of Chaguaramas and the institutions established to give it expression, CARICOM was to face a grave crisis in the period from the mid-1970s until the mid-1980s. This crisis was the product of a number of factors: international economic factors, the emergence of a plurality of social and economic systems, suspicion among leaders of the member states and the general feeling that the hope and promise of the Treaty of Chaguaramas were not being realised.

At the present time, when the global economy seems to be blossoming and small states, especially in Asia, are enjoying the benefits of this expansion, the world economic crisis of the 1970s seems a distant memory. Yet at the time it shook the economic foundations of the Western world, put an end to doctrines such as permanent sovereignty over natural resources, undermined the programme for a New International Economic Order so boldly announced at the Fourth Summit Conference of Non-Aligned States in September 1973 and left a legacy of a heavily indebted developing world beset by intractable economic problems.

A former Secretary-General of CARICOM, Kurleigh King, has pointed to the UNCTAD Report for that period which described this phenomenon as 'the gravest economic crisis since the Great Depression.' Fidel Castro, reporting to the United Nations General Assembly in his capacity as Chairman of the Non-Aligned Movement, gave details of the scope and nature of the crisis. He pointed out that World Gross Domestic Product, which had averaged four per cent in the greater part of 1970s, fell to 3.8 per cent in 1979. In 1980 it averaged two per cent and then dropped to 1.2 per cent in 1981.

The consequences for developing countries, including the states of the Caribbean Community, were critical. Unemployment in developing countries reached levels of 400 to 500 million people. In some states physical hunger, housing and non-existent medical care were the order of the day.

Henry Kissinger in his memoirs, *Years of Upheaval,* described the decision to increase the price of oil as 'one of the pivotal events in history':

The statistics were staggering enough. Within forty-eight hours the oil bill for the United States, Canada, Western Europe and Japan had increased by $40 billion a year; it was a colossal blow to their balance of payments, economic growth, employment, price stability and social cohesion. The Tehran decision (the increase in oil prices) also cost the developing countries more than the entire foreign aid programs extended to them by the Industrial democracies, recreating the desperate conditions that foreign assistance was supposed to cure. But the long-term impact was more grave still. All the countries involved, even the producers themselves, faced seismic changes in their domestic structures.

Such, in summary, was the crisis which confronted the newly formed Caribbean Community. But its visible starting point was the oil crisis of the early 1970s, which had a particularly adverse impact on the economies of the states of the region; this in turn caused grievous damage to the very fabric of Caribbean unity. Most importantly, it undermined public confidence in the efficacy of the integration movement. It is particularly unfortunate that the oil crisis coincided with the creation of the Caribbean Community. Kurleigh King told the Caribbean Development Bank in 1979: 'The ink was hardly dry on the signatures of the Treaty when the full force of the international crisis struck the bottom out of everything we had hoped to accomplish.'

The severe economic crisis, resulting from the sudden fourfold increase in the price of oil, led to a sharp rise in the import bill of a number of major states of the Caribbean Community. Apart from Trinidad, which was insulated because it benefited from the new high oil prices, all member states suffered major budgetary and balance-of-payments deficits and significant increases in the cost of living. These states responded with a variety of stern measures, including high levels of taxation, an intensification of import restrictions and exchange controls, and the imposition of subsidies for vital consumer goods. In their determination to overcome the ravages of the economic crisis, some CARICOM states seemed to have lost sight of the principles and objectives of the Community. Survival seemed to be all. Intra-regional trade, so vital a component to the functioning of the Community, dried up, exacerbating the historical friction with the LDCs.

Once again, the entire integration movement was being called into question. Enrique Iglesias,[7] a keen student of the region's economic affairs, noted that 'by the early 1980s discussion of regional integration was nearly silenced by the overwhelming attention required by the external debt problem, adjustment and national crisis management.' Payne and Sutton[8] argue that the economic crisis confirmed the 'enormous fragility' of the integration schemes of Third World states, and suggest that CARICOM did not seem to 'possess a sufficiently developed sense of regionalism to withstand the impact of the international economic crisis that began in 1973–74.' The crisis, they argued, had cruelly exposed the narrowness of the political base on which CARICOM was built and revealed that the Community's fleeting and initial success had been dangerously dependent on the existence of certain features of the regional movement: namely, an approximate balance of power between the main Commonwealth Caribbean countries, a high degree of ideological consensus within the region, and a good rapport between the Heads of Government. In sum then, the integration movement was judged incapable of maintaining the momentum of its early days and was deemed to have fallen into a state of stagnation.

It has been persuasively argued that the world economic crisis was responsible for the *first breach* of Caribbean unity, and this was given credence in a speech made by Prime Minister of Trinidad and Tobago, Eric Williams, in 1975 at a National Convention of his party. Williams complained that advances in Caribbean integration were being prejudiced by the way in which 'impoverished member states of CARICOM were making bilateral economic arrangements on supplicant terms with wealthy Latin American countries.'

Williams was particularly concerned about the growing economic penetration of the Community by Venezuela's petro-dollars. 'Pilgrimages to Caracas' angered him. He voiced his displeasure over an agreement signed between Jamaica and Venezuela in April 1975, in which Jamaica agreed to supply Venezuela with quantities of bauxite and alumina. A year earlier, subsequent to the signing of the Treaty of Chaguaramas, Trinidad and Tobago, Jamaica and Guyana had agreed to build two smelters which were to be jointly owned. Williams regarded Jamaica's decision as 'a calculated attack' on this agreement.

The truth of the matter was that, faced with the urgent question of survival, member states essayed to do whatever was necessary to escape the full impact of the crisis on their economies and the well-being of their nationals. Guyana and Jamaica, invoking Article 28 of the Treaty, restricted imports from other states of the Community. In a 1977 statement to CARICOM, Burnham said he recognised that the measures taken by Jamaica and Guyana had elicited negative reactions from other member states. But, he insisted, these measures were taken out of necessity and not with any intention to injure the interests of Guyana's CARICOM partners. Guyana's restrictions on intra-CARICOM purchases were occasioned by shortage of funds, not by a lack of commitment to CARICOM.

At the same time, the leaders of Jamaica and Guyana appeared uncomfortable with the manner in which Trinidad and Tobago dispensed what was perceived as its economic largesse to other member states. There was also conflict over transport and education. The upshot of the conflict was a stalemate in which Williams refused to meet with the other leaders. He was quoted in *Caribbean Contact* in the 1970s, as saying that he saw no need for a CARICOM Summit.

Major initiatives of the Community also withered on the vine. The Regional Industrial Programming, the Regional Food Corporation, the Food and Nutrition Strategy, the Regional Energy Programme proposal and the Single Regional Carrier were consigned to the archives of lost causes. At no other time was the fragility of the free trade regime so undermined, the sustainability of CARICOM so vigorously questioned, or the will and determination of member states to proceed with the experiment so severely tested. It was not surprising therefore, that after the Special Summit in 1976 in Trinidad the CARICOM Heads did not meet until the Ocho Rios Summit in 1982. Yet in this long hiatus the institutions of the Community were strong and flexible enough to prevent a terminal decline. There is no other example of an integration movement which has sustained itself without meetings of its highest organs being convened.

Debt Crisis

The economic problems faced by the member states of the Caribbean Community inevitably exploded into a debt crisis. It was a crisis which was long in the making, and was foreseen by Hugh Shearer, Michael Manley's predecessor as Prime Minister of Jamaica, long before it became starkly visible. The crisis mushroomed during the period of the 1970s when developing countries, including CARICOM member states, were encouraged to borrow at low rates of interest and then discovered that as their economies faltered in the oil crisis they could not meet their international obligations.

The developing countries had obtained loans, not from official lenders, but from international commercial banks, which were 'flush with money as a result of the 'petro-dollars' accumulated by the oil exporting countries after the two big oil increases in 1973 and 1979.' The crisis was aggravated in the 1980s by the fall in commodity prices, recession in the industrialised countries, and the unexpected sharp rise in the cost of the US dollar. The crisis came to a head when Mexico could not honour its obligations to the international financial institutions.

Developing countries were caught unawares because, as Susan George has pointed out, '[n]ot only did it cost nothing to borrow – people actually paid you to do so. The average real rate over the decade of the 1970s was –0.8 per cent and in some years some as low as – 3 or – 4 per cent.' [9] There was an orgy of borrowing and by 1985 therefore, when the report of the Socialist International Committee on Economic Policy was published, the debt of the Third World was estimated at US$900 billion.

The Caribbean region's debt in the 1980s ballooned to US$14.5 billion. The largest debtors were Jamaica with US$4.3 billion; the Dominican Republic with US$3.9 billion; Trinidad and Tobago US$2.0 billion; and Guyana with US$1.6 billion. Antigua, the Bahamas and Barbados had accumulated debts of various magnitudes. But it was Guyana and Jamaica which were most severely affected. The political and economic problems resulting from the accumulation of debt led to situations in these two countries which capture in microcosm the economic and social crisis which confronted the Caribbean states.

Servicing these debts was not only a constraint on development but led to problems in the critical sectors of education, health and social welfare. Jamaica's debt service ratio in the 1980s was as high as 39.3 per cent, or almost half of every US dollar earned. The massive imbalances in the economy, of which the country's debt was a reflection, led to agreements with the International Monetary Fund. These agreements invariably demanded programmes of austerity which generated political and social problems. But most significant is that Jamaica's debt crisis led to the curtailment of Michael Manley's programmes for social justice in the 1970s. The Seaga Administration which succeeded the Manley Government in the 1980s seemed to have brought some element of stability to the economy with the help of the IMF.

Guyana too had to end programmes of social justice and shelve plans for the transformation of its economy. It failed to pass an IMF Test in the late 1970s and by 1985 had been declared ineligible to borrow from the IMF. The Economic Recovery Program (ERP) on which the country embarked as a result of this situation brought some measure of balance and vigour back into Guyana's economy. Growth was restored; by 1992 it had reached 9 per cent. But the burden of debt remained. However, with the international climate now more favourable to debt re-scheduling and debt write-offs, Guyana has been able to reduce its debt from US$2.1 billion to approximately US$1.5 billion. But the economic and social costs have been high. Poor economic performance over a considerable period of time has had an adverse impact on the education, health and productive sectors.

Even though the Caribbean states – at least some of them – seem at the moment to have overcome the worst effects of the debt crisis, the crisis itself seems far from over. In 1995, for example, the near financial collapse of the Mexican economy was a powerful reminder that the world debt crisis is still capable of delivering shocks to the international economy. Moreover, the debt of Third World countries between 1989 and 1993 has increased by 23 per cent, or approximately US$1.5 trillion.

For many reasons, the Caribbean has to maintain its vigilance. Adjustment conditionalities imposed by the IMF involving currency devaluation, price controls and wage freezes can lead to a surrender of sovereignty over domestic decision-making. Additionally, the relatively undiversified nature of Caribbean economies limits the bargaining options of these states. The structure of Caribbean debt is also a constraining factor, as it reduces the leverage available to the states of the region. Total Caribbean debt grew by 125 per cent between 1980 and 1988, further increasing its burden:

By the end of the 1980s the Caribbean's debt service stood at 161.3 percent. While the region's debt service was well below those in Latin America that stood at 298.5, Guyana and Antigua exceeded the debt service ratios of the rest of the Latin America and the ratios for Jamaica were comparable. Moreover, unlike Latin America, the Caribbean pays more money to its multilateral creditors than it receives in fresh loans. Between

1986 and 1988, the Caribbean transferred US$1,292 million or 3.7 percent of the region's GNP. [10]

The fact that most of the region's debt is owed to multilateral creditors also reduces its bargaining powers. As Bartilow has observed:

> Another aspect of Caribbean debt that further reduces the bargaining leverage of indebted Caribbean governments, is that the majority of the region's debt is owed to multilateral creditors. By the end of the 1980s, over 70 percent of Latin America's debt was owed to private commercial banks, compared to 39 percent for the Caribbean. Only Cuba, Trinidad and Tobago, Barbados and the Eastern Caribbean countries made significant use of commercial bank credit. Multilateral agencies do not reschedule loans when countries fail to comply with conditionality. The adjustment program is simply suspended and indebted countries must borrow more under increasingly stringent conditions just to maintain a positive net capital inflow. Because indebted Caribbean countries are heavily dependent on multilateral agencies as their primary source for balance of payments financing, their bargaining leverage during debt negotiations is far more limited than their Latin American neighbours. [11]

Ideological Pluralism

Increasing differences in ideology also aggravated the problems of the Caribbean Community. The leaders of the Community could not reach agreement on the ideological model which was most appropriate for the Caribbean. As a result, the consensus on ideology which had been a feature of the early period of the Community disappeared.

A major cause of conflict was that several member states – Guyana, Jamaica and Grenada – adopted socialism as the means of resolving their economic problems. The Community, which had not made provision for this kind of diversity, was faced with the problem of how to mediate and reconcile two different forms of governance, one of which was regarded as authoritarian and the other as liberal and more consistent with the tenets of the Community.

The Group of Experts constituted by the Community in 1980 made an attempt to help resolve these issues. In its Report the Group recognised that ideological pluralism was a shield 'against enforced sameness' but warned that it should not be a 'sword against solidarity.' The Standing Committee of Foreign Ministers in St Lucia in 1980 and the Ocho Rios Summit in 1982 also tried to bring a sense of balance to the situation. The former recognised ideological pluralism 'as an irreversible factor of international relations' which 'should not, [however], constitute a barrier to the strengthening of the mechanism of CARICOM.' The latter also agreed that ideological pluralism was a reality and argued that it should not 'inhibit the process of integration.'

However, despite these pronouncements, it was clear that the Community had reached no consensus on the question of ideological pluralism.

In 1983, at the Fourth Meeting of the Conference of Heads of Government, both Tom Adams of Barbados and Edward Seaga of Jamaica linked ideological pluralism to the question of free and fair elections. Indeed, ideological pluralism has been nothing but controversial. The press in the Caribbean, especially in Jamaica, was hostile to the idea. Jamaica's *Gleaner* ran an editorial in which it declared that it did not consider ideological pluralism to exist when CARICOM countries 'whose Governments had come to power with the aid of arms, which also kept them in power, enjoyed the same membership rights as others. Dictators, it declared, had no place in the 'brotherhood of democracies.'

Nor did the United States find the idea of ideological pluralism a palatable one. The Director-General of the Organisation of Eastern Caribbean States, Dr Vaughan Lewis, in 1983 took it on himself to explain that the United States preferred the 'ideological harmonisation' of the region. Socialist states in the midst of Western-type democracies could not be understood by Washington.

What is clear is that the situation, regarded by Dr Lewis as an ideological stalemate, was very much a part of the economic crisis with which this part of our discussion is concerned. The crisis hurt the economies of the Caribbean as it shattered the ideological consensus and balance of power which had hitherto existed in the Community and had allowed for amicable cooperation on economic and other issues of regional concern. What was affected also, was the close rapport between the Heads of Government and general international interests in the region. These developments were ingredients in the making of the misfortune that was the invasion of Grenada by the USA. More than anything else, the ideological tolerance of which Dr Lewis had spoken gave way to ideological fallout and its consequences.

The Invasion of Grenada

The invasion of Grenada by the United States in 1983, like the economic crisis of the 1970s, proved a stern test for the Caribbean Community. It divided the Community and called into question its tolerance of plural political systems as indicated in, for example, the Declarations of the Foreign Ministers' Meeting in St Lucia in 1980 and the Third Conference of Heads of Government of the Caribbean Community in 1982. It will be recalled that both Declarations expressed the intention to accept the ideologically plural nature of the Community. Whatever consensus was arrived at by the Community on ideological pluralism was destroyed by the Grenada invasion.

The 1979 revolution in Grenada – or the *coup d' état* - depending on one's perspective, had two distinct phases. Under Maurice Bishop, the Caribbean Community seemed to have no particular difficulty in dealing with Grenada. The considered view was that Bishop was a responsible and considerate leader. He had no difficulty in gaining the recognition of Guyana, Jamaica, St Lucia and Dominica, said to be left-wing governments, and participated in all CARICOM conferences, where he affirmed 'firm and abiding commitment to Caribbean regionalism, to the Caribbean integration process, and to CARICOM as our region's foremost integration institution.'

However, with the emergence of Bernard Coard, many leaders in the Caribbean Community and the OECS states, which had seen no threat to their security under Bishop, did not view their situation in the same way when Coard's faction imprisoned Bishop in October 1983. The alarm bells went off in earnest. Bishop had been prepared to leave trade and commerce in private hands, boost tourism and seek accommodation with the United States. Coard was regarded as wanting a total transformation of Grenada along Marxist-Leninist lines. He was also believed to be seeking close ties with the socialist commonwealth, especially Cuba.

The United States had expressed its concerns and fears about the construction of the Port Salines airport. President Reagan in March of 1983 had described the airport as a possible military threat to the USA. Reagan was articulating the position of a class or a group of men who fully endorsed the foreign policy of the USA with the express intention of rolling back Marxism-Leninism and asserting the USA's hegemony in the Caribbean. It is now public knowledge that these men felt that a military strike against Grenada would send warning signals to other Marxist-Leninist regimes and groups in the region. At the same time, the US Administration wanted to make amends to its electorate for the fiasco in Lebanon when eighty-one marines died subsequent to Western intervention in the Middle East led by the United States.

The restraint shown by the OECS during the Bishop Administration was removed when Bishop was killed and a Revolutionary Military Council (RMC) headed by Coard took over. The OECS appealed to the USA, which did not hesitate to intervene. It was the first time that the USA had invaded an English-speaking Caribbean state. They were supported by a number of CARICOM countries which showed no fear of public opinion.

The collaboration between the USA and OECS needs explanation. That the USA had contingency plans for an invasion of Grenada was never in doubt. The problem was to get these plans legitimised by the OECS. The problem was soon resolved when, on October 21 1982, member states of the

OECS, without Grenada, held a Special Meeting in Barbados. The meeting decided that the Chairman, Eugenia Charles, should ask the USA to intervene. Sanctions were imposed on Grenada. Flights from OECS states to Grenada were banned. The supply of currency from the Eastern Caribbean Currency Board (ECCB) to Grenada was stopped. When Barbados' Prime Minister Tom Adams joined this meeting, it became a duly constituted convocation of the Regional Security System (RSS).

The Community felt compelled to act. Its Chairman, George Chambers of Trinidad and Tobago, summoned a conference for October 22–23, 1983. Grenada, as in the case of the OECS Special Meeting, was not invited. The conference eventually decided that Grenada's Governor-General, Sir Paul Scoon, should seek to form a broad-based Government of national reconciliation and hold early elections. CARICOM was to despatch a fact-finding mission. The Grenadian Government was expected to accept a CARICOM peacekeeping force. Grenada's membership of CARICOM was to be suspended and the OECS sanctions reaffirmed.

The inevitable happened. Armed with a written invitation from the OECS (an American demand), 6000 American marines and army rangers, together with 300 soldiers and police from six CARICOM states, invaded Grenada. Guyana, the Bahamas, Belize and Trinidad and Tobago were the only CARICOM states to oppose the use of force in Grenada. It was not the Caribbean's finest hour.

Although the invasion is said to have had popular support, it was denounced by CARICOM's founders. Errol Barrow accused Tom Adams of being 'a victim of the Munroe Doctrine.' Michael Manley said it had not 'either a legal, moral or genuine political basis.' Forbes Burnham and George Chambers roundly condemned the invasion. George Price of Belize called for respect for the principle of non-interference in the internal affairs of states and abstention from the use of force to resolve differences between states.

The post- intervention period was a difficult one, as the future of CARICOM in its current form came in for radical questioning. Barbados and Trinidad and Tobago broke off trade relations. The Heads of Government at their Port of Spain meeting on October 22, spoke of a new CARICOM order and the possibility of a CARICOM II, which would more stringently address issues of human rights and sovereignty, and on specified issues, modify the strict unanimity rule. But Guyana was not interested. Commentators in that country suggested the dissolution of CARICOM and the substitution of a body which would exclude the advocates of intervention and include Haiti and the Dominican Republic.

The debate raged in the international fora. A draft resolution proposed by Guyana in the Security Council condemning the intervention as a flagrant violation of international law, independence and sovereignty was vetoed by the USA, the Bahamas and Grenada (the legitimacy of whose delegate was questioned). In November 1983, Guyana and Trinidad and Tobago supported a resolution in the UN General Assembly sponsored by Zimbabwe and Nicaragua on whether the USA military intervention should be 'regretted.' The meeting of Commonwealth Heads of Government in New Delhi in 1983 expressed 'deep disquiet' over the events in Grenada and directed its Secretary-General to prepare a study on the needs of small states to protect their sovereignty and territorial integrity.

It did not escape the notice of political observers that at a critical moment in its development, the Community did not have an effective central authority to take decisive action in Grenada in 1983. Shridath Ramphal, then Secretary-General of the Commonwealth, attributed this to the failure of the Federation. A Federal Government would have restrained Eric Gairy (Bishop's predecessor, who was seen as having precipitated many of the problems that led to excesses such as Coard's) and crushed the Coard regime. Gordon Lewis saw the invasion as the consequence of a 'fatal absence of any effective Federal or regional authority,' and 'a crisis of self-determination . . . which could be overcome [only] by an intra-regional defence pact, the integration of production and by political Integration.' [12]

The invasion of Grenada, the intrusion of a foreign power into the very heart of the Community, highlighted the weaknesses of the integration movement. It embittered relationships among the Caribbean Heads of Government. The behaviour of a number of CARICOM states did untold damage to the notion of Caribbean unity, when it emerged that they had known about the impending invasion from the time of the Summit in Trinidad and Tobago in 1983 and had deliberately kept their colleagues in the dark. Deputy Prime Minister of Antigua, Lester Bird, captured the impact of this in 1984 by observing that:

By our own actions we have aided the process of external manipulation. We have ignored resolutions laboriously devised and painstakingly negotiated. We have sought relations in contravention of the Treaty establishing the Caribbean Community and we have fallen prey to the lure of external agencies even at the expense of our own solidarity.

The amicable personal relations which had made it easy for the leaders of the Community in the 1970s to work together also suffered a setback as a consequence of the economic and ideological crises of this period. The good personal relations among respective leaders had in fact been one of the noticeable factors in the early days of CARICOM. This was a result of historical as well as educational factors. The early leaders of the Community were deeply conscious of the reasons which impelled them towards unity and laid down conditions that enabled them to work together towards this goal. And when most of them found themselves sharing the same educational experience, particularly in Great Britain, they took the opportunity to forge bonds, deepen personal ties and map out strategies for the integration of their region.

As already indicated, Eric Williams, one of the founding fathers of the Community, was deeply upset by the decisions taken by Jamaica and Guyana to seek solutions to their economic problems outside of the existing framework for CARICOM unity. When Guyana and Jamaica, burdened by chronic balance of payments problems, had invoked Article 28 of the Treaty of Chaguaramas enabling them to restrict imports from the Community, Trinidad retaliated by announcing measures to institute its own system of quantitative controls on the imports of regional goods. Nothing came of all this in the end, as Guyana and Jamaica subsequently undertook to raise the value of their imports to 1975 levels. But all this was not good for the tempers of the leaders of the Community.

The ideological divisions over the socialist systems of government and economic philosophy pursued by Manley, Burnham and Bishop in particular, not only drew sharp criticism from other leaders of the Community, but bred suspicion on both sides of the divide. Some leaders found Guyana's politics, more than any other, particularly troubling. In the attempt to transform internal political and economic structures, Guyana instituted a policy of nationalisation shortly after the country became a republic in 1971. The nationalisation policy placed eighty percent of the economy in the hands of the state. Guyana forged links with a number of radical states (such as Cuba) and movements in the region. The country's activist role in the Angolan civil war in 1976 and its attempt to create a single movement out of a number of leftist organisations, did not find favour with a number of member states, especially those of the OECS. The invasion of Grenada merely accentuated the sharp and painful divides among the leaders of the Community. And one cannot say with any certainty that the legacy of bitterness has disappeared.

One major reason for the establishment of the Caribbean Community had been to rid the region of the burden of psychological dependence and the tendency to seek solutions to vital questions by looking outside of the region. When the Grenada situation erupted, the recommendations and perceptions offered by some of the Community's leaders were a sign, despite the divisions, that the region had retained its will to independence and the ability to follow its own genius. But the lasting pain of that encounter is that instead of adhering to the Treaty of Chaguaramas, individual leaders sought salvation through the intervention of an external power. It is debatable whether the psychological consequences of this course of action do not still affect those who pursue the unity of the region.

The Disenchantment of the Organisation of Eastern Caribbean States (OECS)

While the debt crisis and the invasion of Grenada illustrated CARICOM's problems in dramatic terms, there were continuing problems of a less spectacular but equally serious nature, that constituted a threat to the Community's survival. Among these was the issue of the Eastern Caribbean states.

Smaller states within any economic grouping tend to be sensitive about their positions within it. The states of the Eastern Caribbean have been no exception. They have been sceptical of the ability of each integration body, such as CARIFTA or CARICOM, to protect and ensure their vital interests. The ambiguous relationship between the Community and these smaller states has never been quite resolved.

The fact that the smaller states of the Community had joined the integration process with some degree of caution was articulated by St Lucia's Prime Minister John Compton in the 1960s when he described the relationship between the larger states and the smaller ones, in the context of CARIFTA, as resembling that between 'sharks and sardines.' This scepticism burgeoned into disenchantment when it became clear that the benefits of joining the Community had been dissipated by the economic crisis of the 1970s. The contraction of intra-regional trade in particular hit the OECS states hard. It must have been a difficult period for these countries which had placed their economic eggs in the CARICOM basket. They had come a long way in deciding to hitch their star to the Community.

Even though the Treaty of Chaguaramas had made provision for a special trade regime for the LDCs, by the end of the 1970s, this proved insufficient for the needs of that sub grouping. A number of observers have come to the conclusion that the formation of the Organisation of Eastern Caribbean States was a direct result of the smaller states of the Community not having enjoyed the expected fruits of joining that organisation.

Taking into consideration the issue of the OECS, the economic and debt crises, and the Grenada invasion, there is no doubt that by the middle of the 1980s, therefore, the Caribbean Community presented the spectacle of an institution beset by a number of serious problems and characterised by a leadership which could not find common ground on a number of issues of an ideological and economic nature.

The Seven Year Hiatus

Initially, some obscurity surrounded the events of the period between the Conference of Heads of Government of the Caribbean Community in 1975 and the 1982 Ocho Rios meeting to which we have already referred. However, research and available documentation have contributed to an explanation of what happened during this period. It is now known that although hamstrung by the region's economic crisis and strained personal relations, Caribbean leaders did not withdraw from their commitment to integration. Their political will and determination to forge ahead with the integration movement was not weakened by the severity of the economic crisis. The evidence is there to substantiate this view.

It is interesting that during the seven-year period in which the Heads of Government did not meet, at least three Heads of Government saw the resumption of these meetings as essential to the well-being of the Community and their respective states. Manley, Burnham and Bishop for different reasons recognised that CARICOM was essential to the solution of the urgent problems which confronted them. Manley and Burnham saw a link between a revived CARICOM and a solution to their economic problems, while the search for legitimacy motivated the Grenada Government to press for a Heads of Government meeting.

In November 1977, Michael Manley wrote to the Acting Secretary General, Joseph Tyndall, expressing his concern that 'although we are now in the eleventh month of 1977 it has not been possible to arrange for a Meeting of the Caribbean Commonwealth Heads of Government.' He noted that a number of fundamental issues which had a bearing on the future of the integration movement needed 'to be discussed urgently at the highest level.'

The Government of Guyana under Prime Minister Forbes Burnham expressed its commitment to CARICOM despite the immense economic difficulties it was facing. In his address to the nation in early 1977, Burnham noted that 'CARICOM has undergone severe strain' and that there had been 'dire predictions of the break up of CARICOM and the enemies of CARI-COM have been looking forward with eagerness to its early demise.'

Burnham warned that a solution to CARICOM's problems should not be perceived as merely one country giving aid to another, but as a question of developing inter-territory relations which would benefit all the countries of the region and stimulate industries in all the territories. He felt that complaints against member countries were ultimately self-defeating, and that nothing could be gained from what he described as 'the policy of despair and disengagement.' Burnham placed emphasis on the urgent need for a meeting for the Heads of CARICOM and welcomed the suggestion from the Prime Minister of Jamaica to hold such a meeting at an early date.

Seeking to diffuse the 'confusion' which existed in the region about the 'motives and activities' of some member states, Burnham proposed preparatory meetings of ministers concerned with various aspects of the economy of CARICOM. In particular, he suggested that the lack of a meeting of ministers with responsibility for natural resources had hampered regional integration, and that the resumption of meetings would serve to reopen regional dialogue and foster the climate of confidence and optimism critical to the integration process.

But some of the other Heads of Government remained suspicious of Burnham, as became clear in the subsequent events. Burnham dispatched to the Eastern Caribbean Rudy Insanally, his High Commissioner and one of his top political advisers, to discuss with leaders of the region the possibility of hosting a CARICOM summit in Guyana. In addition, selected Caribbean leaders, including Milton Cato of St Vincent and Tom Adams of Barbados were invited for talks at the National Service Centre at Kimbia on the Berbice River. All indications were that the summit would be held and preparations were undertaken towards this end.

But on June 3, 1982 the Prime Minister of St Lucia, John Compton, cabled the Secretary-General of the Community stating that 'unofficial reports' had indicated that 'plans for the proposed CARICOM Heads of Government Conference in Georgetown, Guyana in July include a caucus of Heads to be held in the area of Guyana claimed by Venezuela.' The St Lucian Prime Minister made the position of his Government very clear:

It is St Lucia's view that the presence of Heads of Government in the disputed area of Guyana may be construed as a show of political force rather than a demonstration on the part of all CARICOM Governments to assist in the Resolution of the Guyana/Venezuela dispute through the machinery of diplomacy.

It was not long thereafter that several OECS Heads of State signalled their unwillingness to attend the summit in Guyana. President Burnham had to withdraw his invitation for the summit. But Burnham would not be denied. At the Third Meeting of the Conference of the Heads of Government of the Caribbean Community in Ocho Rios, Jamaica in 1982, he proposed that the

Community have annual summits. This was accepted. Only his death on August 6, 1985 prevented Burnham from presiding at a summit in Guyana.

St Lucia's reasons for not attending the summit were plausible enough, but senior members of the Burnham administration were convinced that the refusal had more to do with ideological differences and the influential hand of Washington. In this regard it must be explained that Guyana's relations with Washington were at their lowest point, and the latter was reluctant to see Guyana play a leading role in the Caribbean Community.

Predictions of Failure

The crisis affecting the integration movement sparked reaction and debate across the Caribbean. A leading Caribbean journalist, Ricky Singh, opined in the *Trinidad Express* of August 28, 1977, that 'a mood of gloom prevails over the future of the Caribbean Community . . .' as people had lost faith in the idea of Caribbean unity. Former Secretary-General Alister McIntyre, writing in *Caribbean Contact* in July 1977, attributed the Community's slowness in responding to its challenges, to a much diminished infusion of intellectual guidance as to the options open to the region. He argued that the adaptation of institutional structures and modalities to changing development strategies, the determination of CARICOM's ability to survive the plurality of social and economic systems, and the need to face squarely the possibility of continuing difficulties of non-oil producing countries with balance of payment problems, all depended for their successful resolution on the injection and development of intellectually sound options. McIntrye warned:

Recent events indicate that CARICOM is going through a process of profound transition. The impact of changes in the world economy as well as developments within the region itself, have thrown up a new set of questions about the future directions of the Integration Movement. These issues constitute a challenge to the intellectual community to take a lead in the search for technical clarity on the options that are open to the region.[13]

Earl Huntley, writing in the August issue of *Caribbean Contact* that same year, saw the postponement of crucial CARICOM Council meetings and the commissioning of a comprehensive study of the region's economic problems as confirmation that the integration movement was in crisis, which he postulated was fuelled by the general dissatisfaction of the LDCs with their share of the benefits of integration. This dissatisfaction was expressed through rejection of a CARICOM Process List which was proposed at that time. The gloomy forecast by the President of the Caribbean Development Bank,

William Demas, that 1977 was going to be a tough year for Commonwealth Caribbean countries because of the adverse international economic situation, pointed further to the difficult situation facing the states of the Caribbean Community.

Huntley noted that the CARICOM Council, which normally met two to three times a year, could only be persuaded to convene once in September 1977 and once in December 1978. He argued that this, along with other problems internal to the Secretariat, contributed to CARICOM's inability to develop into the deeper form of integration to which the Treaty of Chaguaramas had aspired.

Economist Trevor Farrell, also writing in *Caribbean Contact* in 1977, supported Huntley's position that the dissatisfaction of the LDCs had contributed to the crisis in CARICOM. But he felt that this had resulted from an inherent inequity between the MDCs and LDCs in terms of natural resources and critical technical skills, a factor which, in his judgement, made the LDCs dispensable to the regional movement. The growing discrepancies in development strategies of member states were also seen as contributing to the Community's problems. He concluded that CARICOM as an integration movement was weak and fragile – an outcome which was ultimately traceable to the very rationale officially offered for its existence. Farrell's conclusion was bleak: 'It is important to realise that Integration Movements among underdeveloped countries are notoriously unsuccessful,'[14] he wrote.

In a subsequent issue of *Caribbean Contact* that year, Havelock Ross-Brewster rejected Farrell's view that the LDCs were dispensable. He took the position that perhaps the single most important justification for the establishment of CARICOM was ensuring a commitment to the smaller islands of the region. Ross-Brewster argued that the Leeward-Windward Islands spatially and diplomatically define the Caribbean, their sea space constituting the eastern perimeter of the Caribbean Sea, virtually up to 20 degrees latitude, and the most important access route to and from Europe and Africa. The Bahamas could become a virtually continuous geographic area stretching from the Gulf of Paria to West Palm Beach – an impressive diplomatic theatre of far greater significance than any individual Caribbean state. Like McIntyre, Brewster urged clarity of mind in distinguishing between arrangements which were essential and those which were merely facilitative in dealing with common problems within the parameters set by the existing political authorities.

Clive Thomas saw the problems of the Community in economic and class terms. Thomas wrote that the threatened abandonment by Britain as she pursued entry into the European Common Market should provide the necessary impetus for the Caribbean Community to pursue economic integration. He argued further that the real source of crisis in CARICOM lay in the social contradictions within the organisation. In his view, the first and most important of these was the class basis on which development of the region rested; such a type of 'social structure' was incapable of solving the problems of poverty and dispossession. The second contradiction Thomas posited was that these class interests, although generally dominant, were not necessarily homogenous, since there were sectional interests which conflicted with each other. The third contradiction he suggested was that the ruling *petite bourgeoisie* of the region had a particular style of politics which emphasised manipulation and a marked hostility to mass participation in the political process. Thomas too reached a pessimistic conclusion:

Looking at the range of institutions created, it is difficult to resist the temptation to describe the whole integration edifice as a PAPER TIGER. As the difficulties of integration have been encountered, a new paper institution was proposed as a solution. Many of the paper institutions, e.g. the process list, the aluminium plant, the proposed agreement on foreign investments are yet to leave the files.[15]

Norman Girvan, in a 1978 article 'Three Areas of Our Regional Crisis, like Ross-Brewster disagreed with Trevor Farrell that the LDCs should be excised from the Community. Even so, Girvan observed that academics who were formerly in the vanguard of the development of regional integration had now condemned CARICOM 'to a man.' In these circumstances, he believed, it was unrealistic ' to hold out any short term or long term hope for the Community in its present form.' [16]

Girvan concluded that nevertheless, geopolitical factors dictated that the Caribbean could not attain any degree of real sovereignty without some form of association. This sovereignty was in turn 'indispensable to the internal socio-economic liberation for which our peoples are constantly struggling, no matter how difficult or tortuous the route may seem.'

Brewster, Thomas, Farrell and Girvan, albeit with different emphases, were agreed that the crisis in the Caribbean Community stemmed from its original defects in conception, structure and strategy. The crisis had sharpened at this particular time because of the wider problems in the international capitalist system, characterised by rising oil and falling commodity prices, world inflation and recession. These factors tended to check the momentum of independence and the economic expansion upon which intra-CARICOM trade was premised. These intellectuals also argued that a great many of the problems being faced by CARICOM could be attributed directly to the lack of political will to make the institutions work – a situation which had existed for some time and which was only exacerbated by the developments of this period. What was really required was a theoretical framework that would underpin CARICOM in such a way that its operations and its focus in practice could not continue to be undermined.

Shridath Ramphal, a former Minister of Foreign Affairs of Guyana, and one of the early architects of the integration movement, in his speech at a UWI graduating ceremony as reported in the *Caribbean Contact* of March 1979, told students that it was of particular relevance that they were graduating from a University which had perhaps embodied the most prominent focus of West Indian integration. Yet they were now going out into a society in which the focus on integration as a West Indian concern was now greatly blurred. In his own words, 'regionalism peers as though through a glass darkly.' He lamented that the region was prone to solve difficulties 'by pulling down structures and erecting new ones when the cause of the difficulties may not be with the structures at all but either with the external environment over which we can exercise little control or with the ways in which we manage the habitation.' [17]

West Indian intellectuals and editorial writers of the region were not alone in their predictions that the integration process was in crisis and could not survive. Anthony Payne, in a March 1981 article entitled 'The Rise and Fall of Caribbean Regionalisation' in the journal *Market Studies*, took a similar position. He argued that there were flaws in the design of the Community. In his view the integration movement was not an integration movement at all. Payne also believed that the crisis of the 1970s exposed the fragility of the integration process and changed the balance of power within it. Payne concluded that the experience of the Caribbean Community confirmed the 'enormous fragility of integration schemes established between Third World states.' [18]

Response to the Crisis: The Ideology of Survival

Bearing in mind the recorded failure of other attempts at integration in different parts of the world; for example the East African Economic Community (EAC), it was not difficult to conclude that it was unlikely that CARICOM would survive. And even those who were optimistic about its prospects could not ignore the monumental obstacles to its survival that it was now facing. In retrospect, it can be said that the Community responded to the challenge in a mature, responsible and creative manner consistent with Caribbean tradition. Gordon Lewis has pointed out that ideas as well as human beings crossed the Middle Passage. From the time of slavery the region has always responded with effective ideas when challenged.

The Caribbean Community responded to the crisis of the integration movement and the persistent criticisms by initiating a series of declarations, resolutions and studies, which taken together, constitute a programme and, indeed, an *ideology* for survival. The significant initiatives here were the commissioning of Group of Experts in 1980; the Nassau Understanding of 1984; the Grand Anse Declaration of 1989; the Ocho Rios Declaration of 1982; the Mills Commission of 1990; the Bourne Commission of 1988 and the West Indian Commission of 1992. Taken together, the Reports of the Commissions and the instruments of the Understanding and Declarations, represent a considered response to the crisis faced by the Community in the seventies and eighties and the determination to find solutions to the problems posed by the new millennium. They reflect a resolve on the part of Caribbean leaders to come to terms with the problems posed by the world economic crisis, the ideologically plural nature of the region, and the emerging difficulties of the succeeding decade.

The Group of Experts was mandated by the Sixteenth Meeting of the Council of Ministers of the Caribbean Common Market 'to prepare a strategy for the Caribbean Integration Movement in the decade of the 1980s.' Pending the publication of this Report, meetings of the Heads of Government Conference were postponed. The Report was published in January 1981.

The Group, chaired by William Demas, found that weaknesses at the national level rather than deficiencies in CARICOM as an economic integration instrument were the main reason for the Community's not exerting greater influence on the development of the region. The Experts were convinced that Caribbean integration could not simultaneously cure the economic ills of the region and promote the immediate and particular development of member states. The Group also concluded that revitalisation demanded that the Community 'draw up a fresh affirmation of political and popular will.'[19] They believed that a new public dialogue was necessary. The Group felt that the limited achievements of the Community had resulted in loss of faith and hope in CARICOM both by the regional public and the international community, and saw the renewal of confidence in the regional movement as the major task facing the Community. Heads of Government had a particular responsibility here since they were not only the supreme organ of the Community, but also the custodians of the promises that the Treaty of Chaguaramas had made to the region's peoples. The Group expressed their concern that the Heads of Government had met only three times since 1973 and not at all since March 1976.

The Group also emphasised that the Community was not simply a trading arrangement, but a broader internal effort embracing three major elements:

(1) Economic Integration (through the Caribbean Common Market) consisting of:
  (a) The expansion of intra-regional trade and other economic transactions;
  (b) joint efforts to strengthen production for sale to National, Regional and Intra-Regional Markets;
  (c) joint efforts in extra-regional trade and other external Economic Relations and transactions;
  (d) A special regime for less developed countries.
2. The coordination of foreign policies.
3. Functional cooperation (including common services) in a number of areas; for example, education, health, meteorology, transport, labour relations.

The Group assessed the impact of the ideologically plural nature of the Community to which Alister McIntyre and others had made reference in the seventies and concluded that while the obligations of CARICOM did not necessitate uniformity of domestic political systems, this should not be construed as overriding regional obligations. They pointed to the weaknesses and challenges of the Community such as insularity, a lack of awareness of its resources, the need for joint efforts at production, the need for greater awareness among the people of the true nature of the integration movement, and the need for an assertion of political will. For them, in the final analysis, there was no alternative to integration.

The Ocho Rios Declaration issued at the first meeting of the Heads of Government after seven years reflected the concerns of the Group of Experts. The Nassau Understanding, which was adopted by the 1984 Heads of Government Conference, was based on a Report submitted by the Caribbean Development Bank (CDB) on the structural problems of the Community's member states.[20] It referred to the swift rise in debt servicing, a sudden and sharp deterioration in the terms of trade, abrupt increases in external debt servicing, and continuing declines in the volume of major agricultural exports. Substantial debt relief was seen as a matter of the greatest urgency. The Report warned that the depletion of major natural resources could trigger a loss of confidence between the Government and the population, as people and capital would leave the country and underground economies would come into existence. Control of the economy would therefore increasingly be removed from the hands of government, and the entire economic and social framework of the state would be at risk.

In considering the CDB Report, the Heads of Government agreed that the per capita income in most CARICOM countries remained relatively high, but saw that their economic structures rested on fragile foundations. A large proportion of income, jobs and revenue and export earning depended on one or two exports, and the manufacturing sector still did not have close linkages with other sectors of the economy. The export capacity of this sector was still underdeveloped.

The Nassau Understanding further acknowledged that the productive sector as a whole offered insufficient employment opportunities and as a result unemployment and underemployment were pervasive. School leavers who were affected migrated to urban areas or went abroad. The Nassau Understanding noted that 'such economic conditions breed chronic discontent, crime, violence, and political extremism, putting at risk national cohesion and the democratic process itself.' [21]

The Heads of Government therefore committed themselves to national plans for the growth of the productive and private sectors and agreed to utilise the opportunities for export provided by the Caribbean Common Market. Emphasis was also to be placed on encouraging 'the considerable incipient entrepreneurship' of the people, particularly the young, in rural and urban areas. The public sector, it was decided, should be rationalised for greater efficiency. Financial and fiscal practices should become more disciplined. In the areas of education and training, more planned attention would be paid to the professions, other occupations and tertiary education. Efforts were to be made to introduce technology as a major component in primary, secondary and tertiary education. As the Grand Anse Declaration later emphasised, the proposed directions in education and training, particularly the focus on technology, indicated not only the Community's recognition of the importance of 'scientific and technological capability to the modernisation of the regional economy,' but also its recognition that human resource development was of special value in the exploitation of new opportunities arising in the services sector, particularly through the development of information technology.

The Grand Anse Declaration of 1989 represented a new drive to ensure the implementation of the agreements reached by the Community. The Declaration, a response to the progress Western Europe had made in its own integration attempt, confirmed the need to establish a Single Market and Economy in the shortest possible time. The Heads of Government agreed to specific measures in relation to the Common Market, including the removal of all remaining barriers to trade by July 1991. Agreement was reached for the free movement of skills, professional personnel and contract workers on a seasonal and project basis by January 1991. Member states were also to prepare the necessary legislation to implement a CARICOM Industrial Programming Scheme (CIPS) and the CARICOM Enterprise Regime (CER).

The Heads of Government recognised the importance and special roles of the private sector, the trade union movement, regional universities, religious organisations, women and youth organisations, the professions, non-governmental organisations and 'people of all walks and condition of life.' They agreed on a number of actions to advance the goals of the Treaty of Chaguaramas. These included the establishment of an Assembly of Community Caribbean Parliamentarians and the independent West Indian Commission.

The Mills Report looked at the need to strengthen the Community's institutions. In the process, it dealt with such issues as settling disputes between member states, the need for a Regional Supreme Court, human resource development and the widening of the Community. The recommendations of the Mills Report, especially those which relate to institutional strengthening, are worth re-examination.

The Bourne Commission, as was the case with the Nassau Understanding and the Grand Anse Declaration, was concerned with immediate and long-term economic problems facing the Community. However, it is interesting to note that this Commission, like the Group of Experts and the West Indian Commission, believed strongly that it is the people of the region who will determine the long-term success of the Community:

There are no easy solutions to the immense development problems of Commonwealth Caribbean economies. Long-run development will depend more upon the sustained hard work, ingenuity, productivity and thrift of individuals and enterprises within the framework of sensibly supportive and facilitatory government policies than upon any grandiose schemes or projects. The International environment, although providing sources of support and opportunities for growth as well as constraints on the nature and pace of development, need not be the dominant influence.

The Commission also identified vigorous economic performance of individual states as a priority. It noted, as did the Group of Experts, that economic growth had slackened, and that in some cases there were signs of further decline. The Commission determined that sustained growth at much higher levels; that is, beyond six per cent, was imperative if the region was to cope with the heavy unemployment and looming unemployment problems precipitated by demographic change between 1980 and 1990. The Bourne Commission also emphasised the need to be responsive to globalisation, specifically by the implementation of economic measures to improve CARICOM's credit-worthiness and export competitiveness.

The Bourne Commission Report saw growth opportunities in the following areas: commodity demand; increasing international demand for services; trade with Latin America and the Pacific-rim countries; and the harnessing of new technology for increased production and productivity. Emphasis was also placed on human resources development in the context of the tourism, service-driven aspects of the economy developing in some member states.

The West Indian Commission Report had the urgency of tone and purpose of the Grand Anse Declaration which brought it into being. The Commission sought to prepare the Community structurally and otherwise for the challenges of the twenty-first century. It proposed a CARICOM Commission to ensure the urgent implementation of decisions taken by the Community, and addressed the issue of a Single Market and Economy.

Like its predecessors the Group of Experts and the Bourne Commission, the West Indian Commission advocated greater involvement of the people of the region. They supported the Assembly of Caribbean Parliamentarians which was designed to include representatives of young people, farmers, religious groups, women, labour groups and business groups in the integration process. They also proposed the Charter of Civil Society to ensure that concerns about governance in the Caribbean were addressed. Most importantly, the Caribbean Court of Appeal as the final Court of Appeal for member states was vigorously advocated as one of the important structures of unity.

The West Indian Commission also initiated the Association of Caribbean States (ACS) because they felt that the peoples and Governments of the region needed to expand their thinking beyond the narrow terms of 'the Commonwealth Caribbean.' Other issues addressed were the labour movement, freedom of movement, the environment, culture, human resource development, the maximisation of competitiveness in the global market place and the need for a vision for the twenty-first century. The Commission spoke of the unique contribution the Caribbean could make to world development on the edge of the century:

. . . it is rare, especially in the still developing world – and it may become rarer yet as the decade advances – that a people of many nationalities, many races, many faiths, and different cultural heritages stay together, and indeed grow closer, in a single community. It is an example that is likely to be valuable in the world. The talents which have emerged from our amalgam of peoples have already made a telling and universal mark. This creativity, multiplied through the greater opportunities conferred by closer union, will add stature and a special vibrancy to the example we can expect to offer to our hemisphere and to the world as the new century dawns.[22]

As might have been expected, the Community's efforts to deal with the problems of the integration movement via commissions, special studies and declarations attracted as much comment and criticism as the crises of the 1970s and 1980s had done. Anthony Payne, commenting on the composition of the Group of Experts, described it as an 'in-house team.'[23] He argued that this prevented the Experts from making fundamental criticisms of the ideological thrust of the Community. Havelock Ross-Brewster's criticisms of the West Indian Commission Report were even sharper.[24] He examined several aspects of the Report with regard to methodology, governance, the Community's future, a common currency, a Single Market and Economy, external relations and institutional structures. Brewster concluded that the Commission's methodology was flawed and as a consequence it had treated the question of development policy inadequately. In his view, the Commission also failed to examine with any thoroughness the issues of governance, a common currency and a monetary union. Brewster also argued that a Caribbean Single Market and Economy, including resource complementation and linkage, were unlikely to provide competitive advantages in the changing international environment, which was characterised by widening economic spaces such as NAFTA, the EC, APEC and global corporations.

Brewster concluded his critique of the West Indian Commission Report by arguing for 'an extensive Agenda for the continued life, if not of the West Indian Commission, of a public forum on West Indian, social, and economic futures.' For him, the Report was a 'one-shot preparation of a 'magnum opus' which could not substitute for investment in 'an ongoing- process of deepening, transparent consideration, debate and contention of ideas.'

William Demas: Major Architect of the Ideology of Survival

The Caribbean personality who it can be argued made the most profound contribution to the ideology of integration and whose writings pervaded and continue to pervade the integration process is William Gilbert Demas. In spite of the difficulties which faced the Caribbean Community in the 1970s, 1980s and beyond, Demas remained convinced that integration would succeed. He was Chairman of the Group of Experts, and participated in the work of the West Indian Commission. Demas worked untiringly for CARICOM's success, and understood, as few did, that CARICOM was a political and diplomatic necessity for the region. Vision and care were the twin characteristics of his life's work.

Demas' vision for the Caribbean Community revolved around five main themes: development economics, the special problems of small states, the role of the state in development planning, integration and functional cooperation. Underpinning his concern with these was one broad and overarching objective – the maintenance and protection of Caribbean sovereignty. He campaigned for the introduction of a Pan-Caribbean structure of economic development and planned for medium and long term development strategies by a high-powered core of experts who would take advantage of the cutting edge of technology and trends in globalisation, with an eye to developments in the new millennium.

Demas saw excellence as a critical ingredient in Caribbean development. For him, creative innovation and the design of curricula to ensure tertiary education that was both far-reaching and meaningful to the region, were crucial factors in achieving this. At every opportunity, he stressed the need to inculcate in the people of the Caribbean, from the cradle to the grave, a sense of excellence, which meant never being satisfied with indifferent performance in any field of endeavour. Inspired by his vision of a unified Caribbean, he utilised his connections with Governments of member states to ensure that politically sensitive initiatives were brought to the fore at strategically effective moments to ensure the success of particular programmes. This was part of his characteristic of care.

Demas was deeply concerned about small economies and repeatedly argued that their development necessarily had to be different from that of larger and more mature economies. He thought that self-sustained growth should not be considered independently of a country's size. Fundamental political, social and institutional factors had to be taken into account in the governance of small economies. At the very least, dissimilarities in initial factor endowments and in some cases, the maturity of structures and institutions in small states relative to their larger counterparts, dictated a different frame for analysis. For example, it should be taken into account that smaller economies were characterised by openness and a dependence on external trade and finance for their survival.

Demas' proposal for the care of smaller member states was for an urgent identification of a path of self-sustaining growth, which would hinge on the generation of adequate volumes of domestic savings in both the public and private sectors. In addition to self-sustaining growth, he envisaged a fundamental transformation of the structures of production in smaller economies. Structural transformation, he suggested, should encompass six indices: a politically and socially determined capacity for effecting fundamental change; unification of local markets for goods and services; increased integration of domestic industries and activities; a reduction of dependence on, and change in the structure of external trade and aid; balanced, non-dualistic development; and the emergence of appropriate financial and other intermediate institutions.

Demas constantly emphasised that the process of deeper economic integration must be premised on financial integration at the level of private financial institutions, capital markets, and, importantly, national monetary authorities. He was conscious of the impact of the polarisation of intra-regional trade by which the larger and more developed countries of the Community benefited more than the smaller and less developed ones. He believed that the negative consequences of polarisation could be reduced by redirecting production factors, especially capital, to the less developed areas. Demas also believed that indigenous ownership of regional financial institutions and the regional financial mechanisms aimed at funding trade and investment to the less developed states were critical for their economies. In this context he advocated greater innovativeness in the oversight and operations of central banking in the Community.

Perhaps Demas' greatest contribution to development policy, and by extension, the very survival of CARICOM, was in the areas of economic integration and functional cooperation to reduce the problem of size as an inhibitor to the ability of small countries to achieve economies of scale. He also played a pivotal role in developing and promoting a number of programmes which helped to demonstrate the value of the model he identified for the development of small economies.

The need for a national and ultimately a regional central bank structured to influence the use of financial resources in ways that would contribute to the strengthening of national economies by changing their production structures and patterns of consumption was of critical importance to Demas. He suggested that the assets of these banks and other non-bank financial institutions such as insurance companies should be state-owned.

Without losing sight of the imperatives of integration, Demas was conscious of the need to make adjustments in response to changes in the global environment in which the region had to operate. He made several pronouncements on such issues as NAFTA, the FTAA, the relationship between the ACS and CARICOM and the need for the region to resist a new form of colonialism as evidenced in such proposals as the Ship-Rider Agreement. Ultimately for Demas, the regional movement went beyond mere economics and embraced the questions of identity, community and human rights:

For me, the Caribbean Community is nothing more and nothing less than the efforts of the Caribbean people to create a new and unique political entity that respects the national sovereignty of each individual territory, while at the same time pooling aspects of that sovereignty and pooling aspects of their resources in order to promote and preserve peace, promote and preserve democracy, promote and preserve fundamental human rights and the rule of law, and promote and preserve economic and social development among Caribbean peoples. [25]

Survival Mechanisms

Despite the problems and negative criticisms the Caribbean Community has faced, it must be said that the leaders of the Community not only fashioned an ideology of survival, but created the required structures to sustain it – we have seen that there has been and continues to be an ongoing reform of the Community's institutional structures. And here the Community's capacity to adapt to change is amply demonstrated.

The visionary nature of some of these institutions cannot be denied. For example, the Caribbean Court of Justice, when it comes into being, will have a fundamental bearing on the future direction of the community especially as it relates to the creation of the Single Market and Economy. The Assembly of Parliamentarians allows the people of the region to participate in the process of consolidating and strengthening the Community and by extension the integration process. Through their parliamentarians, the people of each member state and associate state are able to make their views known and to influence specific plans for integration. The Assembly also serves to facilitate more frequent contact in the monitoring of the policies of the Community in order to enhance the foreign policies of member states; and to promote greater understanding among member and associate member states.

Even before these new institutions were created or conceived, the leaders of the Community sought to ensure broad based participation in its work by eschewing a supra-national authority and institutionalising the unanimity rule. This ensured that the interests of all member states were taken into account when decisions were made. Also, from the beginning, the organs and instruments of the Caribbean Community reflected its conception as a community of sovereign states which had agreed by Treaty to pool their sovereignties in order to achieve identified and specific objectives. The Community, following the provisions of the Treaty, sought to facilitate broad areas of cooperation including the establishment of a Common Market, the coordination of foreign policy and the expansion of functional cooperation, while avoiding any implication of supra-nationality.

To this end, the Treaty of Chaguaramas provided for the Community to be controlled by a series of conferences and councils made up of territorial politicians and served by a Secretariat. Decisions were not only to be unanimously agreed on by representatives of member states, but also legitimated by each state in accordance with its own constitutional procedures.

Pollard [26] has also pointed out that this institutional machinery was structured to allow for a process of consultation to take place at each level of decision-making and to include recommendations from the relevant organs or bodies at a lower level. For example, decisions by the Conference of Heads of Government would normally benefit from recommendations of the Community Council and the Secretariat. The decisions of the Community Council would, apart from the national positions articulated by the Minister responsible for CARICOM Affairs, normally benefit from the specialised Ministerial Councils, the Secretariat and the regional tripartite consultative process; and the decisions made by the specialised Ministerial Councils would, apart from the national positions articulated by the relevant Ministers, be informed by the recommendations from the preparatory meetings of officials and the Secretariat.

The Treaty of Chaguaramas also created a number of critical institutions to promote the integration process. These include not only the Conference of Heads of Government and the Standing Committee of Ministers for various portfolios, but also the standing committees for functional and economic co-operation. The institutions for functional cooperation have made a great contribution to the survival of the integration movement in its difficult times. They include the Caribbean Examinations Council (CXC); the agreement establishing the Council of Legal Education (CLE); the agreement establishing the Caribbean Meteorological Organisation (CMO); the agreement establishing the Caribbean Research and Agricultural Institute (CARDI); and the agreement establishing the Caribbean Regional Drug Testing Laboratory (CRDTL).

While some of the institutions established to carry out functional cooperation in different areas have not lived up to expectation, others, such as the CLE and CXC, have been outstanding successes. But there is a more important factor here: *these institutions have functioned whatever the state of the regional integration movement. They have kept the movement alive.* In the words of the West Indian Commission:

The work of co-ordinating regional endeavours, sponsoring and supporting Community institutions, and providing common services across the region continues to be pursued across the vicissitudes of the CARICOM experience. If failure has often been in the headlines, progress continues to be made in the fine print. In any major enterprise the steady and regular accumulation of small successes is of the utmost value. It lays the ground work for major advances in the end.

In the ongoing commitment to responsiveness and reform, the 1999 meeting of the Heads of Government at Chaguaramas took a decision to further review the structure and function of the Community's institutions. The Bureau of the Conference of Heads of Government of the Caribbean Community was charged with the responsibility to oversee the study, the results of which would be considered at the Eleventh Inter-Sessional Meeting in March 2000. That meeting apparently took no further decisions on the matter. But, as Trinidad and Tobago's Prime Minister Basdeo Panday has suggested, the University of the West Indies could be asked to play a major part in conducting this type of project.

The Diplomacy of Survival

The changing international environment demands collective action by the Caribbean to defend its economic interests and participate effectively in the international community. Specifically, it must meet the challenges of liberalisation and threats to its survival. An objective assessment would conclude that CARICOM has the capacity to do this, since at the most difficult period, it has maintained its markets, and has been a training ground for a significant part of the region's manufacturing operations. In effect, this constitutes an economic space from within which member states can consolidate positions and strategies to launch into world markets.

This optimistic view is obviously not shared by all. Payne and Sutton have argued that the Caribbean, as part of the Third World, 'has lost nearly all its content, emptied by the differential achievements of individual states in its various geographical zones during the 1980s.' [27] The region, they suggest, is in danger of becoming a backwater, separated from the main currents of advancement in the twenty-first century. A.N.R. Robinson, as quoted by Payne/Sutton, has remarked that member states must come to terms with the stark reality that there is a new concentration of power in the hands of international capital on one hand, and on the other, a diffusion of power among the core states of the world. [28]

But a vital consideration in assessing the Community's assets in the global arena is that it has remained an important instrument for the preservation of the independence and sovereignty of member states, which they zealously guard. It is a well-known fact, true of any developing country, that given their colonial past, sovereignty is a possession that states will not easily discard.

The case of Guyana comes immediately to mind. The dawn of Independence was darkened by threats to its sovereignty by its neighbours to the east and west. Guyana was able to neutralise Suriname's attempt to invade the New River triangle in 1969 by expelling its forces from that area of its territory, but Venezuela proved to be a more difficult proposition. That country revived its claim to two-thirds of Guyana's territory on the very eve of Independence. It was also successful in blocking major investments in the Essequibo Region. Faced with this situation, Guyana turned to the community of the Caribbean for support. At the Fifth Heads of Government of the Commonwealth Caribbean Conference held in Trinidad in February 1969, the leaders, at the request of Prime Minister Forbes Burnham, officially considered the threat posed to its territorial integrity by Venezuela.

CARICOM has since continued the regional support for Guyana's territorial integrity and sovereignty in the controversy, which arose from Venezuela's contention that the 1899 Award is null and void. Venezuela has continued to reiterate its claim for over a quarter of a century.

Belize also was confronted with a major claim to its territory by Guatemala. It is significant that it was within the councils of the regional community that Belize too raised the issue of the threat to its territorial integrity and sovereignty. At the Conference of the Commonwealth Caribbean Countries held in Barbados in 1967, Prime Minister George Price referred to this situation and informed the Conference that the United States was attempting with the agreement of all parties concerned to find an amicable solution to the dispute.

The threats to the territorial integrity and sovereignty of Guyana and Belize led the Caribbean Heads of Government to articulate the doctrine of mutual assistance against external aggression. At the Eighth Conference of the Heads of Government of the Commonwealth Caribbean countries held in Guyana in April 1973, the Heads determined that political independence and territorial integrity were indispensable to the region's economic objectives and recognised the need for a regime of mutual assistance against external aggression. This doctrine was re-affirmed at the Third Meeting of the Conference of Heads of Government of the Caribbean Community held in Ocho Rios, Jamaica in 1982.

The regional community's support for Belize and Guyana played a fundamental role in ensuring that these states not only achieved Independence with their territorial integrity and sovereignty intact, but also provided an important platform from which they waged an effective campaign to ward off the threats from Venezuela and Guatemala. With the support of the Community, both Guyana and Belize were able to mobilise the assistance of the United Nations and the Non-Aligned Movement.

With the advent of globalisation there has been a tendency towards the miniaturisation of nation states. At the same time, there has been an increased pervasiveness of international governance and the power of multilateral agencies. These developments have had an impact on the sovereignty of the Caribbean people. In these circumstances, CARICOM provides the platform for its member states to increase their bargaining power in the global community. In addition to enhancing Caribbean independence, the Caribbean Community is in a position to provide member states with an increased international presence and an enhanced capacity to influence the global agenda. It is in a position to do this because it can identify and actualise the development objective of all its members and act as a vehicle for the collective will of the region. This can be achieved within the constraints of the present environment 'through the use of the unifying characteristics of language, history and common legal and administrative system, instead of the cultural peculiarities that are present in any single nation state.'[29]

This assessment of the advantages and leverage available to CARICOM States is supported by Clive Thomas,[30] who identifies the region's accession to the chairmanship of the G15 and its participation in the Group of 77, as important strengths of Caribbean leaders and the people of the region. Wise leadership can considerably enhance the status of the South in any global forum. Twenty-five years ago, Shridath Ramphal, speaking in his capacity as Foreign Minister of Guyana, said:

> Our successes over the last 10 years have now imposed upon us responsibilities beyond those which we owe to our Region. Economic integration of the Commonwealth Caribbean has become an integral element of the widening patterns and prospects of Third World economic unity – patterns and prospects which will themselves be diminished by any weakening of our structures or any slackening of our commitment.[31]

Another factor which highlights the importance of CARICOM to the survival of its member states, is the critical need to preserve the special external economic arrangements to attract investors, maintain access to concessional financial assistance and facilitate the export of such basic crops as banana, sugar and rum to preferential markets. As a grouping, CARICOM can negotiate larger markets as well as top foreign investment to assist in the development and export of products from member states whether such products are natural resource based, labour intensive or skills based, and in so doing promote economic stability. It also offers a forum from which member states can lobby for intensified relations with specific groupings such as the European Union, as well as for the promotion of closer trade and economic ties with the Asian Tigers and their associated organisations.

The current emphasis being placed on international competitiveness is necessary if any state is to survive the realities of globalisation and regionalism; it demands also that CARICOM, as a grouping, develop critical cooperation relationships with strategic countries and economic entities. The Community must speak with one voice and pursue a single purpose in relation to the rest of the world. This is an especially salient consideration as there are numerous examples of member states making themselves vulnerable to the manipulations of extra-regional powers and groupings when they chose to operate outside the Community's framework for unity. In the recent issue involving the entry of bananas from the Caribbean into the EU market, the unity of the Caribbean position played a major role in ensuring that some of its vital economic interests were maintained. Also, Caribbean unity was instrumental in guaranteeing the interest of the Region in the discussions and negotiations leading to the successor agreement to Lomé IV.

But also, it appears to be in the interest of the major powers and multilateral institutions, in normal circumstances, to have a vested interest in the survival of CARICOM as a single entity. The United States, Europe, Canada and institutions such as the World Bank and the IMF regard and treat the Caribbean region as a single unit. Increasingly also, the Government of the People's Republic of China has indicated its interest in treating the Caribbean region as a single entity.

The growing importance of the Caribbean Community to its member states in negotiations, security, economic survival, as a shield against the vagaries of the international environment and as an important player in resolving internal disputes cannot be denied. This role of the Community, which has been evident in recent times, will assume greater significance and importance in the future.

The Challenges of the Twenty-First Century

Before dealing with the specific challenges that the Caribbean Community will face in the twenty-first century, it is necessary to deal with two general but highly relevant issues of globalisation which impinge on its survival. These are the creation of the World Trade Organisation (WTO) and the issue of security and world peace.

The creation of the WTO may be regarded in the future as the first step in the creation of a network of institutions which will constitute global governance. A globalised economy cannot function effectively without its political analogue. It is apparent that the world may be on the eve of a revolution in the institutional means by which it is governed. Already, there are efforts afoot to radically transform the United Nations. Specifically, there has been advocacy for the reconstruction of the Security Council to accommodate such newly emerging powers as India, Indonesia and Brazil. It is imperative that in this new dispensation, the Caribbean Community is involved in the creation of the new structures which will have such an important bearing on global politics and economics.

Globalisation will also radically change the nature of the threats to states across the globe and especially the states of the Caribbean Community. In Dominica in the 1980s and Trinidad in the 1990s, it has been demonstrated that, if determined, an armed group or government can undermine the security of the state. But the use of arms is the traditional method. It is becoming increasingly evident that there are threats of a new nature to the security and stability of states. In Colombia, for example, 40 per cent of the territory is held by insurgent groups supported by well-known organisations involved in the narcotics trade. Modern technology will also make it easier for groups within a state to subvert it. If the Caribbean Community is to take advantage of the benefits of globalisation it will have to do so in an environment conducive to peaceful development. One of the important tasks of the Community therefore will be to take the appropriate measures, in conjunction with other states and international agencies, to ensure that the region can peacefully develop and survive in a prosperous manner.

As the twenty-first century begins, the Caribbean Community continues to be consumed by the drive for regional cooperation and its attendant benefits. That is, our peoples are determined to be united in order to exploit our untapped resources for the benefit of entire the region. But the region exists in an environment that is vastly different from the one in which it came into being. The forces unleashed by globalisation are the dominant features of the latter part of the twentieth century and the early part of the twenty-first century. A consideration of equal importance is the increasing role of multilateral institutions and transnational organisations in shaping policies that affect nations large and small across the globe. These institutions and organisations have had and will continue to have a particularly decisive impact on small nations such as those of the Caribbean.

In this context, the need to deepen the process of Caribbean unity cannot be overemphasised. As the West Indian Commission has stated:

As we approach the 21st century we dare not turn aside from each other. Local identities may be in vogue; but we do well to remember that they are invariably being indulged under the roof of regional homes . . . We began to build our regional homes a long time ago. Dismantling will be a malign act.[32]

Prime Minister of Barbados, Owen Arthur has acknowledged in the Barbados Foreign Policy Paper, that:

the confluence of the special economic and political events of the past decade and those which are already looming on the horizon, have heralded and will create such a dramatic change in the conduct and ordering of global affairs as to require fundamental and far reaching changes in all societies, great or small: These global changes which present special and unique challenges for the Caribbean which go beyond anything that it has hitherto had to grapple with in its crisis-ridden history.[33]

In other words, the dawn of the new millennium is witnessing a world undergoing radical and profound changes which have been expressed in such seminal events as the collapse of the Soviet Empire, the emergence of major centres of economic power such as India and China, and the worldwide transformation of economic relations. Commercial barriers among nations are being swept away as a consequence of trade liberalisation and the creation of a truly globalised international economy, based on developments in information technology. All this has brought into being an equally dramatic transformation in global institutions.

As the old system is being dismantled, a new order is emerging which is multi-polar both politically and economically. Nations such as China, India, Argentina, Brazil, Nigeria and possibly South Africa will increasingly become important players in the new dispensation. The Caribbean Community will be constrained to forge strategic relationships with them. Of equal importance is the increasing salience of economic factors which fuel contrasting trends of globalisation. One manifestation of these developments is regionalisation, which attempts to consolidate the benefits of globalisation from within regional trading blocs.

One of the key challenges to the Caribbean region is to enhance its capacity to develop and transform itself structurally in an environment in which sovereignty is less of an important factor than has been the case hitherto. As Peter Wickham argues in *Critical Issues in Caribbean Development 1998*, popular sovereignty is being eroded; a reality which could lead to continued impoverishment and underdevelopment of Caribbean countries.

Globalisation also brings a number of unequivocally negative challenges such as erosion of preferential status, non-reciprocal access to the markets of the developed countries, and non-tariff barriers to trade. These developments present the Caribbean Community with major competitive challenges that effectively alter the context within which regional development must take place.

Barbados' Prime Minister, Owen Arthur, in an address to the Third Media Conference in Guyana on May 5, 2000, made some significant observations on the effects of the forces released by globalisation in the Caribbean. Among these was the loss of the strategic importance of the Caribbean to the rest of the world.

The rest of world no longer sees the Caribbean as a special or unique case, deserving of special treatment and assistance. Our search for empathy or goodwill as we seek stays of execution in carrying out actions arising from our international commitments which can have painful consequences for the survival of Caribbean societies, are now perceived as yet other rearguard actions, not dissimilar from other such actions on our part over the last three hundred years.

Opportunities and Advantages

The Community has planned for the challenges of the new century. We recall that as early as 1989 at Grand Anse, Grenada, CARICOM leaders took action to ensure the creation of a Single Market and Economy. The Bourne Commission of 1986 was specifically mandated to undertake 'a general perspective study on the development prospects of the CARICOM Region in the context of the fundamental and permanent structural changes taking place in the global environment'. The West Indian Commission Report too is an evaluative study of the Community and its institutions, which offers pointers on the way forward in a global context. From these three indicators alone, it is evident that the Community is aware that the globalisation process demands that the Caribbean develop measures that will ensure that it becomes high quality producers of a range of services which meet our resource capabilities. Owen Arthur points out in *Contending with Destiny: The Caribbean in the Twenty-first Century*, that 'the Caribbean's relative political stability, its long standing investment in human resources, its strategic location, all make a strategy in support of the development of "intelligent exports" both feasible and highly desirable.'[34]

Arthur has shown how some of the emerging developments in the global economy are to the region's advantage. He has pointed out for example, that in the new global economy 'information has replaced energy, commodities and natural resources as the basic raw material in the production process.' This has given rise to a plethora of knowledge based, skills intensive and service oriented production possibilities which can readily be exploited by 'all societies that spare the effort to develop the human capital and the institutional capacity required to master the use of information.' In other words, the globalisation process makes available to any number of countries, opportunities for growth and prosperity. The Caribbean is presented therefore with the opportunity of creating an environment which facilitates the efforts to overcome the disadvantages of history, geography, cultural diversity, weak economies, small size and varied and powerful outside influences to which the countries of the region are subject.

Clive Thomas sees the cultural diversity of the Caribbean region as another distinct advantage.[35] He argues that the increase in CARICOM numbers with the inclusion of Haiti and Suriname increases the advantage with which we can participate in hemispheric groupings such as IADB, the FTAA and the OAS. But an even greater advantage, in his view, may be the enhancement of the region's cultural diversity as it faces the challenges of the new liberal order. Bartilow [36] has also observed that the Caribbean's bargaining power will be enhanced if Cuba is ultimately integrated into CARICOM. Bartilow envisages European involvement in a post-Castro Cuba; this in his view could bring the Caribbean the twin advantages of reinforcing its ties with the EU and countervailing US hegemony in the region.

The Caribbean has other advantages. It is true that the region's importance in global terms has been reduced as a result of globalisation and liberalisation. But this situation compels an assessment of the region's negotiating tools and other assets, which could make a distinct and advantageous difference at the international level. These include its relatively good record of governance and its recognised democratic culture, which could distinguish it as a consensus builder - a key ingredient in any New World Order. Indeed, the region's record of maintaining stable democracies could be one important means of leverage the Community has in arguing the case for developmental assistance, market access and new investments.

CARICOM has the capacity, despite its size, to play a role in the emerging global politics. And, as it demonstrated in the 1970s in such areas as the New International Economic Order, the negotiations for Lomé Agreements and now the Suva Agreement, the region has the ability to bargain for its own sustainability and security in international fora.

Conclusion

Our analysis has shown that the Caribbean has not been slow to recognise the challenges and opportunities presented by the globalisation process. The many revisions of the Treaty of Chaguaramas aim to facilitate consultation and negotiation with stakeholders critical to CARICOM's survival in the regional and global environment. Of major significance is the Treaty's Protocol 1, which provides for the establishment of instruments of governance in the Community, particularly as they relate to the strengthening of the regional integration movement. These instruments include the Single Market and Economy to expedite economic integration, and the Regional Negotiating Machinery (RNM), created to enable the Community to present a united front to the rest of the world. Together, these instruments represent a dynamic movement towards a globally competitive integration exercise. The RNM will not only ensure that the process by which the Caribbean speaks with one voice lxvi [INTRODUCTION]

in economic matters is reinforced, but will also be an asset against the high economic cost of participating in the array of complex negotiations currently taking place across the globe.

The people of the Caribbean through a range of activities have forged links among themselves in the areas of trade, education and culture, and have therefore come to view themselves as one. The Caribbean Community has been the expression of this oneness and so has facilitated the integrated efforts of the region, so that the Community and its peoples can effectively function in the environment of the twenty-first century. But the Community is not an entity to itself. It is part of the larger grouping of small and developing countries which are trying to make their way in the world and to face the challenges of the new century as a single coordinating unit in order to guarantee their interests in the major economic negotiations of this period.

The Community exists as the only instrument available to the Caribbean to facilitate the optimal deployment of its human resources. It therefore behoves the region to act as one, to obey the injunction of history. As Shridath Ramphal once put it: 'We have to sing to the same hymn sheet, not only as CARICOM countries but also as individual members of the CARICOM choir . . . only then will the Region's unified approach to negotiations be truly effective.' [37]

As it faces the new millennium, the Caribbean has demonstrated that it has grown not only in its ability to face the global arena, but also in its ability to deal with its internal arrangements and challenges. Unlike its position in the 1970s when it appeared reluctant to manage crises within its member states, the Community has come to the assistance of St Vincent and the Grenadines, Haiti and Guyana. CARICOM's intervention during the crisis in Guyana after the 1997 elections, is of particular interest and significance.

Following the elections of December 15, 1997 in Guyana, demonstrations were organised by the Opposition People's National Congress (PNC). These demonstrations were held to protest against what were perceived to be election irregularities, but soon mushroomed into major political resistance to the ruling People's Progressive Party (PPP), with the PNC refusing to recognise the former as a legitimate government. The size of the demonstrations rapidly escalated. A number of observers in the region and beyond became concerned about the possible irretrievable breakdown in law and order and the possibility that the PPP administration would be severely tested in its efforts to keep the society stable. Indeed, leading officials of the Caribbean Community became so alarmed over the situation that they decided to send a mission to Guyana to seek an agreement between the two parties. On the day before the arrival of the Caribbean Community mission there were some 40,000 people on the streets of Georgetown. It is now incontrovertible that if CARICOM had not intervened, chaos might have overwhelmed Guyana.

The CARICOM mission, consisting of Shridath Ramphal, Henry Forde and Alister McIntyre, arrived in Guyana on January 14, 1998 and held discussions with the two major political parties. The aim of the mission was 'to reduce tensions, promote harmony and lay the basis for political cooperation in a manner designed to restore Guyana to a state of normalcy.'

The mission saw the resolution of Guyana's political problems as resting on three pillars: political dialogue, constitution reform, and new elections. A moratorium was declared on all demonstrations and an election audit was undertaken. Even though the audit had an inconclusive political result and the dialogue between PNC and the PPP did not dispel the ongoing problems, it must be conceded that the intervention of CARICOM has brought measurable political peace to Guyana and helped to ease the threats to the already ailing economy that a major political crisis would have caused.

Jean Monet, one of the fathers of European integration, says in his insightful and informative memoirs 'I have always believed that Europe would be built through crises, and that it would be the sum of their solutions.' [38] Similarly, the thrust of this discussion has been that CARICOM will be built through crises and that its success and survival will represent the sum of its solutions.

Notes

1. Statement attributed to the late Prime Minister of St Kitts, Paul Southwell
2. Gordon K. Lewis, *Main Currents in Caribbean Thought*, (Johns Hopkins University Press, 1983) p. 329
3. Quoted in Lewis, *Main Currents in Caribbean Thought*, p. 93
4. Quoted in Gordon K. Lewis: *Growth of the Modern West Indies*, (London: MacGibbon & Kee,1968) p. 343
5. Quoted in Christoph Müllerleile, *'CARICOM Integration: Progress and Hurdles'*, (Kingston Publishers Ltd, 1996) p. 35
6. Lewis, *Growth of the Modern West Indies*, p. 366
7. Enrique V. Iglesias, 'The New Face of Regional Integration', p. 20
8. Anthony Payne, 'The Rise and Fall of Caribbean regionalisation', *Journal of Common Market Studies*, XIX:5 (1981) p. 279
9. Susan George, 'A Fate Worse Than Debt', (Penguin, 1994) p. 28
10. Horace A. Bartilow: 'The Debt Dilemma: IMF Negotiations in Jamaica, Grenada and Guyana', MacMillan Education Ltd, 1997, p. xii
11. Bartilow, 'Debt', p. xii

12. Quoted in Christoph Müllerleile, *CARICOM Integration: Progress and Hurdles*, (Kingston Publishers Ltd, 1996) p. 166

13. Alister Mc Intyre, 'CARICOM – Setting Records Straight', *Caribbean Contact*, July 1977 p. 44

14. Trevor Farrell 'Why CARICOM Will Fail – What can be done about it', *Caribbean Contact*, 1977

15. Clive Thomas: 'The Community is a big paper tiger', *Caribbean Contact*, December 1977

16. *Caribbean Contact* January 1978

17. S.S. Ramphal, 'The West Indies in Year 2000', *Caribbean Contact*, March 1979

18. Lewis: *Main Currents*, p. 27

19. Report of A Group of Caribbean Experts: p. 3

20. The Nassau Understanding Declaration of the Fifth Meeting of the Heads of Government Conference of the Caribbean Community, July 1984, p. 2

21. Bourne Commission Report: Caribbean Development to the Year 2000: Challenges, Prospects and Policies, Summary, p. 31

22. Bourne Commission Report p. 14

23. Anthony Payne, 'Whither CARICOM? The Governance and Prospects of Caribbean Integration in the 1980s', *International Journal*, XL:2 (1985) p. 208

24. Havelock Brewster, 'The Report of the West Indian Commission – A Critical Appreciation', *Caribbean Quarterly*, 39:1 p. 37

25. Report of the West Indian Commission: Time for Action, p. 467

26. Duke Pollard, 'The Community: Restructuring for the New Millennium', *CARICOM Perspective*, Vol. 68 (1998) p. 25

27. Payne/Sutton: 'The Commonwealth Caribbean in the New World Order: Between Europe and North America' *Journal of Interamerican Studies and World Affairs*, Vol. 34 No. 4, Winter 1992/93, p.71

28. Payne/Sutton: 'The Caribbean' p. 71; Clive Thomas, 'CARICOM and the New Liberal Order', p. 29

29. Peter Wickham, 'Towards recapturing Popular Sovereignty in the Caribbean through Integration' in *Critical Issues in the Caribbean: Elements of Regional Integration: The Way Forward*, (Ian Randle Publishers, 1998) p. 10

30. S.S. Ramphal, Speech delivered at the dinner held in his honour by CARICOM Council of Ministers, Montego Bay, July 5, 1975, 'To Care For Caricom: The Need For An Ethos Of Community', p. 6

31. Duke Pollard, 'The Community: Restructuring for the New Millennium', *CARICOM Perspective*, Vol. 68 (1998) p. 25

32. S. S. Ramphal

33. The Right Hon. Owen S. Arthur, Prime Minister of Barbados: 'Foreign Policy in the Twenty-first Century: Barbados and the Changing World', p. 3. London, September 28, 1995 the West India Committee Lecture.

34. Prime Minister Owen Arthur, 'Economic Policy Options in the Twenty-First Century in Contending With Destiny: The Caribbean in the 21st Century', p. 23
35. Dr Clive Thomas, 'CARICOM and the New Liberal Order', p. 29
36. Horace A. Bartilow: 'The Debt Dilemma: IMF Negotiations in Jamaica, Grenada and Guyana', p. 142
37. S.S. Ramphal, *CARICOM Perspective*, 67:5, 1997
38. Jean Monet, *Memoirs,* (London: Collins) p. 417

[Part One]

Questions of Survival

[I]

CARICOM
Setting the Record Straight

Alister McIntyre

Recent events indicate that CARICOM is going through a process of profound transition. The impact of changes in the world economy as well as developments within the region itself, have generated a new set of questions about the future directions of the integration movement. These issues constitute a challenge to the intellectual community to take a lead in the search for technical clarity on the options that are open to the region.

It is not for me to recount in any detail, the magnificent contribution that West Indian intellectuals made to the development of the contemporary regional movement. Suffice it to say that the progress from CARIFTA to CARICOM owed a great deal to the body of ideas that was developed in the 1960s about development and integration in this region. The work of Lloyd Best and William Demas on the political economy of transformation and the monumental study of the *Dynamics of West Indian Economic Integration* by Havelock Brewster and Clive Thomas stand out as intellectual landmarks that paved the way for later governmental action.

The regional movement badly needs today, another infusion of intellectual work. Indeed, there is a disturbing tendency in many quarters to return to the uncritical use of the metropolitan models formulated to suit the circumstances of different societies and a different age. Moreover, in too many instances, rhetoric and slogans are taking the place of serious analysis. The academic community owes it to the region at large, to set the standard for public dialogue. After the creative contributions of the 1960s, let it not be said that the 1970s were characterised by intellectual laziness and by a return to intellectual dependence.

If I speak with undue bluntness on this subject, it is because I care deeply about this region and have a high opinion about contributions that the academic community can make to its development.

What then are the new issues about integration to which the intellectual community might usefully address itself? First of all, one must face up squarely to the possibility of continuing difficulties with the balance of payments of our non-oil member countries. It is useful to look at this problem in its global setting.

Over the past three years the combined balance of payments deficit of the non-oil developing countries has tended to be in the vicinity of US$30 billion, as compared with the traditional deficit of US$9 billion. The forecast is that, at present prices, the deficit could reach as much as US$50 billion by 1985. One recent study on prospects for the world economy includes the quantitative scenario which indicates that if the non-oil developing countries continue on their present course, the deficit can approximate to US$190 billion by the end of the century. It is unnecessary to caution an academic audience about the reliability of these numbers. Yet they do indicate what the broad orders of magnitude could be if the terms of trade of the non-oil developing countries continue to deteriorate. Agreement for an effective integrated programme for commodities, including a common fund, can make a useful contribution towards reversing this trend. However, in the final analysis the only enduring solutions can come from accelerated transformation of development in the developing countries concerned, including those in CARICOM.

The international arena has sought to carry out rescue operations (with the $14 billion allocation of the IMF), in an attempt to relieve the present balance of payments pressure on development but it is no substitute for a fundamental reform of the IMF, including an increase in quotas, and progressive adoption of the STR with the development link as the world's reserve asset. Action is also required among the Third World countries themselves to ensure that the recycling of the surpluses of oil exporting countries bring greater benefits to both exporting and importing countries within the developing world.

Caribbean economists can usefully study what mechanisms and arrangements could be employed to achieve this objective, at least, within the context of CARICOM. Within CARICOM itself, arrangements are needed which could, as far as possible, insulate intra-regional trade from the adverse effects of continuing balance of payments disequilibrium.

Given the continuing shortage of foreign exchange it must be expected that imports will have to satisfy the test of essentiality. The basic requirement might be to introduce arrangements for building up intra-regional trade around a core of essential commodities in categories such as, food, fuel, clothing and building materials. Contrary to popular impression, over 70 per cent of intra-CARICOM trade is already concentrated on essential categories. Nonetheless, there still remain substantial opportunities for further import substitution and displacement. A second major task for the future is to adapt institutional structures and modalities to changing development strategies in the region. Some member countries are consciously working towards strategies of development based upon satisfying certain basic needs of the population as a whole. Although basic need strategies is the new fashion in development economics, the idea is not new as far as the English-speaking Caribbean is concerned. My own personal acquaintance with it dates back to discussions at (UWI) Mona in the late 1950s, when Lloyd Braithwaite and Lloyd Best in their work on the 'Economic Development of Trinidad', advocated that greater emphasis should be given to the satisfaction of basic needs in sectors such as food and housing. Nevertheless, the adoption of basic need strategies involves a conscious attempt to regulate levels and patterns of demand especially for final consumer goods and services.

Even where there is not an immediate balance of payments problem in the financial sense, it might be necessary to introduce comprehensive import programming to ensure that available foreign exchange is directed towards satisfying priority needs.

It is often not sufficiently appreciated that a country's balance of payments position cannot be divorced from the level of internal activity. If the CARICOM countries are going to create a meaningful impact on the present problem of unemployment then basic needs strategies, including comprehensive import programming, may be required in all of our member countries whether they are currently experiencing balance of payments deficits or not. This opens up a new era for investigation and advice that can usefully be developed by some of our academic economists.

Recent changes in development policies have raised a third question: whether CARICOM can survive the plurality of social and economic systems in the region. This question requires careful study and analysis since certain misconceptions are being allowed to take root in popular discussions. One misconception is that if a country is moving towards a mixed economy or even a centrally planned economy, then this means that it will contract its trade and other economic links with market economies.

This, of course, is at variance with what is taking place in the world at large where trade, economic, and financial relations between centrally-planned and market economies are rapidly expanding rather than contracting. It is also misleading to suggest that the development of trade and economic relations between CARICOM countries and centrally planned economies will necessarily have an adverse effect on the development of CARICOM itself. This might arise only where bilateral trade and economic agreements between a member country and a third country – whether that third country is a market or planned economy – pre-empted opportunities that would otherwise be open for trade and production complementary between the member country concerned and other CARICOM partner countries.

Such difficulties can be averted by the group approach towards trade and economic arrangements with third countries and groupings. It is contemplated by Article 34 of the Common Market annex to the Treaty of Chaguaramas, and certain procedures have already been agreed on, for dealing with bilateral arrangements. The simple point is that all CARICOM countries, irrespective of ideology, have an interest in diversifying their trade and economic relations with the rest of the world. From another direction, the impression seems to be gaining ground that integration is a peculiarly bourgeois instrument of development, and that the problems of CARICOM are largely derived from its being a grouping of market economies. This is also a half-truth.

There is no evidence that the grouping of centrally planned economies has made greater progress with integration than the grouping of market economies. Consider, for example, the number of years that it has taken for COMECOM to work out a scheme of industrial allocation. From all accounts it was only at the recent meeting in Havana that a specific scheme of allocation was agreed – at least a scheme of allocation including its Caribbean member. In this respect we West Indians tend to be our worst critics. The ink was hardly dry on the CARIFTA Agreement before harsh and strident criticisms were being voiced about the failure to include a comprehensive scheme for industrial allocation which requires much technical work and an even greater input of negotiating skill. In other words, it cannot be accomplished overnight.

While it is true that a planned economic system offers some advantages from the standpoint of integrated development, it is also true that all integration groupings tend to face a similar range of problems, irrespective of the social and economic system of their member states.

I would like to turn briefly to a final question, namely the ranking that CARICOM occupies in the hierarchy of external relations of our individual member states. In principle, integration implies greater intensity in relations with partner states than with third countries and groupings. And this principle is becoming manifest within CARICOM in a number of practical ways. If a member country wants financial assistance with the minimum of conditions, it tends to turn first to a CARICOM partner state. The same holds true for concessional purchases of basic foods or for the provision or loan of equipment or expertise to advance a particular development project. All of this tends to take place with a minimum of documentation and procedures, and on the basis of fairly prompt decision-making.

There is a need to set the public record straight on this point. Persons who are close to the day to day process of cooperation are sometimes puzzled by the comparative generosity with which the rhetoric of brotherhood and solidarity are applied to relatively minor acts of cooperation with third countries. By way of comparison, acts of intra-CARICOM cooperation only occasionally secure public acknowledgement. The public cannot, therefore, be blamed for believing that relations with CARICOM are sometimes placed at the bottom, rather than at the top of the list. Here again, academic investigation can play a useful, educative role. I think that I have said enough to indicate that the subject of integration still offers many fruitful opportunities for the academic world.

Note

Keynote address delivered at the Conference on Contemporary Trends and Issues in Caribbean International Affairs in honour of the tenth Anniversary of UWI's Institute of International Relations, St Augustine, Trinidad. The speech was published in *Caribbean Contact*, July 1977.

[2]

Five Major Problems for CARICOM[1]

Trevor Farrell

I raise here what, in my view, are certain fundamental questions about CARICOM and the premises on which it has been constructed. I believe that many of the specific difficulties, that we face, are really manifestations of deep, underlying, intractable problems which have the potential of destroying the regional integration movement.

The first fundamental problem that I believe confronts us arises from the implicit premises on which the Caribbean Community arrangements have been established. The most essential of these is the notion that economic integration among these territories is feasible and best approached through market integration. It is of course quite true that the desirability of resource integration is explicitly endorsed. However the ethos and the focus of the arrangements are on market integration, and the real implications of resource integration have to this day not been seriously confronted. Effective market integration with a reasonable distribution of the benefits from it, requires two conditions, neither of which are met in the CARICOM territories – developed productive structures and the possession of such structures by most, if not all, of the partner countries in the integration movement.

For example, market integration could be mooted in Western Europe precisely because nearly all of the partner countries had well organised and highly developed production systems to which the advantages of scale economies and consequent rationalisation of production structures could meaningfully be offered. The CARICOM territories satisfy neither of these two criteria. They are characterised by a lack of productive systems. In the region as a whole, the quantum of industry is still very small, especially in the LDCs. Everywhere, as well, the agricultural systems are quite underdeveloped. Furthermore, as we all know, the distribution of such production, as there is, is extremely skewed and on top of all this, regional markets are both small and poor.

The result is predictable. Market integration does not work for many of the territories because they do not have the productive systems to take advantage of expanded markets. The imperative for these territories, specifically the Windwards and Leewards, is to get production going but even basic infrastructure is lacking in most of these countries.

The existing production in these territories has, as a result of our history, been organised and oriented towards metropolitan needs and markets. In a few territories, Jamaica, Trinidad and Tobago and Barbados, the productive systems have been a bit more developed, though arguably in the wrong direction. The result is serious polarisation and the attendant train of bitterness, complaints and disintegration, as several territories quickly found that the presumed economic benefits from integration were not forthcoming at the levels expected.

Given the characteristics of the region at this historical juncture, it seems to me that what is required, first of all, is to get production started. This raises the issues of choice of economic activity; investment in infrastructure; development of human resources; and development of the region's natural resources. However, the kind of economic integration that I believe would really make sense in the region at this time, is resource and production integration. For example, the proposal that easily made the most sense in the whole of the last decade was the proposed aluminium smelter in Trinidad, marrying Trinidad's natural gas to Jamaica's and Guyana's bauxite and alumina. Naturally enough, this was aborted.

This argument is reinforced by market considerations. One of the few real implications of our small size, is our need for trade. Apart from the desirability of trade because of the comparative advantage argument, which holds for any country, and the need for trade to transform the malformed economic structures inherited from colonialism, countries like ours also need trade simply because we physically cannot produce for ourselves everything we need, and because to reap economies of scale we must export much of what we do produce.

Only certain lines of production can, and should, be developed for a purely regional market. For these lines, market integration makes a lot of sense. Some examples are cement, some food items, fishing and sugar. But in the overall context of things, this would be relatively minor, though not insignificant. Much of our major lines of production would have to be oriented towards extra-regional markets and the only kind of integration that has the potential of assisting with this is resource and production integration. Resource and production integration among existing CARICOM territories, however, involves at least two fundamental problems: polarisation with respect to known resources and the distributional-political implications.

The possession of natural resources is of course not essential for efficient and successful production at a high level. Nevertheless, it is true that currently known resources in the region are extremely skewed. This is compounded by the fact that the distribution of population and skills is skewed in exactly the same fashion, and that as a result of historical development, only certain territories enjoy the agglomeration economies that come from the concentration of population and economic activity which are critical to the development of production. Therefore, left to 'natural' or 'market' forces, there can be little doubt that promoting resource-production integration, would lead to serious polarisation in terms of where economic activity would get sited; where population and talent would gravitate towards; and where incomes would tend to grow fastest. It would be the more developed countries, the so-called MDCs, Trinidad and Tobago, Jamaica, Guyana and Barbados.

The distributional issues involved in what is arguably the most sensible approach to integration in the region, raise the most profound political problems. In fact, these issues could only be resolved through a political mechanism – decisions on the location of industry or other economic activity as well as decisions on compensatory transfers if these were to be used. The fact that the most effective way of dealing with the distributional problems would have to involve allowing people to migrate freely intra-regionally are all, at bottom, political decisions, and have to be dealt with on a continuous basis. Even if one were to try to go the other way, that is, resist or ignore natural 'market' forces and the resulting allocations and, instead, attempt to programme and locate economic activity on, say, a basis of 'something for everyone', this would not avoid the political problem.

Apart from the questions of efficiency that would arise, and the need to avoid wasteful duplication, the fact is that to develop any kind of serious production in the smaller territories first necessitates the development of their basic infrastructure, and the development of their human resource base. Who will finance this? If it is financed by the wealthier territories in the region, this allocation raises the same political issues. If it is not financed regionally, who will finance it? My belief is that while resource-production integration is the only approach to integration in the region that makes sense, for it to be effective, a political mechanism that is tantamount to political unification, is needed.

I am aware that talking about political unification in the Caribbean today is not just heretical, but invites the suspicion that one is quite dense. Ever since the demise of the West Indian Federation there has been a strong, psychological drive to avoid confronting the question of political unity in the region. I have often suspected that the framers of the Caribbean Community arrangements approached the problem, similar to that of people who have come through the experience of a divorce. It has been well documented that for some time after it occurs, the parties involved in a divorce tend to have distorted perceptions about what really happened.

After the demise of the Federation, there seemed to be a belief developed that political union could not work and that in any event it could not be approached frontally but one had to sneak up on it. Or, for at least a generation, the issue of political unity should not be re-opened. So, functionalism came to be espoused as a doctrine – whether consciously or unconsciously I do not know. That is, there was a notion that by functional cooperation, we could eventually build the webs of cooperation and trust and shared interests and confidence which would gradually and quietly enmesh us in effective political union. In the same way, market integration was espoused. Again, if it worked, economic and political interests would have been built with a stake in the regional arrangements. Of course, there were other intellectual influences at work, and other perceptions, but from what little I have heard or read about the history of those years and the climate of ideas, it seems that these kinds of notions were very widely held. The problem is, that this strategy has not worked. I believe that we have never confronted psychologically why we are really interested in integrating this region – and this particular group of Caribbean countries.

I would like to suggest that our basic motivation is not economic at all. That is, the value of economic integration, whether market integration or resource-production integration is not in fact the real starting point for us. Because from a purely economic point of view, there is more reason for Jamaica to be interested in economic integration with Cuba or Puerto Rico, than with Montserrat or Grenada. There is more reason for Trinidad and Tobago to be interested in arrangements with Venezuela and Guyana (remember, the interest in arrangements need not be mutual) than with Dominica or Antigua. For the LDCs, it is true, there may be logical economic reasons for an interest in integration with some of the MDCs. But for the larger territories certainly, neither the imperatives of market nor of resource integration would logically dictate the choice of partners we have made.

In fact, I believe that subconsciously we chose our partners first, and then secondarily began to worry consciously about the economics of the relationship. In other words, Caribbean integration is a lot like many modern marriages. Arguably, the real basis and impetus for our integration is cultural. It is a sense of commonality, of shared identity, of being the same people. It is also very specific. It does not cover the whole of the Caribbean, just a particular group of territories.

It is true that this feeling is inconstant, it is fitful and it is rather vague. Its strength also varies between territories. It is strongest in the Eastern Caribbean. It is weakest in Jamaica. In fact, if we liken the region to a spread-out hand, Jamaica would be the thumb, joined to the others, but always somewhat apart. But at the same time, this sense of 'Caribbeanness' is enduring. The problem is that failure to identify and articulate the real basis of our relationship has created and will continue to create problems. For example, the CARICOM arrangements though affirming our determination 'to consolidate and strengthen the bonds which have historically existed among us,' in the first paragraph of the preamble [of the Chaguaramas Treaty] ends up emphasising the economic relationship.[2]

It is clear, even to an academic, that the development of an effective regional political mechanism, or of political union is not on the cards at present. It should, however, be equally clear that the present road on which we are embarked is not propitious either. Arguably, it might even be termed a dead end. It is also obvious that the development strategies that we have espoused and tried in the region over the last 25–30 years have not worked. This is not the place to go into why they have failed. What I would like to point out here, however, is what the impact of the present crisis of strategy is, or seems to be.

The failure of the strategy of inviting in foreign capital and espousing domestic capitalist development has led to the rejection, in some quarters, of not just the whole system and the philosophies that provided its intellectual justification, but of the relationship with the international system which had developed, and particularly the nature and forms of the relationship with the West. In some quarters, therefore, (and it is stronger in some countries than in others), there is the search for new forms of social and economic organisation and for new relationships. Thus capitalism is rejected, socialism espoused, the West and imperialism denounced and rejected, and new relationships sought and developed with the socialist countries or with other states. In other quarters the old ideologies and strategies continue to hold sway, and even intensify their hold. The result is intense and even bitter conflict within and between states of the region. Further, and what is even more dangerous, is the form in which the debate is posed – in terms of ideology and alliances. This excites the attention of extra-regional powers and invites increased penetration of the region by them as they seek to influence its direction in their own interests.

Placing socialism in opposition to capitalism and east to west brings the Cold War into the region with seriously invidious consequences. American penetration of the region has, for example, increased sharply over the last year. There is expanded American military activity; more intelligence activity; increased penetration by the foundations and other arms of the American politico-military machinery; and greater manipulation of domestic politics. This is in clear response to the direction that is being taken by some countries in the region and to US perceptions and fears of increased Russian and Cuban influence. For the same reasons Venezuela is showing increasing concern about the region.

I believe this to be a most dangerous development and a very serious threat to the integration of the region. The ideological conflict in the region, which is fundamentally a conflict over developmental strategies produced by the poverty crisis in most of the CARICOM territories, is bad enough. There is group to group opposition within states and now, state to state opposition. We are all familiar with the complex of various conflicts involving Trinidad and Tobago, Barbados, Jamaica, Guyana, Grenada, St Vincent and Antigua over the last year and what this has done to the integration movement. But when the Americans and Venezuelans move in and intensify their attempts at manipulating and determining domestic political and economic developments, in some territories, and the Russians or Cubans do the same in others, the implications are clear.

Historically, the Caribbean has been a place where other people have come to fight their wars. In earlier centuries it was 'peace in Europe, but no peace beyond the line'. The disorganisation, balkanisation, poverty and backwardness of our region today are eloquent testimony to the price we paid for that. Today, the same thing is happening again. The results will be even worse. And one of the first casualties is bound to be the regional integration movements as states fragment, in different ways become enemies and ultimately even go to war with each other. It is imperative that we find a way to prevent this centrifugal force from gaining further momentum if we wish the prospects for integration not to be extinguished.

The last problem with which I wish to deal is the problem of our political institutions in the region. Although I am unqualified to deal with this issue, it has become increasingly clear to me, that our economic arrangements are precariously dependent on a very fragile political base.

To my mind, there are three basic political problems we face. The first is that the regional migration movement is much too dependent on the political will of the region's politicians, who have their own shortcomings. This relates to the second factor – the way in which these politicians come to the fore, as well as the backward political culture of the region. The third problem is that the situation is likely to get worse. The crisis over development strategy, and our failures so far, combined with the weakness of our institutions in many areas, and the backwardness of our political culture, provides all the ingredients for political instability and for the emergence of fascist regimes, totalitarianism and a variety of political excesses. If the integration movement is to survive, I believe much more attention is going to have to be given to the development of our political institutions in the region. It might be noted paradoxically, that political unity would undoubtedly prove to be an excellent prophylactic against some of the political excesses that we have already begun to witness. I do not have the solutions to the fundamental problems I have raised. In one area though, I believe we can do certain concrete things.

Any strategy for making the regional movement more viable, has to address both the centripetal and the centrifugal forces at work. I have no answer for tackling the centrifugal forces identified above. But there is a lot more that we can do to strengthen the centripetal force of shared identity, commonality and cultural integration. In the final analysis, the most potent impetus towards greater integration and greater unification is the power of the *'idea'*. I believe that the regional institutions can quietly and effectively build the idea of the West Indian nation in a variety of ways. Functional cooperation is a good idea, but it is not enough, nor has it been developed as far as it can go.

The first and most basic strategy is to build regional institutions and organisations which are independent of the Governments even for finance. Easily, the most successful West Indian institution is the West Indies cricket team. It is a world-class organisation that is currently the best in the world. A study of the characteristics of the West Indian cricketing organisation suggests the following:

1. It is not controlled by Governments – neither the politicians nor their bureaucrats. It is not subject to day-to-day political whim, or to ignorance or bureaucratisation.
2. It is financially independent and it constantly faces the test of the market.
3. It is a meritocracy – even when personnel choices are unpopular or even if some wrong decisions are made, the guiding ethos for the last two decades has been the pursuit of merit.

4. It is constantly facing outward to the wider world. Its performance is stimulated by the quality of the competition it has to meet. It is in constant contact with that competition, and oriented and motivated to deal with it. It is not protected from competition by any tariff barriers or negative lists.
5. It is an organisation with traditions, with culture, whose top officials while self-perpetuating bear this culture within them.

I believe that as far as possible, this institution provides an excellent model for the creation of Caribbean organisations in art, finance, education etc. The universities of the region (UWI and UG) would operate much better if they were divorced from the Governments, and instead of the Governments paying their bills, they were to charge market rates, while the Governments subsidise students with scholarship awards.

To develop the sense of 'West Indianness', is key to the success of the region; it is important to build people's contacts. I have been very impressed while travelling through Europe in the summer to see the hordes of young Europeans criss-crossing those countries. The implications for the future are profound. The next generation of European political, business, intellectual and cultural leaders will be thoroughly familiar with 'their' continent. The British will be as at home with Germans as with the Welsh; Frenchmen will be as conversant with the British and Belgians as with the French. Italians will know Holland as intimately as they know Rome. This will have a profound effect on their concerns, on their perspectives, and on their reactions to events occurring anywhere in those countries. These are people who have fought each other, and rivalled each other for centuries. They are possessed of distinctive cultures, traditions and histories. They are not one people, in the way that West Indians are one people. Yet, they are moving apace in that direction.

I have also been impressed with the sense of 'Caribbeanness' that one finds in the officials and technocrats of the regional institutions such as the CARI-COM Secretariat, the Caribbean Development Bank (CDB) and the University of the West Indies. It seems to me to be very important to promote cheaper regional travel (student fares for examples), to promote more regional sporting organisations, more regional union activities and more regional professional associations. Over time, the impact will be tremendous. For example, it has become clear to me, that summer internships for university students in territories other than their campus territories, could be enormously useful to all concerned. They can help with things like statistical work – which is very underdeveloped in the LDCs – in return for board and lodge. They will do beneficial work; gain experience and an education; integrate work with study and learn their region. I have seen this work very successfully in Grenada in 1979.

What would be important to fostering the regional movement too, would be for the regional institutions to foster a regional radio station, and/or television network, and/or newspaper. They should be independent of the control of any Government; they should be self-financing and made to face the test of the market; and they should be capable of reaching the entire region. I would suggest too that, at present, it would be prudent to site any and all such facilities in Barbados). Finally, and perhaps heretically, I believe it is time to begin to articulate the idea, the question of a unified West Indies once again. I don't believe it is likely to come about right now, but ideas can become embedded in people's consciousness, and eventually their time can come. And the only way to ever do something is to start.

Notes

1. Excerpt from a presentation titled, *The Caribbean Community – The View of a Heretic* by Dr Trevor Farrell who submitted a memorandum, by invitation, to the Demas team set up to review the functioning of the region's integration movement and to make recommendations for its improvement in the decade of the 1980s. This excerpt was first published in *Caribbean Contact*, March 1981.
2. Treaty of Chaguaramas.

[3]

Three Areas of Regional Crisis

Norman Girvan

As CARICOM enters its fifth year, there are three main expressions of the crisis which, it is now generally recognised, threaten to tear it asunder.

The first is the overwhelming financial pre-eminence of Trinidad and Tobago. The second is the acute financial and balance of payments difficulties afflicting Guyana and Jamaica. The third is the bitterness and disillusionment felt by the Less Developed Countries (LDCs). Of the three, the overwhelming financial pre-eminence of Trinidad and Tobago is the most disturbing because it is breeding an attitude of superiority and arrogance among the ruling groups in that country, both in business and in bureaucratic circles. Call it the arrogance of petro-power. The attitude, as Trevor Farrell outlined in a previous *Caribbean Contact* article, is that 'it serves them (Jamaica and Guyana) right for adopting socialist and Third World posturing; our sensible and prudent policies have brought us prosperity'. The irony, though, as Farrell points out, is that Trinidad and Tobago pursued oil policies that were among the most reactionary of the oil-producing countries and, on the eve of the oil crisis of 1973, was in a position very similar to that of Guyana and Jamaica today.

In any economic community, great disparities in economic and financial power are of course a danger to cohesiveness. In this case there is an additional danger. The danger is that Trinidad and Tobago's oil surpluses under the

guise of financing intra-CARICOM trade, will be used to maintain temporarily, a kind of trade-based integration that is economically unsatisfactory
and, for that reason, politically unfeasible. The aim would be to buy time, as
it were, for a viable model.

It should be clearly understood that Trinidad and Tobago's financial
assistance to its CARICOM partners is in reality financial assistance to its own
manufacturing class – to enable it to maintain exports to the region in the face
of the other countries' balance of payments difficulties. From the point of view
of the recipient countries, it can be seen as the lever used by the transnational
corporations, in alliance with the Trinidad manufacturers, to defeat Jamaica's
and Guyana's restrictions on imports of inessential goods. From the point of
view of the integration process, a far more appropriate use of that country's
petro dollars, would be to invest them in integration industries forged from
agreements on industrial complementarity. These are industries using the
indigenous resources of the region, designed and engineered from regional
technology, and meeting the basic needs strategy through an expanded
Caribbean Development Bank, whose rules and structure would have been
modified to reduce the preponderant influence of its metropolitan patrons.

The balance of payments crisis of Jamaica and Guyana stem from a process
that is common to both – the attempt to pursue socialist policies, that is, the
expansion of the state sector together with populist social welfare programmes, which has been overtaken by an acute crisis in the external sector.
Caught in the grip of rising oil prices and general world inflation on the one
hand, and falling sugar prices and world recession on the other, compounded
with rapidly growing public expenditure, and bloodied by the USA antagonism of 1976, these countries' experiments in socialism, now stand in grave
economic peril. In this context, therefore, their COMECON initiatives cannot
properly be seen as an alternative to their CARICOM ties. They are rather a
last desperate attempt to find additional options at a time when the room in
which to manoeuvre is shrinking fast. These initiatives indicate how marginal
are CARICOM ties to the economic structures of these countries, which
remain overwhelmingly dominated by their relationships with the imperialist
economic system. In that sense, the CARICOM relationships of Jamaica and
Guyana, more specifically their relationships with Trinidad and Tobago,
constitute an aspect of their relations with the metropolitan capitalist countries, for whom Trinidad and Tobago is merely a financial and production
relay station. As long as these islands seek accommodation from the traditional
Western financial capitals, their COMECON initiatives will not progress
beyond the normal diplomatic and economic intercourse of sovereign nations,
as Brewster puts it.

The fundamental problems affecting these countries are therefore neither about CARICOM nor COMECON. Rather, they relate to the political economy of their internal developments and of their relationship with the imperialist countries, especially the USA. The questions are whether Jamaican democratic socialism will survive, or maintain its momentum, within the framework of an agreement with the International Monetary Fund; or if Guyanese socialism is doomed to fail and degenerate in the face of acute racial fragmentation and antagonism. Or what will be the effect of President Carter's initiatives at ending USA's Cold War with the Caribbean, and what alterations does this imply for Jamaica's and Guyana's internal and external stance.

The Less Developed Countries of the region have been the most vocal and bitter critics of the defects of the CARICOM process. A cynic would say that this hardly matters, since the LDCs account for only five percent of the region's production. But the idea of a Caribbean Community goes beyond the economic; it extends to the geopolitical as well. If it fails as an economic community then its geopolitical objectives can hardly be achieved.

The LDCs main hope was to secure the kind of import-substitution, for the regional market, that the MDCs had secured in the 1960s for their national markets through policies of industrialisation by invitation. Instead the opposite occurred. LDC imports from the metropolitan countries were progressively re-routed, under the CARICOM treaty, through manufacture (assembly) in Jamaica and Trinidad, eventually reaching the LDCs, frequently at higher prices. The LDCs have failed to enjoy even the limited, 'finishing-touch' industrialisation secured by the MDCs on a very limited scale. This was predicted by the celebrated Brewster-Thomas study. The CDB's investments in infrastructure are therefore poor consolation to the LDCs, for little industry is coming to use the infrastructure being created.

In spite of this, I cannot agree with my friend Trevor Farrell when he argues that the existence of these island communities makes no economic-technological sense, and that we should face up to the necessity to, in effect, liquidate them as part of a broader rationalisation of population within a Caribbean political and economic union. The evidence of history everywhere is that there are few things to which human beings cling so tenaciously as the sense of community and ethnicity. This is so even after long lasting political union, and in the most technologically advanced societies. Take the case of the United Kingdom. Political union for over three hundred years, a common language and religion, for the most part a single land mass, complete freedom of movement of labour, and two centuries of industrial revolution; yet Scottish and Welsh nationalism remain as strong as ever. Indeed, these forces are growing. Or take the case of the Bretons of France, the Basques of Spain, the

Flemish of Belgium and so on. Nor does socialist revolution abolish the sense of nationality/community: In Yugoslavia, the prospect of Tito's death is viewed with grave apprehension as possibly signalling the break-up of the fragile federation of different peoples. And any visitor to the Soviet Union is immediately made aware of the existence not only of the 15 republics, but also of over 100 different nationalities. To argue that these communities should be 'decanted' because of the alleged imperatives of techno-economics is a form of technological determinism gone mad. There will always be a sense of Vincentian, St Lucian or Antiguan community, and the land base is essential to this sense.

The real alternative, difficult as it might seem, is to import techno-economics to these communities. To devise strategies and solutions for sustainable development – evidenced, for example, in the provision of basic social and public services, food, shelter, full employment, and a basic minimum standard of living – all within the framework of some kind of Caribbean association where larger industries, and a defence capability, are organised. The crisis in the Caribbean Community stems from its original defects in conception, structure and strategy, as Brewster, Thomas and Farrell all underline, albeit with different emphases. But the crisis has sharpened at this particular time because of the wider crisis in the international capitalist system, characterised by rising oil prices, falling commodity prices, world inflation and world recession, all tending to check the momentum of dependent economic expansion upon which depended intra-CARICOM trade and thus the illusion of a successful community. And one must honestly state that the political and economic preconditions for a new initiative in CARICOM-building do not appear to exist as CARICOM enters its fifth year. This is reflected in the weakness of hitherto powerful pro-CARICOM forces in the region.

Michael Manley and Forbes Burnham are preoccupied with their internal problems. The Community's senior regional technocrats, men who have invested a large part of their professional careers in the CARICOM idea, appear depressed and demoralised as the carefully woven fabric of ten years begins to come apart at the edges. The academics, recognised as a vanguard in the development of the regional economic integration concept, now condemn CARICOM to a man. To hold out short-term, or even long-term hope for the community in its present form, in the face of all the evidence, is to fail to face reality and to set oneself up for further disillusionment.

The real danger is that the baby will be thrown out with the bathwater; that the idea of the Caribbean will be discredited in the eyes of the region's population because of the frustrations of CARICOM, coming relatively hard upon the heels of the bitter tragedy of the West Indies Federation. Indeed, it is likely that we cannot avoid a period of disenchantment with the idea of Caribbean association, and an intensification of competitive unilateral actions by the various states. But the idea of Caribbean association, just like the sense of community, dies hard. Historically, it has recurred after every initiative failed to bear fruit. And there is an important reason for this. We are, all of us, relatively small communities sprawled over a large sea, located in the very backyard of the most powerful imperialist nation on earth, and bounded to the south and west by the large Hispanic-American world. We have all been imperialised by the North Atlantic for centuries.

Geopolitical factors dictate that we cannot attain any degree of authentic sovereignty, no matter how modest, without some form of Caribbean association. And this sovereignty is in turn indispensable to the internal socioeconomic liberation for which our peoples are constantly struggling, no matter how difficult or torturous the route may seem.

Note

This article was published in *Caribbean Contact*, August 1977.

[4]

CARICOM's
Soft Belly

Ramesh Ramsaran

Development thought and policy have always been deeply influenced by the experience of the industrial countries. Economic integration, of course, is one of the prominent areas that comes to mind. The formation of the European Economic Community (EEC) was quick to excite the imagination of academics and policy makers in developing countries, who lost little time in trying to adapt the concept to the problems faced in these areas.

Fascinated by the advantages of a larger market, the scepticism of the neo-classicals were easily dispelled, or rationalised away, by the prevailing economic and social conditions, and in the face of the narrow options facing small economies. The packages took different forms depending on the guiding perspectives and the interest involved. The most widespread version varied little from the European concept. However, the pitfalls and weaknesses inherent in this approach, from the point of view of developing countries, did not elude all observers, some of whom sought, where the opportunity provided itself, to fundamentally modify what was essentially a free trade idea by focusing on the area of production. The works done in this respect by UWI economists with reference to the Commonwealth Caribbean is well known, as is the fate they have suffered in the interest of short-term political expediency.

The views on these studies vary considerably; some people argue that many of the ideas put forward, while theoretically sound, are impracticable in the

22

present circumstances of the Caribbean. Others see the approach advocated as not being fundamentally opposed, or in conflict with, what has been used as a basis for launching CARIFTA and later CARICOM. A common argument is that one of CARICOM's objectives, is the eventual integration of production structures in the region, even though the present preoccupation may not point convincingly in that direction. This view persists in some quarters despite conflicting evidence from the recent attempt at industrial complementarity with respect to bauxite.

There is no doubt that some of the leading technicians have worked unceasingly to produce a model that transcends the limits of the free trade idea by proposing measures and drawing attention to the need for coordinated policies which could advance the development of the region. Many of these proposals, however, have remained largely on paper. So, while expectations remain high, in terms of the 'goods' integration can deliver, the structure as it exists is increasingly being accepted as incomplete and unsatisfactory, though often for different reasons. In this connection it is important to point out that the present crisis which has developed within CARICOM should not be viewed purely as the product of external and internal conditions reflecting on the balance of payments position of two of the major member states. This factor may have served to hasten the crisis which has exposed the 'soft belly' of CARICOM. A stalemate, however, has clearly been on the horizon for some time, if we are to judge by the number of unresolved issues and the clear dissatisfaction that exists in some quarters.

A long-term solution to the problems facing CARICOM does not revolve around the return of Guyana and Jamaica to a favourable balance of payments position, (though this would help allay the present difficulties), but upon its willingness to correct some of the obvious deficiencies in its organisation and style, and institute policies which can protect and encourage regional development. For although under the present arrangements, the value of intra-regional trade has expanded, domestic economic conditions in member states have not experienced any significant improvement as a result of this trade expansion. In fact, the more developed countries in the group, particularly Trinidad and Tobago, Jamaica and Barbados, account for the bulk of this expansion. Even leaving aside this unsatisfactory distribution of trade benefits (which was expected given the differences in industrial development among participating states), discerning observers are not prepared to accept this increase in trade as an index of progress in the integration process.

The reason for the dissatisfaction is clear. Such commercial growth as has taken place has not been accompanied by any significant changes in the traditional patterns of the input-output matrices of the countries concerned.

Domestic value added remains minimal in many cases, not only because of the lack of effort in identifying and developing local inputs where they exist, but because of the particular policy framework which continues to encourage the use of foreign material in various stages of manufacture or processing. The business class itself often finds it more profitable to use non-local inputs and peddle foreign goods than to explore local potential. In this environment, foreign firms have found it easy to penetrate the integration market. This has been made even easier in the context of an ethic, in which each member state tries to outsmart the other.

One of the consequences of these dynamics is that the integrated development of the region and the policies required to give effect to this goal have become subsumed in the scramble to protect and advance national interests, or what is perceived to be national interest. This development is not only, in a sense, the logical outgrowth of the present approach to integration, but it also betrays the perceptions and reveals the expectations that underlie the CARICOM undertaking. CARICOM to many, would have served its purpose, if it facilitated the expansion of national industrial sectors which were set up within the protected and limited framework of individual countries. This it clearly did for a time, and up to a point. But it is not surprising that with the first real threats to the simple marketing arrangements, CARICOM is regarded as dead or dying, in some quarters and funeral orations are starting to be prepared.

This situation must cause some consternation in the ranks of those who regard CARICOM as not yet fully out of the womb. It is obvious, however, that the perspectives are different: one rooted in a short-term, opportunistic motive; and the other in the hope that the total structure (yet to be evolved) would measure up to the problems facing the area. The group associated with the latter tends to see the present difficulties largely as teething problems. It would be futile, however, to pretend that there does not exist a real fear in the region that the whole structure, as it exists, is about to collapse. The failure of some of its leading institutions to function, gives credence to this fear.

The noticeable silence of sectors and organisations in the regional community at large, to voice their views on the events unfolding, is disturbing, but in a sense understandable. Trade unions, consumer bodies, professional organisations, and others, have not shown optimal interest in the proceedings so far. Part of this indifference may stem from their own lack of interest in the concept of economic integration. It may be partially explained by the way that the whole exercise has been carried out by officialdom. Another reason may be what is perceived to be the disadvantages inherent in CARICOM.

In the early stages of the movement one of the arguments put forward in support of the integration idea was that it would increase competition among producers, which would in turn lead to lower prices and better quality goods. Longer production runs made possible by the larger market would also assist in this direction. The importance of this expectation can be seen in that from the time CARICOM was launched there have been complaints in all member states about the unduly high prices and the poor quality of goods foisted upon consumers. These complaints, which have both national and regional dimensions, have generated a series of charges and counter charges which have not been properly looked into. The price formation process in the Caribbean, still heavily dependent on foreign sources for a wide range of inputs and final goods, remains a neglected area of study.

To be sure, the integration effort in the Caribbean has had its share of misfortune. The incidence, that prices began to experience an unusual rate of increase (due to a combination of factors) just about the time CARICOM was being conceived, has given rise to the feeling that this institution has created a more established framework for the exploitation of the consumer. The LDCs in particular have been quite vociferous on this point, arguing that the actual changes far exceed the increases warranted by circumstances. And so far, the contentions between suppliers and consumers have taken a minor place in relation to the widening rift between the MDCs and the LDCs. This is a sore area and solutions offered range from exerting greater effort to help the poorer members, to completely jettisoning these islands since they are not of any economic value to the movement, and may well be a drag on the whole process.

Strangely enough, many of the LDCs themselves have often threatened to leave the group. A former Secretary General of CARICOM, Alister McIntyre, has tried to rationalise their participation by saying that the LDCs should not look at their own growth rates in relation to those achieved by the MDCs, but in relation to what their rates might have been had they opted to stay out. But since it is not possible to be in and out of CARICOM at the same time, it is difficult to make this kind of comparison, though one could speculate on the basis of the prospects facing a loner and the deprivation of prerogatives and assistance being received as a member.

The problem of polarisation has no easy solutions. Un-equality, it should be pointed out, is not peculiar to integration movements. It is occurring at the world level where there is a widening gap between rich and poor countries. It is a problem that is endemic to integration movements since it would be difficult to find a group of countries with equal levels of development in the same region. But, it clearly takes on extreme proportions in situations where there is no deliberate planning or serious attempts to control unbridled market forces within the grouping. Mechanisms may be instituted to counter the effects of the forces by giving an artificial advantage to the less advantaged members. These measures, however, can only be pushed so far. In a situation where all members are poor, the relatively richer countries will not easily allow their initial advantages to be lost. In the final analysis the course taken and the strategies adopted will depend on the particular perspective of development embraced, and the political conceptualisation of nation and community building.

The MDC/LDC dichotomy derives from a particular kind of thinking of which we are well aware, and which influences the entire regional effort. The LDCs surround themselves in a web of whims and fancies that sometimes bear little relationship to the reality of social and economic conditions. Out of this situation has grown the kind of insular nationalism and selfishness which now threatens to tear the region apart. It is little wonder that many of the region's intellectuals, who have long advocated and toiled for a regional strategy of development, have withdrawn or exiled themselves from the entire process.

Many of the problems currently being faced by CARICOM can be attributed directly to the lack of political will to make the institutions work. This has existed for some time, and recent events have only served to exacerbate the situation. Although several dedicated persons, bent on saving the integration idea, have called for new theoretical efforts from the region's intellectuals, many others, equally concerned, do not think this is necessary. The options, they argue, are there. They have always been there. Perhaps, quite unconsciously, they surmise that what is being asked for is a theoretical underpinning of CARICOM, not so much as it was conceived, but of how it has been made to operate and to serve ends for which it was not intended.

Note

This article first appeared in *Caribbean Contact*, October 1977.

[5]

The Community is a Big
Paper Tiger

Clive Thomas

Two sets of factors have played determining roles in the formation of
CARIFTA and later CARICOM. Both of these are responsible for the
enduring weaknesses and contradictions of the so-called integration experiment. The first set of factors centres on the political initiative of Guyana in
the establishment of CARIFTA. This is clearly reflected in the establishment
of the Community Secretariat there. The second set of factors centres on the
class and economic interests which have directed the mechanisms through
which the integration movement has unfolded.

Why did Guyana take the political initiative? Shortly after the American
Government had supported the ousting of Jagan and the installing of the
People's National Congress (PNC) regime in Guyana, the Government was
anxious to improve its political position and legitimise its American-backed
seizure of independence. Caribbean integration undoubtedly aided its political position in the region, where because of fears of Marxist attachments, Jagan
and the People's Progressive Party (PPP) were traditionally quite weak. In
addition, within Guyana, the aspiration of the masses for Caribbean integration is widely held. This support cuts across traditional racial and party lines
and the Government no doubt thought that this would speed up its legitimi-
sation. Furthermore, given the racial composition and ideology of the PNC,
Burnham no doubt saw in Caribbean integration, and eventually immigration,
the long-term solution to the minority racial position of the PNC in Guyana.

Initially, the class and economic interests which were to dominate the integration movement were reluctant, if not outright suspicious, of the Guyana initiative. This position was however, quickly reversed and within a short span of time the integration movement was dominated by the need to provide the opportunities for expansion of the transnational corporations of the region, and the local classes in alliance with them. This position was crystallised as soon as the (MDCs) recognised the opportunities which integration would create for the promotion of exports within the region and the consequent rationalisation of the location of their plants and other productive facilities. This meant that Jamaica and Trinidad and Tobago, where transnational capital was most highly developed, exerted the dominant influence in shaping the bread and butter aspects of the integration movement.

One important development, which supported both of these factors, was the threatened imperial-colonial abandonment of the region by Britain, as she vigorously pursued entry into the European Common Market. Consequent upon this action, integration appeared to be more and more attractive in its potential to minimise regional disruption, at this time. Because these two sets of factors dominated the formation of the integration movement, certain features were inevitably and immediately written into the arrangements. The first of these was that from its earliest beginnings in CARIFTA, the integration movement stressed one basic principle. That is, to liberalise trade in order to widen the market, improve the scope for the development of capitalism in the region, and thereby to stimulate private accumulation – both foreign and local.

The subsequent, much publicised attempts to 'deepen' the integration movement by creating CARICOM did not alter this basic feature. CARICOM and other changes led to two essential developments. The first was to ensure a broad uniformity in the regional market for capitalist exploitation. The common external tariff, which CARICOM introduced, was designed to achieve this. The second was to develop a harmonious regional, as against divisive national, system of capital subsidisation. The unsuccessful efforts to harmonise fiscal incentives to capital, reflect this tendency.

Underwriting the position of the transnationals in the region has also meant, at the ideological level, endorsement of the developmentalist ideology which favour capitalism as the only solution to the poverty of the region. This in turn has created a favourable atmosphere for the development and consolidation of the class interests of the rapidly rising national bourgeoisie within the area. The converse of this development has been the total exclusion of worker-peasant interests and ideology in the promotion of the integration movement. This has meant the absence of a socialist perspective and the entrenchment of an authoritarian centralist state-directed process at the service of capitalism.

A further legacy of its origins is the important role that undisguised political opportunism has played in the unfolding of the integration movement. Every state in the region has betrayed this tendency. Guyana, we have already seen. Jamaica's switch from hostility to support for integration has followed the recognition of the scope it offered its growing business class. And recently as it has had to resort to borrowing from Trinidad and Tobago to ease its balance of payments crisis, it has become the most ardent integrationist state! Similarly Trinidad and Tobago's cynicism and arrogance towards its regional partners have grown along with its petro-dollars. All this too is a class phenomenon rooted in the class character of the ruling regimes of the region.

Because the basic emphasis has been on capitalist and market-directed development certain weaknesses of the integration movement were readily apparent. The most important of these was that the so-called rich countries would benefit more from integration than the poorer ones if everything was left to market solutions. As such a development would create the possibility of nationalist reactions, the integration movement has sought to provide a variety of so-called 'compensating mechanisms'. Among the most important of these are: the Caribbean Development Bank (CDB), the Caribbean Investment Corporation, the Agricultural Marketing Protocol and the Guaranteed Market Schemes, the special regimes of tariff reductions for the Leewards and Windwards and so on. Added to these, the integration movement has embraced already existing regional institutions, for example, the University of the West Indies (UWI) and the West Indies Shipping Corporation. It has also created or proposed to create some new ones, such as the Regional Food Corporation, the Balance of Payments Facilities, the Aluminium Corporation, the Process List, and a Common Regime on Foreign Investment.

Looking at the range of institutions created, it is difficult to resist the temptation to describe the whole integration edifice as a *paper tiger*. As the difficulties of integration have been encountered a new paper institution was proposed as the solution. Many of these paper institutions: the process list, the aluminium plant, and the proposed agreement on foreign investments are yet to leave the files. Others such as UWI, the Shipping Corporation, the Agricultural Marketing Protocol are dressed-up agreements from the colonial pre-Carifta period. There is no end of publicity behind each of these institutions. Some even suggest, and I take the opportunity of personally refuting this, that such developments are in accordance with the so-called Brewster-Thomas strategy.

The real source of crisis lies in the social contradictions within CARICOM. The first and most important of these is that the limited class basis on which development of the region is resting and which CARICOM has sought to reinforce, is incapable of solving the problems of poverty and dispossession in the region. The second contradiction is that these class interests, although generally dominant, are not necessarily homogenous. There are sectional interests which contend with each other. Thus the small up and coming bourgeoisie at times resent the dominance of transnational monopolies. Also capitalist interests in commerce may resent restrictions on imports in order to aid import-substitution, whereas the manufacturing class engaged in assembly and fabrication support state restrictions. In some territories the landlords have sought to develop and redirect their capital to commerce and screwdriver industries.

However the sectional difference that is most important of all is that between those who support a state-capitalist form of development and those who favour private capitalist interests. This difference reflects itself in the ideological field principally in the call for socialism in Guyana and, to a lesser extent, Jamaica. State-capitalist oriented development in these countries favours a very active role for the state in economic life. It favours nationalisation by purchase agreement, and state control of external and internal trade. It also favours trade with the socialist bloc. The consequence of these tendencies is to push the market into the background, to substitute state negotiation for open market purchase and also to substitute state production for that of the private firm. This type of development contradicts the CARICOM arrangements which pre-suppose the existence of markets as the basic regulatory form. In this way this contradiction is the source of most of the emerging difficulties at the present stage of integration.

The third contradiction is that the ruling petty bourgeoisie of the region have a particular style of politics. The emphasis is on manipulation, opportunism and authoritarianism. There is a marked hostility to mass participation in the political process and incipient repressive tendencies are strong. Everywhere they can, they subvert the electoral and political process. Such groups contain a natural distrust of other leaders because they see a reflection of themselves and therefore know the depths of political corruptibility which are possible. They find it hard to work on the basis of consensus politics.

The other rule by which the political élites of the region operate, is to minimise their degree of cooperation in maintaining the new political structure by operating as a trade union collective of the established political parties. This does not mean that 'official' opposition parties cannot become ruling parties. On the contrary, they too share in the collective rule, and recent developments in Jamaica, Antigua and Barbados testify to this. What the collaboration seeks to ensure is that those political parties and groupings which are prepared to operate outside of the existing framework of politics, those struggling to create a new political and social order, will have to contend with the mortal hostility of the entire existing, regional, political establishment. It is in this fundamental sense, therefore, that the movement from 'flag' independence to the development of a progressive, socialist alternative in the Caribbean will find the existing CARICOM arrangement a serious, although not insurmountable, political obstacle.

Given this social reality we can anticipate an intensification of three tendencies within the region. The first will be the continued proliferation of paper tigers. Secondly there will be the burgeoning growth of a regional bureaucracy. Experiences in other neo-colonial states support this expectation. The third development to anticipate is attempts to accommodate, redefine, and manipulate the people's struggle to control and own regional resources.

Already a number of policies have been pursued: 'West Indianisation' of senior staff in the multinational firms, localisation through the issue of local shares, state participation in shareholding, the establishment of a competing state-owned enterprise, and in recent times even occasional nationalisation by purchase agreement. None of these policy measures are fundamentally anti-imperialist or pro-socialist. All they seek to achieve is some local variant of state capitalism. To that extent they are part of the measures which serves to sustain the nexus between imperialism and the emerging local bourgeoisie. Dr Eric Williams, a key architect of the present structure, admitted at the fifteenth Annual Convention of the People's National Movement (PNM), just two months after signing the Treaty of Chaguaramas:

It is now clear beyond any possibility of doubt that Caribbean integration will not be achieved in the foreseeable future and that the reality is continued Caribbean disunity and even perhaps the reaffirmation of colonialism.

Note

This paper was published in *Caribbean Contact*, December 1977.

[6]

Trinidad and Tobago
The Rich Cousin

Raoul Pantin

Any doubts about the serious trouble CARICOM now finds itself in were dispelled on December 2, when Trinidad and Tobago Prime Minister Dr Eric Williams, unveiled a record $3.5 billion 1978 budget in Parliament. One of the scores of budget proposals calls for the creation of a Trinidad and Tobago Caribbean Aid Project, a sort of Port of Spain-based technocratic department that will assess and funnel (or turn off?) economic and technical aid to the region. But the launching of the Project does not, for the moment anyway, mitigate Dr Williams' displeasure with the way Jamaica and Guyana, both under pressure for hard cash, have been cutting back on imports from Trinidad and Tobago.

The Prime Minister used the Budget speech to announce that Trinidad and Tobago's 'export trade to its Caribbean neighbours has catastrophically declined, while the position of Trinidad and Tobago's entrepreneurs and workers has been considerably eroded by the increase of imports from Caribbean territories.'

Dr Williams said Trinidad and Tobago's export trade to Jamaica and Guyana had dropped by $16.5 million between 1976 and the first nine months of 1977. But imports from both countries had increased by $10.4 million over the same period. Even worse, there was a decline in Trinidad oil sales to both Jamaica and Guyana and, particularly in Jamaica's case, a corresponding increase in oil imports from outside CARICOM. Jamaica's import of Trinidad oil products dropped from $242.2 million in 1974 to $17.2 million in 1976, the same year, that Trinidad and Tobago loaned Jamaica $184 million. During that same three-year period, Jamaica's imports of oil products from Venezuela jumped from $43.6 million to $112.7 million. Similar increases were noted in Jamaica's oil imports from the Netherlands Antilles and the US.

'We lend only petro dollars. If we don't sell the petro where on earth are the dollars to come from?' Dr Williams queried. He also criticised an unnamed CARICOM territory which he accused of abusing the newly-accepted CARICOM 'Rules of Origin', by 'flooding the Trinidad market' with electronic goods which seemed, in all but name, products of developed countries.'

Though he made no direct reference to it in his Budget speech, the Trinidad and Tobago Government's reaction to the CARICOM 'trade squeeze', has been the appointment of what has come to be known as the 'tit-for-tat committee,' set up to monitor (and apply retaliatory measures where necessary) the CARICOM trade situation. He did not give any hints on the possibility of a CARICOM Heads of Government conference, which both Jamaica and Guyana have been pressing for over the last eight months or so. On the contrary, he was critical of a proposed conference on Caribbean economic needs. He referred to 'the presence of participants who would seem to be neither donor nor beneficiaries, and are mere observers, whatever that may mean.'

However, the Trinidad and Tobago Government had made a proposal to the USA Government about three months before, for setting up a Caribbean Aid Project which would create an $800 million aid consortium to support the weaker economies of the region. Under that proposal, Trinidad and Tobago would put up $200 million, the US Government $200 million, Canada $50 million and other Caribbean Development Bank (CDB) members $200 million. But the USA had given no 'formal response' to that proposal. The Trinidad and Tobago Government would therefore proceed to create its own Caribbean Aid Project.

As for domestic proposals, the budget glowingly reflected the four year-old petro dollar boom, triggered by the 1973 energy crisis and subsequent jump in oil prices. The most dramatic budget announcement was a $332 million welfare programme for the 300,000-plus secondary and primary school students who would get free transportation to school, free meals, uniform and book allowances, a free school medical service (including dental care) – plus the building of a new 100-bed paediatric hospital. Taxpayers also came in for their share of the largesse. Personal income tax allowance moved up from $1,500 to $2,000; the claim for a non working wife from $600 to $1000;

allowances for housekeepers and dependent relatives from \$300 to \$400. Added to a \$25-a-month increase for old age pensioners, the budget also proposed a \$19 million food stamp programme aimed at reducing the rising cost of living for the aged and poor.

In keeping with the Government's long-declared intention to get into housing to deflate rampant land speculation in Trinidad and Tobago, the Budget also announced a \$200 million housing fund which has a target of 6,500 houses a year for low and middle income buyers. Loans from the fund will be made at low interest or 'soft' rates and purchasers will pay only 'pepper corn' land rents. Dr Williams also announced that the Government intended setting up three national holding companies to supervise the substantial state investment in business. The main aim of the holding companies will be to apply stricter financial controls on state corporations.

Initial press response to the 1978 Budget was heady. The republic's well circulated *Sunday Guardian* editorialised, 'With mellowed grace the Prime Minister bestowed upon children, the family, the aged and hard-pressed pensioners of the nation largesse of unprecedented size and scope . . . a Budget that exuded brotherly love.' The Trinidad Chamber of Commerce reacted with more caution. Declaring itself 'favourably impressed with a number of provisions in the Budget', the Chamber, nevertheless, expressed disappointment over the Government's inaction on the matter of reducing Corporation tax (now set at 45 per cent, 50 per cent for oil companies). The Chamber of Commerce also described the increase in personal income tax allowance as 'paltry'. They were concerned 'more and more new plans and programmes are being undertaken while the day-by-day operations of basic utilities are deteriorating instead of improving.'

Two days after Dr Williams presented the Budget, the traditional Parliamentary debate began in the House, but ended prematurely after only a handful of speakers had spoken on both sides.

'Call that a House of Representatives?' the Trinidad *'Express'* asked. To the *Express*, 'It seemed to be more like a bunch of amateurs involved in a public speaking contest.'

Note

This article was first published in *Caribbean Contact*, January 1978.

[7]

The LDCs and
CARICOM

Earl Huntley

In this, its fifth year, CARICOM is still contending, with a situation that has been a constant problem from the inception of the integration movement – the position of the LDCs within the scheme and the perception that they have not been receiving a fair share of the benefits of integration.

The CARICOM Secretariat reports that the position of the LDCs has been under constant review by the Community's relevant institutions, but there is still a strong sense among the LDCs that they have not been gaining from CARICOM. Montserrat's Chief Minister, Austin Bramble claimed that CARICOM has contributed little to the development of the LDCs and that were the community to break up, its passing would make no difference to the less developed member countries. Last year, the debate over whether or not the LDCs had gained from integration was heightened by two principal factors. One is that import restrictions imposed by Guyana and Jamaica, reportedly affected their export trade to those countries adversely, and the second is the postponement of the introduction of a new process list for CARICOM, because of the LDCs' objections.

There are a number of reasons why, in integration schemes among unequally developed Third World countries in particular, problems and crises arise over the distribution of the benefits and costs of integration. One factor is that the notion of what constitutes the benefits of integration, usually differ between the LDCs and the MDCs as a grouping. A country's economic circumstances determine its objectives in pursuing an economic integration scheme and, consequently, its notion of the benefits to be derived. Its economic situation may cause it to desire certain gains in a very short time span, while another may be able to afford longer term development goals. What is benefit or cost for a country may not be so for another.

Over a period of time, one country's objectives may change and, consequently, so would its assessment of the benefits and cost of integration. Over the years, what has been the LDC concept of the benefits they should derive from integration? And has that perspective, and the manner in which the LDCs have presented it, contributed to the continued prominence of the question of equitable distribution benefits in CARICOM? There seems to have been one dominant motive in the LDC's willingness to enter the integration scheme: that is, the acceleration, (in some cases, the commencement) of their industrial development.

It must be realised that when CARIFTA was formed in 1968, it was only the four MDCs (particularly Trinidad and Tobago and Jamaica) which had achieved some substantial level of industrialisation, and therefore they possessed a comparative advantage over the LDCs in manufacturing. While some of the LDCs were increasingly developing their tourist industries, their economies retained basically the traditional undiversified mono-culture pattern and manufacturing was minimal. It was so low that, by 1973, the LDCs contributed only two per cent of the regional manufacturing. Regional integration was therefore seen as a means of raising the level of industrial development in the LDCs.

Although the LDCs realised that they could not immediately capitalise on free trade to the same extent as the MDCs, they were prepared to accept their unfavourable position in trade with their partners, if the latter would help speed up their industrial development. The expectation was that not only would trade in manufacturing eventually be a two-way process, but also that the diversification of production would help solve some of their pressing employment problems. It is for this reason that the location of industries in the LDCs has become the major issue in the LDC's demands for a better distribution of the benefits of integration, and also a sore point between the LDCs and MDCs.

Since there was no quick industrialisation, the LDCs raised the question of the location of industries repeatedly at CARIFTA Council meetings, intensifying their complaints and becoming more rigid in their bargaining position on other issues with each meeting. Such meetings were often deadlocked and lent the impression that the movement was in a state of crisis.

As early as February 1968, prior to a meeting to finalise plans for CARIFTA, the Deputy Premier of St Kitts-Nevis, Paul Southwell, declared that 'sensible' countries among the smaller Caribbean territories knew that they would not benefit immediately from free trade without suitable safeguards. These, he identified as, 'positive action to ensure that industries found themselves in the less developed islands as well, without it the benefits will only come in the long run when most of them are dead.' In 1972, however, when it was being decided to deepen integration by transforming CARIFTA into CARICOM, the LDCs viewpoint was stressed more forcefully. Dissatisfied with CARIFTA, they agreed to further integration only in return for a more effective method of placing industries in the LDC sub-region. At a crucial CARIFTA Council meeting in October 1972, Premier of St Vincent, James Mitchell, stated:

We of the less developed countries share the desire of CARIFTA members for meaningful economic integration. But our people want to see factories – they want to see visible benefits of CARIFTA. I personally do not see our settling at this Summit Conference, the question of transforming CARIFTA into a Common Market . . . But I hope that we can take such decisions that would lead to an acceleration of the economic development of the less developed territories and for us to sell rather than just import from the rest of the region.

A few months later, in 1973, an eight-point proposal by Montserrat on behalf of the LDCs, threw a Council meeting and a Summit Conference into such an impasse that a frustrated Trinidad delegate complained that the LDCs 'want to see the smoke coming from the chimneys of the factories before signing the agreement for the Common Market.' The end result was the Georgetown Accord on a split approach in terms of the timetable for membership of CARICOM, and additional measures to improve the position of the LDCs.

A number of comments by leaders of MDCs and by secretariat officials indicate that the LDC notion of the benefits of integration did not entirely harmonise with MDC thinking. In 1969, Premier Barrow of Barbados, regretting 'the extraneous considerations' of the LDCs, spoke of their complaints as 'threats to push reluctant dragons, into positions to which we do not aspire'.

In 1970, Trinidad's Minister of West Indian Affairs, Kamaluddin Mohamed, blamed LDC dissatisfaction on their 'colonial mentality' and said that if they wished to withdraw from the regional grouping and trade elsewhere they were free to go ahead. If not, they should wait, as they would benefit in the long run. Subsequently, in 'Essays on Caribbean Integration', former

Secretary General of CARICOM, William Demas, said that 'the LDCs should not expect miracles from integration.'

The differing concepts of what constitute the benefits of integration for the LDCs still remain. This polarisation of views, and the manner in which the LDCs tried to force the others to meet the demands (and the fact that CARICOM is composed predominantly of LDCs), led to the prominence of the distribution of benefits question in CARICOM. On the other hand, the LDCs argue that it is not their repeated complaints that have kept the issue alive, but the MDCs' reluctance to comprehensively tackle the problem.

The persistence of the LDC's demands raises some questions: Is it realistic to expect to fulfil their objectives within the integration scheme, as it presently stands? Are the special measures really relevant to them? Shouldn't there be an acceptance of the reality that there will be a permanent imbalance in CARICOM? Is CARICOM providing opportunities for development and is the perspective of some of the LDCs one of the obstacles preventing them from fully utilising these opportunities?

Note

This paper was first published in *Caribbean Contact*, March 1978.

[8]

The West Indies in the
Year 2000

Shridath Ramphal

We cannot be absolutely certain what kind of world the year 2000 will usher in – just 22 years from now – but some projections are reasonably clear. It will be a world, no doubt, in which nations will have grown more truly independent. They will be conscious of the limits of conventional military and economic power; they will recognise with circumspection men's capacity for global self-destruction and will acknowledge the danger of diminishing resources on a more and more crowded planet.

Hopefully, it will be a world less obsessed with sovereignty, which throughout the preceding century was often a masquerade for bigotry and self-aggrandisement. And perhaps, therefore, it will be a world released from the grip of the 'adversary' complex that so often frustrated action; and there will be a move towards a mutually reinforcing planetary order in the second half of the twentieth century.

Assuredly, it will be a world, of giant states: China with 1,150 million people; India with 1,060 million; Brazil, 215 million; Indonesia 240 million; and the former superpowers of the old century still major powers with (USA) 265 million people, (USSR) 315 million, and a united Western Europe of 390 million.

It will also be a world of great regions drawing strength from regimes of cooperation among their peoples. Perhaps it will be a world of burgeoning regional arrangements in West Africa and in Central and Southern Africa; of new economic alignments in West Asia; of integrated economies in Southeast Asia, among the Andean states, and the Central American states of Latin America. Perhaps there will be economic union in Western Europe and in Eastern Europe as well, and new economic linkages within North America itself and perhaps Australia also.

It will be a world, I believe, in which nations great and small will have acknowledged in a variety of ways their essential need for each other. They will perceive that there are no sanctuaries of survival left on Earth, save that of which we jointly make the entire planet.

By the year 2000, all the West Indies will be a region of just over 6.5 million people: smaller as an entire region than the great majority of the world states. Yet, it will comprise sixteen sovereign countries, thus perhaps becoming the highest density of government anywhere on the planet – the world's most intensively bureaucratised, and perhaps politicised region.

We shall greet the new century with something like a parliamentarian for every 11,000 people and a Government Minister for every 34,000. Based on our present situation, we could have an oil refinery for every 500,000 people, while India, with the eighth largest industrial production in the world, could still have one refinery to every 60 million.

On a conservative estimate, by 2000, the West Indies might have six international airlines: one for every one million people. All of Western Europe, pioneers in aero-technology, will probably have one for every 23 million. And, of course, we could continue being exporters of primary products, heedless of the complementarities at hand that only await a regional will to make us attain a more balanced development for the greater economic gain of each state and the region as a whole.

These are some of the choices that we have to make, but there are many others besides. The choices will determine the means, as well as the end. The world order of the twenty-first century will not be the outcome of a natural phenomenon. It will come only as the result of a new planetary bargain struck by man as a basis for coexistence in the face of the inevitable interdependencies of the time. It will be a bargain hammered out through persistent negotiation. It will be derived from consensus achieved through confrontation and a better understanding of the benefits to be derived from change as the perils of the *status quo* becomes more discernible.

What lies ahead in the present century is the process of striking that global bargain. There could be a role for the West Indies, as there was a role for CARICOM in the much smaller negotiations with an enlarged Europe. What is more, the world, and especially the Third World, which persists in seeing us in the West Indies more unified than we often see ourselves, believes that we have in our collectivity a role to play.

The Third World, indeed, looks to us out of our own recent record at forging regional unity of purpose and sustaining regional unity of action to give a lead in the wider process of cooperation among developing countries.

Our own history holds lessons for us that give credence to those expectations. We spent the decade 1948–58 putting together the Federation of the West Indies as the vehicle for freeing the region from colonialism. In the next decade we dismantled the Federation and, leaving our smaller brothers in dependency, hit the freedom trail in isolation.

Yet, in the decade 1968–78, we have felt the need to rebuild the structures of cooperation, this time to our own design. They are not perfect, and their imperfections have been crudely revealed by the harsh, economic winds that have blown against them. But does anyone doubt that if we care enough about being West Indian and if we believe enough that West Indian men and women deserve a place of dignity in the world of the twenty-first century, we can make those structures proof against all weathers or improve our technique for managing them?

We are all too prone in the region, when difficulties arise, to seek to solve them by pulling down structures and erecting new ones when the cause of the difficulties may be not with the structures at all, but either with the external environment over which we have little control or with the ways in which we manage the structures. It is a tendency we shall have to curb.

The alternative is to accept an almost cyclical interpretation of West Indian political behaviour which commits us to breaking down in each decade all we have built up in the preceding – only to acknowledge in the next the imperative of cooperation that our condition imposes, and to commence the process all over again. The trouble with such a regional lifestyle, quite apart from its inherent wastefulness, is that each experience of dismantling renders more difficult, the succeeding process of reconstruction, and in the end, leads to a condition of irreversible disintegration and drift.

Can the West Indies entertain the notion of such an alternative? Are we really to prepare for that newer world of the twenty-first century by retreating each into its tiny enclave with greater or lesser assurance of prosperity and security, accepting with equanimity the need for even tinier corners for our West Indian micro states?

Do we believe that without cooperation among ourselves, we can hope to secure the world's cooperation to meet our individual needs or to influence global development to serve our purposes? It is more likely that we would be exchanging a degree of interdependence, however small, for complete dependence that could easily be more traumatic and destructive of our creative abilities than the colonial dependency so recently relinquished.

I cannot conceive that West Indians are uncertain of what choice to make. But we can suffer by default, the fate we deplore by refusing to act. Being West Indian is worth caring about and working for. The path of regionalism will never be free of difficulty and hazard. To pursue it will always demand, immense patience, compassion and even sacrifice. For our politicians, it will promise further moments of heartbreak and deep frustration, and it will demand of them great courage and steadfastness. But no process of working towards unity is free of such moments. European politicians face no lesser challenges as they work at consolidating their Community.

The real challenge is to keep faith in the importance of being West Indian and to sustain the processes of dialogue that alone can preserve its substance and give it enduring worth. In the end, however, it is the people of the West Indies who must say how much being West Indian means to them. It is they who choose the way forward. Each of you can help to ensure that it is the less travelled regional path that the West Indies takes towards the year 2000.

Note

This was the keynote address by Sir Shridath Ramphal to graduating students of the UWI, St Augustine campus in January 1979 and was published in *Caribbean Contact*, March 1979.

[9]

Major Tasks for the
1980s

Vaughan Lewis

The 1970s began on a note of turbulence for this region with what came to be called the 'February Revolution' in Trinidad. It was a strident signal of the youth rebellion that was to characterise and influence the politics of the region throughout the decade. Then the Trinidad economy appeared to be in a state of decline as foreign reserves persistently diminished. The sense of danger ahead propelled the Trinidad Government to actively pursue and support the politics of regional economic integration (CARIFTA), in search for a wider base from which to reorganise her economy.

The Jamaican economy at that time, however, still seemed vibrant. And the Government, while committing itself to regional integration, was still inclined to maintain a certain posture of isolationism on the assumption that gains could still be achieved from the Western international arena if a degree of Jamaican distinctiveness were demonstrated.

The Guyana Government on the other hand, attempting to shed the cloak of pro-Americanism with which it had achieved office, had begun to make its thrust into the world of non-alignment, while insisting to the other countries of the region that a politically coherent regional base was the only viable mechanism for making an impact on the changing world arena.

For indeed, at least two of these three pivots of the regional movement (Trinidad and Guyana) had begun to perceive that under the influence of the superpower relationship, the world environment was beginning to move towards greater flexibility that might be beneficial to minor states. The initiatives to normalise the position of Cuba in the hemisphere began early in the decade, and crystallised in collective Commonwealth Caribbean recognition of that country when a new regime came into office in Jamaica.

In a sense, the transition from CARIFTA to CARICOM, and the significant role played by the Commonwealth Caribbean countries as a group, with the ACP/EEC negotiations leading to the Lomé 1 agreement, marked the high point of regionalism as a diplomatic and political force in the area. After that, hopes of further progress were to be dissipated.

Today, at the end of the decade of the seventies, regional relations reflect disharmony. Some, with a degree of validity, attribute the change to the distortions in Caribbean economies introduced by the so-called oil crisis of 1973. But whatever the reason, one of the effects of this crisis is clear. No longer are the three pivotal states of CARICOM relatively equal in bargaining strength and financial and political influence on the resolution of problems in the region. A dramatic change in relative status has taken place in the area, with Trinidad and Tobago far outdistancing her partners in financial strength and potential influence in determining the course of events in the region.

In the course of the decade, the Trinidad Government took at least three different initiatives before lapsing into relative quiescence. None of these initiatives, however, has had the success desired.

The Government attempted to move the Caribbean Community in the direction of sectoral production integration with the aluminium smelter arrangement between Guyana, Jamaica and itself. The deal has apparently foundered, with much bad blood between Trinidad and Jamaica. The *casus belli* was alleged by Trinidad to be the different conception of regionalism held by Jamaica as evidenced in the JAVAMEX deal that country worked out with Mexico and Venezuela.

The difference in conceptions of what constitutes the Caribbean region, relates to a second initiative taken by Trinidad – the formation of the Caribbean Committee grouping within ECLA (Economic Commission for Latin America), including the island states of the archipelago plus the former European colonies on the edge of the South American mainland, but specifically excluding Venezuela and the other countries of the so-called Caribbean Basin.

This diplomatic design, masked in the frame of an economic and social development sub-region grouping within ECLA, has not had a successful career. Cuba showed much initial enthusiasm for it, but both Trinidad and herself now appear to have lost interest. Venezuela, with her petro-dollar strength too, has and appears willing to exercise leverage in archipelagic relations which she considers a legitimate sphere of concern.

The third Trinidad initiative was a direct outcome of her new-found financial strength. Following the programme of assistance to Jamaica which Trinidad arranged (joined in lesser roles by Barbados and Guyana) to assist the Jamaican economy's balance of payments situation, Williams, by his own telling of the story, attempted to get the USA involved in a much more substantial arrangement for financial and economic assistance to the weakening economies of the CARICOM area countries.

The Prime Minister has now argued that the USA has generalised the scheme to such an extent – in the Caribbean Group for Economic Co-operation and Development – that it no longer resembles his original conception and intention. Great power interests differ from those of small ones, however substantial in strength the latter may be. The Caribbean Group corresponds to an American global conception in which the Commonwealth Caribbean area constitutes only one element.

The alacrity with which other Caribbean countries have responded to what has become an essentially American initiative, has apparently further deepened the Trinidad Prime Minister's chagrin. His response has been the more minimalist conception of the Trinidad and Tobago Aid Council. This appears aimed at achieving a series of bilateral relations and agreements between Trinidad and other willing CARICOM territories. It is, in a sense, not unlike the Venezuelan approach, though with perhaps more generous terms. Trinidad, however, has now ceased to take initiatives, preferring to make responses when these seem to be in the national interest as defined by the Government.

Whatever the rights and wrongs of the Trinidad view, there does appear to be developing in the region, partly as a consequence of the weakened financial situation of two of the pivotal countries, the psychology of a new dependence on the American metropole. This position persists in spite of efforts still to maintain activist stances in the Non Aligned movement and in the search for a new international economic order.

Politics cannot be separated from economics, and the integral connection between the International Monetary Fund, the World Bank (under whose aegis the Caribbean Co-operation Group function) and the high level of American influence in these organisations, is clearly beginning to have its effect on the course of policy in the region. The initiative appears, at least for the time being, out of the hands of the major CARICOM countries.

The course of domestic politics in some of these countries has, in some measure, had its effect on the development of the new dependence psychology – a psychology which appears so different from the trend evident in the second half of the 1970s. The Guyana Government, for example, unable to derive substantial aid from the Socialist world (since USSR will only grant such assistance to a coalition political system encompassing at least the PPP and the PNC and thereby providing a solid and popular mass base), appears to have decided to reorganise her once-bad relationships with the USA. Of course, this stratagem is intimately connected with the necessity to have recourse to IMF assistance.

One qualification needs to be introduced, however, in discussing the prospects for the development of this new dependence. This relates to the presence, in many of these still-democratic political systems, of a large pool of unemployed and growing, alienated youth populations that form the basis of much of the politics of populism that these countries have experienced during the decade. Politicians, Government and opposition, feel constrained to ride this tiger which they have found easier to mount than dismount. Unless there is a turn to direct authoritarianism (of which there are incipient signs), both internal and external policy, will have to take this force into account.

Grenada

The Grenada Revolution of 1979, in one sense has had the effect of reinforcing this new dependence, particularly among the smaller territories of the area. The revolution initially met with their desire to bring into quick existence what appeared to be a kind of Caribbean holy alliance: a regional security system designed to contain the effects of the behaviour of the new regime within its own borders. The assumption was that it would wish to expand. But this is an assumption historically made in response to events of this kind.

A proper system of Caribbean regional security has long been recognised as a necessity for the emerging independent CARICOM area – at least since the Anguillan secession of 1967 up to the Cubana bombing incident. But the *ad hoc* and narrowly based conception of security that emanated from the LDCs in 1979 suggested no more than a panic reaction based on each island's perception of its immediate needs. Proper regional security requires prior understanding and commitment on rules of behaviour and procedure. The Cubana incident in fact demonstrated that in the absence of these, no systematic regional endeavour is possible.

The reaction of the Eastern Caribbean to the Grenada revolution opened the way to a period of activist American diplomacy in the region. A possible consequence may be the attempt to isolate and contain the Grenadian regime to 'Socialism in one country'.

Such possibilities exist given that at present no CARICOM country seems ready to take the lead in openly discussing and suggesting operational procedures for coping with the problems either of regional security or of the possible development of a situation of ideological pluralism in the area as different economic development options are attempted.

Venezuela and Trinidad

In the Caribbean Basin area, however, Venezuela, with what seems to be a clear conception of the strategic significance of the archipelagic environment for her own national security and commercial interests has recommitted herself under the new regime of the Campins' Christian Democrats to developing a strategy of linking the politics and policies of the Eastern Caribbean, at least, to policies acceptable to herself. We are still in the early stages of this endeavour. The extent of her relationship to the American policy line is still unclear. But as Venezuela's role in the evolution of the Nicaragua civil war indicated, the Government of that country is quite capable of enunciating and implementing a course of diplomatic activity subtly distinct, though not unrelated, to the American diplomatic course.

The open question is how Trinidad, the strongest financial power in this part of the region next to Venezuela, will react to an activist Venezuelan role. So far, Trinidad's political diplomatic position parallels her passive role in economic affairs. This point speaks to the Trinidad doctrine of non-interference and non-intervention enunciated clearly after the Grenadian revolution, but in evidence prior to that event to perceptive political observers.

In this writer's view this stance of non-intervention rests on a mistaken conception of the Mexican doctrine of non-intervention. As Mexico's conduct in the Nicaraguan civil war makes clear, it does not preclude in all circumstances, an activist position. Nor does it suggest that an activist stance be adopted only in the event of a direct affront to the national security of the particular country . . .

Clearly the Trinidad Government is of the view that in the second half of the 1970s, other Caribbean countries have intervened in conflicts in which their political weight and economic strength did not allow them to have a determining role. With too limited a political base from which to operate and limited security capabilities, her policy is to 'keep her nose clean', allow the major powers to run rampant, and have the other smaller powers learn by experience the dangers of mixing in big power politics.

But like it or not, the current disarray and absence of any autonomous collective approaches to resolving extant problems will affect every country in the region. No country is sufficiently powerful to close itself off from the influences of its environment. What we need to identify now, therefore, are some of the unfinished tasks of the seventies whose lack of resolution is at the bottom of the current malaise.

But such problem solving requires periods of long, sustained and systematic endeavour. In the older countries there exist traditions of bureaucratic activity that go beyond the limited lives of the political governments. In our countries this does not exist. The conceptualisation and approach to solution of long term and short term problems is much the province of the political leadership, usually no more than one or two individuals. Jamaica appeared in the sixties and early seventies to be developing a tradition of quasi-autonomous bureaucratic activity, but this inevitably became subject to the rise of charismatic populist politics. In Trinidad it is evident that a certain paralysis of the politico-bureaucratic system exists, at least in the arena of foreign policy-making.

It appeared in the middle of the 1970s that this problem might be partially overcome by assigning a specific role to the CARICOM Secretariat in which the political leadership had confidence. This approach would have allowed the Secretariat to take an initiating role in the identifying, analysing and proposing policies in certain core areas deemed central to regional progress. This should be done in collaboration with the national technocrats. The political directorate would retain the power of decision-making. This approach seemed to work at the Lomé I Convention. But it was premised on common agreement among the political directorate on the core areas of policy. In that context, the CARICOM Secretariat became integrated in certain agreed spheres of decision-making, but not as a supranational mechanism. The latter would have been positively dangerous.

But this practice came to an end as there was disagreement over core areas and general assumptions about regional policy (policies in the national interest that were identified as capable of operationalisation only on a collective basis). This disagreement led to loss of confidence in the system. Fiscal difficulties, partly the result of the oil crisis, and partly the result of mismanagement of the windfall gains of 1974–76, combined with a sense of populist overconfidence, has defeated the possibility of a coherent long-term approach to policy.

Two areas have suffered from this: (1) the process of Commonwealth Caribbean normalisation of relations with Cuba; and (2) the innovation required in working out process of 'integration relations' between the so-called LDCs of CARICOM on the basis of some degree of self-determination and political autonomy. We shall look at these in turn.

Cuba

The political directorate of CARICOM perceived early that it was necessary to come to terms with the existence of Cuba as a substantial force in the archipelago. The collective recognition, which certainly at the time minimised the possibilities of American retribution, seemed to point the way. The pilgrimages of the CARICOM political leadership to Cuba, all expressing their wonder at Cuban social developments, suggested also their awareness of the extent to which the subject of the Cuban development option had become an area of popular consideration.

But the collective approach collapsed. Some countries proceeded with speed to seek particularistic arrangements with a Cuban regime now eager to participate in regional affairs. Others, taking fright particularly after the Cuban intervention in Angola and then Ethiopia, lapsed into withdrawal from the incipient contact.

The difficulties arising, however, cannot be simply attributed to the egos of the political leaders involved. The fact is that CARICOM relations with Cuba cannot be normalised outside of the framework of wider hemispheric relations with that country; in particular the South-Central American countries on the rim of the Caribbean Sea. But that in turn requires the working out by the CARICOM countries of the modalities of their future relations with these countries in such a manner that such relations do not develop on the basis of hegemony.

The Protocol of Port-of-Spain (1970), normalising for a 12-year period, Guyana's relations with Venezuela, has suggested (given Trinidad's participation in that process) that solutions of this kind could more effectively be arrived at if CARICOM countries give themselves sufficient collective weight to balance that of the larger Basin countries. However the peremptory reneging by Mexico on her alumina deal with Jamaica brought that country down to earth, in the realisation that relations between countries of unbalanced financial/political weight can only result in hegemonic behaviour and decision-making by the stronger. The same fate awaits the Windward-Leeward islands now conducting their one-to-one pilgrimages to Venezuela.

Much the same propositions apply to CARICOM relations with Cuba. And this has nothing to do with any of the foolishly attributed malevolence of the Cuban leadership now so current. The fact is that Cuba is a country of undoubted financial, political and military weight in the archipelago. This is an objective situation. Cuba, in spite of her ideology, has been a part of a long tradition of Latin American law and diplomacy. The elaboration of rules of behaviour necessarily involved in any normalisation process makes it necessary that the CARICOM countries work with the Caribbean Rim countries (Mexico, Venezuela, Central America) in this.

This is the basis for adequately balanced relations between the various countries. But it is a long-term task requiring impartial study and analysis of the Latin American traditions of diplomatic behaviour. It is a task for a revitalised CARICOM Secretariat, prior to taking meaningful decisions by the political directorate. It is a fundamental task of construction for the 1980s.

This task is now made more urgent by the fact that Cuba has expressed interest in the development of the independence process in the Windward-Leeward Islands. This has led to the hoisting of panic stations, and frantic efforts to inhibit this development. The present situation was foreseeable. It was described by the *McIntyre Report* (February 1975) on Windward-Leeward Islands independence in the following way:

Four of the independent Commonwealth Caribbean countries have announced policies of trade and diplomatic relations with Cuba. It is just a matter of time before the Associated States will have to make a similar response. It is becoming increasingly recognised that the countries with different ideologies can develop mutually beneficial trade, technical assistance . . . and that much can be gained from the Cuban experience. The Associated States will maximise the benefits if they can, as a group and identify the areas in which they are interested, and make a co-ordinated approach to the Government of Cuba . . .

Not much more can be said about this. (The present writer declares his interest in having been a participant in the preparation of the McIntyre Report). What applies to Cuba, applies with force to Venezuela.

This takes us to the second of the unfinished tasks of the 1970s: the question of relations between the Windward-Leeward Islands. Declarations of intent at integration are no longer enough. We have had our share of these in the last decade. They are no substitute for the fact that time and patience have to be devoted to the operational modalities of co-operation between these countries based on an understanding that a certain degree of flexibility is required for each island Government, to reflect the differing orientations of the Governments. But in any case, the choice of orientations and options is not wide.

Much of what we have been saying so far about failures and unfinished tasks, can be summarised in the following description of CARICOM agenda for the 1980s. The CARICOM countries are faced with achieving complementarity between the strategies required for economic development and their stratagems of regional and international diplomacy. In the current period diplomacy and development strategy are integrally related and feed upon each other.

Such complementarity has to evolve in a world environment characterised by a single global economy, in which two broadly political systems of differing socio-ideological orientations function and inter-relate. The CARICOM countries exist geopolitically within one of these systems, but they are un-avoidably open to currents emanating from the other, to which they have to respond in more than the negative manner of the 1980s.

The evolution of complementarity between regional development and diplomacy can be influenced by a number of factors. The current weakness of Caribbean economies, leading political élites towards subordination to a certain unilaterally devised American political-economic strategy of aid, is one. The minimalist conception of the Trinidad Aid Council based on bilateral arrangements between countries is another. Within this general framework the recently signed Barbados-Trinidad agreement fits. But few outside the arena of official discourse can perceive the regional political implications of this strategy.

Another factor is the increasing role being played by the Caribbean Development Bank in programming economic assistance to the region from wealthy countries and multilateral institutions. This role will be significant in particular for the LDCs, though this writer can perceive the possibility of a larger role for the institution in programmes of assistance to some of the larger countries.

Sooner or later, there must be a degree of co-ordination between the development programmes offered through CDB, and securing technical and economic assistance countries increasingly active in regional and international environment. In that sense the CDB will be performing the kind of role in functional economic integration once attributed to the CARICOM Secretar-iat. The Secretariat has never had, the kind of finance appropriate to such a role, however.

Once a meaningful relationship between development and diplomacy at the level of multilateral assistance is achieved, the need to elaborate further rules of procedure and behaviour within the Caribbean Basin environment will follow. This will clarify the strategies needed to elaborate a system of diplomatic community in this sphere.

These then are the central tasks in regional relations for the coming decade. All the rest is propaganda – propaganda of symbolic political value, but propaganda all the same.

Note

This paper was first published in *Caribbean Contact*, January 1980.

[10]

The University of the West Indies at a Crossroads

Kathleen Drayton

In 1948 the University College of the West Indies (UCWI) was established at Mona, Jamaica as one of the last outposts of that empire on which the sun was already beginning to set. Teaching began at Mona 33 years ago to 33 medical undergraduate students in the medical faculty. In the following year Natural Sciences' students were enrolled, and by 1950 the pioneers of the Faculty of Arts were installed.

By 1950, too both the Extra Mural Department and the Institute of Social and Economic Research (ISER) were in existence. Except for the students, the non-academic staff, some very few members of the academic staff and the physical campus, everything else was transplanted from Britain. Halls had 'high' tables. Students were resident and attended classes and dinner in red gowns. Curricula were shaped on British models and, on the successful completion of a course of study, students were awarded degrees of the University of London. The light all came out of the West!

The Principal of the UCWI was an eminent Englishman, Sir Thomas Taylor, of whom most students and possibly most staff, had never heard. The two most senior West Indians on the staff were men who had been members of the Irvine Commission which had recommended the setting up of the UCWI. Philip Sherlock of Jamaica was the director of Extra Mural Studies and Hugh Springer of Barbados, who had come with a formidable reputation as Secretary of the Barbados Progressive League and of the Barbados Workers' Union, was the registrar.

The UCWI came into being to prepare a selected cadre of West Indian leadership for partnership in the new Commonwealth, which was to be the new colonialist form of the former imperialist economic and political relationship. The rationale for the UCWI was the preservation of colonial attitudes and values.

This writer well remembers an informal conversation with that witty, charming and urbane gentleman and scholar, Sir James Irvine in which he explained that the UCWI had been set up 'to cream off the best and most articulate of West Indians' and to train them to hold the more 'radical and irresponsible elements of the populace in check'. The view that the Commission had of West Indians is partly visible in the following paragraphs of the report:

People of the West Indies unlike those of other parts of the colonial Empire are already literate . . . in English . . . which has for at least 150 years been the mother tongue. It is to Britain they look for practical help and inspiration when they undertake measures of reform and development. Although full use is made of the characteristic British liberty to criticise . . . we found everywhere the strongest loyalty to Britain and a deep affection and respect for British traditions and institutions.

Dr Eric Williams, the leading Caribbean historian of the forties, whose scholarship was, ironically, never made available within the Department of History of the UCWI, was a notable omission from the Irvine Commission. In 1946 Dr Williams had argued in *Education in the British West Indies* for a non-residential, independent, 'university in overalls'. He favoured state control of the university, declaring that 'the governing body of the university should be controlled by representatives of the people'. He thought, unrealistically, that there could be state control 'without interference.'

Until his death last March 30, Dr Williams, Prime Minister of Trinidad and Tobago since 1956, wrote of 'the need for the university to provide knowledge and analysis of the British West Indian condition' and 'of the part it should play in the education of women who are so heavily handicapped by their economic status and the traditional conception of the role of women.' He disagreed on seven fundamental points with the recommendations of the Irvine Commission.

Dr Williams remained critical of the model out of which today's UWI has grown. In 1974, in *The University in the Caribbean in the 20th Century*, he asked:

Can a university whose faculty and students talk glibly about 'involvement' and 'relevance' and 'responsibility to the community' continue to operate on a philosophy imposed by a British Commission a quarter of a century ago anticipating large numbers of expatriate staff in a colonial university?

His views obviously influenced the Trinidad Government's White Paper on *A National Institute of Higher Education* in 1977 whose proposals to restructure UWI are now once again on the agenda of CARICOM governments and the University.

The one department of UCWI which was, so to speak, 'flung' into the Caribbean from the outset to analyse the West Indian condition was the Institute of Social and Economic Research (ISER). Even though some of its staff were English the work produced by ISER was about the Caribbean. This research found its way into the Social Sciences Faculty.

It may be no coincidence that some of the most influential ideas for policy formation and social re-organisation in the English-speaking Caribbean have come from members of the UWI Social Sciences Faculty. It is also, as Dr Williams observed, the Faculty 'denounced by many of (his) colleagues at a Caribbean Heads of Government Conference'. Dr Williams disclosed that at that conference he opposed 'more than one suggestion that the Faculty be closed down.' The thoroughly colonised apparently find decolonisation difficult!

Notwithstanding its colonial nature, the UCWI performed the important function of being a regional institution. It put West Indians in touch with each other, and it tried, not always effectively, to reach out into all the territories of the region. In its members, the UCWI fostered regionalism, even among narrow nationalists. In 1962 the UCWI was finally given its own Charter empowering it to grant its own degrees, instead of those of the University of London. The regional university thus came into being at about the same time that the political federation collapsed. From this time its regional character has been under constant attack in one form or another. In 1963, Guyana withdrew and set up the University of Guyana. Policies of the Governments of Jamaica, Trinidad and Tobago and lately, Barbados with regard to immigration restrictions and work permits have posed threats.

In December 1975, the Pro Vice Chancellor of St Augustine Professor Lloyd Braithwaite commented on this, and as early as 1965, Errol Barrow at a Heads of Government meeting requested the Prime Minister of Jamaica, Hugh Shearer, to ask his Government to reconsider its position in the matter of work permits. Once Guyana left, its re-integration into a regional system became difficult.

Sir Arthur Lewis at the Common Services Commission in 1962 proposed the formula that has preserved the UWI as a regional institution up to this point in time. And the Heads of Government Conference in June 1969 agreed that the UWI should be continued on a regional basis until 1981.

Now another formula for preserving the University of the West Indies is being sought. Many committees have appraised the structure and functioning of the UWI, including an Appraisal Committee that was chaired by Dr Williams in 1969. In 1975 an Inter-Governmental Committee (IGC) under the chairmanship of William Demas was set up and it produced two long reports. The first report dealt with the Committee's first four terms of reference and the second report in 1977 dealt with the last five.

The 'Demas Committee' (as the IGC came to be known through the media), was asked to take into account 'current and projected government policies in relation to the entire system of post-secondary education; to examine and make recommendations on the role, character, functions and orientation of university education in the Commonwealth Caribbean', with special reference to among other things, 'the role of the Caribbean University in promoting national and regional consciousness and commitment; and the need for the Caribbean University to be adapted to the changing development perspective and strategies of the countries which it serves . . . '

Before the IGC completed its assignment, Trinidad 'made its play' with the now famous White Paper on a National Institute of Higher Education (NIHE), which was later approved by the Government of Trinidad and Tobago. The most important proposals in the Trinidad White Paper were that the UWI be decentralised with the cost of its three campuses being borne by the territory and that each campus be given greater autonomy. Trinidad paid 'lip-service' to the regional idea by recognising a central university authority which would have the power to make senior appointments and control exams. But campuses were to control syllabuses, all appointments up to senior lecturer level and finance. 'The function of the central university authority with respect to finance and new developments,' argues the White Paper 'should be advisory, the final decision resting with the campus author-ity'. The proposals in the Trinidad White Paper bore a striking resemblance to Dr Williams' 1946 vision of a West Indian university. In 1977, Edward Seaga supported the Trinidad proposals and plans were afoot to bring together under the umbrella of the 'University of Jamaica', a degree granting institution, CAST, the Jamaica School of Agriculture, the teachers' colleges and the 'cultural schools.'

At a meeting in June this year of the UWI Council and the University Grants' Committee, the Trinidad proposal was discussed and it was sup-ported by Jamaica, but opposed by Barbados and the LDCs. A sub-committee of the Governments and UWI met in the next few months to discuss restructuring. If the Trinidad proposals are implemented the regional character of the UWI would be drastically changed. The dilemma is that while there is general agreement that restructuring is necessary no formula acceptable to all the interested and concerned parties has been found.

The IGC reports are long documents, strong on data and on statements of desirable policies, but weak on practical solutions. The special conference of CARICOM Heads of Government meeting in March 1976 passed a resolution accepting most of the recommendations in the first report – apparently without counting the cost of implementing any.

The Committee agreed that regional 'commitment' was essential but it was unable to define commitment and recommended that research was necessary to determine how commitment was learned! Regionalism, it was thought, could be fostered by extending compulsory courses in the Caribbean in medicine and engineering and by introducing a department of Caribbean creative arts. Some statements sound fairly ridiculous. The committee apparently believed, for instance, that the university could create an ideology.

A regional West Indian university system could help bring about over time a convergence of differing ideologies into a specific West Indian ideology which was not to be either strongly 19th century liberal capitalist or strongly Marxist-Leninist although it must retain some Marxist elements of both classical Liberals and orthodox Marxism in addition to the indigenous elements evolving out of the West Indian experience.

Integrating the world of study with the world of work is among the Committee's recommendations. It is a popular slogan in the English Caribbean, but in this region, only Cuba gives the concept meaningful expression. Dr Williams also favoured it, and proposed that UWI should examine two models. 'Castro's Cuba and Nyerere's Tanzania'. The IGC Report recognises the practical problems, one of them being 'in a region where there is serious unemployment, there is a danger of trade unions seeing it as a form of scab labour.'

The Report makes recommendations on the way the UWI should adapt to changing development strategies. Expansion in 'priority areas' is recommended, so is the 'need' to train more sub-professionals and middle management people, as well as more teachers and to increase the number of postgraduate students. It recommended that the number of science students should be increased. The use of other tertiary institutions for non-degree programmes was discussed and the committee recommended that 'all national tertiary institutions be regarded as regional institutions serving all countries'.

How this 'Alice-through-the-looking-glass' proposal was to be realised was not explained. With the territories fighting over access to and control of the existing regional university, it is difficult to see easy compromises being reached over regional use of national institutions. It is true that a regional programme like the PAHO/WHO Project for the training of allied health personnel uses national institutions, but this is a very different thing from regarding all national tertiary institutions as regional ones!

The Report recommends increasing staff-student contact hours at UWI, although these are already higher than what obtains at British or East or West African universities. Dr Williams would have supported the proposal. Referring once to the staff teaching load of twelve hours a week, the late Prime Minister commented that 'a contributing government would collapse if that was the responsibility of its senior civil servants.' This, as Dr Williams must have known, is an unfair comparison. Twelve hours of teaching in a university must be added to hours for preparation, marking and research, and, in the case of the UWI, numerous committee meetings!

In its second report the IGC presented proposals for decentralisation. They recommended retaining the present formula for financing the university, economic cost per student. They suggested that control of finance should remain with a central university authority, which is in opposition to the Trinidad proposal that the campuses should control finance. They also recommended the replacement of the Royal Charter by an Inter-Governmental agreement. This was opposed by the Vice Chancellor who referred in his memorandum to 'some of the difficulties encountered by the Council of Legal Education established under Inter Governmental agreement.'

The Trinidad White Paper said nothing about the Less Developed Countries, the so-called LDCs of CARICOM. But the IGC Report recommends that tertiary level institutions in the LDCs should have 'capital expenditure, mainly laboratories and libraries' financed either by the University Grants' Committee, or external grants. These institutions should provide first year university education and train middle level people or para-professionals. Other suggestions have included long-distance teaching, on the lines of the 'British Open University'.

What is certain is that many of the IGC recommendations would be costly to implement and the LDCs can afford to pay neither for their needs nor their wants. The LDCs submitted a memorandum which appears as an Appendix in the IGC's second Report. Money, however, always speaks louder than moral suasion, so the voice of the LDCs is a still small one crying in the regional wilderness.

The UWI's response has been to agree that the new structure must 'enable the individual campuses to manage their own affairs within the context of a regional university'. The university has one great advantage over the individual territories in discussions relating to restructuring, since its representatives all speak with one voice. What will happen remains to be seen. Nobody disputes the need for reform of the UWI structure. As far back as 1970, Dr Marshall, then Vice Chancellor, observed that 'the university has carried over a structure from a one-campus university to a multi-campus university. And, he added, 'a defective administrative framework does not distinguish functions of university officers and campus officers'.

From within, the UWI can be seen to be a top-heavy and costly bureaucratic structure with few people understanding either the bureaucracy, or the university's finances. The UWI's current operational costs for the three campuses amount to over J$61 million, (US$1=J$1.78), the bulk of which must be met by the governments of Jamaica, Trinidad and Tobago and Barbados.

Education is a means of social mobility for the individual but modern states do not invest money in education primarily for the development of individuals. Modern states invest money in education with little reservation because formal education is seen as an important mechanism for extending and consolidating the power of the state. The carrot that entices the donkey is 'jobs'.

In small societies the quest for jobs dominates the thinking of all those within the educational system. Through education, skills and certificates attesting to the attainment of skills, are provided and that process of acquiring certificates neatly incorporates successive waves of people into the productive processes of society in which the government has emerged as the biggest employer. In this context the university must be seen as a powerful agency for the extension of the power of the state and as performing a markedly political function. Because it is a tertiary level institution and because it is funded primarily by the Governments of the region, the university, offering programmes that conform to Governments' perceptions of manpower needs, provide the finishing touches on those recruits for the labour force who have successfully survived primary and secondary level education and seek from the university the necessary certification to guarantee them secure jobs.

In the current discussion on re-structuring the university, it is therefore, difficult to see UWI emerging as other than an elitist institution functioning to allocate people to available jobs in the society, and to places in the social hierarchy. It is significant that the initiative for the current exercise was taken by the Caribbean Heads of Government meeting in St Kitts in 1975. It is of further significance that the exercise has been labelled 'Report of the Inter Governmental Committee on Regional University Education'.

From start to finish Governments of the region have been given ample opportunity to ensure that the university serves their interest. The only source of tension arises from the fact that it is proving difficult to find a formula that will enable the university to serve all the contributing territories equally well. But the case for restructuring the university in order to enable it to be a catalyst for societal and cultural change and development has not been stated, and even if it were to be stated, it would suffer from lack of political backing.

This state of affairs serves to remind us of the truism that 'a university is the expression of the social order in which it functions'. In the final analysis therefore, what merits our concern is not primarily the university but, 'the social order in which it functions'.

Note

This paper was first published in *Caribbean Contact,* August 1981

[II]

CARICOM

Successes and Disappointments

Rickey Singh

That all CARICOM Heads of Government, from Guyana's Executive President Burnham to Osbourne of the colony of Montserrat, have been so anxious to proclaim, in their own country, the 'success' of their first Summit in seven years, loudly suggests how concerned they all are to affirm their faith in the regional integration process, in the Community that will be ten years old next July.

In the face of apparent orchestrated initiatives designed to promote discord, this newspaper had urged, before the gathering at Ocho Rios, a high level of maturity on the part of our CARICOM leaders in order to avoid weakening the Caribbean Community. We are encouraged to note the evidence of resilience and the spirit of compromise they displayed in arriving at some far-reaching decisions at this third meeting of CARICOM Heads of Government, even as tempers flared in the cut and thrust of lively debates. There now seems to be cause for hope as Prime Minister George Chambers prepares to host the next CARICOM Summit where the Caribbean Community came into being on July 4, 1973 – Chaguaramas, Trinidad. After all, it was Chambers who told the Ocho Rios Summit: 'Caribbean Unity is Caribbean Strength'.

But let's face, dispassionately, the reality that it was not 'success' for all and that it was simply not possible for any single delegation to get everything it wanted out of the summit. And no one should really be upset because the Prime Minister of Grenada, Maurice Bishop, is today so exuberant over the final outcome of Ocho Rios. He had to work the hardest to convince his CARICOM colleagues about the revolutionary experiment or process of his People's Revolutionary Government and why he could not now go along with some well institutionalised views in the Caribbean Community about human rights. He undoubtedly made quite an impression at the conference. But Chambers, for one, who played a key role, with some essential help from conference host, Edward Seaga, in keeping the peace during those three vital days in Ocho Rios, will be the first to remind Bishop of the request made of him for 'good neighbourliness' and all that this implies. 'Good neighbourliness' of course, is a responsibility of every state.

However, while applauding the spirit of compromise and welcoming the decisions arrived at, in particular the move to establish a high-level ministerial committee to come to terms with the elusive issue of rationalisation of air transport, we must record some disappointments.

First and foremost, is the failure of the summit to declare the Caribbean as a zone of peace. Why this matter had to be referred again to a committee for further consideration after all the initiatives at technical and ministerial committees, is most baffling. Secondly, since our own view of a participatory democracy means more than honestly conducted parliamentary elections once every four or five years, we regret that CARICOM Heads of Government are still not ready to consider amending the Community's Treaty and their national constitution to provide for a Caribbean Court of Appeal within the framework of a permanent Human Rights Commission, with enforcement machinery for securing civil and political rights.

Finally, we endorse the plea – one undoubtedly based on the frustrations he and his colleagues have suffered over the years – made by CARICOM's Secretary General Kurleigh King for the establishment of a ministerial body, 'specially constituted to deal with the strategic and tactical economic survival issues on which critical decisions have to be taken now by all our States'. The Treaty of Chaguaramas does not provide, as King has noted, for the creation of such a mechanism. But we should not let its relevance and importance escape the forthcoming Chaguaramas Summit in 1983.

Note

Published in *Caribbean Contact*, December 1982.

[12]

CARICOM's Dilemma

Contact Editorial

Heads of Government of the Caribbean Community have now met twice in just over three months, having failed to do so in seven years prior to last November's Summit in Jamaica. But even as they were meeting last month in St Lucia with Canada's Pierre Trudeau, amid continuing plans for the forthcoming July summit in Trinidad, the dilemma facing the community was being highlighted by a currency dealings controversy resulting from the Seaga Government's experiment with a two-tiered exchange rate.

The dilemma has to do with member countries' obligations to a workable Community Treaty. As it is, for all the encouraging official words we hear, a basic problem of the Community, still to be attended to, is that it is served by a treaty premised on the operations of a market economy where private decisions of what is produced and sold still dominate. Whenever the state has to intervene, as in the case of Guyana, to centralise trade through a marketing agency or as in the current currency controversy, the Central Banks have to step in to regulate foreign exchange rates, the weaknesses of the Chaguaramas Treaty, signed over nine years ago, are exposed. The reason is obvious enough. The member country concerned can always plead nationalist interests as the overriding factor and relegate, conveniently, its obligations under the Treaty to a secondary priority.

In the circumstances, more than simply emphasising the need to reinforce the Community's mechanism for settling disputes, the scheduled Trinidad's

Summit should strive for a treaty that would ensure that national interests are not so narrowly defined as to exempt member countries from their obligations to the community.

It is felt that the immediate problem flowing from Jamaica's two-tiered exchange rate underscores the need for an agreement, in the short term, on rates of exchange for intra-Caribbean trade. How this is determined must be a matter of priority for the Board of Directors of the Community's Multilateral Clearing Facility, the existing mechanism for financing trade within CARI-COM.

Even so, one of the ironies which the Trinidad Summit itself must recognise, is that the currencies which can be freely used in all the Caribbean territories are the metropolitan currencies, USA dollars, Canadian dollars and British pounds. The currency of the Community's still richest member, Trinidad and Tobago – in terms of foreign exchange holdings – cannot be used for commercial transactions such as paying hotel bills or for shopping, except in some cases, on the basis of CARICOM travellers' cheques. The Community's people, who are being ceaselessly urged to travel more within the region, are only too aware of this particular problem, which existed long before Central Banks were established in this region, and prior to the first dawn of political independence 20 years ago!

Note

Extracted from 'Our Opinion' column in *Caribbean Contact*, March 1983.

[13]

New Vistas for the
Caribbean Community

Havelock Ross-Brewster

Age 21 is not a time for contemplating death. But that's the way it is. CARICOM has not amounted to much in terms of production and trade. Its functional tasks are a classic example of 'spill-around' – a proliferation of low-politic cooperation activities convenient to Governments that can decide neither to go forward nor backward. Foreign policy coordination has been a non-starter.

CARICOM's economic tasks have been overtaken by events which were justifiable at the time of its formation. The economic policy of individual states, as well as recent decisions made by the Conference of CARICOM Heads of Government, reflect a free market stance on integration into the world economy, itself now more open than before. The position is made clear by the stabilisation and adjustment programmes that have been adopted: adherence to the principles of the expanded GATT/WTO; the establishment of the Association of Caribbean States (ACS), trade liberalisation agreements with several Latin American countries; the keen interest on the part of some CARICOM States to join NAFTA; and the commitment that all of them have to participate in the Free Trade Area of the Americas (FTAA) by 2005.

Intra-regional free trade, a common external tariff, the regional enterprise regime and the single market and economy, including a common monetary system and currency have become redundant in this context. Indeed, they make little sense in a situation where intra-regional transactions are a tiny fraction of the total. Integration of the individual states into the FTAA/world economy will more rapidly and effectively lead to integration among the CARICOM states, than will perfection of the present regime pave the way for concerted entry into a liberalised hemispheric and global economy.

CARICOM, as an economic integration mechanism, has failed because it was always a second-best solution, predicated on the acceptance, out of necessity, of substantial protectionist costs and the implementation of effective compensatory mechanisms for mis-distributed costs and benefits. In any event, individual states have always been prepared to defect, in deed, if not in word, for second-best arrangements, as the reality of uneven costs and benefits, have served to curtail the deepening of integrationist ventures. Neo-functionalism also has failed because the strategy lacked coherence and premeditated design on the part of the Community's bureaucracy, and because it was always seen as ceding some of the fruits of state sovereignty for gains that were negligible.

It is thus time to return to the source, to the 'first-best', to the truly authentic rationale for Caribbean integration. Regrettably, the West Indian Commission (1992) missed this opportunity. It sought to avoid commitment, in the foreseeable future, to political integration, and instead, advocated perfection of the economic integration instruments of CARICOM. It attempted to straddle three stools at the same time – West Indian integration, Caribbean regional-wide integration and global integration – and ended up by falling between them. No cogent new directions are discernible in this heavily compromised schema. This is regrettable because, in confining its sights to conventional notions of political integration (parliamentary union) and economic integration (single market) it has not only preserved a false dichotomy between them, but precluded consideration of more creative and fruitful options.

The new rationale must be based more solidly on first-best options, of which cultural identity and kinship are the centrepiece. These are already, to a good extent, part of West Indian reality, and are thus the core of any institutional expression of political unity. Indeed, it may be said that these essential ingredients are far more developed in West Indian society than are reflected in its political institutions. Political expression needs to catch up with social reality. In many ways West Indian society is more united than the present European Union. A more fundamental expression of its identity, as representing a distinctive society, would not only correspond better to reality but would have positive psychological benefits in enhancing our people's pride, self-esteem and confidence. It could bring with it a number of practical benefits, such as those associated with civil society and good governance, administrative economies of scale, enhanced negotiating status and international diplomatic, intellectual, cultural and sporting profiles, and more effective self-protection.

A political expression of cultural identity and kinship is now a real and urgent necessity because CARICOM states have become increasingly peripheral and isolated, with tenuous, virtually non-existent links to external communities – Africa, Asia, Europe, Latin America or North America. The Caribbean may well be the most isolated community of people in the world. Even the strategic, colonial and migrant ties of the recent past have disappeared, while its Diaspora becomes more distant with the passing years. At the same time, even as the nations of the world become more economically open, they are becoming more culturally and racially self-conscious and closed. Of course, if the people of the Caribbean themselves and our political leaders do not share this feeling of identity and kinship, or if they feel it is adequately expressed in a cricket team, and well represented in the barracoons of London and Miami, or if they see themselves as Latino or American or world citizens, then we might just as well call it a day.

The political expression I foresee is a 'Union of West Indian States', incorporating West Indian citizenship, carrying with it generally agreed rights and duties, and coexisting with citizenship of the individual member states. In much the same way as the European Union (Maastricht Treaty) and European citizenship were selectively defined to suit the peculiar needs and limits of the European states concerned so too can a Union of West Indian States be defined to suit our evolving requirements and possibilities. For example, the European Union coexists with the statehood and sovereignty of the individual states; does not provide for a European Parliament with legislative powers or for the elimination of individual member states diplomatic representation and UN membership, or for the immediate and complete freedom of movement of workers. Thus, the West Indian Union can be an indigenous and dynamic concept. Statehood and sovereignty need not, as has been traditionally thought, be fixed, indivisible and wholly externally determined.

Developments along these lines will also ultimately strengthen CARICOM's relations with the non-anglophone Caribbean, Central America and the rest of Latin America. Reaching out, especially to neighbours that are so culturally and geographically cohesive, will enhance self-knowledge, self-confidence and the cultural identity of the people of the Caribbean community.

The economic/functional dimension of the Union would revolve around activities that are inherently first-best. These will be activities that are better pursued regionally than internationally or nationally. They will be activities that are unique and least-cost, and which require regional solutions, as in regional commons, regional public goods and regional resource complementarity. Regional commons are commonly shared goods or 'bads' such as the sea, airspace, weather, disease, pest infestation. Regional public goods are goods and services which, if not provided regionally, would not be provided at all, such as regional security, regional social infrastructure like high technology and advanced scientific training and medical facilities, regional physical infrastructure like sea and air transportation and telecommunications. Regional resource complementarity are combinations of resources that are unlikely to be exploited other than through regional arrangements, such as food demand/arable land, mineral smelting/hydro-electricity, and diversified financial services.

The Community's economic/functional institutions of the future would no longer be fully immersed in the task of managing the instruments that constitute and support the Common Market, for example. Instead, they would be devoted to energising the private sector for its role in region-wide enterprise development; identifying and promoting the development of those truly first-best regional activities, including regional infrastructure and regional services; and supporting member Governments by organising regular, research-based consultations on macroeconomic and national and regional policy assessments and outlook analyses.

Finally, in regard to production and trade, activities that do not meet the test of the first-best on a regional scale, would be left in the future to market forces, and to the dictates of international comparative advantage. This policy would, however, allow for reasonable adjustment periods for critical industries, especially agriculture, that cannot immediately compete internationally, and of course, for a genuine determination that international trading partners are not themselves using protectionist subsidies and other unfair trading practices.

Since individual CARICOM states are progressively moving in this direction, albeit at different rates, some more quickly and comprehensively than others, it would make sense to recognise this reality at the CARICOM level as well. It serves no good purpose to pretend that intra-CARICOM production and trade are being developed under the impetus of Community regimes such as the Common External Tariff, among others, that neither confer common protection nor are effective in promoting resource-based industries and trade within the region.

An approach along these lines would introduce a good deal more realism and flexibility into the increasingly complex situation in which CARICOM finds itself, with overlapping and inconsistent subregional, hemispheric and world commitment, and *de facto* defections by the individual states.

How to proceed is now the question. The political leadership should show the way. Does it have a vision for CARICOM that is anything more than a meeting place for functional cooperation? Can the regional bureaucracy itself orchestrate a truly deepening process, politicians notwithstanding, *à la* Jacques Delors. At any rate, the past and the future are now in collision. And it could mean death, or a new birth.

Note

This paper was first published in *CARICOM Perspective*, No. 65, June 1995, pp. 18–19.

[14]

The Caribbean in 2000
Challenges and Opportunities

Cheddi Jagan

The Caribbean region was described in the early 1980s by the Reagan administration as a 'circle of crisis' among others in the world. This was after upheavals in many Caribbean Basin countries – Trinidad and Tobago, Curaçao, Panama, Nicaragua, Dominica, Grenada, Suriname and elsewhere – following the oil crisis and recession in 1973–74 and, in quick succession, in 1977, after a second oil shock, falling terms of trade and extremely high interest rates.

In early 1976, the former CARICOM Secretary General, Alister McIntyre (later deputy Secretary General of UNCTAD, UN Assistant Secretary General, and Vice Chancellor of the University of the West Indies) told the summit meeting of the Caribbean Economic Community that the region was faced with 'unprecedented difficulties' including a 20 per cent inflation rate, a 'scandalous' food importation bill of US$1,000 million, a worsening balance of payments problem, and the need for 150,000 jobs by 1980. He lamented the shortage of funds for the public sector and 'startling increases' in consumption expenditure.

Today, nearly two decades later, after some trade concessions by USA and Canada; numerous diagnoses by the '12 wise men', over 20 academics and technicians, and the prestigious West Indian Commission; and after structural adjustment programmes, the Caribbean region is again in a serious crisis situation. The food importation bill is now over US$2 billion and less than ten per cent of total trade is between Caribbean Community countries. Unemployment has soared and the 'unprecedented difficulties' have intensified.

The narrowly based Caribbean economy, according to a CARICOM Secretariat study, was not able to take advantage of the free trade provisions of the Caribbean Basin Initiative (CBI) and Canada's Preferential Trade scheme for the Commonwealth Caribbean (CARIBCAN). The statistics showed a bigger trade balance gain for USA during the 'lost decade' of the 1980s. The major Caribbean export products, sugar, bananas, petroleum and bauxite, showed a poor performance because of external as well as internal factors.

Of the 17 Borrowing Member Countries (BMCs) of the Caribbean Development Bank (CBD), the GDP growth rate in 1993 of seven of them was higher than in 1992 – three registered no change from the previous year, and the last two showed only declines. CDB President, Sir Neville Nicholls, told a press conference on February 1, 1994: 'When taken as a whole, the Region's economic performance was still less than satisfactory because the major economies were the most disappointing and the impact of their minimal progress will be felt by the whole Region.' The more developed countries (MDCs) of the Commonwealth Caribbean of the early 1960s have become virtually the least developed countries (LDCs) with negligible growth rates and explosive problems. The slow recovery from recession in the industrialised countries did not greatly assist them.

Banana production and exports which play a vital role in the economies of the Windward Islands (LDCs) fell sharply during 1993, both in volume and earnings. This was due to depreciation of sterling against the dollar and changes in marketing arrangements in Europe. Lower cost Latin American fruit has been given access to the European market, and eventually there will be a phasing of the preferential market access of the African/Caribbean/Pacific (ACP) countries.

Sugar production in the region declined by about three per cent from the 1992 level of 732,000 tons. Reduced quotas in the USA market and a lowering of the world market price tempered returns on sugar. Petroleum production showed a declining pattern in recent years. Output of crude petroleum in Trinidad and Tobago fell by 7.8 per cent during the first three-quarters of 1993, due to a fall in the international prices. The performance of the bauxite industry in the countries of the region continues to be disappointing, largely due to weak international markets.

The only industry making gains was tourism, responding to slow recovery from recession in the industrialised countries, particularly USA. But this service industry is faced with threats from crime, violence, narcotics, high service charges and competition from cruise ships and other attractive tourist destinations.

Social problems are becoming acute. Nearly a decade ago, 'The Twelve Wise Men', headed by Nobel Prize Laureate, Sir Arthur Lewis, had noted high unemployment of nearly 30 per cent in some territories and warned that it could become an explosive problem. Referring to the present grave situation, the CDB's President asserted:

The generally weak performance of the economies did little to relieve the serious unemployment situation. About 200,000 working age West Indians across the region remained jobless in 1993, many of them young people and women. There was the consequential continued rise in social problems and the governments just did not have the resources with which to finance compensatory activities that would have provided more jobs.

Sir Neville recently pointed out that a third of the population of the Commonwealth was living in poverty. This must be viewed in the context of the prognosis made by Secretary General of the Organisation of American States (OAS) that by the end of this decade the poverty of 45 per cent of the population of Latin America and the Caribbean was alarming. Is it the plight of the poor that the Caribbean Conference of Churches (CCC) not too long ago advised churches and their leaders to convert some chapels and church halls into soup kitchens, offices into medical clinics and grounds into playing fields for the children? The situation cannot be allowed to become as explosive as in the late 1970s or at the time of the Great Depression of the 1930s when there were disturbances throughout the Caribbean.

Venezuela, with a very high poverty rate, is a good example of a potentially dangerous situation in the region. Even with abundant natural resources, a high GDP growth rate of 9 per cent and a democratic culture since 1958, two attempts have been made by sections of the military to overthrow the popularly elected government. Guyana, with nearly half of the population below the poverty line, a fragile economy and democracy, must avoid the serious racial/ethnic clashes and strife of the early 1960s. In this regard, and particularly noting the demands of the international financial institutions for speedy privatisation/divestment of state-owned entities, the Report of the IDB study group is relevant. It notes:

Special care must be taken to prevent disruption of the delicate social balance, as winners and losers of the adjustment process are, without deliberate re-distribution measures, likely to run along ethnic lines. Blind application of market forces would result in tangible benefits for the East Indian population group that is strongly represented in agriculture, professional services and commerce, and net costs for Afro-Guyanese, who are highly organised and strongly represented in government, police, military and bauxite mining. Reforms must therefore be designed to spread their impact equitably among the various social strata and ethnic groups: a cost/benefit sharing system palatable to the population at large is a condition *sine qua non* for a successful completion of adjustment process.

The Caribbean economies, particularly the manufacturing sectors, in their quest for export-led growth, are faced with an unfavourable international situation. There is competition from modernised high-tech (computers, robots), production of goods and services in the North with a large internal market; competition from Southeast Asian countries with relatively more competitive labour costs, large domestic population and an educated labour force; dumping of goods; and increased difficulty in funding public sector activities as traditional aid donors shift assistance to Eastern Europe and Africa.

In this era of globalisation and modernised capital-intensive, high- technology methods of production, recession and stagnation will be more prolonged than in the past, and will occur with greater frequency. This is because we are now faced with a cyclical, as well as a structural, crisis. Cybernation and automation – computers and robots – are the hallmark of the modern production process in order to cheapen the product, so as to capture the greater share of the global market. This leads to intense trade competition, trade barriers and protectionism resulting in deepening contradictions between the means of production and the relations of production, the growing social inequality and the widening gap between the rich and the poor.

The continued inability of regional economics to provide sustained improvement in domestic living levels is posing major challenges for the needed change. We are told to embark on structural adjustment programmes that will include increased trade liberalisation, de-regulation, privatisation/divestment, improved climate for private investment and private business activity. We are told there is need for higher expenditure for infrastructure, expanded human resource development activities to improve administrative capacity, and an expanded monitoring and regulatory capacity as private sector activities expand and become more complex. But regrettably, the structural adjustment programmes have proved to be merely a palliative, not a cure. They cannot succeed unless, at the same time, there is debt forgiveness, unconditional aid along with structural adjustments in the industrial countries to which they are inextricably linked in a dependent relationship.

The Standing Committee of Caribbean Finance Ministers noted that the structural adjustment programmes of some member states caused contractions in public sector investment programmes, and limited the capacity of Government to provide funding for viable projects and counterpart funding for externally supported activities. The situation in Guyana is instructive. A virtually bankrupt situation caused the country to be declared ineligible in 1985 for further credits by the International Monetary Fund (IMF).

A structural adjustment programme, though necessary, has been fraught with many contradictions and difficulties. Devaluation of the Guyanese currency, (G$4.15=US$1 in 1985 to G$126 =US$1 in 1992), led to a grave decline in real wages and salaries, increased prices for critical goods and services, higher cost for import inputs, and significant increases in debt payment in Guyanese dollars – amounting to 105 per cent of state current revenues in 1992 and 80 per cent in 1993. This contributed to a huge budget deficit and drastic budgetary reductions in expenditure on subsidies of essential goods, social services and employment costs, which in turn led to massive retrenchment in the public sector and administrative incapacity. A floating currency linked to trade and monetary liberalisation and speculative and trading activities, caused instability, which led to further devaluation of the Guyanese dollar from G$125 for US$1 on December, 31,1993 to G$140 for US$1 in May 1994. Low wages and salaries, despite budgetary support from the World Bank and the British ODA, for an administrative project, led to a ten day strike in the public service which seriously affected steamer and air-transport services. Unsustainably high real interest rates became a disincentive to productive investments and shifted the economy towards speculative and trading activities. It also led to increased inequality with the rich getting richer and the poor getting poorer. A credit squeeze led to overall contraction of the economy, declines in capacity utilisation and an accentuated shortage of critical goods and services. There was lack of administrative capacity to implement projects for which funding had already been secured. A special IDB study notes: 'The task is complicated by the fact that the quality of Guyana public sector has deteriorated sharply . . . The dilemma is that the substantially higher level of remuneration needed to attract qualified personnel is not compatible with the medium term imperative of further reducing the fiscal deficit.

Attaining sustainable development for the Caribbean region with many small island – states demands medium and long-term planning strategies and special consideration. Development, especially human development, must be seen as directly linked to the environment in a positive way. For example, the 1970s destruction of the environment was viewed as a result of economic growth. But in the 1980s the perception correctly changed; environmental degradation was seen as a consequence of stagnation, poverty and hunger.

We need our own agenda. Since the end of the World War II, we have followed a model of flawed growth: the Puerto Rican import substitution model based on wrong premises. A special report, 'Our Own Agenda', prepared by an independent Latin American and Caribbean Commission on Development and Environment, noted that besides problems with direct environmental connotations, other problems of an economic nature include: the outflow of capital from Latin America and the Caribbean to the developed countries; the constant deterioration of the prices of the raw material produced by countries of the region. The report also referred to the fluctuation of interest rates, which worsened the external debt problems, the induction of inappropriate technological patterns and commercial protectionism.

The net outflow of capital from Latin America and the Caribbean in the 1981–85 period was US$36 billion yearly in the form of profits, dividends and debt payments. Commodity price fluctuations particularly for the one-crop and/or one mineral economy had shattering effects. Every one per cent increase in interest rates in the North added nearly US$2.5 billion to the burdensome external indebtedness, which deprived the countries of the capital needed for growth, prolonged the grave economic crisis and exacerbated the conditions of the poor. A prospective EGLAC study for Latin America and the Caribbean for the 1985–95 period predicts, even with a 7 per cent annual growth rate, increased poverty, increased unemployment by nearly 50 per cent and a foreign debt of US$368 billion in 1985 increasing to US$672 billion in 1995.

In the Commonwealth Caribbean, there was a worsening trend in the region's debt servicing. Jamaica, Guyana and Trinidad and Tobago particularly have very high debt service ratios, (the ratio of debt service to export of goods and services) which are not conductive to sustainable economic growth and human development. Structural adjustment programmes, with such huge debt overhangs and an unfavourable international business climate, are unlikely to succeed.

The Standing Committee of CARICOM Finance Ministers sees the need for debt reduction, for write-offs of stock and debt servicing, for repayment programmes of longer duration with the IMF and other FMIs. The recent UN conference of Small Island Developing States for Sustainable Development in Barbados noted that these states, though part of the wider developing world, had peculiar problems, including natural disasters, and thus needed special consideration for the protection of their land and marine resources and the development of their human resources. Industrial countries were criticised for the non-fulfilment of their financial commitments after the Rio Summit on sustainable development and the environment.

The fact is that the developed countries are themselves strapped for cash due to weak economies, fiscal and balance of payments deficits and a greater need for a bigger safety net for the 35 million unemployed in the OECD countries and the 20 million unemployed in Europe. Indeed, 'aid fatigue' is developing in the North and aid to the developing countries is being cut. This is regrettable, as in our interdependent world, the North needs the South in the same measure that the South needs the North. The South must secure debt relief and other forms of assistance so that it can have sustainable economic development and in so doing procure the essential goods and services, especially capital goods, from the industrial countries. The latter needs higher growth rates to end unemployment and poverty, which can be assisted by higher living standards and greater purchasing power of the people in the developing countries.

A New Global Humanitarian Order

Economic recovery in the Caribbean Basin will depend on changes in the international and national arenas. There needs to be a resumption of sustained growth in the global economy and changes in the individual economies to respond competitively with the newly changed world situation. Increased trade liberalisation towards a 'borderless world', free and rapid movement of finance capital, and the technology and information 'revolution' are factors to which adjustments must be made quickly.

Reforms towards a new world socio-economic order is required urgently. It is possible 'to end half of the world's hunger before the year 2000', says the report of the Carnegie Commission on Science, Technology and Government. This needs political will and a new genuine North/South partnership for global cooperation and initiative for development. Science and technology must be harnessed in the service of man to meet the 'basic needs' of the world's poorest as was envisaged by a major revision of the concept of development cooperation in the early 1970s.

Radical reforms of the global system must now be the new agenda for development. During the Cold War era, there was ambivalence about cooperation for development. Political, economic and military considerations were placed before humanitarian concerns. In the developing world, those with higher incomes received the most ODA assistance and the poorest received the least. The top 40 per cent income group received in 1980 ODA per capita US$5 as compared with per capita US$2 for the bottom 40 per cent income group. Two-thirds of the world's 1.3 billion poor live in ten countries that together receive less than a third of the ODA. The ending of the Cold War offers an opportunity for a re-ordering of priorities, for reforms towards a new global humanitarian order of economic growth, good governance, human rights, freedom, equity and development.

During the depression of the 1930s, radical reforms were carried out to alleviate unemployment and hunger. The Swedish Government provided for 100 per cent unemployment relief. The Franklyn Delano Roosevelt New Deal Administration created employment through physical, social and cultural works. In Britain, the Beveridge plan for a welfare state was instituted.

The financial resources for economic growth and human development are not only inadequately distributed but also wasted in vast military expenditure in both the developed and developing countries. World military spending in 1992 was US$815 billion, equal to the income of nearly half the world's people. With a large majority of states facing budgetary and balance of payments deficits, one effective way to mobilise additional funds is accelerated cuts in military expenditures. During the 1987–94 period, decline in military spending resulted in the saving of US$935 billion – a peace dividend – which unfortunately was not used to finance the world's social agenda. With a continued decline in military spending by 3 per cent a year, another US$460 billion could emerge as a peace dividend in the 1995–2000 period. A small tax of 0.05 per cent on global foreign exchange movements – Nobel Prize Economist, James Tobin recommends 0.5 per cent – could yield US$150 billion per year. Such funds can be focused on the priority areas of human development.

The Peace Dividend and other international revenue earning measures can be utilised for debt relief to the underdeveloped countries, especially to the Caribbean small island developing states. Developing countries paid US$160 billion in debt service charges in 1992, more than two and a half times official aid and US$60 billion more than private financial flows. The 1994 Human Development Report says that the debt servicing is hampering developing countries ability to meet urgent human development needs, and suggests cancelling the debt of the poorest countries in return for a pledge that they earmark those same funds for social development.

The Peace Dividend could also be used to increase employment by reducing the number of days or the number of hours worked per week, without loss of pay, or by reducing the pensionable age without loss of benefit. Or it could be used to set up a work programme for physical, social and cultural infrastructure, as in the Roosevelt New Deal Administration at the time of the depression of the 1930s.

The Caribbean region has been variously described in the past as the USAs 'fourth border', 'Achilles Heel' and 'a danger zone'. Crime, drug trafficking, legal and illegal migration make it a volatile area. It is possible to stop the explosion. The people are hungry not because food is not available, but because they cannot afford to buy it. The international community must act urgently to diffuse the time-bomb by enhancing the physical, human and natural capital for development and basic human needs in this beautiful part of the globe. The price for failure will be great, as happened in Latin America and the Caribbean after the oligarchy had rejected President John F. Kennedy's reformist Alliance for Progress. In introducing it on March 13, 1961, he stated:

Throughout Latin America, a continent rich in resources and in spiritual and cultural achievements by its populations, millions of men and women suffered the daily privations of poverty and hunger. They lack decent housing or protection against disease. Their children are deprived of an education or jobs which [open] the door to a better life. And every day goes by, the problems are more pressing. Population growth surpasses economic development – the low standards of living get worse – and the discontent, the discontent of a population that knows that abundance and the elements of progress are at last within reach, that discontent increases.

After the Cuban revolution, President Kennedy wanted reforms – administrative, fiscal, monetary, land – and called for an evolution. Later, in 1962, in a letter to President Betancourt of Venezuela, he said:

The preservation and strengthening of freely elected constitutional government is the aspiration of all the peoples of the Americas and progress in this continent under Alianza para el Progreso in large measure on effecting change through peaceful and democratic means and avoiding violent interruptions of the constitutional process.

Non-implementation of the reforms led to military dictatorship and the 'lost decade' of the 1980s. This must not happen again.

Note

This paper by Cheddi Jagan was first published in *Caribbean Affairs*, Vol. 5 No. 5, July/August 1995, (A Caribbean Information and Systems & Services Ltd. Publication), pp. 155–167.

[P a r t T w o]

Ideology of Survival

[15]

Introduction to

Critical Issues in Caribbean Development[1]

William Demas

The conference of Heads of Government of the Caribbean Community (CARICOM) has accepted many of the recommendations of the West Indian Commission with respect to the strengthening of the Community via the creation of a single market (economic union) and the widening of CARICOM through trade and economic relations in neighbouring non English-speaking Caribbean countries.

This book explores the deepening of CARICOM especially with respect to the goal of the single market. The Commission recommended the acceleration of the process of functional cooperation and the establishment of common services, particularly a West Indian Court of Appeal. It called for greater coordination of foreign policies, including external trade policies, and the setting up where feasible, of joint CARICOM embassies abroad.

In light of the underlying nature of West Indian economies and the trends towards globalisation and regionalism, CARICOM is seen as an essential element in promoting international competitiveness, greater self-reliance and a West Indian identity. The alternatives to a strengthened CARICOM are either 'marginalisation' or *de jure* or *de facto* 'absorption' in a highly dependent mode into one or more much bigger and more powerful country or group of countries.

The positive case for CARICOM is well-known: helping our countries to achieve economies of scale and critical mass in many economic and non-economic activities; the facilitation of extra-regional exports and efficient regional import substitution; functional cooperation and common services in a wide range of fields; and the achievement of greater bargaining power vis-à-vis the outside world.

Development appropriate to the region is defined as efficient economic growth combined with social equity. This includes the promotion of enterprises of all scales combined with the alleviation of poverty and the significant reduction of unemployment.

CARICOM's stance with respect to itself as well as to its long-standing preferential agreements with metropolitan countries must be placed in the context of recent movements towards a hemispheric free trade area. It is considered that for the CARICOM countries the Free Trade Area of the Americas (FTAA) is an alternative to the expansion of NAFTA in that the FTAA permits CARICOM and other sub-regional integration movements to maintain and strengthen the links among their member countries, and between themselves and other sub-regional integration groupings (including NAFTA) in the hemisphere.

Previous trade agreements – for example, with the European Union under the Lomé Convention – would not be seen as being in conflict with the FTAA but as providing a much wider market for export development and competitive strengthening, provided that reciprocity remains selective and not applied across the board.

New relationships such as the Association of Caribbean States (ACS) increase, not decrease, the imperative towards stronger CARICOM integration. Thus membership in the ACS does not negate the importance of CARICOM. The ACS is about cooperation in trade, investment, finance, tourism, transport, science, technology, education, health, culture. Deep integration such as a single market or economic union is not practical at this stage for the ACS. A practical approach, over time, to deep economic integration, involving full membership of CARICOM, might be more feasible between CARICOM and one, two or three of the non English-speaking independent islands of the Greater Antilles.

The 'shield' of CARICOM is necessary to provide some degree of effective sovereignty for the individual CARICOM countries and help them to secure greater benefits from external trade and other economic and diplomatic relationships through joint external negotiations and bargaining. Should CARICOM countries attempt to negotiate individually, the Community might disintegrate. The result would be not only a loss of diplomatic and economic strength but of vital intangibles such as international credibility and a sense of West Indian community and identity.

The question is whether market integration should go beyond a single market, that is, intra-CARICOM free trade; a truly common external tariff, (CET), complete factor mobility in the medium and long term; consultation on and coordination of national economic policies; and financial and monetary cooperation and integration (including the establishment of fixed exchange rates between national currencies and a single currency). The answer is yes. First, there is a crying need for cooperation in joint investments as between the private sectors of the member countries. Second, the need for cooperation in production and in both intra-regional and extra-regional marketing should be emphasised.

Cooperation in investment and, more generally, in production and marketing requires an active private sector and is complementary to a common economic space. This cooperation includes strategies such as the integration of production between national economies, joint ventures across countries as well as a regional industrial and agricultural policy complemented by an appropriate legal and regulatory regional framework. Joint marketing, both within and outside CARICOM, could be undertaken by private sector trading companies.

How can CARICOM in this age of trade liberalisation and open regionalism be of use to its member countries? It should provide an environment conducive to export oriented development policies as well as efficient regional import substitution. These policies should focus on areas such as internal and external macroeconomic stabilisation, increasing productivity, higher levels of domestic savings and productive sector investment, and human resource development. Such policies would enhance the international competitiveness of CARICOM economies which is of critical importance to the strengthening of the productive sectors. It should be emphasised that the most important factor in achieving West Indian international competitiveness is increasing productivity. This involves many policies, programmes and measures, the chief of which is human resource development.

The relationship between deepening and widening is crucial. The deepening of CARICOM must be achieved in order to widen its relationships to make closer trade links with much bigger and more powerful countries, near and far, workable. Widening should take the form of closer relations with our neighbours on the basis of: trade; financial and economic cooperation; collaboration in science, technology, culture, and in education and training. This is bound to develop into an intensive and extensive programme of practical economic and technical cooperation. There may also in the medium to long term be a degree of hemispheric free trade under the FTAA. Full membership of CARICOM over the medium to long term can be envisaged for one or more of the Greater Antilles islands.

Historically, West Indian development has been dependent on the preferences of metropolitan markets (with non-reciprocal preferences) and heavy dependence on external financial assistance. Our economies need to become less externally dependent and more self-reliant, that is to say, more internationally competitive. To effect this, we need to redouble urgently our economic efforts to do everything listed above. But even with tremendous internal efforts, we need a period of transition before we can become internationally competitive. During this transition period, we need external help to promote self-help on our part.

CARICOM should be deepened and become of increasing importance to us while as a united body we develop relationships of cooperation with the larger Latin American and other hemispheric countries and sub-regional groups (including NAFTA), as well as economic blocs further afield, particularly the European Union. Membership of either the ACS or CARICOM is not the issue. CARICOM remains essential to us and there is enormous scope for practical cooperation between a deepened CARICOM and the ACS. Indeed deepening is a condition for the widening of CARICOM.

CARICOM countries need time and continued external support if they are to successfully complete the transition towards being internationally competitive, resilient and more self-reliant. This should be given due recognition by hemispheric and West European preference-giving governments as well as multilateral and bilateral donors. The nature of the West Indian economy as a result of our historical legacy is such that at this crucial juncture we need for another fifteen years continuing non-reciprocal preferences and external aid.

Note

1. This paper was published as the introduction to the book: *Critical Issues in Caribbean Development – West Indian Development and the Deepening & Widening of the Caribbean Community,* by William Demas. (Kingston: Ian Randle Publishers, 1997), pp. xiii–xvi.

[16]

Extract from the Postscript to
Critical Issues in Caribbean Development[1]

William Demas

The fundamental question is what we can do to avoid re-colonisation. Some of the measures have already been discussed in the book. At the risk of some repetition, we put forward the following suggestions.

We should seek further to diversify our trading, economic and political relationships across as many continents as possible. However, because of our geographical location and the size and capacity of the USA economy, we will always have significant trade and other economic ties with that country. It would simply not be possible to effect a substantial reduction of such ties. What we are talking about here is *incremental* diversification for the most part.

The process of constant vigilance, referred to earlier, must obviously include threats and actions which would severely affect or destroy the basis of our economies, as is now the case with bananas. Putting the point more positively, successful efforts to strengthen and diversify our economies are a fundamental means of safeguarding and enhancing our independence.

Heightened concern with our sovereignty and our economic survival will lead to greater efforts at consultation, at both national and regional levels. Our political leaders and ministers of Foreign Affairs, National Security, Finance and International Trade should consult with each other on a continuing basis, on all matters and issues that appear to threaten our sovereignty – whether political, economic or having to do with security.

It is imperative that our leaders scrupulously avoid our countries being played off against each other by much larger and more powerful neighbouring or distant governments, blocs and private entities.

The expansion of the Caribbean Community (both the Community and the Common Market aspects) must also occupy an important place on our agenda. Eric Williams, once referred to by Errol Barrow as the 'philosopher of Caribbean Integration', always envisaged the economic integration of the entire Caribbean Archipelago irrespective of language and constitutional status of the countries and territories. It is, however, easier to start only with the *independent* and possibly near-independent countries. All the independent countries of the Caribbean Archipelago must, after an initial phase of freer trade through trade liberalisation and/or economic cooperation agreements, proceed in the medium-term to come together in a much larger CARICOM Single Market. This would increase our integrated Caribbean Archipelago market from six million to over thirty million people and would obviously greatly enhance our external bargaining-power.

Efforts must also be made by all the Eastern Caribbean members of CARICOM to establish among themselves political unions (of varying degrees of closeness ranging from full federation among some to confederation embracing all). This union should rest on a firm foundation of economic unity – although such political union must transcend purely economic matters. The present extent of, and future potential for, political fragmentation in the Eastern Caribbean is simply scandalous and short-sighted on our part, and invites both drug trafficking and money-laundering activities as well as temptation for political interference and the exercise of crude hegemony by more powerful outsiders.

We return here to the question of incrementally diversifying our trade, economic and political relationships with countries other than the world's lone superpower. Here, CARICOM countries should, wherever possible acting as a group, consciously seek to diversify their trade and other external economic and political relations. This should be done principally through the Free Trade Area of the Americas (FTAA) by trade liberalisation as between the hemispheric sub-groupings, starting with the non-CARICOM Caribbean countries, the Central American Common Market, the ANDEAN Group, MERCOSUR and ending up with NAFTA.

We should also view with the utmost interest the attempt now being made to form a South American Free Trade Area (SAFTA), particularly its relationship to the North American Free Trade Area (NAFTA).

In the context of NAFTA, and also outside of it, our economic, diplomatic and political relations with Canada can provide us with some of the countervailing power we need to avoid an extraordinary degree of dominance by the world's only superpower. Canada has no hegemonic ambitions and understands us and our problems better than the superpower. Much the same applies to our economic and political relations with the Association of Caribbean States (ACS) and with the other Latin American countries (save for the misunderstanding of our banana cost and marketing problem by some of these countries).

For the same general reasons, as well as for more specific trade and economic reasons (such as markets for our bananas, sugar, rice, rum, non-traditional agricultural exports and our manufactured goods; financial aid; access to foreign private investment and technology), we should seek to continue and even to intensify our relations with the European Union, many of whose member states (and its Commission as well) seem to understand our problems reasonably well. Closer trade and economic relations with East and Southeast Asian countries and with India, Pakistan, South Africa and Nigeria also commend themselves.

Diversification of external trade, economic and political relations can be a factor more conducive to a greater degree of effective sovereignty than very close relations with only one or even two superordinate great powers. As the West Indies Commission put it, we now have several 'windows of opportunity' (because of our historical background and our present geo-political situation) and we should make full use of all of them, if only to compensate for our minute size, relative lack of natural resources, and limited individual bargaining power.

There is much to be said in favour of a federation of all the OECS states (both the Leeward and Windward Islands). The British Virgin Islands and Anguilla should certainly be included as well. This federation, which would have only one external sovereignty, could become part of a looser Eastern Caribbean Confederation (where, unlike a federation, individual units retain their separate external sovereignties but agree to exercise them jointly). This confederation would also include Guyana and Trinidad and Tobago. It would be up to Barbados to decide whether it would form part of the OECS Federation or become a separate unit of the wider Eastern Caribbean Confederation; but this country must obviously be directly included in the one or the other. Suriname could consider becoming a unit of the confederation at a later stage, after it has fully settled into the CARICOM relationship.

Needless to say, this confederation, acting wherever possible with their CARICOM partners in the Northern Caribbean, would be vitally concerned with the enhancement of our sovereignty and external security (as well as with our economic and social development, the operation of new common services, human rights and good governance). Essentially, it would complement the CARICOM Single Market and Economy agreed for the economic aspect of deepening the Community – the other two aspects of deepening – (a) Functional Cooperation and Common Services; and (b) the Coordination of Foreign (and External Trade) Policies.

Finally, we discuss a somewhat intangible but most fundamental aspect of the maintenance of our sovereignty – a greater degree of psychological independence. This theme has been dealt with by many twentieth-century West Indian thinkers.

In different disciplines and different contexts, these writers all clearly saw psychological independence as a desirable end in itself as well as a major requirement for achieving and maintaining both formal and effective sovereignty and West Indian identity. Psychological independence, in their view, also entails a certain degree of cultural and intellectual independence. A good example of where we have fallen short in psychological independence is our failure so far to establish the Caribbean Community Court of Appeal with final jurisdiction. The vast majority of other Commonwealth countries – including Canada, India, Pakistan and nearly all the others in Asia and Africa have for some time now had their own Final Appeal Courts. Australia recently announced its intention to do likewise in the near future.

We in the West Indies run the risk of probably being the last set of Commonwealth countries to retain the services of the Judicial Committee of the Privy Council in London.

Another example where somewhat more progress has been made concerns the issue of independence in the form of a monarchy or a republic. Dominica, Guyana and Trinidad and Tobago are now republics and all parties in Jamaica agree that the country should shortly assume republican status under a presidential Head of State. The others are still monarchies. Obviously whether an independent country of the Commonwealth has the British Queen or a national President, as Head of State, is irrelevant to the constitutional independence of that country. It is purely a question of national symbolism and psychology.

But national symbols are of great importance. Recently P. J. Patterson, the Prime Minister of Jamaica, set up a high level National Committee on National Symbols and Observances.

In particular, some measure of intellectual independence is essential in appraising the relevance to the West Indies of the major ideologies of Western European origin – nationalism (constructive or destructive), political democracy and human rights, liberal capitalism, conservative capitalism, varying shades of social democracy and democratic socialism, communism and fascism. Some of these go together, others are mutually exclusive. The issue is to what extent should we draw upon Western European ideologies as against indigenous ones?

This brings us to the question of indigenous West Indian thought in the twentieth century. West Indian indigenous thought and writing from a nationalist, democratic and reformist/radical perspective came into full flowering in the twentieth century.[2] It is useful to think of the contributions in terms of three waves.

The first wave, includes writers born before the First World War – people such as Marcus Garvey, C.L.R. James, Philip Sherlock, Eric Williams and Arthur Lewis (born in 1915).

The second wave, includes writers born between the two world wars. One group – for example, George Lamming, Rex Nettleford, Gordon Rohlehr and Edward Kamau Brathwaite (and to some extent and in a different context Vidia Naipaul) grappled directly with the closely related issues of culture, identity and the other psychological aspects of independence. The other was the New World Group with persons such as Lloyd Best, Kari Levitt, George Beckford, Norman Girvan among others. This group was concerned with psychological and intellectual independence as well as the political economy of West Indian development. (Alister McIntyre made important technical contributions to the subject of Caribbean development, Caribbean integration, monetary economics and trade policy in the early days of the movement).

The third wave, includes those born during and after World War II. There are so many that it would be invidious to select only one or two for special mention.

Obviously, these three sets of thinkers differed among themselves and as between their respective waves in terms of the time in which they lived and their experiences, emphases, preoccupations and disciplines. Nor is it a question of one wave replacing another. Each wave leaves a large legacy for succeeding waves in a somewhat cumulative overall process. For example, the following seems to be more or less common to all three groups: the achievement and maintenance of West Indian self-determination, the basis of which was seen as full internal self-government (later to be called independence). Garvey was the earliest and C.L.R. James the second and most forceful advocate of this; the advocacy of more political democracy internally; C.L.R. James was the first to develop this theme of full, unqualified democracy; the 'economic emancipation' of the masses, to use Eric Williams' term; the need to diversify and strengthen the economic structure; Marcus Garvey, Eric

Williams, Arthur Lewis and all in the second and third waves; greater pride, self-reliance and awareness of their heritage on the part of the masses of African descent. This was strongly emphasised by Marcus Garvey and later on, and continuing up to today, by Philip Sherlock that remarkable West Indian, who in spite of his advanced age, seems to represent all three waves at one and the same time; West Indian political unity – most strongly emphasised by C.L.R. James, Eric Williams and Arthur Lewis. The hope for political union (either of all the West Indian or only the Eastern Caribbean) even after the early demise of the West Indies Federation in 1962 was entertained by Arthur Lewis, Eric Williams and many in the second and third waves. Under the influence of Eric Williams, the New World Group and others of the second wave, favoured economic integration of both the English-speaking Caribbean and the entire Caribbean Archipelago. Michael Manley played an important role in the deepening of CARIFTA into the Caribbean Community (CARICOM) and at the wider Third World level. He also strongly supported economic co-operation among developing countries; a greater measure of psychological independence emphasised by Garvey, James, Sherlock and Williams. It must be stressed that the sub-topic of intellectual independence emerged most strongly and clearly with the second wave of thinkers, both within and outside the New World Group, examples being: Lloyd Best, George Beckford, Norman Girvan and DeLisle Worrell in the former category and Lamming, Nettleford, Gordon Rohlehr, Edward Kamau Brathwaite outside the Group. It is shared by many in the third wave of thinkers such as Hilary Beckles.

One concluding comment on one or two of the leaders of the New World Group. They made the error of unfairly and unjustifiably disparaging the contributions of earlier West Indian thinkers such as Eric Williams and Arthur Lewis. This is most unfortunate – both because of their impiety towards their intellectual ancestors and in conveying the wrong impression to readers that there was little continuity between previous West Indian writers and the New World Group.

Over the last decade and a half, the third wave has mainly consisted of UWI social scientists and some outstanding West Indian commentators such as Rickey Singh, Tim Hector and Raoul Pantin. Suffice it to say that the range of topics is much wider than during the second wave and the number of researchers much larger. Fundamental subjects such as the environment; gender studies; electoral behaviour; international relations; structural adjustment; poverty and the informal sector (and many others) are now being given serious attention. On the other hand during the second wave, the main topics were the political economy of Caribbean development; West Indian integration; the transnational corporation; technology; race, class and colour; labour relations; small farming; the labour market; and savings. Many of the second wave themes are also being examined by the third wave scholars. But the theme of the political economy of Caribbean development is receiving proportionately less attention than under the second wave.

This increased coverage by the third wave is a healthy and very helpful trend and will certainly accelerate. But we cannot afford to reduce emphasis on the history and theory of long-term development and projections of alternative scenarios.

The concern with the past and future long-term development of the West Indian political economy, with West Indian integration and with intellectual independence were the best features in the thought of the New World Group.

This is so not only because we need, as always, a sense of direction but also because of the remarkable progress in technology and the rapid changes which the world economy is now undergoing as both Owen Arthur, the Prime Minister of Barbados, and Edwin Carrington, the Secretary General of CARICOM have recently observed. We must 'factor in' these changes in any vision of the future and in any future development models or scenarios which we construct.

There is a rich legacy of the ideologies of Western Europe some of which are more universalistic and more humane than others. We cannot avoid adopting the ideals and ideas of these universal and humane systems and concepts already laid down in some of these ideologies. We, however, have to add the 'indigenous factor' to make them ideals and ideas meaningful in our circumstances.

My own view is that we have to draw on the ideals and ideas of some of the Western European ideologies and blend them with the dictates of West Indian culture, history, experience and our needs and situation, and with the rapidly changing world economic and technological situation. Bearing all this in mind, I would tentatively suggest as a basis for a model (or vision) of economic, social and political development appropriate to our region for the first few decades of the twenty-first century. The following are ten fundamental points:

1. An efficient, diversified and internationally competitive economy in terms of the production of both goods and services and a just and equitable society dedicated to removing poverty and unemployment.

2. The stimulation of a greater measure of pride, self-esteem and self-reliance among all the West Indian peoples.

3. An efficient and, (where necessary) economically interventionist type state operating in unison (side by side and cooperatively) with an effi-

cient, competently managed and entrepreneurial private sector – the state, the private sector and the trade union movement being dedicated to the well-being of all in the nation particularly the well-being of the truly poor and the unemployed. Popular participation in the development process (as distinct from manipulative populism).

4. Recognition of human development (including human resource development) as an important element both an end in itself and as a means to national development. Recognition of indigenous West Indian cultural growth and development both as an end in itself and as a means to promoting economic and social development. These two points emphasise that development should be 'people-centred'.

5. Greater emphasis on the application of science and technology (including information science and technology and biotechnology) to the development of the region by the state, the other social partners and other relevant groups and a prominent role for these areas at all levels of the educational system.

6. Recognition of the fundamental importance of the preservation and improvement of the environment by the state, the other social partners and all persons and entities undertaking physical development and/or construction or engaged in the ownership or operation and maintenance of production facilities, equipment, infrastructure, or residential facilities. Moreover, there must be widespread understanding that environmental maintenance and improvement are essential not only for aesthetic, cultural, social and health but also for *economic* reasons.

7. An ideology of psychological, cultural, political and economic nationalism which emphasises: West Indian unity and economic integration of the Caribbean Archipelago both as ends in themselves and as means to national development and greater sovereignty. This entails respect in all countries for the equality of *all* West Indian people irrespective of economic and social position, race, colour and particular West Indian country of origin. This principle should, in future, extend to all members of the Caribbean Community to the extent that other Caribbean archipelago countries become members of the Community.

8. Active economic, cultural and intellectual interdependence and interaction with the rest of the world (as distinct from the passive dependence which has prevailed for centuries).

9. The preservation of our *formal* sovereignty and the maximisation of our *effective* sovereignty.

10. Maintenance and strengthening of political democracy should not necessarily involve any far-reaching amendments of present constitutions,

such as modelling them on the American pattern in situations where federalism, an essential rationale for the American Constitution, does not exist. We should also recognise that the excessive separation of powers in the American model is based on a misunderstanding of the then existing British system by the American founding fathers.

One should not forget that the present constitutions strike, on the whole, a sensible balance between speed and reasonable costs in government and parliamentary decision-making on the one hand and the public airing of, and deliberations on, political, social and economic issues of the day on the other. What may be needed in some countries is the devising of new, or the adaptation of existing, political and economic institutions to facilitate more genuine participation by the 'grassroots' in the development process. What also seems to be needed is a greater degree of transparency and accountability at all levels of government. In this connection the establishment of a more select committee of parliament is worth considering. (The issue of retention of the monarchy versus republicanism is not so much a constitutional question as a matter of symbolism and an assertion of psychological independence).

The upholding of human rights – political and civil as well as economic, social, and cultural – should be recognised as being of fundamental importance, as is the recognition of the obligations and duties of individuals and groups to the state and the wider society. Apart from offences against the law being justly and quickly dealt with in an open manner, the grave deficiencies in both the work ethic and business ethics that now exist must be eliminated willingly by both workers and businessmen at fault.

It can be readily seen that the elements outlined above are rooted in a blend of West European and indigenous West Indian thought, history and experience. Moreover, the relative emphases between the elements must take into account the ever-changing situation in the various countries of the region.

With regard to a special ideological label for this vision, I prefer to be concrete and specific and simply use the term 'a West Indian model (or, if one wishes, ideology) of economic, social and political development'.

But in addition to the adoption of an appropriate model of development, specific concrete programmes of action are required in order to achieve a greater degree of psychological, cultural and intellectual independence. Our leaders and our people at large must seek to do the following.

- Generate appropriate national and regional symbols which would inspire and motivate the people.
- Promote the teaching of West Indian and Caribbean history from a Caribbean point of view as compulsory subjects in our educational insti-

tutions – primary, secondary and tertiary. In this approach we need to emphasise our innovativeness and creativity and to stress our achievements in all fields of human endeavours, in spite of the formidable obstacles which we have faced for virtually all of our history;

- Continue material and moral support for the activities of the Caribbean News Agency (CANA) and the Caribbean Broadcasting Union (CBU) in projecting West Indian programmes to all parts of the region, and for further efforts to project such programmes to North and South America, Europe and to other parts of the world. There is much to be said in favour of Ian Boxill's proposals for a West Indian radio station and the establishment of a West Indian film making company. More broadly, in culture, creative arts, and electronic mass media, we should make every effort to project abroad what we have produced and not to be content with being passive importers of what emanates from North America and Western Europe. This is one area where more active effort is needed. We should interact with the rest of the world in culture and the Creative Arts, and not be a one-way importer from the dominant centres in the outside world. For example, Jamaica's reggae music in conquering the world is illustrative and inspiring and the same could be done with regard to the calypso and steelband.

- Finally, we need more activity in disseminating the works of West Indian writers produced by West Indian publishing houses for both the regional and overseas markets.

- Our poetry, creative dancing and drama must also be taken to many parts of the world, as is the case with our novels and the Jamaica National Dance Theatre Company.

- Adopt a style of male dress more suitable to our West Indian climate.

- More actively promote indigenous creative arts, whether of Afro-West Indian or Indo-West Indian origin or the product of our Creole situation and experience.

- Establish creative arts centres along the lines of the one at UWI, Mona, Jamaica, on the two other campuses and in the non-campus territories.

- Make more use of indigenous cultural creations as inputs into the production process and to use such creations as final products for use both within the region and for export to 'niche' markets abroad.

- Promote a regionally coordinated range of external policies and activities. This requires, *inter alia*, the early establishment of a West Indian 'think-tank'. The region has more than adequate intellectual and technical expertise to create for itself a first class 'think-tank' to deliberate on the major challenges facing us in the region today.

Judging from present trends, the real gender problem in the West Indies in the next few decades will relate to males rather than to females. Even casual observation today reveals that, particularly at the teenage level, compared to the young women, the young men are much less motivated or interested in achievement and seem to lack a sense of purpose and direction. Accordingly, gender development programmes must immediately begin to focus on males as well as females. For, if young males do not become better motivated, they cannot become psychologically independent, let alone make an appropriate contribution to economic and social development.

Notes

1.   Extract from 'Postscript' in William Demas, *Critical Issues in Caribbean Development – West Indian Development and the Deepening and Widening of the Caribbean Community*, Ian Randle Publishers, 1997, pp. 93–103.
2.   See Naipaul's novel, *Mimic Men.*

[17]

An Overview of *Essays In Honour of William Demas*[1]

Towards a Caribbean Economy in the Twenty-first Century

M.G. Zephirin

The major theme addressed by contributors to the day's proceedings in honour of William G. Demas was that of effective regional integration and cooperation. This was entirely appropriate, paying tribute as it did to a Caribbean economist who sees the Caribbean regional movement as the primary solution to the constraints of small size and has devoted his professional life to fostering that movement.

Part 1 of the proceedings honours William Demas' personal and professional qualities, as much as his work. In his opening address, Governor Ainsworth Harewood pays tribute to Demas' integrity, committed public service and exemplary role as intellectual and practitioner of Caribbean economists. In his turn, Sir Alister McIntyre speaks about Demas' pivotal roles in the Caribbean integration movement and in the Government of Trinidad and Tobago, his intellect and his endearing eccentricities.

In Part II Laurence Clarke sets the framework for the proceedings by reviewing Demas' landmark writings on the economics of small states and integration, making reference to Caribbean economic thought at the time Demas wrote. He notes Demas' stress on small size as a determinant of the characteristics and performance of economies, and the public policy strategy required to achieve transforming economic development in small economies. Key among these strategies, Clarke explains, is that of economic integration, developed in Demas' 1976 'Essays on Caribbean Integration and Development'. He notes Demas' rejection of the assumptions underlying neo-classical customs union theory, his concern for the unequal distribution of integration benefits among countries and for regional institution-building, as well as, importantly, for human resource development. Finally, Clarke notes, rather sadly, that it remains difficult to judge whether Demas' prescriptions have been effective, in part because they have not been fully implemented.

In Part III the welcoming address by the Honourable Trevor Sudama reflects the fact that the Demas seminar opened the 28th Monetary Studies Conference. In accord with both the themes of the conference and the central banking participation, he discusses financial institution failure and the regulation necessary to foster a safer financial system. Mr Sudama also refers to the ownership issues raised by recent events in Trinidad and Tobago's banking sector and the regulation that may be required to address such issues. Finally, he discusses the complex nature of development and the fact that people are themselves both the origin and the end of economic development.

Dennis Pantin touches on his personal experience of Demas' accessibility to junior economists before briefly summarising and critiquing *The Economics of Development in Small Countries with Special Reference to the Caribbean.* He notes that many of the concerns of that work remain relevant to the Caribbean, although he sees a weakness in its emphasis on manufacturing as the basis for development and a resulting bias in favour of import-substituting industrialisation. Most fundamentally, he questions whether the work provides an adequate analysis of small-island (as opposed to small-country) economics and their ecological vulnerability. This body of analysis is now being undertaken largely, Pantin notes, by economic geographers and is concerned with environmental management, but needs to focus on economic strategies relevant to small-island development. Pantin concludes by suggesting that continuing stagnation and poverty in the Caribbean result from the divide between seminal economic thought of the type produced by Demas and the elaboration and implementation of policy.

Marius St Rose's paper shifts the emphasis, interpreting Demas as political economist concerned with preserving and enhancing Caribbean sovereignty, his personae as development economist and public servant being mere contributors to that goal. St Rose explains this interpretation through a review of Demas' education and career, arguing that he was influenced by the thinking of the then-radical Caribbean politicians and historians who dominated the pre-independence period. He then goes on to discuss five facets of Demas' economic interests: development, the problems posed by small size, the role of the state, development planning and economic integration.

With Carlisle Pemberton's paper, the examination of the work of Demas moves from this broad view to focus on the agricultural sector which Pemberton describes as an unrecognised interest of Demas. Indeed, employing extensive quotes from unpublished addresses by Demas, Pemberton is able to demonstrate that Demas values agriculture as a source of raw materials for local manufacturing and tourism, but recognises that the agricultural sector also competes for labour. Demas sees diversification and regional trade as the required strategies for the sector, a view that is maintained in his current work.

Part IV of these essays turns explicitly to integration, a theme already stressed in part III in the context of Demas' view that the small country constraint could in part be addressed by regionalism. Norman Girvan focuses on this view as a guiding principle of the treaty establishing CARICOM, while noting that it also formed part of a coherent Caribbean body of work on integration. However, the CARICOM integration model is inward-looking and resource-based, giving rise to a number of programmes for joint state-led production which were implemented only to the feasibility study stage. Instead, Girvan argues for a new model, proposed by himself and Samuels in 1993, of private-sector-led regional production integration, with governments serving only a supporting role. He, however, acknowledges continuing failure to progress even on this new front, attributing this to a lack of interest on the part of the private sector and/or the short-term foci of governments. Girvan thus characterises the prospects for regional economic integration as utopian, while clinging to the vision.

Cuthbert Joseph examines the integration movement from the legal viewpoint, observing that the obligations to which member states committed in order to achieve the CARICOM Treaty objectives have not been fulfilled. The Treaty provides no institutional machinery or penalties for the observance of these obligations. He also notes that CARICOM law has not in general been incorporated into country legislation and, where this has been done, individual countries' legislation is not uniform. As a result, CARICOM arrangements do not permit the juridical viability of the Community. Furthermore, CARICOM has no legal personality, unlike other international bodies, because of members' adherence to undiluted individual sovereignty. Joseph argues that, in order for CARICOM to achieve any success, sovereign rights must be limited, albeit in specific spheres, by conferring on the Community the legal means to achieve the treaty objectives.

CARICOM's legal limitations are paralleled by its economics, the subsequent paper by Anthony Gonzales suggests. He reconsiders the rationale for economic integration on the premise that the import-substitution justification has proved a failure. In doing so, he sketches several approaches to integration, concluding that export-oriented integration requires large groups in order to be beneficial to the grouping.

The panel discussion of part V reinforces these rather pessimistic conclusions, with all participants agreeing that the Caribbean continues to face a number of persistent developmental problems, despite the availability of prescriptions such as those of Demas. There is some disagreement over the reasons for the continuing developmental problems, with one explanation based on the failure to implement known remedies of the type proposed by Demas, and the other holding that the diagnostic model and, hence proposed policies are inappropriate to the Caribbean.

Governor of the Eastern Caribbean Central Bank, Dwight Venner, continues the examination of the appropriate analysis to take the Caribbean into the year 2000, by reviewing the requirements for a desired quality of life in terms of production, distribution and consumption, within the context of a changing global environment. Interestingly, his conclusions mirror those of earlier speakers, Girvan and Joseph, for instance, in arguing that CARICOM arrangements should take the form of an 'overriding regional umbrella' under which policies for an improved standard of living within the global environment could be formulated and implemented.

Finally, global changes in the last thirty years of the twentieth century also provide the context within which Laurence Clarke considers Demas' most recent publication. He points out that this work gives Demas the opportunity to revisit his thoughts in a greatly changed environment. Cooperation and coordination within CARICOM remains a major Demas tenet, with caution counselled in deregulating the small states of the Caribbean. Regional institution-building also remains an important theme. Clarke concludes by drawing the parallels between these latest prescriptions of Demas and those reached by other Caribbean academics and public servants participating in the seminar.

The deliberations of the day's activities honouring William Demas can perhaps be summed up by the conclusion that Demas' analysis remains relevant because so little of its vision has been implemented and so few of its objectives achieved. Although no consensus can apparently be reached on the underlying reasons for this deficiency, it is suggested that integration has by and large been ineffective because neither the governments nor the people of the Caribbean seem able to see that its benefits can exceed its costs. At the same time, in striving for sustainable improvements in its standard of living, the Caribbean confronts an increasingly challenging environment in which cohesion, effective government, coordinated regional programmes and effective institutions will be crucial.

Note

1. Extract from *Essays in Honour of William Demas: Towards a Caribbean Economy in the Twenty-first Century*, ed. by Laurence Clark and M.G. Zephirin, Caribbean Centre for Monetary Studies, pp. 1–6.

[18]

Some Personal Reflections on William Gilbert Demas

Alister McIntyre

I feel highly privileged to be given the opportunity to share some personal reminiscences about William Demas at this special programme in his honour.

Let me at the outset congratulate the convenors, the Caribbean Centre for Monetary Studies, for taking this initiative. As Governor Harewood has said 'in the Caribbean, we tend to be remiss in not honouring our distinguished sons and daughters, leaving it to others outside to do that'. Few people deserve the commendation of the region more than William Demas.

William is one of the West Indians for whom I have the greatest esteem, admiration and affection. It was, I think, in late 1957 or early 1958, that I first met him. He had then just assumed, or was about to assume, a position as Trade Adviser to the late Garnet Gordon, then West Indian Commissioner in London. His principal responsibility in that position was to examine the implications for the West Indies of Britain's expected entry into the then European Common Market, in particular the consequences for sensitive exports such as sugar and bananas, and of free reciprocal trade for the industrialisation of the area. In nearly 40 years, much has changed, but nothing has changed: we are still examining the same questions.

I liked William from the moment that I met him. I was impressed by the sharpness of his intellect, the breadth of his intellectual interests, and his commitment to the Caribbean. From the beginning he showed himself to be an excellent conversationalist enjoying topics ranging from the sublime to the ridiculous. One would be certain within a conversation to get a few humorous anecdotes, which often served to lighten up moments of deep reflection.

I saw William most when I came to live in Trinidad and Tobago in 1964. We spoke every day at length on the telephone, and I was often the reluctant guest in one of his long drives through the countryside on a Sunday afternoon. He enjoyed driving, but not, I fear did his passengers. His last minute miraculous escapes from accidents became legendary.

During 1963–64, when I was at Columbia, he at McGill, our thinking began to converge on trade and development issues. I had myself done a piece for the first Conference of Caribbean Scholars on 'Decolonisation and Trade Policy', later to be expanded into a monograph for ECLAC on 'Aspects of Trade and Development in the Commonwealth Caribbean'. William's own thinking was developing along parallel lines in his espousal of economic integration as a way out for small countries dealing with constraints of scale. His book on the *Economics of Development in Small Countries* quickly became a standard reference on Caribbean Economy.

It was a period of intellectual ferment. Lloyd Best and Kari Levitt were then constructing their models of plantation economy which, while addressing a more fundamental and different paradigm, underlined the need to challenge traditional modes of thought.

William used *Aspects of Trade and Development* to encourage some governments to attend an informal seminar at ISER, Mona. It was there that the late Arthur Brown indicated that the Government of Jamaica would support and participate in a Commonwealth Caribbean Free Trade Area, and the commission was given for the integration studies. Best and I served as the Secretariat for that meeting, and wrote the report that went out to governments. The rest is history; but the principal was William's unique ability to bring together the worlds of thought and action.

By that time, he had made himself practically indispensable to the Government of Trinidad and Tobago. It was then said that no major Cabinet decision was taken without his advice. This might have bred arrogance in lesser men. Instead, he remained accessible, especially to younger economists, proving himself to be a good listener, and receptive to new ideas. He was always helping people to advance themselves.

Starting as a member of the now famous group of economists under J. 'Scotty' O'Neil-Lewis in St Vincent Street, William became Head of Planning at Whitehall, and built his own team of people – Frank Rampersad, Frank Barsotti, Eugenio Moore – to name three. Ainsworth Harewood was to come later. That group, together with persons like 'Scotty' Lewis, Dodderidge

Alleyne, Harold Fraser, and Eldon Warner constituted a first class team of officials that gave cohesion and clarity to the government's thrust in the field of economic policy, notwithstanding, the heavy criticism that was directed against particular policies and measures.

William reached the pinnacle of his career as a technocrat when he became Secretary-General of CARICOM. It was for him a labour of love, since he believed deeply in the political and economic unity of the Caribbean. He brought intellectual standing to the Secretariat, and was widely respected by the member governments for his technical competence, and for his devotion to the cause. He was the person most singularly responsible for the development of the regional movement from CARIFTA to CARICOM. Apart from writing himself the basic document arguing for the movement from a free trade area towards a common market, he set out with a group of secretariat officials to sell the idea in each member state through meetings with governments, and in a series of public meetings. By these means, he laid the foundations very carefully for the 1972 Heads of Government Conference where under the masterly chairmanship of Dr Eric Williams, governments agreed to move towards a Caribbean community.

That conference will go down in West Indian history as a major turning point in the life of the region. The proceedings of the conference, the dynamics of the negotiations, and the roles of the respective players, merit a serious book. I hope that one of our younger scholars will rise to the task.

In a sense, his work as president of the Caribbean Development Bank, and later as governor of the Central Bank of Trinidad and Tobago, represents a continuation of his mission as a regional integrationist and development planner.

In all of his various capacities, his prodigious work was legendary. He respected no office hours, or days of the week. Many of the region's leading workaholics – Frank Rampersad, Edwin Carrington, Byron Blake, Marius St Rose – to name just a few – developed under his tutelage.

William's passion for regionalism remains unabated. He is thoroughly convinced, as I am, that economic and political unity represent the best chance for our countries. We may be far from that ideal today, but there are still important voices in the region that are backing the regional idea, however much parochialism and insularity tend to rear their heads in matters both economic and political. William is, in every sense of the word, 'Mr West Indies', and he will long be remembered for his towering contribution to regional unity. He will truly be assessed as one of the great West Indians of the latter part of the twentieth century, and we hope, of the twenty-first, as well.

Moving to a more personal level, William has always been so dedicated to his work as to pay very little attention to the material. He has shown no interest whatsoever in his personal advancement and had given very passing attention to practical matters such as his salary, his wardrobe, and so on. He would often show up for meetings in another country with insufficient clothes or money, so engrossed was he in the substantive matters to be addressed.

In many ways, he is a stereotyped academic don, very absent-minded about the mundane. Some of you may have shared my experience of being invited out by William to a restaurant or to the movies, only to discover that he has forgotten his money. On one occasion, he invited me to the cinema in Port of Spain, but upon reaching the cashier's cage, tried to pay for the tickets in a variety of currencies, many of them being seen by the cashier for the first time. Fortunately, the manager stepped in and invited us to be his guests for the evening.

Anyone so distinguished must be permitted eccentricities. William's own served to endear him to his friends who regard them as a very small price to pay for his monumental contribution to their own intellectual development and to the region.

I believe that he values nothing more than being recognised by his peers. We, who know him, continue to be influenced by his ideas and his unwavering 'West Indianness'. If this Conference does no more than salute his greatness, and the power of his ideas, it would represent a milestone in the evolution not only of Caribbean economic thought, but also in the development of our regional community.

Note

Extract from *Essays in Honour of William G. Demas: Towards a Caribbean Economy in the Twenty-first Century,* ed. by Laurence Clarke & M.G. Zephirin, Caribbean Centre for Monetary Studies, pp. 13–17.

[19]

Tribute to a
Distinguished Son

Lloyd Best

William Demas will always be remembered as a distinguished economist, public servant and revered West Indian and Caribbean leader.

Fate seemed to have dictated his very development from his boyhood days through his university and post university career to the zenith of his achievements – serving West Indian nations, always laced with the respect he had for the common CARICOM citizen. That made him the most popular Caribbean Community Secretary General of all. Demas was a distinguished scholar and critic of West Indian fame.

William Demas, everywhere in the region known as Willie Demas, was born on November 14, 1929 in Trinidad and Tobago. He went on a 1941 college exhibition from the Tranquillity Boys School to Queens Royal College. In 1947, he won an Open Island Scholarship and went to Emmanuel College, Cambridge, in 1948. Young Demas completed the Economics Tripos, after which his graduate research appraised the economies of Barbados, Jamaica and Trinidad in the decades following Emancipation, a singular choice which laid the groundwork for the plantation models conceived in the 1960s by McIntyre, Levitt and Best.

Mr Demas focused his fieldwork on the public finances of the British West Indies territories and emerged as a committed West Indian among a generation of uninhibited regionalists such as Dudley Huggings, Lloyd Braithwaite,

Roy Augier, Elsa Goveia and M.G. Smith. His university days ended happily for him when, in 1957, he was recruited by the West Indies Trade Commission in London headed by Sir Garnett Gordon.

During the years 1955 to 1957, Demas pursued research in public finances at Queen Elizabeth House, Oxford University. He was as prepared as possible to face the challenge, when Dr Eric Williams met him at the Trade Commission, and lured him home to become chief architect of the Public Policy and Planning Office in Port of Spain.

It was a time of hope and golden expectations. Independence and integration seemed indistinguishable. Port of Spain was the Federal Capital; the economics of nationhood – first item on the agenda. At a moment's notice, Demas produced lucid, pointed briefs on complex issues.

Apart from his vast wealth of knowledge and his ability to subdue and quell the most unruly arguments, his greatest asset was a character and personality that caused his colleagues and associates instinctively to shower him with respect. He was recognised not only for his technical competence, but also for his integrity and devotion to a higher purpose. Nowhere is his role as leader and animator generally more highly sung, than in the circle of Sherpas, who saw him at close quarters and could judge him on evidence – Scotty Lewis, Dodderigde Alleyne, Eldon Warner, Frank Rampersad, Frank Barsotti, Eugenio Moore, Edwin Carrington and Ainsworth Harewood.

In successive stages, from different vantage points, Demas, effortlessly, almost instinctively, knitted together teams of technical and policy experts who consistently delivered high quality output, the epitome of public service.

By the end of his career, he caused observers to coin the term 'polycrat', in reference to the low-key but multi-talented, all-purpose, policy-leader on the one hand, and the pragmatic academic in public life who wears the technocrat's face, on the other.

In 1970, Demas took over as Secretary General of the Caribbean Free Trade Area, CARIFTA. Academic commentators have marked him out as the Atlas of the regional movement and its political leaders, in a context where Governments routinely unsupported by politics get little done, save making declarations.

His partners in the venture have been Sir Alister McIntyre and Sir Shridath Ramphal, clearly the main authors, first of the Treaty of Chaguaramas, then of the West Indian Commission Report, and of everything significant in between. In 1974, Demas moved on to the presidency of the Caribbean Development Bank (CDB).

From his seat in Barbados, Demas was tireless in his initiative to achieve Regional Integration. In 1976, he published *Essays in Caribbean Integration and Development* and in 1976 *Consolidating our Independence: The Major Challenge Facing the West Indies.*

Towards the end he seized on the Shiprider Agreements from Kingston, and forced the islands to put their heads together, even when it seemed too late. Demas' was an indefatigable leader with a style that was, incorruptible, and inspiring. Nothing, not even his chronic ill-health, could thwart his efforts.

Those who see Demas as a mere economist scarcely know him. He was certainly a fine, clear, disciplined mind, and a great student of economics and social sciences. He never failed to produce excellent work, but his priority was policy, not theory.

In the end, he gave his life. Few people suspected how young he was, seeming such a venerable, dignified figure. He was a wonderful person to know: a raconteur, a wit, and a volume of encyclopaedia when it came to the zeppo as well as the facts, modern or ancient.

Demas was a well-read man, consuming literature from economists, philosophers, the great literary poets, novelists and critics to entertaining detective stories. He knew Shakespeare, both on stage and on page; and he enjoyed Cantinflas and Fernandel.

Music, much like wine, mainly Spanish and Portuguese, was another love of this loveable human being. Sparrow, Kitchener, Spoiler, Rudder. He loved Bach and Mozart and adored violinists. No aspect of human art, human achievement, human concern did not engage him. His life was full, rich and pleasurable.

Needless to say that he ranks among the great teachers, teaching without effort, without trying, being simply who he was, doing simply what he did, fully, excellently, nobly, so that you only had to notice him to be transported into a world of grace and beauty.

Many who were lucky to have his light shine upon them have fared well.

Note

This article was first published in *CARICOM Perspective*, No. 69, June 1999, pp. 84–85.

[20]

Extract from Caribbean Sovereignty
An Interpretation[1]

Marius St Rose

This paper focuses on five of Demas' economic interests, rationalises his involvement in these and assesses their relevance in contemporary Caribbean.

Development Economics

A few economists are of the view that there is no need for development economics as a separate area of study as the tools of mainstream economics are sufficient to analyse and address the problems of all economies, including developing economies. The argument has even been advanced that treating developing economies differently from developed economies through the use of the theories, techniques and models of development economics may be one of the reasons for the poor performance of these economies. These notions have been debunked on many occasions and as recently as three years ago at a World Bank seminar on the achievements of Development Economics.

In defence of development economics, it is instructive to reflect on one of the better definitions of economics that has been advanced in the literature. Lord Lionel Robbins said that 'Economics is the study of human behaviour in relation to ends and scarce means which have alternative uses'. If we note that 'ends' relate to goals and objectives and that 'scarce means' are really resources, both tangible and intangible, then the critical elements in the definition are study, human behaviour and ends.

What is included in the study of economics, therefore, is not defined but determined by the interests and experiences of the scholars concerned. This is clearly seen in the evolution of mainstream (Western) economics. For example, preoccupation in the feudal days with land and land relations saw land as the source of income, wealth and power, and the question of rent as an important area of study in seventeenth century English and European economics. With the advent of the industrial society came an increased focus on the relations between, and rewards for, labour and capital – wages and interest rates. Later, the notion of an ill-defined enterprise or entrepreneurship was incorporated into the analytical literature. Today, based on that evolution of English and European influences and experience, four factors of production have been identified: land, labour, capital and enterprise. However, such a critical factor as social cohesion and consensus, particularly for tribal societies, has never been even considered or treated as a factor of production even though it can be demonstrated that it is the crux of tribal economies and adds as much value to output as the other heralded factors of production. Similarly, one sees that even the fundamentals of mainstream economics are being increasingly challenged as the economic environment changes or evolves. Romer, for instance, is challenging the established economic notions and principles associated with monopoly based on the workings of the modern day technological and service-oriented economies.

Human behaviour and, therefore, their end are influenced by societies' historical and cultural experiences, geography and state of knowledge. Lewis has shown that classical growth theory applied to developing economies will not work in isolation; growth and development require recognition of, and solutions to, the peculiar historical and institutional situations and constraints and endeavours to address them. Additionally, not all societies see satisfaction, utility and ends only in terms of material progress and necessarily measurable in quantifiable terms. For instance, Guyana, with the lowest per capita income in the Commonwealth Caribbean, objects to the use of the telecommunication system for commercial sex solicitation through voice mail even though the country has a comparative advantage in this area, and the benefits could be used to reduce telecommunication costs to Guyanese consumers. Similarly, many Caribbean countries resist the introduction of casino gambling even though this particular attraction could boost the development of the tourism sector significantly. It is these differences in values, goals and perceptions, particularly between developed and developing countries, that resulted in a recent suggestion by a top World Bank economist that global society would be better off if waste could be disposed of, and other environmentally polluting economic activities could be carried out in the lowest income countries. This raised the ire of developing economies, in particular, even though economists felt that it was an 'economically sound' view.

In summary, the laws, principles and scope of conventional or mainstream economics are determined largely by the experiences and interests of scholars from the developed world. The issues that will be of interest are those that are topical in their contemporary environment; and their conclusions about economic behaviour, based as it must be on observation, empiricism and deductive reasoning must be influenced by the culture and values of the society being studied or observed. To the extent, therefore, that there are fundamental differences in interests and in cultural affinity, then there is the case for the study of economics in the context of particular environments. In addition, there is need for proactive pursuit, analysis and research of the peculiar economic problems of developing countries. This is what Demas and other development economists have been pursuing and advancing.

In the final analysis, however, there may no longer be a special need and role for development economics. Given the role of the media, and the developments in telecommunications and transportation in reducing the world to a global village with instantaneous sharing of experiences, and given the work of the multilateral institutions in standardising values, institutions, approaches and systems, human behaviour and ends and values could, in fact, approach convergence.

Special Problems of Small States

Demas pioneered and highlighted the need for close analysis of the peculiar problems of small states, notably island economies. It is interesting that Demas' work began soon after the failure of the West Indies Federation in 1962, and after he had worked, on the instructions of his Prime Minister, to prepare an economic development plan to include Grenada as part of the unitary statehood of Trinidad and Tobago. His focus on the economic problems of small states coincided with the period that the UK was decolonis-ing its Caribbean countries and had begun to grant associated statehood to the smaller ones, such as the Windward and Leeward islands. It was the period when the UK was experiencing great difficulty and ambivalence in determin-ing whether such small states could be economically viable as sovereign states; it was also the period when the USA was concerned about maintaining stability in its hemispheric area of influence at the time that the Cold War between the superpowers was at its most frigid and tense and saw the Caribbean, through Cuba, as part of the arena or zone of conflict. In fact, there was speculation that consideration was being given by the UK to ceding political responsibility for the smaller islands either to the USA directly or through Venezuela as a surrogate for the USA.

Demas in his *Economics of Development of Small Countries* has highlighted the peculiar problems of small states quite succinctly as follows:

- A very small country can achieve transformation only with a high ratio of foreign trade to GDP.
- Only large economies with varied resources and very large populations can achieve fully self-sustaining growth.
- Small countries, even if their economies have undergone transformation, are placed in serious degrees of dependence in that the momentum of growth is not fully determined by decisions of domestic producers, consumers and the local government.

And, according to Demas, social problems that impact adversely on economic growth issues are generally more acute in small countries than in large ones. The case of India and its caste system is an obvious exception.

Essentially, the basic problems of small states reside in their limited critical mass. This results in a situation where the scope for economies of scale in the production of goods and services is reduced, hence contributing to higher than average per capita costs of production which impact adversely on their international competitiveness. Small size also offers less scope for competitive economic diversification because of small and narrow domestic markets, and because even when opportunities for competing globally exist, the availability of domestic factors of production is not available in a competitive scale or quantity. Small size also results in the economy as a whole becoming more vulnerable to the ravages of any disaster (natural or man-made), and constrains the scope for international bargaining, thus making small island economies largely price takers for the pricing of their goods and services.

Since Demas' pioneering work, the issue of the peculiar problems of small states has attracted the attention of a number of institutions, notably the World Bank, the IMF, the Commonwealth Secretariat, the United Nations and the Inter-American Development Bank. Interest has arisen because of the growing voice of small states in these institutions, their quest for special consideration, particularly in relation to obtaining greater access to concessional resources and preferential treatment in trade relations. In putting forward their case, small states have used the arguments advanced by Demas. As a result these institutions have commissioned a number of studies to analyse the issues and to demonstrate definitively that the typical small developing state is more economically disadvantaged than its much larger counterpart. The studies have all reinforced or reiterated many of Demas' pioneering conclusions but, in general, are somewhat ambivalent on whether the disadvantages may be attributed to small size. In fact, the latest study on this subject by the World Bank has concluded that small states have more favourable relations in global trade arrangements than their larger counterparts. Small states, like many others, can convert some of the weaknesses into strengths. Niche marketing, nimbleness and flexibility, and relative insignificance of their trade volumes can be exploited to advantage.

The Role of the State

Demas has not addressed specifically and explicitly the role of the state in the process of economic management in any of his writings. However, when one reads his work, one gets an impression of his views on the type of activities in which the state should be involved. These include the traditional functions of maintaining law and order; creating a conducive policy, institutional and physical infrastructural framework to induce optimal private sector-led economic activity; and taking care of those who are specially disadvantaged by the development process. Also, on occasions, he has proposed state involvement in initiating and directly participating in essential productive activity where the private sector or the market is not responding appropriately. Today, all of these activities, except the last, are considered legitimate and desirable areas of activity for the state.

Today's orthodoxy, not only sees no role for the state in the initiation, ownership, management and control of direct productive activity, but eschews such involvement under any circumstances. The view is that this role is for the private sector and the market and that the state should simply facilitate that process. In the event that the market is not responding, then the state should examine the market more closely to determine the minimum requirements to facilitate the process. In short, insufficient market involvement in an economy is seen as symptomatic of inadequate and/or inappropriate government facilitation.

At least two arguments defend Demas' position. In the first case, his recommendations were made at a time when most states, irrespective of their ideological orientation, were getting directly involved in productive activity. In an age of 'Keynesianism' and national socialism, all governments, particularly those in Europe, Southeast Asia, North and Latin America and the

Caribbean created, owned and controlled enterprises in the extractive, manufacturing and agricultural sectors from mines to hotels and airlines. This was the existing orthodoxy. Governments extended Keynesianism which stressed control through such policy variables as interest rates, fiscal policy and money supply to include direct engagement in productive economic activity.

While Demas' views on the role of the state was part of the current orthodoxy it was also driven by the existing reality and need. The smaller economies' scope for free market activity was quite constrained and a vibrant private sector was absent. The private sector, in most of these economies, is small, disorganised, family-based mutually suspicious of and risk-averse, with weak management and with limited vision. Even openness (which in any case they did not have) would not have helped because of an international shortage of capital, very limited knowledge about opportunities in the small economies, high per capita costs of production for limited domestic markets, and a perception of higher-than-normal political and economic risks, which would either scare away foreign capital or require premium returns to capital that these economies were not perceived as providing.

In a situation where the market is not developed and the private sector is not equipped to respond to opportunity, there could be need for the state to extend its facilitating role to becoming a catalyst. Take, for instance, the need of these economies to diversify from the traditional agriculture sector to exploit the growing opportunities in the tourism sector. The required tourism plant is capital-intensive and the domestic private sector does not have the resources and/or the organisation to mobilise the required equity capital. In this case, competitive-sized commercial hotels with rooms of 150 or more and requiring capital of over US$25 million, including equity of no less than US$1 million, could only be provided by foreign investors and/or the public sector. This is what the experience has been in the smaller economies. In fact, with the current orthodoxy leading to a retreating role for the state in directing productive activity, and given the increased competition for private foreign capital, there has been very limited activity in the construction of medium-sized hotels in the smaller islands. Only four hotels with more than 100 rooms have been established in the OECS countries in the last five years. Three of these have been built with foreign capital: Dominica with Taiwanese resources, Grenada with Indian capital and/or sponsorship, and St Lucia with Middle Eastern capital. The only regionally-financed, medium-sized hotel project in the OECS countries is in Grenada which was financed by private investors, from Trinidad and Tobago capital and by regional financial institutions. This limited activity compares with a number of resort proposals that are planned for the St Kitts peninsula, and the Rodney Bay Causeway and the Vieux Fort development areas in St Lucia, but are languishing because of lack of sponsorship.

Development Planning

The obvious result of a proactive state role in economic activity and particularly in the productive sectors is the practice of economic planning. In the post colonial period many of the larger Caribbean countries established economic planning units, the main goal being the preparation of annual medium-term economic development plans. Demas was a Caribbean pioneer in this exercise, having spearheaded the preparation of the two post independence plans for Trinidad and Tobago and having commented widely on the subject of planning in his 1965 seminal work on small states.

In this work he defined planning as the 'formulation and execution of a consistent set of interrelated measures designed to achieve certain specific economic and social goals' with the primary goal being 'to achieve as rapidly as possible transformation of the economy' through 'structural and institutional change'. Recognising the limitations of the market, particularly in small developing countries, and the urgency of the need for post-colonial growth, he states that state economic planning 'must encompass the whole economy and take account of, and attempt to influence, decisions in the private as well as the public sector'. Consequently, Demas' concept of planning went beyond the formulation of consistent macroeconomic aggregates into sectoral and even project planning. He wrote:

where the desired rate of growth is faster than that permitted by the balance of payments, there is a very strong case for sectoral programming and use of selective policies because reliance on aggregate instruments of monetary and fiscal policy is inconsistent with efforts to achieve that faster desired rate of growth.

He saw exchange controls as a very important tool to bring about consistency in the balance of payments and to accelerate growth. In his words, 'the absence of exchange and trade controls may deprive the planners of one of the most powerful means of influencing the direction of investment.'

A number of Demas' ideas about economic planning and economic management would be considered inconsistent with current orthodoxy. I.G. Patel, the well-known economic thinker and practitioner, in his keynote address on 'Limits of the Current Consensus on Development' to the World Bank's 1993 Annual Conference on Development Economics, endorsed and summed up the current consensus as follows:

. . . most of us would now endorse a shift away from planning to policy orientation, from discretionary government intervention to a greater acceptance of market forces, from controls and administered prices to transparent fiscal incentives and disincentives, from public to private ownership of the means of production, and from increasing public investment toward some privatisation and lower taxation. Encouragement of competition in all markets and a hospitable attitude to direct foreign investment are now seen to be essential for economic efficiency. Moreover, liberal and competitive policies have, by and large, a positive impact on social equity, and a creation of a climate less conducive to corruption is in itself no small gain . . . If, in spite of all this, I draw attention to the limits of the current consensus, it is essentially because I wish to warn against three dangers: over-simplification, excess optimism, and the neglect of a number of important questions that are beyond economic policy yet at the same time are crucial for growth and the eradication of poverty.

Demas would certainly, then and now, endorse those views.

The issue is how relevant is traditional economic planning today in the context of the small islands of the Caribbean. Caribbean markets remain small and disorganised, their institutional structures are underdeveloped, their domestic private sector is limited and unresponsive, foreign private sector is either ignorant of their opportunities and existence and/or finds them too small and remote to invest in. In this setting, it would appear that the role of the state, as described earlier, is relevant; and that planning should involve defining an appropriate policy orientation, planning con-sistent macroeconomic aggregates, programming public sector invest-ments that are consistent with the broad economic goals and directions and, as a last resort, being involved with the private sector in some sector planning and even implementation in areas where there is obvious poten-tial, but where the private sector by itself does not have the critical mass, the resources, or the inclination to pursue by itself. Obviously, for such initiatives to succeed the government should give autonomy to the oper-ating entity, make its support transparent and non-discriminatory, and allow unrestricted access to any potential new entrant into that area of activity which the state is sponsoring.

The most current view on this issue is that it is not ownership that matters but the presence of deregulation and free competition. As Willig (1993) puts it 'the efficiencies of privatisation stem mainly from the insulation offered by divestiture from public corruption, vested political interests, and arbitrary invention'. It should not be difficult to put appropriate institutional structures in place to allow public sector-owned productive enterprises to behave and perform like their private sector counterparts.

Economic Integration and Functional Cooperation

In addition to introducing the notion of self-sustaining growth as a criterion or indicator for assessing a country's level of development, Demas' greatest contribution to development policy was in the area of economic integration and functional cooperation. His contribution in this regard should be assessed at two levels. Firstly, he attempted to introduce and promulgate a growth model which small countries could use to reduce the constraints of small size by their ability to gain economies of scale. This model stood squarely with such other models as Lewis' unlimited supply of labour and Rosenstein-Rodan's model of the big push, both of which were for comparatively large economies. Secondly, Demas, in his operational roles in the region, was able to play a pivotal role in developing and promoting a number of programmes which helped to demonstrate the value of the model.

Economic integration relates to the process of pooling markets. Departing from the most favoured nation states, the process ranges from a free trade area where goods and services are free to move unhindered by tariffs across national boundaries, but with such movement restricted to a defined but broader geographical area; to an economic union where there is free movement of all goods, services and factors, a common currency and, by extension, considerable harmonisation of economic policy and institutional modalities and arrangements. Between these levels one has customs unions and common markets. Functional cooperation relates to the process of economies and governments sharing services on a pooled basis to gain economies of scale. Such sharing can be in production, distribution, public sector services such as education, health, foreign representation, joint procurement of goods and services, and the list is limitless.

Demas' attempts at fostering economic integration and functional cooperation arrangements in the CARICOM area are legendary. His start with CARIFTA – a free trade area of the ex English-speaking Commonwealth Caribbean was upgraded, if not in substance, certainly in form and nomenclature, to CARICOM, which would allow a partial movement of goods and some factors of production. The success of his efforts was not constrained by lack of vision and energy in designing and promoting programmes, but by his own pragmatism, his keen sense of what was politically feasible and, relatedly, his ability to assess the level of commitment of governments and other decision makers.

At the functional cooperation level, there was more success in establishing institutions, even though many were not self-sustaining. The regional solution to the transportation problem of island economies saw Demas giving strong support for the Leeward Islands Air Transport Services (LIAT) and the West Indies Shipping Corporation (WISCO). Financing needs, particularly in the area of equity financing, led to the establishment of the Caribbean Investment Cooperation, to make equity capital available to the smaller states and to complement and supplement CDB's loan capital resources. Attempts to address agricultural problems resulted in the establishment of the Caribbean Agricultural and Research and Development Institute and the Caribbean Food Corporation to finance self-liquidating agricultural initiatives. And the list goes on. All these initiatives originated with or were supported by Demas during his tenure at the CARICOM Secretariat and CDB. That the performance of many of these institutions did not live up to expectations is not the issue. Nor is their poor performance sufficient argument that there may not have been need for them.

The pursuit of economic integration and cooperation among small countries is an even greater priority today than it was over the last thirty years. Then, cooperation was practised or pursued within an inward-looking, import-substitution, market-protected economic framework. This framework, though it sought to do so, did not necessarily achieve efficiency and cost minimisation because captive preferential markets undermined or removed the efficiencies associated with competition. The structure is different today. A globalised and liberalised economic space with dismantled preferences and an acutely competitive economic environment make economic integration and functional cooperation even greater economic imperatives for smaller economies. These countries have got to find the means to reduce their per capita costs of production and, hence, improve the international competitiveness of their goods and services.

Conclusion

This paper outlined William Demas' economic interests, programmes and preoccupations as revolving around five main themes: development economics, special problems of small states, the role of the state, development planning, and integration and functional cooperation and which all tended to reinforce one broad overarching objective – maintaining Caribbean sovereignty. Even in the current situation, these interests are consistently interdependent and reinforcing of each other and are still largely relevant.

Gordon Lewis asserts that nationals of Trinidad and Tobago show more concern about issues of nationhood than nationals of other English-speaking Caribbean countries, and speculates that this may be due to the heterogeneity of the racial composition of that society. Whatever the reason, this country has spawned such thinkers and activists as Captain Cipriani, C.L.R. James and Eric Williams all of whom have been strong advocates of decolonisation, Caribbean sovereignty and effective self-determination, and who envisioned the benefits of a federal West Indian nation state as a means of achieving and consolidating this objective.

Demas was brought up in that environment and tradition, and embraced the mantle of that vision. He did not use either the route of politics or militant campaigning to try to advance these causes. Instead, he used the economic route, and was as, if not more than, effective as others who used different routes. Despite the breadth and depth of his economic knowledge he focused his economic concerns, programmes and preoccupations around five main themes: development economics, special problems of small states, role of the state, development planning and economic integration and functional co-op-eration. These, in a mutually consistent and coherent way, reinforced each other to achieve one broad overarching objective – maintaining Caribbean sovereignty. It is obvious that ultimate and effective sovereignty is about sustainability of economic self-reliance and self-determination.

He recognised that sovereignty was as much about substance as it was about symbolism, and in his endeavours he advanced both. Just like the 'double entendre' of the calypso which is indigenous to his native Trinidad and Tobago, his economic initiative, in general, had a parallel objective – economic substance, on the one hand, and symbolism, on the other. His economic policy advice was aimed at enhancing the region's growth potential through grouping and the exploitation of broader markets. He wanted such advice to be regionally generated as well as helpful in improving the region's bargaining leverage. For example, tariff policy was as much about protecting CARICOM industry and generating revenue as it was about having a bar-gaining chip for international trade negotiations. His proposals for regional institutional arrangements were as much a means of achieving greater econo-mies of scale through functional co-operation as they were to help the region to create a unified capacity to interface and negotiate with extra-regional countries. His support for a regional food plan had as much to do with exploiting the abundant idle land and labour to create value added and save foreign exchange as it was to minimise the region's vulnerability in being too dependent on the rest of the world for a basic commodity such as food. Simplicity in tastes, and lifestyles that were consistent with the region's resources reflected his passion for self-determination through greater self-suf-ficiency. The special efforts made to fulfil the Southwell statement in the CDB Charter, that the CDB should 'pay special and urgent regard to the needs of the lesser developed members', was a recognition that these countries, the Windward and Leeward islands, could be the 'Achilles Heel' of the regional integration movement. Even the notion of a flag for CARICOM (a symbolism par excellence) was one of his obsessions and gave him much pride when it was erected and flown.

The English-speaking Caribbean in general, and the smaller countries in particular, have made some economic progress since the end of the fifties. Obviously, these achievements are the result of a number of factors and the efforts of a number of people and, hence, cannot be attributed to any one individual. Nonetheless, it is fair to say that Demas' contribution has been more than that of many in that achievement, not least of which is the non-partisan leadership and galvanising role which he played in highlighting the region's affairs.

Demas' life and accomplishments have led to a greater sense of Caribbean consciousness, to an increase in the self worth of Caribbean people and society, and have been a source of considerable inspiration and intellectual leadership to many. He is noted for his economic policy advice, his campaign for economic integration and functional cooperation and the regional institutional arrangements which he helped to engineer. He sensitised society to the dignity and self-respect of Caribbean peoples, and demonstrated that one does not have to leave the region to gain international respectability.

Note

Extract from 'Caribbean Sovereignty: An Interpretation' in *Essays in Honour of William G. Demas: Towards a Caribbean Economy in the Twenty-first Century*, ed. by Laurence Clarke & M. G. Zephrin, Caribbean Centre for Monetary Studies, pp. 55–69.

[21]

Extract from Reflections on the Economics of Development in Small Countries

Laurence Clarke

In his path-breaking 'Small Countries' work, William Demas grappled with the fundamental issue that the economics of development in small countries such as those of the Caribbean must necessarily be different from that of larger economies. He argued that there was a body of factors related to size (physical and population) which hitherto had not been actively captured in the analyses of development. The key implication was that the issues of underdevelopment and 'self-sustained growth' (to use a Rostovian term) could not be considered independent of the consideration of a country's size.

To support this central thesis, Demas argued that the fundamental social, political and institutional complex of factors that must be considered on the governance of smaller economies, differ from those for larger economies. At the very least, dissimilarities in initial factor endowments and, in some cases, the immaturity of structures and institutions in smaller states relative to their larger counterparts, dictated differential analyses. This difference in approach was necessary, especially if development was not defined in the orthodox terms of a sustained rise in incomes (driven in strict Harrod-Domar terms by necessarily related expansions in savings and investment), but in more relevant terms as a fundamental structural transformation of economies and integration of economic agents, activities and means of production.

Smaller economies tended, in Demas' view, to be characterised by 'openness', being dependent on external trade and finance for their survival. The degree of dependence was in the main related to the size of the economy, as partly evidenced by the economic history of today's mature economies. They have also tended to exhibit less balanced growth often reflecting features of 'dualism', or lopsided sectoral development. Typically there was one 'leading', accompanied by several, 'lagging' sectors. Dualism often was also evident in social, political and institutional forms. (The identification in later years of the 'Dutch Disease' phenomenon was another manifestation of the distortions induced by dualism, even for more mature economies). Further, often the presence of the Malthusian constraint in small economies, that is, uneconomically high ratios of population to physical size, was manifestly distorting in its impact on development.

In the face of these peculiar and distinct characteristics of smaller economies, Demas argued that a new and distinct strategy of public policy for development in smaller economies was warranted. Indeed, at the point of economic and political history at which the Caribbean found itself when he was preparing this seminal work, a new strategy was urgently required. His recommended solutions centred on: (a) his notion of a necessary path to the attainment of 'self-sustaining growth', whose attainment hinged on the generation of adequate volumes of domestic savings, in both the public and private sectors, to underpin the desired level of sustained growth over time; and (b), more importantly the fundamental transformation of the structure of production in small economies.

Demas, and a growing body of scholars since he wrote, have argued that conditions 'sine qua non' for structural transformation must include: a politically and socially determined capacity for effecting fundamental change; the unification of local markets for goods and services; increased integration of domestic industries and activities; reduction of dependence on, and changed structures of, external trade and aid;balanced and less dualistic development; and emergence of appropriate financial and other intermediaries.

In attaining sustained development and transformation in small economies, the broad consensus expressed by Demas and other leading economists at the time included the need for serious attempts at integrated development and for macroeconomic planning. Innovative behaviour (technological and institutional) designed to efficiently expand the frontiers of the means of production, was also cited then, as now, as fundamental to sustained development, especially in smaller countries.

Development thought at that time, including Demas', was essentially Keynesian or neo-Keynesian in its approach to economic management and development. In this framework the public sector was perceived as an important factor in post-independence economic stimulation and expansion. As the small countries of the Caribbean evolved to political independence, there was a growing body of opinion, both in this region and in other newly independent countries, that state leadership was required for economic growth, the implementation of which was attempted. The degree varied dramatically in the Caribbean from extremes of state ownership in Guyana and to a lesser extent Jamaica, to more market-based systems in Barbados and Trinidad and Tobago, though even the latter group insisted on strong government oversight and directions. The broad trends at that time were in a way direct responses to the legacies of the colonial era, with which the newly emerging economies needed to quickly grapple. Hence the growing body of literature at that time on unorthodox economics, driving essentially at the need for radical transformation of the old order of economics to more 'command type' models, adjusted for local realities. One common element, however, in orthodox or more radical economic thought in the 1960s and 1970s, was that the only sure way for sustained development for small states such as the Caribbean, was through an integrated multinational approach.

It was in particular on this theme of integrated development that William Demas spent most of his years of active professional life. Indeed, not only has he been an architect in this field, as the first Secretary-General of the CARICOM (at that time CARIFTA) and later the longest serving president of the Caribbean Development Bank (CDB), but he had the distinct advantage of manning these important posts, imbued with the clear personal vision that he himself had earlier articulated and documented. In *Essays on Caribbean Integration and Development* he laid out with unqualified authority and foresight the framework for the integrated approach to which he gave practical expression at the helm of CARICOM and the CDB between 1970 and 1988.

Economic Integration and Development

In *Essays on Caribbean Integration and Development,* published in 1976 but written between 1960 and 1975, Demas argued that an integrated approach to development, especially in small open economies, was particularly required. For small economies it was important to move in practice to this concerted approach to development. Central to the process of deeper economic integration was the need for deeper financial integration, at the level of private financial institutions, capital markets and, importantly, national monetary authorities. Having elected to pursue a multinational course of development, however, it was still vital to ensure planning at the national and regional levels and the evolution of an effective and flexible regional university, continuously adapting to the changing environmental conditions with which the region would necessarily be continuously seized. Such a university was essential to the process of developing in a sustained manner the human and social capital, necessary to the transformation of the region's economy in the long-term.

More specifically, in constructing a theoretical justification for integrated approaches to development among small economies, Demas argued that the classical (and later neo-classical) assumptions of the Vinerian customs union in international trade theory, had only limited applicability to small underdeveloped economies such as those in the Caribbean. In particular he challenged the assumption of full employment and the negative welfare effects attributed to 'trade diversion' as opposed to 'trade creation', in this theory. He reasoned that in conditions of surplus labour, about which Sir Arthur Lewis so deftly wrote, 'trade diversion' may be employment-generating in areas or locations of a customs union or free trade area, with otherwise low economic activity. Demas also pointed out that the high money costs of new trade-diverting activities may be compensated for by the low social opportunity costs of labour (given the propensity for surplus labour absorption in the area to which trade may be diverted as a result of integrated development) and the enhanced social product arising for new or expanded productive employment. In effect, the advantage given to regional producers by trade diversion acts to subsidise employment in an imperfect labour market.

He further emphasised that the key benefits of integration lay in scale economies that may result from such integration, but also referred to the consumption, investment and terms of trade benefits, especially arising from new external markets and from the positive spin-off from regional, as opposed to domestic, import-substituting forms of productive activity. Customs unions, free trade and other forms of integration must, therefore, be seen as first steps towards industrialisation and later expansion into extra-regional markets. This must all be part of a 'truly dynamic theory of economic integration' in which production – its type, focus and location – was in many respects as important, if not more, important, than trade itself. Creation of new investment activity and capacity had to be at the centre of any effort at economic integration.

Demas also addressed the issue of possible 'polarisation' of intra-regional trade and production, the larger more developed countries benefiting more from such activities than the smaller less developed ones, a problem that has indeed surfaced in CARICOM. He was particularly sensitive to this issue, whereby the possible 'backwash' effects could outweigh the 'spread' effect about which James Meade spoke in The Theory of the Customs Union (North Holland, 1995) because of the presence of economies of scale and external economies. Distribution of the activities of expanded trade and production among countries of varying levels of initial and actual development therefore needed to be planned. Demas further argued for measures to reduce the negative consequences of polarisation, including channelling of production factors, especially capital, to less developed areas; export substitutions; deliberate targeting of agriculture products of LDCs for export; and the creation of deliberate poles of growth in these markets. He advocated the harmonisation of incentives with special biases in favour of lesser developed economies, greater infant industry support, longer transition periods for freeing trade completely, and more careful industrial planning by newly created regional institutions. He argued that in the long run a process of systematic planning would promote wider and deeper regional development and more importantly, reduce the region's heavy dependence on the external world, whether in the form of ownership by foreign capital, foreign aid, trade, foreign technical/human 'know-how', or capital consumption or production patterns and norms of behaviour.

Demas was also of the view that indigenous ownership of regional financial institutions and a regional financial mechanism particularly targeted at funding trade and investment flows to the lesser developed poles of the region, were critical in small economies. His efforts and foresight in this area in the Caribbean are well known, resulting partly in the creation in 1970 of the Caribbean Development Bank, whose stewardship he held from 1974 to 1988. The wider question of practical integration among regional financial systems did not escape his attention either. Financial integration via a network of locally owned institutions, was seen as more viable than through foreign owned institutions (given the likelihood that the latter would rotate on the axis of profitability). He attributed this integrated structure of regional financial and capital markets to the need for raising levels of savings ratio in the region, even if this meant challenging, as he did, prevailing wisdom in this area, as articulated by no less a Caribbean personage than Sir Arthur Lewis.

Demas underscored the need for national and ultimately a regional central bank suitably structured 'to influence the use of those financial resources [generated] in ways that would contribute to the strengthening of the national economy by changing its production structures and its patterns of consumption'. Such a central bank would in fact more specifically assume the indigenisation (as opposed to colonisation) of local banking; more active oversight for banks and the facilitating of the efficient mobilisation and channelling of domestic financial resources into more productive use; oversight of non-banks; and the spearheading of the sustained creation and development of national capital markets, to facilitate a greater role in external capital flows, including the important task of deepening regional monetary and financial integration.

William Demas consistently argued that the key ingredient to long term success of a Pan-Caribbean economy, was the development of its human resources. He therefore advocated in this publication and elsewhere, a 'new Caribbean University', a 'scholastic' university, that served primarily as an 'intellectual centre' and the 'real' regional university, which had to serve as a national and regional instrument of development. He argued for excellence among the graduates of a regional university (not separate UWI/UG entities for example); for constant innovation and for curricula designed to ensure tertiary education that was more far-reaching and meaningful to the region. He reminded the region in one of the articles that:

We must inculcate in our people from cradle to grave the right sense of excellence which, properly defined, means never being satisfied with indifferent performance in any concrete task which one has to do – whether in creative or intellectual or artistic work, or in work on the farm, in the factory, at the office desk, in organising and running a non-government association, in sport, in journalism and in other jobs and professions. Excellence means a constant unrelenting striving to be 'one's best self' in whatever specific thing one has to do (p.154).

Today's Reality

Such, therefore, was the economic vision of William Gilbert Demas, twenty to thirty years ago, for a robust Pan-Caribbean economy. The true hallmark of his vision and success in directing the region towards paradigms of meaningful collective development could only be measured effectively over the longer term. Implementation of some of his thoughts and ideas is already underway. But such implementation has not been without its difficulties in practice. To Demas' credit, in no small measure, regional integration has moved in less than three decades well beyond the theoretical principles articulated by Viner and Meade, to successively deeper institutional forms of free trade areas, common market and now towards a single market and economy. Yet, how well the institutional structures have withstood these progressive developments is a matter of some concern to the region, at a time of open challenges from many quarters to the viability and effectiveness of present CARICOM arrangements. The Demas institutional evolution has no doubt taken place but the jury is still out on the effectiveness of these changes, constrained as many have been by factors both beyond and within the control of the key regional operators, in their implementation over the decades following his prescriptions. Indeed, one of the underlining facets of this institutional metamorphosis has been an orientation away from trade integration (trade continues to be less than ten per cent inter-regionally), to one of deepening the integration of production. Demas, advocated such a position but its realisation is still far away, notwithstanding marked progress towards a Caribbean single market and economy.

Some development planning in most Caribbean economies was a positive reality in the 1960s and 1970s. National development plans have, however, become less and less evident in the 1980s and 1990s, when market-based structural adjustment and stabilisation programmes were the norm. The price system was judged paramount in these latter decades and therefore planning was relegated to the back seat. While in principle most CARICOM countries still have medium-term economic plans, perhaps only Guyana has more recently planned for a major economic transformation, with the drafting of a national development strategy with assistance from the Carter Centre in the USA.

Further, according to the Caribbean Association of Indigenous Banks (CAIB), some three-quarters of the assets of Caribbean banks and a great proportion of insurance and other non banks are now owned predominantly by regional nationals, that is, they are indigenised for the most part – a Demas prescription. Yet major problems of management have emerged in the 1980s and 1990s in respect of such institutions in Jamaica (Workers Bank); Trinidad and Tobago (Workers Bank and National Commercial Bank); and Guyana (Guyana National Co-operative Bank; Agricultural Co-operative Development Bank), raising questions about the planning for and operations of these institutions. Most collapses have been due to either political interference, insider dealing, over-expansion of operations, or downright fraud in their operations. On the other hand, virtually no foreign controlled institution, except the BCCI, has failed in decades in the region. The contrast continues to be striking, not only in banking but also in insurance, asset management and related fields.

Much progress has been made regionally in financial integration. Although the indigenisation and local incorporation (localisation) of several hitherto foreign institutions (Royal Bank of Canada; Barclays Bank) in many territories have in a way reduced the degree of financial integration in regional financial systems to some extent, a wave of cross-border investments in recent years by regional financial institutions (for example, the Republic Bank of Trinidad and Tobago; Citizens Bank of Jamaica; Colonial Life Insurance Company of Trinidad and Tobago) have spoken to much progress in this regard. Cross-border tie-ups and activities by the stock-markets in Jamaica, Trinidad and Tobago and Barbados attest to progress in this area also.

Central banking in the CARICOM region has lived up to the Demas vision of less voluntary and more innovative oversight and operations. Apart from the classical functions of money supply and reserve management, currency production, financial system oversight etc., many regional central banks have taken key innovative initiatives at promoting, as well as regulating, financial development in their respective economies. Among these were notably venture capital operations (Trinidad and Tobago), call exchanges (Guyana), Stock Exchange (Jamaica), and secondary mortgage institutions (ECCB and Trinidad and Tobago). A recent spate of revisions of the Financial Institutional and Central Banking Act have conferred oversight of the monetary systems, including the wider financial and non banking systems, to central banks. This applies to new acts in Guyana (1995), Trinidad & Tobago (1993), and Belize (1995). Capital market development, as expressed by Demas, has also been aggressively pursued by the central banks of the OECS states.

Yet Caribbean economies in the mid-1990s are still far from an integrated monetary economy, notwithstanding progress in the OECS. A formal decision by regional Heads of Government in 1992 to move towards a monetary union by the year 2000, has become overdue, though some progress has been made recently on regional currency convertibility, thus bringing the process back on track. Currencies are presently virtually fully convertible throughout the region, with the central banks leading the way in most cases so far, thus promoting monetary deepening regionally. But a dual system of exchange rates persists in regional economies, and there is still no final consensus on full currency convertibility. Trinidad and Tobago, Guyana, Jamaica and Suriname continue to float their currencies, while the OECS, Bahamas, Belize and Barbados – coincidentally the better performing economies – have fixed parities to the US dollar. Renewed efforts at a monetary vision and single currency now underway will have to reconcile these structural contradictions if a new credible single Caribbean dollar is to emerge, with solid backing. The process of economic convergence in the region towards formal monetary integration is being closely monitored, but progress continues to be slow and mixed. Demas would certainly not be satisfied with this.

Moreover, region-wide spending on social services such as education and health is presently lower in the 1990s than it was in the 1980s and 1970s – a dismal commentary on the two sectors that are at the heart of human resource development. The massive brain drain that hit the region in the 1980s in particular, especially Guyana, Jamaica and Trinidad and Tobago, continues to weaken the technical and managerial capacity of Caribbean economies. And the regional university is experiencing probably its worst financial crisis of its near fifty-year history. While serious efforts to reposition the University of the West Indies, reinvigorate its internal structures and respond to the widening gap in the demand for, and supply of, competent graduate output for the region, are being made, this process is a slow and long one, probably stultified by the existing financial constraint. The University of Guyana, in the meantime, continues to operate below optimum, in its own isolated environment, badly strapped for finances, and, no doubt as a consequence, quality Faculty. Some progress has been made in private sector-led development efforts especially in the area of banking, finance and the legal profession, but by and large the Demas dream and vision of excellence in the region's human and social capital is far from a reality at present.

Finally, in more areas than readily meet the eye, the region continues to grapple with the basic problems of small size in a world becoming increasingly less sensitive to the special characteristics and features of smallness that could render such nations particularly fragile and vulnerable. Traditional preferential markets for Caribbean agricultural produce in many of the world's markets have come under severe threat, with no ready evidence of compensatory or other support in the absence of the availability of these markets. Many of the region's economies have been 'graduated' by the multilaterals from concessionary financial terms and are not yet fully ready for accessing international capital markets, though some progress has been made especially by Trinidad and Tobago and Barbados. Natural disasters such as hurricanes, volcanoes and floods persist in our island economies. The difficulties manifesting themselves in the important financial sectors of the region through persistent institutional rigidities and imperfections of small liberalising economies are increasingly manifesting themselves by the divergence and less interdependence between efficient resource mobilisation and efficient investment in real activity. Problems of 'excess liquidity' are emerging from one Caribbean economy to another, reflecting not only fiscal imprudence in several cases but, in virtually all, a basic failure in the monetary transmission mechanisms and the capacities of the region's real sectors to emerge out of a sluggishness into entrepreneurial creativity and innovativeness. Regrettably, these factors are all detrimental to the enhancement of the welfare of the region's people. Thus, the problems of the small state paradigm, persists. Some of the flaws articulated by Demas decades ago are regrettably still relevant for smaller economies such as those in today's Caribbean, at a time when access to exogenous private and multilateral support is being increasingly restrained.

In summary, William Demas' vision for the Caribbean over the years, has been a Pan-Caribbean structure of economic development, planned over medium and longer-term horizons, with a high-powered corps of human resources at the cutting edge of technology, innovations and globalisation, especially with the advent of the new millennium. While the region has broadly progressed over the past three decades, there continues to be sufficiently large complex areas of stagnation, if not retrogression, giving rise to some doubts not as to Demas' prescience, but probably more to the true complexity of the environment within which small-states such as the Caribbean have been forced to, and will continue to have, to evolve. Caribbean political systems and structures, to name only a few key variables, for the most part continue to be unresponsive, if not at odds, with the basic economic perspectives that Demas charted for the region three decades or more ago. The real failure in a way has been the dynamics, not so much macro-economics, but of the political economy of the region. A higher consciousness of this aspect of the region's development will be a necessary and sufficient ingredient for sustained social and economic development in the twenty-first century and beyond. Indeed, it is perhaps out of a realisation of this factor, *inter alia*, that Demas' reflections and prescriptions in his latest publication *West Indian Development and the Deepening and Widening of the Caribbean Community* have been shaped. A summary is made on his current thinking and advice in the 'Postscript' to this publication.

Note

Extract from 'Reflections on The Economics of Development in Small Countries with Special Reference to the Caribbean' and 'Essays on Integration and Development' in *Essays in Honour of William G. Demas: Towards a Caribbean Economy in the Twenty-first Century*, Caribbean Centre for Monetary Studies, ed. by Laurence Clarke & M. G. Zephirin, pp. 22–34.

[22]

A Postscript to Contemporary and Future Caribbean

A Comment on Demas' Critical Issues in Caribbean Development

Laurence Clarke

Since producing *The Economics of Development in Small Countries (1965)* and *Essays on Caribbean Integration and Development (1976)*, both the subject of much review and comment in this publication, William Demas has had to his credit three decades of practical experience in key positions in the region. His recent publication, released in November 1996, *Critical Issues in Caribbean Development: West Indian Development and the Deepening and Widening of the Caribbean Community* has therefore had the benefit of these maturing years of Demas' professional development and formation. In a sense, however, and perhaps even more so than those personal experiences, this latest work may have been shaped and influenced by a number of events and developments that have dramatically redefined the global and regional financial landscape, over the past two decades in particular.

As noted earlier by contributors to several of the presentations in this publication, the main global and regional financial landmarks of the seventies and eighties that are likely to bear on the financial and economic development of the Caribbean are:

(a) the collapse in the early 1970s of the Bretton Woods Monetary System and the consequential move from fixed to flexible rates of exchange;

(b) the oil crises of the early and late 1970s and the impact of petro dollars on financial and credit systems;

(c) the Mexico-driven LDC debt crisis of the early to mid 1980s, precipitated by high global interest rates and reckless lending in the 1970s by private financial institutions in their effort to recycle petro dollars with the resultant 'stagflation' phenomenon;

(d) the growing trend towards technological innovation in real and financial sector activity worldwide and the pronounced implications for global financial integration and fusion;

(e) the pre-eminent re-emergence of the multilateral financial institutions in the context of their renewed emphases on structural adjustment and stabilisation programmes and the realities of poor governance, adverse impact of international trade and fragile local financial environments for the newly developing countries in the Caribbean and elsewhere;

(f) the Mexican financial crisis of 1994–5 revealed new dimensions to the problem of economic management in developing countries (especially smaller ones) over the past 10 years, in an environment of unbridled liberalisation of fiscal, financial, exchange and trade regimes – typical of adjustment and stabilisation programmes and driven by the multilateral financial institutions (MFIs); and

(g) the intensification of the economic integration effort both in Western Europe and North America, and among more progressive groups of developing nations (such as ASEAN and Latin America), at a time of a new global trade order – a rethink of GATT and the emergence of the World Trade Organisation (WTO).

What this all means is that a generation after Demas original seminal thoughts on the economics of development in small economies and on the theory and process of integrated development, the landscape and atmospherics of Caribbean economies have changed dramatically. The environment for small Caribbean and similar economies is, without a doubt, far more complex now than in the early post independence years. It is, therefore, within this changed framework and against a path of tremendous shocks and upheavals over the past three decades or so, that Demas revisits the theme of his earlier writings in his *Critical Issues in Caribbean Development* publication.

Critical Issues

In his latest work, Demas argues that the deepening of CARICOM has to be built on three key areas: economic integration through a single market; common services and functional cooperation; and coordination of foreign policy. Integration however, is merely a facilitating framework and is by itself ineffective. A high degree of political cooperation is vitally necessary for such deepening within the CARICOM integration movement. Further, a strong CARICOM is important because the alternatives are either marginalisation or *de jure* or *de facto* 'absorption' in a highly dependent mode into one or more, much bigger and more powerful country or group of countries.

With reference to increasing regionalisation of trade, he argues that for CARICOM, the Free Trade Area of the Americas (FTAA) is an alternative to the expansion of NAFTA. FTAA will permit CARICOM and other sub-regional integration movements to maintain and strengthen the links among their member countries and between themselves and other sub-regional integration groupings, (including NAFTA), in the hemisphere. The systematic dismantling of the region's Common External Tariff is quite worrisome because of the absolute loss of protective devices and revenue raising import duties. Nor should the recent formation of the Association of Caribbean States (ACS) decrease the imperative towards stronger CARICOM integration; it should increase it. Membership in the ACS must not negate the importance of CARICOM.

In the short and medium term, a CARICOM relationship with one or more English-speaking islands of the Greater Antilles may be more practical than an ACS single market or economic union. CARICOM countries should not try to negotiate anything individually, especially in external relations. CARICOM must go beyond the single market – free trade, CET, complex factor mobility, coordination of national economic policies, financial and monetary cooperation and integration. It must ensure co-operation in joint investments between private sectors of member countries and in production and intra/extraregional marketing.

Demas further argues that CARICOM also has to provide an 'environment conducive to export-oriented development policies as well as efficient regional import-substitution'. Internal and external macroeconomic stabilisation, increasing productivity, higher levels of domestic savings and productive sector investment, human resource development are necessary though not sufficient, for sustained development. Greater integration is necessary for CARICOM to work meaningfully with larger and more powerful countries. However, he said 'we should not take actions that can fragment CARICOM, for example, by each or some CARICOM member state or states entering partial or full trade and economic co-operation agreements with third countries or groupings of such countries . . .' Increased integration would also permit 'widening in the form of closer relations with our neighbours . . . on the basis of trade, financial and economic co-operation; collaboration in science, technology, culture and in education and training'.

At the same time, he argues that enhanced international competitiveness must be accorded the highest priority in replacement of continued external dependence. In the process, Caribbean nationals will have to expend more energy and resources in generating revenues from non-tourism services such as engineering, architectural, economic and financial consultancies, construction contracts, computer software, financial services, telecommunications, informatics, education and medical and recreational services. He stresses that West Indian societies here cannot achieve their ultimate aspiration of self-sustainable development without stabilisation. Sustained physical deficits are unacceptable. 'The IMF is undoubtedly correct in its emphasis', in this area. Demas said while Sir Arthur Lewis' view on the centrality of appropriate trade, exchange rate, incomes and productivity policies was correct, his emphasis on devaluation in a small country in the West Indian context for restoring export competitiveness and wider macro-balance, was questionable in both past and present Caribbean circumstances. In addition, the development of adequate levels of human and social capital in economies is critical, especially in the context of the formation of 'social partnerships' for incomes and price policies, adjustment efforts and other areas.

Advocating continued careful planning in Caribbean economic development Demas cautioned that for micro states such as in the Caribbean, that care must be exercised against:

• too rapid liberalisation of these economies;
• total divestment of state-owned enterprises. Some minority stakes should always be maintained and employees must be offered equity stakes wherever possible;
• total deregulation of price and other controls; deregulation should be accompanied by oversight mechanisms;
• unbridled private enterprises. He believes these must be encouraged to become more efficient and internationally competitive;
• wanton abandonment of economies to the 'magic of the market place'. No such magic exists – the 'market must be given an important but by no means excessive role'. 'The state must intervene sometimes: giving incentives (particularly to foreign exchange-earning activities); providing some

special tariff protection and cheap credit' etc. It also has to increase public sector efficiency.

Demas also emphasises that governance of the institutional aspects of the integration process remains an issue, even after, or perhaps because of, the recommendations of the West Indian Commission's Report (1992) where an alternative was suggested to fill an oversight function for CARICOM.

Although there have been some opportunities and suggested frameworks for political union in the region,[1] none has so far made any substantial progress. A Federal union of all members of the OECS (plus Anguilla and the British Virgin Islands) together with the larger states of Barbados, Guyana and Trinidad and Tobago forming a confederation of four states, might be workable. These might later on be merged into a political union of all the CARICOM members in the Eastern and South Eastern Caribbean. There could be, however, no binding political union without an economic union. It would be 'Like the grin of Cheshire Cat – a grin but no cat!'

Further, Demas reiterates, as he did two decades ago in earlier landmark works, that the region also needs monetary integration, as it 'may be a condition precedent to achieving exchange rate stability and other forms of monetary stability. And once we have monetary integration our future prospects for exchange rate stability will be greatly enhanced'. This process must, however, definitely go beyond simple convertibility of currencies *inter-se*.

Finally, in a postscript to the main thoughts of the publication, Demas strongly opposes adoption of the Shiprider Agreement' being proposed by the USA, and accepted by a few CARICOM states already, pointing out its counter-productive implications for the region in terms of the preservation of the region's national sovereignty, economic independence and basic identity. It is a recipe for recolonisation, he stressed.

In evaluating the overall message and likely impact of this latest book *Critical Issues in Caribbean Development*, there emerge several aspects of the likely environment, policies and structures with which the Caribbean Community will need to grapple.

Firstly, Demas and many of the contributors take the view that both a deepening and widening of CARICOM are necessary and that one cannot proceed without the other, in the twenty-first century. Whether this means a stronger CARICOM that will include other Caribbean Basin countries or NAFTA or FTAA is a matter of detail. What is clear, however, is that integration confined to existing member countries, is a non-starter. As St Rose mentions, this new form of 'open regionalism', with a distinct outward emphasis about which Gonzales commented is critical. The existing CARI-

COM arrangement does not represent an optimum economic space, and must be redefined and expanded with other emerging geographically and economically contiguous arrangements. There appears no alternative.

Secondly, while the private sector in a more deeply integrated and widened CARICOM, will probably have a greater role to play in future arrangements, Demas continues to argue, and other commentators agree (Girvan, St Rose and most of the panellists at the Conference), that the role of the state has to be meaningful. Whether state intervention takes the form of planned national or sectoral activities, through the national budget, or through the regulatory arrangements for the financial and monetary systems, such involvement will be necessary for orderly management of small, open economies such as those in the Caribbean.

Thirdly, the effectiveness of the State's role in the twenty-first century, is circumscribed not only by the capacity of the region's private sector to respond but also by the ability of the region to create and efficiently employ its 'social capital' – a national social contract and cohesiveness that has, by and large, eluded most Caribbean countries in most of their post independence development. It is this critical 'factor of production' that has been, for the most part, missing in national and private production and development functions in the regions.

Fourthly, in different ways both Norman Girvan and Cuthbert Joseph underlined the importance of reinforcing institutional structures to strengthen CARICOM and post CARICOM arrangements. Whether these be 'supranational' judicial structures to more effectively operationalise CARICOM decisions or other forms of structures to stimulate more cross-border activities and flows within and outside of the region, it is common knowledge that institutions are presently weak, at the national and regional levels. Robust structures would need to be built, as Demas himself has come to recognise and admit.

Fifthly, one of the key challenges for the region in the forthcoming years will undoubtedly be its capacity to develop and transform itself structurally, while maintaining orthodox notions of its sovereignty. Demas was right in condemning the implications of the Shiprider Agreement, but many take the view in the region that such sovereignty is already compromised by the strangleholds presently had by 'drug-barons' in CARICOM economies and by distortions that narco-dollars have already introduced into the region's financial systems. They argue that whatever external support can be gained should be welcome and that notions of sovereignty are relative, in a world of a global village anyway. While there is merit in both elements of this argument, in matter of this sort, concerted, co-ordinated, multilateral approaches will always yield greater value-added to the region than any attempt to grapple with these issues on a one-to-one, bilateral basis. Opportunities for exploitation of small by large, are clearly greater in alternative scenarios. In this regard, the key challenge for the region in the next century appears to be generating the capacity to bargain from a position of regional strength, and in a coordinated way.

Finally, when all is told, it is likely that the twenty-first century will present for the CARICOM region even greater challenges than have so far manifested themselves in the region in most aspects of economic, social and political life. As Governor Venner clearly articulated in his presentation, this will require distinct paradigm shifts in the nature and scope of economic responses. High on the agenda for Caribbean economies would have to be the business of what Governor Venner labels their 'socio-economic development'. This implies that Caribbean development priorities must not be purely economic in scope, as the adjustment exercises in the 1980s and early 1990s have so clearly dictated, but must take account of the imperatives of sustained social development. As Demas himself clearly understood thirty years ago and still emphasises, central to such social development must be ample doses of political will. The assurance of better governance, through the creation of more relevant institutions, political systems and administrative frameworks will unquestionably be required. These would appear to be critical ingredients for any new paradigm that could be broadly acceptable for effective Caribbean development in the twenty-first century.

It is, therefore, within such a framework and a reinvigorated capacity of the region to readily rise to the challenges of the next century that the Demas vision of three decades ago must be objectively evaluated.

Under the prescient stewardship and ideas of William Gilbert Demas and his venerable peers, the economic nation of the Caribbean Community has come a far way since political independence. Yet Demas would be the first to admit that the dream of a truly Pan-Caribbean nation – politically and economically – has not yet been realised. His critical contribution in this regard, however, has been the way he has so deftly charted the region's necessary course and carefully signalled the appropriate direction through foresight and experience.

Notes

1. For example, the Mitchell/Compton Initiative for the OECS, the 1991 Manning Initiative for Trinidad and Tobago, Barbados and Guyana; the

Grenada Declaration of 1971; a proposal by the late Dr Cheddi Jagan in a 1996 lecture to the Institute of International Relations (St Augustine) for a West Indian Union, without a single nation-state, federal or unitary, but one with common symbols such as West Indian citizenship, etc.

Earlier published in *Essays in Honour of William G. Demas: Towards a Caribbean Economy in the Twenty-first Century*, Caribbean Centre for Monetary Studies, ed. by Laurence Clarke & M. G. Zephirin, pp. 199–208.

[23]

The Birth of a Vision

Michael Manley

Integration processes which create closer political and/or economic links between nations which have established their historical identities, are complex and difficult. They are difficult because they involve the building of bridges across some part of the divisions created by national boundaries and which give to each nation its sense of identity and capacity for social cohesion. Accordingly, the pursuit of integration can never occur merely in response to the search for greater size for its own sake, much less to political whims or romantic notions about shared destinies.

Geographical proximity and a common cultural background make integration easier to accomplish, yet neither location nor culture is the reason for the pursuit of larger areas within which to seek the benefits of cooperation. This has its roots in economics. However, it has to be pursued through political action because for structural cooperation to occur, separate governments have to agree to some form of common action which will modify the existing structure of relationships between each member of the group. The action itself will reflect the extent to which they feel that some part of their interests will be better promoted by acting together than apart.

The West Indies Federation was no exception and it failed in 1961 because the political action, which it represented, did not convince enough people of being in their best interests. Thus the underlying economic needs which led to the attempt remained unanswered. Therefore it was inevitable that some less ambitious form of political action would have to be undertaken. In due course the idea of CARIFTA was born in 1963 in response to these needs. By 1968 the body was formally established. When CARICOM was formed in 1972, it represented the next logical step forward. And now the decision to form the Association of the Caribbean States in 1994 represents a further advance along the same path. All these steps were taken within an historical context in which nations seek to form alliances with their neighbours to promote economic development and to have a more powerful voice in world affairs.

As one of the founders of CARICOM, I recall that we shared a sense of historical urgency though each had a different view of where the integration process might be headed. For example, Eric Williams was suspicious of Venezuela's intentions towards the Caribbean. Forbes Burnham had border problems with the same country. Errol Barrow tended to see CARICOM as an end in itself, his emphasis being on the development of the English-speaking Caribbean as a discrete element within the wider Basin.

I shared the concerns and emphases of my major colleagues but also felt that the history which had divided the Caribbean into English, Spanish, French and Dutch-speaking components was not made by us. I felt that we should work to build bridges in economics and culture to bring all the segments of the Caribbean into a closer scheme of cooperation than could be provided by the contacts which arose from our common membership in the United Nations.

Accordingly, I saw CARICOM as the first step in a process of necessary cooperation among former colonial territories. It was the easiest step to take because the founding members not only occupy the same geographical basin but also share a common history and easily compatible cultures. But for me, it was only a first step.

As far back as 1969 I had formulated a theory of 'concentric circles' in which former colonial territories would seek closer co-operation with their immediate neighbours while simultaneously building platforms for common action through regional associations and active cooperation with international bodies like the Non Aligned Movement.

In our case I argued that the CARIFTA group would represent the tightest of our circles, the countries of the Caribbean Basin the next and wider area or circle, the Group of 77 in the UN the next; and finally, the Non Aligned Movement as the all-embracing world alliance.

CARICOM was the necessary step to give the first circle greater coherence. For CARICOM itself, the founders foresaw a clear political goal which was to assert our collective voice in a region in danger of sinking into neo-colonialism in the aftermath of the attainment of independence. Giving recognition to Cuba and China in defiance of the wishes of the USA was significant because it represented an early declaration of independence from the more overt pressures of US hegemony.

With respect to the inner workings of CARICOM we hoped it would provide a framework which would promote economic integration in ways not open to CARIFTA with its major emphasis on intra-regional trade. The agenda was widened to incorporate objectives such as common tariff policies and the promotion of intra-regional investment. The construction of multinational systems of production and regionally sound economic infrastructure were part of the new agenda. The unrealised plan for an aluminium smelter based on the flare-off gas of Trinidad and Tobago and the bauxite of Jamaica and Guyana was an example of an attempt to create a joint production organisation. The now defunct regional shipping line incorporating nations outside of CARICOM was an attempt to create a regional infrastructure. It was also significant because it foreshadowed the ACS in its wider membership. In the course of the first few years of CARICOM, Jamaica began to pioneer trading links and other forms of economic cooperation with non-CARICOM states of the Caribbean Basin. This parallel action was deliberate and furthered the theory of concentric circles. Bauxite trading with Venezuela and later the San José accords involving Venezuelan and Mexican oil sales were the forerunners of wider, planned Caribbean cooperation. This provided the background to the formal creation in 1994 of an Association of Caribbean States adumbrated in the recommendations of the West Indian Commission, chaired by Sir Shridath Ramphal.

Looking back across 23 years one can point to considerable accomplishments. Intra-regional trade has increased many times over. The Common External Tariff is at last in place. The work on creating a single market is proceeding. Much cross border investment has taken place and a regional stock exchange has begun, however tentatively, to take shape.

But the outside world has not stood still. The new structure of the world economy barely discernible in 1972, is now sharply in focus. And it is that structure which represents the context within which we must measure our present status and future prospects.

Let us now consider our present and our future at a new moment of opportunity. On August 17 and 18, the first summit meeting of the leaders of the ACS will take place in Port of Spain to examine tourism, trade and transport with special emphasis on the contribution each can make to regional economic development. A conference on these subjects could not be more timely and follows the decision of 25 nations of the Caribbean Basin to create the new regional association recommended by the West Indies Commission and demanded by the logic of history. This is so because as technology makes possible the globalisation of finance, production and marketing in an irreversible process, the nation state is more and more failing to provide a geopolitical unit large enough within which to plan and direct economic activity. Hence, trade blocs are proliferating beginning with Europe, and most recently, NAFTA. That is why it is simplistic to believe as some contend, that the first major blocs have come into existence out of fear of the production tigers of the Pacific triangle. The reasons are more profound and since they are bound up in technology and the globalisation process, we can assume that the trade bloc is not a temporary aberration of history. There will be more, not less of it, as time passes. The question we must ask ourselves in the Caribbean is 'What does this imply for us?'

There are three views: there are some who advocate each Caribbean territory getting into NAFTA on its own, as quickly as possible, and on the best terms which it can secure for itself. Then there are those who see NAFTA as a gobbling monster to be avoided at all costs. They hark back to the 'good old days' when we were able to negotiate special arrangements for sugar and bananas under the Lomé Convention.

As a path, the first may be fraught with peril. The second pursues what will be discovered increasingly to be a romantic illusion. Let us consider each briefly as a prelude to the third which I believe to be the path best supported by logic and common sense.

I will begin with what we may call the unilateralist illusion. It must be conceded that the most advanced of the Caribbean countries could become a part of NAFTA and avoid complete marginalisation. They may have just enough competitive manufacturing capacity and productive diversity to maintain the toehold that they now have in the North American market. But the market is not static. Will they be able to expand rapidly enough to improve their position? And what voice will they have in hemispheric relations?

The question that must be asked is relative. Is unilateral entry in a context of isolation the best position from which to take on the full brunt of open competition within the North American system? Is there a better way, a way more likely to enhance the strength of each country's economy at the moment of full membership in NAFTA? We will explore this when we look at our third path.

The second 'option' we may call the nostalgic illusion. Again it must be conceded that the issue is not cut and dried. The very small territories that are particularly dependent on the protections and advantages afforded under the Lomé Convention are in a position of acute difficulty with respect to

NAFTA. The problem is, however, that Lomé as we know it is not going to survive beyond the year 2000.

Lomé represented a special set of arrangements secured for the countries of the colonial empires at a particular historical juncture. The Independence movement succeeded in a context of historical guilt. This guilt represented a force within the political system of the former metropoles of empire not unlike the guilt which operated upon the consciences of those members of the House of Commons in Britain who voted for the abolition of slavery. But the real driving force behind Lomé, like the real driving force behind the abolition of slavery was not conscience but economic self-interest. Slavery had become an uneconomic method of production. The immorality of slavery provided a brilliant ethical cover for a cunning retreat from a system that was no longer profitable.

In the case of Lomé each colonial system had guaranteed to the producers at the centre of empire a reliable low cost supply of vital raw materials. At the moment of independence it was useful for the former colonial producers within a politically tied system to be spared the search for markets in open competition. But it was even more convenient for the manufacturers at the centre of the empire to be guaranteed a safe supply of raw materials without recourse to general competition. The price supports which were provided under Lomé represented the premium that was paid to guarantee the dependability of the system in a new political environment.

Now more than a generation has passed, production at all levels is increasingly organised outside of particular political boundaries and with absolutely no reference to the desires of Governments or electorates. The claim of conscience, such as it may have been, has long since been discharged. The world of systematic, dependable structures of protection is in its last gasp. To tie the hopes of the future to the prospect of new and better Lomés in the twenty-first century is, at best, romantic and at worst irresponsible.

And so to the third path which I believe to represent a better hope for the most developed Caribbean territories, the best hope for those in an intermediate stage, and the only hope for the most vulnerable. The action we take must respond to two imperatives: an acceleration and deepening of the integration process within CARICOM: and the broadening of that process to include all the countries of the Caribbean Basin under the Association of Caribbean States. The reasons are as simple as they are fundamental. They are to be found in two concepts: economies of scale and specialisation leading to a rationalisation of production. For example, amalgamations involving two or more companies in different countries producing the same things can be hugely beneficial. The new corporate entity will enjoy a large capital base and reduced overhead costs in comparative terms. The amalgamation would also facilitate specialised production for different product lines. All these advantages lead to greater competitive efficiency. Then again, the global marketplace reflects patterns of quality and price that are determined by the latest technology. Increasingly, this technology is expensive and difficult to finance in comparatively small operations. The larger the capital base that can be organised for a particular business, the better the chance that the business can afford the high-cost technology. Without that technology, it will be harder to compete without either painful depression of wages or unaffordable levels of subsidy. The first is not an option in our socially conscious Caribbean. The second, subsidies, is not an option in our cash-strapped Caribbean. Clearly therefore, we have to work for anything that facilitates the process of corporate aggregation. Small may be beautiful but too much of it is too little for survival. Our policies must centre upon widening our immediate markets as the first foundation of the broadening of our capital base.

The same factors apply if we are to accelerate our mastery of the skills which are demanded by the explosion of knowledge-based industries which are now at the cutting edge of economic development.

There are obviously members of CARICOM who can contemplate successful entry into the NAFTA arrangement at this moment. Some may yet succeed in the near future, and in any event, the decision to enter now or not is a purely national one which everybody should respect and which I personally respect. What would, in my view, be an error is to abandon the Caribbean integration process either because an application to join NAFTA succeeded or because it was believed that a particular economy is ready for membership. It is the belief, held by some individuals, that there is no place for the integration process because NAFTA represents a new reality which I describe and believe to be a 'unilateralist illusion'.

The Price of Survival

The political difficulties to be overcome in working for integration are recognised and they are formidable. Nonetheless, the creation of a single market for CARICOM should be pursued with relentless single-mindedness. The challenge to today's political leaders is to sweep aside the impediments and mobilise their societies to understand that the single market is not a regional dream but represents the very price of survival in today's world. Common tariffs, common taxation policies, common investment incentives, represent one part of the equation. An immediate programme providing for the free movement of manpower resources beginning with the more skilled and ending up in due course with a fully mobile labour market is a second element. The removal of all impediments to and the positive facilitation of the free movement of investment capital represent a third element. At the same time, widening the process across the cultural and historical divisions must go hand in hand with deepening integration within CARICOM.

Little of this can be achieved in isolation from the people and what they understand. Indeed this is one more example of the real challenge of democracy. This consists of the education of the people leading to their support of those strategic purposes which lie at the heart of their hopes for a better life for their children. This is why cultural activity and exchange is not to be pursued for the titivation of the elite or the mere entertainment of the masses. We have been so psychologically marginalised by colonialism and by the all-pervasive anaesthetic of United States pop culture that we will lose the capacity for bold action for no better reason than fear. And we will be afraid because we will have lost sight of our own roots and our own capacity for greatness.

There is, therefore, an intimate connection between the logic, which underlies our economic prospects, and the inspiration which our cultural processes can provide. An integrated Caribbean will create more industries which can achieve the scale of operations to be competitive. Each success will provide the surplus for re-investment in an upward cycle of economic development depending on efficiency and self-reliance. This is where our hopes lie rather than in the search for present favour for past ills.

An example of the challenge we face if we are to see reality in a new light is provided by the transnational corporation. The world is still profoundly affected by transnational corporations' behaviour. But this form of economic organisation can no longer be rejected out of hand on the basis of a simplistic, global ethic. We must continue to struggle to make these bodies accountable and reflective of a new form of good corporate citizenship, globally conceived. In the meantime, however, they define today's reality and tomorrow's shape. The truth is that we need our own transnationals which pull together the resources of Jamaica, Trinidad and Tobago, Guyana, Venezuela, Cuba and all the rest and it is our duty to work ceaselessly to make it easier for these things to happen.

The new problems, which we face if the integration process is to be effectively pursued, are commonly seen in one light: as 'difficulties' to be overcome. Certainly, in the context of the present political assumptions and patterns of behaviour the difficulties are very real. At the same time all over the Caribbean there is a growing public unease surrounding political activity and it has nothing to do with the integration process. As unease slides into disenchantment, the level of public involvement in political activity is sinking steadily.

It may well be that the pursuit of the integration process in the vertical and horizontal senses could be one of the causes that re-ignite political interest. The majority of people feel instinctively that the 'old ways' in politics are no longer equal to the 'new needs'. They may not be able to spell out these needs precisely but they know the world is changing radically and they are uncertain of the extent to which traditional political responses can secure their interests in a changing situation.

Integration seen as a challenging opportunity instead of a series of difficulties to be reluctantly overcome may strike chords now missing in the political environment. This is so because integration is a major part of any answer to today's reality. No marriage between political mission and popular interests has ever failed if the synergy is understood and explained.

Note

This paper was first published in *CARICOM Perspective*, No. 65, June 1995, pp. 12–14, 31.

[24]

Awaiting the Dawn of a
Greater Unity

Roderick Rainford

As I reflect upon the period of the 1980s into the early 1990s, when I had the honour of serving as CARICOM Secretary General, it strikes me in a most compelling manner how true it is that CARICOM – in the broad sense of the movement along with its institutional infrastructure – has really been as much a search for an integration arrangement as an actual integration arrangement itself. As such CARICOM constituted a continuity with earlier groupings of the West Indian people's sense of mutual belonging and 'family' for concrete self-actualisation.

In the early 1980s, it was clear that, notwithstanding the existence of a formal treaty setting out the aims, objectives, and operational processes of the Caribbean Community and Common Market, there was a sense that the Governments and peoples of the Commonwealth Caribbean region were still feeling their way around, about how to inculcate in society a workable holistic concept of what CARICOM was about; about consensus on the true limits and boundaries of the West Indian imperative towards unity and on whether these were wider or narrower than the scope of the Treaty of Chaguaramas; about forging a creative dynamic out of the tension between the centripetal pull of oneness and the centrifugal force of separate national tendencies. Answers to this quest, if any were to be found, would depend critically on our

West Indian gift for articulation at all levels of society, animated by a compelling vision supplied by responsible leadership.

Thus there was a kind of hunger in the soul for clarity in the meaning of the CARICOM integration adventure. What were we about in terms of key strategic outcomes? How could we ensure that both process and outcomes have practical relevance for the ordinary people who signify the foundation on which CARICOM integration would have to rest? How to promote the legitimacy of the inter Governmental and people-to-people dimension of CARICOM integration, and connect both in a mutually reinforcing manner without one damaging the integrity of the other?

These were pregnant questions that, implicitly or explicitly, hung on the lips of practically all interest groups as CARICOM prepared to advance into the decade of the 1980s. But, urgent as these questions were, it was not at all clear that an answer, in the sense of an operational concept that commanded wide acceptance and support, would be forthcoming overnight. The question of how to construct consensus was itself a vexing issue. In West Indian circumstances we felt constrained to let hundreds of voices contend – and there never has been a shortage of voices – and hope for consensus to emerge from that magic conjuncture of leadership, luck, social psychology and political and economic circumstances which at times lead to a defining moment that brings a sea of change in human affairs.

As many of us tried in those days to envisage the years ahead that would unfold into the decade of the 1980s, we were acutely conscious of several debilitating circumstances retarding the regional movement. Three of these were particularly prominent. The impact and aftermath of the energy crisis, which erupted in the early 1970s just as CARICOM was being launched, ushered in a period of intra-CARICOM protectionism as various member states scrambled to defend their balance of payments – some grounding their action juridically in Article 28 of the Treaty of Chaguaramas. At the same time there was the challenge to overcome the legacy of the failure to convene the Conference of Heads of Government for some seven years between its second meeting in St Kitts and Nevis in 1975 and its third meeting in Jamaica in November 1982. On top of these, the reverberation within CARICOM of the implosion of the regime in Grenada in late 1983 and the associated intervention by US forces brought added challenges to bear on the resilience of the regional movement.

In this setting, with the imperative for unity still alive but lacking a coherent strategy for decisive advance, it seemed that, the best approach to integration was to go into a kind of holding pattern in the expectation that we would one day burst forth onto the broader uplands of integration. Rightly or wrongly, there was apprehension that trying to force the pace of things prematurely could destroy the still embryonic and fragile machinery that was being constructed to serve the people's sense of connectedness and thus be counter productive in the long run. As one elder statesman of the region observed at the time, the regional movement was constrained to move at the pace of the least common denominator.

So it seemed there was nothing but to resign ourselves, for a while, to a holding pattern and to keep things going at the pace of the least common denominator. Nevertheless there was a conviction that the holding pattern did not necessarily imply lack of growth, and that the least common denominator did not have to remain at one level. There could be credible movement on many fronts while waiting for the decisive big push to take place that would lift the integration movement on to a higher plane. Some might even have surmised that they could awaken one day to realise that the decisive big push had taken place, not with trumpet blasts and shouting from the rooftops, but quietly though the gradual building up of critical mass support, through numerous modest advances across a wide front.

I would say then, that that was the dominant mood in which activities in CARICOM were pursued during the 1980s: keeping the engine of CARI-COM integration turning over in expectation of, and in preparation for, the moment when a critical mass move towards practical commitment would be reached that would put the regional movement decisively on course for a home run. In this context, the decade of the 1980s was a period of broad positive movement across several fronts, though, not unexpectedly there were setbacks and reverses.

One early departure was the ongoing effort to hone the CARICOM Secretariat as the planning and administrative tool of the CARICOM integration regime. During the late 1970s and early 1980s Secretary General Kurleigh King, following a period when the Secretariat had no confirmed executive head, was already working determinedly to streamline and sharpen the management systems employed in the organisation. The initial start-up effort of Cozier, and the strong foundations subsequently laid down by Demas and McIntyre, served the integration process well in their time and continued to do so after they left the Secretariat. However, the Secretariat could not remain on 'automatic pilot' indefinitely, in spite of their outstanding achievements and the management system in the Secretariat had to evolve continuously, even just by keeping the integration engine turning over.

After the initial innovations introduced by Kurleigh King, certain key concerns propelled the drive to streamline the operations and functioning of the Secretariat during the 1980s. One was a concern that the Secretariat reflect the mission of the regional integration movement, in concrete programmes, with clearly articulated goals and objectives to be achieved annually or biennially. Three interrelated approaches were employed to draw the programme boundaries: a close reading of the Treaty of Chaguaramas, careful interpretation of the major mandates of the organs and institutions of the Community over the year, and the application of one's sense of general community policy, even where this may not have been always explicitly stated in the Treaty provisions or in the decisions of the organs and institutions. In an effort to reduce 'ad hoc' unpredictable behaviour every activity had to have its *raison d'être* within the context of a clearly defined programme.

About nineteen basic programmes were identified in this way, with the available staff assigned to specific programmes. Some programmes fitted directly into particular organisational units in the Secretariat, while others were linked to staff resources in two or more units. The definition of programmes and the identification to staff resources was a major aspect of the advance made in the 1980s in programme budgeting, ending the previous practice of setting out annual work programmes section by section. This was a development which, though not without complexities in the special circumstances of the regional movement and the Secretariat, nevertheless served to increase transparency in resource utilisation. Of course, though the political directorate of the Community and the management of the Secretariat were quite settled on the basic thrust of these efforts, it was recognised that this programme budgeting scheme had to be kept under review, with the aim of adjusting and modifying it continuously in the light of experience and new insights. Indeed, each succeeding year did bring modifications and adjustments, either in terms of rationalisation of the number of programmes originally defined, or, in terms of rationalisation of activities within individual programmes.

Beyond the advance into a workable programme budgeting system, other challenges were being faced in the effort to hone the Secretariat as the planning and administrative instrument of the CARICOM integration arrangement. One of these concerned the Secretariat's response to widespread dissatisfaction among governmental and non governmental interests in the region over the frequent failure in the CARICOM integration process to arrive at critical decisions or to proceed with implementation when decisions were made. It was clear that in so far as it lay within the power of the Secretariat to improve the record, this had to be achieved in part through striving for greater and greater technical excellence in the preparatory work that culminates in decisions of the organs and institutions of the Community and Common Market. This meant engaging in preparatory work that established as conclusively as possible the technical, financial and administrative feasibility of whatever proposals were being brought forward for decision. It was obvious that approaching preparatory work in this way would improve the prospects for implementation of decisions, since the challenges of implementation would have influenced preparation from the earliest stages.

Two other considerations were also critical to the prospects for satisfactory decision-making and implementation. One was the issue of political feasibility. It had to be recognised that decisions are always taken in the context of a given political climate which is informed by a host of factors, rational and non rational, national and personal. If there is one outstanding lesson that the CARICOM integration experience has taught us, it is that it is hazardous in the extreme to ignore the issue of political feasibility. This has to do with diplomacy – being able to judge the political climate at the time – to know when a prospect might be accepted through quiet persuasion and consultation and to know when one should withdraw and wait for the right time. The other consideration was the design of the decision itself, since even where technical preparation was adequate, the way a decision was structured could spell the difference between adequate and inadequate implementation.

Secretariat Staffing

These overall concerns focused our attention on the profile of the ideal Secretariat professional. Space does not allow the details of the profile, but it will suffice to highlight a few critical ones. A picture was developed of the ideal Secretariat professional as one with strong conceptual strengths, imbued with a keen sense of how the programmes of the CARICOM integration movement give life to the basic mission of the Community and Common Market. He or she should have a clear notion of the identifiable outcomes being sought, a capacity to plan activities linked to the achievement of these outcomes, and to manage resources needed for the production of these outcomes. He or she needed to show a capacity for acquiring intimate knowledge and understanding of the regional and global context in which programme objectives are being pursued, and must be conscious of resources, financial and otherwise, beyond the Secretariat budget, that can be tapped to support programme development and implementation. The ideal Secretariat professional needed to be conscious that often the Secretariat will be limited to supporting only those programmes that were strategically catalytic. It was accepted that appropriate formal training in institutions outside the Secretariat could contribute much to equipping such a professional but it was also recognised that in the long run nothing could substitute for on-the-job exposure and continuous internal communication in developing these skills.

There was a notion in the 1980s that this approach to the development of the Secretariat would provide a basis for maintaining technical excellence in serving the Community while at the same time limiting budgetary demands on member states which were having to contend with the imperatives of structural and macroeconomic adjustment in their own affairs. There was a vision of a tight permanent establishment of highly developed professionals serving core functions and programmes, along with a wide range of outside specialist experts on a project or the task basis.

This effort at development of the Secretariat needed to proceed pending, and in preparation for, the moment when circumstances were right for CARICOM to take a quantum leap forward. But all possible advances in integration would be made in the meantime. A few such critical areas are worthy of mention.

Among the big issues impatient of delay in the 1980s was the matter of improving the operation of the CARICOM free trade regime and development of the common market envisaged in the Treaty of Chaguaramas. During the first half of the 1980s the level of intra-CARICOM trade dropped from its peak of EC$1.6 billion in 1982 to less than half this amount by 1986. This decline was due in part to a general fall in demand in many of the national markets of CARICOM. But the erosion also stemmed substantially from a surge in intra-regional protectionism. Debates in the Common Market Council and in other fora about where blame for the deterioration should be assigned tended to be emotive and fractious in the extreme. To stem the tide, the Secretariat strengthened its efforts to provide the Council and the Community with detailed quantitative and qualitative analyses of the trends in intra-regional trade, and to explain the precise circumstances relating to specific cases of barriers to trade, in the context of the provision of the common market annex to the Treaty of Chaguaramas. There is reason to believe that this activity broadened the pool of shared information about CARICOM products and the conditions of regional trade in them, and that it turned out to be a confidence building process. This development, which perhaps coincided with the onset of trade liberalisation promoted by what came to be known as the 'Washington policy consensus', most probably played an important part in the resumption of growth in intra-CARICOM trade from 1987 onwards. By the early 1990s, intra-CARICOM trade had been substantially liberalised, and intra-regional trade protectionism was becoming largely a thing of the past.

Also in the second half of the 1980s prompted by growing apprehension about the implications for CARICOM countries of the move towards the European single market, the unfolding of plans for NAFTA within the framework of the EAI, and the anticipated outcome of the Uruguay Round, attention was focused anew on the issue of creating a CARICOM economic space. Relative success in trade liberalisation brought with it renewed emphasis on the need for action on other elements of market integration, and fresh appreciation of the fact that liberalisation of trade in goods alone does not by itself create a single economic space, as the 'Wise Men's Report', coordinated by William Demas in 1981, cogently argued. What should be the aims of the CARICOM integration grouping with regards the intra-regional rolling back of boundaries in relation to trade in services, right of establishment, free movement of capital and of labour, and the unrestrained effecting of payments for current transactions? How to construct a distinctive boundary around this common economic space?

Some serious work was done, in the late 1980s, with regards to the last subject mentioned, as the Secretariat pursued studies and led discussions within CARICOM on the structure and orientation of a Common External Tariff. It is now a matter of record that the exercise of shaping the CET, spearheaded by the Secretariat's technical preparatory work, had to go through successive rounds of complex negotiations, ending ultimately with adoption of an agreed package now in the process of implementation. The momentum had gathered pace towards putting the other elements of a single marketing in place, and this elicited a formal mandate from CARICOM Heads of Government, in the well-known Grand Anse Declaration of 1989, to work towards a CARICOM Single Market and Economy. Here again, the technical analytic work of the Secretariat has been of signal importance in increasing awareness of the implications of a single market, and in guiding thinking about the structure, design and functioning of the single market.

Of course, CARICOM planners have had to contend in more recent times with the emerging view in some influential quarters that there is no longer a rationale for the creation of a distinctive CARICOM economic space in an era of liberalisation of trade and capital flows globally and within regional mega blocs, one of which, being developed on the basis of duty free trade, CARICOM countries are likely to be joining individually or collectively. This is a line of thinking that raises questions about strategic options for CARICOM in the emerging new global and hemispheric trading systems, and adequate evaluation of these options shall test the mettle of CARICOM planners.

Broadly, it can be said that one option that is ruled out by current and foreseeable circumstances is that of pursuing inward-looking integration. CARICOM countries, for better or for worse, are now committed to a path of openness, and the basic question is whether this openness is going to be pursued with or without market integration at the CARICOM level. On the assumption that CARICOM countries will be seeking to link up with NAFTA, the choice will depend at one level on how far they will seek to do so as a bloc or individually, and at another level, on the negotiation dynamics arising from the terms sought and the terms offered. In all this it seems there is much to be said for a scenario in which CARICOM countries join NAFTA as a bloc and on the basis of ample transitional arrangements for phasing into hemispheric free trade, thus leaving room for the creation of an outward oriented economic space within CARICOM. In any case, it is not clear that the present NAFTA partners will be ready to negotiate entry with CARICOM countries anytime soon, and in the interim the CARICOM economic integration arrangements cannot be left in limbo.

In the meantime the great potential for unity in the functional and social areas has always beckoned, and continues to do so. In response, cooperation and joint programmes have been advanced in education, health and human resource development; in information and telecommunications; environmental protection and disaster planning and preparedness; in agricultural development, freer movement of persons and cultural matters; harmonisation of laws and standards, and in sea and air transportation.

But have we come as yet to the big push into strengthening CARICOM integration? *The Grand Anse Declaration* certainly looked like it, with its call for the establishment of a single market and the establishment of the West Indian Commission to help chart the way to greater unity in the region. As the West Indian Commission went the rounds within CARICOM and in the wider Caribbean, conducting its historic hearings, there was apprehension in the minds of many that if this exercise did not lead to a resounding take-off into greater unity it would not happen again for many years and we would return to a pattern of keeping the engine of CARICOM integration turning over until another dawning of another day of inspiration.

But the West Indian Commission exercise, at the level of the report produced, did carry the promise of a far-reaching advance into the greater unity long awaited. It is true that the centrepiece of its principal recommendations, the establishment of a CARICOM Commission, has been sidelined. But there has been broad endorsement by CARICOM's supreme decision makers of the other major recommendations: including the establishment of a Caribbean Supreme Court and an Assembly of Caribbean Parliamentarians [both on the CARICOM agenda from before the setting up of the Commission], the revamping of the CARICOM machinery to provide for a Council of Ministers, the adoption of a Charter of Civil Society, free movement of skills on an initially limited basis, movement towards a common currency and using a deepened CARICOM as the driving force to broaden integration in the wider Caribbean by launching an Association of Caribbean States. There has been follow-up action, with mixed results, in these various areas since the presentation of the progress report and the final report of the Commission. There has been little forward movement with the Caribbean Supreme Court and free movement of skills, but the Assembly is probably nearing implementation; the Treaty is under review with the aim, *inter alia*, of establishing the proposed Council of Ministers, and a draft of the proposed Charter of Civil Society has been approved for circulation for national discussion. For technical reasons, the advance into a common currency will probably be slower than originally thought possible, and there has been good progress in negotiating and agreeing on the formal framework for the ACS.

In general, the jury is still out on whether the overall impact of the formal and substantive operational response to the main recommendations of the West Indian Commission will constitute the big advance into that greater unity that the West Indian people instinctively crave. When we finally hear from the jury on regional sentiment and opinion, we will know whether it is still the case that CARICOM remains as much a search for an integration arrangement, as it is an integration arrangement itself.

Note

This paper was first published in *CARICOM Perspective*, No. 65, June 1995, pp. 67–70.

[25]

Remembering to Score
A Retrospective

Shridath Ramphal

— You see, you see what I tell you,
he playing and missing, I tell you!
— No, no, you don't read the stroke,
He know what he doing, he leaving
the ball alone . . .
that is what I call a indigenous
stroke.

— Edward Baugh

Eddie Baugh's 'View from the George Headley Stand' may well result from the poet's eye, roving beyond Sabina boundary towards wider West Indian playing fields. Anyhow, I offer it as such, highlighting the obvious, that either way – 'playing and missing' or 'a indigenous stroke' – no runs are scored and the risk of getting out is high. This retrospective is about scoring regional runs at another, earlier time, and the need to go on scoring.

To say that the seeds of the Lomé Convention were sown on the lawns of the Prime Minister's residence in Georgetown is perhaps hyperbole – but there is more than a grain of truth in it. On this CARICOM anniversary, it is worth revisiting that occasion in 1972 when we were preparing to advance from

CARIFTA to CARICOM within the Region and to venture forth regionally into Europe.

The first thing to note about those times was our relative freshness and confidence. The times were propitious to innovation and welcoming to creativity. There was a mood of hope at large. Our countries were themselves new to independence: only Jamaica and Trinidad and Tobago were ten years old. Apart from Montserrat which was (and remains) a British Colony, what were to become the OECS countries were still only the Associated States; but they were stretching the limits of that constitutional novelty to free themselves of neo-colonial shackles. We may have lacked experience of the world, but we did not lack boldness or energy.

The times were propitious, too, in another respect which is best described in terms of the difference between now and then. Now, the prevailing sense in Caribbean capitals certainly on matters of trade and economic policy generally, but on other matters as well is one of powerlessness – of constraints, of limitations, of incapacities. Then in the early seventies, there was still a sense of possibility; in our capital cities the political issue was the choice of policy options. In the region, we talked of 'ideological pluralism', and in relations beyond the region, we had a sense of negotiating potential. And that difference between then and now was not merely the difference between naiveté and realism. The realities were different; it was a different time and for us, a better time. The shadow of globalism had not yet fallen across our regional path.

All this had a counterpart at the political level. The region, remember, in 1972 broke the diplomatic embargo against Cuba when Barbados, Guyana, Jamaica and Trinidad and Tobago together established full diplomatic relations with Cuba – American anguish notwithstanding. Caribbean countries at the Conference of Tlatelolco two years later (1974) would tell Henry Kissinger – and encourage Latin America to join in doing so – that a 'Community of the Americas' was not on, since in an association of such unequals, community would mean hegemony. How times have changed! We were being consulted then before Canada was, and we were saying 'no'.

And Caribbean countries were playing key roles beyond the hemisphere in the Non Aligned Movement. That earlier reference to the lawns of the Prime Minister's residence in Georgetown was to the occasion when it was the venue for a reception for Non Aligned Foreign Ministers. It was the first time the Movement had met in the Western Hemisphere outside UN headquarters. And we were prominent too in NIEO discussions in New York and later in the Conference on International Economic Cooperation (CIEC) in Paris. That we mattered in these Councils added to our confidence in all we did in the drive to regional integration and its concomitant of regional negotiations with Europe.

The confidence generated other successes. The reason why my opening words are not far from the truth is that it was our unity in CARIFTA that led to the ACP and the eventual Lomé Convention. Regional unity in CARIFTA allowed us to forge a clear strategy for negotiating a *sui generis* agreement with Europe, and it was in furtherance of that strategy that we were able to play such a leading role in creating the ACP. We had to begin by helping to secure a closing of ranks in Africa itself between its French-speaking and English-speaking countries. It was at the Non Aligned reception in Georgetown that we gathered together African Foreign Ministers, and proposed a joining of hands in the negotiations with Europe. When we spoke with them then, and ever after, we spoke as the Caribbean. And later, with confidence in ourselves, we welded the African, Caribbean and Pacific negotiators into one team speaking with one voice – an African one. When we did that, our unity was actually stronger than Europe's. From these negotiations came Lomé I, not all we could have desired, but a good deal more than Europe had contemplated. And out of the total experience came the establishment of the ACP in its own right – a long way from those first conversations we initiated in 1972.

An extract from a contemporary record explains the depth of this CARIFTA effort:

At the *ad hoc* discussions in Georgetown in August, 1972, it was agreed that a team of Caribbean officials would visit Commonwealth African States for more comprehensive technical discussions. That CARIFTA mission went in September 1972 to East and West Africa, holding talks in Arusha with officials of the East African Community and their counterparts in Lagos, Accra and Freetown – apprising their colleagues of the preparatory work already being undertaken in the Caribbean. What was clearly needed, however, was concerted action among African States, and at Lagos, Nigeria, in February, 1973 a start was made in this direction with a meeting of Commonwealth African Ministers hosted by the Government of Nigeria. It was characterised by a bold and purposeful approach to the questions – whether there should be negotiations with the EEC and, if so, on what basis, and with what objectives.

At Lagos, it was agreed that a further meeting of Ministers should be convened in Nairobi to pursue these issues; but, building on the international links forged earlier in 1972, the Lagos meeting authorised a team of Commonwealth African Ministers to visit Georgetown to hold discussions with Caribbean Ministers at CARIFTA Head-quarters. The meeting, held on 19 March 1973 provided an opportunity for a comprehensive exchange of views on the approach to any negotiation with the EEC, and on the essentials of any possible relationship; a refusal to be confined within the negotiating straight-jacket imposed by the 'options' in Protocol 22 to the Treaty of Accession and a determination to resist European overtures for a free trade area arrangement involving 'reciprocal preferences' emerged clearly and with unanimity from these discussions. Caribbean officials were invited to attend the Nairobi meeting as observers and did so in continuation of the inter-regional dialogue that was now fully established.

Journey to Chaguaramas

None of this would have been possible without the progress we were making at home in developing the fledgling CARIFTA structures into the much larger, more ambitious framework of Community. Indeed the evolution of the 'community' negotiations proceeded side by side with the negotiations with Europe. We journeyed to Lomé in February 1975; four Caribbean countries had journeyed first to Chaguaramas in July, 1973 to sign the Treaty establishing the Caribbean Community. Within a year, all the present member states (except the Bahamas) had joined the group. These processes of ambitious endeavour at home and abroad were mutually reinforcing. It helped us abroad, that we were working together at home. It helped us at home that we were working effectively abroad. Neither was without difficulty for all that. But in each area of effort it became easier to overcome.

The path from CARIFTA to Community has been well chronicled by William Demas and others and I hope West Indian scholars will research with rigour the history of integration. For my part, in responding to this invitation to reflect on things past, I share two lessons from these efforts. The first is the importance, sometimes the essentiality, of starting on a regional cause even if only a few in the region are ready to begin the journey. This may be valid in many contexts: it has a compelling logic in the context of our scattered archipelago. The second is the fundamental necessity for us to act together, particularly when dealing with the world beyond ourselves.

As to the first, where would we have been had CARIFTA not been started in 1965 on the shores of Dickenson Bay in Antigua? I say 'started', but that was hardly what happened or was meant to happen. I can speak with authority only of the Guyana thinking but, as events were to develop, it was that thinking which prevailed. What I can say with assurance is that when Errol Barrow and V.C. Bird and Forbes Burnham signed that agreement they knew they were starting a process; they knew they were not at their regional destination, but just beginning a journey. They may have had differing ideas about the pace of the journey, but not about its direction.

They knew, too, the risk of generating suspicion and division by the action they were taking in the longer-term interests of unity. They were convinced, however, that a start had to be made with economic and functional cooperation and that the simplest way forward lay in agreeing to establish CARIFTA among themselves. They were sure too of the mutuality of their commitment to West Indian unity; they believed it was a commitment shared by the West Indian political leadership generally, and that their colleagues would respond once a start was made.

The critical decision would be when the Dickenson Bay Agreement binding the original parties to establishing CARIFTA would come into force. In effect, its operation was suspended for an entire year after it was signed. That was to be the year of growth; a year in which to persuade others that the Agreement was not for an exclusive trading group but an inclusive reciprocal free trade area. There were predictable initial reactions about going off alone, but it was not difficult to persuade the rest of the region's leaders that the Agreement through its suspension clause offered them an invitation to become partners from the start.

When Eric Williams decided that this was not an invitation for Trinidad and Tobago to turn down, and when the associated states also came on board, it did not take long for the Jamaica Manufacturers Association to persuade Bob Lightbourne that Jamaica should not stand aloof, or the Minister of Trade of the region's largest economy to persuade his colleagues in a JLP government, that regionalism after all had a plus side. True, we were to have many a semantic argument about 'cooperation' and 'integration'. All the same, when the time came to establish the Caribbean Development Bank – a crucial integration institution, as we saw it – Jamaica was a strong contender for its location. It was right to start when there was the will to do so even among a few, especially a few with sense of trusteeship.

The second compelling lesson is how critical it is to pool our resources – political, economic and intellectual – in negotiating with countries beyond ourselves: globally, in Europe, in the Hemisphere, even with the wider Caribbean. The early contemporary record had this to say about the Lomé negotiations:

That process of unification – for such it was – added a new dimension to the Third World's quest for economic justice through international action . . . Its significance, however, derives not mainly from the terms of the negotiated relationship between the 46 ACP States and the EEC, but rather from the methodology of unified bargaining which the negotiations pioneered. Never before had so large a segment of the developing world negotiated with so powerful a grouping of developed countries so comprehensive and so innovative a regime of economic relations. It was a new, and salutary experience for Europe; it was a new, and reassuring experience for the ACP States.

What was true for the 46 ACP countries then is true for our region's 13 countries then and now. Remember, the strength of the 46 had first to be pooled regionally, within Africa, the Pacific and the Caribbean. Separately, no single Caribbean country could have negotiated participation in Lomé. Had we been 13 'associates' merely, we would have acquired nothing but EEC morsels – and even that, with 'reciprocity'. Sugar, bananas, rum, for example, would not have had the preferential markets in Europe they have held over the last 20 years and for that we must work hard together to safeguard now.

As we look not to Europe alone but also to North America, we do well to remember these unchanging realities. The essential, inescapable lesson of the CARIFTA/CARICOM years is that we need each other. All else is illusion and mirage. We must not yield to the siren songs of separateness.

I have mentioned Bob Lightbourne among the pioneer players in the evolution of CARIFTA. There were other ministers as well, not only prime ministers and premiers, who played a part in innumerable Council meetings, sustained by Mrs Ting-a-Kee's crab backs – and much more! Derek Knight, George Mallet, 'Son' Mitchell, Kamaaluddin Mohamed, Lee Moore, P.J. Patterson, Paul Southwell and Branford Taitt were only some of those whose labours paved the way for CARICOM. And the CARIFTA Secretariat itself, with William Demas and Alister McIntyre combining world class profession-alism with passionate regionalism provided the essential infrastructure.

It took all this and more, including camaraderie at all levels among decision-makers, camaraderie that took many forms besides solidarity around the conference table, many forms of togetherness out of which friendships were built and confidences strengthened. Sailing in the Grenadines, duck shooting in Guyana, feasting on curried goat in Antigua, not to mention carnival and cricket and carousing on ferry boats on the Demerara – all this too was part of the story of CARIFTA and its transition to CARICOM.

To set it out this way, may imply there was something special in those who were involved. Perhaps there was to some degree, but not special in the sense that they have no counterparts today. They do and in full measure. Some who were there as ministers are now in the region's leadership: 'Son' Mitchell and P.J. Patterson, for example. And the newcomers among prime ministers, ministers and officials alike are in that same tradition of West Indian region-alists.

The biggest difference between then and now lies not in the people who had the privilege to be there at the start but in the times in which their successors must carry on. In a real sense, these face a harder struggle. They need in larger measure the attributes that helped the earlier team to its successes; they require new techniques and new structures and, above all, a larger vision. The deepening and widening of the Community is a very different matter from the evolution from CARIFTA to CARICOM. But, the region has started down that road. The West Indian Commission has pointed the broad way forward and there is formal political commitment to the deepening process, and actual achievement in the creation of the Association of Caribbean States.

In these more testing times that lie ahead, CARICOM will need to move with determination to mobilise its political, technical and intellectual leadership potential – which is considerable – to create space for the region in the wide world beyond our unity and dividing Sea. Experience may show that CARICOM might ultimately make its greatest mark in building upon and diversifying its already important external economic relations; and, as before, uniting in our Caribbean Community will be both the precondition of such achievement and its own reinforcement.

We cannot afford on the regional field either 'playing and missing' or too many 'indigenous strokes'. Remember, Edward Baugh's West Indian fan warned with anguish:

'. . . that is a damn dangerous way to be leaving the ball alone.
    We need to score.'

Note

This paper was published in *CARICOM Perspective*, No. 65, June 1995, pp. 9–11, 17.

[26]

Dream and Reality of Unity
These Islands Now

Gordon Rohler

'These Islands Now' is an excerpt taken from the paper 'Ä Scuffling of Islands'. The title of this paper is meant to suggest the link between economic necessity, the desperate struggle to survive ('scuffling') and the insular conflicts ('scuffling' in another sense of the word) that have attended all efforts at Caribbean integration. The paper contends that calypsonians and poets have always been aware of both types of scuffle and undertakes an account of their commentaries from the Roseau Conference of October 1932 into the 1990s. Calypsonians had from the turn of the century monitored the movement of the island away from nominated and towards representative government, and were among the first West Indian artists to promote the idea of Federation as a means towards this end. Poets such as Louise Bennet, Eric Roach and Derek Walcott had all shared in the dream of a unified West Indies. In the case of Roach and Walcott, anger and disillusion felt at the break-up of the West Indian Federation in 1961 darkened their portrayals of the post-Independence era.

If Stalin in 'Isms Schisms' ends with a prescription that tells the Caribbean people what they must avoid until the dawning of the new age, Rudder's 'Rally Round the West Indies' (1987) is more positively prescriptive in advising them on what they need to affirm. That calypso is indeed about cricket; but cricket becomes, as in CLR James' *Beyond a Boundary*, whose title Rudder invokes, much more than a game. It becomes a manifestation of the spirit, potential and human excellence of the West Indian people, the perception of which had inspired and ignited the original dream of Federation. It is no mistake that the cyclic rise, fall and rebirth of West Indian cricket are compared with the ebb and flow of the Haitian Revolution

> . . . when the Toussaints go
> The Dessalines come
> We've lost the battle
> But will win the war

Towards the end of 'Rally Round the West Indies', just to make sure that his listeners recognise that cricket is a metaphor for much more, Rudder explains:

> *This is not just cricket*
> *This goes beyond the boundary*
> *It's up to you and me to make sure that they fail*
> *Soon we'll have to take a side*
> *Or be lost in the rubble*
> *In a divided world that don't need island no more*
> *Are we doomed forever to be at someone's mercy?*
> *Little keys can open mighty doors.*

If Stalin advises Caribbean people and states to seek such neutral spaces as might exist between hotly or coldly warring ideologies, Rudder warns them that they will be forced to choose, 'to take a side . . . in a divided world that don't need island no more'. The 'side' that he prompts them to take is their own. The West Indies team has provided them with an example of what that side should be, demonstrating what skilled West Indians, imbued with a collective sense of their own revolutionary history and potential, can achieve.

Early in the decade of the 1980s, Chalkdust, reacting to the cultural and economic penetration of Trinidad and the Caribbean by the United States, concludes that 'the Caribbean belong to Uncle Sam'. Many calypsos of the decade chronicle the steady erasure of anything like a Caribbean conscious-ness by American values, lifestyles, goods and services that are as mindlessly absorbed by Caribbean people as they are resolutely marketed by American capitalism.

Merchant, employing the metaphor of the fete, celebrates the emergence of a unified Caribbean consciousness, an aesthetic in 'Caribbean Connection' (1988) four years after Valentino employs the self-same metaphor in 'Trini Gone Through', his unremittingly negative portrayal of an 'irresponsible and lazy nation', 'running last in their work ethics', 'only conscious of money', 'petty', 'jealous', 'heading in the wrong direction', 'sinking in corruption', 'on a hopeless trip/rocking a sinking ship.'

Chalkdust, with slightly more laughter but considerable acerbity fills out the portrait the next year with 'Rum mania' (1985). Local, regional or international crisis means nothing to the devil-may-care carousing Trini. 'While Guyanese smuggling gold in their bum/all day all night Trini drinking their rum' . . . Similarly, 'While Yankee soldiers eating Grenadian Plum' the Trinidadian remains in a nirvana of blissful intoxication. The fete is again associated with mindlessness, and it is this absence of 'mind' that has made it easy for the American imperialist to fill the vacuum left by the departure of the British imperialist. A sense of the Caribbean is erased in direct proportion to the Americanisation of the region.

Reflecting on the 'Roaring Seventies', Valentino laments the ease with which the entire era seems to have faded from peoples' memory.

> But Trini have this funny funny way of forgetting
> Their history to dem like it don't mean nothing
> The history that went down here in the 1970's
> As though it never was today in the 80's
> But don't care how much they try to tarnish these historic
>   memories
> I will always remember the Roaring 70's

While he resolves to remember, Valentino recognises his society to be a nation of amnesiacs and wonders whether the rebels of the seventies 'gave their lives for a hopeless cause'.

While this question is asked mainly about Trinidad, foremost on Valentino's mind was Grenada, so that the question of memory or amnesia as equal and opposite attitudes towards historical trauma is being implicitly asked of the wider Caribbean region. How can a region that wilfully denies its own heroic effort, that negates and erases even its immediate past, survive? How will it generate dream, idea, or an ideal that's worth the sacrifices that will have to be made?

Valentino holds out no hope in this regard. He ends, rather with a vision of the region's recolonisation and the tragic eclipse of himself as the last survivor of the consciousness of a generation that, already dead in spirit, has passed out of the memory of people; out of history.

> Looking through that era
> Well I see changes develop politically
> Who leave this party and join that party
> And who stole all the oil money

I see conscious black men and women
In the 80s crumble and bend
And the nation gone right back to Europe
On a Western trend

Chalkdust's 'Sea Water and Sand' (1986) counterpoints Valentino's 'Trini Gone Through' of the same year. It acknowledges that the region has redesigned its mechanism, for measuring human and national worth. Caribbean countries are now literally measuring each other according to what their dollar is worth in United States currency. The devaluation of the once proud Jamaican dollar to the North and the struggling Guyanese dollar to the South, is received by those who imagine themselves to be more wealthy, with loud laughter and ribald mockery instead of dread and sadness. 'Sea Water and Sand' questions the wisdom of such laughter, unmasks the same old insularity in each leader, and warns the region that

. . . unless there is co-operation
All o' dem on the same road to destruction

In typical Chalkdust style, the persona cites numerous examples of insularity and arrogant behaviour, beginning with the false confidence that Barbados and Dominica have invested in their status as the favourite mendicant client states of Washington and London, continuing with Trinidad's tariff barriers against CARICOM products and immigration restrictions against Grenadian refugees; Antigua's blockage of BWIA's bid to become the regional carrier and regional leaders' failure to implement treaties that they've signed.

Ingratiating themselves with America, and prostituting themselves to earn whatever handouts they can acquire from the US, the islands neglect their most crucial necessity: that of maintaining meaningful contact, discourse and exchange with each other. Foreign exchange replaces local human interface.

A stream of curious and bitter ironies flows from this anomaly as stanzas II and IV of the calypso illustrate:

All of them Caribbean leader
Instead of pulling together
They prefer to friend with Reagan and Thatcher
Dominicans suffering bad
Their goods can't get to Trinidad
'Cause Chambers ain't giving licences; which is sad
Chambers say he ain't in this big racket
They want flood Trinidad market
With all their cheap inferior goods, and he won't permit it
But he want BWEE register

As the national (sic) carrier
No way sah! Antigua turn down his offer
Some of them Caribbean leader
To get Reagan's dollar
Will denounce their CARICOM friends and neighbour
Eugenia cussing Guyana
Refusing to even go there
And lambasting Chambers for his behaviour
Chambers vetting Grenadians hey
Man as though they cocobey
Cause to travel to Port of Spain
Grenadians need visa
LDC's want Trini money
To build up their economy
Still you can't spend a TT dollar in their country.

So Caribbean unity remains an elusive dream, an idea in the heads of poets and singers that is at every point confounded by the evidence of reality. Each example of a regional institution – the West Indies Cricket Team, BWIA, UWI, CXC, CARICOM – becomes on close examination a forum for the fiercely competing self-centredness of its constituent members, a democracy of opposing views whose effect is to cancel each other out.

The West Indian Federation itself, beginning as a huge dream in the heads of Maryshow and Cipriani, and a slogan that 'The West Indies must be West Indian', foundered with the first serious attempt to translate dream into reality. Fragments of the dream remained lodged in the brain of the region's artists, academics and technocrats, and it is with these fragments that the region's singers still work. The 'crossover' between Jamaican and Trinidadian music which began when Kitchener and Beginner in 1947 and 1948 passed through Jamaica on their way to London, is alive today in Jamaica soca and Trinidadian rapso, and carnivals of one sort or another have blossomed throughout the Archipelago and in every major American city where there is a concentration of Caribbean migrants.

Calypsoes such as Stalin's 'Kaiso Music' (1996), Shirlaine Hendrickson's 'Caribbean Woman' (1997), Rudder's 'Caribbean Party' (1993) and 'Bushyard' (1991), MBA' 'Beyond a Boundary' (1993), Merchant's 'Caribbean Connection' (1988) and Stalin's 'Cry of the Caribbean' (1992), recognise in their various ways the widening and deepening dimensions of the Caribbean cultural interface through movement, exile music, sport and a realisation of common need at home and abroad. The calypsonian continues to perform the roles of warner, adviser and celebrant of the elusive but real dream.

Thus St Lucia's Ashanti in his 'Together in Caribbean Unity' (1992) repeats Chalkdust's critique of Caribbean leadership in 'Sea Water and Sand' and calls for leaders to practise cooperation within their individual islands first and thus gain practice for the harder task of uniting on a regional place. The impression created by all the calypsos on CARICOM is that the premier regional institution is a futile talk-shop. Hear Stalin: 'CARICOM is wasting time. The whole Caribbean gone blind', and Chalkdust:

> And they meeting regularly
> Drawing up all kind o' treaty
> And after they drink their whisky
> The treaty dead already

At their Heads of Government Conference
> Is much shop talk and ignorance
> Lots of talk, but no action ever commence.

and Ashanti
> De claws of the IMF have Jamaica in misery
> De value of de US in Guyana is $120
> But CARICOM in a meeting
> Drink drinking and food eating
> Look de dollar in Barbados too
> Now struggling to keep value, and it's true
> Is either we swim together in Caribbean unity
> Or drown alone in de deep blue Caribbean sea.

The concreteness of distress does not yield to the abstraction of talk.
> De curses of de IMF have Jamaica in social pain
> Guyanese in sore distress travel one way by boat or plane
> But CARICOM dem eh fussin
> Always in some hotel discussion

In another chorus:
> De chores of the IMF have Jamaica in agony
> Guyanese in hopelessness sell their gold for peanuts money
> But CARICOM in a conference
> Paying room and catering expense.

Ashanti, a calypsonian from one of what used to be the Little Eight, the cluster of islands which in Young Killer's *Cry of the West Indies* (1968) were depicted as imploring Jamaica to take them back, now looks in pity at Jamaica and Guyana, two of the original 'Big Four' now in the direst economic distress.

In spite of this sorry scenario, the dream of Caribbean unity is still strong. Ashanti indeed, views the Caribbean as having no choice but to unite. Valentino, even after the crushing disillusionment of Grenada (1983) sings with hope about the prospects of cultural unity in the region. His 'Carifesta Regional Unity' (1992) begins with a dismissal of both CARIFTA and CARICOM, but sees hope in the coming together of the region's artists.

> We celebrating in song and dance
> This family reunion
> The exponents of the Arts
> Will highlight this grand occasion
> Displaying their talents in a way to bring unity
> Where some of the people tried and failed very miserably
> So we have to bridge the gap on a cultural foundation
> If we really want to unite the Caribbean
>
> No CARICOM, No CARIFTA
> It is only sports and our own culture
> No same passport, no same dollar
> It's a waste with political propaganda
> Them fellas on too much tricks
> So no kind of politics
> Could bring the Caribbean people together
> And unite the region like Carifesta

Even as the prospect of a grand reunion of 'the Caribbean family' is being celebrated by Valentino, Pep, his St Lucian counterpart is warning his countrymen:

> An economic Fire is threatening me and you
> It's roasting our neighbours, in a fiscal barbeque
> It burnt right through Guyana, Jamaica followed next
>
> The same West Indian islands who thought they were so big
> Now like vagrants in our market they're begging bread and fig
> That's a moral in this story that Lucians have to learn
> When your neighbour bed's on fire, take water and wet your own.

More clearly than in Ashanti's calypso one hears in Pep's 'Bab Kamawad' (1992) that tone of gloating triumph that economic refugees from the big territories have been seeking refuge and jobs in the once scorned small islands. This triumph is, however, harshly qualified by the apprehension that the IMF fire burning through the more developed countries of the Caribbean will soon scorch St Lucia as well.

> The flames are getting nearer, wake up, get out of bed
> Just look on the horizon, there' s a dangerous glow of red
> Two OECS island have started smouldering
> Antigua and Grenada have their fiscal woes within.

Pep's sense of the Caribbean is strong but negative. The Caribbean territories are invoked as examples of a fate that must be circumvented at all costs, as each island tries via prayer and thrift, to avoid the Debt Trap.

Dreamers of the dream of Caribbean unity are not deterred from their dreaming, merely because of the grimness of social and economic reality that surrounds them. There is no greater realist than David Rudder whose chants in 'Another Day in Paradise' (1995) or the 'Madman's Rant' (1976) are the most harrowing chronicles of social disintegration. Yet there is also no deeper dreamer as his 'One Caribbean' (1994) proves.

> We got so little on our own but as a region we can face tomorrow
> Athletes and artists have shown the way
> And from our roots of resistance and old suffering
> We can rise through this sorrow
> We're much too bright in spirit not to find a better day
> But in this New World all the time we have this common crisis
> For debts won't die away and social tension's on the rise
> From Havana to Georgetown oh the danger, the danger is spreading
> It's time for a common front, it's time that we realise.
>
> I'm saying
> One Caribbean, One Caribbean
> One heart together in a changing world
> One Caribbean, One Caribbean
> One love, one heart, one soul
> Reaching for a common goal

Again the dream, the call. It won't take time. The region has had time. It will require, as Rudder senses when he assumes the role of shaman, chanter and exhorter, magic. Hence the invocation of the 'one love/one heart' spirit of Bob Marley.

Hence the long wild chant, at times in fragmented French and Spanish as well as English, with which the Caribbean people are invited to join hands across the water: hence, too, the final attestation of faith: 'We're coming together', though this is nowhere visible, as the hard-nosed realists illustrate in their own grim songs.

Note

This article was published in *CARICOM Perspective*, No. 68, June 1998, pp. 85–88.

[27]

From Montego Bay
to Georgetown

Cheddi Jagan

The achievable objective of integrating sister CARICOM communities into one regional society which will facilitate charting programmes for the increased prosperity for all our countries is a vision I have carried all my political life.

While recognising the need for the creation of an international marketplace and the formation of a New Global Human Order, we also need to assess and assimilate our own peculiar needs so that our economic sovereignty is not swamped by the economic and trade policies of the more prosperous countries of the world.

We need to address our own socio-economic problems and formulate policies within the framework of our capacity for solution. A united, integrated Caribbean Community can successfully orchestrate ways of solving our problems so that we can stride on the international platforms – not as Third World beggars, but as partners in a global struggle for the survival of the world.

The past six decades have witnessed the Caribbean region passing through several crises of dependency and underdevelopment – the disturbances and 'riots' in the period of the Great Depression of the 1930s; the unrest in the late 1980s resulting in the Caribbean Basin being deemed 'a Circle of Crisis'; the ensuing deep-seated contradictions and problems associated with the structural crisis of modernisation and globalisation. From time to time, various solutions were put on the agenda to deal with the 'unprecedented difficulties.'

In 1942, Professor Arthur Lewis pointed out that the way towards raising living standards was modernisation of agriculture and industrialisation, and the transfer of the surplus population to British Honduras (now Belize) and British Guiana (now Guyana). But this did not materialise.

In the preparations for the Caribbean Federation, the idea was mooted that the way forward was overall planning for the region and territorial specialisation, and a conscious effort to stimulate development in seven of the ten lesser developed territories with less than ten per cent of the income of the region. This also did not materialise.

At Montego Bay, in 1945, the Caribbean Labour Congress (CLC) proposed a Caribbean federation with dominion status and self-government for each territory. But, with the advent of the Cold War, the CLC was dissolved in 1951 and a crown colony type of federation, a 'collective colony', was instituted in 1958. The progressive ideas for an independent Federation were scuttled and the West Indies Federation collapsed in 1962. British Guiana was isolated and became the major victim of the Cold War.

Flawed models of development – 'Puerto Rican', import substitution, regional integration, free trade – and imbalanced economies culminated in the successful Cuban Revolution of 1959.

The 'oil crisis' and recession in 1973–74 and, in 1977 in quick succession, a second oil shock, falling terms of trade and extremely high interest rates led to turmoil and upheavals throughout the Caribbean Basin – Panama, Nicaragua, Dominica, Saint Lucia, Grenada, Suriname and elsewhere. As a result, the Reagan administration deemed the region a 'Circle of Crisis' among others in the world. But President Reagan's Caribbean Basin Initiative (CBI) for non reciprocal trade concessions – duty free entry into the USA of some additional products, proved to be not a cure but a palliative: in the 1982–92 decade, US trade to the Caribbean doubled as compared with a 17 per cent increase of Caribbean exports to the USA.

The major Caribbean export products – sugar, bananas, petroleum, bauxite – showed a poor performance because of external and internal factors. Of the 17 Borrowing Member Countries (BMCs) of the Caribbean Development Bank (CDB), the GDP growth rate in 1993 of seven of them was higher than in 1992; three registered no change from the previous year and the last two showed only declines.

The CDB President, Sir Neville Nicholls, told a Press Conference on February 1, 1994:

When taken as a whole, the Region's economic performance was still less than satisfactory because the major economies were the most disappointing and the impact of their minimal progress will be felt by the whole Region.

The More Developed Countries (MDCs) of the Commonwealth Caribbean of the early 1960s have become virtually the Least Developed Countries (LDCs) with negligible growth rates and explosive problems. The slow recovery from recession in the industrialised countries did not greatly assist them.

The only 'industry' making gains is tourism, responding to a slow recovery from recession in the industrialised countries, particularly the USA. But this service industry is faced with threat from crime, violence, narcotics, high service charges and competition from cruise ships and other attractive tourist destinations.

The Caribbean economies, particularly the manufacturing sectors, in their quest for export-led growth, are faced with an unfavourable international situation.

(1) Competition for modernisation and high-tech production of goods and services in the North with large internal markets.

(2) Competition from South East Asian countries with relatively more competitive labour costs, larger domestic population and a skilled labour force.

(3) Dumping of goods.

(4) An increasingly difficult funding situation, particularly for public sector activities.

In this era of globalisation and modernised capital-intensive and high-technology methods of production, recession and stagnation will be more prolonged than in the past and will occur with greater frequency. The resulting intense trade competition, trade barriers, and protectionism are contributing to growing local inequalities and a widening gap between the rich and the poor in the developed North as well as the developing/stagnating South.

So alarming is the plight of the poor that the Caribbean Conferences of Churches (CCC) not too long ago advised churches and their leaders to convert some chapels and church halls into soup kitchens, offices into medical clinics and grounds into playing fields for the children. The situation cannot be allowed to become explosive as in the late 1970s, or at the time of the Great Depression of the 1930s, when there were disturbances throughout the Caribbean.

Structural Adjustment

With stagnating/collapsing economies, structural adjustment programmes became generally mandatory. These were intended to provide the framework for a development thrust which is in keeping with rational objectives. Regrettably, the programmes have reduced the options and choices available to our countries. In fact, serious social and other stresses have arisen as a result of implementation of these programmes.

The Standing Committee of Caribbean Finance Ministers noted that the Structural Adjustment Programmes of some member states had not only caused contractions in public sector investment programmes, but restricted the capacity of governments to provide funding for viable projects and counterpart funding for externally supported activities.

The situation in Guyana is instructive. A virtually bankrupt situation caused the country to be declared ineligible in 1985 for further credits by the International Monetary Fund (IMF). A structural adjustment programme, though necessary, has been fraught with many contradictions and difficulties.

(1) Devaluation of the Guyana Currency from G4.15 to US$1 in 1985 to G$126 to US$1 in 1992, led to a grave decline in real wages and salaries, increased prices for critical goods and services, raised costs of imported inputs. The significant increases in debt payments in Guyana dollars amounting to 105 per cent of current revenues in 1992 and 80 per cent in 1993, contributed to a huge budget deficit and drastic budgetary reductions in expenditures on subsidies of essential goods, social services and employment cost, which in turn led to massive retrenchment in the public sector and administrative incapacity.

(2) Low wages and salaries, despite current budgetary support from the World Bank and the British ODA for the Public Administration Project, led to a ten-day strike in the public service which seriously affected steamer and air transport services.

(3) Unsustainably high real interest rates, which become a disincentive to productive investments and shift the economy towards speculative and trading activities, leading with high net GDP growth rates to increased social inequality.

(4) A credit squeeze which led to overall contraction of the economy, decline in capacity utilisation and an accentuated shortage of critical goods and services.

(5) An undermining of food production and self-sufficiency, leading to undesirable environmental degradation and the substitution of marijuana for food production.

(6) An erosion of the capacity of infant industries, thereby slowing industrialisation;

(7) A floating currency linked to trade and monetary liberalisation and
speculative and trading activities, causing monetary and other instability
through a further devaluation of Guyana dollars from G$125 to US$1 at
31 December, 1993 to G$145 to US$1 at May 1995.

(8) Lack of administrative capacity in the Forestry Commission leading to
pressures not to grant timber concessions, even though attraction of
private investment is mooted for economic growth and development.

(9) Divestment (not privatisation which can take many forms) of all public
economic enterprises, even profitable ones like banking and sugar, despite historical experience in Guyana with private and public enterprises
under different governments.

As regards the demands of the international financial institutions for a
speedy privatisation/divestment of state-owned entities, the Report of the IDB
study/group is relevant. It noted:

Special care must be taken to prevent disruption of the delicate social balance, as
winners and losers of the adjustment process are, without deliberate redistribution
measures, likely to run along ethnic lines. Blind application of market forces would
result in tangible benefits for the East Indian population group that is strongly
represented in agriculture, professional services and commerce, and net costs for
Afro-Guyanese, who are highly urbanised and strongly represented in government,
police, military and bauxite mining. Reforms must therefore be designed to spread their
impact equitably among the various social strata and ethnic groups; a cost/benefit
sharing system palatable to the population at large is a condition *sine qua non* for a
successful completion of the adjustment process.

CARICOM and its antecedents were set up at a time when the world was
rather different from what it now is. In those days, both high trade barriers to
the markets of the outside world and the dominance of economies of scale, as
distinct from technology and science in manufacturing industries, dictated a
strategy of integration for development based on common external protection
within a liberalised trading area, and promoted by such state instruments as
fiscal incentives and regional agricultural and industrial programming. To this
basic thrust was added interstate cooperation in a number of functional areas
(such as education, health and foreign policy coordination).

But now, after more than 25 years, our community building efforts seem
to have come to a halt. We are now at a crossroads. It would not be a secret
to say we are rather disappointed with the economic progress of the community. We need our own agenda. The Latin American and Caribbean Com-

mission on Development and Environment sponsored by the UNDP and the IDB, concluded that 'more than a half century of flawed development produced total stagnation'.

The CARICOM countries are faced with declining aid and investment flows. In addition, the region has an external debt burden of over US$10 billion, which is the greatest obstacle to real development. Consequently, as a result of 'aid fatigue' and 'donor fatigue' it is necessary to raise additional funds for social progress.

Financial resources for global development cooperation can be found from:

- Demilitarisation Funds – 3% cuts in global military expenditure can yield US$460 billion in the 1995-2000 period;
- A global tax on energy. A tax of US$1 on each barrel of oil (and its equivalent on coal) would yield around US$66 billion annually;
- Taxing global speculative foreign exchange movements. A tax of 0.5 % on the value of each transaction can yield US$12,500 billion annually as proposed by Nobel Prize Winner, economist James Tobin.

Such a fund can be put at the disposal of the United Nations for assistance to countries both in the north and the South for economic growth and human development.

In the north, funds can be allocated for a works programme as in the USA by the Roosevelt New Deal administration during the 1930s Great Depression, and for a reduction of the workweek, as is mooted in Germany and France, without loss of income. In the South, generally, and in the Caribbean region particularly, funds can be allocated for a regional development fund, debt relief, grants and soft loans to accelerate development.

The Caribbean regional integration movement will succeed to the extent that, in keeping with the principles of good global governance, partnership and interdependence, we diligently strive for a New Global Human Order.

Note

This paper appeared in *CARICOM Perspective*, No. 65, June 1995, pp. 15–17.

[28]

Compulsions of Integration

Vaughan Lewis

The Grand Anse Declaration by the CARICOM Heads of Government, encompassing a series of measures in both the economic integration and functional cooperation spheres, indicated a renewal of confidence by the Heads themselves in the Caribbean Community system as a viable mechanism for Caribbean cooperation. However, it indicated also a belief that the integration movement, having, unlike so many others in the Third World, survived over the last two decades, was still a fragile instrument which needed substantial strengthening.

The Declaration was a recognition too, that in spite of a variety of recommendations and decisions made over the last decade and a half, notably the 'Wise Men's' Report and the Nassau measures on Trade and Structural Adjustment, the CARICOM system had not evolved into a vehicle capable of substantially assisting the region in coming to terms with the variety of problems posed by changes both in the international environment, and within the domestic economic systems of many of the CARICOM countries themselves.

As a response to these international and domestic developments, there has been within the region for a period of time, a decisive and almost forced turning inwards by countries in economic difficulty, as they have sought to implement measures proposed by international agencies, measures which have sometimes been in conflict with agreed regional policies and which have served to further augment the process of economic differentiation.

This has resulted in a certain distancing of countries in the region from each other. This has been so both in the terms of policy orientation, and in terms of one or other of the Governments feeling from time to time that the promise of CARICOM – and particularly of the Treaty of Chaguaramas – has not materialised.

Nonetheless, any inclination to turn away from CARICOM as the region's protective umbrella has been inhibited by a felt need for collective action in the face of processes and events emanating from the international environment which have proved difficult to respond to unilaterally or single-handedly.

The challenges faced by CARICOM agriculture as the European Community moves towards a single market are many. There is increasing orientation in the international arena towards negotiations on the basis of regional economic blocs; increasing insistence on the part of some major powers that CARICOM should consider itself part of a wider Caribbean Basin system embracing at least the non Anglophone North Antilles states, and at a wider level the countries of the Central American Isthmus; and increasing insistence by the countries of South America that preferential systems organised in Europe for ex-colonial territories should give way to wider systems of free trade that would give them a share of growing industrial and agricultural markets. There is also the assertion by some of the more northern South American states of the necessity for them to take part in decisions regarding the future of the wider Caribbean Basin; and a concern on the part of CARICOM countries regarding the implications of their very small economic size within Third World negotiating blocks like the ACP. All these factors are forcing upon the CARICOM states a perception of the need to harmonise policies and decision-making strategies, to create a viable regional market and economic space, as a prerequisite for greater economic growth and the preservation of a defined identity in global economic and political relations.

The deliberate choice of the CARICOM political directorate was to take the path to integration laid out in the Treaty of Chaguaramas – the process of economic integration and functional cooperation which, with the gradual but persistent freeing of trade internally and strict adherence to the Common External Tariff, would lead in the first instance to economic unification. That is the creation of a defined economic space in which there is a free flow of the factors of production leading to economies of scale and the growth of viable industries and therefore viable economies. The approach adopted by the CARICOM leadership also suggested the development of an increasingly more coherent network of cooperation in a variety of so-called functional policy areas such as in health, education and transportation. This cohesive network would optimise the use of the scarce financial and human re- sources, and in so doing create viable social and technical institutions (such as for transportation and higher education) that would establish the base of social and institutional infrastructure for intra-regional cooperation and eventually for political integration. The implicit model for this approach was that of the European Community, particularly in respect of the economic sphere.

The main institutions designed to make and execute policy and monitor development of these various processes in the Caribbean Community were the Heads of Government Conference, the various Standing Committees and the CARICOM Secretariat. To these mechanisms was added the Caribbean Development Bank which would ensure a deliberate distribution of financial resources thus bringing about balanced growth and development in the countries within the system which are characterised by varying physical and economic sizes. In this way balanced growth and development would be achieved in the system as a whole.

The approach to integration adopted was cognisant of the desire of countries to exercise and promote their newly achieved sovereignty (inde- pendence) while, due to force of circumstance, subordinating aspects of that sovereignty in certain selected spheres of activity.

As is well known, the Heads of Government Conference, as the central institution of the system failed to function for some years in the 1970s following the signature of the Treaty of Chaguaramas. In the absence of that framework, the system proceeded without the necessary monitoring and mutual consultation needed to ensure the effectiveness of its development. Regionally oriented initiatives by some leading countries, important as they were for the economic survival of countries in the region during the difficult periods following successive oil price increases, could not substitute for the deliberate approach to economic integration intended by the Treaty of Chaguaramas. In addition, the era of 'ideological pluralism' negated the promising beginnings of cooperation in external relations reflected in CARI- COM's approach to the European Community on the elaboration of the Lomé Convention.

However, the difficulties that have been experienced in moving the CARI- COM countries towards viable integration, cannot be solely ascribed to the early fate of the Heads of Government Conference as an institution, to unilateralist initiatives pursued by this or that country in the era of ideological pluralism, or to faulty economic decision-making.

Those days of political and ideological disjuncture are now largely behind us. A 'new realism' has dawned in the region in the face of difficult international and domestic economic circumstances, and in the face of failed experiments in economic policy making. We need now first of all to ask ourselves, even though with the benefit of hindsight, whether the institutional arrangements for integration and cooperation embedded in the Treaty of Chaguaramas were of themselves sufficient and appropriate to attain the objectives stated.

This issue ought now to be placed firmly on the agenda and while it shall be addressed in detail at a later stage we shall preface its consideration by suggesting that the Treaty of Chaguaramas failed to follow its implicit model, the European Economic Community, in some crucial areas that spoke precisely to the question of the need to decisively subordinate sovereignty in certain areas in order to ensure, at least for most of the time, adherence to decisions, and the curbing of natural tendencies to unilateralism and nationally self-interested decision-making. An example of this is the European Court of Justice the significance of which lies not so much in a capacity to ensure enforcement of decisions through penalties, as in the fact that the legal system for which in Europe, as in the Caribbean there was already substantial respect, was now embedded into the sphere of government to government economic relations. The Court of Justice did not commence with the strength that it has today and any considerations to apply this model in our contexts should be encouraged by the fact that it has now found acceptance in 'common law' oriented Britain.

The second question which we should ask ourselves in reconsidering the evolution of the CARICOM system is whether (and again with the benefit of hindsight and the experience of others) we should not have separated the matter of the financial viability and sustenance of CARICOM's institutions from the voluntarist approach financial contributions. An important reason for such separation would be that the taking and implementation of difficult decisions by the central institutions could not then result in non payment by dissatisfied or disgruntled participants, thus resulting in the undermining of the institutions' viability. Such a separation would also have prevented the situation in which, as has often seemed to be the case, the payments of contributions to regional institutions became the last item for consideration in national budgetary expenditure.

In the case of CARICOM's implicit model, the European Community, the imposition of a levy on trade (customs duties), centrally collected and allocated, suggests again, a certain deliberate subordination of sovereignty. But would the European Commission and its agencies have worked without this?

Finally, we need to ask ourselves a third question: whether the extent of time and energy spent in seeking to ensure the development of an adequate intra-regional trade system (up to and including the present concerns with the Common External Tariff), has been adequately balanced by a consideration of matters – equally crucial to a successful economic integration process related to financial and monetary arrangements. The failure of the Multilateral Clearing Arrangement, the decline in consultation among the region's central banks, and the fragility of our input in the sphere of international economic arena and in relations with international financial agencies, all point to a negative response to this question.

Often it is remarked that such deficiencies reflect a lack of 'political will'. This explanation however, seems insufficient to explain the situation. If crucial institutional and other mechanisms which would appear to be the *sine qua non* of political and economic integration arrangements were not put in place, then it cannot be expected that the objectives which those arrangements sought to achieve, would be realised.

The American Federalists, in setting out on their course two hundred years ago recognised the problems of political will – its defects and its periodic over-aggressiveness – and took this as a given of human nature in politics. They argued for 'a government of laws and not of men', that is, a preference for the establishment of binding and balancing institutional and other mechanisms rather than a dependence on personal political volition or the lack of it. The time is now right for CARICOM to ask itself whether the institutions and mechanisms appropriate to the tasks and objectives identified for the future are now in place, and if not, whether some further sublimation of personal (national) sovereignty is required through new collective arrangements in order to ensure effective economic integration, the establishment of a coherent network for social decision-making and social institutional infrastructure development, and thus the realisation of a more effective regional sovereignty than exists today. The consideration of this issue must be at the forefront of our minds during our deliberations at this Regional Economic Conference, the objective of which is the realisation of a consensus on a strategy which would ensure the long-term economic survival and development of the Caribbean region as it faces the challenges brought about by the evolution of the international economic order and the changing nature of international economic relationships.

It is the considered position of St Lucia that the way forward for the Caribbean lies in the reaffirmation of the commitment of our countries to the objectives and the principles enshrined in the Treaty of Chaguaramas. Some of the provisions of the Treaty must now be strengthened to ensure that effective mechanisms are created to accelerate the process of regional integration and functional cooperation and to hold our countries firmly on the path towards the realisation of these goals. There is need for CARICOM countries to adopt a unified and coordinated strategy for development in a world environment in which the stakes for economic survival have been raised to a point where the achievement of critical mass in terms of market size and productive capacity has become a pre-requisite for sustainable development.

The objective of the long-term development thrust of the Caribbean must be to ensure the realisation of acceptable rates of economic growth, the creation of new employment opportunities at a rate which would allow for the minimisation of unemployment levels, and to ensure social equity and improved standards of living for the population as a whole. If these development objectives are to be achieved it is necessary for the countries of the region to integrate their economies to the point where a free, unified internal market is established and where productive potential and capacity merged under the umbrella of a coordinated production strategy. It is the view of St Lucia that unless economic integration of this sort, coupled with high level functional cooperation in key sectors, the Caribbean will not be able to sustain a viable economic existence in a world where large economic and trading blocs have become the norm.

Note

This paper formed a part of *The West Indian Commission Occasional Paper* No. 6.

[29]

Draw Wisdom and Listen
How to Eat and Remain Human

Rex Nettleford

It is the authenticity of the ecology of our landscape that we have helped to shape, or that we have used to help for our survival and beyond. This self awareness has its forging, we know, in the crucible of slavery and plantation, but especially in the period of post emancipation, a period yet to be fully investigated in terms of the intellectual ferment that fuelled the talents of people like J.J. Thomas, Marcus Garvey, C.L.R. James, Norman Manley and the scores of unnamed teachers and preachers who provided a former generation with the courage and will to be. Such will and courage drove so many of our forbears to forms of action that would restore to themselves, their humanity, above all else.

We are right to persist in the search for modes of re-integration, re-affirmation, as well as of the relationship between the micro and the macro, the terrestrial and the celestial; the relationship between the inner space of the mind and the heart and the physical space which we occupy. This battle for space is by no means a postmodern monopoly. In fact what the so-called civilised world is now so anxious about has long been part of the repertoire of Caribbean concerns, since so much of what this region chose to become, was rooted in the exploitation and dehumanisation of a large slice of human kind. That loss of wholeness, of totality, of harmony, which attended the exercise, was to be of concern to the mass of the population a couple of centuries before it became the centre of philosophical discourse and polemics in Western Europe.

Long before Hegel, and long before Karl Marx, the ordinary people of this region consciously grappled with the fragmentation and alienation of man by which I mean persons, at all levels, individual, societal, physical, psychic or cosmic. Our forbears knew that disharmony and confrontation arise out of such lack of wholeness and they turned to what their descendants on university campuses may well do – they turned to the exercise of their creative intellect and their creative imagination, throwing up not only belief systems and expressions of artistic culture, but also organic means of communication, native-born and native-bred – Kamau Brathwaite's nation language – kinship patterns designed to secure the species endangered – but highly renewable – and systems of production, distribution and exchange which our economic planners may do well to salvage from the folklore they have relegated them to, and incorporate them into the mainstream.

The responses to our alienating, dehumanising, homogenising history by those who went before us, remain the best departure for study and analysis in any effort to comprehend our existent reality and to give guidance for an uncertain future. The invention of languages, oral, scribal and that which comes with the non verbal use of the body, including cricket, the invention of religious expressions different from those of yore to contemporary Rastafari, the force of which continues to be misunderstood, and the intellectual discourse was shaped by Christian orthodoxy. The invention of family patterns or the reinterpretation of established ones whether nuclear, extended or matriarchal – we might say that we have grown up in all of these. The invention of new artistic expressions drawing on ancestral rituals and other cultural manifestations to create new classic forms in an unending cycle of creating and recreating the invention of modalities of economic survival and operations with numeracy outweighing literacy among a population of higglers. The per capita formation taking the form of partner or sou-sou. Then there are dubious created forms of hustling, admittedly not always in the best interest of our new nation states. As my great friend and mentor says, 'our hearts are laced with larceny, we thief bad!' There is also the great strategy of demarginalisation, that hit-and-run modality that is part of a psychic inheritance of the oppressed anywhere. The mind is always creatively active to guarantee survival and beyond. Many a Caribbean intellectual, like the Caribbean artist, has got to be a latter-day maroon, ambushing the society under the camouflage of intellectual investigation, analysis and artistic invention. When both these types of maroons find alliance, as individuals or in concert, it is time for action. The fear by some politicians of eggheads and subversives is quite understandable. For nothing can outflank the creativity that underpins all meaningful actions by the human being, themselves all acts of intelligence.

George Lamming is right, the creative artist is high on the list of a civilisation's finest intellectuals, just as the creative intellectual is to be numbered among a civilisation's finest artists. Our ordinary people in this region have known this for a long time, and have bequeathed to us a heritage which we ignore at our peril. Our foreparents learnt how to eat and still retain their humanity. What a challenge confronting our elected representatives! For this takes long distance running, rather than the sprinting which five years at a time in office often dictate. The kind of leadership demanded of them does not mean a monopoly by the state of a function employed to move education, or ensure salvation, which our grandmothers from the canefields knew to be.

The idea of all of us coming from the canefields, is for me, a very satisfying one. I can't understand claims to class, and one being better than the other; when I look at somebody who is invoking that status and realise that even with a little bit of a tar brush, we are all from the canefields. Some would have gotten out a little earlier than others, but that is all.

Least of all must the field of education be hijacked by ministries of education, served by unimaginative pedestrian technocrats, who forget that there are a certain number of human values that need to be activated and kept alive in human scale communities like ours? Values such as the dignity and responsibility of the individual, the freely chosen participation of individuals in communities; equality of opportunity and the search for a common good, cultural certitude, all of which can be realised through the field of education. It is here that a sense of daring is badly needed in any plan or strategy for the way forward; all the actors in the system need to be more alert in the creative response to the challenge that is already upon the region.

The factor of culture and its role in education has apparently given bureaucrats and some teachers more difficulty than it has the very politicians who are frequently bashed and often unjustifiably vilified for being Philistines and myopic. The neglect of culture as integral to education persists among many in the region's public bureaucracy and the teaching profession, despite some of the clearest evidence by many of the people who have had anything of value to say about this region and indeed about humanity – those who have exercised their creative imagination to make sense of the Caribbean and human historical experience and existential reality.

The names of Bob Marley, Jimmy Cliff, Peter Tosh, of the Mighty Sparrow, David Rudder, Lord Kitchner, Louise Bennett, Mutaburuka and other such public poets; of George Lamming, Samuel Selvon, Wilson Harris, Vidia Naipaul, Norma Goodison, Merle Collins, Kamau Brathwaite and Derek Walcott all easily come to mind. They all celebrate the creative potential of the textured resourceful population in the Caribbean from which they spring. And they stand as latter-day maroons, who have successfully fled the terrain of the sort of schooling that still overemphasises rationality alone, technocratic reasoning, restrictive organisational or community structures and an excessive reliance on traditional approaches. They have therefore managed to escape having their creative potential destroyed. Indeed, but for their own determination and the help, as some of them have admitted, of a few far-sighted teachers, they might have fallen on that conspicuous heap of well-trained, but highly uneducated souls who tenant too many positions of trust and power in the region at this time.

Not all is lost however, despite the sorry gap between the arts of the imagination and what is deemed to be traditional and acceptable in intellectual preparation. I like to share this with the audience. Barclays Bank, for all its colonial predilection, once recruited an English literature graduate from the university campus into the banking profession, nurturing him to a high level of decision-making and responsibility in what is now Barclays successor in this country. Another Oxford Classics major presides over the Caribbean Development Bank I am told, and yet another, Head at the Caribbean Tourism Association. Three swallows do not a summer make, but this provides evidence when the creative potential of people are not stultified by unimaginative employment practices and narrow manpower needs. The present Director General of the World Bank is, I hear, a cellist. I myself would prefer if he were a pan player. Either way, the likes of us will still expect from him, some compassion and caring along with the loans and conditionalities.

The educational system, with the help of those who are charged with directing it, especially the Government, should take full responsibility for the promotion of dynamic interaction and co-ordination between artistic creativity and other policy domains such as education itself, working life, urban planning, industrial and economic development strategies, for the benefit of all. Annual national economic reports should stop listing culture in the non productive categories. A child learns the meaning of process and is better able to relate outcome to effort if he is encouraged to create a poem or a song, act in a play, make up a dance, sing in a choir or play an instrument in an orchestra as a normal part of his education. The discipline that underpins the mastery of the craft, the demands made on continuous re-creation of effort and application, the travels encountered on the journey to excellence, the habits of realistic self-evaluation, the capacity for dealing with diversity and the dilemma of difference, whether in the performing arts or in key branches of sport – themselves belonging to the family of performing arts – constitute excellent preparation for learning to be, which is the stock of ontology. For learning to know, the substance of epistemology, learning to live together, the essence of the creative diversity which characterises Caribbean existence, and is about to overtake the entire world, all of this must serve the individual throughout his or her individual life.

It is the opportunity to exercise the creative imagination from an early age that is likely to ensure safe passage throughout that life; and the educational process, in all its modes, whether formal or informal, curricular or non-co-curricular, at all levels – primary, secondary, tertiary or extra tertiary – provides an excellent channel through which this can flow. Adaptability, flexibility, innovativeness and a capacity to deal with the complexity of complexities, are all attributes of the creative imagination which provide yet another route to cognition other than the Cartesian rationalism we have inherited. For if we are because we think, we also exist because we feel. There is much in the Caribbean experience that can set an example to the so-called globalised world.

The separation of these two states of experience into an irreconcilable whole is part of the binary syndrome of a tradition of intellectual discourse and epistemological reductionism which constitute an expensive luxury for people in the Caribbean who have survived these past 500 years on the basis of their creative diversity and the multi-sourced reality in everyday living. The moment we say 'either or', people like us are likely to be on the wrong side of the configuration because we are neither 'either' nor 'or' and, we are some-times in between or both. You know, I have often reminded people that we are just contrary in this region.

The shortest distance between two lines, whatever we might have learnt at school in the Caribbean, is never a straight line. Caribbean educators need to take a look at the long haul of human history, and locate the region where it appropriately belongs, that is, on the trajectory of human becoming, via that process of cross fertilisation which enriched ancient Egypt, ancient Greece, Renaissance Europe, Iberian Spain during the times leading up to 1492, the Americas of modern times, as well as Europe of the immediate future which promises that from the promontory of Asia – a challenging dose of multi-ra-cial, multi-culturalism. Part and parcel of this is the phenomenon of unity in diversity. Here one speaks naturally, or culturally, to a totality of human experience and not simply a little bit of dance, a little bit of music, a little bit of drama, of verse speaking and so on. One speaks to a totality of meaningful articulations, of environmental integrity, the cause, occasion and result of one's culture. The teaching of science would do well to start with this, rather than with the computer.

This bi-focation of knowledge into science and the rest has served to misguide many among the West Indian educated. One has had cause to invite young generations of scholars in this university which is still [a] growing institution, to become engaged in what is one of the most vital and critical of discourses at the end of [the] century, with the result to become original tough-minded, creative contributors – to the exercise for the intellectual and psychic liberation now necessary among us West Indians can be no one else's responsibility to achieve but ours. It is now conceded in large measure that both capitalism and apocalyptic socialism, in their would-be purest of forms have been basically accultural in their approach to development. Neither has had a place for the specificities of experience, culturally determined over time and among particular sets of people.

Development it was felt had to be scientifically determined and pursued universally according to immutable laws, whether of the market, or on the basis of unrelieved class conflict. Any invocation of cultural particularisation or particularities and differences have been considered reactionary or revisionist and although popular cultural expressions have been tolerated, they have been obliged to appear in both dispensations as an ornamental folkloric element. Any who have abandoned this position, objected indiscriminately towards another panacea – the culture of technology. But the task of education has to be to ensure that the source of technology, which is science, finds a central place in the process without prejudice to the humanities, or else we will simply fall into the trap of getting to know the know-how but not the know why!

An editorial from a reputable first world newspaper put it better than I ever could, and I share it by way of warning as I have done in the past to all who have been willing to emulate on the altar of the new panacea:

'The technology card has often been a very useful one to play. Yet, it is no basis for a social vision. What matters is not that all pupils have access to a laptop, but how they use them. Fibre optic technology does not teach children how to spell or add up. '

(I might add they teach undergraduates how to spell or add up).

'nor does it necessarily teach adults how to be better citizens. In the midst of this new political vogue, it is worth remembering that technology is not an end to itself, but one means among many. The celebration of technology does not excuse politicians from the duty to spell out their plans and principles. The hardware is important; it is the software that counts.

Perhaps it is culture that really counts at this time, in the important pursuit of education, defined on traditional lines, but adaptable to the changed and changing circumstances of the temporary world. I see governments, teachers and the institutions of learning at all levels – the institutions of learning in whose name they labour – as major contributors to, and principal facilitators of the cultivation of what Prof. Augier has referred to as 'The Kingdom of the Mind', with branches of creativity sprouting from the exercise of both intellect and imagination, and this, in turn, working in tandem to produce a self reliant, self respecting, tolerant, enterprising and productive community of souls.

I end with a Swahili proverb: '*The beginning of wisdom is knowing who you are. Draw Wisdom and Listen.*'

Note

This article was published in *CARICOM Perspective*, No. 66, June 1996, pp. 4–7.

[30]

Hope for a New Generation
of West Indian Leaders

Havelock Ross-Brewster

While I share Dr Farrell's final conclusions as given in the last two paragraphs of his article in *Contact*, July 1977, I hope he is not as doubtful as I am about the possibility of a 'truly' concerned generation of 'leaders' arising.

I wonder whether we see it in the present over 30 generation and, as far as the younger generation is concerned, do we see something in present society to lead us to believe that such leaders are being moulded out of it? Further, should we not give some thought to the egocentric notion itself of leaders and leadership and its connection to the generation and concentration of power?

There are however, one or two critical reflections which occurred to me as I read the article. I doubt one can impute an official rationale for integration from the official CARICOM documents and statements.

If one were truly seeking for an official rationale in terms of the genesis of phenomena and actual occurrences, it would be rather different from what Dr Farrell perceives really as a scientific rationale. In the context of the origins of behaviour, I believe one would find greater 'rationality' than he does in the interest to engage the smaller islandic countries.

Indeed, I might even venture to say that one might find therein the single most important rationale – the Leeward-Windward Islands; in effect define spatially and diplomatically the Caribbean, constituting as they do, with their sea-space, the eastern perimeter of the Caribbean Sea virtually up to 20^0

latitude, and the most important Caribbean access route to and from Europe and Africa (for example Colombia, parts of Central America and Venezuela, excluding only the mouth of the Orinoco) are otherwise separated from the most convenient passage to and from the Atlantic.

Furthermore, including the Bahamas in the Community part of the Treaty, the Caribbean Community could become a virtually continuous geographic arc stretching from the Gulf of Paria to West Palm Beach, Florida – an impressive diplomatic theatre of far greater significance that any individual Caribbean state.

Such an arc encloses Cuba, Haiti and the Dominican Republic (as well as all of the Venezuelan Caribbean Islands) and thereby lowers their diplomatic significance to Caribbean Community. The single gap is Puerto Rico – hence its latent pivotal importance to a conception of Caribbean Community and potential source of conflict with the United States. Therein lies also the neglected importance of the Caribbean Community taking the initiative in defining its sea space within the perspective of this Caribbean arc and the International Law of the Sea.

In this conception, both Jamaica and Guyana (as well as Belize) are really of peripheral significance to the Caribbean Community – the one being well within the Caribbean arc, the other being outside of it.

Correspondingly, both these relatively large countries ultimately have greater need of Caribbean Community, a fact disastrously unrecognised by Prime Minister Dr Eric Williams in relation to the Federation. This may not always remain an unrecognised fact. For it is perhaps only these geo-security features, together with the symbolism of numbers which confer international status and strength on Caribbean polity.

The so-called more developed countries of Guyana, Jamaica, Barbados and Trinidad and Tobago are a political aberration and economic hodge-podge as a conception of Caribbean Community – points in a pointless eco-political landscape.

It is surely within the power of the smaller islandic countries to use their combined significance to get a better economic deal. The alternative is for Caribbean status to be assumed by Venezuela and Colombia – a possibility apparently already grasped by these countries. The political leaders of the more developed member-countries would seem to be neither irrational nor moved by 'one people' notions in their engagement of the least developed countries.

Moving to the purely scientific rationale of integration, it seems necessary to be clear in our minds what notions of community we are talking about, and to distinguish arrangements which are technically optimal from those which merely facilitate, or, are helpful in dealing with certain common problems within the parameters set by the existing political authorities.

Few would defend a proposition that the Caribbean Community, whether of the more or less developed or of both, defines an optimum economic space. So we are clearly not discussing that and criticisms in that context are, to my mind, not pertinent to present realities. For there are equally important non economic space.

On the other hand, there are clearly many economic matters and other functional tasks which when approached together could be helpful to each country individually and an improvement over what each could do separately – even at such elementary levels as the search for solutions to common problems. This may not be what some people would call integration or a community of nations. What has been taking place in the Caribbean is similar to the 'pre-decisional co-operation' arrangements of the Scandinavian countries.

Part of the problem therefore seems to lie in giving names to situations which inflate and misrepresent their content and stimulate unfounded expectations for cosmetic political advantage. Eventually, reality catches up with symbolism.

The Secretary General of CARICOM was, in my opinion, quite right in saying that CARICOM is now being born. But that birth is long in making its appearance. Surely the Caribbean people, including the regional officials who have worked so hard and against so many obstacles, deserve a better service and sense of responsibility from those now entrusted with the making of political decisions.

Note

This was published as a Letter to the Editor, *Caribbean Contact*, August 1977.

[31]

Making the
Quantum Leap[1]

Hugh Desmond Hoyte

The title I have chosen for my remarks today was inspired by a statement made by Prime Minister A.N.R. Robinson in an address which he delivered in October last year at the Royal Institute of International Affairs in London: 'The Future of the Caribbean'. 'What I am suggesting', he said on that occasion, 'is that we have arrived at a point where we stand to make the necessary quantum leap in the direction of Caribbean integration.' The Prime Minister was revisiting a familiar theme; but the fresh insights he brought to bear on the subject, his perspective analysis and persuasive logic must certainly impress upon us the urgent necessity to take the further practical steps to complete the process of regional integration, if our Community is to survive and achieve its objectives in an increasingly difficult and complex world. I can think of no better point of departure for the remarks I propose to make than the following passage, with which I completely agree, from the Prime Minister's address:

The case (for West Indian nationhood) has been made abundantly clear on economic grounds; the benefit of binding commitments with respect to an enlarged market with freedom of movement of capital and skills; pooling of natural resources; joint exploitation of the Exclusive Economic Zone; coordination and harmonisation of economic development to avoid overlapping and duplication; pooling of scarce management skills in the public and private sectors; general pooling of human resources and of scientific and technological research and development.

To my mind, we have here a clear, concise and accurate summation of the fundamental requirements for the full achievement of the economic objectives of CARICOM, as envisaged by the Treaty of Chaguaramas. These requirements constitute a set of imperatives we can no longer afford to ignore. We must make definitive decisions about them, not at some time in the distant future, but now. Given the emerging world situation, to defer those decisions would be to court disaster.

The world economy is undergoing profound changes at an unprecedented pace. New technologies are emerging almost everyday. These have generated manufacturing processes that require small amounts of raw materials for a given unit of economic output. Certain raw materials are even in danger of being completely displaced by synthetic processes. As industry shifts away from products and processes that are material-intensive, the rate of increase in demand for raw materials has been falling. The steady decline in the raw material intensity of manufacturing processes and products also affects energy, particularly petroleum.

Commodity prices, which collapsed around 1978, continue to be depressed. Indeed, in recent years they plummeted to the lowest levels in recorded history, in relation to the prices of services and manufactured goods. Today, even oil prices, which were so buoyant from the mid 1970s to the early 80s have fallen steeply. Thus, the terms of trade continue to flow against developing countries; protectionist policies reduce their access to the markets of the developed countries; foreign export earnings keep declining; and the problem of external debt remains unresolved and seemingly intractable. Given low commodity prices, reducing importance of raw materials and rampant protectionist policies, the conventional wisdom that developing countries can finance their development by exporting primary materials is hardly tenable today.

These world realities have serious implications for us in CARICOM. They are a jeopardy but, equally, they offer opportunities. It is against this background that we in CARICOM have to make up our minds about the way in which we are going to meet the challenges now confronting us. The decisions we make will determine whether we survive and prosper, or disappear ingloriously and become a mere footnote in the history books.

I believe that the Treaty of Chaguaramas, by which we established the Caribbean Community, provides us with the framework and the mechanisms to make an effective response to those challenges. Both the letter and the spirit of its provisions enjoin us to integrate our activities and cooperate in the way described by Prime Minister Robinson. The things we have in common – make it logical and relatively easy for us to do so within the ambit of a cohesive regional polity – if we have the will. Indeed, history, culture and economics, as well as political and geostrategic considerations, dictate that this is the only rational course open to us.

Global Economy

But even as we seek to strengthen the process of cooperation within the region we must remember that the Treaty envisages that, on major international issues, we will coordinate our approaches and, as far as possible, 'seek to adopt common positions.' Cooperation on the international scene is a necessary complement to cooperation within the Region for, as the founding fathers noted in the preamble to the *Treaty*, the objectives of our community can best be achieved 'by a common front in relation to the external world.'

Perhaps, more than ever before, it is imperative for us to present a common front to the external world. A pervasive feature of international relations today is the politics of economic regionalism which derives from the emergence of powerful economic blocs in the world. The European Economic Community (EEC), primarily a grouping of Western European countries and the Council for Mutual Economic Assistance[2] (CEMA), primarily a grouping of the Soviet Union and the Eastern European States, have long been leading actors in the world economy. The USA, a formidable economic entity, and Canada are about to convert North America into a vast free trade area. This phenomenon of regional economic groupings has also manifested itself in distinct and dynamic ways in Africa, Asia, Latin America, the Middle East and the Pacific.

In 1992, the European Economic Community will be dismantling its internal tariff walls and creating a giant single market. The EEC market is very important to the Region. Our exports to it in 1985 were valued at ECU $1.46 billion. A significant percentage of foreign export earnings of our member states originate in that market. In the case of one country, it was as high as 77.4 percent in 1984. What will the creation of the single market mean for CARICOM? How will it affect in the short or longer term, access to that market for our bananas, rum, sugar, rice and other exports? What demands might be made of us for reciprocity of concessions in return for market access or preferences? The answers to these and other questions are not yet clear but there could be implications that are damaging to our interests. Whatever those are, our best chance of protecting and promoting our national and regional interest lies in coordinating our efforts, adopting a common position and undertaking collective action.

In the meantime, the 'Big Seven' of Western industrialised countries – USA, Japan, Canada, Britain, West Germany, France and Italy – are quietly discussing the idea of coordinating their levels of output, domestic expenditure, interest rates and budget deficits, among other things. The interests of developing countries do not form part of their agenda. I think that the inference to be drawn from all these developments is quite clear: huge economic groupings are going to dominate the world economy and there will be no place for individual countries that try to go it alone. We must avoid the temptation of believing that we could act individually even to protect our individual national interest.

Certainly, the member states of CARICOM cannot face these powerful groupings individually. We have to combine our forces to obtain maximum leverage in any negotiations with them. But if we are to act effectively, in relation to both our intra-regional and external objectives, we will have to strengthen the institutional bases of CARICOM.

All the mechanisms that are essential for institutionalising community economic activities, as the basis for effective integration are identified in the Treaty. From the beginning, the expectation was that we would have put all of them in place. However, we did not adopt and implement the most important of them. For far too long we have approached this crucial issue in a tentative and sometimes parochial manner. We now have to act with greater purposefulness and expedition to give full effect to the provisions of the Treaty.

Initiatives

Over the past three years or so, member states have taken three major initiatives to strengthen the process of integration. They have adopted and brought into force the CARICOM Enterprise Regime, the Protocol on Industrial Programming and the Unrestricted intra-Regional Free Trade Arrangements. These giant steps, taken after fifteen years of hesitancy, were made possible by the climate of trust and cooperation which the Heads of Government were able to create. These three mechanisms are fundamental to the achievement of the purposes and objectives of our Community. Without them our Community marked time: it could not advance further. With them, it now has a real prospect of achieving the 'accelerated balanced development' of which the Treaty speaks.

In commenting on the 1986 CARICOM Summit at which the decision was taken to proceed with the implementation of these mechanisms, one journalist described that meetings as a 'non-event'. Moreover, the media reports on the 1987 and 1988 Summits seemed to miss entirely the historic importance of these decisions. I mention this matter because I think that we need to do more, at the popular level, to explain not only the major advances in the integration movement which the adoption of these mechanisms constitutes, but the extraordinary opportunities which they have opened up to our entrepreneurs and other businessmen for investigating and otherwise doing business in the region. Both government information services and the regional media could help the integration process by disseminating intelligence about business and investment opportunities from a regional point of view.

A knowledge of opportunities is an essential prerequisite of trade, investment, and business generally. One writer observed that an opportunity is as real an ingredient in business as raw materials, labour or finance, but it exists only when you can see it. Businessmen must therefore seek out such opportunities constantly. But the Governments, the CARICOM Secretariat and business organisations should establish appropriate mechanisms to provide the business community with comprehensive, accurate and up-to-date information about trade, investment, manufacturing and other business opportunities that are available. For this purpose, we need to compile a regional directory containing, in relation to each member state, information about business firms, investment policies, applicable laws and procedures and other pertinent matters.

Recent advances in CARICOM have set the stage for the creation of a single regional market. This market has enormous potential, but if we are to reap its full benefits, we will have to work methodically to develop it. For one thing, it will be necessary to increase dramatically the output of goods and services to meet the regional demand; but our manufacturing activities will have to be based firmly on the maximum utilisation of regional raw materials. We are at present just scratching the surface of the regional demand for goods and services. For far too long we have neglected the domestic market. We must no longer do so. Many people speak about the 'Japanese Miracle', but it is important to note that Japan's growth did not depend nearly so much on exports as it did on the development of the domestic market. Home demand not foreign sales, was the main factor driving its economic activity during its many years of high speed growth. We must stimulate regional demand and produce the goods and services to satisfy it.

As a region, we have sufficiently extensive resources to enable us to manufacture a wide range of goods, many of which we currently import, for the domestic market and for export. By doing this, we can escape from the trap of the narrow production basis on which our individual national economies operate. Let us consider that, in the Region, we have fertile agricultural lands and crops and livestock rearing; surrounding seas rich in fish; petroleum;

natural gas; limestone; mineral resources, including bauxite, kaolin and other clays, manganese, gold, diamonds and semi-precious stones, such as agate, jasper, amethyst, high grade silica sand; talc, soapstone and dimension stones; picturesque fauna and flora and the natural beauty of our countries. In addition we have a highly literate, skilled and easily trainable population.

The resources we possess are by no means insignificant; but to exploit them for our benefit we need investment. The scope for investment, then, is very wide. Many of our resources are only marginally exploited; some not at all. Even when they are, we do not establish appropriate linkages to create sufficient added value. We must mobilise the capital, technical expertise and managerial skills to develop our resources.

In all probability, we might not be able to find within the region all the capital or expertise needed for some projects; but we should not balk at joint venture arrangements with those outside of the region. Indeed, I believe that it is in our interest to form alliances with extra-regional entrepreneurs and encourage the inflow of capital, technology and know-how, to supplement our own stock of these assets. Our natural resource endowment and the large regional demand for certain products open up exciting possibilities for large-scale joint-ventures at the national level.

Some years ago, for example, preliminary enquiries were made into the feasibility of joint industrial ventures among Guyana, Trinidad and Tobago, and Jamaica for the manufacture of certain products based upon a combination of our bauxite and hydrocarbon endowment to satisfy our own demand. The products identified included refractory bricks; alumina sulphate; and caustic soda (sodium hydroxide) and its by-product, chlorine – to satisfy the various demands for processing in Jamaica, Guyana and Trinidad and Tobago. The possibility of using Guyana's and Jamaica's bauxite and Trinidad and Tobago's sulphuric acid to produce alumina sulphate for the CARICOM market was also canvassed. The possibilities for such collaboration are as manifold as they are exciting. We must widen our horizon and revive this kind of bold regional thinking. These are large projects requiring, I believe, substantial investments, but we only have to glance at the import list to see the wide range of goods that we import from outside the region, but which we can produce (and should be producing) in the region.

One particular area I would like to emphasise is 'services'. We must develop a greater capability to provide regional services to facilitate and support our development and integration efforts. These include banking, insurance, consultancy, transport and construction services to name a few.

Regional Investment

How do we seize these opportunities that are now unfolding in our region? Herein lies the major challenges. It seems to me that there are two requirements to meet these challenges successfully: one is attitudinal, the other, institutional.

Regional integration like every other idea, begins in the mind. It will flourish only if we have a certain mental attitude to it. At this stage, we cannot afford to entertain any lingering doubts about the value and importance of CARICOM. We have to believe unreservedly in its great possibilities and do more than pay lip service to its purposes and objectives. In our search for business opportunities, we have to see CARICOM as a single economy and a single market, not as an aggregation of separate economies, some deemed large, some small, some more developed, some less developed. We have to shed the habit of regarding ourselves as Trinidad and Tobago businessmen, or Guyanese businessmen, or Barbadian or St Lucian businessmen and see ourselves as regional businessmen with the resources and opportunities of the region at our command. We must learn to see our regional resources as a common endowment and do everything necessary to ensure that they are accessible to our nationals who have the means and the expertise to develop them, in accordance with whatever rules we might prescribe to ensure equitable conduct and fair treatment of all parties.

I would like to say that we in Guyana remain committed as firmly as ever to the regional integration movement and are prepared to do everything possible to advance the process. We have been trying to give effect to the principle that we should treat our resources as a regional endowment, encourage regional investment and promote those intra-regional linkages that are necessary for the development of the single regional market and the single regional economy.

We believe that the private sector has a pivotal role to play in promoting regional integration. We have therefore worked to create a climate of business confidence in the country. As part of this process, we have promulgated and laid in our National Assembly a 'State Paper on Investment Policy'. This document outlines, among other things, Government's attitude to investment. Government welcomes private investment and will do everything in its power to encourage, facilitate and protect it. Such investment includes, of course, investment from our sister CARICOM States. Let me say that if any Trinidad and Tobago businessman wants to invest or engage in other forms of business in Guyana, he will find not only opportunities, but a warm welcome. Government is also prepared to consider any proposal for participation in our public sector enterprises.

I know that I have confined my remarks largely to economic matters, but I am aware of the fact that these constitute just one segment of the life of our community and that in the final analysis, the concept of regional integration must have a wider meaning. Ultimately, notwithstanding what governments do, it is the ordinary people pursuing their private, cultural, professional, business and other interests through regional organsiation who are the cement that will bind our states together in an indissoluble union.

The coordination which we seek at the economic level inevitably leads to cultural and political coordination. In a real sense, we cannot divide these aspects into neat, watertight compartments. They impinge upon one another, influence one another and are mutually reinforcing. The regional economic arrangements are ultimately not self-sustaining nor can they exist in a vacuum. They will wither away and die unless we put in place the institutional mechanisms that will enable them to establish symbiotic links with our cultural and political life. These mechanisms, of necessity, will be administrative, legal and political. We are forced inexorably to acknowledge that the integration movement must rest not only on economic, but also on political foundations among others. Try as we might, we cannot escape from the political factor.

I have always felt that implicit in the provisions of the Treaty of Chaguaramas was the idea that the Community would in time cohere within the framework of a political arrangement. Although we have not yet found the formula, we have really never stopped searching. The idea of a political framework in which we might order our regional affairs has never died. It keeps recurring like a leitmotiv. Already the proposal for a regional Court of Appeal and a Parliamentary Assembly has gained wide support. The OECS countries are grappling with the idea of a political union and Prime Minister Robinson has even speculated on the possibility of some form of political agreement between Guyana, Trinidad and Tobago and Barbados. It seems to me that as we seek to achieve greater regional economic cohesion, the necessity for some form of political underpinning is bound to arise.

The important thing is that we must not be afraid to discuss this issue in an objective and dispassionate way. Moreover, we must not be afraid to follow the path where logic and common sense lead us. We cannot stand still in history. The world will not let us. We either advance or retreat. We are at a stage in the development of CARICOM where these two options face us. If we are to advance, we will have to do some radical readjustment to our mode of thought. We will have to make the transition from stale, hide-bound approaches that mistake dogma for truth to more open minded and flexible attitudes that are not afraid to grapple with new ideas.

What is involved is the abandonment of many a deep-seated and cherished notion and the adoption of some bold, innovative designs for organising our regional affairs. For many, that would be a big chasm to cross. Lloyd George is reported to have once said. 'Don't be afraid to take a big step, you can't cross a chasm in small jumps.' If we are determined to complete the process of regional integration in accord with the Treaty of Chaguaramas, we cannot at this stage do it by a series of jumps. What is required is a quantum leap.

The question is whether we have the courage to make that leap. I believe we have.

Notes

1. This address was made to the Trinidad and Tobago Chamber of Industry and Commerce, Port-of-Spain, Trinidad and Tobago on January 18, 1989. The Speech was originally published in the Book: *Guyana's Economic Recovery: Leadership, Will-Power and Vision, Selected Speeches of Hugh Desmond Hoyte.*
2. The Council for Mutual Economic Assistance (CMEA) is no longer in existence. It became defunct when the Soviet Union collapsed in the 1980's.

[Part Three]

———————

Mechanisms for Survival

[32]

CARICOM
Administration

Kenneth Hall and Byron Blake

It is estimated that in 1976, roughly 70 countries embracing about 40 per cent of the total population of the developing countries participated in regional integration schemes. Among the schemes linking neighbouring countries at the sub-regional level, there were in Latin American and the Caribbean – the Caribbean Community (CARICOM), the Central American Common Market (CACM), the Andean Group and Latin American Free Trade Area (LAFTA); in Africa – the East African Community (EAC), the Customs and Economic Union of Central Africa (UNDEAC), the West African Economic Community (CEAO), the Mano River Union, the Maghreb Permanent Consultative Committee and the Economic Community of West African States (ECOWAS); in Afro-Asia – the Council of Arab Economic Unity; in Asia – Regional Cooperation for Development (RCD) and the Association of Southeast Asian Nations (ASEAN).[1]

Movement towards the formation of economic groupings among developing countries began in the immediate post World War II period as a result of nationalism, the dismantling of imperial systems and the drive to reduce the dependence of the periphery on trade with the metropolitan countries. In recent years, the move has intensified chiefly because of the realisation among Third World countries that the traditional economic order and its associated international development strategies not only failed to solve the problems of mass poverty and economic backwardness, but have imposed fundamental constraints on their developmental endeavours. The prolonged recession and severe inflationary pressures in developed market economy countries, the increases in oil prices, chronic food shortages, fluctuations in primary commodity prices and the consequent financial and balance of payments problems gave rise to the need for developing countries to reduce their dependence on the industrialised centres and to secure interdependent and balanced development through collective self-reliance. As Alister McIntyre, Secretary General of CARICOM puts it, 'economic integration represents a central element in development strategy designed to overcome by joint and concerted action among neighbouring countries some of the basic constraints to development'.[2]

If the new impetus towards regional integration has been primarily economic, the scope of the mechanisms extended beyond purely economic cooperation to include cooperation and joint action in a wide variety of fields – foreign relations and functional activities such as health and education. Whatever the degree of regional integration and cooperation, without effective mechanisms to harmonise the diversity of interests, the attempts to achieve the objectives of the scheme could be inhibited by different circumstances, such as nationalism and the degree of development of the Third World country. To this extent, the success of the integration grouping would be influenced less by the economic and social objectives than by the political will of the states to create the institutional mechanisms which are necessary for their achievement.

From this perspective, the process of regional integration represents

the series of political decisions which the various national states involved in the process of integration adopt in order to define its main objectives, to establish the necessary institutional mechanisms, determine the decision-making power of the community institutions and lay down procedures for the implementation of community decisions in the national states which are members of the multinational organisations'.[3]

The administration of the regional integration involves two essential aspects: the institutional organisation with its mechanisms; and the human, technical and financial resources and its legal administrative and political capacity to ensure implementation of the objectives adopted at the national and regional level. Recognition of the crucial link between the institutional/administrative machinery and the success of regional integration schemes has focused attention increasingly on the administrative organisation and relations within these groupings. Studies have been undertaken in such areas as: the role of national institutions in regional integration; the dimensions of public administration and the process of multinational integration; the interaction between national and regional institutions; the decision-making processes and regional integration; the relations between technical secretariats and the national integration offices; and the internal organisation of states, to safeguard their respective national interest.

The available evidence suggests that while there are certain similarities in the administrative and institutional problems faced by the states involved, there is no blueprint which could be recommended for the solution of the problems. Each regional grouping has responded to its own peculiarities and evolved those mechanisms which are politically acceptable. The paper examines how the Caribbean countries participating in CARICOM have dealt with these issues.

Institutional Framework

The most important feature of the institutional arrangements in CARICOM is their complexity. In legal terms, the arrangements have been regarded as *sui generis* in that there is one Treaty and one Community but legally the Treaty has established two organisations, two legal personae with potentially different membership. These two organisations are respectively the Caribbean Community and the Caribbean Common Market. Institutionally, however, the whole arrangement can be divided into three categories – the principal organs, the institutions and the associate institutions.

In the first category, the principal organs are the Heads of Government Conference and the Common Market Council. The first is the supreme policy making organ of the Community and the second has specific responsibility for the efficient operation and development of the Common Market and its institutions. The second category comprises a wide range of Standing Ministerial Committees which are responsible for the following portfolios at present: Foreign Affairs; Education; Health; Labour; Finance; Agriculture; Mines; Transportation and industry.

In the third category are those institutions which, though established to carry out some of the objectives of the integration movement, function within their own rules and have their own agreements. These are *inter alia,* the East Caribbean Common Market Council of Ministers (ECCM), the West Indies Associated States Council of Ministers (WISA), the University of the West Indies (UWI), the University of Guyana (UG), the Caribbean Examinations Council (CXC), the Council of Legal Education (CLE), the Caribbean Agricultural Research and Development Institute (CARDI), the Caribbean Development Bank, (CDB) the Caribbean Investment Corporation (CIC) and the Caribbean Meteorological Council (CMC).

These regional bodies are supplemented by a wide range of technical groups, including Central Banks and monetary authorities, regional industrial planners, regional agricultural planners and national planning agencies which perform advisory functions. In addition, the organs and institutions of the Community are empowered to set up *ad hoc* committees and working parties to deal with specific subjects, such as, the Working Party on Sugar, the Banana Working Party, the Working Party on the Harmonisation of Company Law.

The complexity of the regional institutional structure is intensified by the existence of the East Caribbean Common Market among seven of the smaller states within the framework of CARICOM. The purpose of the ECCM is not only to promote the development of its members but also to develop and coordinate their positions on CARICOM matters, to compensate for the difference in size and level of economic development between themselves and the MDCs. The efficient functioning of these regional bodies is facilitated by the Caribbean Community Secretariat which is designated as the principal administrative organ of the Community.

In analysing the nature of the institutional framework from the perspective of the balance which should be achieved between the Community and the national organs, attention must be drawn to the factors which have influenced the establishment of that framework. It is only by understanding the interrelationship between the framework and the factors influencing its establishment that the uniqueness of the CARICOM arrangements can be fully appreciated.

Four factors appear to have been crucial in determining the nature of the arrangements – legacies of previous attempts at regional integration, the structure of the national administration, the objectives of the integration process, and the disparity between member states.

The immediate precursor to the integration movement in the Caribbean was the establishment in 1958 of the ill-fated Federation of the West Indies, comprising all the Commonwealth territories except the Bahamas, Belize and Guyana. The Federation collapsed after four years, following the withdrawal of Jamaica and Trinidad and Tobago. This was followed by the Caribbean Free Trade Association (CARIFTA) which came into existence in 1968. In 1973, CARIFTA was transformed to CARICOM with the signing of the Treaty of Chaguaramas by Barbados, Guyana, Jamaica and Trinidad and Tobago. The eight remaining member states, Dominica, St Vincent, St Lucia, Belize, Montserrat, Antigua, St Kitts-Nevis-Anguilla and Grenada acceded in 1974. In 1968, the Less Developed countries (LDCs) set up the East Caribbean Common Market (ECCM) within CARIFTA.

Each of these precursors contributed to the legacies that influenced the CARICOM administrative arrangements. The demise of the Federation left at least five important legacies. Firstly, there was the fear about creating any supranational institution at the political level. Secondly, there were a number of common services, *inter alia*, the University of the West Indies, the Regional Shipping Services and the Meteorological Services, the efficiency of which required the continuation of a regional coordinating machinery. Indeed, the first Heads of Government Conference in 1963 was called primarily to consider the fate of those services. Thirdly, the unsatisfied desire of the non-independent states for political autonomy resulted in a series of attempts at new forms of political integration. The failure of these attempts explains the present constitutional status of the non independent states. Fourthly, a well of caution, derived from anxieties about probable collapse resulted in a preoccupation with ensuring that any regional arrangement did not deprive member countries of the ability to operate effectively in its absence. Fifthly, the failure to deal with economic matters suggested that economic integration should be a focal point in any future regional arrangement.

The reluctance to enter into any new political arrangement and the emphasis on economic integration made it inevitable that CARIFTA would be an economic institution. Furthermore, it was concerned mainly with trade liberalisation. Because the CARIFTA Council dealt primarily with trade, issues of regional interest other than free trade had to be dealt with outside of the CARIFTA framework.

This meant that those institutions which predated CARIFTA continued to function not only independently of the CARIFTA Council but also independently of each other. These included the Heads of Government Conference, the Regional Shipping Council and the West Indies Shipping Corporation, the Meteorological Council, the University of the West Indies and associated bodies, such as the Regional Research Council. Furthermore, new areas of regional cooperation led to the establishment of new institutions, such as the Ministers of Health Conference, the Caribbean Development Bank, the Council of Legal Education and the Caribbean Examinations Council. There was, however, an attempt to link most of these institutions administratively by having the Secretariat for the Free Trade Association act as a servicing unit for them.

From the perspective of institutional growth, these developments influenced the CARICOM arrangements in two ways. The new scheme had to take cognisance of the existence of those institutions. The choice was either to allow them to continue their independent existence with some form of loose attachment within the new framework or establish new organisations to deal with those areas. In all cases, the existing organisations remained and were granted the status of institution or associate institution in the Community.

The main criterion for determining whether an organisation was designated an institution or associate institution was whether the organisation possessed its own charter or treaty. Organisations with such instruments were designated associate institutions. To this extent, the 'Community is largely a normalisation of what already exists'. By allowing these institutions to function independently, moreover, a precedent was established whereby the major areas of regional cooperation were given their own institutions and provision made to establish new ones to deal with each new area of activity. This has resulted in one of the unique features of CARICOM institutional framework – namely, a two tiered integration at the regional level. Not only do the mechanisms provide for the cooperation, consultation and joint action between the member states but direct linkages between the major portfolios of the member states through the institutions of Standing Committees of Ministers.

National Institutional Structure

The peculiar feature of CARICOM derives not merely from the legacy of the past efforts at integration but is closely related to institutional structure in the member states. The areas of Government activity are divided into various portfolios for administrative purposes. There were two options open to take advantage of the range of activities for cooperation at the regional level.. The first was to restructure the national administration by establishing a national organ to deal with regional matters. The second was to retain the existing national administrative structure and regard the regional cooperation as merely an extension of the domestic activity. The first option, with the exception of Trinidad and Tobago, which had the Ministry of West Indian Affairs, was not adopted. Two kinds of explanations might be offered for this occurrence. The tradition of portfolio independence made the creation of a new institution fraught with the danger of competency conflicts. These would undoubtedly have had an adverse effect on the receptivity of the regional integration movement by the existing departments. Equally important was the view that regional integration should have little or no direct impact on the internal administrative structure of Government. This was related to political considerations in some countries as well as the general feeling that should the movement collapse, there would be no adverse effect on the normal operations of Government.

The historical rationale for cooperation among the Commonwealth Caribbean territories was based on the need to improve administrative efficiency and minimise administrative costs. The post World War II era introduced new objectives – the drive for political independence and for economic development. Another factor resulting from the experience of independence, is the realisation that in international relations involving super powers, groups of states and multinational corporations, regional coordination was increasingly a minimum requirement for effective participation. Given the range and relative strength of these forces, it is not surprising that the objectives of CARICOM are diverse and span a gamut of activities undertaken by member states. Specifically, the CARICOM arrangements involve three elements – economic integration, cooperation in functional areas and coordination of foreign policy. These broad objectives influence the institutional structure in that appropriate mechanisms were established through which the achievement of the goals could be pursued. Economic integration would be achieved through a Common Market which provides for trade liberalisation, a common protective policy, the coordination of national development plans and industrial programming. Economic integration also demands the joint development of natural resources, the rationalisation of agricultural production, and cooperation in tourism. There should be a special set of measures for the Less Developed Countries (LDCs), involving preferential access within the regional market and the transfer of financial and technical resources. Regional policies in those areas are formulated primarily in the Common Market Council of Ministers, the Standing Committees of Ministers Responsible for Agriculture, Industry and Mines assisted by the Caribbean Development Bank and the Caribbean Investment Corporation.

Cooperation in functional areas is facilitated by the establishment of the various standing committees of ministers as well as by associate institutions – the Caribbean Meteorological Council, the University of the West Indies and the Council of Legal Education. Coordination of Foreign Policy is the responsibility of the Standing Committee of Ministers Responsible for Foreign Affairs.

Another conditioning factor is the economic and political disparity, between the member states of CARICOM. The economic disparity has affected the institutional structure in two ways. The Windward and Leeward Islands in recognition of the relatively weaker state of their economies formed, as a precondition to their entry into CARIFTA, the East Caribbean Common Market which the CARICOM structure had to recognise and accommodate. Also, the LDCs insisted on the establishment of the Caribbean Investment Corporation as a precondition to their entry into CARICOM and to facilitate the transfer of resources. The CARICOM institutional structure also had to recognise and accommodate this body. With regards to constitutional status, eight of the member states were not independent[1] the United Kingdom was still responsible for their foreign policy. This partly explains why the coordination of foreign policy was identified as a separate area of activity resulting in the establishment of a standing committee with four original members rather than twelve members.

These conditioning factors do not merely explain the institutional framework but they also had a considerable influence on the operational principles of the institutions and the distribution of power between the regional and national institutions.

Concomitant with the view that regional integration should not result in supra-nationality, certain principles have characterised the operations of the organs and institutions of the Community. Firstly, there is the principle of one vote for each member state. Secondly, the decisions require the affirmative vote of each member or the principle of unanimity and there are no provisions in the Treaty for the absence of member states. Thirdly, with the exception of the Heads of Government Conference and the Common Market Council, each institution makes decisions within its exclusive areas of competence and these, with a few exceptions, can only be discussed at the regional level by conference. Fourthly, even though decisions taken at the regional level are binding, they can only be implemented through the constitutional procedures of each member state and have legal effect for nationals only after such procedures have been adhered to. Fifthly, there are no provisions for direct elections to the Community institutions. Sixthly, the Community has no power of taxation and its budget must be unanimously agreed and contributed in agreed proportions by the member states.

Several consequences, which impinge on the administration of the integration movement, flow from these principles. If the administration of an integration movement is seen as a process facilitator who exercises power to achieve specific objectives through specific organisations, it can readily be appreciated that the operational principles of CARICOM would have a critical impact on the distribution of power between the regional and national administrations. CARICOM left all the effective power at the national level. This can be illustrated by an examination of the decision-making process and the functions assigned to the CARICOM Secretariat.

Decentralisation of Decision-Making

It is now generally recognised that one criterion for the success of an integration movement is the nature of the decisions generated by the process. In CARICOM, the organs and institutions of which the relevant ministers and officials represent each country make decisions at the regional level. These institutions are empowered to take binding decisions as well as make recommendations. However, the real decision-making organ is decentralised. With few exceptions, only the Heads of Government Conference is empowered to consider and decide on all aspects of regional integration. Even so, the Heads of Government usually lay down the broad policy outlines while the Common Market Council and the other institutions take the operative decisions in their respective areas of competence.

On closer examination, one finds that the three crucial aspects of decision-making are retained by the member states – initiating, deciding and implementing. It is true that in some of the organs and institutions, the Secretary General of CARICOM has the right to place items on the agenda for consideration, but the member states have the right to refuse to consider them and remove them. In short, it is the member states who decide the matters to be considered by the regional bodies. Furthermore, the requirement that a decision must be unanimous gives each member state the veto over all matters placed before the decision-making organs for consideration. Even after a decision has been taken, the member states retain exclusive control over its implementation.

The pre-eminence of the member states in the distribution of power is further reflected in the functions assigned to the Secretariat. Under the Treaty of Chaguaramas, the Secretariat has the following functions:

(1) to service meetings of the Community and any of its institutions or committees as may from time to time be determined by Conference;
(2) to take appropriate follow-up action on decisions made at such meetings;
(3) to initiate, arrange and carry out studies on questions of economic and functional cooperation relating to the region as a whole;
(4) to provide services to member states at their request in respect of matters relating to the achievement of the objectives of the Community;
(5) to undertake any other duties which may be assigned to it by the Conference or any of the institutions of the Community.

Although the Secretariat has been designated the principal administrative organ of CARICOM with the exception of (3) above, it is not invested with any independent power in the vital stages of decision-making. With respect to its ability to initiate and carry out studies, the Treaty is silent on the destination of those studies. There is no requirement that the studies be considered by the organs and institutions of CARICOM with a view to influencing decisions or accepting any recommendations in those studies. Furthermore, the Community's control over the Secretariat's budget and work programme provides the Governments with effective control over the number of studies which can be undertaken.

Viewed purely from the perspective of institutional organisation and legal procedure the balance of power between the regional and the national administrations is overwhelmingly in favour of the latter. For this reason the national, Governmental and administrative structures play a crucial role in the regional integration because they form 'the main protagonists, the pillars, the transmission mechanisms and the executing agencies of the common enterprise'.[4] These structures perform the functions of co-ordination, conceptualising , representation, promotion, consultation, evaluation and execution. In this connection it is often posited that an efficient national coordinating body to serve as the focal point between various national governmental bodies and as the channel for communication with regional institutions, is a minimum requirement for the successful administration of an integration movement.

A unique feature of the administrative organisation of CARICOM is the absence of any such national coordinating agencies primarily responsible for regional affairs. Instead, the Minister and officials within whose portfolio they fall deal with each area of activity at the regional level. In the absence of a national coordinating body the quality of CARICOM administration is therefore intimately related to the national administrations. This raises questions of how representative is the national administration of the national interest; how efficient and effective it is; how honest it is; how politically stable it is; and the question of the level of dependency and underdevelopment in each member state.

One of the critical problems of developing countries is the shortage of trained personnel with the technical and managerial skills to effectively manage national affairs. Associated with the shortage is the problem of continuity as the few capable technicians, especially in the fields of development planning, undergo rapid promotions and transfers. Another administrative constraint is the problem of the requisite institutions to effectively coordinate aspects of national policies.

Recent studies on public administration in CARICOM countries suggest they experience all the problems and characteristics of public administration in developing countries. These studies have stressed the lack of adequate preparation for self-government, notably the failure 'to equip the public services with the skills, competence and attitudes required to maximise the benefits of self-government or to overcome the complex administrative problems likely to arise in the early years of statehood. Public servants are uninitiated in law and order procedures, are unprepared to be involved in policy formulation and are more concerned with income as against output. The heritage of paternalism, the shifts in bureaucratic power resulting in conflicts between Ministers and officials and the unrepresentative nature of the bureaucracies result in the decisional machinery of Governments being dominated by elite groups.[5]The view advanced by Mills and Robertson about the Jamaican Civil Service could equally be applied to that of all member states in CARICOM. According to them

Jamaica has a Civil Service which was and remains a construct suitable for colonial status rather than for independence. In terms of behaviour the service is uncoordinated and hampered by red tape and inflexibility . . . Incumbents seek to opt out of the service rather than attempt to change it. Finally, the members of the Jamaican Civil Service lack creativity and basic ideas and are generally weak in their behaviour'.[6]

Adding responsibility for regional affairs in this situation, creates an additional dimension to the problem from at least three perspectives. First, there is the competition between regional and national institutions for capable staff. Secondly, there is need for the senior administrative and technical officials to attend regional meetings which adversely affect the day-to-day efficiency of the national administrative machinery. Thirdly, the practice of member Governments hosting regional meetings, especially in the LDCs, requires a considerable amount of organisation with the result that the resources of several departments have to be tapped to service any of the bigger meetings.

Some member states, especially the More Developed Countries, have attempted to cope with the additional dimension of regional affairs by assigning the responsibility for regional affairs to particular officers within each department. In the LDCs this solution has been difficult at the individual state level because of the shortage of manpower. They have, however, sought coordination through the establishment of the ECCM and WISA Secretariats.

The reluctance of CARICOM member states to invest regional institutions with decision-making and executive powers has left some of the regional institutions without the capacity to undertake regional activity requiring these powers. The result is that a new phase of regional integration movement – the emphasis on productive activity – raises new administrative problems. The pattern, which appears to be emerging, is that each area would be administered by its own organisation and its own rules. In this regard, the Caribbean Food Corporation set up to manage production, processing and marketing in the agricultural sector, and the regime of CARICOM Enterprises designed to establish companies between member Governments to facilitate regional development projects, points a new direction in regional administrative organisation and relations.

Analysis of the nature of the administrative organisation and relations should not, however, be confined to the purely legal institutional structure.

Equally important is the performance of those institutions at the level of concrete activity.

Notwithstanding any weaknesses in the decision-making process, a number of decisions which have fundamentally lent body to the integration movement have been accepted and implemented by the various organs and institutions of the Community.

Alister McIntyre, Secretary General of CARICOM, in his recent address to the Sixth Annual Meeting of the Board of Governors of the Caribbean Development Bank, identified 'seven areas where substantial progress has been registered' viz the arrangements for intraregional trade; monetary and financial cooperation; development of a regional food plan; arrangements of intra-regional transportation (shipping and air); arrangements for improving the special measures for the LDCs; sectoral integration; and foreign policy.[7] In addition to the areas identified above, progress has also been made in the functional areas of health, education, social security, information (the establishment of the Caribbean Broadcasting Union and Caribbean News Agency), tax administration, meteorology and harmonisation of laws.

These decisions have given rise to, *inter alia*, a new Origin System for the Common market to take effect from January 1, 1977. This is a regional food plan to be implemented primarily by a multimillion dollar intergovernmental food corporation and an intra-regional clearing scheme and a balance of payments mutual support facility which is a multimillion dollar investment programme for the regionally-owned West Indies Shipping Corporation. The decisions have led to the making of a regional standards council; and a joint position in the negotiations with the European Economic Community culminating in the Lomé Convention.

In addition to decision-making and implementation, the organs and institutions have functioned effectively in the solution of the various kinds of conflicts which have arisen in the integration movement. One study has identified three types of conflicts of interest which arise in integration groupings – conception, application and organisation.

Conflicts of conception are those which stem from a breach between the global or partial conception of the project and its original juridical formulation on one hand, and the idea one or all the parties have about what the project should be, the changes that should be introduced in it, or the manner in which its development should be considered, on the other. The essence of this type of conflict lies in the fact that one or several parties believe that in its present state the common project does not satisfy any longer their national interests.[8]

Conflicts of application arise when one of the parties believes another is not adhering to certain common rules and therefore preventing the attainment of the objectives of regional policies.

Conflicts of organisation arise from the operation of the institutional mechanism. Such conflicts may arise between a member state and one of the organs, between two member states in respect of the institutional mechanism itself, or between two or more organs. They may be due to a divergence based on opposite views on aspects such as the competence of the organs, their personnel, their operations and the like.[9]

The frequent meetings of ministers and officials in CARICOM provide forums through which conflicts can be settled both at formal and informal levels. Furthermore, the personal contacts between the national officials establish a mechanism where conflicts between two member countries can be settled directly. In this regard it is significant to note that the arbitration machinery provided in the Treaty has only been invoked on one occasion.

In spite of its relative lack of power vis-à-vis national administrations, the Secretariat has exercised considerable influence on the process of regional integration. Apart from its normal functions, the Secretariat has played a crucial role in bringing before the organs and institutions, proposals designed to advance and regulate the process of integration, and ensuring the proper functioning of the regional arrangements. In fact, nearly all of the technical work and background papers resulting in decision-making, were done in the Secretariat.

The growth in the Secretariat's influence derives less from its power than from a number of peculiar features in the CARICOM arrangements. First, in recognition of the shortage of technical expertise and manpower in some of the national administrations, member Governments have been inclined to allow the Secretariat to undertake technical studies and submit proposals to the organs and institutions for decisions. In undertaking studies, the Secretariat often works along with the national technicians in various working parties. These technicians in turn attend meetings at which decisions are taken. To this extent the administrative relations at the level of concrete activity permits the development of an alliance between these national power centres and assist in securing their link with, and support for, the regional programmes and projects. Secondly, the Secretariat has been initiating studies in areas of direct relevance to the national development policies. Thirdly, an atmosphere of confidence in the Secretariat has been built up in member Governments because of the response to their request for assistance. This has been facilitated by the presence in the Secretariat of a number of senior civil servants on secondment from member Governments. These officials not only brought the national perspective to bear in performance of their functions but assisted in retaining direct and cordial relations between the Secretariat and the civil service of member states.

Conclusion

A clearer picture of the administrative organs and relations within CARICOM can be presented if they are evaluated against the criteria suggested by the UNCTAD Seminar on the institutional framework of economic integration among developing countries.[10]

Emphasis was placed on the importance of the institutional framework in relation to the short-term objectives that led to its establishment as well as the stimulating activities leading towards the attainment of the longer-term objectives that the grouping set for itself. It should be flexible enough to adapt itself to changing circumstances and needs. The institutional arrangements of the Caribbean Community satisfy this criterion in that the principal organs and institutions cover all aspects of the integration movement. These institutions have the capacity not only to deal with short-term objectives but also to initiate action for longer-term objectives. This is particularly important since CARICOM is largely based on a set of agreements to agree. Furthermore, there is provision for additions to the list of institutions, if circumstances warrant this, as well as to the function of each institution.

It was recognised that it would be necessary to seek the advice of experts in the resolution of highly complex and technical issues. The CARICOM experience has utilised heavily the institution of regional and international experts in the elaboration of projects both at the national and regional levels. It was further posited that the active cooperation of private entrepreneurs, autonomous public entities, trade unions and other professional associations with the activities of the regional grouping is important. CARICOM has provision for consultation with the business sector, consumers and trade unions.

Furthermore, the provisions from the very inception, of a permanent Secretariat with high technical capability or its equivalent was essential to assist in the elaboration of common or regional action programmes, the preparation of projects, the control and evaluation of their implementation and in-servicing negotiations. The Caribbean Community has had a permanent Secretariat which performs all of these functions. The member states of the Community have recognised the need for highly qualified personnel to man the Secretariat and have taken steps within their limited capabilities to ensure that the terms and conditions of service are sufficiently attractive to permit recruitment from all member states.

It was also suggested that the intensification of the cooperation process will necessitate either the creation of new regional bodies or the strengthening of the existing regional Secretariat and the enlargement of their powers to include taking the initiative to make binding decisions, and implementing these decisions. The Caribbean Community has strengthened its Secretariat but has not yet vested it with powers of initiative (other than studies), of making binding decisions, nor of controlling the implementation of decisions (as distinct from monitoring the implementation of such decisions). It is interesting to note that the member states have recognised the need for new institutions with additional powers and have commissioned the elaboration of a system to achieve those objectives. Emphasis was laid on the principles of unanimity or consensus and equitable representation of all member countries.

The seminar also emphasised several other criteria, the most important being the principle of unanimity, equal representation of member states in the higher-level posts of the common institutions, the establishment of permanent training programmes, appropriate institutional support for regional projects, with special agreements permitting some countries to delay participation until they are able to do so, and permitting regional projects to be implemented even if one member state withdraws. The Caribbean Community has accepted these mandates to a greater or lesser extent.

Another important action was the establishment of intergovernmental bodies at a political level to make decisions binding on partner states. All the organs and institutions of CARICOM are at the ministerial level and are endowed with decision-making powers. Decisions, which do not require any constitutional procedures, are binding. The organs and institutions also allow for the participation of officials.

In summary, the CARICOM institutional arrangements do satisfy most of the important criteria suggested by the UNCTAD Seminar.

It should not be concluded, however, that the CARICOM arrangements are ideal or that it has fulfilled all the criteria suggested by the UNCTAD Seminar. The two most obvious omissions are the absence of an efficient national coordinating body and the failure to create new regional bodies or strengthen the existing regional Secretariat and enlarge its powers to include initiatives, the taking of binding decisions and control over the implementation of decisions.

These omissions resulted in some dissatisfaction with the decision-making process and has led to some proposals for strengthening the decision-making machinery.[11] At the national level proposals have been made to improve the quality of administration by creation of national co-ordination machinery with sufficient authority to ensure effective representation, of the interest of the member states and implementation of decisions. It has also been proposed that in the LDCs their effective participation in the regional movement might be enhanced by the establishment of common services.[12]

At the regional level two sets of proposals have been advanced: first, that new institutions should be created to speed up the decision-making process and ensure the implementation; secondly, to assign the Secretariat sufficient power to bring before the organs and institutions proposals which will enable the integration process to advance and correct any imbalances or malfunctions.

Notes

1. A.F. Mohr, 'Statement on Economic Co-operation among Developing Countries' (UNCTAD IV, Nairobi, May 1976).
2. A. McIntyre, 'Evolution of the Process of Integration in the Caribbean and the Current Situation and Perspectives of CARICOM', (Statement to the IBRD Washington, June 1976).
3. H.H. Godoy, 'Public Administration and Multinational Integration', (Seminar on Administration of Multinational Integration in Latin America, Barbados, 24–28 May. 1976).
4. D Sidjanski 'Comparative Study – National Decision-Making Processes and Regional Integration', (UNCTAD, September 9, 1975).
5. G.E. Mills, (ed.) 'Problems of Administrative Change in the Commonwealth Caribbean', *Social and Economic Studies*, Special number, Vol. 19, March 1970, ISER Jamaica.
6. Mills, 'Problems'.
7. Mills, 'Problems'.
8. McIntyre, A: 'Evolution of the Process of Integration in the Caribbean and the Current Situation and Perspectives of CARICOM', Statement to the IBRD Washington, June 1976.
9. M Casanova, 'Institutional Aspects of Problems Related to the Processes of Integration: Interaction Between National and Multinational Sectors', (Seminar on Administration of Multinational Integration in Latin America, Barbados, 24–28 May 1976).
10. Casanova, 'Institutional Aspects'.
11. UNCTAD, Seminar on the Institutional Framework of Economic Integration among Developing Countries.

12. S.S. Ramphal 'To care for CARICOM: The Need for an Ethos of Community'. (Speech delivered at the Dinner held in his honour by the Common Market Council of Ministers, Montego Bay, July 5, 1975).

References

M.A. Ajomo, 'Regional Economic Organisations – African Experience' in the *International Comparative Law Quarterly*, 25:1, 1976, pp. 58–101.

O.P. Amare,.:'National Interest and Decisions Control in an Integration Process (with special reference to the Andean Group)', Simposio sobre aspectos de organización institucional interna para la integración en países miembros de agrupaciones económicas; San José, Costa Rica, 22–27 September 1975.

A. Brown: 'Planning as a Political Activity: Some Aspects of the Jamaican Experience', *Social and Economic Studies*, Vol. 24, No. 1, March 1975, pp 1–14.

J. I. Burgos, 'The Effectiveness of Public International Law', (Report on the Subject and Present State of the Matter), Simposio sobre aspectos de organización institucional interna para la integracion en países miembros de agrupaciones económicas; San José, Costa Rica, 22–27 September 1975.

F. Byabato, 'Institutional, Administrative and Infrastructural Framework of the EAC', Seminar on Administration of Multinational Integration in Latin America, Barbados, 24–28 May 1976.

B.W. Blake, 'The Caribbean Common Market – The Development from a Free Trade Area to a Common Market'. CARICOM and its effects on the Guyana Economy – Opportunities and Challenges', Text of a Lecture to the Management Development Course organised by the Booker Group of Companies, Georgetown, Guyana, 4–9 April 1976.

B.W Blake, 'Anti-polarisation and Distribution Mechanisms in CARICOM', Georgetown, Guyana, June 1976.

Caribbean Community Secretariat: 'Problems of the Lesser Developed Countries of the Commonwealth Caribbean', Twelfth Caribbean Regional Conference Commonwealth Parliamentary Association, Guyana, July 1976.

Caribbean Community Secretariat: 'The Caribbean Community – A Guide', Guyana, 1973.

Caribbean Community Secretariat: 'Progress in Caribbean Integration during 1973', Guyana, 1974.

Caribbean Community Secretariat: 'Treaty Establishing the Caribbean Community', Guyana, 1973.

Caribbean Community Secretariat: 'A Manual for the Administration of the Scheme for the Harmonisation of Fiscal Incentives to Industry in CARICOM Countries', Guyana, 1975.

Commonwealth Caribbean Regional Secretariat: 'CARIFTA and the New Caribbean', Guyana, 1971.

Commonwealth Caribbean Regional Secretariat: 'From CARIFTA to Caribbean Community', Guyana, *1972*.

Commonwealth Caribbean Regional Secretariat: 'Regional Co-operation in Education: The Caribbean Examinations Council Comes into Being', Guyana, 1972.

Commonwealth Caribbean Regional Secretariat: 'Agreement on a Technical Assistance Programme', Guyana, 1970.

A.Z Castedo, 'Administration of the Agreements of Industrial Complementation of ALALC', Seminar on Administration of Multinational Integration in Latin America, Barbados, 24-28 May 1976.

M Casanova, 'Institutional Aspects of Problems Related to the Processes of Integration: Interaction Between National and Multinational Sectors', Seminar on Administration of Multinational Integration in Latin America, Barbados, 24-28 May 1976.

W.G Demas, 'Change and Renewal in the Caribbean', Barbados, CCC Publishing House, 1975.

W G Demas, 'West Indian Nationhood and Caribbean Integration', Barbados, CCC Publishing House, 1974.

W.G Demas, 'Some Thoughts on the Caribbean Community', Caribbean Community Secretariat, Guyana, 1974.

H.H Godoy, 'Public Administration and Multinational Integration', Seminar on Administration of Multinational Integration in Latin America, Barbados, 24–28 May 1976.

Information Division, E A Community: 'The East African Community – A Handbook', 1972.

INTAL: 'The Methods for Settling Conflicts and Ensuring the Enforcement of the Law in the Processes of Economic Integration or Co-operation', Seminar on Administration of Multinational Integration in Latin America, Barbados, 24-28 May 1976.

E Jones, 'Tendencies and Change in Caribbean Administrative Systems', *Social and Economic Studies*, Col. 24, No. 2, June 1975, pp 239–256.

L. L De Kubes 'The Administration of the First Sectorial Programme of the Metal-Mechanics Industry in the Andean Group', Seminar on Administration of Multinational Integration in Latin America, Barbados, 24–28 May 1976.

A Linares 'Synthesis of the Sub-Regional Processes of the Integration of Latin America and the Principal Characteristics of their Financial Institutions', Seminar on Administration of Multinational Integration in Latin America, Barbados, 24–28 May 1976.

A. McIntyre 'Recent Developments in CARICOM', Speech to the St Lucia Chamber of Commerce, St Lucia, 12 November 1975.

A McIntyre 'CARICOM To-day', Speech to the Top Executive Convention organised by Caribbean Management Consultants, Trinidad, 15 January 1976.

McIntyre, A: 'Evolution of the Process of Integration in the Caribbean and the Current Situation and Perspectives of CARICOM', Statement to the IBRD; Washington, June 1976.

A McIntyre Statement at Sixth Annual Meeting of Board of Governors of Caribbean Development Bank. Basseterre, St Kitts, 12–13 May 1976.

Mills, G E. (Ed.): 'Problems of Administrative Change in the Commonwealth Caribbean', *Social and Economic Studies*, Special number, Vol. 19, March 1970, ISER Jamaica.

G E Mills 'Issues of Public Policy and Public Administration in the Commonwealth Caribbean', *Social and Economic Studies*, Vol. 23, No. 2, June 1974, ISER Jamaica.

A.F Mohr 'Statement on Economic Co-operation among Developing Countries', UNCTAD IV, Nairobi, May 1976.

E Noel 'How the Institutions of the European Community Function', Seminar on Administration of Multinational Integration in Latin America; Barbados, 24–28 May 1976.

A V Oviedo,: 'Administrative Problems in the Solution of Controversies in the Andean Group', Seminar on Administration of Multinational Integration in Latin America, Barbados, 24–28 May 1976.

F.R Ramos 'The Relations Between Technical Secretariats and the National Integration Offices', Seminar on Administration of Multinational Integration in Latin America, Barbados, 24–28 May 1976.

S. S. Ramphal 'To care for CARICOM: The Need for an Ethos of Community'. Speech delivered at the Dinner held in his honour by the Common Market Council of Ministers, Montego Bay, 5 July 1975.

J Sancho 'How States Organise Internally in Matters of Integration for the Safeguard of their Respective National Interests', The National Preparation of the Community Decision, San Jose, Costa Rica, October 1974.

D Sidjanski 'The Role of Institutions in Regional Integration among Developing Countries: Current Problems of Economic Integration', UNCTAD, 1974.

D Sidjanski 'Comparative Study – National Decision-Making Processes and Regional Integration', UNCTAD, 9 September 1975.

UNCTAD: Seminar on the Institutional Framework of Economic Integration among Developing Countries.

[33]

Revisiting Chaguaramas
Institutional Development in
CARICOM since 1973

Duke Pollard

From the outset the founding fathers of the Caribbean Community determined that the Treaty of Chaguaramas, 1973, would have to be complemented by related legal instruments in order to achieve the objectives identified in Article 4 of the Treaty. In the submission of the present author who was privileged to participate in the elaboration of the relevant constituent instrument, the instrumentalities:

devised for the achievement of the Caribbean Common Market . . . (were) not exhaustively dealt with in the Treaty Establishing the Caribbean Community including the Common Market Annex. Several supplementary instruments had been elaborated and signed before July 4, 1973, and most of these have created binding relations in international law for the parties concerned. These instruments include the Georgetown Accord, the Agreement on the Harmonisation of Fiscal Incentives, the Agreement on Double Taxation, and the Agreement Establishing the Caribbean Investment Corporation. These Agreements were concluded either in anticipation of obligations to be assumed under the Common Market Annex or in fulfilment of various objectives of the Common Market.

Since that time, a multiplicity of legal instruments have been concluded by the member states of the Caribbean Community whose cumulative impact has been an impressive enlargement of the institutional arrangements of the regional integration movement, especially in the area of functional cooperation. These instruments include: the Agreement Establishing the Caribbean Examinations Council (CXC), the Agreement Establishing the Council of Legal Education (CLE), the Agreement Establishing the Caribbean Meteorological Organisation (CMO), the Agreement Establishing the Caribbean Agricultural Research and Development Institute (CARDI), the Agreement Establishing the Caribbean Regional Drug Testing Laboratory (CRDTL), the Agreement Establishing the West Indies Shipping Corporation (WISCO), the Agreement Establishing the Caribbean Food Corporation (CFC), the Agreement Establishing the Regime for CARICOM Enterprises (CER), the Agreement Establishing the Environmental Health Institute (CEHI), the Agreement Establishing the Caribbean Regional Centre for the Education and Training of Animal Health and Veterinary Public Health Assistants (REPAHA), the Agreement Establishing the Caribbean Disaster Emergency Response Agency (CDERA), the Agreement Establishing the CARICOM Foundation for Art and Culture, the Agreement for the Avoidance of Double Taxation and Prevention of Fiscal Evasion, the Agreement Establishing the Caribbean Investment Fund (CIF), the Agreement for the Establishment of the Assembly of Caribbean Community.

The record of achievement of the institutions established by the above mentioned instruments has been mixed with some depressing failures like the West Indies Shipping Corporation and the Caribbean Food Corporation, and some outstanding successes like the Council for Legal Education and the Caribbean Examinations Council.

Most of the institutions identified above are technical bodies designed to pool regional resources for the achievement of common objectives perceived to be required for enhancing the quality of life of the peoples of the Caribbean Community. Seen in this light, the Agreement for the Establishment of an Assembly of Caribbean Community Parliamentarians was a radical departure in terms of institutional profile and stated regional objectives. But the novelty of the concept and the calculated risk of political fall-out did not dissuade the Conference of Heads of Government from determining at its tenth meeting in Grenada in July 1989, that the Assembly should be established as a consultative and deliberative body for the deepening of the integration movement. The objectives of the Assembly set out in Article 4 of the Agreement are:

(a) to involve the people of the Community, through their representatives, in the process of consolidating and strengthening the community;

(b) to provide opportunities for involvement in the issues of the integration process by Members of Parliament in each Member State and Associate Member, in addition to those who now participate;

(c) to provide a forum for people of the Community to make their views known through their representatives;

(d) to provide more frequent contact in the monitoring of the policies of the Community;

(e) to provide enhanced opportunities for the co-ordination of the foreign policies of Member states;

(f) to promote greater understanding among Member States and Associate Members for the purpose of realising and safeguarding the ideals and principles of democratic governments in the Community and facilitating the economic and social advancements of their peoples;

(g) to encourage the adoption by the Governments of Member States of the Community of a common policy on economic, social, cultural, scientific and legal matters deliberated upon by the Assembly.

The functions of the Assembly are set out in Article 5 of the Agreement, which identifies the institution as 'a deliberative and consultative body for the discussion of policies, programmes and other matters falling within the scope of the Treaty.' The Assembly does not have any power to make determinations committing member states to obligations but may 'make recommendations to the Conference, the Council, Institutions, Associate Institutions and the Secretariat'. An extremely important limitation on the deliberative competence of the Assembly is to be found in paragraph 4 of Article 5, which forbids it

to discuss or adopt any resolution on any matter which is exclusively within the domestic jurisdiction of a Member State or Associate Member of the Community and any question whether any matter is within the competence of the Assembly for the purposes of this paragraph shall be decided by the Speaker of the Assembly.

Only time will tell whether the concept of domestic jurisdiction will be interpreted in a dynamic manner similar to the concept set out in the relevant provisions of the United Nations Charter.

Based on the objectives and functions of the Assembly, some of its detractors in the media have been quick to dismiss the institution as another talk shop, of marginal relevance to the critical developmental problems plaguing the region, and unlikely to do more than constitute an additional financial burden on the deprived peoples of the community. In the present submission, however, it is strange logic to question the relevance of the Assembly at a time when an issue of primordial concern is good governance – an important aspect of which is open debate on issues of importance to the general populace. One of the criticisms of policy makers of the region is their overwhelming concern with national issues and their diffidence in enlightening their populations about developments in the regional integration movement. These criticisms are likely to continue, since issues on the regional agenda are rarely seen to impact one way or another on the outcome of the electoral process with which decision makers are quintessentially concerned. In the premises, the Assembly must be perceived as remedying this inadequacy in the regional integration process by involving the representatives of the people of both government and opposition in regional issues of importance.

Disparaging perceptions of the Assembly are, no doubt, influenced by the competence of the European Parliament, which has an important element of democratic accountability within the legislative and executive system of the European which has been enhanced by the holding of direct elections to this body. The European Parliament enjoys wide advisory powers and many provisions of the EEC Treaty require it to be consulted on draft legislation prepared by the Commission before consideration and adoption by the Council. Most importantly, the European Parliament can oblige the entire Commission to resign by approving a motion of censure (Article 144). Finally, the European Parliament can challenge the legality of actions by the Community institutions before the European Court of Justice. As yet, however, our Assembly is a fledgling institution whose first session is yet to be convened at the end of May1997 and, consequently, public perceptions of its relevance or usefulness are still an issue for future resolution.

Unlike the Assembly, whose establishment was initiated by the Prime Minister of Barbados, the Charter of Civil Society was conceived by the West Indian Commission which perceived it as contributing to good governance in the region and recommended its elaboration and adoption by the member states of the Community. Consequently, the Conference of Heads of Government, at their special meeting held in Port of Spain in October 1992, adopted the recommendation of the West Indian Commission. In their determination, the Conference agreed that the Charter

would deal *inter alia* with matters such as free press, a fair and open democratic process, the effective functioning of the parliamentary system, morality in public affairs, respect for fundamental civil, political, economic, social and cultural rights, the rights of women and children, respect for religious diversity, greater accountability and transparency in governance.

Since that time, the draft Charter has been subjected to several revisions based in part on submissions made by participants in some national consultations on the draft. It is proposed that the Conference of Heads of Government will formally adopt the Charter at their forthcoming meeting in Bridgetown during

July 1996. The Charter has 28 Articles encompassing, among others, the areas identified in the guidelines established by the Conference mentioned above.

In the present submission, the underlying theme of the Charter provisions is provided in paragraph 1, Article 1, which clearly establishes that the fundamental rights and freedoms of the individual are 'subject to respect for the rights and freedoms of others and for the public interest'. This qualification should operate to restore some balance to the human rights activists' seemingly exclusive preoccupation with the rights of the individual completely oblivious to the correlative obligation which the enjoyment of such rights impose. In their ordinary signification, rights are legal entitlements enforceable by tribunals of competent jurisdiction and do not exist in *vacuo*. In the submission of some eminent jurists, the enjoyment of a right is normally a function of the recognition of a pre-existing obligation corresponding to such a right. And it is important that the Charter of Civil Society, by ineluctable inference, recognises this axiomatic juxtaposition of rights and obligations subsisting together.

Not unlike the Assembly, the Charter has its fair share of detractors. One general criticism of the Charter is that it breaks no new ground and merely repeats much of what has been enunciated by various human rights instruments elaborated by one or another organisation within the United Nations System. Further, it is argued that the Charter must aspire to nothing more than a motley compendium of pious platitudes, given the absence of any binding commitment on the part of its signatories, and the absence of any credible monitoring mechanism and enforcement measures to secure compliance with its prescriptions. In the present submission, these criticisms are either uninformed, misconceived, or both. In the first place, it is simplistic to assume that compliance with moral or ethical prescriptions is necessarily a function of an effective sanctioning process. Men were not all created in Hobbes' image requiring social intercourse, inevitably, to be nasty, brutish and short. Indeed, man's inherent rationality leans towards the observance of norms of conduct intuitively or experientially perceived to inure to the general good. In the premises, the Charter, once adopted by the Conference, will constitute a moral commitment to observe its prescriptions, prescriptions which, over time, will be internalised by policy makers and constitute a standard of conduct to which they will adhere in performance of their functions.

The Agreement Establishing the Caribbean Court of Appeal is the last of a trilogy of instruments which the Conference of Heads of Government may be required to address at their forthcoming Meeting in July 1996. It was as early as 1988 that the Heads of Government had agreed to establish a

Caribbean Court of Appeal with appellate jurisdiction similar to that of the Judicial Committee of the Privy Council. Subsequently, the Standing Committee of Ministers Responsible for Legal Affairs approved a draft intergovernmental agreement establishing the Court. At its special meeting mentioned above, the Conference of Heads of Government took note of the recommendation of the West Indian Commission for the establishment of a CARICOM Supreme Court with original jurisdiction in respect of matters arising under the Treaty of Chaguaramas. Perusal of Article X of the Agreement Establishing the Caribbean Supreme Court does appear to confirm that the Court will replace the appellate jurisdiction of the Judicial Committee of the Privy Council. And, here again, there appears to be no regional consensus about the need to replace the Privy Council.

Detractors of the proposed Caribbean Supreme Court express scepticism about the willingness and readiness of the regional governments to provide the funding necessary for the Court to perform its functions effectively. Concern has also been expressed about the manner of appointing the President of the Court, that is, by

unanimous vote of the Heads of Government of the Contracting Parties after such consultations with such persons or bodies of persons or organisations, and in such manner as the Heads of Government of the Contracting Parties may deem fit, including consultations with the Heads of the Judiciary and other members of the legal profession in the Member States of the Caribbean Community. (Article IV (5)).

Other judges of the Court are to be appointed by majority vote of all the members of the Regional Judicial Service Commission. Article VIII, which addresses the tenure of office of judges, appears to accord them the required degree of security from political interference in the performance of their duties. Earlier drafts of the Agreement had provided for a reserve fund to secure the salaries of judges, but this provision disappeared from the final text which requires the contributions of the contracting parties to the expenses of the Court to be a charge(s) on their consolidated funds or other public revenues.

Despite the provisions of the Agreement concerning the conditions of service and tenure of judges of the Court, and which appear to insulate them from undue political influence, there persists in various quarters of the region a nagging apprehension that abolition of appeals to the Judicial Committee of the Privy Council would, in some measure, compromise the right of the individual to a fair hearing in the tribunal of ultimate resort. The initiative to establish a Caribbean Supreme Court should not be perceived as grounded in insular chauvinism, and harbouring discarded vestiges of an outworn anti-colonial sentiment. Indeed, recent judicial determinations of the Privy Council would appear to underscore a crying need for a more indigenous jurisprudence, albeit rooted in the common law but having constituent norms adapted to their environment of control.

Norms, to be controlling, must reflect the essential ethos of a people, their collective conscience, no less than their collective consciousness of moral prescriptions of what constitutes right or wrong conduct. All of which must be viewed as social imperatives defining, in the ultimate analysis, the Caribbean reality which both prescribes, and is a function of, generally accepted standards of conduct. Assuming the validity of the foregoing submissions and the existence of an ethos operating to define our Caribbean reality, then repatriation of the Court of last resort would appear to be an axiomatic requirement of good governance in the region. But, in all of this, the issue failing to be resolved is: Is there a Caribbean social reality reflective of a regional ethos collectively shared by peoples of the area? Indeed, the decision to repatriate or not to repatriate the Court of last resort will effectively determine the issue, given that the relevant determination must be, in the final analysis, one that is politically inclusive.

In the present submission, the case for the Caribbean Supreme Court must be based on the need for a regional Court of last resort to apply laws incorporating a collective regional ethos, reflecting the moral imperatives of the Caribbean social reality, and amenable to interpretation by judges who would have internalised the values informing the content of that social reality. And advocacy of such a position must not be construed as an uncharitable appraisal of the legal luminaries gracing the chambers of the Judicial Committee of the Privy Council. Suffice it to say, however, that judicial determinations intended to have validity for a social reality far removed from Westminster in time and space must fall somewhat ineptly from the lips of their authors.

Note

This paper was published in *CARICOM Perspective*, No. 67, June 1997.

[34]

Progress Report of The Independent West Indian Commission

Shridath Ramphal

As promised in its initial statement 'Let All Ideas Contend', the Independent West Indian Commission has published a Progress Report at the halfway point in its work. The final report of the Commission is not due until mid-1992 as requested by CARICOM Heads of Government; but the Commission believes it important to keep Caribbean publics, as well as governments, informed of its progress and particularly, of the nature and out turn of its wide ranging public consultations.

The Commission emphasises that the report is not a draft of its final report but an interim report on progress. While keeping its options open in terms of its final recommendations, the commission's Progress Report identifies the themes, concerns and issues which have dominated its consultations and points some directions for policy and structural changes in furthering Caribbean integration.

The Commission highlights inadequacies in the integration process and warns that it is already evident that 'the West Indies cannot afford the luxury of marking time, mistaking it for progress'.

Warning that 'regionalism is not on its own a panacea for the region's problems', the Commission emphasises that CARICOM itself 'stands or falls' on the degree to which it 'contributes to an improvement in the lives of people'.

In this context, the Commission's work has covered a wide range of civil, political, economic, social and cultural matters, including more open government, participation in governance beyond the ballot box and increased opportunities for social and economic achievement for the average West Indian.

The Commission emphasises the need to involve the younger generation more deeply in the process of development in every area and warns that if this is not done the best and more dynamic will join the West Indian Diaspora or increasingly reject the social and political order. It speaks out on the need for 'hassle-free' travel within CARICOM, on the problems of currency distortions within the community, about disquiet over declining standards in primary and secondary education in many places, of deteriorating health care and growing unemployment.

The Commission especially notes the need to correct the disadvantaged position of women in the region. It directs attention to the need for the integration process to be seen to be addressing these issues, no less than to the need for putting in place the machinery necessary to ensure the development of economic integration.

The Commission also signals the need for the region to look beyond structures of economic integration to the ethical basis of 'community' in the Caribbean, including such matters as free elections, the functioning of the parliamentary system and the need to root out corruption in public life, particularly, that deriving from the illicit drug trade.

The Progress Report highlights the 'virtual absence of effective machinery for implementation of regional decisions as a major impediment to the process of the integration movement'. It gives credit to regional government for the decisions that have been taken; but deplores the record of unfulfilled expectations and broken promises. It points to the need for 'effective implementation machinery' as a precondition of progress towards Caribbean integration.

The report also underscores the sense of alienation resulting from impediments to free movement of West Indians through the region and the implications of massive cultural penetration from North American television. The Commission calls for a positive response to this challenge in terms of a more purposeful approach to enlarged information flows within the region, including a major increase in Caribbean programming – using communications technology – along the lines already begun with CANA's 'Caribbean Today', Caribbean Broadcasting Union's 'Carib Scope' and 'Carib Vision' and now 'Caribbean Eye'. The Commission promises that its final report will deal with such related matters as the democratisation of state-owned media in the region and instruments of people participation in the process of governance.

Looking to the economic environment of the region, the Commission's Progress Report concludes that 'Caribbean nations have so far failed in their ambition to steer the course of their economic fortunes', and calls for joint regional efforts to tackle vital issues of economic development and reduction of unemployment.

The Commission concluded that the record of success in many areas of economic endeavour on a country by country basis was not encouraging. The Commissioners contended that the Caribbean would have 'much brighter prospects if we design adjustment programmes jointly for the Caribbean, collaborate in negotiations with the international financial institutions, and introduce a Caribbean monetary system with stable currencies'. It sees this as especially relevant to the prevailing acute external debt payment problems of some countries of the region.

The Progress Report highlights the impact of external factors on the region with particular emphasis on the threat to bananas in the context of the European Single Market in 1992. It draws attention to the wide range of studies already commissioned which will influence the final report.

In its Progress Report the Commission gives special attention to the question of the 'deepening' of CARICOM among its current membership and the 'widening' of the Community beyond the English-speaking countries of the Caribbean Basin. The Commission is convinced that the region must both deepen the process of integration to which it has set its hand, and reach out to a wider Caribbean at appropriate levels of cooperation'. It is a dual track approach which the Commission believes CARICOM can pursue, 'confident of both our identity and our capacities, and ready to take a lead in the creation of a real Community of the entire Caribbean'. The Report projects circles of association that start with the intimate West Indian non-English speaking islands of the Caribbean, and a still larger circle of closer relations with countries of the Caribbean Basin that includes territories of the South and Central American littoral.

The Commission's Progress Report concludes with a call for 'Immediate Action' in a cluster of six areas which the Commission feels demand such urgent attention that a response should not be postponed until after its Final Report in 1992. They relate to:

(1) hassle-free travel by West Indians within the CARICOM region with simplified procedures including the use of ID cards; also the positive promotion of Exchange Visits within the region especially involving high school students;

(2) a start with the free movement of CARICOM nationals within the community beginning with 'all Graduates of the University of the West

Indies and other recognised institutions' and 'of duly accredited media workers'. 'Communications', the Commission emphasises, 'is essential to community'; it believes that 'the right of West Indian journalists to be assigned anywhere within the region will significantly enlarge the capacity to improve communications and advance the realisation of the aims of the Community;

(3) the first steps towards a common Caribbean currency. The Commission proposes a phased approach to a common currency. It sets out specific proposals for beginning the process with the new Caribbean dollar operating alongside existing currencies;

(4) action to establish a Caribbean investment fund on the basis of proposals already developed by the Commonwealth Secretariat at the instance of CARICOM. It envisages an investment fund of a minimum of US$50 million raised on external capital markets or investment in new and existing businesses throughout the region immediate action to implement agreements already reached on creating the CARICOM Single Market;

(6) special measures for mobilising the region's political and technical re- sources for international negotiations in relation to a swiftly changing external environment with individual Heads of Government being as- signed 'Portfolio responsibilities for specific negotiations' such as those involving, for instance, the survival issues of environment and develop- ment which will be discussed at the 1992 United Nations Earth Summit in Rio de Janeiro.

Visits to all 13 CARICOM countries – greatly facilitated by the regional airlines BWIA and LIAT –have been made by the Commission. Throughout the Progress Report, the Commission refers to the encouragement it received from the West Indian people in all walks of life, including those encountered during the Commission's first visit to the West Indian Diaspora in Britain.

Noting with understanding the initial scepticism of West Indian publics in relation to the Commission's assignment, the Progress Report, nevertheless, records how the process of consultation has enlarged hopes 'for new energies flowing from the Commission's efforts, for more effective ways of regional co-operation and for more workable regional arrangements that reflect the reality of a single Community'.

The Commission emphasises that its Progress Report is directed to both people and governments. It has been widely released in the region and formally presented by the Chairman of the Commission to CARICOM Heads of Government at the St Kitts and Nevis Summit on July 2, 1991.

Reference

1.   The West Indian Commission Occasional Paper No. 3, 'To Be a Canoe', a presentation by the Chairman of the West Indian Commission Sir Shridath Ramphal to the Twelfth Meeting of the Conference of Heads of Government of the Caribbean Community, Basseterre, July 2, 1991.

[35]

More Shadow than Substance

Peter   Wickham

This paper attempts to chronicle the main activities of the Independent West Indian Commission (WIC), with emphasis on its report, Time for Action. The focus is predominately placed on the recommendations that have a political import, and should not be seen as an attempt to discuss the entire WIC report. The paper places Time for Action in the context of the mandate of the WIC since this has implications for the eventual outcome. Important also is the discussion on the reception of the WIC report at the levels of the leadership and people of the region, which is also chronicled, as far as was possible.

The Independent West Indian Commission can be seen as being comparable only to the Moyne Commission in importance. It commanded the attention of Caribbean people between 1989 and 1992, and culminated in a report which was intended to be the blueprint for the region for the next few decades. The magnitude of this report, and indeed the WIC itself, invokes closer scrutiny. Here, attention will be paid to significant events surrounding the WIC, but especially to the report *Time for Action*, and reactions to its publication. The intention is to highlight deficiencies in the WIC report and suggest possible reasons for their occurrence. Thereafter the treatment of the WIC by the Governments and people of the Caribbean can be examined to assess the adequacy of the reaction that the report has received.

The identification of deficiencies in the report employs a multi-faceted approach, utilising foundation documents, the report itself and various assessments in newspapers, and scholarly comments. The reactions are assembled in much the same way, but include the judgement of the Heads of Government. The examination of the report proceeds by isolating important 'Political Recommendations' individually, and making a judgement on each area. This allows for an analysis of each recommendation's value or lack thereof.

The reactions to the WIC, broken down to the levels of Government and the people, form the final part of this paper. Here, the reactions are not surprising especially in the case of Government. These reactions largely reflect disappointment and a lack of support for the proposals. The paper however stops short of suggesting alternatives open to the region to achieve the unfulfilled objectives of the WIC. While this is an important area of investigation, certainly it would be better treated in a separate discourse.

The West Indian Commission (WIC) arose out of a paper presented by the Prime Minister of Trinidad and Tobago Hon Arthur N. R. Robinson, to the tenth conference of the Caribbean Community and Common Market in July 1989. The paper entitled 'The West Indies Beyond 1992', articulated the potential dilemma of the West Indies. This is that the trends of world interdependence place the small Caribbean islands in the precarious position 'of becoming a backwater, separated from the main current of human advance into the twenty-first century'. The paper noted changes occurring in Europe and the proposal for the North American Free Trade Area (NAFTA) as factors urging an evaluation of :

How best to bring about real betterment in the condition of life, to achieve their full potential . . . and to improve their region's place in the community of nations.

The paper concluded by proposing that the CARICOM Heads of Government establish the West Indian Commission to ascertain from the people of the West Indies their desires, and to help them prepare for the twenty-first century. The Robinson paper was adopted and embodied in the Grand Anse Declaration. The Commission was formed under the chairmanship of Sir Shridath Ramphal and given an extensive mandate in relation to regional integration. This mandate reproduced at Appendix IV shows that in addition to the substantial mandate, the Heads sought to extend the WIC's mandate to include issues which arose during the WIC's existence.

The instructions given to the WIC were generally to conduct consultation among the Caribbean people and recommend a way forward for the region in relation to Caribbean integration and general development. Important in the mandate is the expectation that the Commission should formulate proposals 'for advancing the goals of the Treaty of Chaguaramas' giving the Commission's work a secure grounding within CARICOM. Furthermore, it was stated that efforts should be taken to improve CARICOM's public relations and where possible widen the institution. The internal operations of CARICOM as an institution were also to be considered while fully appreciating the Mills report on this matter.

Social Class

The Commission of 15 was chosen to represent a broad cross section of eminent Caribbean personalities in many areas and was headquartered in Barbados. The eminence of this body was apt to be problematic since it predisposed the WIC towards particular norms identifiable with the social class to which they belong. Edwin Jones identifies this as an ongoing predicament the Caribbean Commission of Enquiry faces.

So long as the Commissioners originate from a particular class this will be reflected in any number of recommendations that they make. This trend can be traced back to the Mordecai Sugar Commission of 1966 (Jamaica), where the highly academic team of Commissioners contradicted themselves by identifying many socio-societal problems within the Jamaican sugar industry, but at the same time recommending a technocratic-bureaucratic problem solving strategy. Certainly this theory can be extended to other inherent biases of the WIC. Reference is made here to the average generation, gender and educational background of the Commissioners. The report of the WIC, composed of people of similar background and predisposition can be expected to possess similar trends, a feature which would act to severely restrict its usefulness.

In an effort to ensure the WIC was financially independent of the Caribbean Governments, funding was sought from extra-regional sources. As envisaged in the *Grand Anse Declaration*, the Commission carried out its work by visiting each country and consulting with 'the Governments, political parties, trade unions, the private sector, religious bodies, professional groups, academics [*and*] the average West Indian'. Also included were consultations in the West Indian Diaspora, namely West Indian communities in the UK, Canada, and the USA.

Public opinion at the launch of the WIC did not appear to deem it an exercise which would yield any significant results. Worse still, some sections of the West Indian Community saw it as merely another opportunity for eminent persons to travel and gain whatever benefits were to be derived. There was also a feeling, which was tantamount to the view that the Commissioners held fixed positions on specific issues, positions that were not going to be influenced by the hearings.

However the activities surrounding the Commission's launch substantially modified this cynicism, and West Indians began to adopt a slightly more anticipatory attitude, in the hope that some change would come as a result of the consultations. This was evident by the attendance at the Commission hearings which according to the WIC, included 'people of all ages and from all walks of life'. . . . . These persons spoke freely on issues directly related to Caribbean integration. Indeed, the Commission noted that there was hardly 'any theme or issue, concern or problem, that was not aired'. So intense and honest were discussions that it appeared as though the Commission was being viewed as a 'court of last resort to which . . . [*people*] . . . felt able to bring their grievances and frustrations'. The consultative process was also helped by the preparation of many papers in related subjects by eminent persons.

The expectations that were being aroused in the minds of people were further stimulated by the publication of the Progress Report of the West Indian Commission immediately upon completion of their first round of deliberations. This document was published so soon after consultations were completed, that it is unlikely that it could have benefited very much from the opinions gathered in the consultations. The report was nevertheless a concise discussion of many pertinent issues and helped stimulate public interest in the work of the Commission.

The strength of the Progress Report lay in its succinct identification of thirteen critical areas in which CARICOM has made agreements and failed at implementation. This highlighted the serious nature of the implementation problem within CARICOM, an issue the WIC would later address. The report then sought to identify six areas where immediate action was required to provide the necessary 'morale boost to the spirit of regionalism.' These recommendations concerned action in the general areas of:

a)   Travelling in the region
b)   Free movement of skills
c)   Towards a Common Currency
d)   Enlarging investment
e)   Creating the CARICOM Single Market
f)   Mobilisation for international negotiations.

In each area, the WIC outlined a series of proposals which they believed could be 'agreed upon without difficulty or delay and their adoption in word and deed would advance the goals of the Treaty of Chaguaramas'. The interim report was well received by the West Indian leadership and population because of its straightforward approach in dealing with the issue at hand. In keeping with this pattern of forthrightness the final report would now be expected to surpass this interim one.

The final report of the WIC represents a well-written and compiled document, which gives the reader more than just a judgement on the future of the regional integration movement. The report gives a useful history of the movement, reviews CARICOM, and looks at various activities taking place, and organisations seeking the furtherance of Caribbean integration. There is also an element of completeness to it by the inclusion of appendices which supply relevant documentation. The only presentational shortcoming was the fact that the voluminous 592-page publication appears intimidating to all but the most enthusiastic reader. This problem was skilfully overcome by the simultaneous publication of a summary document which highlighted and isolated the major issues for the reader requiring a more concise document.

The WIC at various points in the report identified the circumstances which made their work necessary. These circumstances could be said to lie within the general categories of the increasing pressure of external events in the world economy, and the need to address urgent internal needs of the Caribbean. These conditions necessitated the WIC, and as a result were the issues which the WIC report ultimately hoped to address. This aspect of their work, which is largely descriptive, was well articulated at various points throughout the document.

The report suggests that the problems which the WIC sought to address had their solution in the regional integration movement. Hence the Commission appeared to propose integration as a panacea for all the social, political and economic ills of the region – an assumption which was only partially justified. This created a perceived parameter within which the WIC's consultations took place, and the consultations were, hence, influenced by the intrinsic inclination of the WIC towards promoting integration. The WIC's work therefore appeared more like a Caribbean Integration Public Relations crusade throughout the region, rather than an investigative exercise. It is therefore not surprising that in the publication of the report, the ‘way forward’ was anchored securely within a framework of closer cooperation. While this assumption is not without merit, the importance of a neutral commission was violated here. The commissioners were all known to be sympathetic to Caribbean integration and surely this preference must dilute the credibility of the exercise.

As a result of this assumption, there was an intense focus on CARICOM, since this organisation was seen as the key to the advancement of the regional integration movement. There was the implicit assumption that CARICOM was the proper forum within which regional integration initiatives should be focused. While the WIC was careful to point out that they were not constrained in their deliberations by any concept of CARICOM, their predisposition to it can be inferred by an approach which assumed CARICOM would be the basis of future initiatives. Moreover, the WIC did not find it necessary to outline any justifications for CARICOM's centrality in this issue, and why it should not be dissolved altogether, or replaced by a more suitable institution.

CARICOM in the Shadow

This fondness for CARICOM can be partially attributed to the fact that this 1973 institution would have emerged during a period when many of the commissioners were able to contribute directly to its formation. Certainly, in at least one instance, a commissioner, acting in another capacity, was a catalyst to the formation of CARICOM. It would therefore have been unlikely that the WIC would recommend anything detrimental to CARICOM, as they know it.

In relation to conclusions of the WIC, it was noted that the advancement of Caribbean integration was for the most part being retarded by both the slow process by which CARICOM came to decisions, and thereafter, the inability of CARICOM to implement that which it has decided. The WIC postulated that this has led to a situation where people perceived that CARICOM leaders are good at rhetoric as an end in itself but not meant to be taken seriously. They are well versed in making decisions which stay on paper.

This is a perception which I agree was not 'misguided'. This assertion is supported both in the WIC's review of CARICOM and the critique of CARICOM discussed above. Here the experience with the CET, deadlines for which were set and broken on two separate occasions, and the CMCF for which a reintroduction date was later ignored, and, finally the experience with the CER which suffered a fate similar to the CET all served to illustrate this point.

The WIC suggested that this was partially due to the fact that there was no implementation medium within CARICOM, a role that the CARICOM Secretariat and the Secretary General were neither intended nor equipped to perform. Thus, the report noted, with reference to T.S. Elliot:

between the idea and the reality, between the motion and the action, between the emotion and the response – falls the shadow.

This is a shadow dually referred to by the WIC as the inertia of regional commitment overtaken by national preoccupation which makes implementation unreliable within CARICOM. This is a postulation which can hardly be contradicted. Certainly, CARICOM has made some lofty commitments, such as those in the Grand Anse Declaration which have later been reneged upon.

While this is the case, the solution to the problem proposed by the WIC is highly questionable. They recommended putting in place, a permanent 'CARICOM Commission'. This new body was to supplement the machinery of CARICOM, concerning itself essentially with the implementation of 'decisions taken by [*the*] CARICOM Heads of Government under their authority'. The WIC proposed that this be a three-man Commission of 'persons with high-level public and political experience in the region'. Their mandate would be to 'initiate, mobilise, facilitate and secure action.' This machinery is without a doubt the 'bedrock' of the WIC proposals and is inextricably woven into their mosaic structure of unity. This body would fall just below the Council of Ministers, but above the Secretariat, Supreme Court and Assembly.

This proposal has met with some serious opposition. Of major concern to the Heads of Government must have been the cost of this new machinery since, these persons of such 'high-level public and political experience' come at a relatively high price. This high cost factor would seem sufficient to rule out the feasibility of the Commission, in a cash strapped CARICOM. To achieve this implementation, the WIC made no attempt to modify the present CARICOM machinery but, instead, supplemented it with a costly structure.

Apart from the cost and placement of the Commission, the question of how exactly the Commission was expected to implement its decisions is improperly addressed. The WIC envisages that the Commission would facilitate implementation of CARICOM decisions by a procedure outlined in their structures of unity discussion. This procedure basically upgrades the present status of CARICOM decisions to that of a 'Community Law' that the members agree to give 'effect to' upon their agreement to sign the Treaty of Chaguaramas.

Treaty Obligations

The actual mode of implementation of these decisions now given the status of Community Law, whether administrative or political, is to be embodied in the 'instruments of implementation' which the Commission draws up with the full consultation of the Heads. Failure to implement them after these instruments are drafted, would result in referral to the CARICOM Supreme Court which was also proposed. Upon consideration of the matter, the court could issue an 'implementation order'. Any further action forcing implementation would be taken by the Heads who could exercise the powers to 'suspend an area of treatment' or impose any other political sanction.

This exercise has merely recommended the upgrading of the decisions of CARICOM to the level of Community Law and superimposed two bodies to clarify and urge implementation. On the WIC's own admission: *'In the last resort CARICOM cannot prevail against a member state whose Government defies Community Law by reneging on a decision properly taken and basically breaching its treaty obligations.'*

This remark highlighted the fact that notwithstanding the new 'imposed' structure and commission geared towards the task of implementation, that power still ultimately rests with member states who may wish not to implement. The two proposed bodies will only act to clarify law and articulate instruments, the implementation of which is still left up to the member states. This is essentially no change over the present situation.

The WIC has sought to suggest that their proposal will work so long as there is a commitment on the part of the members to discharge their 'Treaty obligations in the utmost good faith', a commitment without which they assert the movement cannot proceed. This assertion ignores the fact that the Treaty of Chaguaramas mandates members to: 'take all appropriate measures . . . to ensure the carrying out of obligations arising out of [*the*] Treaty . . . [*and to abstain*] . . . from any measures which could jeopardise the attainment of the objectives of the Treaty.'

This is a similar 'good faith' assumption which has proven insufficient to ensure action by CARICOM presently. Therefore, while identifying the problem correctly, the WIC has not been able to advance the region towards a solution. The reason for this lies within a foundation principle they indicated would be guiding their proposals. This was that CARICOM should continue to be a 'community of sovereign states' and as such, any implementation would have to be discharged locally. To interfere with and force such implementation would tinker with the members sovereignty and would 'strain the foundation [*of sovereignty*] by trying to guard against a breach of treaty obligations', such being to them an unworthy exercise.

This observation raises one of the fundamental misunderstandings that the WIC sought to encourage. This concerns sovereignty and the division thereof. The WIC falsely identified sovereignty as a commodity which: (a) the maintenance of it is indispensable to Caribbean islands' development; and (b) can be maintained and shared at the same time.

Thus, the Community of Sovereign States is proposed as a community with which the members, by Treaty, agree to the pooling of certain of their sovereignties and to exercising them collectively in very specific aspects. This sharing, they assert, is preferable to a total transfer of sovereignty such as happens in a federation, a structure which they are not proposing.

The absurdity of this postulation unfolds further as we recall that even in specific areas when sovereignty is shared, still one cannot trespass on the individual state's sovereignty which is seen as the 'foundation' of the Community. The WIC has herein identified the indivisible nature of sovereignty but at the same time tried to suggest that some patchwork can take place by declaratory pronouncements.

It is illogical that the sovereignty which the WIC conceded is 'less than substantial', is given this level of importance within CARICOM, when it is this very commodity (sovereignty) which makes a mockery of attempts at implementation of community decisions and progress. Furthermore, if members are to agree to share this sovereignty within 'specific' areas which were identified, why then is the national sovereignty still seen as the 'foundation' of CARICOM. This is an admission that in the final analysis CARICOM will be subject to (or inferior to) the member states, a postulation which undermines the Treaty, and impacts on any institutions derived therefrom, such as the Commission, the Charter of Civil Society, and, the CARICOM Supreme Court.

The WIC gave no discussion to the concept of a single CARICOM governmental structure into which all these flagging individual sovereignties could be thrown, since that resembled a federation – a concept that was ruled out from the start. This would have addressed the implementation problem in a way which is concrete and not contradictory. The WIC did not go this road since they believed that at present 'the political climate for it does not exist, either at the level of Governments or people'. This conclusion was based on consultations with people who raised the idea from time to time but were reminded that the WIC was 'not advancing proposals along these lines'. This killed the idea of a full political union at the inception as regards the WIC's consultations. Interestingly enough this was not a limit placed on the WIC by their terms of reference, therefore if the idea came up from among the people, it should have been allowed to flourish for what it was worth. It would appear however that the idea of full political union was not 'politically correct' in the Commissioners' eyes and was discouraged. This serves to validate the point that the WIC went into consultations with fixed ideas on a number of issues which would have made their recommendations predetermined. What they recommended could only vary within fixed outer limits which were either expressly or implicitly agreed among the members of the WIC. This invalidates their suggestion that their recommendations were not limited in any way by the existing structures or preconceptions, and that made them qualitatively different from previous reviews.

The WIC proposals to establish the CARICOM Commission amounts to an admission of defeat. The WIC correctly identified the problem but failed in providing a solution. If, as it was stated, the problem within CARICOM was implementation, it was incumbent for the WIC to lay the blame squarely for that in the quarters of the Heads of Government. They needed to suggest that it was Government insularity that was responsible for the state of inertia within CARICOM. Instead, the WIC put the matter to the Heads in so diplomatic a fashion, they were convinced that a new institution could overcome their lack of sincerity to the tenets of CARICOM. Certainly, the degree of freedom given to the WIC enabled them to advise the Heads that CARICOM could only properly function if they were committed to it. Anything short of total commitment would facilitate a continuance of the problem they have identified. This cannot be overcome by a Commission, of either a temporary or permanent nature, but by a genuine commitment of the individual Governments.

It should be explained that assumptions identified above were not so much stated assumptions but existed, moreso, because of the comparability of the members of the WIC. It was noticeable that the WIC reflected an under-representation of *women* and *young* people. Hence, the entire WIC would have had some experiences under the federation of 1958, and their recommendations would have been framed against this background. This is indeed unfortunate since the work of the WIC would better impact on future generations who would care little for the fogies of the past.

The Integration Process

In addition, the members of the WIC all originated from a similar background. They can all be considered middle class, and have all been educated to a tertiary level, and all this combined to fix the opinions and perceptions of the WIC in a typically conservative middle class way.

The recommendations relating to the Council of Ministers essentially reaffirms the Treaty of Chaguaramas. The WIC recommendations in this regard are noteworthy since they quite rightly indicated the need for a minister with responsibility for CARICOM affairs. This clearly identifies the person in member states with whom CARICOM needs to relate. The CARICOM minister is a key element in the WIC's proposals, since he has a specific role on the Council and in relation to the furtherance of the integration process. This is one proposal requiring local action which can be expected in the fullness of time within an institution such as CARICOM.

The construction of the 'CARICOM Structures of Unity' is also a cause for some concern. The Structures of Unity places some institutions in positions that contradict their importance or lack thereof and the position given to this Commission demonstrates this. The new Commission was expected to ensure implementation of Heads of Government decisions, yet this body is itself subservient to the Heads of Government. Furthermore, the body to which the Commission prefers to have implementation orders issued, the CARICOM Supreme Court is even lower on the totem pole. This creates a peculiar situation where 'underlings' would be expected to exercise influence over their superiors.

In relation to the CARICOM Assembly, the placement is consistent with the role that this body is expected to play. It is given prominence on the level of other associate institutions such as the CDB and the UWI. This reinforces the point that the Assembly will essentially be a discussion forum which will have very little impact on, or influence over the Heads of Government.

The inclusion and primacy of the CARICOM Charter of Civil Society in the WIC report under the chairmanship of Sir Shridath Ramphal can only be described as a curious irony. The proposal laments the widespread 'disaffection with governance' in the region and the 'increasing incidence of corruption in public life and the particular contribution of the illicit drug trade to this process.' As a result the WIC called for the establishment of a 'normative structure of the Community through which member countries commit themselves to respect for the fundamental elements of civil society like free elections and fundamental systems of democratic governance, and social and economic justice.'

This would set an important normative framework against which accepted standards of behaviour could be measured. It is instructive that the Charter is given a high placement in the Structure of Unity. This reflects the prominence and importance of the norm which they are seeking to establish. Thus every action emerging from within CARICOM could be expected to be in furtherance of this deal.

The NGO review has however noted that this apparent prominence is at direct variance with the WIC's chosen developmental basis, which is itself responsible for much of the irregularity which needs to be addressed. It is suggested that due to the closer inter relationship of the social and political facets of integration, the attempt to move the civil society into paramountcy with an incompatible developmental orientation makes the entire concept a mere statement with little meaning. It would be tempting to suggest that the middle class bias of the WIC is responsible for this peculiarity, causing the WIC to want to acknowledge the importance of this group for political reasons, but not necessarily empower it in terms of its recommendations.

However, full credit needs to be given to the WIC for having identified the importance of a social pillar at all. This brings the work of the WIC to a level where people can relate to it and at a level which the movement must increasingly operate. It is a level not usually identified as important and this makes the movement less politically acceptable.

The WIC also gave some exposure to the social pillar in other areas of the report. The inclusion of the NGOs in the proposal for the Assembly of Caribbean Parliamentarians is another such. This refreshing disposition was also manifested in the importance the WIC attached to ease of travel, and freedom of movement within the region, emphasising that personal contact was an important precursor to greater Caribbean integration. This represents an aspect of thought absent from the three previous reviews of CARICOM.

Realistically, the Charter is not dissimilar to the various conventions to which the individual CARICOM states are signatories. Certainly a recommitment is always welcome especially if it is given pride of place within the revised CARICOM structure. A substantial weakening however comes from the lack of enforceability which is a feature of the WIC's chosen structure. The Charter is thus relegated to the status of a declaratory instrument.

While the WIC sought to strengthen CARICOM they also proposed the establishment of the Association of Caribbean States. This was based upon their acceptance of the Mills Report, that the continued centralisation of CARICOM around a mere 15 per cent of the Caribbean population, 'is not only a travesty of Caribbean history . . . [but] . . . also a prescription for certain failure of such a Caribbean in an emergent 21st century'. The WIC therefore identified Caribbean integration as a means to an end and not an end in itself. This manifested itself elsewhere in the report where the WIC called for a greater articulation of CARICOM with the non-English speaking Caribbean, as well as other hemispheric groupings. This addresses the misconception that the English-speaking Caribbean has the potential to be a powerful bloc within itself. The WIC helped to place the movement in context in a way which can only be beneficial to the region.

The CARICOM Assembly of Parliamentarians is not an original idea of the WIC; instead it has its origins in a proposal of the Right Honourable L. Erskine Sandiford. It is anticipated that this Assembly would be 'a regional forum that can deliberate on Community matters'. This forum fills a void in CARICOM, giving it its own political apparatus to ventilate views, opinions and the like. It is however unfortunate that in borrowing the proposal from its original conceptualiser, the WIC did not take the opportunity to modify it and remove its regressive aspects. These deficiencies retard the political efficacy of the Assembly.

In relation to the former, the NGOs could have taken great comfort by the inclusion of some of their kind in the Assembly. Thus they proposed that the Assembly allow for NGO participation. This embraced the 'NGOs, the private sector, the labour movement, the academic community, [*and*] even representatives of the West Indian Diaspora'. The method by which these persons are to be chosen, is however in question. The WIC advocates a process of selection which is nominative among national parliamentarians firstly, and they hoped, among other social partners. In so recommending, the WIC missed the opportunity to create a truly *representative* forum with a democratic base secured within the people of the Caribbean who elected them. Instead they choose persons, nationally elected, and suggested that they be imposed upon the regional arena, thus utilising them in a capacity and for a purpose which was not intended.

This calls into question the democratic moorings of institutions such as the said Assembly and the Charter of Civil Society, and reflects yet another contradiction of the WIC proposals. A true democratic base for any regional institution would negate the provision of guaranteed seats for politicians or NGOs. Similar representation can be secured from social, and indeed all partners, by active participation of the electorate in elections to this assembly. Instead the WIC recommended what is akin to a Senatorial type selection which would inherently be biased in favour of the selectors' preferences.

The last point on the work of the assembly is less strong. It is predictable that an assembly within the WIC structure would not be a powerful body. As expected, the Assembly's role is envisaged to be deliberative. Thus what is proposed is essentially what CARICOM is accused of being presently, a *talk shop*. It can however be hoped that a ventilation of numerous views and opinions in a deliberative forum, initially, could lead to the evolution of a powerful organ in the future and this is reflected in the WIC report.

There is little more that can be said about the proposal, which reiterates the benefits of a CARICOM Supreme Court. However the WIC sought to add to this Court's responsibility the expectation that they would, 'interpret the Treaty of Chaguaramas, resolving disputes arising under it . . . declaring and enforcing Community Law, [*and*] interpreting the Charter of Civil Society.

These duties would be a logical consequence of the structures established. The Community Law aspect has already been discussed and its dubiousness identified. The declaratory nature of the Courts' judgements is however questionable in the sense that they offer a very biased concept of what law is all about. The court would be treading upon the sacred ground of sovereign-ties, an area it would need to avoid running afoul of. Like the Assembly, however, such a beginning may lead to some evolution of substantial and enforceable law in the future.

The WIC observed that the Mills report had the right idea when it criticised the unanimity rule. This feature could be blamed for the painfully slow movement of CARICOM. However, in an effort to resist the temptation to go full-scale into a majority rule, the WIC recommended that 'the unanimity rule [be] relaxed save for cases where it was considered essential'. This allows for an argument similar to that of a constitutional regime, where basic concepts and structures are held constant by virtue of unchangeable agreements except by consensus, while less significant matters lead the region along a path to closer integration.

Immediately upon publication, the WIC report was greeted with sharp criticism from almost every conceivable angle. This criticism took the form of personal attacks on the integrity and motives of the commissioners, as well as their recommendations for restructuring CARICOM and developmental bases used. Both the leaders of the Caribbean as well as the general population of the region joined in this onslaught.

In looking at the criticisms that the report received, it is important to place them in the context of the expectations of various groups. The leadership had outlined an extremely wide mandate for the commissioners. This was further widened after the second intersessional meeting in 1991 where the Heads added a consideration of the Mills report, the issue of remoteness, the need to foster greater public awareness of CARICOM and decision-making within the Community to the WIC list of issues to be examined. The addition of new issues as they arose, for instance, the application of the Dominican Republic for membership in CARICOM, made it appear that the Heads were throwing in any contentious issue which surfaced at the time at the Commission. This was, without doubt, a prescription for disappointment. The expectations of the region's people were not defined by a document. As the commissioners themselves noted, all sorts of issues were brought before them and the people actually believed that they were in a position to recommend solutions to make things better for them.

One of the first regional citizens to react to the report of the WIC was Tim Hector. Hector noted that the report was 'the most important document about the region issued in the last 50 years', and certainly 'a high-water mark of West Indian intellectual contribution to our own self-propelled development'. However, he took issue with the Commissioners due to their proposals in major areas, which he rejected outright. One such was the prominence given to the retention of sovereignty, and the rejection of any notion of a Caribbean state. He saw these as prerequisites for sustainable Caribbean development.

According to Hector, by rejecting any federal concept, the WIC was left with little room to manoeuvre and hence proposed a weak form of confederation doomed to failure. As a result of that, the Commissioners were restricting themselves to the traditional models, and consequently the WIC missed the opportunity of suggesting indigenous Caribbean models of Government.

The general consensus of a large section of the Caribbean population was far less elegantly conceived and expressed than Hector's opinion. People across the region accused the WIC of merely creating employment for themselves. Reference was being made to the proposal for the CARICOM Commission of three *'eminent'* persons to act as the implementing arm of CARICOM, a powerful body with security and financial trappings. People were generally disappointed because amid all of the cynicism that prevailed, they actually believed that the WIC was different, that they were being listened to, and the outcome would not be typical of other Commissions as they had come to know them.

Much less personal was the critique offered in the *Trinidad and Tobago Review* which criticised the WIC proposal not so much for its content but, because of the dubious feasibility of a Commission of that nature. The editorial noted that the WIC erred in assuming that these all-powerful Heads of State, who for 20 years had not been implementing their own decisions, would somehow be capable of devolving such responsibility to others.

This promotes the question of whether the WIC was unable to anticipate the rejection of their proposal in light of present economic, social and political conditions. Certainly they should have, since the WIC were all persons of considerable public experience. A major component of any proposals like theirs has to be the potential to gain acceptance. If this is absent, then the architects are obviously lost in a sea of theory, an inexcusable condition for commissioners of that calibre. By failing to propose a solution that the people and leaders would buy, the WIC did not achieve what should have been their prime objective.

The reaction of the various Governments in the region ranged from the ridiculous to the sublime. For example, regional issues, have been for some time the sole preserve of the JLP. The JLP leader the Right Honourable Edward Seaga, condemned the minimalist position of the WIC as trying to introduce Federation through a 'back-door or side-door', and indicated that he would have nothing to do with it since for his party, the future of Jamaica was better secured in the North and not in the South'. Seaga went on to add that what is done today can be undone tomorrow, sending a warning to the PNP, less they felt inclined to go along with any such moves. At the same time, however, he effectively made a case for Jamaica not to be the forerunners in any regional integration initiatives of the future.

In the realm of the sublime, Prime Minister of Barbados Right Honourable Lloyd Erskine Sandiford made a surprising critique of the recommendations by suggesting that we should not be creating another level of bureaucracy not anchored in the electorate of the Caribbean but selected through some specific process.

Minor Changes

This statement is described as surprising because he then went on to discuss the virtues of his proposed Assembly of Caribbean Parliamentarians, the members of which were to be identified by such a specific process.

Junior Minister, David Thompson, went even further by suggesting that the issue of Federal Political Union should have been addressed by the WIC. The absence of which he suggested 'questioned the very effectiveness of the report'.

The Heads of Government were united in their response to the recommendations from WIC. They realised that caution was necessary as the recommended CARICOM Commission was a key factor in the WIC's revised structures, whose implementation was critical to the Community. And a rejection of this new Commission would substantially reduce the impact of the WIC's other proposals. The Heads at their special meeting, did not actually articulate a position on the WIC's Commission, but instead noted the need to 'strengthen the institutional capacity of, and improve the implementation process in, the Community' and to this end agreed:

to establish a Bureau, comprising the Chairman in office of the Conference, as Chairman, and the incoming and outgoing Chairmen of the Conference, assisted by the Secretary-General, in the capacity of Chief Executive Officer. The Bureau shall have competence to initiate proposals, update consensus, mobilise action and secure implementation of CARICOM decisions in an expeditious and informed manner.

The Heads, by this approach, conveniently substituted the Commission with a body with which they were more comfortable. In discussing their rationale for this, Chairman of CARICOM, Prime Minister Patrick Manning noted that 'the prospective $5 million cost had influenced the final decision' to veto the Commission proposal.

The Heads gave a general acceptance of all the other major recommendations of the WIC. Among these were a reaffirmation of the Community of Sovereign States concept, pursue greater co-operation in foreign representation abroad, and the acceptance of the need for a CARICOM Charter of Civil Society. The proposal to form an Association of Caribbean States was given support as the Heads saw the need to widen the scope of the Community, and increase their influence overseas. Important also was the agreement to revise the Treaty of Chaguaramas to give the Secretary General executive powers.

Despite criticisms levelled at the Commission above, the rejection of it is still unfortunate for CARICOM. This is because it has been replaced with a body which will no doubt be less productive and effective than the Commission. The Heads have opted for a committee of three Heads who are all national leaders in their own right, and as such can only be part time CARICOM officials. In addition, the rotating nature of their appointments makes them all transitory, and ensures that Heads, whose commitment to CARICOM is questionable, will from time to time be on the Bureau. This serves as a recipe for a similar inertia that already exists within CARICOM. It is unlikely that CARICOM will conduct an exercise similar to the WIC for another 20 years, hence, little change can be anticipated as regards the most critical area of CARICOM's failure as identified in the report.

In the final analysis the decision on the Commission can only be described as an opportunity missed by CARICOM. The Commission represented an, albeit, imperfect institution but one which could have stimulated some activity within CARICOM. The attention focused on this body, and the interaction of them with the Heads of State, could possibly have created a renewed interest in integration, which, while unproductive, could have led to productive activity in the future. This sentiment was strongly expressed in the editorial appearing in the *Sunday Express* of November 1, 1992 which observed that, 'Caribbean leaders (*sic*) have failed to rise to the occasion. Where courage and vision were required they have demonstrated an inability to meet the demands of a new and unpredictably dangerous internal and external reality'.

The imminent danger that procrastination on this issue has led to, is well articulated in this excerpt.

The WIC can only be seen as a disappointment, both in terms of its report, and the lack of action that it inspired. The foregoing has sought to demonstrate that this is the result of many factors ranging from overly high expectations of the WIC to its composition. Certainly the bias of the commissioners is one of the more significant limitations. Here, due to an accident of composition, a commission was assembled which was in the main middle class, highly educated, predominantly male, mature, and highly supportive of Caribbean integration. This established many parameters into which the recommendations of the WIC would necessarily have to fit. The WIC would therefore not reflect public opinion, but in a sense impose an opinion on the public. This combined with other factors, such as an unduly wide mandate, served to limit the scope of the WIC.

The major weakness of the WIC report centred around the imposition of a CARICOM Commission on the present structure of CARICOM. This role of implementation that the Commission is intended to perform is seen as critical to the future of CARICOM. The Commission has, however, encountered the stumbling block of sovereignty, a hurdle previously faced by CARICOM, and the manner in which the Commission is expected to get around these difficulties appears optimistic, to say the least. In addition, the cost factor appears prohibitive, and induced the Heads of Government to oppose that particular recommendation, while supporting others. This action negatively affects the efficacy of some of the remaining WIC proposals and leaves the major problem within CARICOM unresolved.

Reactions to the WIC report have confirmed a degree of dissatisfaction with its recommendation, from both the Governments and the people of the region. It is evident that much was expected of this body, indeed too much and this has set the stage for massive disappointment. What is more, the circumstances which gave rise to the WIC have already begun to impact negatively on the Caribbean as seen with the Windward Islands Banana situation. The WIC must therefore be seen as an excellent opportunity which has been lost. It however provides an opportunity for the region to learn useful lessons from the entire WIC debacle. These experiences, negative as they are, can yet be instructive for the future development of CARICOM.

Note

This paper was published in *Caribbean Affairs*, Vol. 7 No. 3, July August 1994, pp. 38–61.

[36]

Amending the Treaty of Chaguaramas

Duke Pollard

At its Special Meeting held in Port of Spain, Trinidad and Tobago in October 1992, the Conference of Heads of Government decided to establish the CARICOM Single Market and Economy (CSME) and set up the Inter-Governmental Task Force to supervise the revision of the Treaty of Chaguaramas for the purpose. Recognising that to be effective, the required Treaty revision process, would be a protracted exercise, involving extensive consultations and national participation at every stage of the process, the Inter-Governmental Task Force, at its third meeting, decided to revise the Treaty by a series of protocols. This incremental approach would ensure discernible progress, periodically, toward the agreed goal – the CSME, and facilitate external donor funding from various sources for each phase of the exercise.

The only other credible alternatives to the incremental approach adopted by the Inter-Governmental Task Force are, firstly, a comprehensive treaty revision process involving extensive national consultations by interested stakeholders and extending over a period in excess of five years, or secondly, a plenipotentiary conference with multi-disciplinary participation from each CARICOM member state and extending over a period in excess of three months. Given the known budgetary constraints of member states, the significant expenditure likely to be involved in such an exercise, and the possible indisposition of interested donor agencies to commit the funding required, conventional wisdom argued against revision of the Treaty by plenipotentiary conference. Negative perceptions in the wider community about the delivery of CARICOM decision-makers appeared to argue against the comprehensive treaty revision process extending for a considerable period.

CARICOM Heads of Government, by signing Protocol 1 at the Eighth Inter-sessional Meeting of the Conference in St John's, Antigua and Barbuda in February 1997, indicated both their willingness and readiness to take the bold steps required establishing the CARICOM Single Market and Economy. Protocol 1 addresses the organs, bodies, institutions and procedures of the CARICOM Single Market and Economy. In this context, it is important to bear in mind that the Community as transfigured, in terms of the quality and intensity of anticipated economic interactions among the member states, continues to enjoy the status of an association essentially of sovereign states. Consequently, the principle of unanimity, the juridical expression of sovereign equality, continues to determine decision-making in the Conference, the supreme organ of the Community. However, as a departure from the process of decision-making in the old regime, other Organs of the Community, which, collectively, replace the Common Market Council and the Standing Committees of Ministers, make decisions by qualified majority vote. Further, in deference to the perception that consultations are critical to an effective decision-making process, Protocol 1 provides for an appropriate regime.

In its celebrated report, the West Indian Commission concluded that implementation was the bane of the integration movement and implied that the lack of implementation was a function of, among other things, inadequate consultation in the Community. Informed by these perceptions, the Inter-Governmental Task Force determined that each draft protocol must be the subject of in-country consultations with national multidisciplinary stakeholders from both the public and private sectors. These consultations on various draft provisions of the protocols were to inform the relevant deliberations in the Inter-Governmental Task Force and the orientation and definition of relevant instruments. In this connection, Protocol II was the subject of in-country consultations with multidisciplinary teams in Belize, Jamaica, Barbados, Trinidad and Tobago, Guyana and Suriname. One general consultation was conducted with national representatives of the OECS as a group in order to benefit from the cross fertilisation of views tendered by national representatives and to contain expenditure overruns.

In all these consultations, it was agreed that competent officials would adequately brief national representatives on the Task force, and that deliberations in the Inter-Governmental Task Force would be faithfully reported by national representatives to their institutional superiors in detail. In this connection, Protocol II was the subject of detailed discussion at the following meetings of the Inter-Governmental Task Force: sixth meeting, Guyana, October 2–4 1996; seventh meeting, Barbados, December 16–19 1996; eighth meeting, Antigua and Barbuda, February 24-26, 1997; ninth meeting, St Lucia, April 22–26 1997; and tenth Meeting, Barbados, May 5–6, 1997. In addition, Protocol II was tabled for discussion at the 44th meeting of the Common Market Council, Guyana, January 30–31 1997; the second Special Meeting of the Standing Committee of Ministers responsible for Legal Affairs, Dominica, May 12–13 1997; and the seventeenth Special Meeting of the Common Market Council, Guyana, June 5–10 1997. The Standing Committee of Ministers responsible for Legal Affairs and the Common Market Council, all commended Protocol II to the Conference of Heads of Government for signature at its eighteenth meeting in Montego Bay, Jamaica in July 1997.

Objectives of Protocol II

In a very real sense, Protocol II, which addresses the right of establishment, the right to provide services and the right to move capital in the community, is a microcosm of a wider movement towards liberalisation and globalisation in the international community –a process which is enveloping all CARICOM states. Protocol II may be seen as the most important single instrument in establishing the CARICOM Single Market and Economy (CSME) which would create a single economic space for the collectivity known as the Caribbean Community. In this space, all factors of production would be able to be efficiently employed in a manner designed to enhance the international competitiveness of regional producers from both LDCs and MDCs.

In making their commitment to the right of establishment, the right to provide services and the right to move capital in any part of the community by any community national on a non discriminatory basis. Member states are undertaking, by way of Protocol II: (a) not to impose any new restrictions on the rights mentioned above; (b) to remove such restrictions as exist according to relevant programmes to be established.

As such, the Protocol is designed to establish enabling conditions only in respect of the removal of the restrictions mentioned above. The identification of specific restrictions to be removed and the time-frame for their removal, have to be established and *agreed* by member states in the competent organ at the material time. And in establishing any such programmes, Article 38c requires the special needs of the LDCs to be taken into account. In effect, even after the Protocol enters into force or is applied provisionally as contemplated, the rights to be accorded and the obligations to be assumed by member states are still to be negotiated and agreed. It is further understood and agreed that the OECS States, in signing on to Protocol II before Protocol VII on Disadvantaged Countries, Regions and Sectors has been completed, would enjoy the same favourable conditions in the CARICOM Single Market and Economy (CSME), to be established, as they did, in the Common Market.

The Protocol implicitly recognises that the economies of member states differ in strengths and structural rigidities and therefore establishes conditions to take care of transitional problems of weaker, inflexible economies. Thus, Article 37c(bis) provides for derogations by member states experiencing balance of payments problems resulting from removal of restrictions on the exercise of rights. Similarly, Article 38b provides for waivers for member states not in a position, at the material time, to remove one or another restriction within the contemplation of the Protocol. In effect, the Protocol attempts to go as far as it must to satisfy the requirements of an exclusionary integration process desiring compatibility with relevant provisions of the WTO Agreement. Any further concessions to protectionism and discrimination in the community can place the CSME outside the exceptions recognised by the WTO.

Protocol II must also be read in conjunction with relevant provisions of Protocol I and, in particular, Articles 17(4) and 19 (3) and (4). Article 17 (4) contains an opting-out provision, not unlike the Luxembourg Resolution of the European Union, while Article 19(3) and (4) gives member states a veto power in organs other than the Conference, provided that specified conditions are satisfied. This is designed to ensure that genuine concerns of member states are not lightly ignored by others not in similar circumstances.

The scheme of drafting adopted in elaborating Protocol II is similar to that employed in the Rome Treaty. The Protocol requires a standstill by member states on the imposition of new restrictions upon entry into force of the instrument. This is followed by a requirement to notify the competent organ of relevant restrictions in place upon entry into force of the Protocol. The most important phase in this process of removing applicable restrictions is the establishment of relevant programmes for the purpose. And it is at this stage that member states, as an attribute of sovereignty, will determine the types of restrictions to be removed, and the number, manner and time-frame for their removal.

Some concerns have been expressed by representatives of some OECS countries with regard to signing Protocol II without knowing the specifics of the Protocol on Disadvantaged Countries, Regions and Sectors. It is felt, however that these concerns have been taken into account in the drafting of this protocol. In the first place, specific safeguards and waivers have been inserted into the protocol at Articles 38c, 38c(bis) and 38b as well as in the relevant provision of Protocol I as cited above. Furthermore, the proposal is to apply all protocols provisionally, pending their definitive entry into force through the satisfaction of relevant conditions including ratification by member states in accordance with their respective conditional procedures. And, if during its implementation, Protocol II is perceived to be operating adversely on the economies of the LDCs despite the safeguard mechanisms and waivers mentioned above, appropriate remedial measures could be provided in the Protocol on Disadvantaged Countries, Regions and Sectors, to ensure that the LDCs continue to enjoy their comparative advantage *vis-à-vis* the MDCs in terms of distribution of benefits from the integration movement.

Note

This paper was published in *CARICOM Perspective*, No. 67, June 1997, pp. 62–63, 71.

[37]

CARICOM in the new Millennium

Duke Pollard

As we approach the 21st century, we dare not turn aside from each other. Local identities may be in vogue; but we do well to remember that they are invariably being indulged under the roof of regional homes. We began to build our regional home a long time ago. Dismantling it would be a malign act. And it is dismantling that we will face if integration is not perfected, but allowed to begin the inevitable alternative process of unravelling. There is no way for us but forward. It should be for us the natural way. It is for us the best way. Thus the Report of the West Indian Commission, which might have gone on to conclude: It is the only way.

Six eventful years have elapsed since that inimitable constellation of regional luminaries analysed with remarkable poignancy and unerring aplomb the West Indian condition and delineated the way forward to the next millennium. During this brief period, Europe has edged closer to economic and social cohesion as a prelude to political unity; the North American Free Trade Area has become a reality and the Free Trade Area of the Americas stretching from Alaska in the north to Terra del Fuego in the south has been announced; MERCOSUR has been formed and the Asian tigers have begun to lose their economic fangs even as the Pacific Rim countries contemplate closer cooperation in trade and finance.

In the meantime, world leaders assembled at Marakesh in 1994 and appended their signatures to the Agreement Establishing the World Trade Organisation. All of these developments in one form or another heralded the twin phenomena of liberalisation and globalisation in the international community. For the fragile economies of CARICOM, liberalisation and globalisation are perceived as the new bully on the block, especially since the attendant erosion of preferential trading arrangements previously enjoyed in Europe and North America, has become a stark and discomforting reality. In the meantime, the USA brandishing its current statute as dominant superpower with vaunting military, economic and political capabilities, has opted not only to speak loudly but, simultaneously, to wield a big stick in its political interface with other participants in the WTO, including minuscule economic actors like the states of the OECS.

In order to confront and manage emerging global developments, competent decision-makers in CARICOM have been constrained to devise new structures of governance based in large measure on the recommendations of the West Indian Commission, whose reflections quoted above provide the point of departure for this discourse on the emerging structures of the Caribbean Community.

The new dispensation for state interaction in the Caribbean Community in the twenty-first Century must be perceived as an unqualified rejection of the mind-set which traced its genesis to the demise of the West Indian Federation and determined for decades the functional parameters of regional political intercourse reflected in the arrangements emerging from Chaguaramas in 1973.

The preferred paradigm of regional political cooperation in the post Federation era was approached with hesitancy and diffidence by the policy makers and was also bedeviled by an ethic of sanctimonious insularity. Small wonder, therefore, that in the interplay of developments at the regional level, political accommodation was interpreted to be the compromising of endogenous notions of autonomous decision-making. Consequently, the Caribbean Community, as an association of sovereign entities symbolised by the legal requirement of unanimity for critical decision-making in both organs and institutions, tended to be buttressed by the conspicuous absence of sanctions for non-compliance with decisions, including those relating to the primordial obligation to contribute to the regular budget of the Community.

Predictably, the West Indian Commission determined that implementation of decisions was the Achilles heel of the integration movement. Implementation of decisions requires knowledge based on appropriate consultations with various stakeholders and an in-depth study of relevant issues, coupled with an unqualified commitment to the achievement of shared values and objectives. The regime emerging from Chaguaramas was not designed to accommodate these essential ingredients.

In 1997, the Conference of Heads of Government, at its Ninth Intersessional Meeting in St John's, Antigua and Barbuda, signed Protocol I amending the 'Treaty of Chaguaramas Establishing the Caribbean Community'. This instrument constitutes a significant point of departure for the establishment of structures of governance in the Caribbean Community, particularly as they relate to the deepening of the regional integration movement.

Protocol I addresses, in an innovative way, the organs, bodies and procedures of the Community, including the proposed CARICOM Single Market and Economy. The new arrangements seek to accommodate tradition, continuity and change for the achievement of dynamic stability in advancing the integration process. Thus the unanimity principle remains entrenched in the voting procedures of the Conference, but has been dispensed with for decision-making of other organs save in the exceptional circumstances identified in Article 19 (3) and which relate to issues 'determined to be of critical importance to the well-being of a Member State'.

Any such determination is required to 'be reached by a two-thirds majority of Member States' in order to pre-empt frivolous claims in that behalf. Further, even where the unanimity principle prevails, it is qualified, and not absolute, since 'abstentions shall not be construed as impairing the validity of decisions required to be reached by unanimity provided that Member States constituting not less than three-quarters of the membership of the Community vote in favour of such decisions' – Articles 19 (5) and 18 (2) of the Treaty as amended by the protocol.

Another important innovation in the new dispensation was the attempt to effectuate the submissions of the West Indian Commission which stated that 'we must not proceed at the pace of the slowest; that those who are ready to move must do so – reserving a place for the others when they are ready' . . . Consistent with this position, Article 17 (4) which addresses voting procedures in Community organs states:

Subject to the agreement of the Conference, a Member State may opt out of obligations arising from the decision of competent organs, provided that the fundamental objectives of the Community, as laid down in the Treaty, are not prejudiced thereby.

It is important to note that the right to opt out is subject to two important conditions – the agreement of the Conference and the requirement to preserve the integrity of the Community's fundamental objectives. What is envisaged here is a scenario in which some groups of member states may decide to integrate at a quicker pace than others without compromising the integration process as a whole.

Reacting to the West Indian Commission's finding that implementation was the Achilles heel of the regional integration movement, competent decision makers in the Community sought to remedy this defect in relevant institutional arrangements. In this context, Article 16 of the revised Treaty of Chaguaramas expressly provides for a consultative process to be established and maintained by the Community Council of Ministers in collaboration with competent authorities of member states. Paragraph 2 of the Article requires the system of consultation to be established to be so structured as to 'ensure that determinations of Community Organs and the Legal Affairs Committee are adequately informed by relevant information inputs and are reinforced by consultations undertaken at successively lower levels of the decision-making process'.

In keeping with the provisions of this article, measures would need to be taken at the regional level for a flow of information/consultation between and among the Secretariat, other regional organisations, the social partners and national officials culminating in structured intersectoral consultations at the level of the ministerial councils. At the level of the Community Council, major tripartite consultations are contemplated periodically, on a regional basis. The inputs for such consultations would come from intersectoral consultations held at national and regional levels.

The process of consultation should extend at each level of decision-making to include the recommendations flowing from the relevant organs or bodies at a lower level. For example, the decisions by the Conference of Heads of Government, apart from the national positions articulated by the Heads of Government, would normally benefit from recommendations from the Community Council and the Secretariat. The decisions of the Community Council would, apart from the national positions articulated by the Minister responsible for CARICOM Affairs, normally benefit from recommendations emanating from the specialised ministerial councils, the Secretariat and the regional tripartite consultative process. And the decisions made by the specialised ministerial councils would, apart from the national positions articulated by the relevant subject ministers, be informed by the recommendations from the preparatory meetings of officials and the Secretariat.

At the national level, it is envisaged that consultations between and among the social partners, the national ministries/agencies, the regional organisations including the Secretariat, coordinated and organised by the Ministry of

CARICOM Affairs, would choose national representatives to deal with matters relating to regional decision-making.

In terms of organisational structure, the Conference retains its status as the supreme organ for the collective responsibility, ultimately, of determining and providing strategic direction for the policy of the Community. The composition and procedures of the Conference operate to underscore the juridical status of the Community as an association of sovereign states based on the principles of consent and the sovereign equality of states.

As the supreme organ of the Community, the Conference is competent to make determinations on any issue affecting the policy of the Community, and in so doing, is subject to the unanimity principle. The Bureau allows continuity in the discharge of the responsibilities of the Conference between Meetings of this organ. The Community Council is the second highest decision-making organ and is designated as such in Article 6(1) (b). According to Article 8 (2), the 'Community Council shall, in accordance with the policy directions established by the Conference, have primary responsibility for the development of Community strategic planning and co-ordination in the areas of economic integration, functional co-operation and external relations'.

Assisting these two principal organs are four other organs, namely, the Council for Finance and Planning, charged with primary responsibility for economic policy coordination and financial and monetary integration of member states; the Council for Trade and Economic Development, charged with responsibility for the promotion of trade and economic development in the Community; the Council for Human and Social Development, charged with responsibility for the promotion of human and social development in the Community; and the Council for Foreign and Community Relations, charged with responsibility for determining relations between the Community and international organisations and third States.

Complementing these institutional arrangements are three important bodies, namely, the Legal Affairs Committee, the Budget Committee and the Committee of Central Bank Governors, whose nomenclatures are a clear indication of their function within the scheme of things in the Community.

Protocol I, which addresses the organisational, institutional arrangements and procedures of the Community, including the CARICOM Single Market and Economy, is merely one of nine integrating instruments envisaged to amend the Treaty of Chaguaramas in order to establish the CARICOM Single Market and Economy. The other instruments are; Protocol II (Rights of Establishment, Provision of Services, Movement of Capital); Protocol III (Industrial Policy); Protocol IV (Trade Policy); Protocol V (Agricultural Policy); Protocol VI (Transport Policy); Protocol VII (Disadvantaged Countries, Regions and Sectors); Protocol VIII (Disputes Settlement), and Protocol IX (Rules of Competition).

In the final configuration of the Treaty as revised, each protocol will constitute a discrete chapter. It is contemplated that, with the elaboration and implementation of these instruments, a single economic space will be created within which the factors of production, including labour, would be able to locate to countries, regions or sectors where they can be optimally employed, and, in the process, improve productivity and the efficient allocation of resources while enhancing the quality of life and the standard of living of citizens of the Community.

Of these instruments, the most sensitive in terms of compromising the autonomy of decision in national economic development policy would appear to be Protocol II, which establishes the broad parameters for the conferment of national treatment in the areas identified. The importance likely to be attached to Protocol VIII, which addresses disputes settlement, will depend on the willingness of interested member states to confer on the Caribbean Supreme Court original jurisdiction in respect of the interpretation and application of the Treaty as revised.

In addition to the above, the Conference of Heads of Government agreed on the establishment of other critical structures designed to enhance the process of governance in the Community with probable positive impact on the sustainability of democratic norms and the quality of life for ordinary citizens of the Community.

The celebrated report of the West Indian Commission, in its section entitled 'Time for Action', names a CARICOM Assembly of Parliamentarians, a CARICOM Charter of Civil Society and a CARICOM Supreme Court as some of the important institutions to be established to take a revitalised Caribbean Community into the twenty-first century. Of equal importance but not readily recognised as a critical integrating instrument is the CARICOM Agreement on Social Security, which would allow Community citizens to maintain and transfer their social security benefits from one CARICOM jurisdiction to another. In the absence of such a facility, the, much hoped for, mobility of skills in the Community will never be realised. This instrument has now been ratified by the prescribed number of CARICOM States and is now in force.

The Community Secretariat is currently spearheading initiatives to have the Agreement implemented by the parties and to operationalise the regime. Of importance, too, is the Agreement for the Avoidance of Double Taxation intended to facilitate the provision of services and the right of establishment by Community nationals in member states.

The Assembly of Caribbean Community Parliamentarians has been established and already convened its inaugural session in Barbados in 1996. The objectives of the Assembly are set out in Article 4 of the Agreement and read as follows:

(a) to involve the people of the Community, through their representatives, in the process of consolidating and strengthening the Community;

(b) to provide opportunities for involvement in the issues of the integration process by Members of Parliament in each Member State and Associate Member, in addition to those who now participate;

(c) to provide a forum for people of the Community to make their views known through their representatives;

(d) to provide more frequent contact in the monitoring of the policies of the Community;

(e) to provide enhanced opportunities for the co-ordination of the foreign policies of Member States;

(f) to promote greater understanding among Member States and Associate Members for the purpose of realising and safeguarding the ideals and principles of democratic governments in the Community and facilitating the economic and social advancements of their peoples;

(g) to encourage the adoption by the Governments of Member States of the Community of a common policy on economic, social, cultural, scientific and legal matters deliberated upon by the Assembly.

The composition and powers of the Assembly have elicited unfavourable comments from various quarters. In the perception of the West Indian Commission, the provisions of Article 5 of the Agreement unduly restrict the deliberative functions of the Assembly, which, if it is to improve the delivery of governance in the Community, must be competent to discuss issues of concern to the vitality of the body. The Commission's concern was not an invitation to the Assembly to meddle in the internal affairs of member states, but must be seen to be supportive of the Assembly's competence to deliberate on issues relevant to the CARICOM Single Market and Economy, on functional cooperation among member states and the external relations of the Community. In the Commission's submission, the composition of the Assembly is too restricted and should have been configured to accommodate representatives of the social partners – the private sector, NGOs and labour. It was also submitted that the Assembly should have been entitled to receive reports on the work of the Community to enable the peoples of the region to be informed about the community activities.

Based on the objectives and functions of the Assembly, some of its detractors in the media have been quick to dismiss the institution as another talk shop of marginal relevance for the critical developmental problems plaguing the Region and unlikely to do more than constitute an additional financial burden on the deprived peoples of the Community. In the present submission, however, it is strange logic to question the relevance of the Assembly at a time when an issue of compelling concern is good governance, an important aspect of the open debate on issues of importance to the general populace.

Indeed, one of the criticisms of policy makers of the region is their overweening preoccupation with national issues, and their diffidence in enlightening their populations about developments in the regional integration movement. These criticisms are likely to continue, since issues on the regional agenda are rarely seen to impact one way or another on the outcome of the electoral process at the national plane with which decision makers are quintessentially concerned. In the premises, the Assembly must be appreciated as remedying this inadequacy in the regional integration process by involving the representatives of the people of both government and opposition in regional issues of importance.

Disparaging perceptions of the Assembly are, no doubt, influenced by the competence of the European Parliament, which has an important element of democratic accountability within the legislative and executive system of the European Community and which has been enhanced by the holding of direct elections to this body. The European Parliament enjoys wide advisory powers and many provisions of the EEC Treaty require it to be consulted on draft legislation prepared by the Commission before consideration and adoption by the Council. Most importantly, the European Parliament can oblige the entire Commission to resign by approving a motion of censure (Article 144).

Finally, the European Parliament may challenge the legality of actions by the Community institutions before the European Court of Justice. As yet, however, the Assembly is a fledgling institution whose first session was not particularly eventful in terms of controverting important regional issues, and, consequently, public perceptions of its relevance are still an issue for future resolution.

Unlike the Assembly, whose establishment was initiated by the Prime Minister of Barbados at the material time, the Charter of Civil Society was engendered by the West Indian Commission which perceived it as contributing to good governance in the region and recommended its elaboration and adoption by the member states of the Community. Consequently, the Conference of Heads of Government, at their Special Meeting held in Port of

Spain in October 1992, adopted the recommendation of the West Indian Commission. In their determination, the Conference agreed that the Charter,

would deal, inter alia, with matters such as a free press, a fair and open democratic process, the effective functioning of the parliamentary system, morality in public affairs, respect for fundamental civil, political, economic, social and cultural rights, the rights of women and children, respect for religious diversity, greater accountability and transparency in governance.

Since that time, the Charter has been subjected to several revisions based in part on submissions made by participants in some national consultations on the draft.

The Conference of Heads of Government formally adopted the Charter at their meeting in Bridgetown during July 1996. The Charter has (28) Articles encompassing, among others, the areas identified in the guidelines established by the Conference mentioned above.

In the present submission, the underlying theme of the chapter provisions is provided in paragraph 1, Article 1, which appropriately establishes that the fundamental rights and freedoms of the individual are *'subject to respect for the rights and freedoms of others and for the public interest'*. This qualification should operate to restore some balance to the human rights activists' seemingly myopic preoccupation with the rights of the individual, inexcusably oblivious to the correlative obligation which the enjoyment of such rights must be seen to impose. In their ordinary signification, rights are legal entitlements enforceable by tribunals of competent jurisdiction and do not exist in *vacuo*. In the submission of some eminent jurists, the conferment of a right is normally a function of the recognition of a pre-existing obligation corresponding to such a right. And it is important that the Charter of Civil Society, by ineluctable inference, recognise this axiomatic juxtaposition of rights and obligations subsisting together for social cohesion.

Not unlike the Assembly, the Charter has its fair share of detractors. One general criticism of the Charter is that it breaks no new ground and merely repeats much of what has been enunciated by various human rights instruments elaborated by one or another organisation within the United Nations System. Further, it is argued that the Charter must aspire to nothing more than a motley compendium of pious platitudes, given the absence of any binding commitment on the part of its signatories, and the absence of any credible monitoring mechanism and enforcement measures to secure compliance with its prescriptions.

In this context it is important to note that the Charter is not a legally binding instrument. In the present submission, these criticisms are either uninformed or misconceived, or both. In the first place, it is simplistic to assume that compliance with moral or ethical prescriptions is necessarily a function of a coercive sanctioning process. Men were not all created in Hobbes' image requiring social intercourse, and in the absence of authoritarian intervention, to be nasty, brutish and short. Indeed, man's inherent rationality leans towards the observance of norms of conduct intuitively or experientially perceived to inure to the general good. In the premises, the Charter, which has been adopted by the Conference, will constitute a moral commitment to observe its prescriptions – prescriptions which, over time, will be internationalised by policy makers and constitute a standard of conduct to which they will adhere in performance of their functions.

As early as 1988, the Conference of Heads of Government agreed to establish a Caribbean Court of Appeal with appellate jurisdiction similar to that of the Judicial Committee of the Privy Council. At its special session held in Port of Spain in October 1992, the Conference of Heads of Government took note of the recommendation of the West Indian Commission for the establishment of a CARICOM Supreme Court with original jurisdiction in respect of matters arising under the Treaty of Chaguaramas. At its first special meeting held in Kingston, Jamaica, from February 16–18 1998, the Legal Affairs Committee requested the Conference of Heads of Government to address, in particular, the issue of the proposed Caribbean Supreme Court having original jurisdiction. At this meeting, the Legal Affairs Committee completed the draft Agreement Establishing the Caribbean Supreme Court, subject to minor drafting changes.

The draft agreement, as approved, allows parties to the regime to enter reservations to Article X with the consent of the contracting parties mentioned in Article XXII. This provision is intended to facilitate the participation of the Republic of Trinidad and Tobago in the regime in respect of criminal appeals only.

Presumably, however, if a decision is reached to accord the Court original jurisdiction in respect of matters relating to the Treaty of Chaguaramas, Trinidad and Tobago will concur in this enlargement of the Court's jurisdiction and agree to be bound by the relevant provisions of the agreement as amended. The present agreement also attempts to insulate judges of the Court, including the President, from direct political influence by making their appointments and removal subject to an affirmative recommendation of the Regional Judicial and Legal Services Commission acting on the advice of a tribunal to be constituted, as the case may require, to examine allegations of judicial misconduct.

There are indications, however, that the private bar in several jurisdictions entertains serious reservations about the ability of the Court to dispense justice in a manner consonant with the requirements of due process and of a quality commanding the respect of the legal community.

One major concern expressed in various quarters is the political will of participating Governments to finance the operations of the Court for the effective discharge of its responsibilities. But in the submission of the West Indian Commission, this is an investment member states cannot afford not to afford. Reservations are also made about the legal erudition of prospective aspirants to judicial office and the quality of delivery of services. And, here again, the West Indian Commission begged to differ about the quality of our judges.

The most important reservation, however, relates to the ability of judges of the Court to perform their functions free from political influence, despite reassuring institutional arrangements for their appointment and removal. Some of these reservations have been addressed by the West Indian Commission as set out below.

In the submission of the West Indian Commission, the case for a Caribbean Supreme Court is compelling, both in terms of enhancing cohesion among the participants of the regional integration movement and in providing an appropriate final Appellate Court in the region. In terms of enhancing the regional integration process, it is important to note that the establishment of the CARICOM Single Market and Economy creates important rights and obligations for member states and which must impact importantly on the economic well-being of individuals in the Community, both natural and juridical.

In particular, Protocol II, which addresses the right of Community nationals to establish and provide services in any jurisdiction of member states and to move capital freely from one jurisdiction to another, must be the subject of interpretation and application in the daily lives of citizens. Given the status of the Community as an association of sovereign States, implementation of the Treaty, as revised, will be amenable to as many judicial interpretations as there are jurisdictions in the Community. Absence of uniformity in the interpretation and application of relevant norms must, in the present submission, be seen as a prescription for business uncertainty and retardation of the integration movement.

In the characterisation of the West Indian Commission,

integration in its broadest economic sense – involving a Single CARICOM Market, monetary union, the movement of capital and labour and goods, and functional co-operation in a multiplicity of fields – must have the underpinning of Community law. Integration rests on rights and duties; it requires the support of the rule of law applied regionally and uniformly. A CARICOM Supreme Court interpreting the Treaty of Chaguaramas, resolving disputes arising under it, including disputes between Governments parties to the Treaty, declaring and enforcing Community law, interpreting the Charter of Civil Society – all by the way of the exercise of an original jurisdiction – is absolutely essential to the integration process . . .

In terms of the appellate jurisdiction of the Court, the Commission submitted

that a Caribbean Supreme Court manned by distinguished West Indian jurists and in which litigants have confidence, is likely to attract a larger number of appeals from countries of the Region than the Privy Council now does. Its knowledge and understanding of regional problems, language and culture, coupled with its identification with the very ethos of the Caribbean Community, at once invests it with intrinsic qualities which the Privy Council, despite its great learning, does not and can never hope to possess.

Postulated in other terms, the case for a Caribbean Supreme Court could be based on the need for a regional Court of last resort to apply laws incorporating a collective regional ethos, reflecting the moral imperatives of the Caribbean social reality and amenable to interpretation by judges who would have internalised the values informing the content of that social reality.

Note

This paper was published in *CARICOM Perspective*, No. 68 June 1998, pp. 25–32.

[38]

Aligned for Global Change
Restructuring in the
Caribbean Community

Joseph Farier

More than ever before, perhaps, we have become conscious, that *change* rather than permanence is the fundamental reality of the world. It often takes highly symbolic events to drive this fact home and encourage examination of the root causes and patterns of this change, its implications and available options and strategies.

The fall of the Cold War systems and postures, including command type economies in Eastern Europe around 1989, have helped to crystallise aware-ness of certain fundamental trends referred to as globalisation. Within these trends it is clear that technological innovation is a dynamic force, and that political and social systems insufficiently flexible to channel and use it effec-tively, will not be able to keep their societies in the mainstream of development – and may implode.

Those systems, on the other hand, with superior capability and more pragmatic philosophies will also have to adapt, but may do so with less catastrophic consequences. We live in a world where hegemonic systems more open to change adapt quite frequently by bringing other societies in line using cross-border pressures to open up possibilities that will enable their internal dynamics to be fruitful. Even where they do not feel the need to pursue 'possession' or 'strategic denial' goals, they are not safe or successful until they project their values to other societies thereby opening up wider operational spaces.

The world has changed in such significant ways that successful products and services which were once a source of growth have to be examined from the perspective of whether they are not now a source of stagnation – impeding effective management with an eye to the future. The advantages of large size and centralisation for improving chances of success of an organisation have paled in comparison with their vulnerabilities in today's environment. Large companies/organisations in both command and market oriented economies have suffered from inherent inflexibilities and staying too long with what made them at one point undoubtedly successful. This awareness is a major source of pressure for restructuring worldwide.

Turning to our region, any organisation that wishes to be vibrant should also seek to be open to self-criticism and analysis. In this regard, the Secretariat undoubtedly has its track record of institutions it has nurtured to sustainability, programmes that have impacted beneficially on the people, successes in liberalising trade and protecting traditional exports. Nevertheless, the challenge is to review these very achievements in the light of changing circumstances and to identify what would now make it into an organisation that is more fundamentally rooted in the needs of its 'customers and stakeholders' for 'tomorrow'. Like products, organisations are best seen as going through growth cycles and need to be examined in terms of their potential for viability and securing strategic scope for renewed growth.

The pressures of globalisation have led to the emergence of new coping strategies and conceptual tools – how to seek competitive advantage, establish core competencies and building the corporate unit into a learning organisation. Other skills are the ability to exploit the value-chain in production/services, reengineer and restructure the organisation to create a more customer-driven focus for continuous improvement.

The need for the Secretariat to revisit itself and undertake appropriate restructuring, is part of the broad trend of organisations today. It is no longer time to lie on their laurels, but rather, to test how well they are aligned to global trends: customer needs, competitive pressures, future value and service.

It has been suggested that the principal tasks in managing today's organisations include:

- defining distinctive competencies;
- establishing a mission supported by an appropriate strategy, supportive policies and budgets;
- building an organisation capable of carrying out strategy successfully;

- motivating people to pursue target objectives (implementation) and aligning recognition and reward structures to the achievement of results;
- creating a culture conducive to strategy implementation;
- installing appropriate support systems;
- instituting best practices for continuous improvement (managing human skills and databases); and
- exerting strategic leadership to drive implementation forward.

The Secretariat's review of its operations and management is perhaps best done with these considerations in mind.

Restructuring in the Caribbean Community

At the start of the 1990s, the Independent West Indian Commission (the Ramphal Commission), whose work was supported by a number of donors, played a significant role in examining various aspects of the regional integration process and evaluating advances made against global trends, as well as in the light of the very dramatic changes that had taken place in the world especially since 1989. A broad set of recommendations across many fields resulted from the Commission's work.

Among others, the report of the Commission, 'Time For Action', addressed issues of widening and deepening the integration process as well as attacking its 'Achilles heel', that of non-implementation. Recommendations were also made to streamline the institutional framework of the Community by creating a smaller number of new bodies to replace a range of ministerial bodies and standing committees. The thrust of the recommendations on institutional change was broadly supported. Certain of them however were modified for implementation. Thus the proposal for a high level Commission System was replaced by one aimed at the establishment of a Bureau of the Conference of Heads of Government.

In the last three years much effort has been expended on work to implement or underpin the process of restructuring. Work has advanced on the revision of the Treaty of Chaguaramas so that the new organisational structure (envisaging new Community councils) and the thrust towards a Single Market and Economy could be appropriately reflected in new, approved, legal provisions. Four important protocols have been drafted, as part of a process in which they will have been subjected to scrutiny and consultation at the national level prior to examination and refinement at intergovernmental meetings. The work on Treaty revision includes the revisiting of the issue of the unanimity rule and new models of decision-making in the new organs of the Community, based on the premise that, on agreed issue areas within the purview of ministerial organs, it could be feasible and progressive to proceed by way of qualified voting. In a supporting process at the national level, some governments have taken to heart the recommendation that there be a focal Ministry for CARICOM Affairs with appropriate processes for inter-ministry coordination and consultation.

It would appear that many people consider that if only things could be rearranged institutionally so that the unanimity rule is abandoned all will be well for decision implementation. There is, in this view, certainly a large dose of misperception. It underestimates the effect of bureaucracy and officialdom in delaying decisions taken with political will and good faith at the regional leadership level. It underestimates the divergence of national agenda priorities from the regional agenda in focus, orientation, and timing. One has to bear in mind that, after all, intra-regional imports is less than ten per cent of total imports and that this limited weight by itself is not persuasive enough to place regional issues at the top of the 'national interest' agenda. Also, the national constituencies within which CARICOM must root itself are pulled in other directions by more powerful allegiances and interests. Additionally, it might be noted that the budget to support CARICOM programmes is part and parcel of the Foreign Affairs budget in major contributing countries, thereby directly competing with other priorities within limited or shrinking national allocations. Moreover, a large part of the problem resides in the preparatory phase of the decision process where inadequate mechanisms and processes obtain in respect of consultations with important stakeholders at the national level, and where there is inadequate provision to analyse the implications of costs and benefits, before important decisions are taken. Thus, inadequate decision-making processes at national and regional levels have also played a part in hampering decision implementation.

Technical Action Services Unit (TASU)

Within the Secretariat, there now exists as part of its operations, a special unit, The Technical Action Services Unit (TASU), to provide assistance in support of decision implementation to member states. TASU has responsibility for promoting consultative processes at national and regional levels preparatory to decision; documenting, analysing and generally tracking regional decisions; for identifying hindrances to implementation capable of being alleviated or removed by providing technical assistance; and for orchestration and provision of appropriate assistance. This may take the form of short-term expertise, attachments, specific studies, training or exchange of information and model documents. Establishment of the Single Market and Economy is the primary area of attention at this point.

Among the important changes that have taken place has been the institutionalisation of a Bureau of the Conference of Heads of Government. This body is essentially a management committee of the Conference comprising the outgoing chairman, the incumbent chairman, and the prospective chairman of Conference along with the Secretary General. The mechanism is designed to monitor the decisions of the Conference between sessions and secure progress in their implementation through follow-through consultations aimed partly at tracking implementation and updating consensus. It might be noted that in the restructuring, it is contemplated that executive authority would be attached to the position of Secretary General.

Since 1994, the Secretariat has embarked on processes internally to strengthen its performance as a results-oriented and implementation-conscious organisation. Executive management positions have been filled at the Assistant Secretary General level, introducing a level of strategic management as part of a restructuring plan (1994–1996) approved by the Heads of Government. Under this plan target ceilings were set for meeting the annual financial requirements although there has been significant slippage as a result of the financial situation of some governments. Programmes have been reduced from 24 to 15 to help provide for a more integrated approach.

A smaller number of thematic priorities have been identified in the overall work programmes for 1995 as well as for 1996 and 1997 to encourage Programmes to work more synergistically to achieve results in the thematic areas of concentration. Budgets and work programmes have become progressively more integrated. In addition to an executive management committee with responsibility for providing strategic direction, technical leadership to the Community and taking decisions on corporate issues, new consultative and advisory structures have been implemented. These are aimed at strengthening processes of staff involvement in corporate administration, programme development, management, implementation and review by allowing for a broader catchment area for staff views, suggestions and technical inputs.

These consultative or advisory mechanisms include a General Management Committee and a Committee for Programme Review and Evaluation, with specific mandates being given to a Work Programme and Budget Committee and an Organisational Advisory Committee.

Organisation change has been supported by the creation of a special programme with responsibility for organisation development. This programme, among other things, has spearheaded work with respect to a study of work processes and procedures, as well as a survey of competencies in the organisation. Complementary work is underway to train staff in, and implement a new results-oriented performance development and review system. A number of areas have already been identified through an internal organisation dynamics survey, as requiring attention in order to build an organisation culture and strengthen practices conducive to optimising the involvement and contribution of staff. In all of this, the Secretariat is pursuing an option of a single building in the host country, considering the involvement of the private sector and some revenue generation capacity for these interests.

In its efforts to prepare for a more effective role in support of decision implementation, the Secretariat now enjoys dial-up facilities enabling member states to tap more easily into industry and trade databases. It is also engaged in a project to establish an information network to promote information and macro-economic data between member states and with other regional secretariats.

From the foregoing, it is clear that work is proceeding to revamp Community institutions and fashion them into more effective instruments for member states. On the issue of decision implementation with respect to widening, Suriname has become part of the decision structures as a member of both the Community and Common Market. All CARICOM states have opted to be part of a process of developing new structures aimed at widening the base of economic and functional co-operation with other Caribbean Basin states. They have actively participated in shaping the structure, defining the scope of work and bringing into force the Association of Caribbean States (ACS) by ratification of the relevant inter-governmental agreement.

Making Restructuring Effective

William Barton, a Canadian diplomat, in discussing reform of the United Nations, made a number of points that are equally relevant to 'restructuring' in the Caribbean Community Secretariat. For restructuring to be effective, a number of processes must be congruent and supportive. Governments should continue to examine their own internal coordinating mechanisms. The Secretariat's personnel policies should continue to work to secure the recruitment of competent staff with more of its staff having second languages, but also to have adequate geographic representation.

The organisation should be able to examine which problem areas of the past could lay fewer claims on resources, in order to allow refocusing of programmes in light of new challenges. The organisation can benefit from paying particular attention to the principle of accountability so that it could be demonstrated to member Governments, that its programmes are fulfilling their purposes by responding to challenges with economy, efficiency and effectiveness. And to show that it has instituted mechanisms to fulfil its obligation of delivering value for money. Governments on their part should ensure that resources are available for the initiatives and programmes they approve.

At this juncture, however, there is a growing feeling that it would be unwise to regard the CARICOM 'restructuring' to date as settling matters once for all. In respect of the Secretariat itself, a number of persons see the need for a review of the strategic plan for its restructuring and the testing of its emphases and priorities in the light of ever clearer global trends. In this view, under the twin constraints of limited resources (owing to constrained contribution from member states and diminishing aid from donors), and the need to reposition the Community in a highly competitive, aid-and-preferences-averse world, there is continuing need to revisit basic questions such as:

- What should be the long-term direction of the collective membership (including its strategic space)?
- What business therefore should the Secretariat gear itself to be in, based on the expectations of its stakeholders?
- What should be the scope and mix of its programmes?
- What new core skills competencies and capabilities need to be built?
- What new services should it promote?
- How can it better focus its efforts so that it is geared to critical *future* Community success factors and help promote strategies that protect its stakeholders against external threats and internal weaknesses?

It would be useful then if the Secretariat can look again at the region and itself in the light of greater awareness of global trends. In terms of broad posture, the Secretariat can do well to address the challenge posed by Prime Minister Owen Arthur of Barbados in his recent address at the Institute of International Relations, Trinidad and Tobago. Mr Arthur recommended a review of our priorities and goals in developing strategies to deal with a reciprocity-driven trading environment and in securing new capital for enterprise development and increasing credit-worthiness. He suggested that a new look be taken at the approach to technology-driven change and competitive advantage, and appropriate human resource development (bearing in mind our potential for development of service industries).

Thus, we may begin to ask fundamental questions:

- If the Secretariat were to be found to be a successful, vibrant, relevant organisation five to ten years from now, what would its profile, priority programmes, internal processes have to be, working back from that desired future image?

- What should be the optimum breadth and mix of its service products?
- How should it position itself regarding other organisations (including the ACS), technology-related success factors, promotion of capital and entrepreneurship, skills-related success factors, image and organisational capability, and the marketing of the quality of its services?
- What are the critical four or so driving forces making for fundamental change and what might be done to address them structurally and programme-wise?

In other words, effective future-driven restructuring should address the issue of decision-making at two levels: whether strategic mission and priorities are properly aligned with major trends; and whether structures and processes to deal with priorities are likely to lead to improved quality of decisions and effective results.

This would seem to call for appropriate sourcing of strategy and well focused activity; building appropriate organisational capability in terms of skills, behavioural and managerial competencies required; appropriate organisational learning and information sharing environment; building of supportive networks nationally, regionally and in the West Indian Diaspora as sources of expertise, technical assistance and capital, as well as opportunities for cross-fertilisation of value-creating knowledge.

Internally, the Secretariat will need to continue to spend considerable time building an organisation with a forward looking organisational culture, emphasising openness and information sharing, building technical skills, promoting interactive and interpersonal skills (even moreso), encouraging innovation and ownership of results further down in the organisational strata. Organisational change would require persistent efforts to build in-house coalitions for new and appropriate managerial behaviours and to regenerate levels of trust between managers and their knowledge workers especially. This is work that has begun, but would require sustained effort to be really beneficial.

Finally, there must be scope for the organisation and its senior executives to devote more time to looking outward, and *forward,* five or more years into the future. The organisation must give time to building a shared corporate perspective on needed strategic space, as well as a transformation agenda that presents alternatives to the limited sovereignty, or 'shiprider' solution, proposed in some quarters as a reasonable model for prosperity and security for certain small states in the Caribbean.

Note

This paper was published in *CARICOM Perspective,* No. 66, June 1966, pp. 89–92.

[39]

The Caribbean Court
of Justice
Challenge and Response[*]

Duke Pollard

. . . the case for a Caribbean Supreme Court could be based on the need for a regional Court of last resort to apply laws incorporating a collective regional ethos, reflecting the moral imperatives of the Caribbean social reality and amenable to interpretation by judges who would have internalised the values informing the content of that social reality. (Duke Pollard, *CARICOM Perspective,* 1998).

The draft agreement establishing the Caribbean Court of Justice must be perceived as constituting the measured institutional response of competent decision makers in the Caribbean Community to a challenge which persisted in the region for several decades. This challenge is multi-faceted, comprehending dimensions which include juridically misconceived appeals to sovereignty, genuine concerns about autonomous judicial decision-making, the legal erudition of potential incumbents and the financial insecurity of an indigenous Court of last resort. All of these issues were ventilated by both members of the judiciary and the private bar at a symposium organised and sponsored by Caribbean Rights in Bridgetown, Barbados on November 28, 1998 and will be employed as the point of departure for much of the discussion which follows.

Among the more ardent proponents of the argument that an indigenous Court of last resort is necessary to complete the independence of member states of the Caribbean Community is Mr Justice Telford Georges. In his characterisation, the learned judge maintained:

(s)tarkly put, it appears to me that an independent country should assume the responsibility for providing a court of its own choosing for the final determination of legal disputes arising for decision in the country. It is a compromise of sovereignty to leave that decision to a court which is part of the former colonial hierarchy, a court in the appointment of whose members we have absolutely no say. The counter argument is that . . . on achieving independence the countries (of the Caribbean) had a choice of either allowing appeals to an external court to continue or of abolishing them. It is therefore not a derogation from sovereignty to allow appeals to continue. It was in effect an exercise of that right. I think this is the type of argument, which the average person would call a lawyer's argument. It asserts that it is an exercise of sovereignty and of independence to choose a situation of dependency. In real life, any one who behaved in that way would evoke pity and exasperation, like the grown man who demonstrates his independence by continuing to live free at home.

However, from the perspective of the norms applicable to state interaction in the international community, it appears to be in the nature of an axiomatic juridical postulate that the essence of sovereignty is the faculty to compromise it. And, as postulated, the sovereignty argument is based on the wrong conclusion for the wrong reason.

As the quotation at the commencement of this article suggests, the case for an indigenous Court of last resort may be persuasively advanced without an appeal to popular sentiment by reference to our colonial past. Nor should lawyers resile from employing lawyer's arguments to demonstrate the relevance of legal rules. Indeed, the layman's inability to appreciate such arguments should not be more a cause of concern than the lawyer's inability to grasp the mathematical complexities of Einstein's theory of relativity nor the scientific implications of Newton's corpuscular theory of light.

And in this context, it does appear to be less a construct of Cartesian logic, than an incident of special pleading, to introduce at this juncture of the debate, a simile whose pertinence for addressing socio-attitudinal phenomena appears to be unimpeachable but which is not likely to be accorded any persuasive value in analysing inter-state relations governed by generally accepted norms of international law.

An issue of considerable and continuing concern to the private bar in the Caribbean Community is the insulation of the Caribbean Court of Justice (CCJ) from political manipulation. In the present submission, this concern is common to politics the world over.

In the present submission, it would be disingenuous to assume a greater disposition in the Caribbean to interfere with the judiciary than exists among the states of the European Union. Despite this, the appointment of judges to the European Court of Justice and to the Court of First Instance of the European Community is made by the political directorate. Thus Article 167 of the Rome Treaty provides that:

The Judges and Advocates General shall be chosen from persons whose independence is beyond doubt and who possess the qualifications required for appointment to the highest judicial offices in their respective countries or who are jurisconsults of recognised competence; they shall be appointed by common accord of the Governments of the Member States for a term of six years . . . and shall be eligible for reappointment . . .

In order to address this concern of the private bar in the Community, the political directorate has agreed to remove the appointment of judges of the Caribbean Court of Justice from direct political control. Thus Article V(I) of the Agreement provides for the establishment of a Regional Judicial and Legal Services Commission, and Article V(2)(1) charges the Commission with responsibility for the appointment of judges other than the president (Article IV(5)).

The President is to be appointed or removed by a qualified majority vote of the Contracting Parties on the recommendation of the Regional Judicial and Legal Services Commission. The President of the European Court of Justice is elected by the members of the Court from among their number for a term of three years and may be re-elected (Article 167). Thus in both cases the appointment of the President is one removed from the political directorates of the European Union and the Caribbean Community.

In either case, the temptation to compromise the independence of the Court is likely to be a function of the relevant political culture and the viability of the perception of the role of the justice sector in the overall development of national economies. In this connection, it does appear to be pertinent to submit that as a general rule the political directorate in the Caribbean Community underrate the contribution of the judicial sector to national economic and social development. But, in the present submission, its contribution must be seen to be critical. Suffice it to comment that investment decisions by potential investors are not unrelated to perceptions of the effectiveness of judicial remedies in one or another jurisdiction.

In the submission of Mr Justice Telford Georges, one distressing fact is that the opposition of the private bar in the community to the establishment of an indigenous Court of last resort is the quality of judges before whom counsel are constrained to appear. However, this perception of the private bar has been vigorously contested in informed quarters.

In one submission, the validity of this perception is brought into question by the fact that most appeals to the Judicial Committee of the Privy Council from the Caribbean are dismissed. And, in any event, it has been observed that there is no requirement established by the relevant provisions of the Agreement Establishing the Caribbean Court of Justice that members of the Court be appointed from among sitting incumbents. Moreover, the argument should be advanced that, more often than not, the quality of judicial pronouncements is a function of the quality of the submissions of counsel in the relevant case. Indeed, the West Indian Commission, in its celebrated report, submitted that:

In the matter of judicial talent for staffing the Court, there can be no room for doubt. Some of our own highest judicial officers have sat on the very Privy Council itself; the Caribbean has now provided a judge of the world's highest judicial tribunal – the International Court of Justice at the Hague; several of our lawyers have been in demand as Chief Justices and Judges of Courts of Appeal in jurisdictions like The Bahamas, Bermuda, the Seychelles and several countries of continental Africa. When Commonwealth countries look for legal talent, it is often to the Caribbean that they turn. What ails us that we lack the confidence to go forward.

And competent decision makers are in no doubt that the required expertise can be accessed from among qualified persons in the Community.

Concerns expressed by the private bar and one or two opposition political parties in the region about the willingness and ability of governments of the Community to provide the funding necessary to establish and maintain the Caribbean Court of Justice are not without considerable merit. In the characterisation of Mr Justice Telford Georges:

. . . if Great Britain had given a grant on the dissolution of the Federation for the construction of buildings and the provision of a basic library for a Caribbean final Court and had agreed for a period of ten years to make available judges paid by them, one may today have been looking forward for the celebrating of the 40th anniversary of that Court rather than being timid about setting it up if not downright opposed.

In the submission of the West Indian Commission:

. . . A CARICOM Supreme Court will require the provision of resources but, in one sense, this is like straining at a gnat when we have already swallowed a camel in terms of national expenditure on the judicial system. Even so, we should find ways of reducing costs. One way, we feel, is to locate the Court in one place. We have already referred to the generous offer by Trinidad and Tobago; that is a great help. Another device might be to allow some of the members of the Court to remain in their home locations

– other perhaps than the Chief Justice. Communications have improved so greatly, both physical communications and telecommunications, that savings can be explored in new and imaginative ways. Where the resources will be most needed will be in attracting and retaining the very best of our judicial talent for service on the Court. On this we cannot skimp; but it will be one of the most productive investments the Region can make in the interest of making CARICOM work and in the wider cause of civil society throughout our Region.

It does appear that the countries of the OECS have resolved the problem of the financial security of their Court by agreeing to an arrangement by which the Eastern Caribbean Central Bank is responsible for funding that institution, including the payment of the emoluments of judges. There is no guarantee, however, that an agreement by the other member states of the Community to have their central banks provide the funding for the Caribbean Court of Justice would yield the same result. The central banks of other member states are not independent of their political directorates and any such arrangement is unlikely to afford any greater comfort than the currently proposed arrangement to make the expenses of the Court a charge on the national consolidated fund.

As concerns the issue of jurisdiction, competent policy makers have responded positively to the recommendation of the West Indian Commission to invest the Caribbean Court of Justice with original jurisdiction in respect of the interpretation and application of the Treaty of Chaguaramas as amended. In his excellent presentation on the Caribbean Court of Justice, the learned Mr Justice Telford Georges expressed doubt about such a course of action. In his submission, Articles 11 and 12 of the original Treaty were adequate to address the issue of disputes among member states concerning the interpretation and application of the Treaty. In his submission, disputes arising between Member States on issues of unfair trading practices will be disputes similar to the one between the European Union and the United States on the scheme of preferences afforded bananas from ACP territories as contrasted with bananas from Central and South America.

. . . and the sense of bitterness may be no less . . . (and) it would be unwise to permit the possibility of exposing a Caribbean Court still building its reputation to a divisive dispute of that sort among the members where there is an allegation of unfair trading.

In the present submission, it would be foolhardy to disregard lightly submissions of the learned Justice, especially in view of his acknowledged erudition and vast experience on the bench. This observation notwithstanding, it is pertinent to indicate some issues of considerable importance which might have been overlooked.

Foremost among these is the fact that whereas the regime of rights and obligations established by the original Treaty of Chaguaramas was relatively meagre on rights and weak on obligations, the new dispensation contemplated by the far-reaching revision of the Treaty, creates a qualitatively different regime in which extremely important rights are being conferred and equally important obligations are being imposed on member states. In this new dispensation, it cannot be business as usual and relevant decisions cannot remain unimplemented if the stated objectives of the Caribbean Single Market and Economy are to be realised. An immediate task confronting all member states once the revised Treaty comes into force would be its implementation by the enactment of relevant legislation. The practical effect of such enactments would be to endow national courts with jurisdiction to interpret and apply the Treaty, thereby facilitating a Pandora's box of interpretations which are not required to be consistent with one another.

The case for investing the Court with original jurisdiction was persuasively argued by the West Indian Commission in its celebrated report 'Time for Action'. In the characterisation of the Commission:

... there is now another reason for establishing a court of high authority in the Region, and that is the process of integration itself. Integration in its broadest economic sense –involving a Single CARICOM Market, monetary union, the movement of capital and labour and goods, and functional co-operation in a multiplicity of fields – must have the underpinning of Community law. Integration rests on rights and duties; it requires the support of the rule of law applied regionally and uniformly. A CARICOM Supreme Court interpreting the Treaty of Chaguaramas, resolving disputes arising under it, including disputes between Governments parties to the Treaty, declaring and enforcing Community law, interpreting the Charter of Civil Society – all by way of the exercise of an original jurisdiction – is absolutely essential to the integration process. It represents in our recommendations one of the pillars of the CARICOM structures of unity.

Essentially, our recommendation is that the Court should have an original jurisdiction in matters arising under the Treaty of Chaguaramas (as revised) and that any CARICOM citizen (individual or corporate) and *any Government of a Member State of the* Community or the CARICOM Commission itself, should have the competence to apply for a ruling of the Court in a matter arising under the Treaty. This will include, perhaps prominently so, matters in dispute between Member States in relation to obligations under the Treaty, particularly under the Single Market regime; but it will also provide for clarification of Community law as it develops pursuant to decisions taken within the CARICOM process. As already indicated, we envisage that that original jurisdiction should also be exercisable to a limited degree in the context of the CARICOM Charter of Civil Society which we have separately recommended.

We believe the arguments for the Court to be unassailable. It needs only to be added as an important footnote to what we have said about the establishment of the CARICOM Supreme Court that the process of development of Community law in the future will be part of the equally necessary evolution of reform of our legal systems themselves. The point we make here is that we can now look for return on the investment the Region has made in the development of law as a major discipline in the University of the West Indies.

The foregoing submission of the West Indian Commission touch on three important issues which have been addressed by the draft Treaty articles and the draft Rules of Court of the Caribbean Court of Justice relating to the original jurisdiction of the Court. These relate to the following:

(a)   uniformity in the interpretation and application of the Treaty;
(b)   *locus standi* for both public and private entities in matters for which the Court is seised; and
(c)   development of Community law pursuant to decisions taken within the CARICOM process *(stare decisis)*.

Before examining these issues, however, it is proposed to offer some clarification on the term 'Caribbean Community' and 'Community law' as they are employed in the CARICOM context. As a first step in any such examination, it is important to bear in mind that despite its misleading nomenclature, to wit, 'Caribbean Community', the regional integration movement from its very inception and, indeed, up to the present time, remains an association of sovereign states.

This status was clearly established by the voting procedure employed in the Conference of Heads of Government. Article 9 of the original treaty provides: 'The conference shall make decisions and recommendations by the affirmative vote of all its members.'

Article 18 (1) of Protocol I which amends the Treaty provides: 'Save as otherwise provided in this Treaty and subject to paragraph 2 of this Article and the relevant provisions of Article 17, the Conference shall take decisions by an affirmative vote of all its members and such decisions shall be binding'. Paragraph 2 of Article 18 provides that abstentions in an amount not more than one-quarter of the Community's membership shall not operate to impair the validity of decisions of the Conference, while Article 17(3) provides that decisions on procedural issues, of all organs of the Community, including the Conference, shall be reached by a simple majority of the member states.

In effect the unanimity rule, which is ordinarily perceived by international lawyers as the legal expression of sovereign equality of states, operates to deprive the highest organ of the Caribbean Community of any attribute of supra-nationality which is a standard ingredient of communities in the juridical sense. Further, the Caribbean Community possesses no organ like the European Union and the Andean Common Market, whose acts create legally-binding rights and obligations directly for private entities, that is, without the intervention of national legislatures.

In short, the term 'Community law' appearing in the West Indian Commission's submission quoted above is ordinarily employed to characterise norms arising from or under relevant international instruments and which create rights and obligations directly for private law entities. *Stricto juris,* therefore, the term 'Community law' is juridically misconceived in its application to the Caribbean regional integration movement.

Uniformity in the Interpretation and Application of the Treaty

The objective of uniformity in the application and interpretation of the constituent instrument of any integration movement would appear to be as axiomatic for its successful development as it would be for the efficient functioning of the CARICOM Single Market and Economy. Given that the Treaty of Chaguaramas creates rights and obligations for member states only, and has to be implemented by national law before private entities can benefit from its provisions, it would be reasonable to assume that, in the absence of an agreed mechanism for authoritatively and definitively interpreting and applying the Treaty, the aphorism *quot homines tot sententiae* would prevail. Such an eventuality would, in the present submission, constitute a prescription for legal uncertainty with daunting adverse consequences for foreign direct investment, and the structured development of the CARICOM Single Market and Economy.

Postulated in other terms, not only should the proposed Caribbean Court of Justice have jurisdiction to interpret and apply the Treaty, but that jurisdiction must either be exclusive or final if legal certainty, which is indispensable for the successful development of the CARICOM Single Market and Economy, is to be secured.

The founding fathers of the European Union, buoyed by similar sentiments, crafted Article 177 of the Rome Treaty to read as follows:

Article 177

The court of Justice shall have jurisdiction to give preliminary rulings concerning:

    (a) the interpretation of this Treaty;

    (b) the validity and interpretation of acts of the institutions of the Community;

(c)   the interpretation of the statutes of bodies established by an act of the
Council, where those statues so provide.

Where such a question is raised before any court or tribunal of a Member State, that
court or tribunal may, if it considers that a decision on the question is necessary to
enable it to give judgement, request the Court of Justice to give a ruling thereon.

Where any such question is raised in a case pending before a court or tribunal of a
Member State, against whose decisions there is no judicial remedy under national law,
that court or tribunal shall bring the matter before the Court of Justice.[1]

It does appear from an ordinary reading of these provisions that the
European Court of Justice is the final, though not the only, tribunal competent
to rule on the interpretation and application of the Rome Treaty. The ultimate
objectives of legal certainty and uniformity in the applicable norms are,
however, the same. Similar considerations appear to have informed the
establishment of the Court of Justice of the Cartagena Agreement, whose final
preambular paragraph reads as follows:

Certain that both the stability of the Cartagena Agreement and the rights and obligations deriving from it must be safe-guarded by a juridical entity at the highest level,
independent of the governments of the member countries and from the other bodies
of the Cartagena Agreement with the Authority to define communitarian law, resolve
the controversies which arise under it, and to interpret it uniformly...

Consistently with the foregoing, the provisions of the said Agreement on
Advisory Opinions read as follows:

Article 28. It shall correspond to the Court (sic) to interpret, through prior advisory
opinions, the norms which comprise the juridical structure of the Cartagena Agreement, in order to assure uniform application in the territories of the member countries.

Article 29. National judges who have before them a case in which any of the norms
comprise the juridical structure of the Cartagena Agreement must be applied may
petition the Court for its interpretation of such norms, but provided that the ruling is
subject to appeal within the national judicial system. In the event that it is necessary for
the national court to issue its ruling before receiving the interpretation of the Court,
the judge must proceed to decide the case.

In the event that the ruling is not subject to appeal within the national judicial system,
the judge shall suspend the proceeding and petition the interpretation of the Court, ex
officio in all cases, or upon the petition of an interested party, if so required by law.

Article 30. The Court shall restrict its interpretation to defining the content and scope
of the norms of the juridical structure of the Cartagena Agreement. The Court may
not interpret the content and scope of domestic law nor judge the substantive facts of
the case.

Article 31. The judge hearing the case must adopt the interpretation of the Court.[2]

The approach adopted by the draft Articles is to invest the Caribbean Court of Justice with exclusive jurisdiction in respect of the interpretation and application of the Treaty. Indeed, this was the only rational approach open to the drafters if the objectives of legal certainty and uniformity in the applicable norms were to be secured. The decision of the Conference to invest the Caribbean Court of Justice with original jurisdiction, as distinct from exclusive jurisdiction, would not operate to deprive municipal courts within the Community of concurrent jurisdiction in respect of the interpretation and application of the Treaty. In the premises the objectives of legal certainty and uniformity in the applicable norms would only be secured if the Court were also invested with final appellate jurisdiction in respect of the interpretation and application of the Treaty.

Since, however, the relevant decision of the Conference was confined to an original jurisdiction only, the objectives of legal certainty and uniformity in applicable norms, which appear to be the subject of a compelling inference from the context informing the decision, could only be secured by making the jurisdiction of the Court exclusive as well.

The foregoing considerations appear to explain the thrust of the draft Treaty Articles which read as follows:

Article IX (a)

The Court shall have (exclusive) jurisdiction to hear and deliver final judgement on:

(a) (actions) (applications) by Member States parties to this Agreement;
(b) referrals from national courts of Member States parties to this Agreement, disputes between Member States parties to this Agreement and the Community concerning the interpretation and application of the Treaty.

Article IX (c)

Where a national court or tribunal of a Member State Party is seised of an issue whose resolution involves a question concerning the interpretation or application of the Treaty, the court or tribunal concerned shall, if it considers that a decision on the question is necessary to enable it to deliver judgement, refer the question to the Court.

Consequently, even though the Conference did not pronounce on the exclusive jurisdiction of the Court, the Legal Affairs Committee will need to advise the Conference that in the absence of such exclusivity, the exercise of an original jurisdiction by the Court will not operate to secure the objectives of legal certainty and uniformity in applicable norms, both of which are required for the efficient and successful development of the CSME.

Locus Standi for both public and private entities

Since traditional international law only recognised states and state entities as subjects of international law, only such entities were recognised as capable of espousing a claim in an international forum. Consequently, there was no machinery in the international domain by which persons, natural and juridical, could have asserted a claim against foreign states and their nationals.[3] In the submission of the Permanent Court of International Justice, predecessor to the International Court of Justice (ICJ), the claimant state, in espousing the claim of its national, was in effect asserting a right with respect to a wrong committed against the state in respect of its national.[4]

When a state determines that an international delinquency has been committed against one of its nationals or his property, the foreign office of the State concerned normally makes a claim against the offending State, initially, by diplomatic representation designed to secure an *ex gratia* settlement, and ultimately, by judicial settlement if the parties so agree.[5] In the absence of consent, an international tribunal is not competent to determine the claim. For the claim to succeed, the claimant state must establish:

(a) the nationality of the claim, or its legal entitlement to espouse the claim;
(b) the exhaustion of local remedies in the jurisdiction of the delinquent State; and
(c) the jurisdiction of the tribunal to hear the claim.

And, in the absence of a contrary agreement, the state espousing a claim must establish continuous nationality, or that the person aggrieved was its national at all material times, that is, both at the time of the incident grounding the claim and at the date of espousal of the claim.

Where the claim is by a state for breach of treaty provisions respecting its nationals, the injury is considered to be a breach of good faith and an injury directly to the state itself.

Only in the rare instance where the treaty is intended to confer rights directly upon the individual can it be said that the individual is also injured . . . Even where the national has rights directly under the treaty, the contracting State alone should have the competence to bring suit and this competence should be independent of any change in nationality.[6]

Where the national aggrieved is a company or corporation, the nationality of the claim will be determined by one or more genuine links such as the place of incorporation,[7] the place of domicile,[8] the place of the *siee social* or administrative direction, or the disposition of effective control.[9]

Consonant with traditional international law, the statutes of the International Court of Justice (ICJ) accord *locus standi* to states only. Article 34(1) of the Statutes of the ICJ reads as follows: 'Only States may be parties in cases before the Court'.[10] These provisions are in sharp contrast to the provisions of Article 173 of the Rome Treaty which reads as follows:

The Court of Justice shall review the legality of acts of the Council and the Commission other than recommendations or opinions. It shall for this purpose have jurisdiction in actions brought by a Member State, the Council or the Commission on grounds of lack of competence, infringement of an essential procedural requirement, infringement of this Treaty or of any rule of law relating to its application, or misuse of powers.

Any natural or legal person may, under the same conditions, institute proceedings against a decision addressed to that person or against a decision which, although in the form of a regulation or a decision addressed to another person, is of direct and individual concern to the former.

The proceedings provided for in this Article shall be instituted within two months of the publication of the measure, or of its notification to the plaintiff or, in the absence thereof, of the day on which it came to the knowledge of the latter, as the case may be.

Similarly, the Court of Justice of the Cartagena Agreement accords *locus standi* to both public and private entities as provided in the following Articles of the Treaty creating the Court of Justice of the Cartagena Agreement:

Article 17

It shall correspond (sic) to the Court to decide the nullification of Decisions of the Commission and Resolutions of the Junta adopted in violation of the norms which comprise the juridical structure of the Cartagena Agreement, including *ultra vires* acts, when these are impugned by any member country, by the Commission, by the Junta, or by natural or juridical persons as provided in Article 19 of the Treaty.

Article 18

The member countries may only bring an action of nullification against the Decisions approved without their affirmative vote.

Article 19

Natural and juridical persons may bring actions of nullification against Decisions of the Commission or Resolutions of the Junta which are applicable to them and cause them harm.

It is important to note, however, that in both cases where private entities have *locus standi* in matters before the courts, such entities are directly affected by the acts of competent organs of the integration movement. In both integration movements, provision has been made for legislation with direct effects. Thus, Article 189 of the Rome Treaty which addresses Community legislation, provides as follows:

In order to carry out their task, the Council and the Commission shall, in accordance with the provisions of this Treaty, make recommendations or deliver opinions.

A regulation shall have general application, It shall be binding in its entirety and directly applicable in all Member States.

A directive shall be binding, as to the result to be achieved upon each Member State to which it is addressed, but shall leave to the national authorities the choice of form and methods.

A decision shall be binding in its entirety upon those to whom it is addressed.

Recommendations and opinions shall have no binding force.[11]

Similarly, the relevant provisions of the agreement creating the Court of Justice of the Cartagena Agreement provides as follows:

Article 2

Decisions are obligatory for the member countries as of the date they are approved by the Commission.

Article 3

Decisions of the Commission are directly applicable in the member countries from the date of their publication in the Official Gazette of the Cartagena Agreement, unless the decision provides for a later date . . .

The question now to be examined and determined by competent decision makers is whether, given the broad objectives of the CARICOM Single Market and Economy as set out in the various protocols, and the role the private sector is required to play in this new paradigm of economic development, private sector entities should not have *locus standi* in matters before the Caribbean Court of Justice. At its Second Ordinary Meeting held in the Bahamas from September 7–10, 1998, the Legal Affairs Committee, *inter alia*, 'noted the recommendation that a procedure should be considered to afford individuals, institutions or other private entities, the opportunity to appear before the Court in special circumstances'.

The draft articles, consonant with traditional international law, do not accord private entities *locus standi* in matters before the court. Consequently, a private entity aggrieved by a member state or any of its nationals must have its claim espoused by the State of nationality. Alternatively, the party aggrieved may institute legal proceedings in the national courts of the delinquent party and secure a ruling of the Caribbean Court of Justice on any issue relating to the interpretation or application of the Treaty through a reference by the national court to the Caribbean Court of Justice. In both instances, therefore, access to the Caribbean Court of Justice by private entities would be indirect. The issue falling to be determined is whether, in the considered view of the Legal Affairs Committee, such access should not be direct.

Unlike the Treaty of Rome, which legislates directly and derivatively for private entities in the European Union with direct effects, the Treaty Establishing the Caribbean Community, as revised, does not create rights and obligations directly for private entities within the Community. Nor does any organ of the Caribbean Community like the Council and the Commission of the European Union or the Commission of the Andean Common Market, have the competence to create rights and obligations for private entities within the domestic jurisdiction of member states without the intervention of national legislations. The rights and obligations created by the Treaty of Chaguaramas are both primary and derivative, issuing either from the Treaty itself or from competent organs established by the Treaty *and which have legal incidence for member states only.*

Rights and obligations enjoyed or endured by private entities in the Caribbean Community and expressed in the Treaty have legal incidence for such entities where the relevant Treaty provisions have been enacted into local law. It would appear to follow, therefore, that all claims of private entities arising in connection with the Treaty would have to be espoused by the country of nationality or made the subject of a reference to the Court by national courts seised of the issue. For example, where the Treaty as amended provides for the removal of restriction on the right of establishment, the provision of services or the movement of capital in the Caribbean Community, enjoyment of such rights by private entities is contingent on:

(a) the enactment of Protocol II into local law by member states;
(b) the establishment of the relevant programme for the removal of relevant restrictions by the Council for Trade and Economic Development (COTED) or the Council for Finance and Planning (COFAP) as appropriate;
(c) compliance by member states with the programme established for the purpose by appropriate legislative or administrative measures.

On the basis of the foregoing submissions, the Attorneys General of the region have determined that private entities should be accorded *locus standi* in proceedings before the Caribbean Court of Justice by special leave of the Court on the satisfaction of specified conditions. Consonant with this determination, Article IX(n) of the Draft Agreement Establishing the Caribbean Court of Justice reads as follows:

Article IX (n)

Locus Standi of Private Entities

Nationals of a Contracting Party may, with the special leave of the Court, be allowed to appear as parties in proceedings before the Court where:

(a) the Court has determined in any particular case that the Treaty intended that a right conferred by or under the Treaty on a Contracting Party shall inure to the benefit of such persons directly; and

(b) the persons concerned have established that such persons have been prejudiced in respect of the enjoyment of the benefit mentioned in sub-paragraph (a) of this Article; and

(c) Contracting Party entitled to espouse the claim in proceedings before the Court has:

    (i) omitted or declined to espouse the claim, or

    (ii) expressly agreed that the persons concerned may espouse the claim instead of the Contracting party so entitled; and

(d) the court has found that the interest of justice requires that the persons be allowed to espouse the claim.

Development of Community Law Pursuant to Decisions taken within the CARICOM Process

'Although no international decision is binding on subsequent tribunals, there is a natural reluctance to depart from principles and rules which have proved satisfactory in the past for the settlement of legal issues. Hence a tendency towards *stare decisis* is most marked'.

This submission of O'Connel[12] eloquently adumbrates the current position in international law where decisions of international tribunals create rights and obligations only for the parties to the dispute and constitute a *res inter alios acta* in respect of a third state or party. And it would appear to follow from the doctrine of sovereignty that decisions of an international tribunal involving third parties cannot operate to establish rights and obligations for a state in the absence of the state's consent. In effect, the doctrine of *stare decisis* is perceived to have no place in international law but is a doctrine of municipal law associated with common law jurisdictions. The foregoing notwithstanding, publicists like Hersh Lauterpact[13] detect in the practice of international tribunals a *Jurisprudence constant*, or a tendency for such tribunals to be influenced by judicial decisions of one another even though adherence to such decisions is not a legal requirement.

Since, therefore, it is proposed that the Caribbean Court of Justice should apply international law in the exercise of its original jurisdiction, the Court, in the absence of a contrary intention, would be precluded from being constrained in its determinations by the doctrine of *stare decisis*. But given, as mentioned above, that legal certainty was required for the successful operation of the CARICOM Single Market and Economy, the question to be decided is whether such certainty was possible of achievement in the absence of the application of the doctrine of *stare decisis* in the Court's determinations. The draft Articles have opted for the application of the doctrine of *stare decisis* in the determinations of the Court. Proposed draft Article IX (e) reads as follows:

Member States parties agree that decisions of the Chamber shall create legally binding precedents for parties in proceedings before the Chamber, unless such judgements have been revised in accordance with Article IX (j).

   Alternate Formulation

Decisions of the Court are binding on the parties in respect of the particular case; they constitute binding precedents for parties in subsequent proceedings before the Chamber unless such judgements have been revised in accordance with Article IX (j).

The Legal Affairs Committee will be required to examine and formulate a recommendation on this issue for the Conference.

Notes

1.   The Articles relating to the European Court of Justice are set out in Appendix I.
2.   The Agreement Creating the Court of Justice of the Cartagena Agreement is set out at Appendix II.
3.   D.P. O'Connell, *International Law*, Vol. II 2nd Edition 1970, p.1029.
4.   The Mavrommatis Concession Case (Jurisdiction), P.C.I.J., Sec. A. No.2, 1924.
5.   For international responsibility and the protection of the property of aliens, see D.E. Pollard, *Law and Policy of Producers' Associations*. Oxford University Press, 1982, p. 283.
6.   D.P. O'Connell, *International Law*, Vol. II 2nd Edition 1970, pp.1036–7.
7.   *Standard Oil Co. of N.Y. (US) v Germany*, UN Rep., Vol. VII, (1926) p.301.
8.   *F.W. Flack (G.B.) v United Mexican States*, UN Reports, Vol. V, (1929) p.61.
9.   *Daimler Co. v Continental Tyre and Rubber Co.*(1916), 2 A.C. 307.
10. See Articles relating to the International Court of Justice at Appendix III.
11. See *Treaty Establishing the European Economic Community*, Rome 25 March, 1957, London, HM Stationery Office. (See Appendix IV). Also

Richard Plender, *A Practical Introduction to European Community Law*, Sweet & Maxwell, London, 1980, p. 7.

12. *Treaty Establishing the European Economic Community*, Rome 25 March, 1957 p. 32

13. *The development of International Law by the International Court*, (1998).

References

Brownlie, *Basic Documents in International Law*, 3rd Edition, (Oxford: Clarendon Press, 1983)

D.P. O'Connell, *International Law*, Volumes I & II, (London: Stevens & Sons, 1970).

R. Plender, *A Practical Introduction to European Community Law*, (London: Sweet & Maxwell, 1980).

D.E. Pollard, *Law & Policy of Producers' Associations*, (Oxford: Clarendon Press, 1982).

International Legal Materials, Volume XXIII, No. 2, March 1984.

International Legal Materials, Volume XXIV, No. 4, July, 1995.

★Article featured in CARICOM Perspective, No. 69, June 1999, pp. 24–34.

[40]

The Caribbean Single Market and Economy
The Legal Implications

Duke Pollard

Set out below for general information is a synopsis of the measures taken to implement the Caribbean Single Market and Economy (CSME):

(a) *Free Trade in Goods*

Three member states have not yet dismantled their licensing regimes, while five have not ratified Article 29A of the Treaty to facilitate the unimpeded trade in agricultural products. Two member states have not ratified the revised Schedule IX to facilitate trade in oils and fats while three member states have discriminatory regimes for the treatment of CARICOM salesmen.

(b) *The Common External Tariff*

The structure of the Common External Tariff (CET) to 1998 has been determined and agreed for manufactured products and a basic rate held for agricultural products. With respect to the first phase of implementation of the CET to have been effected by June 1993, two member states are in default. In respect of agricultural products, technical work is to commence early to facilitate negotiations in 1996 with a view to establishing revised rates for 1997.

(c)   *Common Customs Legislation and Uniform Practices and Procedures*

CARICOM Member States are working towards an implementation date of 1995.

(d)   *Common External Trade (Import) Policy*

Consonant with a decision of Conference as early as 1984 that the CET must replace quantitative restrictions as the principal instrument of protection, most member states have eliminated QRs.

(e)   *Elimination of Internal Border Control on Goods and Persons*

Members states have decided to defer work on the free circulation of goods within the region and to take specified measures to promote hassle-free travel in the region. Six member states have not yet accepted forms of identification other than passports for entry into their territories.

(f)   *Harmonisation of Incentives to Investors*

The original Harmonised Scheme of Incentives to Industry has been the subject of intensive study by competent regional experts. The Common Market Council, at its Meeting in February 1994, approved a schedule of activities to advance implementation of a new scheme.

(g)   *Avoidance of Multiple Taxation and Application of a Single Rate of Tax*

Eight member states have signed a Double Taxation Agreement which is due to take effect on January 1 1995. No agreement has yet been reached however, on a uniform rate of taxation.

(h)   *Right to Establish, Own and Manage Production Facilities and to Provide Services on the Same Basis as Nationals*

The right of nationals of member states to establish enterprises and provide services in other member states on a non-discriminatory basis is constrained by aliens landholding legislation, specific legislation in relation to the provision of services like banking and insurance, and legislation requiring work permits. Some member states have enacted remedial legislation in respect of aliens holding land and graduates of regional institutions requiring work permits for gainful employment in their territories.

(i)   *Right to Transfer Capital, Dividends and Profits and to Trade on Stock Exchanges*

Three member states have put arrangements in place for cross listing and cross trading on their respective stock exchanges. The CARICOM Enterprise Regime (CER) is also technically operational although no such enterprise has been established. In July 1994, the Standing Committee of Ministers responsible for Finance directed the Secretariat to undertake an assessment of the CARICOM Enterprise Regime to determine its continued relevance, the requirements to make it operational, and the feasibility of such requirements.

(j) *Common Standards for Goods, Common Legislation for Plant and Animal Protection, Equivalency or Mutual Recognition of Qualifications or Standards*

The Caribbean Common Market Standards Council (CCMSC) had been established to develop and recommend regional standards. However, only one member state has in place the legal and administrative structures to implement regional standards. The CARICOM Export Development Project (CEDP) has provided significant in-country assistance to Member States to enhance their capability in standardisation.

(k) *Harmonisation of Internal Tax Regimes*

No action has been taken by member states in this area.

(l) *Coordination of Macro Economic Policies*

Divergence in monetary, exchange rate and interest rate policies are greater now than in 1993 and minimal efforts have been made to coordinate them. A study commissioned by the Secretariat in 1993 on Macro Economic and Trade Policies has been completed and is being studied by the technical team.

(m) *Payment Arrangements and a Common Currency*

The CMCF remains in abeyance since 1983. Further, three member states have floated their currencies but there appears to be agreement on the free convertibility of CARICOM currencies.

(n) *Caribbean Industrial Programming Scheme (CIPS)*

Member states have all signed the CIPS Protocol which still remains to be effectively operationalised.

(o) *Caribbean Investment Fund*

The Agreement establishing the Caribbean Investment Fund has already entered into force, but the absence of liquidity has militated against its early operationalisation.

(p) *Institutional Arrangements for Decision-Making and Management of CSM&E*

The restructuring of the Secretariat has been completed and a draft Protocol on the new organs and institutions of the CSM&E has been elaborated under the direction of the Intergovernmental Task Force established by the Conference to oversee revision of the Treaty of Chaguaramas. A second draft Protocol on the Right of Establishment,

Movement of Capital and Provision of Services is under examination in the Secretariat.

(q) *Action to Develop a Regional System of Air and Sea Transportation Including a Pooling of Resources by Existing Air and Sea Carriers*

No significant progress has been recorded in this area. In point of fact, the achievement of a regional transport policy which is critical for the success of the CSM&E has been complicated by failure to attract regional participation in recently privatised national carriers and by the emergence of rival carriers in the region. Despite this, the elements of the CSM&E proposed for consideration and adoption below, provide for the establishment of a transport policy for the Single Market and Economy.

The Way Forward

Notwithstanding the attainment of several objectives in that behalf, the establishment of the proposed CSM&E has not been attended by any significant measure of success. As mentioned above, this lack of achievement appears to have been due in large measure to bureaucratic insouciance and inadequate capabilities at the national and regional levels, which were aggravated by the enlargement of institutional responsibilities issuing from the need to respond to unforeseen and unforeseeable significant developments in the hemispheric and global economies. Ironically, these developments while exerting inordinate pressure on national and regional resources have simultaneously underscored the urgency to move towards the establishment of the CSM&E.

At its third meeting which convened in Georgetown, Guyana, October 18–20, 1993, the Intergovernmental Task Force, having considered options for effecting the revision of the Treaty of Chaguaramas in a practical, expeditious and efficient manner, adopted a two-phased approach involving, in the first phase, the elaboration of a protocol to effect the agreed institutional and organisational changes in the Community and, in the second phase, the elaboration of a second protocol to establish the proposed CSM&E at an early date as mandated by the Conference. Pursuant to this determination, the Task Force approved and adopted a draft protocol on the proposed organs, institutions and decision-making procedures of the CSM&E and this was distributed to member states and the OECS Secretariat for comments. It was envisaged that at its fourth meeting scheduled for January 9–12, 1995, in Georgetown, Guyana, the Task Force would have considered and approved the draft protocol for submission to the Common Market Council and the

Attorneys General of CARICOM Member States for consideration and approval. The proposed meeting of the task force was aborted, however, due to the expressed inability of several member states to attend or to submit their comments on the draft protocol to the Secretariat.

In view of the resulting delays in the time-frame for effecting the transition from Common Market to the CSM&E, and, given the urgent need to deepen the CARICOM integration movement, compounded by the inadequate capabilities at the national and regional levels, the Secretariat should consider the establishment of the proposed CSM&E through a revision of the Treaty of Chaguaramas by a series of protocols, as a viable option. In this context, elements of the CSM&E could be established according to the priorities determined by the competent authorities. Such protocols, incorporating amendments to the Treaty of Chaguaramas, would create enabling provisions for competent organs of the Community and constitute a necessary first step for the establishment of the CSM&E. In this way the Treaty, as amended, would operate to establish at the international plane a framework of legal obligations within which competent Community organs could proceed with confidence to adopt required measures for implementation at the national level. The approach canvassed here is consistent with that set out in chapter six of the study entitled, 'CARICOM Single Market and Economy: Concept, Objectives, Elements and Work Programme' which was commissioned by the CARICOM Secretariat, approved by the Common Market Council at its thirty-ninth meeting, and endorsed by the Conference of Heads of Government at its thirteenth meeting in Port of Spain, Trinidad and Tobago in July 1992.

Chapter six of the Study states, *inter alia*:

The elements agreed for the introduction of the Single Market and Economy would be given legal effect in a legal agreement establishing the CARICOM Single Market and Economy. This legal agreement would be an amendment/ replacement of the Common Market Annex to the Treaty of Chaguaramas ... The Treaty having made provisions for the various elements of the Single Market and Economy, it will then be necessary to put in place the various measures that would operationalise the new Treaty provisions. These measures would be designed, agreed upon and implemented in accordance with the arrangements set out in Chapters (iv) and (v) above.

Chapters four and five address the work programme for the introduction of the CSM&E and the decision-making and implementation process.

Set out below are some proposed elements of the proposed CSM&E which, collectively, subsume the various issues identified to be addressed in the approved Work Programme of the CSM&E mentioned above:

i)   elimination of Tariffs, QRs and other restrictions on intra- Community trade;

ii)   establishment of the CET and a Single Market and Economy Trade Policy *vis-à-vis* third states;

iii)   elimination of constraints on free movement of persons, goods, capital, services, and technology;

iv)   establishment of a Single Market and Economy Agricultural Policy;

v)   Industrial Policy;

vi)   Transport Policy;

vii)   Social/labour Policy;

viii)   Investment Policy;

ix)   Economy Taxation Policy;

x)   Human Resources Development Policy;

xi)   coordination/approximation/harmonisation of economic, fiscal, monetary, and financial policies;

xii)   regulation of competition in the Single Market and Economy;

xiii)   harmonisation/unification of legislation of the Single Market and Economy;

xiv)   establishment of the organs and institutions of the Single Market and Economy;

xv)   establishment of a special regime for disadvantaged regions in the Single Market and Economy;

xvi)   promotion of research and development in the Single Market and Economy;

xvii)   disputes settlement/sanctions in the Single Market and Economy;

xviii) establishment of a Single Market and Economy Environment Policy.

It is important to emphasise that the approach to the revision of the Treaty will not necessarily interfere with the structure or content of the Work Programme on the CSM&E, as approved by the competent organs, nor with the various projects which have so far been identified for completion. On the contrary, the proposed paradigm for establishing the CSM&E will facilitate completion of the exercise within a comprehensive and structured framework of treaty obligations as intended by the Secretariat's Study mentioned above. In addressing the establishment of the CSM&E through the elaboration of a series of Protocols and the adoption of appropriate measures at the regional level for implementation at the national plane, the relevant provisions of the draft Protocol on the proposed new organs and decision-making procedures in the CSM&E should also be borne in mind. One objective of these provisions is to allow interested groups of CARICOM member states to integrate their economies at faster rates than others.

This information is not necessarily exhaustive and does not presume to prioritise the elements identified. However, consideration should be given to addressing the issues at [iii] as a matter of priority for completion in 1995. It is not improbable that the provisions of a draft Protocol which was elaborated in this context could be made available for examination and discussion at a multidisciplinary public/private sector workshop on trade and investment aspects of the CSM&E, scheduled to be conducted in 1995. And assuming the adoption and ratification of the two Protocols mentioned above in 1995, consideration could be given to the elaboration and adoption of other protocols on the issues identified in paragraph 5 above.

Note

1.   This paper was first published in *CARICOM Perspective,* No. 65, June 1995, pp. 83–85.

[41]

The OECS and Closer
Political Union

Vaughan Lewis

Since the USA-OECS initiative in October 1983 to intervene in Grenada after the assassination of Prime Minister Maurice Bishop, the orientations and characteristics of the countries of the Eastern Caribbean constituting the Organisation of Eastern Caribbean States have come in for relatively close scrutiny in both academic and political circles across the globe.

The intervention, while giving rise to varied views as to its legitimacy, the role of the USA in the Caribbean at this time, and the extent of autonomy of the OECS member states, did have the positive, longer-term effect of focusing policy makers and others on the question of the roles and viability of very small states in the contemporary international system.

The extremely lively debate that took place at the November 1983 Commonwealth Heads of Government Conference in India was of particular significance in this regard. It led to a substantial policy study, initiated by the Heads of Government on the subject of the vulnerability of small states in the global society, and to a more practical appreciation by the Governments of larger states of the specific problems of the varied kinds of small and very small sovereign entities now in existence.

This paper seeks to discuss some of the problems of a particular set of very small states in the Caribbean, and their current orientations, in the context of

301

a greater global awareness of the need for the international society to focus more directly on this category of countries.

The Organisation of Eastern Caribbean States (OECS)

The OECS (among whom are Antigua and Barbuda, Dominica, Grenada, Montserrat, St Kitts-Nevis, St Lucia, St Vincent and the Grenadines and the British Virgin Islands as an associate member) and other Anglophone Caribbean states bear a general similarity to most Third World states, to the extent that they tend to be, in one economist's phrase, 'small, open, early-state developers . . . not rich in natural resources.' Though some of the larger Caribbean states do in fact possess mineral resources in substantial quantities, they still can be said to fit the general category to the extent that such resources tend not to be diverse. Further, they tend to dominate the economies of these countries in such a way that their economies exhibit characteristics of trade dependence and single source (market) dependants for deriving foreign exchange.

At least two characteristics are readily observable, which distinguishes these states from many other Third World states: the physical characteristics of many of them as island states; and the fact that the majority of them are what are sometimes called in the classification systems of many international agencies, 'middle income' countries or economies (economies of per capita income of between US$500 and US$2000).

As island states, they fall within a group largely concentrated in the Caribbean, the Pacific and the Indian Ocean, and which in recent years some United Nations agencies have decided are worthy of special attention. But even within this category, the Caribbean island-states can be differentiated to the extent that they do not display the characteristic of remoteness (from major land masses) that is normally the case of the majority of contemporary island entities. The Caribbean archipelago lies, as is often observed, in the immediate shadow of a major power, the USA, which exercises legal jurisdiction over some of the territories in the area. In addition, the Caribbean countries are somewhat more spatially concentrated than the island-states of the Pacific and the Indian Ocean. This gives rise constantly, both among the states themselves, and in the major metropolis, to the conclusion that they constitute a geopolitical unity, with the potential for political and policy harmony.

Caribbean political leaders, as is well known, have not in practice found such a conclusion particularly easy to operationalise. And even at the level of mere diplomatic (interstate) relations, difficulties have arisen that indicate a tendency to divisiveness, rather than harmony, in the resolution of problems arising in part from geopolitical proximity. Similarly, given their proximity and the geophysical formation of the sea in which they are located (the Caribbean Basin), Caribbean Governments have not found it easy to take advantage of the Law of the Sea Convention's delineation of a 200-mile Exclusive Economic Zone, in the way that other states and more spatially isolated islands have been able to. (It is noticeable that at the Law of the Sea Conference, most of the participating Caribbean states characterised themselves as 'disadvantaged').

Nonetheless, particularly since the end of the World War II, there have been continuing discussions among the political élites of the Anglophone part of the area about the possibilities for the formation of some kind of political integration of the separate island-territories that might enhance their prospects for economic development and provide a sufficient political space for the maintenance of democratic political freedom.

These discussions quickened as it became apparent that the colonial power, the United Kingdom, was, as it surveyed its own postwar prospects, willing to countenance in various parts of its Empire, the independence of territories within a structure of federalism. An important consideration here certainly was the possibility for more effective maintenance of regional, and therefore global order, if existing entities were aggregated into what were assumed to be viable economic and administrative units. For the Caribbean, such discussions resulted in the formation of the Federation of the West Indies under the experimental status of a self-governing Dominion in 1958. With the secession in 1962 of Jamaica, and its progression to the status of a fully sovereign state, however, this experiment came to an end.

Those, in particular, economic analysts, who have given some consideration to the implication of the 'special characteristics' of islands have concluded that they do not differ substantially from those deriving from the characteristics of smallness, defined in terms of physical size, population or size of economy (GNP). There has now been a fairly substantial discussion in the economic literature of the economic implications of size, and even a casual comparison of the OECS and other Caribbean States will indicate that by any of the relevant criteria these states are small.

Any compilation given the 'size' characteristics of the Caribbean countries, indicates that all the OECS countries fall at the lower end of a listing of small countries in terms of population. On the other hand, none of the countries fall within the category of either island states or underdeveloped states that are in United Nations terminology, least developed or low income countries. All have GNPs per capita that are well over US$500, thus putting them within the category of so-called middle income countries. This means that, in a period in which the emphasis of international aid donors, is on the least developed countries, the OECS states (like other CARICOM countries) find themselves in a dubious position.

Within the category of middle income countries (generally taken as having a per capita income of over US$500), a fairly clear differentiation exists between most of the OECS countries and countries like Trinidad and Tobago and Barbados (and, until the devaluations of the 1980s, Jamaica). The latter, while having much larger population sizes – and in the case of Trinidad and Tobago a much larger land area – all have per capita incomes well in excess of US$2000; while in the case of the former, only Montserrat can claim this. But we might note, while considering per capita income as a criterion, the existence of entities like the British Virgin Islands and the Netherlands Antilles which have managed to acquire fairly substantial per capita incomes – in excess of larger OECS states.

Because of population size, physical size, and per capita income, the general assumption is that many of the Windward and Leeward Islands, as well as the Virgin Islands and Netherlands Antilles, could not survive as independent nations. It is felt that they would be deficient in their external representation systems, and security systems because of inadequate remuneration for the bureaucratic system to ensure minimum efficiency in economic management.

Yet successive attempts at forming an integrated political unit came to nought and were put to a decisive end in 1974 when the Government of Grenada came to agreement with the United Kingdom Government that that country should become fully independent. The Windward and Leeward Islands had, after the independence of Barbados (1966), in an attempt to maintain the coherence of the existing areas of functional cooperation, decided to organise the West Indies Associated States Council of Ministers, as a politically-directed sub-regional management institution. Allied to this was the formation of the Secretariat of the Eastern Caribbean Common Market. And in the framework of that structure most of the other territories proceeded to sovereign status in the late 1970s and early 1980s.

The Organisation of Eastern Caribbean States was then established in June 1981 as the mechanism for enhancing economic, political and functional cooperation among the countries of the Leeward and Windward islands of the Caribbean, after the majority of them had gained full sovereignty following a period as Associated States of the United Kingdom. Independence dates were: Grenada 1974, Dominica 1978, St Lucia 1979, St Vincent and the Grenadines 1979, Antigua and Barbuda 1981, St Kitts and Nevis 1983. Montserrat is still a Crown Colony and cannot participate in matters pertaining to defence, security and foreign affairs without the express consent of the United Kingdom Government. All the full members of the OECS are also members of the Caribbean Community and Common Market. All of them, with the exception of Montserrat, are also signatories to the Memorandum of Understanding establishing the Regional Security System for the Eastern Caribbean whose other member is Barbados. (This was established at the end of 1982 with St Kitts-Nevis adhering to the Memorandum after its assumption of independence in September 1983).

Principal Objectives

Article 3 of the Treaty establishing the OECS provides that the principal objectives of the organisation shall be:

(a) the promotion of cooperation among OECS member states and at the regional and international levels;

(b) the promotion of unity and solidarity among the member states and the defence of their sovereignty, territorial integrity and independence;

(c) to assist member states in the realisation of their obligations and responsibilities to the international community;

(d) to seek to achieve the fullest possible harmonisation of foreign policy among OECS member states; to seek to adopt, as far as possible, common positions on international issues and to establish and maintain wherever possible arrangements for joint overseas representation and/or common services;

(e) to promote economic integration among member states through the ECCM agreement (which became incorporated into the OECS Treaty); and

(f) to pursue these purposes through its respective institutions by discussion of questions of common concern and by agreement and common action.

On the basis of these objectives, the member states of the Organisation have, since 1981, sought to further the economic integration process through a number of measures, the most recent being a decision to liberalise all trade within the Eastern Caribbean Common Market by January 1988. Allied to this has been a revision of the scheme for the allocation of industries among the countries of the grouping; the establishment of the Eastern Caribbean Investment Promotion Service (ECIPS) in the USA which is designed to increase the flow of investment capital into the sub-region; a decision to establish an Eastern Caribbean Export Development Agency (ECEDA) to promote a harmonised approach to increasing exports of agro-industrial and industrial commodities, and to ensure appropriate quality and standards of such exports. But it is increasingly being recognised that the effort at trade liberalisation (given especially that the OECS countries already have one single currency and monetary authority) will accelerate the move towards harmonising customs arrangements, and give more coherent political direction to ensure that potential imbalances arising from free trade are not damaging to the interests of particular countries within the OECS itself.

The point here is recognition that free trade within the market system, along with the relatively free movement of capital, requires at a certain point a degree of organised political coordination – though the form that such political coordination takes can be open to debate. This is the point at which the OECS economic integration process appears to be free market-oriented; economic integration systems never stand still, and economic integration does not, of itself, bring about the political cooperation necessary to sustain the economic integration process.

Some passing remarks might be made here on the question of strengthening the OECS internal market as different from the wider CARICOM region and Common Market, in which these countries also exist, and of which they are an active part. The more coherent organisation of the OECS countries, in recent years, has undoubtedly had an impact on building up the OECS interest in the CARICOM system. On the other hand, the trade depression in CARICOM in recent years, with its effect of diminution of OECS industrial and agro-industrial exports to the more developed CARICOM countries, has made the OECS countries more conscious of the need to further exploit the opportunities for mutual trade within the OECS sub-region and common market itself. This was a part of the context in which the decision was made to liberalise all trade within the OECS Common Market beginning in January 1988. This, however, does not mean that the OECS countries do not recognise the value of doing their best to develop and expand exports to third countries within CARICOM and beyond.

The view can also be asserted, however, that as the process of coordination among the OECS countries proceeds, the OECS system will need for its survival, strategies from, and practical support of the larger countries of the region, especially those of the Eastern and Southern segment of the Caribbean community. It is well recognised that, particularly in respect of economic relations, and of the protection of the OECS country interests in the current unstable international economic environment, the optimal framework for activity is the CARICOM framework. This lesson has been well learnt in our dealings with the European Economic Community, and it is becoming clear, too, in respect of the current discussions on re-organisation of international trading relationships taking place within the GATT system.

The OECS countries have also entered into a number of arrangements for functional cooperation designed to maximise the potential benefit from economies of scale, given their small size. Thus the Eastern Caribbean Drug Service is concerned with the bulk procurement of pharmaceuticals for the public health sectors of member countries; the Multi-Island Project for Technical and Vocational Education is designed to derive technical and financial resources from the international community for the furtherance of activities for these fields; the Fisheries Unit seeks to establish a joint approach to exploitation of the marine resources in the exclusive economic zones of the countries; the Sports Desk undertakes a coordinated approach to the development of sports and physical education in the area; the Directorate of Civil Aviation seeks to ensure appropriate civil aviation standards in the sub-region.

It should be noted too that there has existed for some time among these countries a single judicial system as indicated in the Eastern Caribbean Supreme Court; a common currency and monetary authority in the Eastern Caribbean Central Bank; and for some member countries of the organisation, a joint system of diplomatic representation in the United Kingdom and in Canada.

This kind of cooperation within the OECS has indicated one thing in particular: that as small countries, with small populations subject to extensive migration of skilled personnel, a way must be found to mobilise the human resources of those countries more efficiently, so that a central core of technical expertise can be politically coordinated and directed for use in strategic developmental activities over the sub-region as a whole. It is recognised that for small countries, the key to economic development is: the appropriate mobilisation – training and organisation – of their limited human resources at all levels. The experience of the political leadership, as well as the experience of others in the sub-region, has indicated that mobilisation and coordination within a framework of closer political union, now appears to be a necessity.

Specialists working in the major metropolitan centres and who come into contact with the limited number of diplomatic and technical personnel representing the interest of OECS countries abroad, will surely be aware, as are OECS political and technical cadres, that a system of joint representation in the world capitals and international fora, should result in a more effective representation of OECS country interests there.

None of the OECS countries has anything near the capacity, in their diplomatic establishments, to deal with, for example, the intricacies of the American Congress – so increasingly influential in the decision-making of the

US Government. The political leaders now seem to believe too, that political union, bringing in its train the aggregate of diplomatic talent as exists, would substantially enhance the present situation, through division of labour. It should be noted, too, that two of the so-called More Developed Countries of the wider Caribbean Community, Barbados and Guyana, recently requested the Caribbean Heads of Government Conference to consider the possibility of sharing representation in international conferences and organisations. One of the arguments made for this is the more cost-effective use of the financial resources at present available to the CARICOM states.

Political Integration Revived

Now, almost 30 years after the initiation of a West Indies Federation that failed, the question of political integration has been raised again, this time in the context of the political-economic co-operation process encompassing the smaller and less developed states of the Eastern Caribbean. It would appear to be the feeling of the majority of the political directorate of the OECS that the prospects for a beneficial political union among these islands are better than in the past, since such a union can now be built on a recent experience of relative success in interstate cooperation – that of growing communication, growing harmonisation of decision-making and of implementation of decisions and laws of the OECS states.

This cooperation process is still a fragile one, based on slim human and financial resources; and on the necessity for the political leadership to gradually learn methods of communicating with each other and making difficult decisions based on compromise, consensus and reciprocity within a framework that sustains amicable interstate relations.

Thus at the Eleventh Meeting of the Authority of the Organisation of Eastern Caribbean States held on May 28–29, 1987, the Heads of Government agreed, following a discussion on the question of closer union among the OECS countries, that while they favoured this,

(1) member Governments would engage in a process of comprehensive consultation within their countries, including a Referendum before deciding on further appropriate steps;

(2) that Heads of Government would take the opportunity of their presence in St Lucia for the CARICOM Heads of Government Meeting (June 30–July 3, 1987) to hold further discussions on this matter, including discussions on an appropriate question to be simultaneously put before the peoples of member countries; and

(3) that in preparation for those discussions the Legal Unit of the Secretariat would prepare draft enabling legislation for holding a Referendum.

On July 3, 1987, the Heads of Government of Dominica, Grenada, Montserrat, St Kitts-Nevis, St Lucia and St Vincent and the Grenadines further discussed this decision in St Lucia and issued a statement in which it was noted that a Union of Eastern Caribbean States 'would increase the benefits which had already been gained by the present cohesion of Member States in the OECS'. (Antigua and Barbuda, the other full member of the OECS, indicated that it would not wish to participate in such a union, and the participation of the British Virgin Islands was not discussed at this meeting.) The Heads of Government of the countries named also indicated that as 'guiding principles', such a union should be 'fully democratic, governed by the rule of law and be constitutionally bound to respect the protection of the basic human rights of all citizens'; and that in each constituent unit of the proposed union 'there should be a form of administration which will ensure responsiveness to the local concerns of the people'.

While recognising the significance of existing cooperative activities, the Heads of Government in their statement of July 3, 1987, also asserted the view that a closer political union of their countries would bring further benefits to the peoples of their countries. These benefits could be achieved through:

- better utilisation of expertise in the region which the countries cannot afford on their own;
- much larger market access for the goods produced in the member territories, which would move freely within the proposed Union;
- free movement of capital;
- freedom of movement of all persons;
- more effective and wiser joint representation abroad making it more efficient and less costly, at the same time affording the territories increased access to international financial institutions;
- more effective joint marketing of agricultural produce thus building on the achievements of such organisations as the Windward Islands Banana Association (WINBAN);
- enhanced status within CARICOM and particularly within the international community;
- opportunities for more effective joint promotion and marketing of tourism.

While the Heads of Government of the interested countries have agreed to hold a referendum within a short time, to seek a determination from their peoples on whether there was a popular desire for a union, it is also the case that there are certain constitutional requirements for effecting a merger of the sovereignties of these states. The constitution of each state requires that to amend or remove the entrenched clauses of the constitutions, there must be first, a referendum on the form of new constitution proposed, and secondly, this constitution must receive the support of a substantial majority of the members of the Legislature. (The particular majority requirements in the case of the referendum as well as the vote of members of the Legislature differ among the countries).

The Heads of Government have therefore recognised that in respect of both a preliminary referendum and a formulation of plans for effecting any political union, extensive preparatory work would have to be undertaken. They have therefore agreed that, given their own limited resources, assistance in the form of both technical and financial resources would have to be sought from sympathetic Governments and institutions within the international community.

Specialist Task Force Groups

In respect of the preliminary referendum, it is accepted that extensive preparation of information and documentation materials will be required in order to effectively inform the communities of the states of the present arrangements pertaining to the functioning of the OECS and the rationale for closer political union, so that an appropriate judgement can be made. A technician from the Secretariat has initiated work in this respect and is to be joined by external expertise as the required support becomes available. To date, therefore, as far as the technical work required for the establishment of a political union is concerned, the Heads of Government have established an oversight working group of recognised Caribbean public servants under whose aegis will function a number of specialist task force groups which will cover the following areas:

(1) the preparation of legal documentation on the Constitution, including matters relating to citizenship and immigration, and arrangements for appropriate electoral machinery;

(2) fiscal and financial arrangements;

(3) the organisation structure and functioning of a unified administration and of the civil administrations which will exist at the island level, including the necessary financial costings;

(4) arrangements for external representation and the organisation of defence and security; and modalities for harmonising economic development policies, especially in fields relating to investments and external trade.

The initiative for closer union among the interested OECS States has received the support of the membership of the Caribbean Community. At their Conference in July 1987, the Heads of Government of the Community made the following observation:

The Heads of Government were pleased to receive a report on the decision taken at the Eleventh Meeting of the Authority of the Organisation of Eastern Caribbean States held in Tortola, British Virgin Islands, on 28–29 May, 1987, to work towards the establishment of a Political Union of OECS Member States.

Confident that this initiative is of importance not only to the aspirations of the people of those States concerned, but also to the strengthening of wider integration movement in CARICOM, the Heads of Government of the MDCs expressed their strong support for any action towards unity among those States.

Following a statement made by one of the OECS Heads of Government to the Meeting of the Heads of Government of the Commonwealth in Vancouver, Canada, in October 1987, the initiative of the OECS countries was welcomed. Member countries and the Commonwealth Secretariat were encouraged to give assistance where this was requested and was possible.

The decision of the interested Governments to first hold a referendum to settle the question of whether the population of their countries wished, that discussions and negotiations should commence to form a political union, has meant, for the political directorate, that work on a specific form of any political union should await the peoples' response on this matter. Thus while there have been recommendations from one or other of the political directorate of forms of union, there is as yet no collective consensus on this matter. However, at the Twelfth Meeting of the OECS Authority held in November 1987, the interested Heads of Government did agree that some technical work should proceed which would indicate the possible forms of union that should be considered and of the institutional apparatus that might under-pin any of these.

In this paper, therefore, we simply make some suggestions as to areas of economic and political decision-making which seem to require an institution-alised and centralised approach if the OECS countries are to derive the desired benefits from the regional and international environment.

If the Eastern Caribbean territories are to be able to borrow funds and to draw financial (equity) investment on a substantial scale they will need to demonstrate that any union system possess sufficient financial base for repayment of funds over the medium term. To plan and raise funds for large-scale prospects, it is necessary to demonstrate a capacity for the system of raising counterpart revenues; this in turn requires an organised financial system across the current boundaries of our countries, rather than the somewhat segmented systems that we now possess. This is particularly important in the light of the situation that the OECS States now have to face: that they shall soon, in spite of the reprieve that has recently been obtained, be 'graduated' from receiving concessionary funding from the International Development Agency, the soft-loan affiliate of the World Bank. The skilful negotiation and mobilisation of funds on a substantial scale will require a centralised system for adequate representation in major capitals and financial and monetary institutions.

As tourism increasingly becomes one of the leading sectors, the countries will require coordinated systems for marketing and promotion and for organising adequate and diversified tourism attractions encompassing multiple islands. However, if the countries are not to be played against each other, a coordinated capacity for making aviation policy and for negotiating route rights appropriate to their tourism needs in particular will be necessary.

The countries now require a centralised system for determining higher education policy; for making adequate arrangements for higher education for OECS nationals within the region and beyond; for maintaining curriculum standards among the small tertiary institutions of our small countries, and for economically viable preparation of appropriate text books and teaching materials. Also the protection and advancement of OECS training arrangements will require a centralised core of technical resources.

There will be required a centralised system capable of quick response for ensuring adequate arrangements for the security, and in particular the maritime security, of the sub-region, and for negotiating assistance for this; this would in fact entail a streamlining of the existing regional security system arrangements.

Underpinning these centralised systems would be a re-organised public service apparatus, based on a new division of labour between central and island administrations, and involving the judicial/legal system, customs, audit and taxation arrangements.

Conclusion

The participating Governments in this venture are well aware that this question of whether there should be 'a merger of the sovereignties of these islands' into a closer union, is a strategic one, both in the sense that the answer to it will determine the fate of the peoples of the Eastern Caribbean islands well into the twenty-first century; and that unlike other attempts at such mergers, it involves reduction of powers, which as mainly sovereign entities, they have become accustomed to wielding.

On the other hand, the Governments' inclination towards political integration is informed by an awareness of trends in the international environment which propel them towards a more closely coordinated policy making among themselves.

Among these trends is the increasing integration of the countries of the European continent, including the United Kingdom, and the clear inclination of these countries and the European Economic Community to relate to the Eastern Caribbean countries on a collective basis. Additionally many donor countries and institutions are unwilling to bear the administrative costs of dealing with the negotiations and transference of aid on an island by island basis, given the small sizes of these states. There is need for integration to deal with an increasingly protectionist international environment and to achieve the required economies of scale for cost-effective negotiation and a meaningful presence in international markets. Other significant factors are the increasing tendency among contiguous major countries to rationalise their trading agreements and to form free trade areas and common markets among themselves, and the need to have a 'viable' presence in international aid and monetary institutions increasingly inclined to direct their assistance to the 'least developed' countries of the developing world. The paradox is that the Eastern Caribbean States, though still having serious infrastructural deficiencies and characterised by easily damaged 'monocrop' economies, are increasingly considered 'middle income' economies capable of sustaining themselves through participation in the private capital markets. Finally, of consequence too, is the sense of vulnerability, which in some measure pervades these states with relatively large maritime zones to protect and patrol, while not having the financial resources to sustain the physical and mechanical facilities required for this.

The effort at closer union, if it is approved by the Eastern Caribbean populations, will at various stages require assistance from the international community for the consolidation of the process. Firstly, OECS Governments will be requesting from major countries and international institutions technical and other material assistance to help with the preparatory technical work that is required to be undertaken to effect a new political/institutional arrangement among these countries. Secondly, the Governments will wish to make a substantial effort to persuade major donor countries and institutions that there is beneficial significance for Western Hemisphere order, in increasing Caribbean coherence and stability; that an important mechanism for achieving this is closer political integration of the constituent states of the region; and that to this end support for a number of large-scale economic projects which will assist in consolidating the integration and in advancing economic growth is necessary.

Thirdly, in spite of the well-known unwillingness of large countries to make exceptions to their general policies and arrangements, particularly in the area of trade, Eastern Caribbean Governments strongly believe that, given their own relatively small size and minimal potential impact on major country markets, more flexible and favourable arrangements should be worked out in respect of the Caribbean Basin Initiative, the Canadian CARIBCAN Initiative and the ACP-EEC trading and investment arrangements.

Finally, the current effort at political integration in the Eastern Caribbean seeks to reverse the balkanised geopolitical situation that is the legacy of European colonialism, and to create a new coherence out of the incoherences and the divisions that characterise the present-day Caribbean and are the result of metropolitan attempts to create the New World. Many other very small territories in the wider Caribbean – unsure of their own fate in the future – will be looking at how this initiative proceeds and whether it can be for them a useful model in tomorrow's world.

Notes

1. Dr Vaughan A. Lewis is Director General of the Organisation of Eastern Caribbean States. This paper was originally prepared for the Colloquium on 'The Geopolitics of the Eastern Caribbean' at the Maison Française, Oxford University, in England on January 8–9, 1988.

This paper was first published in *Caribbean Affairs*, Vol. 1, No. 3, July/September 1988, pp. 160–173.

[42]

The Assembly of Caribbean Community Parliamentarians

Erskine Sandiford

The integration movement of the Caribbean Community (CARICOM) secured its first parliament when on August 3, 1994 the legal inter-governmental agreement to establish the Assembly of Caribbean Community Parliamentarians received the required number of signatories from CARICOM member countries. The Assembly held its inaugural meeting between May 27–29, 1996, in Bridgetown, Barbados.

The idea of a parliament for the Caribbean integration movement was conceived by me, following on the break up of the West Indies Federation. In 1963, I had commented: 'In the case of the West Indies one possibility is that upon the independence of the Eastern Caribbean group, the three powers could federate.' This possibility seemed remote.

The second possibility was that the territory could increase the number of common services among themselves, and extend this cooperation to include British Guiana.

Twenty years later, and seven years before the West Indian Commission was set up by the CARICOM Heads of Government, noting a disconcerting weakening in the underpinnings of CARICOM, I introduced a resolution in 1982 into the House of Assembly of Barbados calling for the establishment of an Assembly of Caribbean States composed of parliamentarians chosen from the national parliaments on a proportionate basis to party strengths in those parliaments.

One of my early actions upon becoming Prime Minister of Barbados in 1987, was to suggest to the Eighth Conference of Heads of Government of CARICOM in St Lucia that an Assembly of Caribbean Community Parliamentarians, composed of representatives from both Government and Opposition members in the Parliaments of CARICOM states, should be created.

The paper was presented at the Tenth Meeting of the Heads of Government of CARICOM in 1989 in Grenada. The proposal, *inter alia*, was based on the following premises:

(1) that CARICOM states all subscribe to the principles and goals of democracy, peace and development;

(2) that each CARICOM state possess representative and deliberative parliamentary institutions, all of which are essential elements of a modern democratic state;

(3) that executive, administrative, legislative and judicial organs are necessary in any efficient modern democratic system, and that within CARICOM, the executive functions are performed by the Heads of Government, the Common Market Council of Ministers, and the meetings of various groupings of Ministers;

The administrative functions are performed by the CARICOM Secretariat headed by its Secretary General, but the legislative functions awaited the establishment of an Assembly of Caribbean Community Parliamentarians, and the judicial functions awaited the establishment of the CARICOM Court of Appeal.

The conference welcomed the proposals and agreed in principle to the establishment of the Assembly of Caribbean Community Parliamentarians. The next stage consisted of the preparation and approval of a draft inter-governmental agreement for the establishment of the Assembly. That process was completed on 3rd August 1994.

The creation of the Assembly of Caribbean Community Parliamentarians is one of the significantly notable decisions taken within the Caribbean integration movement in recent years. For what that decision did was to take the entire movement closer to the masses of people in the Caribbean community from whence popular authorisation, true empowerment and mandating authority in CARICOM and in any democratic community should emanate.

It is regrettable that an Assembly, directly elected by the people, could not have come into being in full panoply at the outset. CARICOM member states were not yet ready for that step. Rather, the parliamentarians are chosen indirectly from among the membership of their respective parliaments. It is expected that in due course the Assembly will call for the direct election of its members. After all, the West Indies Federation (1958–62) had a directly elected parliament.

The powers of the Assembly are at this stage somewhat modest. It is a deliberative and consultative body for consideration of matters falling within the CARICOM Treaty, and for passing resolutions on such matters. It can also consider matters passed to it by CARICOM organs, it can request information from such organs, and it can make recommendations to those organs.

These powers should give the Assembly scope to bring the values, insights, aspirations and sensibilities of its members to bear on the issues affecting CARICOM. At the same time the existing powers should enable the Assembly to begin the process of holding the CARICOM executive, the Heads of Government, accountable to the people of CARICOM with respect to CARICOM matters.

The Assembly is composed of representatives chosen from the parliaments of CARICOM member states. Each member state is entitled to not more than four representatives, while each associate member state is entitled to not more than two associate members.

The Assembly is required to meet at least once in every year, with other meetings being convened by the speaker with the assent of the majority of Assembly members. Alas, it is now almost two years since the inaugural meeting of the Assembly was held, and no meeting has been held since then. The CARICOM authorities must take the blame for that.

It is shocking that this new institution should be stymied in its operations even before it has properly got its teeth into its work. The vigorous promotion of the democratic experience of CARICOM; transparency and public accountability within CARICOM; the human rights of CARICOM people; the expression of popular sentiment through the voice of CARICOM parliamentarians specially selected for that purpose – all of these possibilities have been stultified through the infrequency of meetings of the Assembly of Caribbean Community Parliamentarians. That institution must now claim and establish its place as an independent institution within CARICOM, with control over its administration and budget.

The Caribbean integration movement is seen as the best means for the disparate, small territories of the Caribbean Community to achieve greater political, social, cultural and economic fulfilment. Cooperation and integration are seen as the key elements for achieving the fulfilment of the aspirations of Caribbean people rather than the false gods and mirages of separatism and isolationism. Yes, there are some functions which we wish to perform and have control over as separate states. But there are other very important functions which we should perform and have control over as a coordinated and integrated entity.

The Caribbean is our fatherland and motherland. The Assembly of Caribbean Community Parliaments is a vital institution to help bring us into that patrimony. The Secretary General and staff of the Community Secretariat have played a significant role in getting the Assembly off the ground. Their role is not yet ended.

The problems facing the regional integration movement now and into the foreseeable future are, and will be, varied and complex. Some of these problems will relate to CARICOM, its institutions, mechanisms and modalities. Some will relate to the movement and its relationship with the wider Caribbean, the Americas, Europe, Africa, the Middle East, and the Asia-Pacific region.

The problems include the need to increase total output and real per capita incomes within the movement; the need to enhance the performance and competitiveness of export sectors, particularly agriculture, manufacturing, and services resulting in greater intra-regional and extra-regional trade. There is need to deal with issues of sustainable development and health conditions; to come to grips with globalisation and the new trading regimes and to develop more rapidly the human resources of the region. Further, the rates of savings and investments must be increased thus resulting in greater job creation and increased flows of foreign direct investment and debt, economic and financial matters must be better managed.

These problems certainly present grave challenges to the CARICOM integration movement. But they also present opportunities for the application of prudent policy interventions. It would be fallacious to think, however, that Governments or technocrats alone can resolve these issues: for they raise serious issues of governance requiring the understanding and involvement of people and their representatives.

The Assembly of Caribbean Community Parliamentarians is expected to grow into a key institution within the regional integration movement. As such it will be called upon to play a focal role in the deliberation of the problems identified as well as on others not mentioned.

Above all, the Assembly of Caribbean Community Parliamentarians will have to make an important contribution to the issue of ensuring that an adequate regime evolves for the Government of the integration movement.

It is clear that responsibility is being placed upon the movement for which it has neither the legal nor constitutional framework, the financial ability, nor the human resources to cope with them. The approaches set out and implied in the Treaty of Chaguaramas of 1973 have played themselves out, and revisiting them now will not help. New approaches are required, a process that calls for the input of many streams of thought, including the thinking of the Assembly of Caribbean Community Parliamentarians.

Note

This paper was first published in *CARICOM Perspective*, No. 68, June 1998, pp. 73–75.

[43]

Social Partnerships and
New Modes of Governance
The Barbados Experience

Patrick Gomes

Growing concerns in Caribbean Community (CARICOM) member states to strengthen democracy and pursue more inclusive relations for national policy making might benefit from critical reflection on recent experiments in social partnerships and the quest for social contracts.

One of the most frequently cited references in the social partnership approach within CARICOM member states is the evolution of the Barbados experience during the last eight years, beginning with an Incomes and Prices Protocol in 1992. Two subsequent protocols were to result in the current Social Compact on the Implementations of a Social Partnership 1998–2000. A follow-up protocol is expected to be signed for a subsequent two-year period.

It would be useful to identify the contextual realities of the early 1990s in Barbados within which the inaugural Protocol was formulated and the subsequent development of the social partnership approach. This brief analysis is a contribution for the guidance of member states who may want to pursue a critical examination of the fundamental philosophical principles, and may be applicable to advancing a debate on social contracts elsewhere in CARICOM.

The Barbados Context

With a substantial financial deficit in 1991 and a spate of industrial unrest, intensified by an IMF-linked Structural Adjustment Programme (SAP) that required a reduction in public servant wages and salaries by eight per cent, the Barbados dollar with its exchange rate ($2.00=US$1.00) came under severe pressure for a devaluation. The industrial unrest was extensive and mass public demonstrations demanded that the cut in public service pay be restored. Unemployment was already as high as 20 per cent and thousands of temporary workers were being severed.

Retention of the exchange rate in its current state was an inescapable imperative, in the view of the majority of the population. Currency devaluation in an economy extremely dependent on imports for basic necessities, particularly major food items for the domestic population as well as the tourist sector, would amount to economic and social dislocation. Such circumstances of enormous national significance could not be adequately addressed by partisan responses. Neither the trade unions continuing demands to reverse programmes of severance and reduced pay nor the government opting for an IMF imposed solution, requiring the currency devaluation, would be effective as a means of arresting the fiscal crisis.

A response based on a recognition of a collective responsibility by both labour and government was, therefore, essential if the national interest was not to be imperilled.

Intense and innovative discussions were initiated to explore ways to contain the crisis. With public sector wages already reduced, a proposal to the unions, representing private sector workers to also undergo a cut in salaries, was rejected with a counter-proposal that a freeze on wages could be entertained, if controls on prices were instituted. It was, therefore, recognised that involvement of the private sector would have to be integral to any national adjustment process. This was evident on account of two main factors. The reduction of salaries and retrenchment of public sector workers implied a slow down of demand for goods and services and reduced capacity to purchase basic necessities on the part of a significant proportion of the working population. By convention, such a situation would have prompted a reaction by the commercial class to increase the price of goods, placing further pressure on the cost of living for that section of the working population whose livelihood is predominantly derived from wage labour. This did not happen.

The prevailing circumstances, fortunately, were encouraging enough to inspire a tripartite approach, with a view to ensuring that mutual gains were derived on the basis of enlightened negotiations for the overall management of the economy by the state; the avoidance of industrial disputes and wide-spread hardships on the working population; and the survival of local business with modest returns from commercial transactions.

The negotiating of a national adjustment process was perceived by all the stakeholders to be the only viable option for an economy so heavily dependent on foreign imports for basic necessities, and so reliant on a tourism market that could not allow uncompetitive prices for its services. A period of pro-tracted negotiations had been initiated late 1991 to 1992. It was to the credit of the leadership of the labour movement that, faced with a proposal for a cut of private sector employees wages and salaries, comparable to the eight per cent settlement with public servants, the counter-proposal from the unions was the acceptance of a wage/salaries freeze. Simultaneous with that offer was a mutual understanding to have productivity as the central criterion for future increases in wages and salaries.

The bare-bones of an Income and Prices Protocol with an essential link to productivity, were now advanced as central guiding principles for macro economic stability and a new approach to collective bargaining. Efforts were undertaken to garner experiences from outside of Barbados, on productivity-related pay schemes and mechanisms by which to promote and measure productivity. The subsequent establishment of a National Productivity Board is a direct outcome of this enlightened tripartite approach in cooperation between the social partners.

Protocol One (1993–95)

A period of protracted negotiations and public debate in 1992 and early 1993 reached a critical watershed in August 1993 when the Parliament of Barbados adopted a resolution in support of a protocol for the implementation of a Prices and Incomes Policy, endorsed by the social partners.

For the purposes of the protocol, the social partners referred to were the Government, the employers' representatives and the workers' representatives. It was explicitly stated in a August 1993 resolution that:

the Prices and Incomes Policy shall have as its major objectives the safeguarding of the existing parity of the exchange rate and the creation and expansion of a more competitive economy which would provide for greater employment opportunities and make Barbados goods and services more competitive at home and abroad.

Attention should also be directed at the very distinct and precise objectives which had been agreed upon viz. safeguarding the existing parity of the exchange rate and measures for a more competitive economy. The latter was of course not an end in itself but to provide greater employment opportunities.

It may be instructive to note here that despite public protest demonstrations of almost two years previously, national consensus had been hammered out on a common objective for the larger good of the society, as a whole, – a fixed exchange rate of the Barbados dollar, and employment creation.

Seven years later, the Barbadian society can reflect, with understandable relief, that the exchange rate has remained constant and unemployment, almost 20 per cent in 1992, has declined in 1999, to less than 10 per cent. In general terms, the fundamental objective and intention of the 1993 Protocol has been realised in an admirable manner. The broadening of the basis of governance by means of a protocol binding by mutual consent and for the common good, above partisan interests is an enormous tribute to the social partners of Barbados, given the record of eight years of macroeconomic stability and substantial increase in gainful employment.

A distinctive feature of the political maturity in the society must be also recognised. The core tenets of the inaugural 1993 protocol not only continued after electoral defeat of the government in 1994, but also received a reaffirmation for commitment and consolidation in a successor arrangement that brought into existence an expanded protocol.

Protocol Two (1995–97)

The encouraging success of what amounted to a national adjustment process, in rejection of an IMF demand for a currency devaluation, provided an attitudinal platform on which to explore the main tenets of Protocol 2. The preamble of this protocol stated that the tripartite approach to industrial relations has been a vital component of a Barbados macroeconomic pro-gramme for the realisation of sustained economic growth and development through increased competitiveness.

Among seven factors in the protocol, responsible for reversing the gradual erosion of Barbados competitiveness, four should be highlighted for their significance and applicability, as prerequisites for sustainable economic growth and development, in all CARICOM member states. These are:

- Establishment of an environment of greater dialogue among the Social Partners within which fundamental issues of economic and social policy may be discussed;
- Stability and sustainability of the industrial relations climate. Opportunities for improved access to employment, thereby reducing the risk of social dislocation, particularly among young people;
- National commitment to improve productivity increase efficiency, reduce wastage and enhance performance in the economy.

Such factors should not be treated as hard and fast rules or magical principles. They were the outcome of a process of building national commitment, in the context of a vision for sustained economic growth, and development of a service economy which was being restructured for competitiveness in the face of intense, international trade liberalisation.

The capacity to resolve the conflicting demands of a traditionally strong commercial class and dominant tourism sector, with the majority of Barbadians occupying low-paying jobs on the one hand, and a dynamic and well-organised union movement, on the other hand, was severely tested. Business interests were represented by a private sector agency, as an umbrella body, while the labour movement had been consolidated under the Congress of Trade Unions and Staff Associations of Barbados (CTUSAB)

For Protocol Two, the social partners made explicit references to circumstances in which the contrasting interests of business and labour had to make a clear commitment to work together in the national interest. The commitment should be based on mutual respect for each other, discipline, and a commitment to security of tenure on the one hand and reduction of labour disputes on the other.

The details of such a framework are not necessary for this discussion. It is sufficient to note that Protocol Two recognised that the entire process was to be understood in the context of the country's search for a new mode of governance. It stated that:

. . . the implementation of all aspects . . . will be undertaken in a manner that fully acknowledges the spirit into which it has been entered and which honours the principles of transparency and objectivity.

Acknowledging that this protocol marked another stage in the advancement of a process for alternative modes of governance, the social partners accepted and agreed that: 'Steps will be taken to effect the deepening and widening of the social partnership.'

Protocol Three and Beyond

With the signing of Protocol Two in August 1995, a major step towards institutionalisation of the restructured relations of governance in Barbados, was the agreement to administer the protocol by a sub-committee of the social partners who would meet once per month or as often as necessary. This became *the first line of consultation regarding all aspects of the implementation* of the protocol. The sub-committee comprised six Government representatives, two of whom are Ministers, with an equal number of representatives from the umbrella bodies of unions and employers.

The organisational basis for the current Protocol Three (1998-2000) has proven to be an effective tripartite mechanism in that there has been no major industrial dispute of a protracted nature. Quarterly meetings, under the chairmanship of the Prime Minister have been maintained, close working relations have developed and a prominent role is carried out by the National Productivity Board.

Nevertheless, instances have arisen to test the tenacity of purpose and the capacity for participatory democracy, on the matter of securing national consensus on wage restraint and a prices policy, sensitive to unavoidable or legitimate cost increases. In early 1999, for example, a strike at a state-owned corporation was vigorously supported by the largest union in the Congress. Despite public differences and harsh language in heated exchanges between union representatives and management, consultation at the highest level of government, and the spirit of the social partnership prevailed.

It would be naive not to expect incidents, in the future, that will test the nature of the relations that require partisan interests to be subordinate to the preservation of a macro policy framework of economic and industrial stability. It appears however, that the understanding of governance that is participatory, and premised on inclusion, has become an integral element of the public consciousness in Barbadian society.

The formulation and upholding in practical circumstances of the current Protocol for the Implementation of a Social Partnership 1998-2000, capture the spirit and modalities by which the record of economic and social advancement has been demonstrated.

At least four indicators are instructive. The rate of growth of the economy over the last five years has been consistently 3.5-4.0 per cent; per capita GDP is US$8,200. On the Human Development Index of UNDP, in 1999, Barbados was the only Caribbean country rated among the top 30 countries of the world, on the basis of quality of life on a composite index, reflecting life expectancy, adult literacy, school enrolment and per capita GDP. Also the fixed exchange rate has been maintained at Bds$2 = US$1.00.

With the observance of Protocol Three, relations among the social partners have evolved into a formal structure governing their continued collaboration and consultation on fundamental issues affecting their individual and collective contributions to all aspects of national development. This has been entered into as a Social Compact for a two-year period. Now it is being considered for further extension.

The document has a format which begins with a preamble, acknowledging a mutuality of interests among the social partners and the evolving process of the preceding five years, as well as a restatement of the intent on which a policy of industrial harmony is grounded.

The seven-year success of Barbados social partnerships cannot necessarily be taken as a blueprint or template for other CARICOM member states to achieve similar economic and social results. But what Barbados has demonstrated is a capacity to pursue a vision for sustained economic growth and development, predicated on specific major objectives. These objectives include political and economic values that are indispensable to the survival of every CARICOM member state. They should be debated nationally, formulated and incorporated as basic tenets without which the likelihood of maintaining even a modicum of current survival patterns might be questionable. These tenets are imperatives of the conjuncture of the external environment and internal polarisation of inequities to which most member states are subjected. Therefore, the Barbados protocols offer useful guidelines and lessons for adaptation in the search for alternative modes of governance in the rest of the region.

The necessity of a stable industrial relations climate; the pursuit of sustainable expansion of the economy through its *competitiveness;* reduction of social disparities through *increased employment;* national commitment to increased *productivity;* and consolidation of the *process* of tripartite consultation should not be dismissed with cynicism, and Barbados' success seen as being merely fortuitous. On the contrary, one should hope that the lessons of consistent and deliberate efforts to make participatory democracy a reality in a small Caribbean State can, and will, bear fruit that will enhance the life of the individual.

Note

This paper was first published in *CARICOM Perspective,* No. 69, Vol. II, July 2000, pp. 65–67, 69.

[44]

A Vision for **CARICOM** and The Caribbean Development Bank

Neville Nicholls

The origins of the CDB are closely interwoven with those of sovereign governments in the English-speaking Caribbean. It must be recalled that the last years of the 1960s and the early years of the 1970s were a time when it was thought that the economic fortunes of a people were largely, if not totally, determined by their inheritance of raw materials.

This dichotomised us into a group comprising Guyana, Jamaica and Trinidad and Tobago on one hand and on the other, the rest of us. Not surprisingly, there was a tone of urgency and near impatience when the colonial and other imperial governments met to analyse the prospects of the countries in the Eastern Caribbean in the last half of the 1960s. The establishment of the CDB was, perhaps, the major product of those various deliberations. Let us recall that they took place against a background of extreme pessimism about the prospects of those economies that were poor in resources, such as this country and the others in the Eastern Caribbean, excepting Trinidad and Tobago. The recent failure of the Federation heightened those feelings of despair.

We were hardly launched when the whole of the developing world was engulfed in the crisis brought about by the massive changes in the terms of trade caused by changes in the structure of commodity prices. In some ways the developing world has never recovered from that crisis even though the fortunes of the nations it comprises have been marked by remarkable twists of irony. In all of this, the resource-poor nations of this region have performed much better than they must have been expected to three decades ago. To this extent, their survival can be dubbed a success. CDB shares in this achievement. We share also in the new set of anxieties that now confront all our Borrowing Member Countries (BMCs), not least the strikingly prosperous members. What do I mean?

When CDB came into existence more than a quarter of a century ago, the Cold War had become part of humanity's consciousness. There were a few thinkers who claimed that Soviet society was artificial and could not survive very long. But most of us thought that those were the views of ultra reactionaries who could never come to grips with the reality of socialist success. Few would have wagered whatever the odds, that the powerful Soviet empire would have expired before the century had. Today I speak to you against the backdrop of that reality. The traditional Cold War has ended and less than a handful of governments admit to being socialist in any form. Therefore, the circumstances that gave strategic importance to the Caribbean region as recently as fifteen years ago, have vanished.

We are now in a situation, where our prospects are going to be determined by our own efforts. We have got to start working on this understanding right away. The reality that now confronts us causes us much anxiety, but it should do much more.

Caribbean people demonstrate a remarkable example of the survival instincts of humans. Most of our ancestors came from considerably distant parts. They spoke a wide variety of African, Asian and European languages and to one another must have seemed to possess a vast range of strange habits and mores. Most of our people have a history of one sort or other of bondage and a legacy that could engender generations of bitter hatreds. Notwithstanding all this, we have learned to live together in quite harmonious patterns.

Our cohabitation is not perfect and we often fret about how well we are doing. Judging ourselves by our own standards or those of regions that do not share our heterogeneity, we seem as failures. Yet, judged by more realistic standards, we remain the envy of most other regions of this planet. And that certainly helps to explain the success of our tourism product.

Once we focus on the human resilience that has characterised our societies over the last few centuries, we are bound to see that the circumstances that cause us some anxiety and foreboding now should be seen as new challenges to be faced.

There is nothing in the ordinary sense of things that is remarkable about one year over another. For some members of the human race the year 2000 will have a significance that is bound up in their peculiar history. But even among Christians, that year will vary in emotional appeal according to which calendar is used to date events. Notwithstanding that, for all of us in this region, the concept of the millennium is steeped in meaning. We can therefore use it to inspire in us a resolve to meet future challenges with a positive attitude.

Because we are small, our economic fortunes and our production patterns have always been determined by the demands of the global market place. The emphasis that was laid on various staples is now replaced by the services our people can perform for the rest of the world. We are doing quite well in conventional tourism, and are learning to be good at eco-tourism, for which Dominica is very suited. Recently we expanded our financial services market and our countries are finding credible niches.

But because I think the human factor is important, for me the development of human capital must be at the forefront of our economic development efforts. This includes the effective motivation of our people. I know that there are many facets of motivation, but an important aspect is the cognitive dimension. We must know where we wish to take people if we are to lead them effectively. We must be able to convince them that they should go with us. We should be able to explain the sacrifices they might have to make to achieve national or regional goals, and the length of time that might pass before those sacrifices begin to pay off. I think that this is the kind of leadership that will be required in the new millennium.

What I think is going to be most important is that we set our own goals and define them as much as is reasonable and the socio-economic path for reaching them. This is what I wish to call repatriation of our economic policy making. I think that this will always be a matter of pride for a people who have had a long experience of social bondage and colonialism. CDB can make a substantial contribution to the effort of this region to reach this very crucial stage in our national development.

This is why in the last few years I have been so insistent, that under my charge, CDB will take a pragmatic approach to becoming a viable institution, but, at the same time, exhaust our research capacity. Our Board of Directors has agreed that we should begin work on this aspect of our portfolio, and already we have begun to recruit staff and to develop the modalities for commencing a serious programme in economic research.

The change in the global circumstances is not a necessary precursor to the condition that we are getting too accustomed to calling marginalisation, making it seem that we need to depend on the goodwill of others for our successful integration into the modern dynamic global economy.

We must stop thinking like this and we must start thinking positively about our life chances and the developmental path we must take to secure them. Sound indigenous economic research, that identifies clearly our options and warns us of dangers to avoid, has a major role to play in our further development as a people. The current difficulties besetting many of the developing economies in South East Asia have many lessons to teach us. One we must not miss, is that no region should leave its economic research and policy prescriptions entirely to others, regardless, as in this case, how favourably disposed they are to its good fortunes. The CDB will be an important player in this arena.

If our region is going to make its way in the new global environment and banish the fear of our marginalisation, it will need more than sound policy advice from an indigenous source it can safely trust. There is yet more to be accomplished in our traditional role of financing development for our BMCs, paying special regard to the LDCs.

We have a challenge as a development bank, to focus our new lending strategy in the direction that improves the competitive dynamism of our countries, and prepare them for successful docking on to whatever hemispheric trading arrangement emerges soon in the new millennium.

I shall be submitting to our Board of Directors at its next meeting the initial draft of a strategy for CDB which, when it is fully formulated after consultation with our directors and other members of our regional public, will guide the lending activities of CDB in the early years of the millennium. We anticipate that in our new environment, in which countries such as Dominica, will have to move away from a dependence on banana cultivation to a more diversified and service-oriented development strategy and in which also, small countries will continue to lack easy access to global capital markets, CDB will have to increase and diversify its lending.

The initial forecast by our staff is that in the five-year period between 1999 and 2003 CDB will be lending its current set of BMCs an average of about US$141 million per year. The expectation is that lending in the social sectors, including for human resource development, will expand substantially in this period. We shall also intensify our efforts to help eliminate structural poverty from within our BMCs.

This new lending recall, will be accompanied by well researched policy advice and focused on avoiding the danger of marginalisation of any of our BMCs. We intend to offer BMCs whatever reasonable support can help them overcome present implementation difficulties, so that they can take advantage of our increased activity. A major feature of our new approach will be the partnerships we shall strive to foster with a wider range of institutions in our BMCs.

Notwithstanding our increased activity, we will still be expected to fund only a relatively small part of the Public Sector Investment Programmes of the larger BMCs that have access to larger multilaterals and the private capital market. But we intend to participate in those countries in sectors where our resources will generate considerable leverage and where our policy advice will be most relevant.

We shall continue to pay special regard to the LDCs in our BMCs but we intend to remain the development bank of all our BMCs. As our charter prescribes, we will be committed to regional integration. This will, in some ways, become an easier goal to achieve, but in others a greater challenge as the forces of globalisation impinge on our traditional bonds. CDB intends to help our region preserve these bonds in a way that does not inhibit its successful integration into large economic entities, such as, whatever the Free Trade of the Americas eventually evolves into, and the larger global economy itself. I believe that CDB will have to explore lending for the new communications industry. We are beginning to search for an appropriate niche. However, that industry too will have to embrace a research and development orientation if they are to become and remain competitive in this new globalised environment.

In the years I have led CDB, I have had the wonderful support of all our members both in our region and beyond. I have been able to build on the splendid achievements of two distinguished predecessors with both of whom I had the privilege of serving. It is because they achieved so much that I am now able to think of these other things I would like to see CDB start to accomplish before the end of this century and carry on beyond. I am proud that under my leadership we could access the international capital market and retain our favourable rating after several market transactions. This has been a tribute to the whole of our region and it has justly shared our pride. There are still other things CDB can do to enhance access to global financing for the Caribbean and we have started to work on some new initiatives.

I do understand the anxiety that some feel about our present chances in the global economy, especially in the wake of so many changes in the preferential arrangements which were previously negotiated with us. For us this could be a crisis, but in every crisis there is an opportunity. I believe I have pointed to a vision of how our region could grasp this new opportunity.

Note

This paper was first published in *CARICOM Perspective*, No. 68 June 1998, pp. 33–35.

[45]

The Future of Development Banking in the Caribbean

Compton Bourne

Development Banks are now a prevalent feature of the Caribbean economic landscape. Created as instruments of economic development policy, they have functioned with varying degrees of success.[1] There are many signs that their operating environment has changed and that the ethos of state-led economic development which informed their creation and conditioned their economic context is being jettisoned. The question therefore arises about their future.

This paper analyses the future of development banking in the Caribbean. It restates the original roles assigned to development banks and then addresses the issue of their future by appraisal of the current and evolving conditions as they influence the purpose and functioning of development banks. Attention is paid to national development banks as well as the Caribbean Development Bank.

The Original Role of Development Banks

Development banks were established in the Caribbean, as indeed elsewhere, to accelerate economic development essentially by the provision of financial services. Several elements lie behind this statement. It is premised on the historical experience of slow and unstable economic growth in these small, open economies with highly specialised production structures. Economic development thus entailed broadening and deepening of production structures and diversification of international trade. These efforts are conditional upon substantial capital investment and upon the identification and exploitation of economic opportunity. There is also the presumption of adequate knowledge systems and technology.

At the time of the formation of development banks, Caribbean economies were short of investment capital. Domestic savings ratios were low relative to desired investment rates and savings were concentrated in the few commercial banks which comprised the financial system. Stiglitz has reminded us that among the principal roles of financial markets are intermediation between savers and borrowers, agglomeration of capital, selection and monitoring of projects, and risk transference, sharing and pooling.[2] Caribbean financial markets performed most of these poorly. Banks were long on deposits and short on credit. Financial lenders remained strongly risk averse; shunning those risks inherent in long-term lending, associated with new ventures and new customers, or intrinsic to production and marketing. Financial market imperfections, especially information asymmetries and oligopolistic conditions, typically combined to create divergences between net private returns and net social returns inimical to the financing of economic development, both in terms of the cost of finance and access to credit by potential investors.

Development banks were created to provide services not provided by private financial institutions. Their niche was investment finance. Their strategy was concessionary credit accompanied often by supervision and technical assistance. In these respects development banks have a closer affinity to the banking traditions of Europe and Japan than to English banking outlook and practices, with the important difference that development banks typically refrained from managerial intervention and equity participation.

A unique role of development banks is their mobilisation of investment capital not from domestic savers, but from the international financial community and official development assistance agencies. International capital sourcing has a clear justification in terms of aggregate savings-investment gaps which are equal to foreign exchange gaps under certain conditions. However, there is a further justification to be found in some of the terms and conditions attached to financial resources provided by bilateral and multilateral agencies. Extremely long loan maturities, below market rates of interest, and lengthy grace periods confer considerable cost savings to development banks thereby facilitating their own concessionary interest rate policies and long-term asset portfolios.

Development bank lending may generate positive externalities in the financial sector. Through portfolio demonstration effects on other less venturesome financial institutions, development banks may increase the overall supply of funds. Furthermore as the clients of development banks establish themselves as viable entities, they enter the mainstream of private commercial finance. The gain redounds to the rest of the financial sector.

Although direct contribution of investment finance is the principal traditional role of development banks, they have occasionally been assigned other roles such as the promotion of entrepreneurship, dissemination of technical knowledge, and improvement of the size distributions of national income and wealth. Development banks have had limited success with the technology dissemination function mainly because of the insufficiency of their own human resources and the tendency of their organisation to give little priority to this aspect of their mandate. Distributional objectives are also not a success story of development banks. The ability to achieve distributional goals depends upon how effectively the banks manage to apply equity criteria in loan allocation decisions, the subsidy element in loans, and the distributional incidence of the tax system used to finance credit subsidies. Political and social influence sometimes prevent effective application of equity criteria. The tax system itself has often turned out to be regressive despite its progressive intent.

The leadership roles ascribed to development banks accord with the state's assumption of the role of leading sector. It is one facet of interventionist public sector strategies. Complementary strategies are equity participation and management of production and distribution enterprises, industrial development promotional agencies, and export marketing institutions.

The issue of whether development banking has a future may be approached by examining whether the initial conditions and problems persist substantially, and then proceeding to analyse how development banking may be affected by the contemporary evolution of economic structures and policies. This section deals briefly with initial conditions and problems.

Few would doubt that there is still an urgent need for structural change in Caribbean economies. Industrial development projected for the 1960-1990 period has proceeded at a much slower pace and with less national and regional coverage than envisaged. Moreover, traditional economic sectors exhibit signs of long-term secular decline or face drastically changed international market conditions which threaten their viability. Even within newly emergent industries, such as tourism, changes in the product mix and the competitive repositioning of countries, such as Cuba, would necessitate fundamental restructuring. At the same time, deceleration of economic growth during the past four or five years gives a fresh urgency to the challenges of achieving sustained economic growth and minimal unemployment.

More debatable, perhaps, is the extent to which entrepreneurship is a continuing problem. There is ample evidence in the form of new ventures and new entrants to the business sector of a strong and growing entrepreneurial impulse. Doubts arise in relation to entrepreneurial achievement, that is, the creation and spread of viable business ventures. A time series study of start-ups and closures is likely to reveal proportionately numerous failures which would be an indication that entrepreneurship is weak. Human resource development plans for the region have placed a great deal of emphasis on the training of managers and executives, but little attention has been paid to business development and product development, that is, to the core entrepreneurial skills.

Financial markets have improved significantly. Term lending has increased: the term structure of credit portfolios has lengthened and the production sector and new ventures are financed to a much greater degree than, say, two decades ago. There is a greater degree of risk pooling and risk sharing. These improvements are attributable to several developments. New, specialised financial institutions, such as merchant banks, entered the financial industry providing new services, carving out niches for themselves, and in the process demonstrating to others latent profit opportunities to be exploited. The growth of the older, well established financial institutions contained its own dynamic for financial innovation since new ways of sustaining and expanding profits and corporate growth had to be found. On the borrowing side, improvements in business capabilities made financial risks smaller and more acceptable. However, the experience of financial institution closure in several Caribbean countries has served as a caution to commercial banks, restricting their involvement in development finance.

The establishment and growth of stock markets is often seen as an important way of providing long-term capital to enterprises. This has happened to some extent in the Caribbean. New issues have raised capital for business enterprises. However, the records of the more active Exchanges (Jamaica and Trinidad and Tobago) reveal only a few new issues over a ten-year span and the predominant allocation of these funds to financial institutions. The stock market has therefore not been a major source of investment capital for the non-financial business sector.

Reasons are to be found on both the issuing side and the stock acquisition side of the market. They include the reluctance of firms to raise equity capital, the preference for debt capital, informational deficiencies which militate against investor preferences for equity of non-financial corporate enterprises, high transactions costs, and weaknesses in corporate reporting and account-ability. There is another fundamental reason to be considered, namely, the predominance of price margin transactions on the stock exchange. Most stock market transactions are motivated by short-term price considerations of either capital loss avoidance or capital gains. Trades in existing stocks predominate. The existence of facilities for trade in stocks is of great importance to long-term investors because it makes risk transference and liquidation easier and less costly. However, a better balance must be struck between new issues and trading in old stocks if the capital investment function is to be effectively performed. Stiglitz (1993) exaggerates when he states that: 'The stock market . . . is perhaps more a gambling casino than a venue in which funds are being raised to finance new ventures and expand existing activities'. But he is certainly right in concluding that . . . 'new ventures typically must look elsewhere' for investment capital.[3]

Caribbean economies must still source international capital. For a variety of reasons, aggregate investment expenditures exceed aggregate national savings in all countries other than Barbados and Trinidad and Tobago in the current decade. There were no country exceptions in the decade of the 1980s (World Bank, 1994).[4]

The conclusion to be drawn from the analysis in this section is that several of the important conditions and problems, which stimulated the establishment of development banks, remain with the Caribbean today. *Prima facie*, there is still need for development banking.

Changed Context for Development Banking

It appears that three major trends will define the shape and structure of Caribbean economies for the rest of this decade and much of the coming one. The first is the increasing adoption of economic liberalisation of markets for goods and for services as a principal set of economic policies. With respect to the foreign sector the elements of economic liberalisation include removal of non-tariff barriers to goods and services, progressive reduction of protective tariffs, and elimination of restrictions on financial transactions in the current and capital accounts of the balance of payments. There is discernibly less enthusiasm or liberalisation of foreign trade in labour services. For non-trade-able goods and services as well as for tradeable goods and services, economic liberalisation also entails deregulation of production, markets and prices with residual safeguards for the public interest and social costs.

The second major trend is reduction of the direct participation of govern-ment in the economic system. In several countries, governments have discontinued ownership and management of economic enterprises and have instead begun a process of equity divestment and contracting out of management functions. Reform of regulatory controls on enterprises is another facet of the changing role of government. These trends have been reinforced by fiscal downsizing – lower taxes and subsidies as proportions of gross domestic product. Several factors contribute to fiscal downsizing: social welfare promotion and achievement of distributional justice as responsibilities of government command less influential support now. Furthermore, there has been a revision of the mainstream economic consensus about fiscal influences on economic growth. In particular, Keynesian orthodoxy of fiscal propulsion has been replaced by neo-classical orthodoxy of fiscal retardation with its explicit policy prescription of lower tax rates. An additional factor is the adoption of balanced budget or zero deficit principles in contexts of limited fiscal revenue generating capacity. Policy announcements and recent movements in public sector employment indicate that another feature of the redefinition of the role of government is disavowal of employer of last resort responsibility.

Pedro Aspe, a recent former Mexican Minister of Finance, describes the changed conception of the role of the state in terms that have resonance but not full agreement in the Commonwealth Caribbean. He remarks that:

> during the early phases of development, when an economy is no more than a collection of fragmented markets and regions, the establishment of government institutions, the construction of infrastructure and the direct participation of the State in some areas of the economy are not only desirable but indispensable preconditions for the growth process.[5] (Aspe, 1992, p. 9).

However, in the present times, state participation eschews subsidies and nationalisation, and emphasises 'the elimination of institutional constraints on competition, the creation of new markets and the generation of opportunities for all members of the population' (p. 9).[6] The maxim is creation of a propitious climate for individuals and enterprises.

The third major trend influencing the nature of Caribbean economies is regionalisation. The creation of sub-regional and regional economic groups of varying sizes – ACS, NAFTA, European Union – is of far reaching importance, with potential effects on the total fabric of Caribbean society. For present purposes, only economic aspects are germane. The salient feature is the expansion of economic borders. To a greater or lesser degree, depending upon the completeness of coverage in the regional agreements or treaties, national political borders cease to be economic borders. Economies become more open and more like localised economies or economic districts. There is *potential* enlargement of the scale of economic organisation and scale of the markets. There is *potential* integration of factor markets. Competition may increase in the local economy, both from other parts of the region and from entities within the local economy faced with threats to their accustomed market sizes and market shares. Regionalistion is incompatible with economic insularity and weakens the ability of small nation states to insulate their economies from external shocks. Spillover effects from strong local economies within the region are more pronounced.

Effects on Development Banking

The operating environment of development banks becomes more challenging as a consequence of the major trends outlined previously. Economic liberalisation and the new regionalism make domestic enterprises more open to competition. Risks increase in domestic markets and in export markets because of the greater availability of competing goods and services and the loss of trade preferences. On the plus side, regionalisation offers potential market expansion. Economic liberalisation also enlarges the scope for enterprises to improve their production efficiency by sourcing factors from outside the nation state and to improve their cost efficiency by acquiring production inputs at more economical prices. Development banks in their project selection and monitoring activities would need to pay more than customary attention to market risks. Macroeconomic and global development would feature more prominently since industries would be less insulated nationally and would be more affected by changes in the global environment.

Economic liberalisation and regionalisation expand the potential scale of enterprises, reinforcing and building upon existent tendencies. A source for expansion of Caribbean enterprises within national borders is conglomeration through mergers and acquisitions. Diversification through divisional strategies is another. Holding companies in which divisional firms span several industries exist in most countries. Many of them are of recent origin. Enterprises have also become trans-Caribbean within the framework of the CARICOM integration movement, but mainly because of economic liberalisation in both home countries and host countries. The conglomerates are too large to be clients of the national development banks. Providing for their capital investment requirements would violate prudential guidelines and restrictions such as maximum proportion of the portfolio to be allocated to a single client. National development banks would not have the asset base to exert significant leverage on the operations of conglomerates or many of the large firms. The exclusion of the large, successful firm from the portfolios of development banks marginalises the banks somewhat, but keeps their focus on the smaller, emergent enterprises which it was their original mission to service.

Within the financial sector itself, private financial firms have greater latitude with respect to the range of financial services they provide. In particular, financial enterprises have become more involved in capital finance. From one perspective, these activities are competitive with development banks. The superior quality of service which private financial institutions are reputed to have may induce improvements in development bank operation, especially in notorious problem areas such as loan appraisal and disbursements. From another perspective, competition should be seen as a desired outcome of development bank lending – a measure of their positive demonstration effects and externalities on other financial market participants. There is yet another possibility, namely the prospect of co-financing of projects. Financial joint venturing, while not unknown in the Caribbean, has involved only private financial institutions acting on a purely local basis or in syndication with foreign financial enterprises.

The diminished economic role of the state has three implications of special significance for development banking. First, the removal of protection and subsidies increases business risks and therefore increases lending risks for development banks. Second, the privatisation of state-owned enterprises creates an initial problem of valuation of existing debt to the banks if government guarantees do not extend to the new corporate entities. Third, the issue must arise as to why privatisation should not extend to development banking. In other words, if divestment of state-owned enterprises has been applied to non-financial businesses, why not to the government-owned development banks.

The Caribbean Development Bank

The trends and developments described thus far enhance the role of the Caribbean Development Bank (CDB). The traditional role of the CDB may be summarised in three categories. The first is to provide investment capital to its member countries on terms and conditions consistent with the time trajectory of costs and returns in capital investment projects of a developmental nature. This entails striving to effect economies in lending and funds mobilisation so as to minimise loan charges and to provide long-term capital. The second is to mobilise international investment funds complementary to national efforts. It performs this function by intermediating with regional and multilateral development banks and with foreign governments. The third function is the promotion of economic integration through preferential loan portfolios that counteract economic polarisation, for example, the special treatment of CARICOM LDCs, through the financing of regional projects, and through its contribution to regional economic decision-making.

Individual Caribbean countries experience a greater level of difficulty now in sourcing commercial loans and official development assistance than they did previously. The World Bank (1994, p.31) reports that '. . . multilateral and bilateral financial flows to the Caribbean have declined substantially since the early 1980s'.[7] Net lending from multilateral sources fell from US$546 million in 1982 to $72 million in 1992, and net bilateral lending from US$597 million to negative US$44 million over the same period. Private credits to public sector fell from US$214 million in 1983 to negative US$27 million in 1992. Various reasons are suggested for this adverse trend: the shift of aid to Eastern Europe; unacceptably high country exposure and risks; diminution of aid budgets; development assistance fatigue are the more prominent. A new element in realistically pessimistic scenarios is the imminent diversion of financial aid from CARICOM countries to Haiti and Cuba. The global outlook is itself not promising. The Institute for International Finance is reported (*The Economist*, April 22, 1995, p. 79) to predict that private capital to emerging economies will fall from US$159 billion in 1994 to US$82 billion in 1995, while official lending will rise from US$15 billion to only US$51 billion resulting in a net contraction of US$41 billion in just one year.[8]

Access to international equity markets is also problematic. The small scale of transactions, volatility of returns on corporate equity, imperfect information, poor corporate accounting and reporting practices, foreign exchange risks, and official restrictions on capital movements are some of the main obstacles to successful mobilisation of bond and equity finance. Even when capital market liberalisation and institutional development have helped in establishing emergent capital markets as good portfolio investment outlets for international investors, the volatility of foreign capital poses acute danger to the macro economic performance of those developing countries. The collapse of Mexican stock prices and its contagious effects on other parts of the Mexican financial system, and the financial systems of major Latin American countries dramatically exemplifies this type of danger.

The existence of a sub-regional development bank such as the CDB confers some advantages. The bank is itself a country risk pooling entity. By having an asset portfolio consisting of credits to individual Caribbean countries, it minimises the sum of the individual country risks. It can therefore offer to the foreign portfolio investor a risk superior liability. Furthermore, the scale of its international transactions can contribute to 'reductions of transactions' costs for both the foreign investor and the borrowing institution. CDB debt is also not subject to cross-border payment restrictions which discourage foreign portfolio investors. More important perhaps, the CDB, by virtue of its potential influence on national economic policies, may have conferred upon it the role of principal mobiliser of official financial aid. Altogether, it is unlikely that a high proportion of funds disbursed by the CDB will be highly subsidised. Not only is there the likelihood that private market funds at higher interest rates will be a larger proportion of its liability portfolio, there is also a trend towards less concessionary terms on official development assistance.

The trend towards less direct state involvement in the economy has several potentially problematic implications for the CDB. If privatisation extends to the state-owned development banks, governments may no longer be willing to guarantee the financial obligations of those banks to the CDB. The CDB's risk exposure would automatically increase. The divestment of state-owned non-financial enterprises has a similar implication.

On its assets side, the CDB has virtually confined itself to financing public sector entities. It may therefore have to shift its orientation towards the private sector since the national trends are in favour of private sector growth. This itself would confer some advantages. In particular, the CDB, unlike national development banks, would be better able to deal with the large non-financial enterprises as clients, and may also be more prone to enter into co-financing arrangements with large Caribbean financial enterprises.

The conclusion to this analysis of the future of development banking in the Caribbean can be very brief. There is still a strong case for development finance. Private financial firms have begun to perform development finance functions. Nonetheless, the magnitude of the development challenge and the relative paucity of the private financial response signal a continuing need for development banking. Major changes in the economic environment, especially those pertaining to markets and the role of the state, convey the need for changes in the way development banks function at the national and regional levels and in the business relationships they forge with other financial institutions. The future of development banking will depend upon how well the current institutions adapt to the new economic environment and evolving trends.

Notes

1.   Pedro Aspe and Jose Angel Guerra: *The State and Economic Development: A Mexican Perspective,* (Proceedings of the World Bank Annual Conference on Development Economics, 1992.) pp. 9–14.
2.   George Abbot, *The Caribbean Development Bank,* ed. by Worrel, Bourne, Dhodia (Chapter 9).

3. Compton Bourne, *The Role of Development Finance Corporations in the Caribbean,* ed. by Worrell, Bourne, Dhodia, (Chapter 10),

4. Compton Bourne, 'Challenges and Prospects for the Caribbean Development Bank in the 1990s', in *CDB to the Year 2000* (Proceedings of the 20th Anniversary Symposium, May 1990) pp. 22–29.

5. Elaine Buckberg, 'Emerging Stock Markets and International Asset Pricing', in *The World Bank Economic Review,* 9:1 (1995) pp. 51–74.

6. Joseph E. Stiglitz, 'The Role of the State in Financial Markets' (Proceedings of the World Bank Annual Conference on Development Economies, 1993). pp. 19–52.

7. World Bank, *Coping with Changes in the External Environment,* (Report No. 12821 LAC, May 1994).

[46]

CARICOM in Education

CXC a Success Story

Lucy Steward

Since its establishment just over 25 years ago, the Caribbean Examinations Council (CXC) has contributed significantly to regional cooperation in education. In all aspects of its operation, CXC has brought together teachers, university and college lecturers, subject specialists and resource persons from the public and private sectors to participate in activities such as syllabus development, paper setting, marking and grading.

The Council is now well known for the high quality of its syllabuses, thoroughness in its procedures, and valid and reliable examinations to meet the needs of a changing environment regionally and internationally. However, the journey has not always been easy. But the determination and vision of educators across the region have helped in the introduction of several innovations that mark the Council's work in carrying out its main regional mandate: 'to conduct examinations as it thinks appropriate and award certificates and diplomas on the results of examinations so conducted'.

Sixteen countries participate in the Council's activities. Membership of the Council includes the Vice Chancellors and representatives of the Universities of the West Indies and Guyana, representatives of the participating countries and of national teachers associations. The work of the Council is conducted through the Administrative and Finance Committee (AFC) and the School Examinations Committee (SEC) and its Sub-Committee (SUBSEC). In addition, the constitution provides for national committees established by each participating government. Subject panels are appointed to prepare and review syllabuses and examination committees set question papers, prepare mark schemes and supervise the marking by examiners and assistant examiners.

This very extensive network reflects a regional commitment to a consultative process for the management of the affairs of the Council and for ensuring quality and relevance in education provisions.

CXC offers examinations for the Caribbean Secondary Education Certificate (CSEC) at the end of the five-year secondary cycle. The Council also offers the Caribbean Advanced Proficiency Examinations (CAPE) at the post CSEC level. Currently the examinations are available in 33 subjects for CSEC and 17 subjects for CAPE, introduced as a pilot in seven subjects in 1998.

The number of candidates has also increased. For the first examinations in June 1979, 30,194 candidates registered for the examinations, and 58,708 subject entries were received.

With the increase in candidates and in subjects offered, in 1998, the Council examined nine subjects in the January examinations: 71,127 candidates registered, and 26,235 subject entries were received. In June 1998, 116,465 candidates registered, and 440,301 subject entries were received.

The Council, in its formative years, in particular, worked very hard to gain acceptance and credibility in a region where British education traditions and examinations were deeply entrenched. The Council's work was not made any easier by the fact that it sought not merely to replace overseas examinations, but to indigenise curriculum and modify the ways of conducting assessment.

The main changes, radical at the time, were a switch from norm-referenced testing to criterion-referenced testing; the introduction of internal assessment or school based assessment; reporting performance by grades and profiles and the integration of technical and vocational subjects with academic subjects.

These changes were new to teachers, parents and employers, and the Council embarked on intense teacher training workshops in collaboration with Ministries of Education across the region. Further, the Council had to put in place controls and procedures that give all stakeholders assurance about international recognition of certification.

In order to do this, when the first examinations were introduced, the Council contracted chief examiners from the UK and mainly from Cambridge. The Council also obtained assistance from the Education Testing Service in Princeton, USA. Through this collaboration, the Council was able to equate grades awarded with those awarded by overseas bodies. In addition to the grades, the Council provided information on candidates' strengths and weaknesses using profiles.

Perhaps the most innovative feature introduced by the Council was the School Based Assessment (SBA). This was a proud banner under which the Council marched, since the Council was way ahead of many other examining bodies in taking the plunge in this area. Two former chairmen, Sir Roy Augier and Dr Dennis Irvine (1998) noted that:

> It was a frequent boast and pardonable exaggeration that in implementing the idea, the CXC was ahead of the English boards. However, the innovation required Council staff to engage in demanding forms of moderation, and teachers have grown increasingly restless as the number of subjects demanding school-based assessment has grown. The teachers claim to be burdened beyond tolerable limits by the number of assignments they have to mark and record. However, the Council remains fully committed to school-based assessment, and efforts are constantly made to assist schools and teachers with its implementation. (p. 154)

The Council is looking very seriously at the demands of the SBA since the number of subjects has increased significantly. In addition, in responding to the need to provide educational opportunities for persons outside educational institutions, the Council has been developing alternative examinations for these candidates.

Presently, private candidates can take examinations in 12 subjects in the January sitting. The introduction of examinations for private candidates is in keeping with a regional thrust to provide persons with opportunities for life-long learning.

The Council continues to respond to changing demands and is determined to improve the quality and range of its services and products. For example, before 1998, candidates' performance was reported on a five-point grading scale. However, educators identified a need for greater distinction between grade boundaries. The Council has addressed this issue and, since June 1998, performance is reported on a six-point grading scheme with Grades I, II and III in the new scheme equivalent to Grades I and II in the old scheme. Other examples of the Council's sensitivity to the needs of the region are in its current efforts to reduce the demands of internal assessment and to work with governments to provide national examinations for a wider range of abilities.

Now that the examinations for CSEC are well established, the Council has embarked on activities at the post CSEC level in response to a mandate from Ministers of Education for a new developmental model at this level. The mandate is clear that the model should not be a replica of GCE 'A' level examination but rather should provide flexibility in subject options and in access to programmes.

Between 1980 and 1988, the Council reported to the Standing Committee of Ministers, responsible for Education (SCME) on the progress of work done in the development of an alternative to the 'A' Level examinations.

With funding from the Commonwealth Secretariat, a study was done which showed wide support for a regional examination, equivalent in standard to the 'A' level, but differing from it in its philosophical assumptions and, consequently, in its structure. In addition to the study, consultations were held with the University of the West Indies (UWI), the University of Guyana (UG), other tertiary institutions including community colleges and key educators across the region.

The Caribbean Advanced Proficiency Examination (CAPE) was, therefore, born out of the same set of diagnoses that gave birth to the establishment of Community Colleges; innovative curricula at the post-secondary level; open access to learning opportunities; and, the push for a regional accreditation system that enjoys full support within the region, and convertibility across the international community.

CAPE is intended to provide assessment and appropriate certification for a diverse and rapidly expanding population. It is envisaged that the members of this population will prepare themselves for the examinations, using a variety of delivery modes and in different sequences.

The primary objective of CAPE is to provide a coherent and transparent certification, which is recognised regionally and internationally, and which establishes equivalencies across upper secondary and lower tertiary education in the Caribbean with a view to: clarifying routes to educational advancement; and promoting better articulation between educational pathways.

CAPE is designed to:

(a) satisfy entry requirements to universities and other tertiary institutions regionally and internationally;
(b) assess achievement in courses that are equivalent in standard to the 'A' level;
(c) include courses that are less narrow and specialised in nature to the 'A' level;
(d) provide assessment in technical/vocational subjects as in traditional academic subjects;
(e) provide for assessment of core skills;
(f) satisfy the educational needs of a larger percentage of the post CSEC population;
(g) cater to a wider range of abilities and interests than the 'A' level;
(h) allow for flexibility in choice of subjects and in time and place of study;
(i) address the manpower needs of the region.

Table 1:   Subjects Examined for Caribbean Secondary Education

Subject	Proficiency
Agricultural Science (Double Award)	General
Agricultural Science (Single Award)	General
Art	General
Art and Craft	General
Biology	General
Bookkeeping	Basic
Building Technology	Technical
Caribbean History	General & Basic
Chemistry	General
Clothing and Textiles	General & Basic
Craft	General
Electrical/Electronics	Technical
English A	General & Basic
English B	General & Basic
Food and Nutrition	General & Basic
French	General & Basic
Geography	General & Basic
Home Economics: Management	General & Basic
Information Technology	General & Technical
Integrated Science (Double Award)	General
Integrated Science (Single Award)	General & Basic
Mathematics	General & Basic
Mechanical Engineering Technology	Technical
Metals	General & Basic
Office Procedure	General & Basic
Physics	General
Principles of Accounts	General
Principles of Business	General & Basic
Religious Education	General
Shorthand and Typed Transcription	General
Social Studies	General & Basic
Spanish	General & Basic
Technical Drawing	General & Basic
Typewriting	General & Basic
Woods	General & Basic

Table 2:   Caribbean Advanced Proficiency Examination (Up to 2000)

Subject	Units
Phase I	
Caribbean Studies	1 unit
Communication Studies	1 unit
Functional Spanish	1 unit
History	1st unit
Information Technology	1 unit
Mathematics	1st unit
Statistical Analysis	1 unit
Phase II	
Accounting	2 units
Applied Mathematics	1 unit
Biology	2 units
Chemistry	2 units
Electrical and Electronic Technology	1 unit
French	2 units
Functional French	1 unit
History	2nd unit
Literatures in English	2 units
Mathematics	2nd unit
Physics	2 units
Spanish	2 units
Phase III (for 2000)	
Art and Design	2 units
Computer Science	2 units
Economics	2 units
Geography	2 units
Geometrical & Mechanical Engineering Drawing	2 units
Law	2 units
Management of Business	2 units

The provision of tertiary education in the Caribbean region is a source of great concern. At their meeting in Montego Bay, in July 1996, Heads of Government, recognising the imperative of tertiary education and training for the development of the region, set the target for an increase in the enrolment of graduates to tertiary institutions from the secondary education system at 15 per cent to be achieved by the year 2005. CAPE responds to this mandate by providing flexibility and the opportunity to increase access to quality education at the post CSEC level.

Flexibility in CAPE is realised through a structure of One and Two-Unit courses. A One-Unit course requires 120 contact hours; a Two-Unit course requires 240 contact hours.

A candidate can opt for breadth by selecting several 1-Unit courses and for depth by doing 2-Unit courses. For example, a person wishing to specialise in the Sciences can take the 2-Unit courses in the Sciences but may also wish to take a I-Unit course in Functional Spanish or in the Management of Business.

Quality is achieved through inputs from experts and other resource persons in the various disciplines, so that the syllabuses have the required breadth and depth, reflect current thinking in the disciplines and incorporate elements to meet current and anticipated needs of the region within a global context. The programme is also enhanced by the inclusion of six core courses: Caribbean Studies; Communication Studies; Statistical Analysis; Information Technology; Functional Spanish; and Functional French.

The purpose of these core courses is to provide opportunity for persons to acquire generic skills. They also allow candidates to pursue ancillary, complementary or contrasting subjects without prejudice to the main area of specialisation.

Because of the need for assurance about international recognition, the stipulated content for an 'A' level offering is incorporated in the 2-Unit courses. At all stages in the development of CAPE, extensive consultations and regional and international scrutiny take place in order to ensure quality, thoroughness, relevance and marketability.

The Council is collaborating with the tertiary education institutions in the region in the development of CAPE, in order to realise economies, increase enrolments and maintain high standards. The present Chairman of Council, Sir Keith Hunte (1999), noted that:

In the light of the severe economic pressures that are being exerted on the budgets of our respective governments, we should always be exploring the best ways to achieve our objectives in the most cost-effective mode.

In several areas the lack of critical mass leads to the incurring of the high unit cost for development, test construction and administration of examinations.

In the areas where we have a common agenda in relation to the courses that should be offered, we ought to assume joint responsibility for syllabus construction and development but consider redefining the benefits to be gained by common regional or sub-regional examinations. (p.13)

The Council is at the service of ministries, institutions and public and private sector enterprises. The established practices, wide network of educators at regional and international levels and the investments in appropriate technologies are assets on which the various bodies can draw. For example, in order to realise economies and ensure regional and international currency of certification, the Council can assist at national level in syllabus development, provision and administration of examinations, training local persons in assessment procedures, and analysis and research necessary for improving the quality of education at all levels. In recent times, the Council has undertaken some of these activities. It is hoped that this collaboration and partnership will increase as the region makes a concerted effort and takes systematic short and long-term measures to ensure that it has the human capital to meet its developmental needs in a highly competitive global environment.

As a CARICOM institution, CXC has benefited from the guidance and intervention of the CARICOM Secretariat and from the support of governments. Despite economic pressures, regional governments remain firmly committed to education provision at all levels. CXC has also benefited from the hard work of education officials, lecturers, teachers and other educators, and a pool of resource persons from across the region.

Thanks to the policy makers and to all stakeholders across the region for the invaluable contribution to this regional effort, and to what is certainly a success story in regional cooperation for human development.

Notes

1. Caribbean Examinations Council (1999). Caribbean Advanced Proficiency Examinations. CXC Barbados.
2. R. Augier, and D. Irvine, 'Caribbean Examinations Council' in *Examination Systems in Small States*, ed. by M. Bray and L. Steward (Commonwealth Secretariat, London, 1998).

This paper was first published in *CARICOM Perspective*, No. 69, June 1999, pp. 65–69.

[47]

The West Indian
University Revisited

Alister McIntyre

I am very delighted to be back here in Port of Spain. I consider it a signal honour to be invited to deliver the Sixth Dr Eric Williams Memorial Lecture. I have chosen to speak on 'The West Indian University Revisited' in order to take this opportunity to express some very preliminary thoughts on certain issues connected with the future development of the University of the West Indies.

The University will, this year, be celebrating its fortieth anniversary. This provides an appropriate occasion for review, assessment and projection. I am, therefore, gratified to note that public consultations are taking place here in Trinidad and Tobago on the University. I hope that this timely initiative will be emulated by other contributing territories to the University, so that a full exchange of views can result on the University and its future.

On September 1, I shall assume duties as Vice Chancellor of the University having left the institution 14 years ago, and the region itself 11 years ago. My long absence handicaps me in speaking about this subject. Prudence will normally dictate that I hold my tongue until I have fully re-acquainted myself with the University, and with the conditions in the region to which it must relate.

I feel compelled, however, to share some of my perceptions with you this evening, because of the urgency of taking action on many of the matters related to the development of the University.

Over the 40 years of its existence, the University has chalked up a solid record as a regional centre for teaching, research and outreach activities. I must also sincerely compliment my colleagues for their achievements over the years, despite the many difficulties that they have had to surmount. It is no chauvinistic remark to say that compared with other institutions of similar origins in different parts of the Third World, the University of the West Indies stands out for its stability, growth and resilience. This is in no small measure due to the quality of its staff and students and to the substantial and steady support which contributing governments and external sources have provided over the years.

The University has progressed from a single campus at Mona planned for 600 students, to three campuses with a total student body of almost 12,000 students, with a School of Hotel Management and Tourism in Nassau, and with University centres in all 14 of its contributing territories. A total of about 35,000 students with first degrees, higher degrees, diplomas and certificates have graduated from The University of the West Indies.

The research record of the University is equally noteworthy. Every single faculty and department of the university has major publications to its credit reporting on advances made in understanding and solving important problems, more often than not of the region itself. The research record of the university is reflected in the fact that outside grants – principally for research and related activities – account for over 20% of the institution's budget.

A similar situation prevails with respect to outreach activities. University people are to be found in every sector of community service: advising governments and serving in their various standings and *ad hoc* bodies; participating and assisting civic groups; arbitrating labour disputes; contributing to the print and electronic media – to name a few examples. It would be difficult to imagine any major event taking place in the region today with which the University would not be associated in one form or another.

Dr Eric Williams himself, were he alive today, would have taken some satisfaction from the University's achievements although it would be characteristic for him to view the institution with an incisively critical eye, and to come forward with innovative ideas. Many of the directions which the University has taken over the years were foreshadowed in his seminal speech at the Institute of Jamaica in August 1944 on 'The Idea of a British West Indian University'.

In that speech, Dr Williams placed much emphasis on the role of the University as an agent for development and for strengthening Caribbean identity. In both respects, UWI has much to its credit, but it will have to respond to formidable challenges in the years ahead. Of particular importance will be the University's contribution to resolving the development problems with which the region will be faced.

The basic challenge facing the countries of the Caribbean is to find and utilise opportunities for vigorous growth, after a decade or more during which several countries have experienced stagnation, and even negative growth. This is not the place to engage in an analysis of recent economic performance. Suffice it to say that the CARICOM countries may be moving into the last decade of this century and into the next one, with a serious accumulation of unmet development needs, and with a diminished capacity to provide for them.

The Caribbean must take full stock of its reality. More than ever before, recognition has to be given to the limited growth potential of the traditional sectors, whether of mining or export agriculture, partly because of poor international demand prospects and with respect to petroleum resource depletion. Even in the case of tourism where market prospects are better, the outlook for the industry depends upon the region's capacity to diversify both its tourist attractions and its sources of tourists.

Despite all of the efforts that have been made, the region is still a chronic importer of food. The manufacturing sector remains at a rudimentary stage of development. The services sector and the physical infrastructure in many countries require significant rehabilitation and upgrading.

The critical question is what can be the new sources of growth. Without attempting a detailed answer to this, let me just say that in my view, future growth will very much depend upon whether we can successfully make the transition from a pattern of development principally dependent on natural resources, to one dependent on human resources and knowledge. This will require a major strengthening of our capacity to acquire, adapt, develop and utilise technology. We have to look increasingly towards science, technology, management, and organisation, as key ingredients of the development process.

Meticulous attention must be paid to updating the technological content of production. Greater use must be made of biotechnology in modernising the agricultural and fishery sectors; the development of engineering industries oriented towards exports have to be speeded up; information technology must be harnessed for the production of both goods and services; sophisticated management must be trained and the entire labour force inculcated with values that assign the highest importance to hard work, discipline and achievement. Merely to state this requirement is to illustrate what a considerable gap separates aspirations from current performance.

There are no overnight solutions available. Experience elsewhere indicates that a significant enhancement of technological capability will depend on sustained efforts lasting perhaps over several decades. But just as one looks back over the last 40 years with some satisfaction, it is imperative to develop a vision of the next 40 years, and to begin a response to the prospects and challenges that lie ahead.

The University faces a major task in contributing to the more sophisticated manpower needs associated with strengthening the region's technological capacity. At an aggregate level, in all but one of the contributing territories, enrolment ratios at the tertiary level (that is, the number of students enrolled at the tertiary level as a percentage of the age cohort 20–24) is currently five per cent or less. This can be compared with a figure of about twelve per cent for Hong Kong and Singapore; of over thirty per cent for the Republic of Korea, which is roughly the figure for a large number of Western European countries and Japan; and over fifty-seven per cent for the USA.

In the field of science and technology itself, the region is far behind. To give one example: according to the UNESCO Statistical Yearbook for 1987, Trinidad and Tobago with a population of 1.1 million, had in 1985 a total of 1,226 students enrolled at the tertiary level in Science, Mathematics, Computer Science and Engineering. Compare this with Singapore, which with a population of 2.6 million, had in 1984 over 18,000 students enrolled in those fields. This may be a rather dramatic comparison, but examination of available data for other fast-growing developing countries confirms that the region is lagging behind.

The issue which the university and the region as a whole will have to face is how to remedy these deficiencies. I suppose one ought to start by seeing how far numbers can be increased through a fuller utilisation of existing capacities. I am not on firm ground here, but based upon some recent information that I have seen, it appears that the University is already pursuing, and needs to be encouraged to pursue further, some important possibilities.

One is to step up the provision of University teaching through outreach activities, particularly in the non-campus territories. Here the UWIDITE system and the challenge examinations can be important vehicles for increasing the access of students to University campus.

Governments in the non-campus territories are already making efforts to mobilise resources for first-year and non-degree teaching in subjects such as Mathematics, Science, and Management. However, these needs also exist in areas distant from the campuses in the campus territories themselves. There are several such areas in Trinidad and Tobago. We must all welcome the initiative taken by the Commonwealth Heads of Government to establish a Commonwealth Distance Teaching Facility which can give a major impetus to our own programmes of distance teaching.

The University is also discussing how far an expansion of numbers can be achieved through more systematic networking with existing tertiary level institutions in the region. Virtually all of the contributing territories have one or more tertiary institutions which can be upgraded to provide at least first-year work in some subjects and certificate and diploma training in certain fields. Some of them may even be suitable for extension to second and third-year courses. It is obvious that full advantage should be taken of these possibilities in order to cut both the cost and time involved in securing a University education, and to bring the University into a closer relationship with the communities that it serves.

It is necessary, however, to guard against the dangers of institutional proliferation. In tertiary education, critical minimum size and economies of scales are extremely important considerations. Experience, even in the Caribbean itself, shows that it is extremely difficult to provide high quality instruction on a sustained basis in national institutions operating under the handicap of small teaching units.

It is inevitable that such institutions find it difficult to recruit and retain high quality staff, if they are to be restricted to teaching a limited range of general courses with very little opportunities for intellectual interaction, and with a poorly equipped infrastructure in the form of libraries, laboratories, and equipment. The University of the West Indies itself is struggling against great odds to maintain its academic standards in the light of financial constraints.

The idea of consolidating existing tertiary units into a single national institution may be a good one, if the new structure is linked to a strong support system. Without the latter, it might end up as a mere exercise in re-labelling. Such support can best come from an institution with experience of local conditions and needs. In any case, it should come from an institution of substantiated academic standing.

I echo the concern of those who have expressed the view that the region is sometimes too easily tempted by access to the facilities of institutions of comparatively low standing. One should not have to make the trite observation that the young people of the region deserve nothing but the best. A second-rate education cannot produce anything other than a second-rate performance.

One of the services that the University can provide is to assist national tertiary institutions in establishing relationships with outside academic institutions. Too often, because of a lack of initial information and insufficient local experience, these arrangements fail to satisfy the objectives for which they were established.

A situation can be envisaged where the University develops progressively systematic arrangements for supporting the delivery of undergraduate programmes at the general degree level by national tertiary institutions. However, to overcome constraints of critical minimum size and economies of scale, it may be advisable to organise a regional network of mutual support. The national institutions concerned could aim to achieve a measure of complementarity in their programmes of study. They could engage in regular staff and student exchanges. They could also co-operate in developing teaching materials and in conducting examinations. In other words, serious thought needs to be given to the feasibility of developing a regional tertiary network with the University of the West Indies as the main support and feeder institution.

I would like to encourage the CARICOM Governments to arrange for a comprehensive feasibility study of such a network. I feel certain that the University would contribute fully to such an effort.

From the perspective of the next 40 years, who knows whether the University of the West Indies might not emerge as principally a 'topping-up' and graduate institution at the apex of a network of associated undergraduate colleges? This is an exciting prospect, but for it to be realised, the foundations have to be carefully laid through preparatory work and planning.

The expansion of access can also be facilitated by the introduction of semester and credit systems, as well as by the establishment of a comprehensive Summer School programme. These are all currently under study in the University, and I am hopeful that positive recommendations will be forthcoming shortly.

I am myself particularly interested in a Summer School programme, not only because it will increase access for West Indian students, but also because it can provide a useful source of additional income for the University, if students from overseas can be attracted. There are a number of fields such as history, literature, linguistics, the social sciences, and education, where overseas students of West Indian origin or persons who are working with West Indian communities abroad, such as teachers, might wish to take advantage of summer programmes at the University of the West Indies. A well developed Summer School could be beneficial to both the faculty and regular student body of the University itself, as well as enhance the international standing of the institution.

Apart from the increases in numbers which have to be achieved, thought has also to be given to curriculum reform in the light of changing development requirements and educational advances worldwide. On previous occasions, I expressed my belief that the University needs to introduce a core programme of work for all of its students which exposes them to science, technology and management disciplines.

In particular, I feel that the aim should be to make every student computer literate. I should add to this the need to adopt a problem-solving approach in courses, and to provide students wherever appropriate and feasible, with hands-on experience. This leads me to mention the growing importance worldwide of sandwich programmes involving alternating periods of study and work, and of 'fast-tracks' where students can complete their degree work in a comparatively short period of time by year-round attendance. This is relevant to what I have just mentioned about the introduction of a Credit System and Summer School.

The short point is that the University of the West Indies has to develop consciously a greater development orientation into its teaching, trying among other things, to reduce the gap between the world of study and that of work. This will necessitate changes not only in the content and orientation of programmes and courses, but also improvements in work habits. The entire range of academic activities must give prominence to the importance of hard work, discipline and achievement. The University must view itself as a pacesetter for the society as a whole in promoting high productivity and cost-effectiveness.

Let me hasten to recognise the point made by those who are concerned that such practical approaches run the risk of turning the institution into a degree factory. This is not a problem unique to the University of the West Indies. Universities in many countries are, in the face of stiff competition for resources and public questioning of their relevance, making strenuous efforts to improve the practical orientation of their teaching, while endeavouring to build on their reputation as centres of reflection and intellectual innovation. To put the matter at its extreme, the plain reality is that under contemporary conditions, if universities were to function simply in the style of medieval cloisters characterised by leisurely intellectual activity, they should expect no more from that than medieval levels of resources.

A principal test of an institution's capacity to reconcile the practicability of its work with intellectual depth and innovation is the quality and reputation of its research, both within the area that it serves and outside. As I have said before, the University of the West Indies has a good research record, and could do more if the resources were to become available.

The strengthening of research and postgraduate studies is a need common to all of the University's campuses and faculties. They will not be able to retain high quality staff and students, let alone undertake the investigative work required for problem solving in the region, if regular budgetary provision is not made for their research and postgraduate work. Up to now, nearly all of the University's research is financed from outside, and postgraduate programmes are being maintained on a shoestring basis.

The Caribbean needs a substantially stronger and more sustained research effort by the University of the West Indies with a focus on research and development, if the technological thrust about which I spoke earlier is to have any chance of success. Research and development must become a regular part of the operation of all sectors of the economy.

One way in which the University can give some impetus to these activities is by the establishment of enterprise and technology parks, in a triangular partnership with governments and the private sector. I have in mind centres where management training packages can be provided for local business as well as a range of support services, such as Data Processing, Financial Analysis and Accounting, Laboratory Testing, Market Research and Design, Engineering and feasibility studies. These can be of particular value to start-up enterprises. Based on experience elsewhere, the establishment of a cluster of such services can serve as a magnet for the location of companies, particularly those utilising 'state of the art' technologies.

There is already some institutional capacity for this in the region, two examples being CARIRI here in Trinidad and Tobago, and the Scientific Research Council in Jamaica. However, I feel sure that these and other similar institutions would welcome a greater involvement by the University, with as many faculties as possible associating themselves with the effort. Here again, the University can conceive of itself as the principal feeder institution for building up a network of mutually supporting organisations and companies working in the field of Research and Development. This is also a matter that I would commend to governments of the region for full consideration with the University.

The idea of Caribbean identity is sometimes dismissed as a sentimental notion associated with past attempts at federation. It is true that when Dr Williams spoke about the University over 40 years ago, he discussed the evolution of Caribbean identity in terms of federation. But much more fundamentally, the idea of Caribbean identity has to do with survival in a complex and rapidly changing world.

The basic question is how can the tiny states of the Caribbean survive and retain their shared social and cultural values, in a world becoming less heterogeneous under the impact of satellite communications, and more intricate partly because of the emergence of major economic groupings and new centres of economic power.

Can the Caribbean states aspire to be more than lilliputian entities in the twenty-first century, with some standing in the international community?

Without the underpinning of a solid grasp of their history, their culture, and the articulation of a world view, will it in the years to come mean anything to be called a West Indian, or for that matter, a citizen of Trinidad and Tobago, Grenada, St Lucia and so on? What will those designations represent to those who use them and to the outside world?

I pose these questions not to provoke tendentious debate, but rather to illustrate the exercise in self-appraisal and understanding that still needs to be done, despite all of the work accomplished over the last four decades. In some respects, the Caribbean appears to be more vulnerable now than it was in the early 1960s at the time of Independence. I hope that I am not misreading the situation, but there seems to be less certainty about our place in the world, what we are trying to achieve, and how to set about securing it.

In a certain sense, we have also become more inward-looking, preoccupied with immediate local problems, and setting aside the larger picture. This is to some extent understandable, because many countries in the region have been going through very difficult times. But we cannot keep our eyes closed for too long. The world outside is changing rapidly, and we have to get a better grip on those changes and see what they portend for our future.

I myself would like to see very active programmes on regional and world affairs in all of our campus and non-campus territories. In addition to the formal academic training provided by the Institute of International Relations and the Faculties of Social Sciences, there is considerable scope for a regular series of open lectures, seminars, panel discussions and short courses. Given the new technologies that are now available, the University should be encouraged to produce a wider range of programmes and publications targeted towards the non-specialist public. It should mobilise and develop regular radio and television material on regional and global issues for its ongoing programmes of public education. I shall be inviting contributions, in particular, from external sources, to develop some of these activities.

In this context, the University needs to go further in developing area studies. Considering the extensive relations the region has with the USA and Canada, it is surprising that we do not yet have a regular programme of American Studies. One can make the point even more strongly in relation to Latin America, from which we are still relatively isolated. It is not too visionary to look forward to the day when Spanish can become the second language of our institution, thereby giving our students greater access to the richness and diversity of Latin America. I hope that we can progress along this road by increasing academic contacts with Latin American universities; arranging more exchanges of staff, students, and publications, and more systematic cooperation in research.

In this rather cursory overview of some possible directions for the University's development, I have strayed over a rather heavy agenda of issues which is by no means exhaustive. To recapitulate, they are as follows:

- Regional networking and development of national tertiary institutions.
- The establishment of Semester and Credit Systems and a Comprehensive Summer School. Curriculum reform, by providing students with a greater exposure to science, technology and management disciplines, and to a practical orientation.
- Substantial strengthening of research and post-graduate studies, with an emphasis on research and development activities.
- Extending the work on international affairs and area studies as part of the University's ongoing contribution to the evolution of Caribbean identity.

In order to respond adequately to these challenges, the University needs a substantial increase in its resources. The governments of the region are already stretched in its resources. They are already stretched in providing support for the University. However, I must urge them to fulfil their present financial commitments and in particular, to clear their arrears of contributions. The arrears outstanding to the University reflect themselves in a run-down physical plant, which is endangering the maintenance of academic standards. Governments are aware of the concerns about Faculties such as Medicine and Natural Sciences, of general overcrowding, and of the poor state of the library system and student amenities. If the University is to do the job required of it, these and other deficiencies have to be remedied immediately.

I myself shall be encouraging the University to launch a public appeal for financial support in all of our contributing territories as well as overseas. Let me start here and now in Trinidad and Tobago by asking you to respond as much as possible when the appeal is launched. There are difficult times, but it is precisely because they are difficult that we have to make the extra effort.

In general, I very much hope that through the appeal, the University and the communities as a whole can come closer together in tackling the region's manpower and development problems, and in trying to realise its full potential. I hope that our alumni will play a leading role, not only in fundraising, but also in developing a wider involvement. Some of our alumni, many of them abroad, are well placed to make part-time or occasional contributions to the University's teaching, research and outreach activities. Systematic machinery needs to be set up for the purpose. I hope the occasion of the anniversary will encourage a start along these lines.

May I end by expressing once again my great pleasure to be here, and by pledging all of my efforts – and I am sure that I can do likewise for all my colleagues at the University – to the further growth and development of the University and of the region.

Note

Address delivered at the Sixth Dr Eric Williams Memorial Lecture Series on June 18, 1988.

[48]

Health and Caribbean Development

Perspectives and Challenges

Stanley Lalta

A basic right, a fundamental asset – such is the language used to define good health for individuals and the population as a whole. As middle income developing countries, health indicators in the Caribbean are more favourable than most comparator countries and, in fact, are more reflective of health status in industrialised countries. With one or two exceptions among countries, the standard indicators reveal the following:

- Crude birth rate   25 per 1000
- Crude death rate   8 per 1000
- Infant mortality rate   20 per 1000
- Fertility rate   2.8 per woman of child-bearing age
- Life expectancy   70 years

Generally, the morbidity/mortality profile has changed considerably. The critical health concerns are now the chronic, non-communicable diseases – cancer, cardiovascular conditions, diabetes, hypertension, accidents/violence and sexually transmitted diseases/AIDS as against the infectious diseases such as typhoid, tuberculosis, measles, malaria and yellow fever. This 'epidemiological transition' in the health profile of Caribbean countries means that more attention has to be focused on services which emphasise caring and comforting, health promotion and illness prevention as well as rehabilitation.

These impressive health achievements reflect a combination of social, economic and educational improvement; public health and communicable disease control measures; maternal and child health programmes; investment in primary and secondary care; ongoing regional cooperation as well as visible political commitment to health over the last three decades.

In terms of the impact of regional cooperation and integration on health successes, Caribbean countries have collaborated in such major initiatives as:

- the adoption of the Primary Health Care Strategy in 1982 to achieve Health for All by the year 2000;
- the Caribbean Cooperation in Health Programme in 1986 which articulates strategic actions in certain priority areas – environmental health, human resource development, care for chronic and non-communicable conditions, strengthening health delivery systems, food and nutrition, maternal and child health and control of AIDS/STDs;
- the adoption of the Regional Programme for Health Promotion in 1994.

In addition, countries have received significant benefits from the activities of regional institutions such as: the University of the West Indies; Caribbean Epidemiological Centre; Caribbean Food and Nutrition Institute; East Caribbean Drug Service; Commonwealth Caribbean; Medical Research Council; Regional Drug Testing Laboratory and the Caribbean Environmental Health Institute.

Traditionally, the state has played the dominant role in the provision and financing of health services. In recent years however, this role has been seriously affected by economic difficulties particularly the inability of the public sector to guarantee adequate and high quality care to all. The old dictum that 'it takes cash to care' is a major factor defining the current realities and policies in the health care of all countries.

Financial flows to the sector are heavily constrained by uncertain public health budget and dwindling foreign aid – this is evident in the difficulties of retaining professional staff, in inconsistent supplies of equipment and drugs, in the deterioration of the capital stock, and the rapid growth of the private health care market. At the same time, the demand for and cost of health services are growing exponentially due to: the ageing population; the prolonged treatment expenses for chronic care patients; increasing urbanisation; the technological imperative; patient expectations; persistent inefficiencies in the delivery of health services and the normal requirements to upgrade working conditions and employee benefits.

Unless early and systematic action is taken, this increasing gap between resource demand and resource needs will threaten and possibly roll back the improvement in the region's health care, so painstakingly achieved in previous decades. Already, some countries like Jamaica, Trinidad and Tobago, St Lucia, St Vincent, Montserrat and Dominica, with assistance from regional and international organisations are implementing or are contemplating a package of reforms to consolidate and expand their successes in the health sector. It is still quite early for rigorous evaluation of these reforms.

In a real sense the basic challenge facing the health services in the next decade is the same as before – how to add years to life and life to years for everyone through provision of a mix of services at the least cost. In designing specific and innovative strategies to meet this multifaceted challenge, there are five key elements to be considered:

- The role of social and individual responsibility
- The involvement of all sectors – public, private and NGOs
- The provision of a basic package of services for all.
- The sharing of health services as an efficiency strategy.
- The need for continuous monitoring, evaluation and research.

Shared Health Services

The benefits of good health or the costs of bad health are felt by individuals and society. A major factor in reducing the demand for health services is the encouragement of life style changes through health promotion. At the same time there are other health-enhancing activities which require the involvement of the entire society, for example, clean environment and the training of health professionals. Greater emphasis has to be placed on sharing the responsibilities for future health successes by individuals, communities and the society as a whole.

Health is too diverse, multifaceted and expensive for any single sector in the country. Mechanisms and programmes have to be designed which can maximise the skills and resources of the public, private and the non-government sectors (NGOs). The fact that most governments feel ultimately responsible for the health of the population does not mean that they have to finance and provide all services. This has implications for all health planning and programme development.

Despite the optimistic rhetoric in all countries, the level of one's income affects the accessibility to and quality of health services received. At the same time that governments are spending large sums of money on health services which benefit the few, other services which benefit sizeable segments of the population are ignored or under funded. With rising levels of poverty and increasing income differences between the have and have-nots in most countries, efforts must be made to provide a basic guaranteed package of services for everyone. This ensures that equity in health becomes a reality rather than remain an elusive principle.

Given the relatively small size of the population in most countries and the need to maximise resource use in the region, the sharing of services should be seen as a critical efficiency strategy in the provision of health services. There are three components to this: moving patients to where the skills and facilities exist; moving professionals (for short periods of time) to where the patients are; and developing regional Centres of Excellence for particular services. Each of these should be systematically explored and properly administered to optimise health outcomes.

Continuous Research and Evaluation

If the overall objective of the health system is to achieve equity and efficiency (*value for money*) there must be ongoing evaluation, innovation and customer research. The casual assumption that some good is being done or that some health professionals are working assiduously is inadequate.

In summary, as a basic right or fundamental asset, health for all is a social imperative and is feasible. The cost of not achieving this is the lives of countless persons who are deemed expendable.

Note

This paper was published in *CARICOM Perspective*, No. 65, June 1995, pp. 76–77.

[49]

Disaster Management in
CARICOM Countries

Jeremy McA Collymore

The Caribbean has had a long history of hazard impact and disaster experiences. The region is exposed to three of the worst kinds of natural hazards: hurricanes, volcanic eruptions and earthquakes.[1] Loss of life resulting from the impacts run into the thousands whilst property losses and other damages have reached billions of dollars at present day values. Almost every city in the region has been devastated in the last 300 years.

In the 120 years between 1871 and 1999 more than 130 named systems have traversed the Eastern Caribbean sub-region within which the OECS states fall. Between 1944 and 1980 an increase in the average number of hurricanes was noted; a slight decrease in frequency but significant increases in magnitudes have been observed.

In the last ten years CARICOM states have been exposed to at least seven major hurricane systems. Most of the OECS states in the Leeward Islands and the northern Windward islands have been severely impacted by at least two major hurricanes in the last decade. Jamaica was severely affected by Hurricane Gilbert in 1988 resulting in approximately US$4 billion in damage. The Bahamas suffered the ravages of Hurricane Andrew in 1992 and Hurricane Floyd in 1999. Every year since 1979, Jamaica has experienced severe flooding in at least one local community. In recent years, drought has become a more common phenomenon in many CARICOM states.

Volcanic eruptions in St Vincent and the Grenadines (1979) and Montserrat (1995) have reminded us of the potential physical and economic dislocation that may result from this hazard. Recent activity in Dominica reminds us of the geographic distribution of the threat.

Earthquakes, though not as prevalent as other hazards, are still a threat. The Antigua and Barbuda experience of 1974 is a reminder that must not be ignored. Trinidad and Tobago and Jamaica are also as exposed to this threat.

The landslides that have taken place in Dominica (1997), St Lucia (1999) and more recently throughout the sub-region as a result of Hurricane Lenny, pose severe threats to our infrastructure and general lifeline systems. The landslide related devastation in Jamaica is well documented.[2] (Ahmad 1989).

Impact on Development Aspirations and the Caribbean

The more than US$0.7 billion of dollars loss as a result of Hurricane Lenny related damages alone in the Eastern Caribbean has set back the development agenda of the sub-region. Losses and reconstruction costs associated with Hurricane Lenny alone are estimated at EC$712.5M. Similar levels of loss have been associated with hurricane events in the region.[3] See also Collymore 1996.

It is worthy to note that critical sectors of the economy – tourism, housing and agriculture are being repeatedly devastated; critical facilities such as schools and hospitals are repeatedly affected; and the losses appear to be increasing. This suggests that the sustainability of our development interventions will largely be determined by our willingness and efforts to manage our hazardous environment.

Disaster Management Interventions

It can be safely argued that disaster management at the national level has been focused primarily on preparedness and response, has been hurricane centred and event driven.

CARICOM member states have been making efforts to better their arrangements for improving disaster preparedness and response. A comparison of basic elements of commitment suggests that since 1991 some process is discernible. However preparedness audit from the Caribbean Disaster Emergency Response Agency (CDERA) in 1997, indicates that the core elements of resourcing of programming and training are still to be supported by national governments.[4] (SCL 1997).

The most noticeable area of inaction has been the articulation of policies and incentives to promote disaster loss reduction in our critical sectors and facilities. Our development interventions, by being generally indifferent to our susceptibility to hazards have, through design and location, contributed to the region's increased vulnerability.

Following the devastating events of Gilbert 1988 and Hugo 1999, Governments of the Caribbean Community created CDERA whose objectives are:

(1) To make an immediate and coordinated response by means of emergency relief to an affected member state;
(2) To secure, coordinate and channel to interested inter-governmental and non governmental organisations reliable and comprehensive information on disasters affecting a member state;
(3) To mobilise and coordinate disaster relief from governmental and inter-governmental organisations for affected member states;
(4) To mitigate or eliminate, as far as practicable, the immediate consequences of natural disasters in member states;
(5) To establish, enhance and maintain on a sustainable basis adequate disaster response capabilities among member states.

This preparedness and response mechanism was seen as essential to facilitating the regional efforts in better preparing for and responding to disasters in member states. The agreement establishing the Agency also expressed some minimum expectations of the member states to make this system effective (Article 15). A recent regional preparedness audit has indicated that there is still much basic work to be done.[5] (SCL 1997)

Indeed it is the desire to promote some common institutional capability among its participating states that has informed the programming agenda of CDERA since its inception.

The following have been initiated or established:

- Multi-Hazard Contingency Planning
- Emergency Telecommunications Manual and Plan
- Emergency Operations Centre Management
- Relief Supply Policy Guidelines
- Donations Management Policy
- Relief Supply Management System
- Shelter Management Programme and Policy Guide
- Work Programme Planning Guide
- Damage Assessment and Needs Analysis Protocols
- Mitigation Planning Guide

- Donor Group Support Guidelines
- Institutionalising of Disaster Training and Research
- Community Disaster Planning
- Recovery Planning Framework and Guide

Much of the above has been attained through cooperation with regional and international partners. But the major challenges to date have been the high variability in support for disaster offices at the national level; the high turnover of national disaster coordinators and the event-focused support for the disaster management agenda.

Enhancing the Institutional Capacity for Disaster Management

There is no doubt about the considerable efforts of the Caribbean Community to improve our response readiness. If we are to make any significant reduction in the losses we have been experiencing from recent hazard impacts there will be a need to refocus our capacity building interventions. Vulnerability reduction, in its widest sense, must become the centre of our disaster management capacity building efforts.

Capacity building centred on a vulnerability reduction agenda must quickly and radically move away from our present approach where interventions have taken place outside of the definition of an overall disaster management policy framework. There will also be need to reassess capacity enhancement initiatives, which are centred almost entirely on post-event recovery and rehabilitation needs and/or donor interests.

Future and ongoing efforts to improve institutional capacity in disaster management in the Caribbean, and indeed elsewhere must focus on 'institutionalization' itself and the implications for the nature and framing of the policy we wish to purpose. At least one must be clear about 'capacity for what' and 'capacitation from whom'. Equally important is ensuring that the process elements which inform the institutional capacity enhancement efforts are indeed empowering. Attention must therefore be given to technology transfer, training methodologies and cooperation infrastructure.

A critical first step in our institutional capacity reform efforts must be the determination of the policy framework, which is significantly influenced by our articulation of the environment-society relationship. One needs to know whether there is a commitment by the state to the removal of natural hazard related risks. There will also be a need to be clear about who is vulnerable, the causes and how this vulnerability is generated. Our policy framework will also be informed by the solutions we anticipate, whether this be technology application or structured management interventions.[6,7] (Healey 2000, Collymore 2000).

CDERA and its regional disaster management partners agree that institutional capacity building and reform in disaster management must begin with the definition of a policy framework for a comprehensive and integrated approach to disaster management. This must have full political endorsement at the national and regional levels and be integrated into the programming agenda of critical institutions of the Community.

The UNDP/USAID support for CDERA's strategic programming for CDB will allow for the engagement of major sector players, such as, tourism, agriculture, education and utilities in the consensus building process.

The capacity enhancement policies and programmes in the Caribbean Community will need to emphasise more, the development of self-reliance infrastructure. Training and public education initiatives must become end-user directed and economic preparedness planning must be incorporated into investment and economic forecasting mechanisms.

More importantly, there is need to embrace a concept of economic preparedness planning where explicit consideration is given to socio-economic impact of an event and the development of policies and instruments to support relief assistance, recovery/reconstruction and mitigation. The intent is to ensure that relief assistance expectations are known and shared and better costed, as well as to facilitate time-sensitive recovery.

CDERA has already prepared and shared model guidelines on a Relief Assistance and Donations Management Policy with its participating states. A paper on linking emergency assistance to mitigation sensitive reconstruction has also been prepared and widely distributed with notable policy changes emerging among the Multilateral Financing Institutions.[8] (Collymore 1996).

In essence, it must be acknowledged that disaster loss reduction has to be a national agenda embedded in the considerations of key sectors and actions.

Opportunities for Enhancing Disaster Management

In the region there are several development intervention plans that provide excellent opportunities for operationalising the principles of a comprehensive disaster management programming, that is, multi-sectoral, interdisciplinary and integrated. Coastal zone management programmes, sustainable development councils and poverty alleviation programmes provide great potential for partnering towards a common goal, the improvement of the quality of life of our people.

Opportunities for supporting and promoting disaster reduction and sustainable development at the regional level may be considered within the framework of incorporation of disaster management considerations in regional institutions and programmes and consultation and consensus to inform lobbying in international fora.

The intention is for each regional organisation to examine how its programmes may contribute to increased vulnerability on one hand and how to support vulnerability reduction on the other. The expected outcome is an increase in the stakeholders and actors promoting disaster loss-reduction without changing mandates or augmenting resource needs.

The Caribbean Development Bank has started this process through its Natural Disaster Management Strategy and Operational Guidelines. The Organisation of Eastern Caribbean States has already embraced proposals from CDERA in this regard and committed itself to having the subject of disaster management on the agenda of regular meetings of the Authority and Ministerial Meetings. It is also seeking to identify how its various programmes can contribute to the promotion of vulnerability reduction.

Sourcing disaster management is essentially political. The nature of our political articulation of support for resources to promote disaster management will be critical to the attention it receives. The following may be considered:

(1) Regional commitment to securing a debt relief protocol for SIDS based on a level of impact or series of impacts measured in relation to some measure such as GDP. May need to join forces with SIDS partners in AOSIS.

(2) Regional Approach to Development Financing Institutions and Agencies for the Establishment of Contingency Rehabilitation funds that would allow time-sensitive restart of the economy. Already CDB and IDB have articulated a policy that addresses the contingency fund. The World Bank is in the process of doing the same. Our goal is to focus on time-sensitive access to these resources.

(3) Exploration of EU/ACP Post Lomé IV Agreement to build on support for loss reduction and reconstruction interventions especially in general infrastructure development and specifically in key economic sectors.

(4) Development of a common strategy on promoting loss reduction measures in private sector investment.

(5) Collective political support of appeals for emergency assistance by member states.

(6) Promotion of the interfacing of environmental management, poverty and disaster reduction initiatives.

(7) Lobby of multilateral and bilateral organisations for resources to promote vulnerability assessment.

(8) Endorsement and promotion of an integrated and comprehensive approach to disaster management.

The centre piece of our international lobbying process can be the development of a vulnerability index that gains acceptability as an alternative to PCI based consideration for grant assistance or concessionary financing. This requires that the Caribbean states must take responsibility for doing the hazard assessments and vulnerability analysis required to operationalise the proposed models. Political support is therefore required for the mobilisation of resources to carry out structured vulnerability assessments.

It must be noted that the credibility of the programme will be significantly influenced by what we do for ourselves. Every effort must be made to ensure that in each state there is a defined programme for capacity enhancement with the level of local and regional support clearly articulated.

Our articulated approach to institutionalisation of capacity in disaster management is captured in an understanding that we are seeking to influence the more enduring features of social life.[9] (Giddens 1984). Specifically we are referring to the embedding of specific practices in a wider context of social relations that cut across the landscape of formal organisations and to the active processes by which individuals, in given social contexts, construct their way of thinking and acting.[10] (Headley 2000).

Experiences suggest that most vulnerable societies are those unable to have great economies and normal lives after a disaster. It is also informed by a recognition that changes in the frequency of the event do not have to occur for vulnerability to increase. Development aspirations and interventions have tended to increase exposure and vulnerability, and technology transfer often disconnects communities from their coping capacity and increases dependency on systems that they cannot manage or afford.

What we are reaffirming is that capacity building is more than the creation of organisations or the execution of activities. In the context of disaster management it calls for a greater interface among the actors in development control, economic planning and environmental planning. Disaster management is a critical cross cutting development issue and must be approached as such. Our position is informed by an observation that the amount of damage associated with a disaster is largely a function of decisions made in the course of development.[11] (Munasinghe and Clarke 1995).

Vulnerability assessment interventions pursued within the framework of institutionalisation as articulated here, would therefore have to go beyond examining the physical structures and demographics of our communities. Careful consideration would have to be given to the resilience of our communities. In this context the capacity to prevent or mitigate losses, minimise social and economic disruption associated with an impact or threat and the management of the recovery process are critical.[12] (Buckle et al 2000).

More and closer attention must be addressed to the peculiar social, economic and cultural factors of our region. It is these elements that will better allow us to define the uniqueness of small island developing states in the context of hazard related vulnerability.

Notes

1. A. Rafi, 'Geohazards in Jamaica and the Caribbean: The Landslide Problem', *UNESCO Courier,* 3:5, (1989) pp. 2–4.
2. Caribbean Development Bank Policy for Natural Disaster Management, Bridgetown, Barbados, (1998).
3. Buckle et al, 'New Approaches to assessing Vulnerability and resilience' *Australian Journal of Emergency Management,* 15:2 (2000) pp.8–24.
4. J. McA. Collymore, 'Disaster Management in the Caribbean: Possibilities for Critical Policy Links and Consolidation'. (Paper prepared for the Forum of Ministers of the Environment of Latin America and the Caribbean, Barbados, March 3–6, 2000).
5. J. Collymore, 'Emergency Assistance as a Critical Catalyst in Future Loss Reduction Planning', (Hemispheric Congress on Disaster Reduction Sustainable Development, Miami, Florida 1996)
6. A. Giddens, *The Constitution of Society,* (Cambridge, UK: Policy Press, 1984):
7. O. Granger, 'Geophysical events and social change in the Eastern Caribbean' in *The Tropical Environment. Proceedings of the International Symposium on the Physical and Human Resources of the Tropics,* ed. by L. Nkemdirim, (Working Group on Tropical Climatology and Human Settlements of the International Geographical Union, Calgary, 1988) pp.78–84.
8. P. Healey, 'Institutionalist Analysis, Communicative Planning and Shaping Places', *Journal of Planning Education and Research,* 19:2 (2000) pp. 111–22.
9. IADB, 'Facing the Challenges of Natural Disasters in Latin America and the Caribbean', (Washington, March 2000).
10. IADB, 'Bank Response to Emergencies from Natural and Unexpected Disasters'. (Washington DC, May, 1998).
11. M. Munasinghe and C. Clarke, 'Disaster Prevention for Sustainable Development: Economic and Policy Issues', (A World Bank Report from

the Yokohama World Conference on Disaster Reduction, Washington, D.C. 1995).

12. Systems Caribbean Ltd. (SCL), Final Report – Regional Disaster Management Survey, (Prepared for the Disaster Emergency Response and Management System Project (DERMS), CDERA, Barbados, 1997).

[Part Four]

Diplomacy for Survival

[50]

Diplomacy for
Survival

L l o y d   S e a r w a r

Until the fundamental change in the international system which marked the ending of the Cold War, the foreign policies of CARICOM member states responded far more to international issues than to national and regional interests. How did this come about?

The Cold War system in 'freezing' the international system against major change, including economic change, provided the CARICOM states despite the achievement of independence, with the 'safety' net of the old colonial economic system characterised by preferential markets.

At the same time, the Cold War international system provided a range of diplomatic opportunities for small states. While the superpowers confronted each other, small states were able to manoeuvre, so to speak, in the interstices of power and indeed could play at the game of securing benefits by appearing to favour one superpower over the other. As the Caribbean was perceived by the superpowers as being of high geo-strategic significance, the CARICOM states readily found themselves the focus of superpower attention. With their comparatively high levels of diplomatic skill and endowed with a number of leaders, both at the level of Heads of Government and Foreign Ministers, who had a particular inclination for the global stance, the CARICOM states exerted an influence on global issues out of all proportion to their size and resources.

Responding in important part to the superpower conflict and partly to their own urgent development imperatives, the developing world had at this time established the great Third World movements, the Non Aligned Movement and the Group of 77. The small, but diplomatically active CARICOM states soon began to play major roles in these movements. Guyana for example, hosted a Non Aligned Foreign Ministers conference in 1972, which fundamentally reshaped the agenda of the Non Aligned movement, while Jamaica was to provide a president for the G77 in New York.

At the same time, the dominant UN body, namely the Security Council, was largely immobilised by superpower conflict and the consequent exercise of the veto by one side or the other. In this situation, the running could be made in the United Nations General Assembly which came to dominate UN diplomacy and in which very small states on the basis of equality, one state one vote, could exercise pervasive influence. The range of issues on which, at the UN, CARICOM states took the initiative or were front runners was quite remarkable, ranging from Southern African issues through the New International Economic Order, to Antigua and Barbuda's vanguard role on the question of Antarctica.

In short, the Cold War international system provided situations and institutions which could be exploited by CARICOM small states diplomacy.

It is nevertheless true and not to be passed over lightly that CARICOM diplomacy was focused at this time on certain security issues, namely the defence of the territorial integrity of Guyana and Belize. However, it is generally true to say that regional diplomacy was by far more concerned with global issues which attracted diplomatic prestige than with the regional and national interests of the CARICOM community itself.

But, the avoidance or evasion of regional issues did not derive altogether from the opportunities presented by the Cold War international system or the proclivity of some CARICOM statesmen to strike global poses. There was also a profound internal problem which dictated, in terms of the choice of issues, the external orientation of regional diplomacy. It was the fact that there was between CARICOM states, sharp divisions in the choice of internal systems with several member states affecting to one degree or another Marxist/socialist approaches to political and economic development. This was particularly true of Grenada under Bishop and Guyana under Burnham. And one must not forget at one stage US decision-makers were said to perceive an axis of hostility running from Kingston through Havana to St George's and Georgetown and Paramaribo.

This situation of profound division on internal strategy within the region, led CARICOM Foreign Ministers to adopt the doctrine of so-called ideological pluralism, in an effort to maintain the fabric and integrity of the CARICOM Community. In terms of this doctrine, one started off by maintaining that each member state was free to choose its own way, this in studied disregard of the fact that integration is truly only possible when there is a high degree of commonality in internal systems. Nevertheless, it was the case that precisely because of ideological differences it became unrewarding and unsafe for foreign policy to concern itself too closely with the bread and butter issues of the region. It was far easier and more prestigious to deal with apartheid and Southern African issues or indeed the question of Antarctica.

However, there were two other factors which enabled the region to preoc-cupy itself with global issues. One was that, despite the radical rhetoric, the region continued to make its living through the old colonial economic arrange-ments, however dressed up in the Lomé Convention, with traditional com-modities being exported to preferential markets. We were safe with our colonial markets and were therefore free to strike global stances and to speak the global rhetoric of change to a New International Economic Order.

The other factor was that, despite the membership of most CARICOM member states in the OAS, our diplomacy paid little attention to relationships with the neighbouring Latin American states. Indeed, differences in language and constitutions apart, the territorial disputes led us to perceive these states as unfriendly, if not hostile. Instead, we emphasised our Afro-Asian identity which gave us legitimacy in the Third World movements and the consequent distribution of CARICOM diplomatic missions showed that there were only two or three established in Latin America, while at the same time, there were missions in Addis Ababa, Lusaka, Cairo, New Delhi and Moscow and Beijing.

Bread and butter issues

Alas, the entire context of CARICOM diplomacy as outlined above has been subject to profound change amounting to the ushering in of a new system. We are still to come to grips with such change. The region is no longer of any geo-strategic significance. Only one superpower exists and its attitude to the region borders on indifference and disinterest. The Security Council has recovered its dominant role and little attention is now paid to the deliberations of the UN General Assembly. The once great Third World movements are in disarray and are searching for new agendas. We have become what we had forgotten we were – very small states in an uncaring world. There is no longer the possibility either in terms of resource or opportunity to affect global stances, and we are beginning to learn the hard way that bread and butter issues such as the preservation of the European Union market for the bananas of the Eastern Caribbean must profoundly shape our diplomacy, and the issues with which it deals.

CARICOM diplomacy must now urgently identify new issues for coordination and joint action. These must be the issues for economic survival, issues which will ensure for the CARICOM peoples acceptable standards of living with reasonable autonomy.

We start with one major advantage – either as a matter of electoral change or pressure from donor countries and the Washington finance institutions – all member states are now committed to market economies. Hitherto, co-ordination of foreign policy has been the stepchild of the CARICOM integration arrangements. The Common Market, soon to be deepened into a single market, has been perceived so far as the major institution. It is at least doubtful whether the new international trade insistence on reciprocity and the steady pressure for the reduction of tariff walls will permit, in the future, measures of closure such as a single market. Coordination of foreign policy must now become central to the integration arrangements.

Foremost among the issues with which we must come to grips is the building of relationships with the neighbouring Latin American States. These are very much larger continental states with huge populations and different cultures and institutional patterns. A major step has been taken in this direction with the establishment of the Association of Caribbean States (ACS) with its Secretariat in Port of Spain. Now, we have to devise, as a matter of urgency, a relationship which will ensure that the ACS does not engulf or erode the integrity of CARICOM.

We must now find issues which provide leverage in our relationship with our giant neighbour to the North. Two such issues are migration and the flow of narcotics. Experience has shown that there is no way in which legislation can bring to an end the porousness of borders. Similarly, the mixture of sophistication and discontent with high levels of unemployment make the Caribbean very vulnerable to the narcotic trade. There is the further possibility, as shown from time to time, by eruptions and disorder, of which the last was the Muslimeen attempted coup in Trinidad and Tobago, that even with communism out of the way, there could be instabilities which cannot be tolerated in this hemisphere.

Such issues should provide the occasion for arguing the case for the expansion or restoration of assistance for CARICOM states and the safeguarding of access to the North American and European Union markets.

The OAS should be seen in the future, as the Third World movements once were, an important focus for CARICOM diplomacy. CARICOM already provides the largest grouping of the members of the OAS. We share with Latin America the problems of underdevelopment and with the USA and Canada, a language and similar institutions. It should not be too difficult to develop a diplomacy based on mediation and interpretation.

Except in the case of the United Nations in New York, we have tended to give scant attention to the resources available in international institutions. In addition to bilateral diplomacy, there is need for a diplomacy directed to the decision-makers of international institutions. CARICOM diplomacy should in future try to ensure that assistance available from such sources caters for the special needs of small states including in particular small island states with special vulnerabilities.

But, as the traditional preferential markets are eroded, far more important will be diplomacy directed to finding un-utilised technology and to discovering and maintaining niches for our new export products including services in the international markets. In short we need a practical diplomacy which, on the one hand will help us to identify technological opportunities especially in the emerging services sector, and on the other, to sell our products in the increasingly competitive global markets.

In the global arena, thought might also be given to cultivating a new international role of leadership of the small developing states (many of them like the majority of CARICOM states being island developing states) which now number one-sixth of the international community.

CARICOM diplomacy in the future, will almost certainly not yield the global prestige in which our regional leaders once basked, but it can help us to maintain reasonable autonomy and improve standards of living in this grouping of small states which has already produced two Nobel Prize winners.

Note

This paper was first published in *CARICOM Perspective*, Issue No. 65, July 1995, pp. 20–21.

[51]

The New Realities of
Caribbean International
Economic Relations

Owen Arthur

In a very special sense, the long-run has arrived for the Caribbean. Our region has, throughout its entire history been a theatre of constant change and an exemplar of crisis intervention and crisis management. Indeed, there have been instances in the past where the region or individual nations have been forced to respond to crises of major proportions, arising from cyclical fluctuations in the international economy, or from problems originating in the performance of a leading economic sector.

The region has also experienced its fair share of political and social crises, and has been challenged, time and again, to find new and ingenious ways to accommodate the conflicting ends of various social classes, to democratise its political structure and institutions, and to amend its political and economic relationships with partners within and without our region, as circumstances warranted and have dictated.

In all of this, the Caribbean has never been lacking in its capacity to devise home-grown methods to respond to international challenges, and to participate effectively, and to its advantage, in the shaping of an international economic environment with a view to securing for this region special and unique advantages and concessions to compensate for the disadvantages of its small size and to redress the inequities of a sordid colonial past.

As a consequence, the Caribbean has evolved with a dependence on the special relationships which have been arranged with its main trading partners to conferring on the region special trade, economic and financial advantages commensurate with its geopolitical significance in the old political order, and its status as an underdeveloped colonial regime.

In the process, the economic systems of Caribbean societies have come to be shaped, both in terms of structure and functioning, by an extensive network of special preferential trade and financial arrangements, designed to insulate vulnerable Caribbean economies from the real pressures of having to compete on free market terms internationally, and to underwrite a large part of our development by affording these economies access to substantial volumes of financial resources, at concessional rates.

In many respects, the Caribbean has faithfully internalised and institutionalised the economic and financial effects of this old economic, and political order. As such, many traditional industries have been created whose entire survival has been predicated on the existence of high and preferential tariff barriers. Old and long-standing forms of economic activity have been perpetuated on the presumption that a system of international trade preferences will continue to underwrite their survival and their viability.

In its wake, there has been the conviction that trade negotiations, designed to secure and perpetuate the existence of preferences, rather than to bring on stream new and innovative measures to engineer international competitiveness, will be enough to maintain the economic *status quo* and the fortunes of long established, but hopelessly uncompetitive Caribbean industries.

In such a milieu, many Caribbean states have therefore eschewed policies which, if resorted to, would have improved their international competitiveness and their credit worthiness.

Indeed, it may be fairly said that the Caribbean has been passively incorporated into the international economy and society; depending heavily on preferential trade arrangements, concessional aid and capital flows and on access to foreign technology and entrepreneurship on terms set largely by foreign entities.

In fact, a form of acquiescence has set in, in which the success of the region's international economic relations effort has come to be measured in terms of its ability to exact more and more concessional resources and preferential trade arrangements from an increasingly disgruntled international community.

In the interim, the Caribbean economies have stagnated, or at least stalemated; while countries which were on a lower rung of the development ladder than the region at the turn of the 1960s have, by pursuing policies entirely at variance with those practised in this region, prospered and have secured for themselves unshakeable niches in a rapidly changing international economy.

The long-run has arrived for the Caribbean because the economic policies and postures, deriving from our passive incorporation into the international economy as the recipients of preferences and concessional financial flows, have now been overtaken by powerful and irreversible international developments, and it would be fatal for the region not to take cognisance and to accommodate the new realities in its contemporary international economic relations.

In a word, the Caribbean must come to grips with a new and challengingly different economic order which has not, and will not, reserve for us the economic space which has been our lot in the old, but vanishing global economic order of the post World War II period.

The long-run has arrived because it would be fatal for us to resile from making the economic adjustment nationally and regionally which can no longer be postponed if the region is to respond appropriately to irreversible and fundamental changes at the core of the international economy. This situation becomes even more compelling because even more far-reaching changes are likely to take place in the foreseeable future, creating a drastically new and dynamic global economic system.

This new global economic order will make nonsense of the system of preferences on which the Caribbean region has hitherto depended. It will render obsolete the instruments of the Caribbean economic integration movement and challenge us to revisit the concept and practice of integration in the Caribbean.

Moreover, the new realities of this new international economic order will fundamentally challenge the way in which business is and has been conducted in the Caribbean, and will bring about a new economic culture in the region having as its central features increased competitiveness and credit worthiness as the keys to survival, viability and prosperity in the Caribbean states.

This evening's exposition acknowledges that there is a new international economic order which is unfolding and which will be manifested in the drastically new trade and financial arrangements confronting the Caribbean societies.

The exposition will, therefore, first evaluate the forces which are and have been shaping the evolution of the new international economic environment, and the manner in which they depart from shaping influences of the past. We will next examine the special challenges to be faced by the Caribbean in its future dealings with the European Union, NAFTA and Canada. Finally, we will offer suggestions as to how the Caribbean should seek to respond to the new realities of its new international economic relations.

The New Global Forces

The international economic environment in which the Caribbean will have to operate in the closing years of the twentieth century and the first decade of the twenty-first century will be remarkably different from that which has existed since the end of World War II.

A predominant influence has been the end of international tensions generated by the end of the Cold War between the East and the West. An equally important influence has been the impact of technological change.

As John Kenneth Galbraith predicted in his seminal work *The New Industrial State*, the imperatives of new technology rather than the workings of political ideology have come to be the shaping influence on industrial behaviour, as well as a critical determinant of the participation of sundry and various economies in the new global order. It is safe to say that everywhere there has been an accommodation to the Galbraithian view of things. There is now very much a new global order shaped in large part by new technological imperatives.

The new technological imperatives in this evolving global economy have and are rapidly redefining the comparative advantage of respective regions and economies. In this new order of things, a premium is being placed on the possession of skills and the ingenuity of human capital, rather than the mere possession of abundant natural resources as one of the key considerations in determining a country's competitive position. The evolution of skill-intensive knowledge-based industries, related to this process of change, has considerably widened the economic horizons of those economies which rise to the challenges of their new technological age.

We can reasonably expect that this new technological imperative in international economic relations will remain in place, redefining and improving the prospects of technologically dynamic societies, and by the same token, constraining the expansion of those which do not make the necessary adjustments.

In a similar vein, the Caribbean, like all other regions of the world, has been caught up in a process of global economic integration which has been taking place simultaneously at three distinct but integrated levels: the level of the spread and pervasiveness of transnational corporations, the evolution of new and major trading blocs and economic communities and thirdly, in the radical transformation of the multilateral trading system.

Havelock Brewster, in an insightful piece entitled 'The Caribbean Community in a Changing International Environment: Towards the next Century', has alluded to this phenomenon and its implications for the Caribbean.

In this respect, he has observed that transnational corporations are increasingly taking over their local operations – providing financing, raw materials, services and technology, production and assembly facilities, marketing and distribution opportunities and research and development skills on the basis of what is advantageous to them (the corporations) on a worldwide basis. These developments have been facilitated by the revolution in information technology which has caused all these operations to be feasibly and profitably linked up and controlled on a global basis.

This phenomenon, which has come to be referred to as the globalisation of production, has also featured the merger of companies, the dismemberment and reconstitution of companies and their re-establishment for production purposes in various host countries as a means of achieving the lowest unit costs or of circumventing protective tariff and non-tariff barriers.

Japanese companies have typically shown the way in this process, and many developing countries have entered multilateral free trade arrangements, or have negotiated treaties for the avoidance of double taxation and investment treaties, as a means of enhancing their attractiveness and competitiveness as locations for such mobile production.

Many Caribbean countries would find it impossible to plead innocent to being used as preferred locations of transnational companies, intent on exploiting the countries' special tax or wage advantages as a means by which these companies penetrate markets which they would otherwise find difficult or impossible to enter. The globalisation of production in this fashion has been accompanied and assisted by the creation and expansion of regional economic and trading blocs.

It can safely be argued that the creation of mega trading blocs, whether in the form of the North America Free Trade Area, the single market of the European Community and the European Economic Area incorporating the EC and the EFTA, the Asia-Pacific European Co-operation Council, the South East Asia Free Trade Area, and the proliferation of new groupings in Latin America like the MERCOSUR and the Andean Group, to say nothing of the African Economic Community, have served to create an interlocking network of communities committed to free international trade. This, in turn, has facilitated the operations of transnational corporations and the creation of a 'global economy' in which efficiency and competitiveness are the principal hallmarks of the main economic actors.

The Commonwealth Caribbean itself has contributed to this reconfigura-tion of the global economic landscape by being party to the formation of the Association of Caribbean states and in establishing new trading relations with the principal economies of Central and Latin America.

It has been urged, with some compelling force, that the Caribbean needs to enter or relate to these new economic groupings, in order to broaden the trading horizons of our enterprises and to improve our prospects of achieving competitiveness and greater efficiency through the achievement of economies of scale. An even more powerful influence on the contemporary and future structure and functioning of Caribbean societies has been the changes effected recently to the world's multilateral trading system.

Ever since the mid 1940s under the aegis of GATT, the structure of world trade has been subject to continuing reform, aimed at liberalising trade, reducing the adverse effects of punitive tariffs, establishing rules, not only of free, but also fair and reciprocal trading arrangements, while protecting the interests of the poorest societies and trading blocs. Successive rounds of multilateral trade negotiations culminating in the Tokyo Round have resulted in the substantial lowering of tariffs, principally on industrial goods.

The Uruguay Round, which has recently been successfully concluded after extensive negotiations reaching back into the 1980s, has extended the scope of international trade reform. It has led to a further reduction of tariffs on industrial goods and, in so doing, has reinforced the tendency towards trade liberalisation globally. It has also created an environment for the tariffication of non-tariff barriers; and has fundamentally reduced the capacity of developed countries to buttress their agricultural sectors by export subsidies and domestic price supports. Above all, it has brought within the ambit of the multilateral trade regime the governance of activi-ties in services and intellectual property rights and the like. In addition, it has prescribed new rules for the phasing out of limitations to free trade, such as the multi-fibre agreement.

As more and more nations have subscribed to the GATT and have ratified the new World Trade Organisation, the purposes of non-reciprocal trade arrangements have been challenged, while trade liberalisation, support for non-discriminatory trade practices and a commitment towards free trade, not only in commodities but also in services have grown apace. Everywhere, there is now the resolve to apply GATT compatible approaches to the administra-tion of multilateral and bilateral free trade regimes. This has and will entail the application of more 'most favoured nation status' whereby what is extended to one in the form of trade concession is extended to all, the increasing recourse to reciprocity in trade relations between countries and trade blocs, and the insistence of non-discrimination in the application of trade-related practices and policies.

GATT compatible solutions to trade matters will have an enormous bearing on the fortunes of those countries, not excluding the Caribbean, which have hitherto sought to develop their societies behind high and protectionist tariff walls, have benefited from discriminating but favourable treatment from regional trading blocs, and have resisted the international impulse towards trade liberalisation in all its various forms.

The end of the Cold War too has also exerted its own special and peculiar effects on the functioning of Caribbean societies. It is beyond reasonable doubt that, as a result of the end of the Cold War, the Caribbean has declined in geopolitical significance in the eyes of those countries to whom ideological rivalries mattered, and who saw the region as a potential location of international tension arising from the clash of conflicting ideologies.

In practical terms, it has resulted in a substantial reduction in bilateral aid flows to the region, and, in general, to the application of a policy of polite indifference and benign neglect on the part of some of the region's principal partners. It has also given rise to a redefinition of the purposes to which such development assistance as is provided can be put, and the terms and conditions attached to access to such resources. Indeed, concern has radically shifted from the provision of concessional resources primarily for purposes such as infrastructural development towards the financing of 'structural adjustment programmes' to create a market-driven, private sector-led approach to the region's development. There is also now equally the tendency for matters such as the respect for human rights, good governance, the observance of strict environmental standards, gender issues and the like to be foremost on the agenda as points of issue in our contemporary international relationships.

The Caribbean region, with its long tradition of commitment to the practice of democracy, is wonderfully well positioned to accommodate many of the new political nuances that are now infusing its contemporary international economic relations arising from the end of the Cold War. It is, however, less well positioned to cope with the reduction in its access to concessional financial resources. In this respect, there is documented disinclination on the part of some major donors to expand their contributions to the Special Development Fund of the CDB. In addition, most Caribbean economies have also now attained the per capita income level to graduate from access to soft loans from the World Bank; and Barbados, Antigua and Barbuda and the Bahamas have graduated from access to World Bank loans in any form. The direct implication is, for the future, a greater proportion of the region's development which will have to be financed by loans raised on the international capital market than has been the case in the past.

Creditworthiness, and the capacity to negotiate and manage complex financial transactions, have thus become some of the new realities of the Caribbean's international economic relations of today. This makes it all the more compelling that the countries of the region prudently manage their monetary and fiscal affairs and attach greater significance to the pursuit of export-led development strategies; considerations which have not always been features of our economic management in the region in the past.

Measures to enhance international competitiveness, to improve creditworthiness, and the capacity to adapt to changing international demand and rapid technological change, will be the great challenges facing Caribbean countries as a result of the new directions in the global order. However, these challenges are modest compared to those which have to be met in our dealings with our traditional trading partners and the relationships which must now be forged with the new and evolving regional trade blocs during the next decade. It is to this matter that our attention will now turn.

The Caribbean and its new trading relationship

One of the dominant features of the Caribbean's international relations, historically, has been its overwhelming dependence on special trade arrangements with a few major partners, specifically the European Union, the USA and Canada. These have been formalised as preferential trade arrangements, exhibiting relatively similar features, and intended to confer on Caribbean producers, special duty and market access concessions beyond those contained in the Generalised System of Preferences, or afforded to most other developing countries.

Briefly, and as is very well known, the various Lomé Conventions, the CBI and CARIBCAN, all extended to Caribbean countries a preferential trade arrangement in the form of duty free access for most of the region's exports on a non-reciprocal basis.

This one-way, non-reciprocal, duty free arrangement was supplemented by special quota arrangements and pricing mechanisms for some exports not allowed duty free access, or special market access provisions (as has been the case with special USA tax provisions). These special tax provisions allowed duties on garments, electronic products and the like assembled from USA inputs in the Caribbean, only on the value-added originating outside the USA. The special relationship implied by these arrangements was amplified, particularly in the case of the Lomé Conventions, by very generous financial arrangements which put large sums at the disposal of Caribbean societies in the form of soft loans and grants.

The Lomé conventions also include special financial mechanisms to protect and stabilise the foreign exchange earnings accruing to the region from agricultural exports and the export of mineral products. In the case of the USA, the preferential trade arrangements were supplemented by arrangements to facilitate the region's access to 936 Funds, and special concessions to enable the Caribbean to become a prime location for the staging of conventions. In the early 1990s Canada embellished its special preferential trading relationship with the region by pioneering the extension of debt relief to the Caribbean as an instrument of international cooperation and goodwill.

These mechanisms, the CBI, Lomé and CARIBCAN were all intended to be of finite duration but subject to extension; and in the case of the CBI, it was eventually agreed that the agreement should be of indefinite duration. In all of this, the Caribbean enjoyed a special relationship with the leading countries in the developed world, designed to facilitate Caribbean development by enabling the region to draw on a package of concessional resources and arrangements, the core of which was a one-way, duty free trade pact in favour of the region, on terms not similarly made available to most other developing countries.

There is now such rich and voluminous literature on the details and aspects of these special relationships that there is no need here to indulge in repetition. This literature has, however, drawn attention to the fact that these various trade arrangements, while providing duty free access to the largest proportion of Caribbean exports, somehow failed to extend that special duty free access to those lines of exports such as textiles and garments, leather products, rum, petroleum and petroleum products that the region can most easily produce and sell in abundance. It has also drawn attention to the fact that the extension of preferential trade arrangements has not resulted in a surge of Caribbean exports to the countries extending the concessions themselves.

The value of Caribbean exports traded under preferential arrangements has fallen, the Caribbean's relative market share in these preferential markets has declined, the trade deficit of the region with its special trading partners has widened and, ironically, countries which have not been awarded any preferential trading concessions have expanded their exports in the markets of our special trading partners in both absolute and relative terms.

In such circumstances, the question, which necessarily arises, is that as to whether trade preferences, per se, serve the purposes for which they were intended. It may be argued that preferential trade arrangements, involving one-way, duty free concessions, can only be a fillip to development where it can be demonstrated that the existence of tariffs, even low tariffs, serves as the chief hindrance to market penetration by the recipient country.

However, where countries to whom such preferential treatment has been extended have more fundamental problems relating to supply capacity, as has been the Caribbean's case, the provision of one-way, duty free access for their exports and the countries' inability to exploit it only serve to dramatise and magnify their inability to compete internationally. It also sends the signal that the focus of these countries ought to be directed towards effects to enhance their international competitiveness and the efficiency of their production rather than on negotiations to perpetuate the existence of trade preferences for their own sake.

The main thrust of this address is to substantiate that the special relationship, and, moreso, the preferential trading arrangements which the Caribbean has enjoyed with its principal trading partners, whether through CBI, CARIB-CAN or the Lomé Conventions are set to be diluted by the responses of the countries concerned to the new realities of their own new international economic relationships.

The Caribbean faces the danger of being entirely marginalised and having the problems related to its inherent international competitiveness compounded by the stripping away of the unique preferential arrangements which have hitherto featured so much as a factor in the region's development. They face the danger of being caught in a unique no man's land, of being unable as yet to effectively compete internationally and not daring to hope that preferences will be extended.

What would be, in any event, a difficult process of transition is aggravated by the fact that the period within which the Caribbean region has to make the transition to a new set of international relationships is not only finite but is also very short. Indeed, it may amount to no more than a decade at most. The process of change is also likely to involve irreversible developments which will, for the foreseeable future, not only drastically and adversely affect the region's relationships with its principal trading partners, but will also set in train once and for all a new and more competitive relationship with the global economy as a whole.

To make matters worse, there is no organised body of evidence to suggest that the Caribbean has prepared itself properly to secure its best interests in the evolving new global order or in the new relationships which it must forge with its principal trading partners, as they, themselves, undergo fundamental restructuring.

On the contrary, there is everything to suggest that the region will hang on, for the wrong reasons, to arcane, outmoded and anachronistic forms and forces of integration; few, if any of which, come into contact with the new modalities of a transformed global economic system. The Caribbean region is not properly prepared to cope with the new realities of its contemporary international economic relations. And there is the very grave, present and pressing danger that the new integrating forces of a radically transformed global economy will effectively bypass the Caribbean and render it even more exposed as the world's smallest and most vulnerable group of nations.

The Caribbean would do well to recognise and to act on the presumption that the age of preferences is over, or at least will be over by the turn of the century and that it has to put a new dispensation in place, both in relation to its own domestic and regional economic processes, and in relation to the character of its relations to the rest of the world. The imperatives for change in our international dealings over the next decade can be portended from the adjustments that our principal trading partners proposed to make to their relationships with the Caribbean.

The Lomé Convention

It would be instructive to start with an evaluation of our relationship with the European Union, as it is likely to evolve.

Since 1975, the Caribbean has been the beneficiary of a special relationship with the European countries through its membership of the ACP. Since the negotiations of Lomé IV in 1989, the Lomé partnership has come under pressure from a number of sources and directions. This has been prompted chiefly by the fact that the European countries' evaluation of their interests in the post-Cold War international order had led to a radical change in the European Union's definition of its pyramid of privileges in favour of its new partners in Eastern Europe and the Mediterranean and at the exposure of its traditional trading partners.

While the European Union will not abandon its ACP partners, the consensus among its member states is that the privileged relations between the European Union and the ACP have evaporated in line with new post-Cold War realities. In this context, the 1996 Draft Budget of the European Union is predicated on a significant budgetary increase in favour of Central and Eastern Europe and Mediterranean countries; an important sign of the times. In addition, since 1992, the European Union has signalled its intention to move towards a more global development policy and this has placed significant pressure on the preferential and exclusive relationship which the ACP group of countries has enjoyed with Europe for over 20 years.

Lomé's present exclusive membership formation is not consistent with the new directions in the European Union's development policy which accentuates aid for the poorest of the poor within the context of a new global development strategy and approach. There is also grave disillusionment among members of the Union and the usefulness of the Lomé Convention in its present form. There is especially the feeling that twenty years of preferential relations have not engendered a significant improvement in the fortunes of the ACP countries.

The evidence originating out of the recently concluded mid term review of Lomé IV substantiates that the European Union is in favour of a substantially changed relationship with the ACP after expiry of the present Convention in the year 2000. The European Union's Commissioner has confirmed that the present Convention will be 'the last of the Conventions as we have come to know them'.

In such a context, it is very likely that the guaranteed preferential access afforded to the agricultural and manufactured exports of the ACP to the Union will not be continued in the present exclusive form once the Convention expires in the year 2000. It also seems to be the case that the European Union will wish to depart from the policy which causes it to relate to the ACP as a group as presently constituted, and move towards a new policy within which it can adopt *region specific* approaches to its economic cooperation with the respective regional areas of the ACP.

Given the move towards a more global rather than an exclusive ACP-related development policy, it is likely that the European Union will wish to broaden the range of countries to which it extends trade and other concessions after the year 2000. It has already started to forge relationships with countries in this Hemisphere and has accorded a special place to Cuba in this new dispensation.

The Commonwealth Caribbean's special relationship with the European Union that has been effected through the various Lomé Conventions and in partnership with a selected range of ACP countries is set therefore to undergo a dramatic transformation after the year 2000. The Caribbean has already seen the pressure brought to bear by forces outside the European Union to secure the annulment of the Banana Regime which confers special market access privileges on Caribbean banana producers. This is indicative of the kind of pressures that the region will have to adhere to, in order to maintain a special preferential status in a new age of GATT-related trade liberalisation. By a similar token, the results of the Uruguay Round will also create revenue problems for Caribbean sugar procedures to the European Union.

It is well known that while the Sugar Protocol of Lomé allows the Caribbean to meet supply quotas on an indefinite basis, the price paid to Caribbean sugar exporters bears a relation to that paid to European producers of sugar under the Common Agricultural Programme (CAP). The Uruguay Round prescribes reduction in the domestic price supports that countries can grant to their domestic agricultural producers.

In consequence, it is envisioned that the price paid to Caribbean sugar exporters to the European Union is set to decline *pari passu* with the reduction in the domestic price support allowed by the Union to its agricultural producers. In general, the Caribbean has but a limited time, therefore, to recommend a new *modus operandi* with the European Union.

It is quite clear that the special preferential arrangements embodied in successive Lomé Conventions will not be extended after the expiry of Lomé IV. It is equally clear that the European Union will wish to subsume the Commonwealth Caribbean in a region specific, new relationship, that it has already begun to construct and to treat the CARICOM sub-region within the context of its broader relations with Latin American countries. In such a context, preferences will be extended to the poorest of the poor in the region only, rather than across the board as has been the case in the past.

The Commonwealth Caribbean will have to strain its every diplomatic sinew to ensure that its peculiar interests are not glossed over and obfuscated in the European Union's new general development policy relationship with the wider Caribbean and Latin America. It is likely to face even more profound repercussions in its efforts to access NAFTA and the wider North American Free Trade Area of the Americas.

NAFTA presents the Caribbean at the most superficial level with the enigmatic challenge if you do, you are damned, or if you don't, you are even more damned. This enigma arises from the fact that in keeping with the prevailing GATT-related trade provisions, access to NAFTA will require Caribbean societies to confer on other NAFTA countries, reciprocal duty relief in circumstances where the existing trade relationships between the Caribbean and the USA and Canada are on the basis of one way duty free arrangements in favour of the Caribbean region.

This raises many delicate and complex problems as regards the nature that such reciprocity should assume and the way in which it should be negotiated. It raises equally complex issues regarding the application of reciprocity, as a governing principle, in the trading relationships between unequal trading partners.

A related matter is that if the Caribbean enters a reciprocal trade arrangement with the developed countries of North America under NAFTA, it would be duty bound under Section 174 of the Lomé Convention to grant similar reciprocal arrangements to its European partners, with whom it now enjoys the advantage of one-way, duty free trade.

The third issue is, of course, the fact that the subscription to all NAFTA entails involving not only a reciprocal duty free trade arrangement but acquiescence in its provisions regarding the relaxation of controls on the free movement of services and capital. This will involve the Caribbean region in a relationship with extra-regional countries that is more liberal than that which it has as yet managed to effect among its own, and create pressures for changes to our new integration processes.

At a minimum, NAFTA will make nonsense of the provisions of the proposed CET in the Caribbean which is intended to maintain a 20 per cent tariff on the value of extra-regional consumer goods after 1998. However, not to accede to NAFTA would confer special advantages on Mexico, reinforcing scale, locational and wage-related advantages which it already enjoys. As was stated earlier, the CBI excluded from duty free coverage, textiles, garments and certain other goods whose production can easily and profitably be undertaken in the region. Under NAFTA, Mexico will be allowed duty free access for these very goods. In the absence of some special legislation which will endow the region with parity with Mexico, the result would be a significant diversion of investment and trade from the region in Mexico's favour.

Our concern here with the likely effects of NAFTA goes beyond trade matters. While the agreement aims at the reciprocal liberalisation of trade, it is not only a trade arrangement in the traditional sense of reducing tariff and non-tariff barriers. NAFTA also incorporates new matters such as trade in services, intellectual property, labour and environmental issues. Its scope is such that major matters of domestic policy are now to be placed on the table as part of negotiating an international trade regime.

NAFTA is also premised on an ideological bias which requires countries seeking to access it to meet stringent conditionalities to create a private sector-led, market-driven model of development. It requires as conditions the enhancement of the privatisation process, the institution of market-determined interest and exchange rates, and the formulation of investment treaties sufficient to accord foreign investors equality of treatment in the domestic arena of Caribbean economies with Caribbean investors.

It should be enough to point out that the Caribbean has not yet created the conditions within the region for the free flow of capital regionally; nor do all Caribbean economies subscribe to the notion of freely floating exchange rates, and on the weight of evidence, they should not be in a panic to do so. A decision, has, however, already been taken that Caribbean countries should seek to access NAFTA and to be part of the wider Hemispheric Free Trade Area to be put in place by the year 2005.

The very real issue that arises, therefore, is the nature of the negotiating strategy that the Caribbean should employ to protect its best interests in this process of trade and general economic restructuring.

As regards our relationship with Canada, we would all do well to study carefully the report of the Standing Senate Committee on Foreign Affairs, published in 1995, entitled *Free Trade in the Americas*. It clearly affirms that while Canada ostensibly wishes to preserve its 'special relationship' with the Caribbean, it recognises that it has much more to gain from broadening and deepening its relationships with the newly-emerging market economies of Latin America. In this respect, it is instructive that Canada is now awaiting World Trade Organisation (WTO) ratification of its request to waive the rules of trade to permit the extension of CARIBCAN.

In every respect, Canada would seem to have defined its new relationship with the Latin American and the Caribbean region using the same criteria as the European Union. The relationship will perhaps still be special, but certainly not unique. We can, therefore, anticipate a relative decline in the priorities attached to the development of economic and financial relationships with the Commonwealth Caribbean by Canada while it pursues broader hemispheric goals.

The Way Forward

In light of the foregoing, it would be evident that a Caribbean strategy to effectively relate to the new and evolving global order must be informed by the following considerations. Generally, the strategy has to accept the reality of the globalisation of economic forces rather than hanker after a less complicated but very impoverished past.

The strategy must also recognise that the Caribbean countries, singly and as a group must make the transition from the old age of preferences to the new age of reciprocity in its international economic relationships. In so doing, a strategy must be designed to minimise the costs and dislocations associated with the transition, and to put in place mechanisms that can allow the region to exploit the market opportunities which are being created by the international liberalisation of trade and the formation of mega trade blocs.

As a first step, the region, acting through CARICOM, has to synchronise the development of transitional mechanisms for assessing these blocs, and do so in short order. Given the relatively short period for the transition – less than five years – it is amazing that this has not yet been accomplished.

To be more precise, and as our relationship with the various Lomé Conventions has demonstrated, the Caribbean should act in concert and as a group, in accessing the new trade grouping, and pay particular attention to the specific requirements of the Lesser Developed Countries within its midst.

Within this group approach, it should be agreed that countries should negotiate accession to the new groups such as NAFTA when they are ready to do so. The group approach, however, should entail cross-Caribbean collaboration in negotiating investment treaties and meeting the other stringent conditionalities that attended participation in groupings such as NAFTA. The regional approach should also obviously recognise that reciprocal trade relationships do not require equal terms for all the parties concerned, but rather a commitment to liberalised trade on a phased basis.

It is therefore crucial that the Caribbean follow the Mexican and Canadian approach to minimising the transition costs associated with joining NAFTA, and determine the sensitive industries regionally that should be protected from the brunt of free trade, and define an appropriate phasing-in period of the new reciprocal duty relationships.

Above all, the Caribbean, as a group, should negotiate for its Less Developed Countries to avoid having to engage in full or even partial reciprocal trade relationships with the new large mega trade blocs of the world.

While adequate arrangements are being made in the transition for sensitive agricultural and manufactured products, the Caribbean should, as a deliberate strategy concentrate its development efforts on those activities for which there is a strong and growing international demand and in which the Caribbean has done well in open, international competition. The export of services, especially tourism and financial services immediately spring to mind in this respect.

Effective participation in the new global economy will also require fundamental changes in the region's economic integration processes and mechanisms. Instruments such as the Common External Tariff will be rendered obsolete by the turn of the century as mechanisms of integration because of the reciprocal trade arrangements to which the region will become a party. Equally, the fascination with mechanisms to promote intra-regional trade, while important, must come to be seen in the true perspective as impacting only on less than ten per cent of Caribbean economic activity.

The focus of Caribbean integration must, therefore, shift from tinkering with measures to deal with intra-regional trade, to measures which can enhance the region's international competitiveness and creditworthiness in line with the new dictates of a transforming global order. Efforts to build a strong regional financial and capital market and to properly capitalise enterprises capable of competing regionally and internationally must become a crucial priority of the regional integration process.

So too, must mechanisms to promote the development of the human resources of the region, in line with the new dynamics of international technological change. The region's integration process must also be informed by the recognition that in a new world, shaped increasingly by technological imperatives, the underdevelopment of a country's or region's technological capabilities is fatal. The creation of institutional mechanisms to support technological development through the region must become a part of the region's integration response. Above all, the mechanisms of CARICOM, which have been designed to be inward looking in support of regional import substitution must now be refashioned to an export culture at both the national and regional levels. It also goes without saying that there must be a changed role for the regional private sector in the new international dispensation. The new global economy is characterised by a commitment to market-driven, private sector-led solutions.

The environment must therefore be created within which the region's enterprises can be adequately capitalised and acquire the critical mass to compete at home and compete internationally. Widespread encumbrances and the high cost of doing business in the region must be systematically reduced. And wherever possible, systems must be put in place to allow the private sector to acquire its inputs at international prices and thus to compete internationally on a level playing field.

The Caribbean has, through its history, known only the necessity to respond to crises. The changes taking place in the global economy do not constitute a crisis to which the region cannot appropriately and successfully respond.

The sad irony in all this is that at a time when our international economic relations will matter so much in shaping the region's destiny, the future of the Institute of International Relations is subject to much uncertainty. It might very well be that this Institute may enjoy a reincarnation, not just to train the region's diplomats as has been its principal role in the past, but to design and help the region implement a new international economic relations strategy consistent with our times, our requirements and our purposes.

Note

This is an address made by the Rt Hon Owen Arthur on the occasion of the Ninth Annual Lecture in the Distinguished Lecturer Series, Institute of International Relations, the University of the West Indies, St Augustine, Trinidad & Tobago, 1996.

[52]

Caribbean International Relations in the Year 2000

Anthony Bryan

In many respects the twenty-first century is already here with us. The old assumptions, the seemingly immutable structures and intellectual constructs which underpinned the functioning of the international system since the end of World War II have been shattered and swept away by the tidal wave of far-reaching changes, political and economic, taking place in many areas of the globe, particularly in Eastern Europe. The international community has thus found itself thrust abruptly in the post-Cold War era.

Trends Shaping the Future

There are a number of factors presently at play whose influence will have an impact, to varying degrees, on the shape of the international system of the early years of the twenty-first century. The USA/USSR rapprochement has led to a relaxation of East/West tensions and to the creation of an atmosphere propitious to the successful conclusion of arms reduction treaties between the two superpowers and to the resolution of several long-standing regional conflicts. The fear of a nuclear holocaust precipitated by the superpowers may have receded somewhat. Nevertheless, the issue of conventional weapons and of their increasing proliferation, and use, in the Third World are moving closer to the top of the disarmament agenda. Another connected concern is the acquisition of certain military technologies (nuclear and chemical) by 'outlaw' states. As their level of technological sophistication improves and as the relaxation of controls on prohibited materials and technologies continues apace in a world where the Soviet Union and the USA are perceived less and less as threats, a new approach to the problems of disarmament and of proliferation may be required.

With regard to regional conflicts, it should be noted that though they are exacerbated by super power interference, many of these conflicts have their origins in purely local conditions. As such they are less amenable to the coaxings of the powers and, consequently, are not necessarily influenced by the atmosphere of détente which is taking hold. This will continue to be an area of potential danger for the evolving international system of the twenty-first century.

The reform policies of President Gorbachev in the Soviet Union and the demise of the Brezhnev doctrine, coupled with massive popular demonstrations for liberalisation have, in a matter of months, swept away the seemingly all-powerful communist régimes of Eastern Europe. These dramatic changes which present both opportunities and challenges have radically altered the post-war structure of Europe. They are of crucial importance to the reinforcement of détente between the superpowers and between the military alliances in Europe. They will also be instrumental in bridging the divisions in Europe and in helping to make a reality, the vision of a Europe which is united in its multiplicity.

Nevertheless, the transition from communist dictatorship and a centrally planned economy to democracy and a market economy involves fundamental changes. It is legitimate to ask the question whether these newly liberalised societies will be successful in satisfying the rising material expectations of their peoples. Also, to what extent will these societies which have grown accustomed to a high level of social equity in the distribution of goods and services (health care, education, etc.) accept the social and material inequities which are part and parcel of the market economies which they are adopting? The answers to these questions will be vital to the management of change and to the avoidance of convulsions which, added to the ferment of nationalism, could jeopardise the security of Europe.

The democratisation of Eastern Europe is but the most spectacular example of a move away from authoritarian and military rule which has affected other parts of the globe, in particular Latin America and Asia. The continuation, and the deepening, of this trend will be of critical importance to international relations of the twenty-first century. It should, however, be observed that two contradictory factors will impinge profoundly on this development. In its favour is the perceptive observation made by one scholar on democratisation, who notes that 'for the first time in recorded history, throughout almost the entire globe, the main alternatives to democracy lack legitimacy'.[1] Militating against it is the suspicion that true democracy will not survive very long in conditions of austerity, frugality and inequality, that is to say in conditions which are the lot of the majority of the Third World and which could perhaps soon become that of the newly-democratised societies of Eastern Europe.

Another major factor which will be instrumental in determining the future structure of the international order is the formation of mega-trading blocs on a regional basis. The establishment of a common internal market by the 12 European Community countries by December 1992 will create a unified market with 320 million consumers and a combined GDP of USA$4.6 trillion. Already the world's largest trading bloc, the economy of the Single Market will be slightly larger than that of the USA and double the size of Japan's. West European integration will no doubt be the vital cornerstone in the eventual creation of a pan-European entity incorporating the European Free Trade Association members and the newly-liberalised states of Eastern Europe.

In like manner the USA and Canada have formed a free trade area. Mexico has very recently agreed to consider negotiations for a free trade agreement with the USA. Such an agreement would pave the way for a North American common market. It may also hold incalculable and grave consequences for the preferential trading arrangements between the Caribbean and the USA and between the Commonwealth Caribbean and Canada.

Japan and other rising economic powers of the Pacific Rim cannot afford to be left out of these moves towards regional economic integration. It therefore seems only a matter of time before a modern-day equivalent of the old 'sphere of co-prosperity' is recreated in the Pacific.

Despite the expressions of concern over the possible negative effects of these developments on their respective trading positions, Third World countries have been slow to react in a coordinated manner to international economic integration movements among the western industrialised states. This is perhaps not surprising in view of the increasing political and economic differentiation among the countries comprising this group. Both the Non Aligned Movement and the Group of 77 stand more divided today than previously, incapable of agreeing on a common political platform or on a common programme of action. Some scholars have concluded that mobilisation of the Third World is most likely to take place in smaller regional groups. The outcome of these moves towards economic integration, especially if they facilitate the parallel development of political integration, could well be a regionalised international system.[2] The fact remains that whatever form it takes, South-South integration and cooperation are imperative if the developed countries are to avoid being marginalised.

Consequences of Present Trends

The dominant role once played by the two superpowers in the international system is being progressively reduced by internal and external factors of a political and economic nature. The energies of the Soviet Union will be absorbed for some time to come in resolving its considerable social, political and economic problems brought about by its stagnant economy and the policies of Glasnost and Perestroika. It will also be distracted by the need to manage the consequences of the dramatic changes which have transformed its former empire in Eastern Europe. Not least among these preoccupations is the forthcoming reunification of East and West Germany which will create a rival economic and military power in Central Europe.

The future development of the USSR, and the repercussions therefrom for several regions of the world, is one of the important question marks at present. The USSR is in an era of weakness from political, economic and strategic perspectives. The possibility of a rapid and chaotic disintegration of the present Soviet Union is a possibility. Yet in the worst case scenario, the nation of Russia alone will still have a population of more than 150 million. Even a truncated USSR will still be a military superpower in the 1990s; but the Soviet Union (whether in its present dimensions or in truncated form) will remain economically weak for some time to come in the market economy of the world.[3]

It also remains to be seen how quickly the United States can meet the challenges to its global economic and financial prominence. The USA today is by far the economy with the greatest quantum of international debt. At present the huge USA budgetary deficit is being financed with capital and credit imported from Japan, Germany, Holland, Switzerland and, in part, from Latin America (which because of the debt situation, is a net contributor to the capital supply in the USA). It is estimated that by 1992 the USA debt to the rest of the world will be one trillion dollars net; and at an interest rate of 7 to 8 per cent it could result in a potential capital transfer from the USA to the rest of the world of some 70 to 80 billion dollars annually. In the meantime, the debtors are in the process of buying the USA patrimony in the form of real estate, shares, hotel chains, firms and factories. Unless the budgetary deficit is corrected, protectionism and trade conflict will be characteristic of USA trade strategies in the 1990s. However, the resurgence of the USA as an economic superpower seems likely and in all probability it will remain as a military superpower.

The economic and financial pre-eminence of the USA is also being increasingly disputed by Japan which has become an economic superpower in its own right. Its economy is responsible for 15 per cent of the world's gross national product. Seven of the world's ten largest banks are Japanese and its companies dominate some of the most important advanced and military-sensitive areas of technology. In 1989, Japan became the largest donor of aid to the developing world. Through massive investment and its domination of the USA bond market it has become an influential actor in the USA economy itself. As a result, Japan is emerging from its habits of timidity and parochialism and has begun to search for a more assertive and influential role in world affairs. This is being facilitated by the USA which wishes to see Japan assume a greater share of international responsibilities.

More critically, Japan's economic prowess and the perception that it has taken unfair advantage of the international trading system have generated anxiety and frustration in the USA which are damaging the important USA/Japan relationship. This rivalry is perhaps all the more galling to the USA as it comes at a moment when domestic economic problems, in particular the budget deficit, have placed severe limitations on its capacity to influence events and developments overseas. This is vividly illustrated by the ongoing debate in the USA as to how best to apportion the foreign aid pie at a moment when the transformations in Eastern Europe have placed greater and unforeseen demands on this vital foreign policy tool.

The diminishing Soviet military presence in East Asia and the Pacific also has an impact on the future of Japan. The need for an enlarged Japanese military budget will disappear (it now has the world's third largest) as will the necessity for any defence pact between the USA and Japan. In the final analysis, Japan which is today the greatest international creditor in the world will remain an economic power in the twenty-first century and will have become an international power broker. Perhaps it will abstain from becoming a 'military' superpower as well.

The emergence of the EC of 1992, and the recent far-reaching political and economic changes within Eastern Europe, are fundamental elements in the transformation of the character of the international environment in the 1990s and for the early years of the twenty-first century. Economics is still the driving force behind the European Communist and the Single European Market; but calls for 'political union', have already been issued by Germany and France. The basis of a united Europe would rely on monetary union (ECU as the common currency), a common foreign policy and security arrangements, and European citizenship including the protection of fundamental rights. The integration of Europe at the present moment is all the more important in view of the changes that have taken place in the East.

The revolutions in the countries of Eastern Europe are however not a victory for capitalism but rather a victory for democracy and for self-determination. The European Community is envisioned as the anchor necessary to stabilise the emerging democracies through economic and financial cooperation or aid. An investment bank and a version of the Marshall Plan are but two of the instruments to accomplish this. Eventual association with or incorporation into the European Community once their economies are strengthened, is a goal. Now that the Soviets will no longer stand in the way of a united Germany, provided the security arrangements are satisfied, the present Federal Republic of Germany will play a crucial role in the context of the new Europe. It is a major trading partner both of the USSR and the Eastern European countries, with which it had traditionally had close ties. As former German Chancellor Helmut Schmidt has noted, the most appropriate way of abating French and British fears about the size and economic power of a united Germany is 'to ensure that it becomes an inseparable part of a confident and dynamic European Community'. [4]

The future of Europe will depend on prudent policies of economic integration and less on military security arrangements. Currently, the countries of Europe have been able to increase their international decision-making capacity in the design of the new Europe with minimal superpower involvement or interference. In the future, policy issues identified by the European Economic Community (EEC) can be expected to carry significant weight on the global economic and political agendas.

By the end of this century there will be three main mega-bloc centres of economic power:

(a) North America, comprising the USA, Canada and possibly Mexico;
(b) Europe, excluding or including the USSR;
(c) The Pacific, comprising Japan, China, Australia, New Zealand and nine rapidly growing East Asian developing countries.

One characteristic of these economic groups is that they will include countries at various stages of growth and development. For example, in the Pacific grouping, China will be weak economically but powerful militarily. The European Community may eventually incorporate some of the poorer countries on its Eastern and Southern flanks, either through full membership or associated status. The North American Free Trade Area will exert an even stronger magnetic pull on many countries of Latin America and the Caribbean. However, the fate of countries that do not have strong trading and investment links with any of these regional groupings is by no means clear. What will happen to many of the countries of sub-Saharan Africa and South and West Asia in this new dispensation? A likely scenario is the emergence of a two track development process among these states, that is, a 'growth' track and a 'stagnation' track, depending on the particular country's capability to adapt to the new economic changes. But the prospect for many is increased marginalisation in the global economy.

One of the most influential, though underestimated, forces of change in the international system is the impact of technology. The advent and the application of new techniques are creating new lines of change, shattering long-standing certitudes and upsetting old balances of power. The information revolution has not only made the services sector one of the most successful industries in the global economy, but it has also brought about profound structured transformations in the economies of the most technologically advanced nations. Japan's primacy in the area of semi-inductors, the brains of sophisticated weapons systems, has given it a strategic advantage over the USA. Information systems and telecommunications have made the world a gigantic electronic financial market through which billions of dollars move at the touch of a button. Developments in one market have immediate repercussions in the others, vividly illustrating the concept of interdependence while at the same time negating the notion of sovereignty.

Impact on the Third World

As the international system evolves, new issues are rising to the top of the international agenda – the environment, drug trafficking, international migration. But once again the priorities and the approach to these issues are being determined by the western industrialised countries.

Not too long ago dismissed as the hobby horse of fringe groups, the 'environment' has shot to the forefront of the international agenda. Increasingly sensitive to quality of life issues and, more recently, perceiving a lessened military threat from the USSR, public opinion in the developed countries has been placing greater emphasis on issues such as acid rain, the disposal of hazardous waste, air and water pollution, and the greenhouse effect. A recent poll in the USA indicated that 84 per cent of the American public believe that pollution is a serious national problem which is getting worse.[5]

This new international emphasis on the environment is perceived as having a detrimental effect on the development efforts of the Third World. As the industrialised countries move from the polluting smokestack industries of

yesteryear to the service industries of tomorrow, they are starting to insist that
the developing countries undertake environmental safeguards with respect to
development projects being carried out with their financial or technological
assistance. These safeguards can be quite costly and can render certain
projects unfeasible. Many developing nations such as Guyana, have been
warning against the tacking on of environmental conditionalities to assistance
from the developed world.

Notwithstanding the above, economic development and protection of the
environment are not mutually exclusive nor in conflict. What is true is that
the profligate use of natural resources can lead to irreversible damage being
done to entire ecosystems. In like manner, poverty can lead to the destruction
of the very resources which are needed for survival, as the experience of Haiti
and the countries of the Sahel region in Africa so tragically underline.
Consequently, the concept of sustainable development seems destined to gain
greater currency as the international community increasingly accepts the fact
that 'population and physical capital cannot continue to grow forever on a
finite planet.'[6]

Another, and more immediate, problem of particular concern for the
developing world is the dumping of hazardous and toxic wastes. As the
disposal of toxic wastes in the industrialised nations becomes increasingly
difficult (opposition of neighbouring communities) and costly (environmental safeguard regulations), the developing world has become an easily
available depository for these wastes, a most insensitive and cynical type of
exploitation. This has unfortunately been facilitated by the venality and
ignorance of Third World officials. This issue will become a sub-item on the
environmental agenda as more information and data become available on the
limitations of the planet to absorb the wastes of all types created by human
wants and activities and as awareness develops of the threats to security posed
by environmental degradation.

The illicit trafficking of drugs across international borders has become a
modern-day scourge which is capable of eroding the physical, moral, economic and political health of society. The example of Colombia where the
established government is locked in a battle to the death against the all-powerful drug cartels is but an extreme illustration of what is being experienced,
albeit more subtly, in other developing nations. This issue is of particular
concern for the Caribbean as its geographic location places it in the centre of
the drug transhipment activities between the major production areas in Latin
America (Peru, Bolivia, Colombia) and the major market, the USA.

In a study of the problems experienced by the Caribbean in this area, Ron
Saunders a former Antiguan diplomat, has identified six broad types:

the lack of financial resources to mount an adequate general response to the problem of drug trafficking; the insufficiency of resources to effectively police territorial waters or borders, ports and airports; the corruption of officials; threats to the security of states from external forces and internal instability; the lack of know-how to vet offshore enterprises and casinos; and coping with the interventionist policies of the USA. [7]

The basic problem, as Saunders has pointed, out is 'how to reconcile their fear of being swamped by the USA with their need for help in dealing with the drug problem'. There is no doubt that this dilemma will become an increasingly critical foreign policy issue in the Caribbean's international relations, especially as the USA has begun to use drug interdiction as a pretext for intervening in the international affairs of Latin American countries (Bolivia, Colombia, Panama and most recently Peru.)

Another issue which will figure prominently on the international agenda of the twenty-first century relates to *international migration*. The greater openness of international borders of the global village as well as the international flow of information have facilitated the freer movement of capital, trade, services, technology and people. The flow of persons across international borders has been accelerated by other factors which are intrinsic to the developing world – poverty, high unemployment, national disasters, political repression and internal and/or regional conflicts. The latter factor is responsible in particular for the staggering number of Third World refugees (2.7 million in 23 countries in Africa in 1985, five million in 16 Asian countries. Another 674,000 refugees were in Western Europe.[8]

It is therefore not surprising to learn that the proportion of immigrants in the labour force of many receiving countries is quite high: 45 per cent in Oman, 71 percent in Kuwait, 81 per cent in Qatar, 85 per cent in the United Arab Emirates, 24 per cent in Switzerland, 9 per cent in France and the Federal Republic of Germany.[9]

At present the problems related to international migration are treated for the most part as national and not international problems. In certain Western European countries, for example, France and West Germany where the so-called 'tipping point' has been attained, these problems have taken on a racial dimension. In the poverty-stricken Third World countries whose resources are clearly unable to cope with the unprecedented number of refugees swarming across their borders, the problem has been put in the hands of international and charitable agencies.

In this area, as in so many others, if this item is placed on the international agenda by the developed nations, the focus will not encompass the full sweep of problems which are felt most acutely by the developing world. More hermetic barriers and repatriation could place intolerable pressures on many a developing nation for which migration has been both a safety-valve and a source of foreign exchange. As Myron Weiner has pointed out:

No state is prepared to accept the unrestricted entry of people, but most governments believe in the right of emigration. In this normally ambiguous situation one thing is clear: states are no longer able to make decisions about migration oblivious of their international consequences.[10]

However, what is already apparent is that preventing the entry of migrants, whether in the form of illegal migrants or as refugees, has proved to be problematic both in Western Europe, the USA and in the developing states which are less capable of controlling their borders. As the disparities between a rich and dynamic North and a stagnant and deprived South increase, as disasters, natural or manmade, continue to afflict the South, there will be even greater flows of migrants across international borders. Some of the consequences will be of a far-reaching nature. It is already projected that by the year 2050 the USA will cease to be a predominantly white Eurocentric country. What will this signify for the strategic interests of one of the key players in the international system? The problems of assimilation and ethnic pluralism will have to be confronted by West European states which have always viewed themselves as homogenous societies. The costs for Third World societies will also be tremendous – both in terms of the loss in human and intellectual resources as well as the pressures placed on their inadequate infrastructures and material resources by refugee and immigrant flows.

When the global demographic variable is factored in, the potential dangers of this problem are cause for even greater concern. In 1950 the ratio of poor to rich was under two to one. Today, it is almost four to one. By the year 2000, 80 per cent of the world population will belong to the countries of the South. If, as present trends indicate, the developed countries increasingly turn their attention away from the developing nations to the South, the already great disparities between the two will increase dramatically. It is inconceivable that four-fifths of humanity could be living in a state of poverty and deprivation without such a situation becoming a factor of destabilisation for the international system of the future.

The cumulative effect of the trends identified above will radically alter the shape and the functioning of the international system of the twenty-first century. Some of the major characteristics of this evolving system are already starting to emerge, some more sharply than others.

The focus of attention of the western industrialised countries is going to shift nearer home, to the newly liberalised countries of Eastern Europe. The reasons for this shift are easily understandable. The 'cousins' of the European Community as Mr Jacques Delors, President of the European Commission, calls them, share a common history and civilisation. More critically, because of their proximity, the very security, stability and continuing prosperity of the European Community could be affected by the failure of the reform movement and by any convulsions and crises in the Eastern European countries. Consequently, even less attention will be paid to the major concerns of the developing nations which, in any case, have been consistently rebuffed over the past decade, as is seen in the neglect of the call for a New International Economic Order; the deterioration of the terms of trade; the practice of protectionism and the absence of a more equitable international financial dispensation. We have already witnessed the alacrity with which the European Bank for the Reconstruction and Development of Eastern Europe with substantial funding was established. We have also witnessed the diversion of USA assistance funds from Jamaica to Poland. Having suddenly lost their 'internationalistic outlook', the East European countries are also repatriating their experts in the Third World. Africa alone stands to lose the expertise of thousands of those cadres. This sudden vacuum will have incalculable consequences for the countries affected.

It seems to be just a matter of time before the East/West rift is replaced by the North/South divide as the major antagonistic relationship in international relations. One of the major consequences of such an evolution is that the Third World will lose the political support, in international fora, and elsewhere of its former 'natural allies', the communist countries of Eastern Europe. This will substantially weaken the bargaining power of the Third World in the only forum where it still has a modicum of influence – the United Nations. It will also lead to the virtual isolation of radical and socialist Third World countries such as Cuba and Ethiopia which will be hard put to resist external pressure for political and economic reform.

However, of greater significance is the possibility of greater marginalisation of the Third World in an international environment where the concerns of the South are neglected by a North increasingly turning inwards on itself. Deprivation, poverty, disease and hopelessness will certainly increase as a result. So will the threats to international security and stability unless concerted efforts are made to address the root-causes of underdevelopment. There must be a new awareness by the developed countries of the North of the danger to world peace and order posed by the destabilising effects of non-military threats to security such as underdevelopment and environmental degradation.

Another of the major characteristics of this evolving system would appear to be the pre-eminence of economic issues over international political matters. In a world of regional trade blocs it will be difficult to avoid the temptations of protectionist trade reflexes. Trading frictions could easily escalate into trade wars that would do irreparable damage to the entire system.

As far as the Third World is concerned, the shift in emphasis from the political to the economic could have unforeseen consequences. Political issues such as decolonisation, anti-imperialism, the struggle against apartheid and nuclear disarmament have in many ways been the mobilising forces which have helped to forge Third World solidarity, to determine a Third World point of view and to cement a semblance of Third World unity. Deprived of these great political rallying causes and confronted with increasing economic differentiation, the Third World will have great difficulty in retaining a veneer of common purpose and in identifying common goals and objectives. One may even ask whether the concept of Third World will survive in this new dispensation.

The creation of a multi-polar world and the subsequent diffusion of power and influence among a multiplicity of states will permit greater freedom of initiative for regional powers as pawnbrokers in their own capacity. India, Brazil, Indonesia and South Africa are prominent candidates for such roles. This could in turn lead to new forms of hegemony, thereby creating added threats for small states.

There is, however, the possibility of another and more troubling scenario emerging. In a world where power will be measured increasingly by economic and financial clout, the twenty-first century will undoubtedly witness the emergence of a tri-polar world economy built around a united Europe, a rejuvenated USA and Japan. However, none of these poles may be in a dominant enough position to provide the leadership for the world economy. Theoretically, Japan should have the attributes to provide this leadership; but the western industrialised countries may not willingly accept the primacy of Japan. The fear and resentment already mounting over the success of Japan Inc. and its perceived unfair and selfish trading practices could well lead to attempts to isolate Japan.

Efforts to keep Japan out of the two largest markets could have unintended consequences of the greatest import for the international system. Japanese money, technology and capital will require new and substantive outlets. The Soviet Union and China, increasingly marginalised by the pace of economic developments will desperately require foreign capital, technology and capital goods. With the withdrawal of the protective USA military umbrella, Japan will have to come to terms with the Soviet Union or to rearm! Could we therefore witness the emergence of a Moscow-Beijing-Tokyo axis comprised of these three relatively authoritarian societies? Would it present a danger for the stability of the international order? Perhaps it could be a beneficial development for the Third World, permitting it to exploit to its own advantage the political and economic rivalries which would arise.

What seems quite likely is that there will be less predictability in the new international system. This could be a source of danger if a higher level of statesmanship than that which pertains at present is not forthcoming to skilfully manage and overcome the new challenges.

Regional conflicts may diminish in intensity, but they will remain a fact of life in the Third World until a certain level of development and democratisation is attained. In view of the increasing emphasis being placed on the respect for human and political rights, it would seem to be just a matter of time before human rights conditionalities replace purely political considerations as the yardstick for determining the provision of assistance by the industrialised nations to the developing countries. At a recent conference in Paris to discuss 'The Impact of Change in Eastern Europe on Africa,' the former Nigerian Head of State, Olusegun Obasanjo, observed that 'safe political conditionality' was being applied for western aid to the East, requiring rule of law, human rights, free elections, multiparty systems and a market economy. He expected the same to be applied to Africa.[11]

Such an international environment would seem, however, to underscore the usefulness of multilateral organisations such as the United Nations. It seems inevitable that many of the responsibilities previously taken on board by the superpowers will be devolved to the United Nations. The rapprochement between the superpowers over the past two years has resulted in increased peace-making and peace-keeping responsibilities for the world body. This is a welcome trend which could allow the UN to fulfil finally the role it was intended to play. Thought will, however, have to be given to strengthening the political and technical mechanisms at the disposal of the UN if it is to carry out these responsibilities meaningfully and on a wider scale.

The critical importance of the UN will also be underscored when it is fully realised that the real security problems of the future – drug trafficking, inequities in the international economy, growing poverty in the midst of increasing prosperity, environmental degradation, global climate change and the population explosion – cannot be resolved by one state or one group of states in an increasingly interdependent world.

The abatement of regional conflicts and the reduction of ideological tensions will not necessarily provide the Third World with the 'peace dividend' so eagerly awaited. Indeed, the domestic economic concerns of the industrialised nations will take priority. Also paradoxically, arms races are heating up, squandering the potential benefits from peace. The countries of ASEAN, as well as Japan, South Korea and Taiwan will spend about $40 billion on arms in 1990. When China, Indian and Australia are taken into account, the figure rises to $60 billion. Analysts expect that spending on arms in Asia will rise to $130 billion by the end of the decade.[12]

A number of factors are influencing this trend. As a result of the disappearance of leftist insurgencies, armies are being reorganised and modernised to deal with external threats. In addition, the need to police resource-rich territorial waters requires increased naval and air power. Western manufacturers of weapons, trying to find new outlets to replace their dwindling markets in the West as the focus of security shifts from military to economic concerns, are encouraging these developments. The arms industry of Eastern Europe will also look with favour on these trends in order to perpetuate one of their lucrative export industries.

Current Status

The trends and characteristics of the new and emerging international order have been underlined in this paper, because they suggest a distributing fluidity and uncertainty about the future, brought about by rapid and often unpredictable changes. The Caribbean region, like much of the Third World, is still a spectator to these transformations. At this stage, there can be no clear and precise vision of the consequences of these changes. Who will gain? Who will lose? As indicated, many of them will affect either adversely or positively, the future of the Third World and the Caribbean. But an awareness of the implications and discussion of strategies to cope with the changes or take advantage of them, seem to be appropriate, bearing in mind that historically the gift of foresight has been in very short supply. At this stage any statement or analysis can only be holistic, painted on a broad canvas not cast in concrete and reflective of what might be termed 'conventional wisdom'.

Perhaps the most important dynamic of Caribbean International Relations has been the dichotomy between formal statehood and actual power. The contemporary landscape of 16 independent states, three associated states and nine dependencies are all weak by definitions of power employed in the analysis of international relations. They have had to struggle with an international system in which they have not and cannot demonstrate much power, be it economic, military (with the exception of Cuba), or diplomatic. In fact, the main arena in which some power resources have been evident is that of diplomacy in international and regional organisations.[13]

Some of the people of the ongoing issues of international relations for the Caribbean have largely begun to disappear or lessen in importance over the past few years. Issues of decolonization, secession and boundary disputes are hardly likely to be part of the active agenda for much longer. As far as the 'decolonisation' issue is concerned, of the six remaining British dependencies (Anguilla, Bermuda, the British Virgin Islands, Monsterrat, the Cayman Islands and the Turks and Caicos Islands) the only movements for independence are in Montserrat and Bermuda. Colonial status, and accompanying political stagnation, may be considered anachronistic in the modern world; but unless there are firm guarantees of economic development and sustained prosperity, to compensate for limited physical resources and small size, Britain will remain as a colonial power in the Caribbean for the foreseeable future.[14]

Since 1946, the French Caribbean territories of Martinique, Guadeloupe and French Guyana, have been named overseas departments (*départments d'outre-mer*, or DOMs). Sporadic demonstrations of discontent have been tempered by additional financial resources rather than any political concessions toward independence. Since 1986 President Mitterrand has appeased some of the demands for autonomy by instituting mechanisms for decentralisation. Since the departments belong to the European Community proper, the POSEIDOM programmes specifically aimed at furthering their integration into Europe was finally approved by the European Council of Ministers in December 1989. The result will be the greater integration of the DOMs into the Community, and the undermining of nationalistic and independence movements.[15]

In the case of the Netherlands Antilles (comprising Aruba, Curaçao, Bonaire, Saba, St Eustatius and part of St Maarten) the willingness of the Dutch Government to grant independence to all six islands has met with a positive response only from Aruba. The Arubans, (who are mostly meztizos and whites and suspicious of the Government in Curaçao) obtained separate status within the Netherlands Antilles from January 1986 with the option of independence by 1996. However, economic difficulties and local reluctance in all of the Netherlands Antilles may leave the issue of independence unresolved for the future.[16]

The United States Government granted the USA Virgin Islands a measure of internal autonomy in 1954. Subsequent attempts to expand it have been rejected by referenda. Political opinion in Puerto Rico has been divided since 1952 over those who favour continuing that island's Commonwealth status, advocating statehood, or struggling for independence. Even though Puerto Rico's constitutional status was placed before the UN Committee on Decolonisation in 1972 by Cuba, the USA has consistently denied that Puerto Rico is a colony. Until the status question is firmly resolved, Puerto Rico's interest in the Caribbean remains as a function of USA policy toward the region.[17]

The issue of *secession* in the Caribbean is the result of multi-island arrangements, rather than ethnic conflict (though the latter has not been unknown in Trinidad and Tobago and Guyana). The concessions to Aruba, Anguilla, Barbuda and Nevis took place during negotiations for independence from states of which they were a part. However, no independent Caribbean nation has so far lost any portion of its territory through secession.

The major maritime and boundary issues are also being resolved, or put on the back burner. A maritime delimitation agreement between Venezuela and Trinidad and Tobago is a reality. Steps are being taken by the UN Secretary General to resolve the Guyana-Venezuela boundary dispute. Relations between Guyana and Suriname have improved in spite of their boundary dispute. Meantime, the British still guarantee the security of Belize in the face of Guatemala's territorial claim. None of the boundaries of these states have been altered by force, although the foreign policies of Belize and Guyana in particular have been shaped by the disputes.[18]

In a more global context during the 1990s, the traditional Western European colonising powers will have lost their distinctive personalities by integration into the new Europe. Anti-imperialist slogans and rhetoric will have to find new antagonists since historical adversaries such as USA and USSR may become disinterested in traditional displays of crude economic determinism, or techniques of political and military destabilisation as demonstrations of power assertion or hegemonic management. Ideological differences will remain, but there will be room for more political convergence and new international paradigms. Most importantly, perhaps, the Caribbean, like other regions, will lose political leverage and room for bargaining if the influence of the Soviet Union in the world community is severely weakened.

Future Prospects

In the emergent era of the nineties, the focus for developing countries will have to be economic. In fact, the importance given to international politics in foreign policy and international relations will have to be reconsidered. In turn, strategies will have to be devised to discern, diagnose and respond to the challenges and opportunities which will arise from the process of global economic change.[19]

When one looks at possible trends for the year 2000, several major factors may be responsible for uncertainty in the region. One factor is the emergence of a new Europe and the possible consequences for the Caribbean in loss of development flows and assistance, bank credits, foreign investment and preferential trading arrangements. There will possibly be economic marginal-isation of the region, because of the emergence of new trading mega-blocs, and doubts about Caribbean competitiveness in a global context.

Trade mechanisms such as the Caribbean Basin Initiative, CARIBCAN, and the Lomé Convention might fail to achieve sustained export-led growth in non-traditional economic sectors in a more integrated world economy. There might be added competition in the marketing of traditional crops and industrial products as technological changes bring about more efficient use of raw materials and the substitution of synthetic raw materials for resource based industry. The inability of the region to offer sophisticated financial services and the uncertain environment in which capital flows take place, will prove a threat to possible investments and trade.

These trends point to urgent need for structural changes in the relation-ships between the Caribbean and the world economy, as well as the structure of the Caribbean economy itself. The impact of these trends is particularly difficult for the very small states of the region.[20]

The foreseeable security concerns of Caribbean countries derive from location, historical factors and for many the intrinsic disabilities of Island Developing Countries (IDCs) and Small Island Developing Countries (SIDCs).[21]

Territorial claims, maritime delimitation, and policing the territorial waters are still complex issues which will require resolution. The vulnerability to natural disasters (hurricanes and earthquakes), the destruction of fragile ecosystems, demography, food supply, are all concerns of basic security. Other security concerns of IDCs and SIDCs, in particular, will include policies and measures to cope with natural disasters, regional migration, resource limitations and the vulnerability of ecosystems.

The trends in the emerging international environment, as outlined in the background paper, may seem to have adverse implications for the future of the Caribbean by the year 2000. What it really presents, however, is a challenge and opportunity to thoroughly re-examine the role which the region can and should play in the new international context. The most important mechanisms to meet the challenges and the opportunities is the adoption of coordinated strategies and coordinated foreign policy responses. There is no doomsday scenario!

The policy responses that can be regionally coordinated will require study – identification and assessment of the options which should be pursued in order to influence international events. Such studies are already underway in the relevant institutions of the region and major conferences are planned in the near future to deliberate on the possible scenarios.

Some of the relevant considerations which might point to resolving the issue clusters are: how to cope, despite lack of resources, with the problems of effective and relevant representation at bilateral, regional and multilateral levels; how to cope with the special security and development problems of small states, most of them island or multi-island states and how to secure diplomatic coherence in the wider Caribbean including the Hispanic states of the littoral. There is the need to know how to manage traditional economic relations so as to ensure that such relations are supportive of new development objectives at a time of change; how to influence international commitment to developing countries; and promote change in the international system which would make it more supportive of the security and development objectives of small developing states. Consideration must also be given to how to cope with new areas of global concern of special relevance to the small states of the Caribbean such as the management of the resources of the sea, the preservation of the environment and the dumping of waste; and how to capitalise on potential growth opportunities such as international demand for services (tourism, telecommunications, transport); and trade and investment opportunities, particularly in parts of Europe and Latin America.

The major challenges and opportunities which will be presented to the Caribbean do not only require detailed analysis, but also the creation of appropriate mechanisms and policy implementation. As one major study on the future of the Commonwealth Caribbean has indicated, the international environment 'although providing sources of support and opportunities for growth as well as constraints on the nature and pace of development, need not be the dominant influence.'[22] The ability of strong nations to define the nature of international relations is one aspect of power. The potential for other states to get their definition of the situation accepted might be another.

Notes

1.   Scott Heron, 'A Brief Window of Opportunity', *The Daily Journal*, March 29, 1990. (Statement attributable to Robert H. Dahl at a symposium at the University of Dayton).

2.   See Robert Keohane: 'Beyond Hegemony', Boston: Little Brown, 1986; and Bruce Moon, 'Political Economy and Political Change in the Evolution of North-South Relations', in *Political Change and Foreign Policies* ed. by Gavin Boyd and Gerald Hopple (London: Pinter 1948) pp. 225–250.

3.   Helmut Schmidt, 'The United Nineties', *The Listener* (London), May 10, 1990.

4.   Schmidt, The United Nineties.

5. *The New York Times*, April, 17, 1990.
6. Boyce Richardson, 'Time to Change: Canada's Place in a World of Crisis', *Peace and Security*, 5:1 (1990) pp. 2–5.
7. Ron Sannders, 'Narcotics and Corruption', *Caribbean Affairs*, 3:1 (1990) pp.79–92.
8. United Nations Population World Survey, 257–262; 465.
9. Myron Weiner, 'Immigration: Perspectives from Receiving Countries', *Third World Quarterly*, 2:1 (1990) pp. 140–165.
10. Weiner, Immigration.
11. *The New York Times*, 6 May 1990.
12. *The New York Times*, 6 May 1990. (Malaysia for example signed a $1.6 billion Memorandum of Understanding with Britain in September 1969 to purchase fighter aircraft, anti-aircraft missiles, naval corvettes and possibly submarines).
13. Anthony Payne, 'Equal States – Unequal Powers: Independence in the Contemporary World – The Caribbean', (Paper delivered to the British International Studies Association ISA Conference, London, 1989).
14. Tony Thorndike, 'The Future of the British Caribbean Dependencies', *Journal of Inter-American Studies and World Affairs*, 31:3, (1989) pp. 117–140.
15. Tony Thorndike, 'Europe and the Caribbean: Threat or Opportunity', (Paper delivered at 15th Annual Conference of the Caribbean Studies Association, Port of Spain, 1990).
16. Rosemarijn Hofte and Gert Oostindie, 'Upside Down Decolonisation', *Hemisphere*, (1989) pp. 28–35.
17. See Jorge Heine, 'Puerto Rico in the Caribbean', *Caribbean Handbook*, (London, 1989) pp.26–27; and Juan M. Garcia Passalacqua, 'The Caribbean in the 1990s and Beyond: The Role of Puerto Rico', (Paper delivered at the World Peace Foundation Conference, Montego Bay) 1990.
18. On the disputes see Anthony Payne, 'The Belize Triangle: Relations with Britain, Guatemala and the United States', *Journal of InterAmerica Studies and World Affairs*, 32:1 (1990) pp.119–135; and Jacqueline A. Braveboy Wagner, 'The Venezuela-Guyana Border Dispute: Britain's Colonial Legacy in Latin America', (Boulder, Colorado: Westview, 1984).
19. Several of these trends in economics and security, and possible implications for the small state have been the subject of analysis in the following: 'Vulnerability: Small States in the Global Society', Report of a Commonwealth Consultative Group, London, 1985; Lloyd Searwar, 'Peace Development and Security in the Caribbean Basin: Perspectives to the Year 2000', A Conference Report (ISER, IIR, IPA), 1987; *Peace and Security in the Caribbean*, ed. by Anthony T. Bryan, J. Edward Greene and Timothy M. Shaw, (London: Macmillan, 1990); Compton Bourne, 'Caribbean Development to the year 2000; Challenges, Prospects and Policies'

(Report for the Caribbean Community Secretariat, 1988); Ramesh Ramsaran, *The Commonwealth Caribbean in the World Economy*, (London: Macmillan, 1989). See also Anthony P. Gonzales, 'The Changing International System and Caribbean External Strategy' (Mss); Henry S. Gill, 'Economic Implications for Latin America and the Caribbean of Changes in Eastern Europe' (Mss) Papers presented at a Conference on the Crisis in Eastern Europe) 'The Emerging New World Order and its implications for the Third World', (Institute of International Relations, UWI, Trinidad, May 9 and 10, 1990).

20. The most thorough analysis, from which the following trends on security, and policy responses are extracted is the document written by Lloyd Searwar, 'Studies in the Management of the Foreign Policy of the Small State: An Analytical Framework', (Institute of International Relations, UWI, Trinidad, May 1989). The original framework was reviewed by a group of Caribbean regional experts who met at the Institute in October 1988.

21. The most recent analytical study on this question is the document by Lloyd Searwar, 'Intrinsic Disabilities of Island Developing Countries and National, Regional and International Measures for Reducing Vulnerabilities', (Mss. done for the UNDP 1990).

22. Compton Bourne, 'Caribbean Development in the Year 2000; Challenges, Prospects and Policies', (Report for the Caribbean Community Secretariat, June 1988).

[53]

The Future of CARICOM
in the Global Economy

Alister McIntyre

It is well known that the growth of the world economy, which stayed at a level of about 3 per cent per annum for most of the 1980s, slipped in 1990 to 1.8 per cent, and then in 1991 to -0.4 per cent – which is the first occasion on which world GDP declined since the end of the Second World War. Despite optimistic forecasts both by governments and the private sector in the major countries, the upturn from the recession has not yet taken hold. At best, growth this year is likely to be weak. The United Nations world economic survey predicts a 1 per cent rate, while most forecasts project no more than a return in 1993 and beyond to the 3 per cent growth of the 1980s.

It should be recalled that several commentators made the point at the time, that 3 per cent growth in the major countries was insufficient to generate satisfactory rates of growth in the developing countries.

It is true that in 1990 and 1991 developing countries, taken as a whole, grew faster than the world average at 4.7 per cent and 3.4 per cent respectively. However, this was largely due to the performance of Asian countries, especially China, which grew at the impressive rates of 5 and 7 per cent respectively. A few Latin American countries – Mexico, Chile, and Argentina, in particular – recorded relatively high rates of growth, but this was not generally the case in the countries of the Caribbean.

We are facing a situation, therefore, where the global economic environment is unlikely to provide much general impetus to our growth. The rate of growth of world trade itself has declined from the peak of over 8 per cent attained in 1988, to just over 3 per cent in 1991. In such a context of slow growth, the only way we can perform above average is to increase our market shares, both with respect to traditional and new products.

The Traditional Exports

There is very little to say about the traditional products. The bauxite and alumina market is unsettled and over-supplied at the present time. Petroleum production is declining in Trinidad and Tobago because of the depletion of reserves. In the case of the traditional agricultural exports – sugar and bananas – the challenge is to retain market shares. Given present costs and quality there is only limited hope of increasing them.

Tourism is probably the only product where some positive growth is taking place, but it is patchy. The all-inclusive hotels are doing well, as are some of the newer destinations in the Eastern Caribbean. But certain traditional destinations are in trouble. It would seem that major investments are called for to refurbish the hotel plant and to improve the quality of attractions and service. There is no doubt that international competition in tourism is intensifying, with new destinations coming on stream, and with the inroads being made by the cruise ships.

Developing new exportables

It is already well understood that the CARICOM countries need to find new exportables, both of goods and services. The multilateral financial institutions and important bilateral donors have been pushing for institutional and policy reforms to make the economies more competitive and to remove export biases. The missing element has been a well-targeted effort to build up the knowledge base for exports. Experience elsewhere shows that this will not happen spontaneously. A deliberate government/private sector effort, backed up both by local and external resources, seems to be indicated.

We stand our best chance of improving our export performance through product development and innovation. In the agricultural field, despite long standing recognition of the need for it, insufficient attention is being paid to product development in areas such as fruit and vegetables, aquaculture, and marine culture. Individual countries lack the critical mass of expertise to do all of the research and development needed on their own. It has long been recognised that we need to organise regional research and development teams to undertake the investigative work, but action is slow in coming.

The same thing is true with respect to traditional manufactures, such as garments and furniture, where informed commentators have long made the point that our best bet may not lie in labour-intensive mass production, but rather in going up-market with smaller scale custom-tailored production. The point needs to be made here, again, that in tourism we need to work harder on product development and innovation, in areas such as local dishes and beverages, health and eco-tourism.

Services

A field of great promise for export development is services. Some banks, building societies, and insurance companies are already beginning to set up subsidiaries, affiliates, and offices abroad. At least one accounting firm is selling software services as far afield as Southeast Asia. There are opportunities, too, for exporting services in areas such as engineering and construction, design, medical diagnosis, legal advice, agricultural technology, and education, to name only a few.

If we are not careful, despite our potential in these fields, we may end up in the future as net importers, not net exporters, of these services. Subject to what I shall say later, it is not too fanciful to project the establishment of a worldwide regime for open multilateral trade in services, following the conclusion of the Uruguay round. If we do not make strenuous efforts now to improve our competitiveness in the services trade, we shall find ourselves in a disadvantageous position when that time comes.

The era of knowledge

It is clear that we are living in an era where knowledge is increasingly becoming the key to economic progress. We have to take action now to develop much greater capability than ever before in knowledge-intensive production of both traditional and new exports of goods and services. As several people have argued, this requires unprecedented efforts to modernise the education system at all levels.

In their report entitled 'Time for Action', the West Indian Commission has set out a number of areas where CARICOM countries can work together to their mutual advantage. Colleagues at the University of the West Indies (UWI) and I have stressed repeatedly what needs to be done to increase access to the University and to improve the quality of its graduates. Today, I underscore the urgent need to improve access and the quality of tertiary education as a whole, by drawing attention to the grave situation with respect to intermediate level technicians and technologists.

The World Bank report on 'Access, Quality and Efficiency in Caribbean Education', makes depressing reading on the subject. The report shows that the annual output of craft-level graduates in CARICOM, as a whole, is between 1200 to 1500 technicians. This level of output means that improvements in the quality of the labour force are very slow. For example, as a percentage of the projected labour force by the year 2000, the annual addition of workers at this level ranges from 0.2 per cent in Barbados to 0.1 per cent in Trinidad and Tobago, 0.04 per cent in the OECS and 0.06 per cent in Jamaica. In other words, at present levels of output, it will take between five years in Barbados, ten in Trinidad and Tobago, 25 in the OECS, and over 30 in Jamaica, to achieve a 1 per cent increase in the proportion of technicians in the labour force. This situation is clearly untenable.

The UWI cannot do the entire job of knowledge development, but it is ready to play its part in strengthening the knowledge base for exports. We have undertaken in our current development plan to achieve a 50 per cent increase in our enrolment by the year 2000, with an emphasis on science and technology. We have secured a US$66 million concessional loan to upgrade our facilities and staff in science and technology.

We hope to discuss with government and the private sector our plans for establishing a science park, and reorganising and upgrading our consultancy services.

UWI is also working to become an export earner. We are embarking on a very substantial expansion of our summer programme, with international summer schools in Caribbean studies and multicultural education, to which we expect to attract students from many countries. We are looking at the feasibility of introducing summer programmes in English as a second language, targeted towards the non-English-speaking Caribbean and Latin America. We are developing, with encouragement from the Commonwealth Fund for Technical Co-operation (CFTC), short courses for students from other developing countries, particularly in Africa and the Pacific. We are already making a start with courses in plant tissue culture, solid waste management, and gender studies.

Caricom as an integration scheme

CARICOM countries need to mobilise all of their companies, firms, and institutions, to work on export development. The world economy is in an anaemic state, but as the fast-growing developing countries are showing, there are still possibilities for expanding exports. Small countries, like our own, should be particularly favoured, since our needs are modest in global terms.

I turn now to the second question: the future of CARICOM as an integration scheme in the light of trade policy developments in major countries, and the evolution of the international trading system itself. There continues to be great controversy over whether regional and sub-regional groupings are building blocks or stumbling blocks to the reestablishment of an open system of multilateral trade. Article XXIV of the present GATT rules permits the formation of customs unions and free trade areas, and part IV of the agreement recognises the value of economic integration to developing countries. However, GATT has never in its history approved an economic integration scheme, since in every case there was a division of opinion as to whether the scheme was leaning more towards creating trade rather than trade-diverting.

It is possible that the rules emanating from the Uruguay round would be stricter on integration schemes. This was foreshadowed in the Leutwiller report on the world trading system which was negative on the matter. The negotiation text of GATT's Director General makes no mention of these schemes, except in relation to trade in services. Nevertheless, it is not realistic to suppose that given the many schemes around the world, especially the larger ones, such as the European single market and NAFTA, they could be completely excluded from consideration in any final negotiated text for a new world trading system. Accordingly, it is doubtful whether the continued existence of CARICOM will be in conflict with any future regime for international trade.

Integration and export-led growth

Nevertheless, the substantive point is whether an integration scheme is appropriate for countries following strategies of export-led growth. There is a point of view which sees integration schemes as essentially protectionist arrangements designed to support import-substitution strategies of development. Those who hold that view argue that countries pursuing strategies of export-led growth should liberalise their trade as much as possible since import tariffs are essentially export biased. In a fully liberalised economy exporters can identify sources for their imports from the cheapest suppliers without incurring a duty penalty. If other countries reciprocate, they can also export to them on an equal footing with other exporters and with their domestic producers.

This line of reasoning cannot be contested in conceptual terms, but, in reality, the world is very far from a regime of universal free and open trade, notwithstanding the genuine efforts being made in the Uruguay round to roll back protectionism. Some are even arguing that managed trade is gaining ground as major countries revert to protectionist devices to deal with their trade imbalances and disputes with other major countries. Agriculture is a particularly difficult sector where quite recently decisions have been taken to increase the sale of subsidised products.

Timing trade liberalisation

In that scenario, the CARICOM countries will have to judge very carefully the extent and timing of trade liberalisation. Advocates of unilateral trade liberalisation by developing countries tend to say that even if developing countries get no reciprocity from such liberalisation, their consumers will benefit from cheaper imports. But as a very distinguished economist used to say, it is cold comfort to an unemployed man to tell him that the cost of living has declined.

CARICOM agricultural producers have a problem competing with producers from other countries who enjoy producer-subsidy equivalents of 50 percent and more. While cheaper food for the CARICOM consumer is an important consideration, this must be set against the need to sustain production in the region. It is quite possible that unilateral trade liberalisation with respect to agricultural products could generate a wave of subsidised imports that would force regional producers to cut back production, if not to go out of business entirely.

Accordingly, tactical considerations alone suggest that an appropriate protective tariff be retained on a transitional basis, both for bargaining purposes and to provide temporary protection for sensitive products such as agriculture, until the process of liberalisation has definitely taken hold.

A CARICOM single market and economy

It is sometimes not appreciated that CARICOM is likely to become more than a scheme of market integration. CARICOM heads of government committed themselves in 1989 to establish a single market and a single economy by 1994. If that decision is implemented, CARICOM would go beyond the freeing of trade in goods to include: (i) freer trade in services; (ii) freer movement of people for purposes of work, starting with university and professional graduates and media personnel; (iii) freer movement of capital, including the development of a regional stock exchange, and the establishment of a Caribbean investment fund for the mobilisation of venture capital; (iv) steps towards the creation of a common currency; (v) more structured efforts to negotiate jointly on international economic matters and, where appropriate, joint external representation.

In other words, CARICOM would progressively become a single economic space within which goods and services and raw materials will move freely. This could significantly improve the climate for investment and export development in all countries of the region. Entrepreneurs will be able to meet their requirements for management, highly skilled personnel, and finance from throughout the region.

Production, cooperation and production sharing

Companies and firms can enter into production cooperation and sharing whereby they can package large volumes for export and achieve critical mass in vital areas such as research and development, marketing, and market development.

A single economic space can also provide a solid base for reaching into the non English-speaking Caribbean. Trade and economic cooperation with the non English-speaking Caribbean can eventually represent a vast enlargement of the potential for production sharing, as well as the size of the market open to CARICOM producers. Jamaica will be exceptionally well placed to take advantage of such developments.

It is no accident that the Dominican Republic and Venezuela have applied for membership in CARICOM, rather than sought bilateral trade and economic agreements with individual CARICOM member states. Neither is it an accident that under the Enterprise for the Americas Initiative (EAI), the US administration has pointedly indicated its willingness to negotiate with groups of countries rather than individual countries.

The fact of the matter is that it is easier for countries to deal with a group rather than negotiate separately with 13 mini-and macro-states. This has been the region's experience through the Lomé Convention, to CARIBCAN, CBI, and now the EAI.

We have to be hard-headed about this. CARICOM is a starting point into a wider world. As the West Indian Commission has argued, we have the advantage of multiple entry points into that world. We must try to utilise all of them so that we can respond to opportunities as they arise.

NAFTA

The North American Free Trade Agreement (NAFTA) is perhaps the development to which we must give the keenest attention. The prospect of eventual hemispheric-wide free trade is breathtaking, but it will not happen overnight. Considerable time must necessarily elapse before over 20 countries and groupings can gain access to the free trade area, because of the protracted negotiating and legislative processes involved. This is not to argue for delay in opening a negotiating dialogue with the three NAFTA partners. To the contrary, it is to say that the earlier one starts, the better the chances of bringing an arrangement within reach.

The complexity of international economic negotiations

International economic negotiations are by their very nature time-consuming; they require substantial inputs of diplomatic and technical expertise; and are vulnerable to the ebbs and flows of politics, governmental changes, and the shifting influence of special interest groups. In charting a course for the future we have to be realistic and flexible, and prepared to adapt and fine-tune our strategies as developments unfold. We should not delude ourselves into thinking that substantial benefits are just around the corner. It is only through a sustained effort that success can ultimately be achieved.

To conclude: I do not have a crystal ball; I do not know what the future of CARICOM might be; but based upon the considerations I have outlined, I see nothing emerging in the global economy that would negatively affect its continuance as it moves towards a single market and economy.

What West Indians need to show is a determination and capacity to stay the course; to implement plans and decisions which have been agreed; to eschew delusions of grandeur which can lead us to misjudge our importance to other countries; and to work resolutely to transform our economies into high growth, internationally competitive countries that can take advantage of the many opportunities that are arising in different parts of the world for greater trade, investment, and production.

Note

This paper was first published in *Jamaica: Preparing for the Twenty-first Century*, Ian Randle Publishers Limited, Kingston, 1994, pp. 241–249.

[54]

Economic Integration with Unequal Partners
The Caribbean and North America

DeLisle Worrell

Situated at the pivot of North and South America, the Caribbean is inevitably swept up in the wave of economic – and perhaps political – change that has seized the Americas. 'Time for Action' from the report of the West Indian Commission set up by the Heads of Government of CARICOM,[1] began the process of conditioning the Caribbean to a new economic and political reality. The region, and its leaders, are still working out the implications of the direction in which the report points. Neither leaders nor populace are confident that the Caribbean can achieve meaningful self-determination in a world dominated by sophisticated industrial nations. The fear of economic, cultural and social oblivion lies deep in many hearts. The apprehension that the Caribbean will be overrun by the US, losing its identity, sovereignty and the means of a satisfactory livelihood, is understandable, considering the relative size of the US and the Caribbean, and the recent geopolitical changes that have shifted focus, it seems, exclusively towards Eastern Europe and the Far East. However it is a misapprehension that the Caribbean faces a hostile monolith, intent on consuming it entirely. The interrelationships between the Caribbean and North America (Canada as well as the US) are subtle with nuances from both directions, and currents determined as much by historical influences and associations as by economic and political dictates. Moreover, there are many shades of opinion in the US, Canada, Mexico, the Caribbean and the rest of the hemisphere, and the relationships are evolving in unexpected ways.

Background

The history of Caribbean-North American economic relations goes back over 400 years. The trade between the eastern seaboard of the Americas and the Caribbean, in which food and building materials for the Caribbean were exchanged for rum and molasses, started very soon after the establishment of slave plantations, and was a source of conflict and contention between the Caribbean and Great Britain for 200 years or more. There was also a fair amount of travel and migration between the Caribbean and the eastern seaboard, particularly with the southern states/colonies. The Caribbean, like Canada, was a haven for refugees from the newly independent US in the late eighteenth century. Haiti established close ties with the US after it gained independence in the early nineteenth century. Links between the Spanish Caribbean and North America were officially severed when Spain lost its colonial footholds in Florida, but informal commerce continued, intensifying with the weakening of the Spanish colonial Government in the eighteenth century.

The nature and intensity of north-south commerce varied over time. Political changes had an effect, with attempts to suppress trade with the US after its declaration of independence, and divert to the Canadian provinces. The US civil war saw Caribbean sympathies with the south, for the most part, though slavery had been abolished in the British colonies a generation earlier, and the rebel states were aided in attempts to evade the union blockade. The abandonment of mercantilist doctrines in Britain in the late nineteenth century brought an end to restriction on Caribbean-US trade.

The construction of the Panama Canal set up a large current of migration across the Caribbean, and there was subsequently a smaller influx into the US of ex-canal workers. These movements accelerated flows of remittances from the US to the Caribbean. The twentieth century has seen the development of Caribbean minerals for the North American market, especially oil and bauxite. There has been considerable penetration of Caribbean financial markets by Canadian banks and insurance companies; US financial institutions have a much smaller presence because they have, until recently, been hindered by states' laws that give them an overly parochial focus.

However, Europe remained the dominant influence on Caribbean economies until the end of the nineteenth century; for the English-speaking Carib-

bean, that dominance lasted until the 1960s. The base of Caribbean economies was the production of sugar and other agricultural staples – rice, cotton,
cocoa, coffee, spices – for export to Europe. Finance for this investment came
mainly from Europe, and surpluses and windfalls were repatriated there.
Migration patterns were biased heavily towards Europe: it was the source of
management and technical skills, and the destination of youth in search of
education beyond the basics.

The European connection was reinforced by Britain's maritime power and
dominance in world trade, and supported by the spread of British financial
institutions. The Colonial Bank, established in the Caribbean in 1837, continues in operation, as part of Barclays International. (Barclays Bank, 1991).
The economic foundations of the European colonial empires were undermined in the late 1800s, but the empires themselves, and the economic
relationships they created, lingered for as long as 150 years in some parts of
the Caribbean.

European colonialism determined the pattern of economic and political
integration and fragmentation within the Caribbean. The islands and some
adjacent mainland areas were divided into language blocs in a haphazard
pattern, reflecting the spoils of war rather than the logic of geography.
Trade links were mainly between colony and imperial centres; even among
colonies of the same power, trade was not very great. However, among
colonies of the same allegiance there were political, administrative and
non-trade links of varying importance. Public servants were mobile between colonies, as were managers and a select body of professionals in the
private sector. Many financial institutions served all colonies of the same
power, and many shared common currencies. A few territories were
administered jointly.

Although there was some interaction between colonies of different allegiance it was insignificant for the region as a whole. Moreover, even for
colonies of the same power, interaction among themselves was nowhere on
the scale of colonial relations with Europe.

Time, events and technology have destroyed the foundation of the old
economic relationships between the Caribbean and the wider world. For
almost a century Europe has not had a compelling economic interest in the
Caribbean, and the region's patterns of trade and commerce have shifted
northward. Since the 1960s Europe has no longer felt able to sustain the cost
of strategic and political reach across the Atlantic. North American firms have
stepped in to exploit the new products and services which the Caribbean
supplies to the modern world – tourism, bauxite, oil and the assembly of
manufactured goods. At the same time the US economy has grown enor-

mously in relation to the world economy, to cast a huge economic shadow over the Caribbean and Latin America.

US interventions in the Caribbean have been motivated by geopolitical concerns such as the security of the Panama Canal and resistance to the spread of what were perceived to be ideologies hostile to the US. These interventions have strengthened US-Caribbean links in some cases, and have resulted in the incorporation of some Caribbean territories (Puerto Rico and some of the Virgin Islands) into the US in the twentieth century, under special arrangements that do not carry the full privileges and responsibilities of statehood. However, in other instances intervention has severed economic relationships for periods of time, and has left a legacy of hostility and resentment towards the US. The most conspicuous example is Cuba, but interventions in Haiti and the Dominican Republic have also created lasting suspicion of US power, a sentiment which is not far from the surface elsewhere in the region.

As will appear later the evolution of Caribbean-North American economic relationships is less influenced by world economic currents and the debate over trade liberalisation than the intense focus on the North American Free Trade Area (NAFTA) and the possibility of a western hemisphere free trade area would suggest. In the postwar period the US has initiated three programmes to bring the Caribbean closer into its economic ambit, two of them involving Latin America as a whole. In the 1960s the Alliance for Progress was conceived, arguably still the most fruitful of the initiatives. The provision of technical assistance, and the establishment of multinational institutions has made a difference to the quality of decision-making in the region, and provided durable mechanisms for economic, political and social cooperation.[2] The Caribbean Basin Initiative (CBI) has been the source of intensive assessment, inconclusive because it is impossible to say with confidence what might have been the pattern of trade in the absence of the CBI. The fact that the CBI does not affect services, and that garments are excluded, means that its effects have not been far reaching.

The nature of Caribbean-North American relationships is also influenced by the characteristics of the European withdrawal. The French did not withdraw at all: their colonies have been incorporated into the French republic, with the status of 'department'. The British withdrew altogether (though the process is incomplete: a few colonies remain) and the former colonies are fully independent politically. The terms of the Dutch withdrawal lie somewhere in between, with the establishment of independent administrations in the Caribbean, and retention of some functions by the Hague. The Spanish Caribbean achieved its independence in the nineteenth century, and for much of the twentieth has been under US tutelage. Because of their continuing responsibility France and Holland remain more of a counterweight to US economic dominance in the parts of the Caribbean with which they are associated than does the UK in the English Caribbean.

The nature of the Caribbean-North American economic relationship has to some extent been influenced by Caribbean responses to the above currents. The extent to which the Caribbean has been able to alter the outcomes, and the degree to which individual countries can exercise economic sovereignty are the principal questions to be addressed in this study.

The current circumstances raise questions, not simply of the Caribbean's future economic relationship with North America, but about the very identity of the Caribbean. It may be argued that the Caribbean is as much a part of US economy as is Florida; the Caribbean cannot choose its rate of growth, rate of unemployment, inflation rate or interest rate independently of the fortunes of the US economy. This is to the Caribbean's disadvantage: if for some reason Caribbean economies decline relative to the US – an economic slump causes a disproportionate fall in air travel, for example – Caribbean workers are not free to migrate to more prosperous regions of North America, as would be the case for residents of Florida who might be similarly affected. Moreover, the Caribbean benefits from none of the fiscal transfers which moderate income disparities between states of the US.[3]

It does not therefore follow, as has occasionally been suggested, that the Caribbean should reject pretensions of independence and sovereignty and seek accession to the US. There is little sympathy for that idea either in the US or in the Caribbean. In the US it is regarded, unreasonably, as a threat to living standards, through job losses to the Caribbean and through federal transfers. In fact the Caribbean labour force is too small to have any noticeable impact on labour market conditions in the US. In the Caribbean the notion is rejected as a return to a hated colonialism.

The potential benefit from accession to the US may be overstated. Migration, a major avenue of equalisation of Caribbean and US incomes in theory, is inhibited in practice because social costs such as the dislocation of schooling, re-negotiation of mortgages, disruption of family and community ties inhibit migration, except in extreme cases.

There is considerable resistance to the loss of Caribbean identity. Caribbean people, at home and in the Diaspora, have a strong sense of home which finds expression in the arts and in links of family and community. The loss of Caribbean identity would depress the quality of life, not only for Caribbean people, but for many North Americans, Africans and Europeans for whom Caribbean music, cuisine, street festivals and literature are sources of enrichment.

In any case there are variations among states, nations and regions, in the Americas and worldwide, in the extent of economic integration, due to geography, differences in legal and administrative systems, differential taxation, transport costs, natural phenomena and individual and group preferences. Legal and political boundaries do not identify homogeneous economic units; political divisions determine the nature of many economic transactions (because of trade restrictions and border taxes) but there are many other transactions – especially tourism and services – which may not be affected. Economic relations between some nations may resemble links within large countries more nearly than they do relations with other nations.

Both the US and the Caribbean are in search of an economic relationship of mutual satisfaction; the old relationship has been superseded, the current situation is fluid and evolving. Further changes are inevitable. The Caribbean remains apprehensive about the direction and implications of that change. The US seems not to have a systematic strategy, as yet, beyond NAFTA; there is a vague notion that the NAFTA provisions will be extended to the rest of Latin America and the Caribbean. Things will probably not work out that way.[4] I hope in this essay to explore what is likely, and to suggest what might be desirable, by looking at the circumstances and the prospects.

One clue to the probable evolution of the Caribbean-North American relationship is the strength of the Caribbean sense of identity. Section two describes how the Caribbean describes itself, using the English-speaking countries as a point of reference. It discusses evidence of a Caribbean identity, and whether it covers English, Dutch, French and Spanish-speaking countries. Spanish Central America is excluded, but Belize is included because it is a member of CARICOM; Venezuela and Colombia are excluded, but Guyana, Suriname and Cayenne are included because of their strong affinities to the islands of the Eastern Caribbean.

Section three explores the ways in which the desire for regional association might be realised in terms of economic links. It draws insights from theories of economic integration.

The majority of people in the Caribbean consider the rate of economic development and the quality of life unacceptable, and feel that their opportunities fall short of their aspirations. Section four examines the roots of this disaffection, and the successes and failures of economic strategy in the post-war period. Section five reviews efforts in the English-speaking Caribbean to set up regional political and economic structures that would give voice and vision to the common Caribbean identity.

Section six discusses relationships between the English-speaking countries and the rest of the Caribbean. Section seven documents Caribbean-North

American links, and section eight does the same for Caribbean relations with Latin America.

Section nine describes how global changes have affected North American policies and attitudes towards the Caribbean. Section 10 is devoted to inferences for regional integration and suggestions for Caribbean policy.

Defining the Caribbean

For historical reasons the Caribbean has always defined itself in linguistic groups, contrary to what the map would suggest. Language grouping has been reinforced by patterns of travel and migration, shared institutions, common traditions and initiatives for integration among Caribbean territories. There is very little travel between islands belonging to different language groups, their legal systems, political and social institutions vary and attempts to unify the Caribbean have, up to the present, all taken place within language groups. Cultural links have tended along similar lines until recently, but modern telecommunications have led the Caribbean to uncover strong cultural affinities that transcend language barriers. Trading links within the Caribbean remain weak, based on geographic proximity and special products and markets, for commodities such as petroleum.

Literature and education have developed largely within separate language groups. Remarkably strong literary traditions have grown in the English and French Caribbean and in Cuba, but with few exceptions – Nobel laureate Derek Walcott, Aimé Césaire, Nicolas Guillén – the protagonists are known only to those who share their language. English speakers from Belize to Guyana have recognised a commonality of upbringing, social structure and value systems in novels (*Beka Lamb*; *In The Castle of my Skin*; *Annie John*; *Miguel Street*; *Summer Lightning*), theatre (*Dream on Monkey Mountain*; *I, Marcus Garvey*), essays and criticism (*The Girl of the Sea*; *Beyond a Boundary*) and poetry(*Omeros*; *Sun Poem*). A common education system in the English Caribbean has produced a single examining and certification body for high school achievement for the region, and supports a single university of international standard.

Literature in other languages reveals many of the same concerns and sentiments, suggesting the basis for cultural fusion. However, the works have not been translated and disseminated across the language barrier - except for a handful of authors who have attracted wide readership in metropolitan countries (Walcott, Naipaul, Césaire, Condé, Carpentier).

Language separation has been aggravated by travel patterns. The overwhelming direction of travel and migration is to and from North America and

Europe, and where travel within the Caribbean is significant it is within the same language group. This pattern is self-perpetuating because travel costs vary with the volume of business.

Major initiatives for multilingualism would be needed to erode the language barrier. At present only the Dutch speakers are multilingual, typically with mastery of Dutch, English, Spanish and their native Papiamento. None of the other countries has mounted an educational effort of the magnitude necessary to achieve a general command of a second language.

There are very few political institutions for integration among Caribbean countries now remaining, but the region boasts an impressive array of institutions for cooperation in particular areas. Although the majority of these bodies are centred in the English Caribbean there is great diversity in their coverage. Among the strongest and most influential are the University of the West Indies, funded by CARICOM countries; the Caribbean Development Bank, whose membership includes Venezuela, Colombia and several industrial countries along with its English-speaking Caribbean borrowing members; the East Caribbean Central Bank, the monetary authority and financial regulator for six East Caribbean states; the Caribbean Tourism Organisation, whose membership covers all the language groups; the Secretariat of the Caribbean Economic Community; the Caribbean Examinations Council, for CARICOM countries; the Caribbean Association of Industry and Commerce, and the Caribbean Congress of Labour both with CARICOM membership.

The language divide tends to define legal, judicial, and to some extent, social and political institutions and systems. Legal and judicial systems tend to mimic those of the United Kingdom and Holland, in their former colonies. Martinique and Guadeloupe are incorporated into mainland France. Political upheavals in Haiti and the Spanish Caribbean have left these islands with some distinctive legal and judicial forms.

Colonial patterns remain imprinted on the religious landscape, somewhat attenuated by large scale immigration in the nineteenth century. Former British and Dutch colonies are mostly Protestant, except for Muslim and Hindu descendants of East Indian migrants; other countries are mainly Catholic.

These distinctions are reflected in the political culture: the former British and Dutch colonies have established stable democracies – except for Suriname. The former Spanish colonies and Haiti have had a more chequered history of government. The legal and judicial systems of the English and Dutch speaking countries betray their colonial roots; there has been much more innovation and borrowing from American systems in other countries.

Social systems tend to be quite similar right through the region, despite religious and ethnic distinctions. They feature extended family structures, informal income support, the importance of festivals and socialising in small stable groups, often centred around the church.

It is in the area of culture that the Caribbean is most uniform, although until recently the cross-Caribbean contact was so intermittent that this may not have been readily appreciated. The development of the electronic media and the growing ease of travel have brought the strands of Caribbean cultural development together, producing an exciting mix, born of their common roots, which continues to evolve. The result has been a flowering of music, drama, painting, skilled craftsmanship, athletics and street festivals. This cultural resurgence has reached far beyond the Caribbean Sea, and in music its influence is worldwide.

Perhaps the weakest area of integration within the Caribbean, even among countries of the same linguistic group, has been trade. The predominant direction of trade continues to be with North America and Europe. There are few complementarities that would make for intra-regional trade, and the efforts to develop them have not been successful. Such intra-regional trade as there is has resulted, not from language affinity or tariff policy, but from cheap transport and cost differentials between close neighbours. These factors explain the relatively high volume of trade between Barbados and Trinidad and Tobago during the oil boom years, and the trade between relatively high income, Martinique and Dominica, where average incomes are much lower.

Discussion of Caribbean integration, and of links between the Caribbean and North America, has paid excessive attention to tariffs and other measures affecting visible trade, which have little effect on the structure of economic relationships either within the Caribbean or between the Caribbean and the wider world. Intra-regional trade is unlikely to assume major proportions, and it will continue to be dictated by relative prices and transport costs, notwithstanding the level or structure of tariffs and trade regulations. Inevitably trade will be mainly with the rest of the world, its pattern and growth determined by skills, investment, productivity and the rate at which the region adopts new techniques, the critical factors in international competitiveness.

In certain important ways, particularly with respect to culture, the Caribbean sees itself increasingly as a single unit. In many other areas Caribbean leaders seem to understand the need for unity, particularly as a means of accelerating the region's economic development. These perceptions, it may be argued, form the basis for building the Caribbean nation. As world events have recently illustrated, nations are not natural phenomena; they begin with a sense among a collective of populations that they share common roots, interests and aspirations but thereafter the sense of national identity must be carefully nurtured.

There is little institutional infrastructure that spans the entire Caribbean region. Only among the English-speaking countries do institutions exist to affect policies in defined areas, that may deepen the sense of nationhood and the degree of integration. A useful approach seems to be offered by the West Indian Commission, which looked first at the nature of the integration process in the English-speaking Caribbean, broadening the analysis to the wider Caribbean and the patterns of integration between the Caribbean and North America.

Economic Integration

Until about ten years ago most economic theories of integration were concerned with the effects of the removal of tariffs and the liberalisation of trade. Largely in response to the issues that have taken centre stage in the consolidation of the European Community (EC) a more comprehensive and useful literature has emerged, which pays attention to transaction costs, monetary union, economies of scale, factors that inhibit the mobility of labour and capital, the convergence of fiscal and monetary policies among members of an economic union, and mechanisms for the transfer of finance between members.[5] The effects of trade liberalisation are rather innocuous, compared to those of the other factors, even in the case of the EC (Emerson *et al*, 1992; De Melo, Panagariya and Rodrik, 1993).[6,7] Because intra-regional trade in the Caribbean is so small a proportion of the total, and the trade links to North America so embedded in the structure of Caribbean economies, trade liberalisation is an even more trivial issue in the Caribbean.

According to what must now be considered old-fashioned theory, a customs union or a free trade area – involving trade liberalisation among members but the maintenance of tariffs and restrictions against non-members – may have good or bad effects on the union, depending on assumptions about the competitiveness of markets, the universality of technology and information, transport costs, the use of imported inputs in production, the extent to which unit costs fall with rising output and the extent to which large scale producers provide benefits or impose extra costs on the rest of the economy. The result familiar to readers of elementary economics — that the union benefits if cheaper partner imports are substituted for dearer home production and loses if dearer partner imports are substituted for cheaper non-member imports – holds only under very special conditions, which correspond in no way to the reality of intra-Caribbean and Caribbean-North American economic relationships.[8]

A realistic estimate of the impact of intra-CARICOM trade liberalisation should begin by subtracting from total intra-regional imports of goods and services the value of petroleum products, services (principally tourism) and resource based items (mainly primary agricultural goods that can only be commercially produced in the large mainland countries). That leaves about half of intra-regional imports that may be affected by trade liberalization.[9] Intra-regional trade in goods and services is about 8 percent of the region's total imports,[10] so that at most 4 percent (one-half of 8 per cent) of the total may be affected by trade liberalisation. The size of the impact depends on the amount of effective protection before liberalisation and the price elasticities of supply and demand. The cost of transporting some of these items from the cheapest source to potential markets within the region is so great that the landed product is not competitive with most expensive home production, or with the landed (duty paid) cost of goods obtained even more cheaply from outside CARICOM. Disaggregation is required to determine whether the results would, on balance, be favourable, but it is already clear that they will be insignificant. The results for the wider Caribbean are even more innocuous: for reasons of history, language, transport and transactions costs, and commerce among the wider Caribbean is even lower than for CARICOM, in relation to total external transactions.

Trade liberalisation between the Caribbean and North America is affected by the extent of substitution of local production for goods and services which are more cheaply available from North America, after deducting freight and insurance costs. Caribbean exports already enjoy free access to North American markets under the provisions of the Caribbean Basin Initiative and the CARIBCAN Agreement with Canada (see section 7). Trade liberalisation will be effective only if the exclusions from those agreements are removed.

Import patterns are determined by the size of Caribbean economies, which limits the variety and range of goods they can produce. Whatever the trade regime, imports from outside the region remain very high in relation to the national income, and the Caribbean must export most of its output to pay for these imports. Economists accustomed to markets of the industrial world, Latin America and East Asia find it difficult to appreciate the limitations to import substitution in the Caribbean. A medium sized garment factory produces enough men's shirts in a month to supply the retail needs of the entire Lesser Antilles for a given style for at least one year.

The ratios of imports to GDP, and the direction of trade between the Caribbean and North America owe very little to tariffs and trade restrictions.

They are determined by the import content of domestic production, the need for variety in local consumption, and the limited range of these items for which domestic production is conceivable. The clearest evidence is to be found in the efforts that have been made to induce import substitution in the Caribbean. The most far reaching were undertaken in Guyana from 1974 to 1980, when draconian restrictions prohibited imports even in cases where no good domestic substitutes were available. The import ratios for Guyana remained unchanged for that period, compared with the periods before and after. Rather than finding substitute for imports the protective measures depressed output and drove activity from the formal markets underground. One observes a similar outcome during the period of severe import restriction in Jamaica (1974–1980).

Further evidence of the limits to import substitution in the Caribbean may be gleaned from the CARICOM experience. The existence of CARICOM has made no measurable difference to the pattern of trade with North America: the ratio of North American trade in goods and services to the regional total has remained unchanged since 1973 (the date of CARICOM's establishment), and that ratio has increased relative to the region's GDP.

The gains which economic integration may bring in terms of greater efficiency of production are potentially greater than the benefits of trade liberalisation *per se*. Efficiency levels may rise because of the larger scale activity which allows greater specialisation and increased productivity. The projection is that large scale activity will encourage a wider scope and range of allied activities in relation to inputs or by-products. On the distaff side are potentially harmful spillovers.[11]

The policies that might raise efficiency in the Caribbean are labour mobility, capital mobility and currency unification. Large firms could tap a larger resource pool for talents appropriate to their needs and technology, and the costs of moving staff and of accessing finance from a variety of sources would be reduced by the elimination of currency risk. There are potential benefits from economic integration within the Caribbean, as well as between the Caribbean and North America. Unfortunately, policies to realise these gains have presented great difficulty in implementation. Within CARICOM there is a plan for currency unification, but the domestic policies of some countries may not yet be compatible with it; the first steps have been taken to improve capital mobility, but agreements on limited labour mobility have yet to be implemented. There are no similar initiatives for the Caribbean as a whole. If Caribbean currency unification were achieved the prevailing sentiment would favour arrangements that formally or informally integrated the financial system with that of the US, preferably with fixed exchange rates, large foreign exchange reserves and regulations only on large financial trans-actions (to inhibit speculative activity). However the prospect of labour mobility with North America, which would have a major impact, is remote.

Furthermore, one cannot say a *priori* that efficiency gains would outweigh efficiency losses, if one includes environmental effects, and efficiency may be bought at the expense of regional polarisation. Some cities, countries or regions of the union may attract a concentration of activity, reducing job opportunities elsewhere. If the integrated region is wealthier as a result of the union, everyone may benefit, provided there is a mechanism for transferring some of the wealth from the centres of concentration to depressed areas. In CARICOM the Caribbean Development Bank's operating practices provide such a bias, to a limited extent, but a more automatic mechanism is clearly preferable. There is nothing of this kind for the Caribbean as a whole, and the possibility has not even been raised in the context of discussions with the US, Canada and Mexico. If, contrary to the position argued in this paper, Caribbean trade liberalisation does significantly improve North American access to the Caribbean market, North America should offer to share a portion of the rewards with the Caribbean, to assist with the ensuing changes in Caribbean production.

Integration may bring changes in the Caribbean's comparative advantage, and therefore in the activities that attract investment. But because of size disparity, integration will have no effect on North American production. To the extent that comparative advantage is determined by natural resources the areas of Caribbean specialisation should not change much. The region has already geared investment to its mineral resources, tourism and extensive agricultural potential. Beyond this, comparative advantage may depend on historical developments, government subsidies and regulations, population concentrations, geography and even pure accident.[12] However, the Caribbean does have an advantage in the quality of its labour force, which, with the exception of Haiti, is better educated and housed, and enjoys better health than does the labour force of countries at an equivalent level of per capita income (Evidence for Jamaica, the Dominican Republic and Trinidad and Tobago appears in IDB, 1993; see also UNCTAD, 1993).[13,14] This should encourage skill and knowledge intensive activity, provided firms are free to bring together the mix of talents needed for each activity. The growth promoting effects of the development of health and educational services are increasingly emphasised in the economic literature. The potential benefit to the Caribbean may increase with greater mobility of labour within the region.

Trade liberalisation does not help to change comparative advantage to the benefit of Caribbean economies. It has been suggested that energy supplies available cheaply in Trinidad be used for the smelting of alumina from Guyana and Jamaica (Girvan, 1967).[15] However, the inhibiting factors are not trade restrictions and tariffs but transport costs and weak aluminium markets.

The effects of economic integration – within the Caribbean and with North America – on the competitiveness of Caribbean markets are indeterminate, though they may well be very considerable. Again, because of size disparity, the effects in North America will not be noticeable. Such effects derive from capital and labour mobility, which remove barriers to the growth of regional firms. Competition increases if a much larger number of strong regional firms emerge in areas like banking, insurance, professional services, business services, tourism, food processing, agriculture. But it is quite possible that fewer firms will dominate each of these activities (I discuss this more fully in Worrell, 1992).[16] It is not clear that that would be unfortunate, from the point of view of maximising potential growth. The debate over the direction of the relationship between competition and growth remains unresolved.[17]

Mobility of labour and capital will emerge as the major instrument for realising benefits from economic integration. It permits exporters and potential exporters to operate on a scale which yields efficiencies from specialisation, allied activities and spill-overs. Such firms may draw on specialised skills scattered throughout the region and may tap financial resources from any member country, providing the best returns on investment. Labour mobility might also improve the quality of public administration, leading to a better economic environment and faster implementation of productive investment. It should reduce the emigration of skilled personnel, as more challenging job opportunities become available in the Caribbean.

Labour mobility might also lead to better matching of wage levels and skills, which should improve efficiency and produce stronger firms with better growth potential. However, firms with the wrong mix of skill, technology, wages and quality might be forced out of business.

Stable nominal exchange rates within the union and with the rest of the world yield significant benefits. They improve investment incentives by eliminating a major source of uncertainty, they reduce the cost of international business because currency risk premiums are unnecessary, they eliminate the incentive for capital flight, they remove the major source of inflation in small open economies, and they lend credibility to fiscal and monetary policies that are compatible with the stable matrix of exchange rates. For the Caribbean these benefits may be realised only by implementing domestic policies that maintain the values of domestic currency in terms of the US dollar.

If there is no parallel market in foreign currency, Caribbean countries may stabilise their exchange rates by adjusting fiscal and monetary policies to produce a sustainable balance of payments, characterised by adequate official reserves of foreign currency, a low external debt service burden and absence of short-term debt accumulation. If there is a parallel market in foreign exchange, the policy régime will need to be altered, foreign exchange or long run credit secured to bring foreign exchange reserves to an adequate level, and a realistic market exchange rate adopted, along with the removal of exchange controls on current account transactions. It will usually be necessary to adopt a new budget and monetary policy, with interest rate policies that are geared to the expected nominal rate of inflation after the effects of the devaluation have worn off.[18]

There is no need for further integrating mechanisms if each country always satisfies the conditions for exchange rate stability, but inevitably circumstances arise that raise questions about the sustainability of policy in one country or another. They may be a response to differential external shocks in different countries, manifestations of the election cycle, lax controls on government spending or an unsupportable surge in consumer demand. Also, countries that have had a history of changing unsuccessful policy régimes find it difficult to gain credibility for any new initiative, and the expected response to a policy régime based on economic fundamentals fails to materialise. Because of such problems monetary union may be essential for exchange rate stability in some parts of the Caribbean.

Monetary union involves the establishment of institutions for joint management of monetary policy and currency. It requires an independent central bank or banks with a strong anti-inflationary mandate. Its credibility may be enhanced by keying the money supply to the central bank's holding of foreign assets. To expand the money supply, both government and private financial institutions must supply foreign assets to the central bank. They may acquire foreign assets only by running down their deposits with the central bank – thereby reducing the money supply – not by obtaining credit from the central bank. Accession to a monetary union with an independent central bank, endowed with adequate foreign exchange reserves, may be the only credible régime change available to countries with a history of economic instability.

There continues to be inconclusive debate in Europe over the degree of convergence of the economic performance that is necessary for monetary union among potential members. On one hand it is argued that insufficient convergence dooms the union, and the UK's precipitate exit from the EMS is cited as an example. On the other hand it may be that commitment to monetary union accelerates the convergence of members' economies. A

Caribbean monetary union is unlikely to suffer the strains of the EMS because the anchor of the Caribbean currency system – the US – is so large compared to the countries of the region. Caribbean countries do not have monetary or fiscal instruments that can hold their rates of inflation much below that of the US, and efforts to boost economic growth through inflationary spending are frustrated by the supply of foreign exchange. The issue of accepting a higher rate of inflation in order to secure faster growth therefore does not arise. The only way to accelerate growth relative to the US is to maintain faster productivity growth. Policies which are more inflationary than those of the US may create a temporary gain in employment, particularly the public sector, but that employment is soon lost when external imbalances cause a devaluation. The result is an inflationary spiral, with no growth in employment. Efforts to obtain a lower rate of inflation than for the US may cause much unemployment or little abatement in inflation, unless wages can be reduced with little difficulty. The motive for the Caribbean to accept US inflation rates is very strong, and there is virtually no sentiment in favour of deviation from US inflation rates even when they are relatively high.

Nonetheless countries often deviate from policies that are consistent with achievement of US inflation rates, because the penalty for such deviation appears only after an interval which may be as long as three or four years. This should make monetary union highly desirable because it removes the opportunity to engage in what are ultimately futile policies. However, it also makes for reluctance to adopt monetary union rules, precisely because they outlaw short-sighted behaviour that may be to the temporary advantage of influential lobbies.

The above arguments point away from the removal of tariffs and other obstacles to intra-regional free trade as important economic expressions of a Caribbean identity. The vital mechanisms for integration are labour mobility, capital mobility and monetary union, and they all require sound macro economic policies that produce a stable balance of payments. The frustrations that CARICOM has experienced with trade policy were unfortunate, but intra-regional trade is not very important, and trade disruption is inevitable if macro economic policies do not stabilise the economy.

The analysis also has implications for Caribbean-North American economic relationships. Although the US is outside the Caribbean it is to US economic performance the Caribbean economies tend to converge. In this respect the Caribbean differs from the EC and the former USSR, where the focus of convergence is a country within the union. To a degree this facilitates economic union, since all members have similar concerns in respect of international policy.

Caribbean convergence on US economic performance creates fears of a loss of Caribbean identity, as economic links are reflected in social, cultural or political influence. The Caribbean is drawn into the US sphere of influence through capital flows, tourism, the growing sector of international business services, the emulation of US lifestyles (frequently experienced first hand through visits to North American relatives and friends) and the predominance of US goods in the import basket.

There are, at the same time, measures on both sides to slow the pace of integration and to contain its scope. They include US barriers to labour migration, resistance both by Caribbean countries and the US to the elimination of Caribbean currencies, US non-tariff restrictions on Caribbean exports and measures to combat threats of dumping and predatory practices by US firms.

The following generalisations emerge from the discussion of this section:

- The removal of tariffs and non-tariff barriers does not much affect the degree of integration, either within the Caribbean or with North America. Transport and transactions costs are the principal factors that separate one market from another.
- Freedom of movement of capital and labour are very important instruments for deepening integration and expanding the Caribbean's capacity to produce and grow.
- Fixed exchange rates make for faster integration and more rapid gains because uncertainty about the future of the exchange rate is the principal reason for high transactions costs.
- Monetary union, with a single currency and an independent central bank, can yield additional benefit by lending credibility to future government policy, linked to a promise of future exchange rate stability.
- Integration involves the convergence of economic trajectories; in the case of the Caribbean the US is the focal point. Neither the US nor the Caribbean in general would regard the US and the Caribbean as an integrated union, but in many important economic respects North America and the Caribbean do form an entity with respect to trade in goods and services, currency and the movement of finance. Policies are required to make this an equitable relationship, in view of the fact that neither side wishes to allow full integration, with freedom of labour movement and automatic mechanisms for fiscal transfers from the US to disadvantaged regions of the Caribbean.

Caribbean Achievements and Failures

A significant cause of the Caribbean identity crisis is the sentiment that Caribbean countries have failed to achieve their economic objectives, and that living standards are below the expectations and aspirations of the population. Countries are in search of a better economic strategy, at the same time fearful that, should such a strategy involve much deeper integration with North America, it would result in a loss of identity.

The Caribbean sense of economic failure is not necessarily a faithful reflection of the actual circumstances. The region has recorded a wide range of achievement and failure in the postwar period, judging by per capita incomes, education, health and sanitation, inflation, employment, income distribution and the elimination of poverty. Countries may be divided into broad categories according to economic performance as follows:

- Good performers with good prospects – Belize, Bermuda, Cayenne, Cayman, Guadeloupe, Martinique, Netherlands Antilles, Puerto Rico, Saint Lucia, St Kitts-Nevis and Virgin Islands.
- Good performers with major adjustment problems – Antigua and Barbuda, Bahamas, Barbados, Jamaica, Trinidad and Tobago.
- Good performers with poor prospects – Dominica, Montserrat, St Vincent.
- Poor performers with good prospects – Dominican Republic, Guyana.
  Poor performers in difficulty – Cuba, Grenada, Haiti, Suriname.

The good performers made considerable gains in per capita income, improved income distribution and showed major improvement in health, education and sanitation in the postwar period. Economic expansion which made these improvements possible was the result of factors such as new technology, extensive agriculture, newly exploited natural resources, improved quality of the labour force, improved infrastructure, capital flow and foreign expertise.

Tourism provides the most dramatic example of technology-based growth. The advent of jet aircraft reduced the time and real cost of travel so dramatically as to bring the Caribbean within reach of the holiday maker who had only one or two weeks to spend, and brought the cost of a tropical vacation within reach of the working classes of industrial countries. It transformed the Caribbean from a preserve of the wealthy tourist, and tourism from a minor activity to a major export and source of employment. An important if less dramatic example of technological change is the mechanisation of agriculture, which has significantly increased labour productivity.

Notable increases in agricultural production came as a result of the opening up of previously uncultivated areas, in Belize and Guyana. The exploitation of newly discovered natural resources opened new export sectors and caused dramatic expansion in bauxite and alumina in the Dominican Republic, Guyana, Jamaica and Suriname; petroleum in Trinidad and nickel in the Dominican Republic.

Focus on educational improvement over many years has brought higher overall levels of achievement and a larger proportion of skilled workers in the labour force. This has contributed to growth through increases in average labour productivity, and improvement in the quality and variety of Caribbean output.

Another significant contributing factor is the improvement in infrastructure, in particular transport and public utilities. The difference between the transport, electricity, water and telephone services of the good and poor performers is marked.

Private foreign investment has made a major contribution to the growth of Caribbean economies. It has brought expertise in foreign market structure and requirements, quality control and resources, as well as finance for establishment costs and the purchase of imported materials. It has proved relatively easy to attract the attention of potential foreign investors when labour costs are very low relative to those in well established competing centres. More active domestic investment strategy is needed as living standards rise closer to those of industrial countries.

Judicious official foreign borrowing helped to stimulate growth, but excess foreign borrowing caused instability which eroded previous improvement in some countries. Where governments kept external debt service ratios low and used the proceeds of foreign loans to build infrastructure the results were improved quality of life for citizens and a stronger incentive for investment.

The countries that have good prospects of continuing growth are characterised by one or more of the following: they are in the early phase of tourism development and the introduction of modern technology; they have political links to metropolitan countries to ensure a continuing stream of transfer payments; they have sustained investment to improve quality, develop new markets and increase the productivity of labour and capital they employ; their labour costs are still very low.

Tourism usually grows very quickly in the early stages of the development of new resorts. The latest examples are Aruba, the Dominican Republic and St Lucia. Thereafter expansion slows, as may be seen in mature resort destinations such as Jamaica, the Bahamas and Puerto Rico.

Puerto Rico, the Virgin Islands, the French and Dutch Antilles retain some form of link to metropolitan countries which gives access to financial transfers into these countries.

Labour costs remain very low in the Dominican Republic and Guyana, making for an obvious incentive to labour intensive industry. However, poor infrastructure reduces considerably the competitive edge offered by low labour costs. Moreover, should these countries experience rapid growth they will be confronted with the challenge now facing their more prosperous neighbours, as the work force feels able to express its repressed demand for a better quality of life.

Pessimism about the outlook for the Caribbean seems justified to some extent by the fact that very few countries in the region base their prospects for growth on continuing investment in quality enhancement and greater productivity. In many countries there are pockets of such investment, but overall this seems to be the driving force only in the tiny countries of Bermuda and Cayman. The other engines of growth may be viewed as elements of a catching up strategy which can serve to bring new players and countries where living standards have lagged behind. The only strategy which can improve the Caribbean condition, apart from dependence on unrequited transfers, is one that depends on improved productivity, quality and variety.

Countries that have major adjustment problems suffer from one of the following: low policy credibility because of repeated changes of strategy; domestic aggregate demand too high relative to levels of export production; and external debt service commitments that absorb too large a proportion of foreign earnings.

Jamaica is the Caribbean country whose Government suffers most from a lack of credibility, after close to two decades of changing policies, from extremely interventionist to extremely liberal, with no lasting improvement in the quality of life for the average worker, no containment of inflation and no reduction in unemployment. There is, at the time of writing, very little confidence that current economic policies will stabilise the economy and set the stage for renewed growth.[19]

High foreign debt service is a problem for Guyana, where debt service commitments exceed foreign earnings, and Antigua and Barbuda, where arrears continue to build. Jamaica has been successful in reducing its debt service to one quarter of foreign earnings from almost 50 per cent, but further reduction is desirable.

In Barbados and Trinidad and Tobago the levels of domestic demand, fuelled by the size of Government's deficits, are too large in relation to the country's national output. Because of the openness of the economies this results in a balance of payments deficit and, if not contained, a depreciation of the nominal exchange rate. Efforts in both countries to address the problem by fiscal adjustment have not definitively rectified the imbalance.

Dominica and St Vincent have doubtful prospects because the export of bananas to the UK, which has been the foundation of their economic growth, will not be viable if the special marketing arrangements now in force come to an end. The banana protocol of the Lomé agreement between the EC and African, Caribbean and Pacific (ACP) countries is being challenged by lower cost suppliers in Central America, with the support of Germany and other members of the EC. Unlike other banana producers, Dominica and St Vincent have been unable to diversify into tourism and the assembly of manufactured components. Montserrat's fortunes depend on the market for resident retirees, which no longer seems to be growing.

The poor performers have suffered from inappropriate economic policies, persisting over many years, as well as political instability. Studies of economic change in developing nations are unanimous in finding that political stability is essential for economic development(Nelson *et al*,1990). The processes for democratic transition either did not exist, or broke down for an extended period during the postwar period in all the poorly performing countries. In the Dominican Republic, Grenada and Guyana functioning democratic processes have now been restored, and unrealistic regulation, restrictions and state intervention have been eliminated. The Dominican Republic and Guyana have encouraging prospects, but Grenada's future is clouded by its dependence on the banana marketing arrangement with the EC.

This brief survey has uncovered the roots of Caribbean pessimism. Of the countries with good performance and prospects, only two of the very smallest seem to have developed the internal capacity to drive their economies forward, by initiating productivity-enhancing investment. The other growing economies depend on unrequited transfers from rich countries, paid for by the surrender of political autonomy; or they have recently begun to exploit some major resource such as tourism, and will eventually have to face the problems of maturity which have already overtaken their Caribbean neighbours; or they are so poor that their prospective growth still leaves them well down the development ranks.

However, the problems of most countries may be addressed by economic policy measures available to Caribbean countries, so long as there is a functioning democracy in place. Independent monetary policy to contain aggregate demand and stabilise the balance of payments would lay the foundations for growth oriented policies in most Caribbean countries. The credibility of such policy would be buttressed by monetary union and a fixed exchange rate in terms of the US dollar; supported by sufficient foreign reserves to meet contingencies, counter speculation (with the help of controls on large capital transactions only) and to accommodate normal seasonal activities. Mobility within the Caribbean would help in the evolution of firms with the knowledge and flexibility to reach international standards of competitiveness.

Moreover, economic development in the postwar period has endowed the Caribbean with relatively advanced infrastructure and comparatively rich human resources. The indicators of the human condition for Caribbean countries are always higher than average income levels would lead one to suspect. Some pockets of destitution remain – most of Haiti, some rural districts of the Dominican Republic, Guyana and Jamaica and the Kingston ghetto –but the majority of the Caribbean population enjoys a healthy lifestyle. Since the prospects for development depend, more than any other factor, on the quality of the workforce, the Caribbean is better placed in the international competitive race than its citizens realise.

Cuba is the Caribbean's special case. So long as the Soviet Union existed Cuba's economic circumstances paralleled those of Puerto Rico and the French Antilles, with average income boosted above the average product by transfers from the Soviet Union, mainly through marketing arrangements for Cuban sugar and the supply of petroleum from Russia. The collapse of the USSR devastated the Cuban economy, interrupting the supply of fuel, machinery and essential inputs, forcing Cuba to seek alternative markets for sugar and eliminating all elements of subsidy, all in a haphazard process of unmet commitments, rather than through formal abrogation of pre-existing arrangements. The rest of the Caribbean views the prospect of Cuba's inevitable integration into the North American economy with apprehension, and expects an even greater challenge to its competitive position than is anticipated from Mexico.

However, the impact of Cuba-North American integration should be seen in the perspective of the size of the North American market, compared to the productive capacity of the Caribbean. Although Cuba accounts for about one third of the Caribbean population, the addition of its production to Caribbean capacity still leaves the region with a miniscule potential share of the North American market. There will, however, be major transitional problems, in the mass tourism market and in the competition for investment in labour intensive production.

Integration in the English-speaking Caribbean

If the economic benefits of integration are real, it is surprising that so little progress has been made towards an economic union in the Caribbean. Various attempts at integration, dating back to earliest colonial times, all encountered difficulties because of parochial sentiment. Sometimes the economic motivation was evident, because integration threatened the advantages of a privileged and powerful group, but integration has also been resisted because of colonial loyalties, linguistic barriers, and religious and ethnic differences. Still, the surprise may be that so many regional arrangements do exist, when one takes account of the divisiveness of the region's history, the complexity of Caribbean society and the idiosyncrasies of human motivation.

The end of World War II saw the beginnings of change in the colonies of European nations, including all of the Caribbean except the Spanish-speaking countries, Haiti and the Virgin Islands. Fortunately for the Caribbean there emerged a generation of political leaders with a vision of a united Caribbean that might one day include all linguistic groups. However, that was regarded as a distant ideal. The immediate goal was greater political autonomy for the colonies, and the alleviation of the terrible poverty characteristic of most of the region. The Moyne Commission report, the most comprehensive documentation of the Caribbean condition just prior to World War II, recorded generally poor health, widespread unsanitary living conditions, low educational achievement, dilapidated housing, average incomes below subsistence levels and high levels of joblessness.

Because of colonial fragmentation the agenda for political and economic reform came to be tackled on a linguistic basis, with British, French and Dutch colonies moving on different tracks and often in different directions. The Spanish-speaking Caribbean and Haiti, underwent a series of upheavals of their own which had far more revolutionary effects. Puerto Rico embarked on a strategy, based on US investment, which at one time was expected to be the model for economic development in the rest of the Caribbean.

The French colonies were incorporated as departments of metropolitan France, which effectively cut them off from subsequent developments in the rest of the Caribbean. The most influential integration mechanisms depend on the existence of national decision-making institutions which can enter into mutual arrangements. No such institutions – legislatures, taxing authorities, central banks, autonomous judiciaries – exist in the French Antilles. These services are all directed from Paris. The immigration and travel restrictions of metropolitan France inhibit interaction between the French Caribbean and its neighbours. Puerto Rico and the US Virgin Islands are similarly compartmentalised, but less severely. They both have more local government, which has facilitated commercial links with the rest of the Caribbean in recent years.

The English-speaking Caribbean has produced most of the analysis of integration possibilities in the Caribbean, and has done the most to implement forms of integration. Efforts in the immediate postwar period aimed towards a federation of the English-speaking Caribbean. A federated nation seemed the minimum size of unit required for economic and political viability in any post colonial arrangement. A series of conferences leading up to the establishment of the Federation of the West Indies in 1958 was arranged to work out the structure of the federal government, the powers of the centre and the make up of the legislature. The Federation was dissolved in 1962, soon after Jamaica seceded. In hindsight it has been argued that insufficient attention was paid to the economic underpinnings of the Federation, but focus on the political arrangements was inevitable. The major concern was to bring an end to colonial relationships while preserving and reinforcing the traditions of parliamentary democracy which were inherited from the British.

Moreover, there was considerable economic analysis, even though much of it seems not to have informed popular debate. There were recommendations for the establishment of a central bank, and for an analysis of the extent of labour mobility in the region (Roberts and Mills,[20] 1958; Reubens [undated]).[21] However, analysis of the probable transfers of jobs and finance, and the provision of funds to offset regional disparities, might have allayed some fears and provided better ammunition against the anti-federalist lobby.

Concerns about the implications of monetary, fiscal and other stabilisation policies seemed unimportant in these early debates, compared with the problem of growth. Economists worried about securing finance sufficient to accelerate economic growth rates in societies where the propensity for domestic saving was thought to be very low, even negative in some cases. Moreover, since the colonial relationship permitted free capital flows to the metropole, it was feared there would be insufficient incentive for growth promoting, but potentially risky, investment in the Caribbean. Policies were recommended to attract foreign investment and to ensure there would be no cut-throat competition to offer more attractive régimes of tax and other incentives. It was recognised that investment might not be distributed among the members of the Federation in the same way that it might be for individual countries, but there was little sentiment for individual country independence prior to the 1960s, so the issue was not considered crucial.

In fact colonial arrangements provided some integration mechanisms which have subsequently been lost. All colonies were members of the sterling era, within which capital could be moved without exchange controls. Countries of the East Caribbean from the British Virgin Islands to Guyana used a single currency; there were three currencies in use in the English-speaking countries of the West Caribbean, but the Jamaica currency dominated. West Indians could migrate within the region with relative ease, though labour movement was subject to restrictions. In all these areas the end of the Federation and the establishment of independent nations has been retrogressive: fierce restrictions have at one time or another been put on intra-regional capital movements, there has been a proliferation of regional currencies, the majority of which have proven unreliable stores of value, and there are severe restrictions on the movement of skilled persons, along with a virtual ban on the legitimate migration of the unskilled.

The demise of the West Indies Federation threw the question of political integration off the agenda for 30 years. Attention shifted to economic aspects, driven by a perception that the Federation's failure was largely to be blamed on an inadequate economic foundation. The new efforts bore fruit first in the form of the Caribbean Free Trade Area Agreement (CARIFTA) of 1969, which was superseded in 1973 by the Caribbean Community (CARICOM) Treaty.

The arguments for economic integration were that the creation of a single regional market, the temporary proscription of some imports, the zoning of new enterprise and the development of major industry that combined regional natural resources would attract additional domestic saving into investment in import substitutes, and raise the local value added in export industry.[22] It was expected that the removal of intra-regional tariffs would significantly increase the degree of integration of the CARICOM market, but it was recognised that high transport costs would remain a major factor in market segmentation. Studies were commissioned on the regional transportation systems (Keirstead and Levitt, 1963;[23] De Castro, 1967),[24] but they had little impact. No attention was paid to the potential disruption of markets by rising transactions costs. At that time there were few currencies in circulation in the English Caribbean, and they were all members of the sterling area, eliminating the major cause of high transactions costs in later years.

The strategy envisioned a role for government in providing fiscal incentives for investment and that fiscal saving would be used to make direct investment in large scale industry such as a proposed aluminium smelter. Governments were also expected to enter mutual agreements for the zoning of industry, distributing activities around the region to ensure greater complementarity between the economies and to combat tendencies for regional polarisation.

The Treaty of Chaguaramas, which established CARICOM, provided for a common external tariff (CET) to be introduced in stages, with a longer phasing-in period for those members who were deemed less developed. However, the tariff remains so riddled with exemptions and special provisions, even after major revision, that it is of little consequence. This has occasioned great distress in the popular mind in CARICOM, but failure to implement the CET seems of little consequence for the economic future of the Caribbean. The CARICOM Treaty includes provisions for the marketing of agriculture B which have had only sporadic effect, and for the zoning of industry B a dead letter which has at last been abandoned as impractical and unproductive. A new outward-oriented industrial strategy is recommended in Girvan *et al*, 1993.

The most influential and useful provisions of the Chaguaramas Treaty initiated a network for regular consultation among members at the technical and policy level, together with a secretariat to service these functions. There is now a 20-year tradition in the English Caribbean of collaboration, not only in economic areas such as trade, finance, industry, tourism and agriculture, but also in health, education and labour. This collaboration has been extended to women's affairs, the environment, the arts and sports. Much to the disappointment of the CARICOM public, these networks do not often produce unanimous policy decisions, but they have played a crucial though little recognised role in framing the policy agenda for the Caribbean, and in sharpening perceptions of the options available. The institutional arrangements of CARICOM have fallen far short of intentions, but critical analysis – which remains to be done – might reveal a degree of cohesiveness in decision-making that would probably not have been possible without CARICOM (See *Time for Action* chapter 2 for one evaluation of CARICOM's achievements and failures).

CARICOM's efforts at collaboration are given high profile by meetings of Heads of Government, originally intended as annual affairs, but more recently held twice a year, with more frequent subcommittee meetings. These meetings may have produced more contention than agreement, and agreements reached do not have a good record of implementation, but that has itself intensified pressures for more effective enforcement, rather than for dismemberment.

CARICOM is supported by a wide range of institutions and associations, some of which predate the Treaty of Chaguaramas, which are official and private, technical, professional and voluntary. They include the University of the West Indies, the Caribbean Development Bank, the Caribbean Tourism Association, the Caribbean Association of Industry and Commerce and a variety of professional bodies.

By the late 1980s CARICOM members had developed a profound discomfort with the regional arrangements, mainly because they seemed to have been of little assistance in overcoming the region's widespread economic malaise. There was little real progress on the CET, a régime to encourage regional enterprise, and other agreements, and there were no sanctions to prevent beggar-thy-neighbour policies (which invariably proved self-destructive for the implementing country, as well as harmful to other members). The search began for ideas to provide new impetus for integration that might enhance economic performance.

Another motive for strengthening regional ties was to resist increasing intrusiveness of externally determined policies. Many Caribbean countries enjoyed only a brief interlude when local policy makers were at liberty to determine fiscal and monetary policy independently of the opinions of the international institutions for economic surveillance: the IMF, World Bank and Inter-American Development Bank. As the views of Washington prevail over local opinion on interest rates, trade liberalisation, exchange rates, fiscal strategy, the privatisation of state enterprises and financial regulation, the perception grows that Caribbean economies now suffer a new form of dependency which condemns the majority of their populations to frustration of their ambitions. It is hoped that regional collaboration will restore to economic decision makers a greater degree of autonomy. The example of the EC has encouraged interest in strengthening of the CARICOM arrangements. Europe's problems have renewed interest in regionalism and have given prominence and respectability to the notion, providing ideas and examples from which the Caribbean may borrow.

Yet another influence is the threat of marginalisation of the Caribbean in the consolidation of regional trading arrangements. The establishment of NAFTA is seen as a major threat to Caribbean economic interests,[25] and Caribbean exports to the EC face challenges. There is a strong sentiment that the region's common interest in resisting marginalisation should be reflected in stronger arrangements for collective action.

In response to these sentiments the CARICOM Heads of Government commissioned a group of prominent administrators, businessmen, technicians and scholars to hold public consultations, develop background papers, evaluate the CARICOM arrangements and make recommendations. The Heads of Government are now trying to come to terms with the report of this West Indian Commission (WIC), which was presented in August 1992.

The WIC report is the most comprehensive and influential of recent efforts to develop a new paradigm for Caribbean integration. There was one previous evaluation of CARICOM (Group of Experts, 1981); it did not depart from the original objectives which had informed the Chaguaramas Treaty, nor from the mechanisms that were expected to achieve them. However, the failure of many aspects of that economic strategy pointed to the need for a re-evaluation.[26] The West Indian Commission's report 'Time for Action' is the culmination of efforts to redefine the objectives and strategy of CARICOM. These efforts include analyses of social and economic issues by Bourne *et al* (1988)[27] and Beckford and Girvan (1989)[28] economic assessments by Bourne and Worrell (1989)[29] and Worrell, Bourne and Dodhia (1991);[30] economic policy analysis by Worrell (1992);[31] and a number of reports specially commissioned by the CARICOM secretariat (Field-Ridley, 1991[32] and Blake and Sanatan, 1991).[33]

The main economic elements of the new paradigm of integration for development would seem to be the following, though policies may sometimes appear to deviate from them:

- Growth to depend on exports, tourism and internationally traded services;
- Tax systems to provide incentives for investment in these areas;
- Regional mobility of skilled labour and capital to enhance production capabilities;
- Monetary union to reduce transactions costs within CARICOM (and the wider Caribbean), and to reduce uncertainty;
- Independence of the monetary authorities, so as to achieve greater credibility for policy;
- Currency stability to reduce expectations of high inflation.

Some weaknesses also remain in the policy framework. There is lack of investment incentives because of inflation uncertainty, absence of a credible policy and short term horizons. All of which is sometimes viewed mistakenly as financial insufficiency. This results in a misguided faith in high nominal interest rates as an instrument to increase finance, which themselves become a major source of inflation. Another weakness is the continued over-emphasis on the importance of tariffs in regional trade. The notion that tiny Caribbean home markets may form the basis for companies that may later expand in the extra-regional market diverts too much energy to local markets and import substitution. On the other hand there is very little initiative shown in the pursuit of a monetary union, which is potentially the most powerful instrument for regional convergence.

CARICOM and the Wider Caribbean

Because of economic and political circumstances the non English- speaking Caribbean has devoted less effort to integration, and there are no institutions similar to CARICOM elsewhere in the region. The issue did not arise in the

French-speaking Lesser Antilles and Haiti and the Spanish-speaking Caribbean were preoccupied with the search for political stability. The Dutch-speaking Caribbean suffered a degree of disintegration, with the withdrawal of Aruba from the joint Netherlands Antilles administration.

In recent years interest has grown in the establishment of links between CARICOM and the rest of the Caribbean. Initiatives have been motivated by recognition of shared features and problems, and the sentiment that cooperation might offer the best outcomes.

Private investors from CARICOM countries have sought out investment opportunities in non-CARICOM countries, as the relaxation of capital account controls by CARICOM countries has made such investment possible. There have been major tourism investments from CARICOM in Cuba, and the private sector has shown interest in selling to non-CARICOM countries; but the principal barriers are high transport costs, and the low average spending power of Haiti and the Spanish Caribbean.

The leadership of Puerto Rico and some French Caribbean intellectuals are reaching out to their neighbours, perhaps as a way of acknowledging and sustaining their Caribbean identity. They are sensitive to their dependent status, their lack of influence in regional affairs and the fact that they have no forum for a voice in international affairs. Puerto Rico has actively sought to develop regional links through its development bank and its Department of State. There are also a number of business, sports and professional groups with an active Puerto Rican membership. The participation of the French-speaking Caribbean in regional organisations is very low, where it is in evidence at all. They do not have institutions such as the Puerto Rican Development Bank at the Caribbean level, and there is nothing to counter their professional and business links to France.

Fear of beggar-thy-neighbour policies has motivated efforts to link CARICOM and the rest of the Caribbean. There is, inevitably, competition among Caribbean countries for investment and markets, because of their many similarities. Countries have an incentive to collaborate in setting environmental standards establishing regulations for financial probity and agreeing to a régime of tax concessions. There remains considerable variety in the tax régimes existing in the Caribbean, but collaborative efforts in environmental protection and financial regulation embrace the majority of the Caribbean, of all language groups.

A recognition of shared heritage, traditions and cultural practices is uniting the Caribbean across language barriers. Collaboration in music, festivals, sports and the performing arts is increasingly common, with practitioners and performers borrowing freely from each other, blending styles developed in their different communities (see, for example, *Caribbean Festival Arts, Caribbean Style*).

The Netherlands Antilles has been drawn to CARICOM in particular because their political problems very closely mirror those of the English-speaking Caribbean, with the danger of political fragmentation at a time when the region needs to consolidate and strengthen alliances. The Netherlands Antilles participate in many economic and business fora of CARICOM, though they are not members of the Community.

CARICOM and other Caribbean countries have begun to reconcile their interests in external economic relations, particularly in negotiating agreements such as the Lomé Accord with the EC and trade arrangements with North America. This collaboration is too episodic to be satisfactory, and there continue to be differences of policy, opinion and interpretation. The most recent example pitted the Dominican Republic and Haiti against CARICOM banana producers in discussions with the EC.

The Caribbean is being driven together by a common fear of marginalisation and loss of identity, as world trading blocs develop. The fear may be exaggerated, and the trading blocs less homogeneous than at first appears, but the sentiment is a powerful motivation for deepening regional ties.

In time these motivating factors may produce more influential links among all the countries of the Caribbean, but at the moment there are relatively few institutions that serve the whole region. The Caribbean Tourism Organisation does research, coordinates marketing, and acts as liaison between individual country tourism organisations; there is a region-wide programme for bank supervision, which acts as liaison and supervises training; and there are *ad hoc* bodies for international economic relations. Non-governmental organisations dealing with environmental issues have wide coverage (Caribbean Natural Resources Research Institute, Caribbean Conservation Association), and so do some professional organisations (Caribbean Library Association, Caribbean Studies Association).

The most significant regional initiative involving the non English-speaking Caribbean is the special provision under the Caribbean Basin Initiative (a programme of trade liberalisation, debt relief and investment promotion launched 1982-83) for surpluses of multinational firms accumulated in Puerto Rico to be invested anywhere in the Caribbean Basin (including Central America) free of US federal taxation. Significant investment resulted, mainly in the Dominican Republic, Jamaica and Trinidad and Tobago,[34] but the overall amounts fell well below the expectations of the scheme's Puerto Rican supporters. The provisions are to be phased out within five years.

The Caribbean Community has developed a number of linkages which reach out to the wider Caribbean. They take the form of joint working parties on issues of interest such as the negotiation of trade agreements with the EC, participation in joint trading and investment missions, and provisions for non-CARICOM countries to attend CARICOM meetings as observers.[35]

There are limited traditional trade, travel and migration links between Caribbean countries of different linguistic groups. English-speaking Dominica and Saint Lucia have strong links with French-speaking Martinique and Guadeloupe, born of their proximity and the fact that the English-speaking islands were for a long time part of the French colonial empire, and the four countries now share a common indigenous dialect, which is based on a French vocabulary. The US Virgin Islands attract tourism workers from nearby St Kitts. Guyana-Suriname trade is a product of their shared and easily accessible border, and their common Dutch heritage. Trinidad and Venezuela also share a linguistic inheritance (Spanish) and close proximity. The volume and value of these transactions is small in comparison with the total of any one of these countries' external transactions.

There is more significant growth of informal and illegal trade of more recent provenance. Trade between Guyana and Suriname grew to important proportions because of restrictive Guyanese policies, from the mid 1970s, which provoked a large expansion of informal activity. (See Thomas, 1989;[36] Hope, 1990).[37] Informal activity resulting from unrealistic policy was also responsible for the expansion of Jamaica's trade with Haiti and Puerto Rico. These informal transactions have declined in importance in the 1990s, as the Guyanese and Jamaican economies have been liberalised.

CARICOM, the Wider Caribbean and North America

North America is by far the most important source of earnings of foreign exchange for Caribbean countries, and it has increased steadily as a source of foreign exchange, relative to other areas. A similar pattern can be seen with respect to the Caribbean's imports of goods and services. The Caribbean's trade in goods, tourist services and other services is equal to the region's GDP,[38] so the dominance of North America in the region's trade implies a pervasive influence on all economic activity. Moreover, the strength of that influence has been growing in the postwar period.

North America has been the primary source of private investment in the Caribbean, with major investments in tourism, minerals, utilities and light manufacturing. The UK, France, the Netherlands, the Far East and Venezuela have all been sources of major foreign investment in the Caribbean, but their contribution all together falls well short of the level of investment from North America. Levels of private foreign investment fell after peaking in the 1970s, but the proportionate contribution from North America continued to increase.

The decline in official bilateral finance for the Caribbean since the 1970s has been precipitate, and in many years net flows have been negative. Nevertheless, the dominance of North America is reflected here as well, in net flows in both directions. Such information as is available on the source of remittances to the Caribbean confirms the importance of North America as the principal source of foreign exchange.[39]

The operations of financial markets in the Caribbean provide further evidence of Caribbean integration into the North American economy. Attempts to insulate Caribbean financial markets from the US have all come to naught, and have had to be abandoned. Several countries attempted in the 1970s and early 1980s to increase the domestic money supply and keep interest rates low by imposing exchange controls on financial flows, but the controls were circumvented with impunity, and capital flight depleted the money supply, frustrating the authorities' intentions. More recently countries have acknowledged the link between the financial systems of the Caribbean and North America by keying domestic interest rate policy to US dollar rates and the rate of domestic inflation.[40]

Largely because of the ease of financial flows, the Caribbean rate of inflation is closely linked to US inflation. The rates deviate significantly only where there is a depreciation of the local currency. Imports dictate domestic pricing because of the high import content of consumption and domestic production (Downes, 1992[41]; Holder and Worrel, 1985).[42]

High levels of migration between the Caribbean and North America contribute to the strong ties between the regions. Caribbean migration to North America, relative to the size of Caribbean populations, has been significant throughout the postwar period, though there have been periods when flows diminished or increased from one country or another, and Cuba's isolation makes it a special case (Pastor, 1985, p.7).[43] The extent of migration is reflected in the size of remittances to the Caribbean. In addition, there is considerable remittance in kind. For the poorest Caribbean countries remittances have for some years been the most important source of foreign exchange.

The Caribbean is already highly integrated into the North American economy, in trade, services and labour and capital movement. Whatever the fate of Caribbean economies, that process seems set to be a permanent feature. The scope for autonomous policy in the Caribbean is thereby circumscribed:

interest rate policy must take US monetary policy as its point of departure, while the rationing of foreign exchange, non-tariff barriers and exchange rate manipulation prove ineffective.

Caribbean countries should allow their economies to converge on the US rates of inflation and interest. Attempts to deviate lead to stagflation. Over the medium term the Caribbean may better use growth rates of real output by upgrading the use of technology and modernising techniques, improving quality and the mix of products, so that total productivity, of capital and labour, rises more quickly than it does in the US.

The limited choice of domestic policy options need not inhibit growth potential if the right choices are made from the available options to improve productivity. A policy régime which has been popular in the Caribbean, but which is to be avoided, expands domestic demand to create jobs, coupled with devaluation and/or trade controls to divert expenditure away from imports. The policy is stagflationary because the domestic suppliers to whom demand is to be deflected cannot expand their output unless they are able to increase their imports, in countries where the import ratios are as overwhelming as they are in the Caribbean.

Caribbean Governments should invest in education and social amenities that improve the quality of the work force, in finance and expertise for development of new markets and in incentives – fiscal and administrative – to promote investment which specifically raises the productivity of labour and capital. Furthermore, barriers to the regional movement of capital and skills should be eliminated so as to improve the efficiency with which skills and capital are employed.

Impact of Trade Arrangements on Caribbean-North American Integration

Arguably the most significant North American trade policy change affecting the Caribbean has been the reduction in the size of the US sugar import quota. It has resulted in a significant decline in Caribbean agricultural exports to the US, in spite of the increase of citrus products, vegetables and other food products. The impact on the Dominican Republic was especially severe, giving urgency to tourist development in that country. It remains unclear whether the loss of a dependable market in the US contributed to the decline in overall sugar supply in much of the rest of the Caribbean, though cost factors are probably the most important reason for the decline.[44]

The persistence of non-tariff barriers continues to be the most significant obstacle to the growth of Caribbean exports to North America. Exports of clothing may be subject to maximum amounts under the Generalised System of Preferences, and to limits on their source of materials, under special tariff provisions that are the basis for duty free access for most Caribbean clothing exports to the US. Any level of Government in the US – federal, state or local – may obstruct trade with arbitrary changes in standards of health, quality and content. State and local regulations have been known to conflict with federal policy; legal battles to prove this are long and costly, and the knowledge that such a challenge may be mounted is enough to deter potential exporters. [45] Prohibitive US legal costs cause exporters to the US to acquiesce in trading practices that put them at a disadvantage. US firms, which are usually many times the size of their Caribbean counterparts, may use their muscle to deter entry in markets they dominate. International patent and copyright laws may also encourage monopoly. These non-tariff barriers are the greatest actual and potential brake on Caribbean-North American trade.[46]

The Caribbean Basin Initiative provides duty free access to the US for the exports of the Caribbean and Central America, along with some debt relief and promotion of US investment in the region. However, the largest items in Caribbean trade with the US were excluded, and continued to be subject to the conditions of access which predated the CBI. Among the excluded items were petroleum, which accounts for about a quarter of Caribbean exports to the US, and remains subject to a 3 per cent tariff; textiles, clothing and footwear, where restrictions mentioned in the last paragraph remain in effect; and sugar. When we take account of the fact that tourism, which is now the Caribbean's largest 'export', and other international business services, which are important exports for several countries, are not affected by trade policy, there is little benefit that may be attributed to the CBI. Exports of manufactured goods to the US have risen in the 1980s[47] but they grew no more rapidly than in the 1970s, and total foreign earnings have grown less rapidly in the 1980s.[48]

The Enterprise of the Americas Initiative (EAI) for Latin America and the Caribbean, announced by the US in 1991, was not a significant improvement on CBI from the Caribbean viewpoint, though it was enthusiastically welcomed in South America, as reassurance that US attention would not be fully diverted by the unfolding events in Eastern Europe. There are few additional benefits for the Caribbean: some additional debt relief for Jamaica and the Dominican Republic, and entitlement to a portion of the small fund set up to make grants to hemispheric countries for support for private sector development. Provision is being made for consultations on non-tariff barriers and other contentious issues, but it is not yet clear what arrangements will be made for resolution or what procedures and powers there will be for enforcement.

The disappointing experience of Canada with conflict resolution arrangements under CUFTA does not give reason to expect the current situation to change very much. The EAI does bring threats for the Caribbean: the rules about the minimum domestic content for goods to qualify for free access to the US may be less favourable than under the CBI; and earlier accession to a free trade agreement with the US gives Mexico an advantage over the Caribbean.[49]

Canada has had provisions allowing duty free access for a range of goods from the English-speaking Caribbean since the 1920s. They were updated in the Caribbean-Canadian Agreement (CARIBCAN) of 1986, which also contained provisions for official financing 17 items. The agreement mirrors the CBI in excluding textile products, and its impact on Caribbean exports to Canada has been attenuated by non-tariff barriers such as provincial regulations on the standards for alcohol and regulations over how it is sold, which have inhibited sales of Caribbean rum.

In light of this experience the following observations may be made about Caribbean-North American relationships:

- Economic links between the Caribbean and North America remain very strong however institutional links and tariff arrangements evolve.
- This imposes constraints on Caribbean economic policy options, but there is still scope for the Caribbean to accelerate its growth by suitable economic strategy.
- The principal issues for Caribbean negotiators ought to be the removal of non-tariff barriers, compensation for the losses that may result from the exercise of monopoly power by US corporations and payments for additional costs, including compensation for accelerated polarisation of activity that may result from faster integration of the Caribbean and North America;
- Following a path of convergence on the US economy facilitates integration within the Caribbean, reducing transactions costs within the region, eliminating exchange rate uncertainty, and facilitating mobility of capital and skills. That increases the region's viability, reduces the incentives for polarisation that will draw industry away from the Caribbean and thereby lessens the tensions inherent in the Caribbean-North American relationship.

The Caribbean and Latin America

Economic links between the Caribbean and Latin America are few and isolated. Each has a specific motivation and history, and carries no implications for the trend in Caribbean-Latin American relationships. They are unlikely to intensify with present trends and current policies. The Caribbean's geographical location suggests that it might attract financial and trading services for commerce between North and South America. Panama and Miami, at the southern and northern ends of the Caribbean, have developed these markets extensively. Only a few Caribbean countries have the institutions, legal framework, telecommunications and linguistic skills to attract such business. Significantly, the US dollar is the domestic currency in both Panama and Miami.

Oil is by far the most important product in Caribbean-Latin American trade. Crude oil from Venezuela is processed in Curaçao and Trinidad, while Venezuela and Trinidad are the principal suppliers of oil to the insular Caribbean. Oil is the only significant Mexican export to the Caribbean.

Other Caribbean-Latin American trade is small. Between Guyana and Brazil there is a little trade in beef, gold and consumer goods, but Guyana's communications with Brazil are poor, and confined to the Amazonian state of Roraima, where the population is sparse. Belize, among the smallest of Caribbean economies, imports a small portion of its consumption needs across its border with Mexico. Venezuela exports foods to Curaçao in colourful wooden boats which are a tourist attraction in Curaçao. Argentinian processed meats are imported throughout the Caribbean, but seldom directly from Argentina.

Latin American tourists to the Caribbean comprise mainly Venezuelans visiting Barbados and the Netherlands Antilles. Their numbers fell dramatically with the decline in oil prices in 1981, and the subsequent fall in the value of the bolivar. Close family links between Venezuela and Trinidad have produced some migration between them, but the flows are not large. There has been no other migration of note between the Caribbean and Latin America in the postwar period.

Curaçao and Cayman are hosts to financial and trading companies which have a substantial Latin American clientele. However most of this business from Latin America favours location in Panama and Miami.

Both the Caribbean and Latin America have shown an interest in strengthening economic links. Venezuela has been most active, initiating a Caribbean Oil Facility jointly with Mexico in 1975, to provide credit for oil purchases by Caribbean countries. Credit accumulated in bolivars or pesos can be used to finance purchases of Venezuelan and Mexican goods and services, at favourable interest and repayment terms. The fund has financed low cost housing in Barbados and Jamaica.

In 1992 Venezuela announced free trade access for exports from CARI-COM members. It is too early to assess the impact. Venezuela maintains a network of cultural and language institutes throughout the Caribbean, and its universities have established a tradition of Caribbean scholarship. Colombia has made efforts to strengthen economic and cultural links with the Caribbean, to a much lesser extent than has Venezuela. Arrangements have been made for trade credits for exports from Caribbean countries to Colombia.

Colombia, Mexico and Venezuela provide finance to the Caribbean through the Caribbean Development Bank (CDB). The Caribbean also has access to finance from BLADEX, the Latin American bank for export finance, with headquarters in Panama.

There are numerous meetings and interchanges among officials and policy makers of the Caribbean and Latin America, often through such agencies as the UN Economic Commission for Latin America and the Caribbean (ECLAC), the Centre for Latin American Monetary Studies (CEMLA), the Latin American Integration Secretariat (SELA) and the Organisation of American States (OAS). CARICOM has established ongoing contacts for discussion of mutual concerns such as GATT and hemispheric free trade with Latin American integration groups such as MERCOSUR (Argentina, Brazil, Paraguay and Uruguay) and the Andean Group (Bolivia, Colombia, Ecuador, Peru and Venezuela).

None of the current strands of the Caribbean-Latin American relationship is sufficiently robust to promise a deepening of the relationships over time. If the Caribbean is to take advantage of its geography to become an important centre for commerce between the Americas, countries of the region will have to take major initiatives. Treaties to eliminate liability to double taxation on a single source of income must be negotiated. More widespread linguistic versatility is needed, particularly in English-speaking countries. A major effort to inform Latin America of the Caribbean's capabilities and the services being offered is also required.

Global Changes affecting Caribbean-North American Relations

The advent of floating exchange rates among major international currencies in the 1970s created dilemmas for the Caribbean and strengthened their link to the US. At that time the currencies of the Dominican Republic and Haiti had their values fixed in terms of US dollars, but those of the rest of the Caribbean were linked to European currencies. With the exception of the French Antilles they all switched to pegging their currencies to the US dollar during the 1970s, because that was the currency of most of their external transactions. That reinforced the bias towards the North American market, away from the swings and uncertainties of commerce with Europe. Traditional exports such as sugar and bananas continued to be sold to Europe, and the Caribbean's share of European tourists increased, but the receipts from these transactions were subject to wide exchange fluctuations. There was very little expansion of agricultural and manufacturing exports to Europe or other non-US destinations. Non-US markets in all activities, including tourism, were seen as a form of export insurance, in case of a depressed US market, rather than as the primary market for any export or service.

Lacklustre US economic performance in the 1980s reduced the official and private financing made available to the Caribbean, but appears to have had little effect on trade and services. The growth of US holiday making abroad remained robust, and the Caribbean retained its share. The Caribbean's share of US imports of minerals, agricultural produce and manufactured goods is so small that no correlation may be detected between the performance of the US economy and the volume of Caribbean trade. However, the amount of US official financing to the region was reduced as part of the effort to reduce the federal budget deficit (even though the amount of US financing to the Caribbean was so small that savings would have made no measurable impact on the deficit). The crisis over sovereign credits by US banks led to a general cutback of financing to all Caribbean countries, even those whose payments record remained impeccable.

The fact that the US has lost some of its pre-eminence in the world economy does not materially affect the Caribbean's economic options, as is sometimes suggested. The North American market more than exhausts the Caribbean's productive capacity, so the relative performance of Europe and Japan hardly matters. The Caribbean continues to have more than ample marketing opportunities, and can therefore attract the investment needed to take advantage of them, from North America as well as from Far Eastern and European entrepreneurs eager to gain access to North America.

The end of the Cold War has no meaningful implications for the level of North American official finance for the Caribbean. The battle with communism for the hearts and minds of the Caribbean people was lost almost before it began; communist parties never held the allegiance of more than a handful of people in any Caribbean territory, with the exception of Cuba. The communist People's Progressive Party of Guyana, the only one to have any substantial following, based its support on racial solidarity rather than on political ideology. The popular belief that perceived threats of communists gaining power motivated the US to provide extra finance to the Caribbean is not supported by evidence. The per capita official development assistance for countries such as St Kitts and Barbados, where there was never any suspicion of a radical government, was no lower than for Grenada and Guyana, where unstable and undemocratic governments held power for some time.

There has emerged competition from the Eastern bloc countries for official development assistance and technical skills. This is a potentially serious threat, particularly as the technical skills deployed for the analysis of Caribbean problems is scarce in any case, because of the countries' small size. Able and experienced technicians, researchers and policy makers tend to move on from the Caribbean to larger countries and areas relatively quickly, leaving the field to a succession of the young and inexperienced. This has led to superficial analysis and policy error. The situation is aggravated by the pull from Eastern Europe and the former Soviet bloc, but the impact should not be exaggerated. Caribbean specialists have no comparative advantage in Eastern Europe and the lure of working in that part of the world has already begun to wear off, in the harsh light of social and political condition in those countries.

The revolution in telecommunications looks to have a very profound impact on the Caribbean. It has created a vast new market in information services, making what were formerly domestic services into tradeable commodities. Some of the technically feasible services have shown more promise than others, but processing of forms, publishing and design are areas of rapid growth where the Caribbean may provide competitive services. The telecommunications revolution has reduced the importance of the Caribbean's proximity to North America, but the region's relatively high levels of education and skill give it a competitive edge in this field. The telecommunications revolution also has begun to affect the way firms are structured, with greater dispersion of function and the spin-off of service activities. Both trends may offer greater opportunities for the Caribbean.

The Future of Caribbean-North American Integration

There will inevitably be a high degree of trade integration between the Caribbean and North America into the indefinite future. The ratio of imports from North America to Caribbean GDP when projected into the future implies continuing high import penetration, even if there is no change in policy. Lowering of tariffs results in no measurable intensification of North American import penetration. High variability of the exchange rate of the dollar to other international currencies should strengthen the trade link to the US, but Caribbean preferences may mitigate against that tendency. A preference for Japanese automobiles has persisted despite the wide fluctuations in the US dollar value of the yen in the past decade.

No change in the destinations of traditional Caribbean exports is expected, but traditional exports are set to decline because of the contraction of volumes under the negotiated marketing arrangements for these products. Manufactured and non-traditional exports are almost exclusively for the North American market; the potential for growth in this area would expand significantly if arrangements for a Caribbean-North America FTA resulted in significant lowering of the present non-tariff barriers, but the prospects are not encouraging. The specialisation in exports for the North American market continues under any scenario, with or without NAFTA, whether or not the Uruguay round of GATT negotiations is brought to a successful conclusion. NAFTA threatens to slow the growth of non-traditional exports if the Caribbean fails to achieve immediate parity with Mexico, however.

The North American share of tourists to the Caribbean has not declined, despite the opening up of new business from Europe in the 1980s. In addition to growing numbers of conventional 'long-stay' visitors the Caribbean has seen phenomenal growth of cruise tourism. The emerging information services industry in the Caribbean serves the North American market almost exclusively. Other international services such as banking, trusts, insurance and trading have some European and Latin American clients, but their business is preponderantly North American.

Investment is coming to the Caribbean from the Far East and Europe, but as far as one may tell the majority of investment continues to originate in North America. North American investment covers all major areas of new investment in the Caribbean – tourism, manufacturing, agriculture, minerals, services. Investment from the Far East gravitates towards manufacturing, while most EC investment is for tourism.

No change is likely in the pattern of migration and remittances, both heavily biased towards North America. Ties of family and history, and Puerto Rico's political link with the US, ensure that migration will continue to be an important link between the Caribbean and North America. Remittances should decline in relative importance if overall Caribbean economic performance improves, but the actual amount should continue to increase.

Travel and telecommunications reinforce the trade bond to North America. They foster aspirations to the artefacts of the North American lifestyle, and the variety, styles, products and services that go along with it.

The extent of Caribbean-North American integration, for all countries except the French Caribbean (but including Haiti), will continue to strengthen, whatever the fate of NAFTA or world trading arrangements.

NAFTA does have the potential to slow Caribbean exports, if it contains provisions that benefit Mexico at the Caribbean's expense, but it will not weaken the Caribbean's links to North America or divert exports elsewhere. In the Uruguay round of international trade deliberations the proposed agreements on services are of special interest to the Caribbean because they are a potential growth area for the region. There should be no regulations to protect monopolies that would deny the Caribbean access to technology needed to be competitive in services. This is another source of danger of loss of export potential, but it will not affect the degree of integration into the North American market.

The concept of the Enterprise of the Americas, with which the Caribbean reluctantly acquiesced, is that countries of Latin America and the Caribbean would successively join NAFTA, the free trade core. Tariffs would be removed bilaterally, subject to special provisions for sensitive items; there would be guidelines on non-tariff barriers and procedures for resolving conflicts over them; and some additional finance and technical assistance was provided for.

Whether NAFTA develops into LAFTA or not is of little consequence for the Caribbean, but the region has specific interests for which it should lobby in every available forum. Interests include the elimination of trade restrictions on clothing; liberal and equitable stipulations about the domestic content of duty free imports and an effective framework for eliminating unwanted non-tariff barriers. Both the provisions of CUFTA and bilateral treaties the US has negotiated with Caribbean countries have been ineffectual. The Caribbean should also lobby for greater financial flows from the US to the Caribbean, to combat the danger of economic polarisation away from the Caribbean as the integration of the northern part of the hemisphere intensifies.

Except for the last item, the Caribbean might be better served by negotiations within the GATT framework. There the Caribbean does not face the dilemma that confronts Lomé signatories in negotiating entry to North American free trade. Under the provisions of Lomé the EC would be entitled to free trade access to Caribbean markets as well. As it stands the EAI is a poor bargain for the Caribbean. The additional finance and debt relief offered are very small, in relation to the needs of all of Latin America; the proposed mechanisms for resolving conflicts over non-tariff barriers are unconvincing and exceptions for clothing are to be retained. Caribbean countries would need to restructure their tax systems as a result of accession to the FTA because they would lose a major source of revenue, which would have to be replaced.

Free trade in the Americas is to the advantage of the Caribbean only if it leads to greater free trade globally. Many supporters of NAFTA, CUFTA and LAFTA argue that this succession of agreements is the least painful progression towards global free trade, serving to condition US public opinion towards an outward orientation, away from an isolationism that impoverishes the US and reduces growth prospects for the rest of the world. The detractors of the NAFTA are represented as protagonists of an ineffectual protectionism. But many supporters of openness and global free trade remain profoundly suspicious of the EAI and LAFTA, as attempts at isolationism on a grander scale. The motivation for the EAI, in apparent reaction to the threat of 'Fortress Europe', gave cause for this concern, though that initial motivation seems to have receded with Europe's economic difficulties.

The establishment of a 'Fortress America' in competition with 'Fortress Europe' was never practical. Europe is much less a policy making entity than casual observation and the texts of formal agreements would suggest. This has now become clear, with Europe's dithering over every major political crisis since the Gulf War, and the recent economic conflicts within the alliance. The history, economics and politics of American societies make for even greater difficulties in engineering an American economic community. With fewer rich countries and very large and populous poor countries like Brazil and Mexico the prospect that the Americas will emulate the European example of free movement of capital, labour and commodities is remote.

There is therefore no foundation for the argument, advocated by the US State Department and supported by some Caribbean intellectuals, that the Caribbean must climb quickly aboard the EAI/LAFTA train for fear that the region will be left stranded and alone. So far is the train from departure that its makeup, cargo and destination have yet to be determined – indeed, it remains uncertain whether there will be a LAFTA train or not. More to the point, the Caribbean is already on the march, LAFTA or no, and has been for generations, through migration, exports, tourism, business connections and imports, and this commerce continues unabated.

The Caribbean should focus on cooperative mechanisms to address their joint interests with North America, and on the development of institutions for collaboration and interchange, many of which have existed for decades: the Pan American Health Organisation, the Organisation of American States, the Latin American Centre for Monetary Studies (CEMLA), the Inter American Development Bank. The establishment of regional coordinating mechanisms is the fastest way to make real progress on the issues material to the ongoing relationship between the Caribbean and North America, and this process is helpful in the deepening sentiment towards an outward orientation for the US, since all these organisations form part of global networks.

The removal of Caribbean tariffs on imports from North America will have no noticeable impact on US exports. Exports to the Caribbean total less than the margin of error in US trade statistics. The removal of Caribbean tariffs is clearly not vital to US interests. It may harm some Caribbean industries where tariffs are high. However, most protection in the Caribbean is by way of non-tariff barriers in agriculture, where genuinely free world markets do not exist and the prices quoted on international exchanges reflect a considerable element of national subsidy for producers in industrial countries.

The Caribbean may take unilateral action to intensify integration with the US by instituting policy régimes that fix their currency values to the US dollar. This strategy keeps inflation as low as in the US, reduces the cost of US-Caribbean commerce, encourages investment in the Caribbean and removes the incentive for capital flight. There are no meaningful disadvantages. In theory a flexible exchange rate offers scope to adjust to temporary export shortfalls by temporary expansion in government spending, but in practice government expansions are never temporary. Removing this possibility is therefore a benefit to the economy.

The free movement of capital and labour holds out the prospect of faster growth for the Caribbean. Unfortunately the US will not permit free labour movement for countries which are independent of its political jurisdiction. Caribbean countries should however aim to maximise labour mobility within the region. The degree of labour mobility will ultimately be determined by a complex of factors, including shared language, economic disparities, size, the degree of economic concentration in a few locales, political divisions and cultural affinities. The strongest currents will continue to run between the US and Caribbean nations, rather than within the Caribbean. However, the volume and direction of labour flows will be influenced by policies which Caribbean nations put in place. Policy should aim for the fastest trajectory for removing restrictions on labour movement within the region, compatible with political reality.

Exchange controls on capital movements might also be removed, except for a monitor on large transactions to discourage currency speculation. However, the changeover to a régime of liberal controls should be undertaken only after the external value of the currency has been stabilised and the central bank's foreign exchange reserves are adequate to sustain it. Liberalising the capital account with an unstable exchange rate institutionalises hoarding in foreign currency.

The Caribbean has at its disposal powerful measures to deepen integration among members and with North America, to the region's benefit. Currency stability, capital mobility and labour mobility within the region do not involve negotiation with the US, Canada or Mexico. Policies for currency stability are now fairly well understood; for some English-speaking countries monetary union and a common currency will make them more easily attainable. Stable currencies make free capital movement possible without the danger of exchange rate crises. Labour mobility may be introduced in incremental fashion to take account of the political realities of the region, beginning with the proposal for the English-speaking Caribbean recommended by the West Indian Commission.

The principal issues for negotiation with North America are effective mechanisms to remove remaining barriers to Caribbean exports, soliciting additional finance to develop human resources and infrastructure in the Caribbean, and measures to accelerate technology transfer. No progress has been made on the removal of non-tariff barriers or protection for garments, either in the CUFTA or NAFTA. The laboriously negotiated provisions for ensuring fair trade in the CUFTA have proven a dead letter, and the same may be expected of comparable provisions in NAFTA.

The Caribbean abounds with evidence of the benefit of expenditure on infrastructure and human development. Further investment is required, especially in areas where there is the greatest disparity with North America and therefore the greatest danger that economic integration, which is inevitable, will intensify motives for emigration from the Caribbean. Investment that reduces the deficiencies in Caribbean economic and social infrastructure – hospitals, transport facilities, schools, public utilities – helps promote return migration to the Caribbean. Returning migrants are fewer in number than emigrants, but they boast much higher levels of skill, on average.

The Caribbean cannot be on the cutting edge of technology, but it needs to employ modern methods, which make most effective use of its relatively skilled workforce. Incentives should be biased in this direction, and technical assistance sought from North America to speed up the transfer of knowledge, techniques, market developments and new systems of organisation.

Notes

1. CARICOM is the economic community of English-speaking Caribbean countries, comprising Antigua and Barbuda, the Bahamas, Barbados, Belize, Dominica, Grenada, Guyana, Jamaica, Montserrat, St Kitts and

Nevis, St Lucia, St Vincent and the Grenadines, and Trinidad and Tobago. The British Virgin Islands and the Turks and Caicos Islands are associate members.

2. Theodore Mesmer, 'The English-speaking Caribbean and the Alliance for Progress Years', (Washington, DC: Friends of the Alliance for Progress 1992).

3. Barry Eichengreen, 'One Money for Europe? Lessons from the USA Currency Union', *Economic Policy*, April 10, (1990).

4. John Whalley, 'ACUSATA and NAFTA: Can LAFTA be far behind?', *Journal of Common Market Studies*, 30: (1992).

5. Peter Robson, 'The New Regionalism and Development Countries', *Journal of Common Market Studies*, 31:3 (1993).

6. Michael Emerson, D. Gros, A. Italianer, J. Pisani-Ferry and H. Reichenbach, *One Market, One Money*,(Oxford: Oxford University Press, 1992).

7. Jaime Melo, A. Panagariya and Dani Rodrik, 'The New Regionalism: A Country Perspective' (World Bank Working Paper, 1993).

8. Unfortunately, the few empirical analyses of Caribbean integration which have so far been attempted failed to incorporate realistic assumptions, leading to misleading results. See World Bank, 1990, critically analysed in Hilaire *et al*, 1990.

9. Intra-CARICOM exports for 1990 were US$526.8 million (Marshall, 1992, Table 4). Intra-CARICOM travellers accounted for an estimated 13 percent of tourists and we assume they account for the same proportion of total expenditure by tourists in CARICOM, estimated at US$1.918.4 (Estimates calculated from CTO, 1993 and IMF, 1992). Exports of oil and related products from Trinidad to other CARICOM countries were US$101.5 million (SITC sections 3 and 7, Trinidad and Tobago Central Statistical Office, 1993). The proportion of exports and tourism that might have been affected by tariffs works out at 55 percent. This is overstated because of the exclusion of traded services other than tourism.

10. The higher figures often quoted – in excess of 10 per cent – are arrived at by omitting services, an extraordinary oversight in a region where tourism is the principal traded commodity.

11. These effects are known in the economic jargon as economies of scale, economies of scope and external economies.

12. Paul Krugman, *Geography and Trade*, (Cambridge, Mass: MIT Press, 1991)

13. Inter-American Development Bank, *Economic and Social Progress in Latin America: Report*, Washington, DC., 1993.

14. UNCTAD, 'Human Development Report', New York: United Nations (1993)

15. Norman, Girvan, *The Caribbean Bauxite Industry*, Kingston, Jamaica, Institute of Social and Economic Research (1967).

16. DeLisle Worrell, 'A Common Currency for CARICOM', St Michael, Barbados: West Indian Commission (1992a).

17. Elhanan Helpman, 'Endogenous Macroeconomic Growth Theory', *European Economic Review*, 36:1&2 (1992).

18. Too often in the Caribbean, interest rate policy has been targeted on current rates of inflation which are high during the period of transition to the new régime, either because of the devaluation needed to eliminate the parallel market or because of the unrecorded inflation that preceded the adjustment, where controls had driven activity underground. This results in very high nominal interest rates – implying very high real rates if the adjustment measures prove successful in curbing inflation – which themselves become a source of ongoing inflation, undermining confidence in the adjustment strategy.

19. *Money Index*, 28 September 1993, p.3, Kingston, Jamaica.

20. G.W. Roberts and D.O. Mills, *Study of External Migration Affecting Jamaica, 1953–55*, (Kingston, Jamaica: Institute of Social and Economic Research, 1958).

21. Edwin Reubens, *Migration and Development in the West Indies*, (Kingston: Jamaica, Institute of Social and Economic Research, [Undated]).

22. Havelock Brewster and Clive Thomas, *The Dynamics of West Indian Economic Integration*, (Kingston, Jamaica: Institute of Social and Economic Research, 1967)

23. B.S. Keirstead and Kari Levitt,), *Inter-Territorial Freight Rates and the Federal Shipping Service*, (Kingston, Jamaica: Institute of Social and Economic Research,1963)

24. Steve De Castro, *Problems of the Caribbean Air Transport Industry*, (Kingston, Jamaica: Institute of Social and Economic Research, 1967).

25. Richard Bernal, 'Caribbean Nations need NAFTA too', *The Washington Times*, October 1, 1993.

26. The weaknesses of the overly interventionist approach to economic development, which informed CARICOM, was pointed out by some economists and policy makers at the time (Blackman, 1982; Worrell, 1980). Many CARICOM member countries deliberately made no effort to implement strongly interventionist policies.

27. Compton Bourne *et al*, *Caribbean Development to the Year 2000: Challenges, Prospects and Policies*, (London: Commonwealth Secretariat, 1988)

28. George Beckford and Norman Girvan, (eds.), *Development in Suspense*, (Kingston, Jamaica: Friedrich Ebert Stiftung,1989).

29. Compton Bourne, and DeLisle Worrell, *Economic Adjusttment Policies for Small Nations*, (New York: Praeger 1989).

30. DeLisle Worrel, Compton Bourne and Dinesh Dodhia, *Financing Development in the Commonwealth Caribbean*, (London: Macmillan, 1991).

31. DeLisle Worrel, 'Economic Policies in Small Open Economies: Prospects for the Caribbean', (London, Commonwealth Secretariat 1992b).

32. Desireé Field-Ridley, 'Toward a CARICOM Single Market and Economy', (Georgetown, Guyana: CARICOM Secretariat 1991).

33. Byron Blake, and Roderick Sanatan, (eds.), 'Profile of Caribbean Services for International Trade', (Working Paper, CARICOM Secretariat, Georgetown, Guyana, 1992).

34. An amount of USA$537 million to end March 1992, with the largest beneficiaries being Jamaica ($248.7 million), Trinidad and Tobago ($135 million) and the Dominican Republic ($76.1 million) (CANA, 1992).

35. The following countries have observer status in various organs of the Caribbean Community: the Dominican Republic, Suriname, the Nether-lands Antilles, Puerto Rico, Mexico, Colombia and Venezuela. At the time of writing (December 1993) full membership for Suriname is reported to be imminent. Haiti's observer status with CARICOM institutions has been suspended because of the coup against President Aristide.

36. C.Y. Thomas, 'Foreign Currency Black Markets: Lessons from Guyana', *Social and Economic Studies*, 38:2, (1989).

37. Kempe Hope, 'The Subterranean Economy', *Caribbean Affairs*, 3:2. (1990).

38. GDP for CARICOM countries for 1990 is US$15.7 billion (calculated from Marshall, 1992, Table 1). Exports are US$15.7 billion and imports $6.4 billion (Marshall, Table 6). Tourism receipts are $3.5 billion and other service receipts $0.8 billion (IMF Balance of Payments Yearbook, 1992), for a total of $15.2 billion of foreign transactions.

39. Pastor gives North America as the principal source of remittances in a survey for Barbados and St Kitts and Nevis. (1985, p.76) For Saint Lucia and St Vincent, the other countries in the survey, the most important source was other Caribbean countries, followed in the former by North America and in the latter by the UK. The study confirms the magnitude of migration to North America, with one estimate of the migrant population as high as 10 percent of the resident population in the Caribbean (p. 12), which suggests the importance of remittances from North America.

40. I discuss the nature of the link between Caribbean and USA financial markets more fully in Worrell (1992). Financial policy in the Caribbean is discussed in Farrell (1986), Danns (1990) and Bourne and Worrell (1987). See Steward and Payne, 1988 for additional references.

41. Downs 92.

42. D. Holder and Worrel.

43. Robert Pastor, (ed.) *Migration and Development in the Caribbean*, (Boulder, Westview, 1985).

44. Samuel Indalmanie and Hygenus Leon, 'Supply Response in the Sugar Industry', (Kingston, Jamaica, Consortium School of Graduate Studies, 1993).

45. Ricardo Grinspun and Maxwell Cameron, 'The Political Economy of North American Free Trade', (New York: St Martin's Press, 1993).

46. Refik Erzan and Alexander Yeats, 'USA-Latin America Free Trade Areas: Some Empirical Evidence,' in Sylvia Saborio and contributors, *The Premise and the Promise: Free Trade in the Americas*, (Washington, DC: Overseas Development Council, 1992).

47. This is the basis for most claims for the benefits of the CBI (Congressional Research Service, 1992; Coppin, 1992).

48. Logically the argument requires a counter-factual, about which views may diverge widely.

49. If the Caribbean joins a North American free trade area that advantage will be lost to Mexico, but by then Mexico may have established a reputation that makes it difficult to attract the attention of new entrants, who might gravitate to the centre which had already established itself, where there would be external economies to be had.

50. See Institute for Research on Public Policy, 1986).

[55]

Caribbean Integration in
Today's World

Sidney Weintraub

Despite much handwriting about the fate of the Caribbean region, GDP growth was satisfactory for the majority of countries during the 1980s, certainly as compared to Latin America. The region's average rate of growth was 2.2 per cent per capita on an unweighted basis[1]. The smaller countries did relatively well, but the larger ones did not. It is clearly premature to proclaim the end of history for the region. (The countries included in the Caribbean as defined here are shown in note 1.)

However, the global situation faced by the countries of the Caribbean is changing rapidly. In the trade field, the Uruguay Round will reduce margins as preference in their main market; and the North American Free Trade Agreement will erode preferences even more in the USA and Canadian markets. The Lomé Convention, while it still has five years to run, is under review and its extension on current terms is questionable. The banana regime in the European Union is under attack and while it may survive for now, its longer-term prospects are not good. Aid flows are declining and increased reliance for capital will have to be placed on domestic savings and foreign investment flows.

The discussion that follows will focus on balance of payments issues – trade in goods and services and capital flows, although these matters cannot be separated from domestic policies. The balance of payments emphasis is justified by the high ratio of exports and goods and services in the generation of GDP of these small countries, coupled with the deep reliance of most of them on capital inflows to finance large current account deficits.[2]

While it is clear that a transformation in external policies of the Caribbean region will have to take place, it is not apparent how much breathing space the countries have to make changes. The policy trajectory of the countries undoubtedly will combine efforts to retain current benefits, while also preparing for their diminution. The adjustments needed vary among the countries and this detail is not easily captured in a brief essay designed to deal generally with the region.

The next section of this essay will lay out the range of views that have been expressed about this combination of policy retention/reform. This will be followed by my own views, differentiated by short and long-term demands. The final section would pose questions about key issues and then provide brief answers that come from the earlier discussion.

Views on Policy Reform

The most extensive and carefully laid out views regarding Caribbean participation in the emerging international economic structure are those of the World Bank. These can be found in a series of studies prepared for the Caribbean Group for Co-operation in Economic Development (CGCED)[3]

The World Bank programme has three core elements:

- World trade is becoming more open, thereby reducing Caribbean preferences in its main markets and Caribbean countries must themselves become more open to imports and cease thereby to burden exports of goods.
- Export emphasis should be placed on non-factor services, particularly tourism, but also such other services as health care, education (particularly higher education), financial, software programming, and information. The World Bank points to past successes in this field, the increase in the share of services in world trade (about 21 per cent in 1991), plus the inclusion of the General Agreement on Trade in Services (GATS) in the Uruguay Round.
- This strategy requires increased reliance on mobilising domestic and foreign savings, led by private sector initiative. However, public sector savings must also be increased. The Bank's proposals call for the public sector to move away from activities that compete with the private sector and to focus instead on the policy framework for development, and to provide the means for the expansion of service exports. The latter include more extensive human resource development, improving infrastructure, and devoting increased attention to environmental protection.[4]

These themes are elaborated in considerable detail in a number of World Bank publications. They are buttressed in detailed studies of each of the countries. There is no reason to repeat the argument here, but the overall World Bank position has an inner coherence that makes it quite persuasive.

The World Bank is equivocal about what it calls the 'NAFTA option,' that is whether or not, Caribbean countries should join the Agreement. However, after listing arguments against seeking membership – few trade preferences over and above those already granted under the USA Caribbean Basin Initiative (CBI) and Canada's Preferential Scheme for the Commonwealth Caribbean (CARIBCAN); the loss of all import protection over a reasonable transition period, and the sacrifice of Lomé preferences – the World Bank concludes that 'the costs of not joining NAFTA would clearly outweigh these considerations'.[5] The basis for this conclusion is that NAFTA membership would prevent erosion of current USA and Canadian preferences and, equally important, reduce the danger of investment diversion.

The 'NAFTA option' is not an immediate issue. The Agreement at the Summit of the Americas does not call for a Free Trade Area of the Americas (FTAA) until the year 2005, and there is no evidence that USA is prepared at present to expand NAFTA beyond Chile, assuming the Congress permits the Administration to go that far.

The World Bank has provided a separate study on the Organisation of Eastern Caribbean States (OECS), for which recommendations must take into account the special conditions in these countries.[6] For the Windward Island countries, other than Grenada, banana exports constitute 50 per cent or more of total merchandise exports (figures for 1992): Dominica 57 per cent, Grenada 17 per cent, St Lucia 60 per cent and St Vincent and the Grenadines 49 percent.[7] Each of these countries exports more goods to Europe than to all other regions combined, whereas for the Caribbean countries as a whole, North America is by far the dominant export destination. In other words, continuation of the banana regime is seen as a *sine qua non* in this region.

It is not necessary here to go into the details of the European Union's revised banana policy adopted as of July 1, 1993, except to note that it is under international challenge.[8] However, because of its importance to the economies of the three main banana exporting Windward Island countries there is every reason for them to fight for continuation of this preference. The World Bank has estimated that the Windward Islands banana exports constitutes close to 20 per cent of GDP in 1992 but the thrust of its position, however, is that Windward Island governments must prepare for a transition to a non-preferential banana regime.

Unlike the recommendations for Caribbean countries generally where a reduction in the level of foreign aid is assumed to be inevitable, the Bank suggests that financial aid to Windward Island banana exporters be increased in their transition away from a preferential regime. This may eventually be accepted because the amounts are modest, but is by no means assured in this era of aid reductions. The other recommendations, however, are similar to those for the Caribbean generally – movement into other economic activities, particularly services, even as efficiency and productivity improvements are sought for the banana industry.

Richard Bernal

Richard Bernal has been quite forceful in seeking some immediate variant of the NAFTA option.[9] Bernal's position encompasses a series of steps eventually leading to full accession to NAFTA by Caribbean countries. 'Orderly accession', is what he calls this. The central feature of the proposal is to give Caribbean countries full access to the markets of NAFTA countries while they, the Caribbean countries, provide reciprocity only over an extended period. The rationale for this gradual reciprocity is that Caribbean countries are not able to provide full reciprocity at this time.

The technique he suggests for accomplishing this is for NAFTA to devise a form of associate membership under which associate members would reach agreement with NAFTA on 'selected issues, sectors and products', while GATT rules would govern other areas.[10] There is a Jamaica-centred aspect to Bernal's discussion. What he proposes is most germane for the bigger English-speaking Caribbean countries, Jamaica and Trinidad and Tobago.

Much of what Bernal proposes may come to pass even without associate membership in NAFTA. Thus, if CBI preferences are broadened to make them more comparable to benefits which Mexico receives under NAFTA, particularly for apparel and other manufactured goods, this would ease much of the potential trade diversion problem of major Caribbean exporters of these products, including Jamaica. The CBI mechanism would provide one-way preferences in the USA market in favour of the CBI countries and not compromise the preferential relations under Lomé that many of these countries now enjoy. What Bernal proposes is essentially a free-trade area under which there is no explicit or reasonable plan and schedule for the elimination of substantially all import barriers among member countries. He wants delayed and unspecified reciprocity on the part of the Caribbean countries. This suggestion, unless modified, would not conform to Article XXIV of the

GATT. Nor would special arrangements on particular sectors be applicable if the preferences were reciprocal.

The CBI legislation proposed in 1994 by the USA Administration, and which is likely to be incorporated in any CBI bill that has a chance of congressional approval, includes some reciprocity on the part of CBI countries for improving conditions for foreign direct investment and protecting intellectual property. If this is done on a Most Favoured Nation (MFN) basis, this would not contravene provisions of GATT.

Consideration of CBI legislation is pending in congressional committees of the USA House of Representatives and Senate as this is written. There is no certainty that such legislation will be enacted by this Congress, or that its final form will be identical to what is now in the separate bills. As now configured, CBI countries would receive import treatment in the United States comparable to what Mexico receives under NAFTA for apparel and most other manufactured and agriculture products now excluded from benefits. In return, CBI countries would have to provide more favourable treatment for foreign direct investment and protection of intellectual property on an MFN basis. Finally, one of the pending bills sets forth procedures for completing negotiations for accession to NAFTA by CBI countries no later than 2005, the date set at the Miami Summit of the Americas for establishing the FTAA[11] provides the beginnings of a plan and schedule missing from Bernal's proposal.

Nevertheless, the bills as now structured would move a long way toward what Bernal proposes, at least with respect to USA treatment of merchandise imports from Caribbean countries. They would not, however, cross over into more ambiguous territory of preferential sectoral arrangements or setting out a free-trade area without a definite plan and schedule.

R. DeLisle Worrell

A somewhat different vision of greater Caribbean insertion in the world economic system is provided by Worrell.[12] Worrell's position is that tariff and non-tariff barriers hardly affect intra-Caribbean integration or integration with North America. He gives primary stress to reducing transportation and transaction costs and freedom of movement of capital and labour within the Caribbean region. He goes beyond this by advocating not only fixed exchange rates for Caribbean countries, but also monetary union among them with an independent central bank.

In this vision, the nature of the integration between the Caribbean and North America is presented more by what is not possible than by what is.

Some form of equitable relationship is needed, but Worrell states that it must take into account 'that neither side wishes to allow for full integration, with freedom of labour movement and automatic mechanisms for fiscal transfers from USA to disadvantaged regions of the Caribbean. [13]

Worrell also asserts that free trade in the Americas will benefit the Caribbean only if it leads to free trade globally. He expresses concern over the growth of USA isolationism leading to a 'Fortress America' competing with a 'Fortress Europe', although the evidence for this outcome is skimpy, particularly now that the Uruguay Round has been completed. His central argument is that the Caribbean can by itself, without negotiation with NAFTA, deepen its integration through currency stability and capital and labour mobility within the region.

There are some common themes in these various visions of greater Caribbean insertion in the world economy. Worrell devotes special attention to coordinated policies in the English-speaking Caribbean, but all the other proposals, either explicitly or implicitly, make clear the importance of coherent and economically sound national and regional policies for foreign economic policy to succeed. Worrell, however, gives much more attention to monetary union in the English-speaking Caribbean than to do the other commentaries listed here. The others focus much more directly on trade and investment links.

Both the World Bank and Bernal argue for eventual accession of Caribbean countries to NAFTA. Bernal is more specific on the path to this objective, namely associate membership, but his presentation is less complete than that of the Bank on how smaller countries should move in this direction. The Bank, Bernal, and the Lande-Crigler paper, all cover the possible trade diversion, coupled with investment diversion, that could affect Caribbean countries as a result of more ample preferences to Mexico under NAFTA than exist in the CBI. The issue, as all of them agree, is how to mitigate these adverse effects on the Caribbean until the countries are ready for accession to NAFTA.

The differences are largely in their selective emphases, but these are crucial in that a particular emphasis implies a de-emphasis of another aspect. Where should the primary emphasis or emphases be placed?

On building up the ability to export services, as the World Bank proposes? This requires attracting much foreign investment.

Focusing for now on improvement of the CBI and leave questions of NAFTA accession for a later day?

Or, instead, focus on the path to eventual accession and thereby seek to alter the CBI from a unilateral USA grant of benefits to a contract in which the Caribbean has a voice when the United States seeks to make changes in CBI provisions?

Face head-on now the choice between continuing Lomé preferences or obtaining NFTA accession? This is a sub-category of the NAFTA-CBI priority issue.

For countries which export substantially to the EU, such as the main Windward Island banana exporters, how to combine retaining these benefits while also making a transition leading to their eventual loss?

Focus now on the monetary, capital, and labour issues that Worrell recommends?

Finally, should we exercise the great power that lies in inertia – to continue what is now being done, at least for those countries for which it has worked in raising per capita incomes.

The foregoing are listed as competing emphases, although there are overlaps. Many of them require decisions not just from Caribbean countries, but also negotiation with others, particularly USA, but also NAFTA as a whole, the EU with respect to Lomé and bananas, and within the Caribbean. However, it is important for the Caribbean countries to know what are their negotiation objectives. They may not be fully achieved in an actual negotiation but then, any participant in a negotiation must establish a set of priorities. It is to this that the paper turns next.

Setting Priorities

Four considerations must loom large as Caribbean countries consider actions for greater insertion into the world economy. These are the following:

The world-trading situation is changing. Margins of preference, where they exist, are declining for Caribbean countries, whether under CBI, CARIB-CAN, Lomé, or the various systems of preference of the industrial countries. NAFTA even reverses many Caribbean preferences in that these countries, formerly favoured by the CBI and CARIBCAN, now face discrimination as compared with Mexico.[14] The new EU banana regime is an exception in that rather than narrowing the scope of preferences, it has extended them to EU countries where they did not exist before, especially Germany. One country's preference is another's discrimination. This is an important reason for the adverse international reaction to the EU action.

Official capital flows to Caribbean countries clearly are declining and the region must rely increasingly on private flows. Two other features of financial flows should be highlighted. These are the importance of foreign direct investment (FDI) and the substantial level of remittances from persons of

Caribbean origin living outside the region. The level of national savings is quite low in many Caribbean countries, which means that it is imperative to attract foreign savings.[15] Current account deficits in relation to GDP are also quite large throughout the Caribbean, which also brings out the importance of capital inflows.[16] Policies that impede financial inflows into the Caribbean are clearly self-defeating.[17] The World Bank analysis is surely correct, that prospects for greater insertion into the world economy are more promising in the service sector for most Caribbean countries than in the goods sector. The most promising service activities require a great degree of openness – to FDI, the movement of personnel into the Caribbean countries for providing many services, and extensive interconnections with the outside world. The last is evident in tourist services, and for communications, education, health, record keeping, and others. A highly educated national population is an imperative for success in many of these service activities.[18] The major market for Caribbean exports, whether of goods or services, is North America. The main exception to this statement is for banana exporters who benefit from EU preferences. North America, if anything, is likely to grow in importance as the destination for Caribbean exports. This leads to the inevitable conclusion that as export policy is fashioned, the emphasis for most countries should be on North America – USA in particular.

The last of these considerations should perhaps be analysed first because this forces consideration of a number of choices: North America versus Europe; Lomé versus NAFTA; continuation of the CBI versus something more in the nature of a contract with the rest of North America; the short term versus the long term.

For the important banana producers of the Windward Islands, there is little choice in the short term other than to fight for continuation of the EU preferences. It does not follow that these preferences must be fashioned as the EU recently chose to do under which the benefits go primarily to EU middlemen rather than to producers in the Caribbean. But unless, and until, the resources from banana exports can be replaced by something else, the exporters have little option.

However, the international clamour against the current banana preferences may force change in the longer term, regardless of the desires of the Caribbean exporters. These countries, even as they fight for continuation, must also consider their extrication options. Even if the revenue from banana exports were to be replaced by foreign aid, as the World Bank analysts suggest, this would not be a long-term solution. Foreign aid is likely to be limited in time.

Short-term/long-term options arise as well as for other countries in the Caribbean. The most important short-term option for their export aspirations is improvement in the benefits of the CBI to reduce the preferences in favour of Mexico for their most important merchandise exports especially apparel.[19] There is already some evidence of export diversion away from the Caribbean to Mexico for apparel and this is likely to increase as investors take advantage of Mexico's depreciated exchange rate and expand investment there. But parity with Mexico in this sector is a short-term solution – a ten-year solution as import quotas under the multi-fibre arrangement in the GATT are phased out. Then the competition from low-cost Asian producers is likely to become more intense than it is today, despite tariff preferences that will remain.

However, the most important short-term/long-term issue centres on the unilateral decision-making that exists under the CBI. Currently USA need not consult with CBI countries as it adds or removes items from benefits, or even as it removes countries for some infraction of the USA legislation. This is seen against having another kind of contract under which the two sides, the CBI countries and USA have a voice in decisions. For the short term, improvement of the CBI is really the only feasible option for more beneficial access to the USA market. Neither the Caribbean countries nor USA is ready for NAFTA accession negotiations.[20] For the long term, NAFTA accession – a contract, not a grant – may be an option for the Caribbean countries.[21]

The World Bank endorses the NAFTA option. So do Bernal and Lande-Crigler. Worrell is equivocal. The value of NAFTA accession is not self-evident for the Caribbean countries. Worrell correctly points out that USA and Canadian import barriers against most Caribbean exports are not onerous. Indeed, most enter duty free under CBI and CARIBCAN. The USA general system of preferences (GSP) gives further beneficial treatment to many imports from the region. If CBI benefits can be improved, why undertake the wrenching liberalisation that NAFTA would require?

The response of the NAFTA accession proponents is that a comprehensive free-trade agreement of this nature is about much more than border barriers, whether tariffs or non-tariffs measures. A contract assures continuity of policy, both on the import side by current and future NAFTA members, and on the export side in favour of the Caribbean countries. The lack of a precise contract has in fact made liberalisation within CARICOM slow and uneven because, if there were a contract, equivocation tactics would be less acceptable. NAFTA is not just a trade agreement. One can argue that from the Mexican viewpoint, the more relevant aspect is the incentive it gives to direct investors – domestic, North American, or other. This would be true for Caribbean countries as well.

Even this distinction between trade and investment is artificial because the two are inseparable. The attraction of Mexico for corporations in the United

States and increasingly those in Canada is the ability for co-production, in maquiladoras and elsewhere. Proximity facilitates the production of components in any location for eventual assembly in other locations for marketing in any of them. The Caribbean would have this attraction as well.

And even this attraction is hardly the complete story. Entry into a free-trade agreement demands national macro- and microeconomic policy measures that do not frustrate investors or producers. The cost of incorrect policies can be high – as Mexico is now learning – but the benefits of correct policies can be more substantial for the smaller countries than for the large. NAFTA accession, whatever its pitfalls for Caribbean countries, would demand discipline for them that does not now exist.

It is here, really, where I part company with Worrell. He asserts the following: 'The principal issues for negotiations with North America are effective mechanisms to remove remaining barriers to Caribbean exports, soliciting additional finance to develop human resources and infrastructure in the Caribbean, and measures to accelerate technology transfer.'[22] Fair enough, but why divorce these objectives from Caribbean accession to NAFTA? Will the additional finance to develop human resources and infrastructure come from more aid or from foreign investment? Under what circumstances will this investment be optimised, within or outside of NAFTA? Will technology transfer be more likely if NAFTA provided the certainty of treatment that is now lacking? Will the investment in the kinds of service industries the Caribbean countries should seek – particularly those involving technology transfer – be more likely if they were members of NAFTA than if they were not?

Worrell argues that the Caribbean countries already have at their disposal powerful measures to integrate their economies to achieve currency stability and capital and labour mobility, and he divorces these from NAFTA negotiation. Why haven't the Caribbean countries taken these measures already? The question he should ask himself, I think, is whether NAFTA membership would provide incentives for the very internal integrative measures he advocates.

The issue of Caribbean accession to NAFTA is not a burning issue in the USA. It may never be from an economic viewpoint because the markets are small.[23] NAFTA accession may not be a burning issue in most Caribbean countries either, but many of them have a greater stake in the NAFTA option than does the USA. In any event, to repeat what was stated earlier, the question of NAFTA accession is not an immediate one for either side. But as we move from the short to the longer term – as we move toward 2005 and the possibility of concluding negotiations for an FTAA – plans must be set in motion for

NAFTA or a related option. The initiative for this will rest more with the Caribbean countries than with the NAFTA countries.

Should the decision be made to plan for NAFTA accession, this of course will require some consideration of the preferences the Commonwealth Caribbean countries now enjoy in the EU. Few critics have been prepared to face this issue head on, at least not now.[24] Neither am I. A positive decision on the NAFTA option means the end of Lomé unless the Caribbean countries were prepared to eliminate substantially all import barriers on an MFN basis – which is unlikely. Giving up Lomé preferences surely is not an option that countries of the Windward Islands are prepared to consider, certainly not now while they enjoy banana preferences.[25] Giving up the Lomé preferences would be less of a wrenching issue for many other Caribbean countries, such as Antigua and Barbuda, The Bahamas, and Trinidad and Tobago. Only 17.5 per cent of Caribbean exports went to Europe in 1990, and the percentage was lower for the three countries mentioned.

A few points can be made, however. To the extent that service exports are expanded, Lomé preferences become less important for the generality of Caribbean countries. In any event, even for goods, margins of preference are diminishing. If the EU were prepared to provide general preferences to Commonwealth Caribbean countries, as the United States now does for African-Caribbean-Pacific beneficiaries of Lomé, the cost of giving up Lomé preferences would be further diminished. If banana preferences were phased out as a result of international pressure and replaced by official aid, it would be desirable for USA to share in providing this assistance so that it is not seen as something that requires a trade *quid pro quo* to the EU from the Caribbean countries.

Relevant Questions

As stated repeatedly in this essay, Lomé banana exporters must battle for continuation of their preferences in the absence of any tangible alternative.

Caribbean countries generally must seek improvement of CBI benefits in the light of potential trade and investment diversion stemming from superior preferences to Mexico under NAFTA.

The future of most Caribbean countries is more promising in expanding and developing service industries – tourism, finance, teleports, record keeping, health, education, and various professional activities – than for goods. This, of course, does not mean advances are not possible in the production of agricultural and manufactured products.

Finally, none of this obviates the need to begin planning for a world structure of trade in goods and services that will be radically different from what exists today. The following questions elucidate this:

Where should be the focus on Caribbean insertion into the world economy?

The answer, is on USA and, because of what is happening in North America, on NAFTA.

Should the Caribbean countries begin now to prepare themselves for NAFTA accession?

Yes. This does not mean foregoing improvement of the CBI in the short term. Indeed, the reciprocity that is certain to be asked of CBI countries if USA legislation is enacted will include placing fewer restrictions on FDI and increased protection of intellectual property. These commitments will be necessary in any event in negotiations for accession to NAFTA.

What does preparation for NAFTA accession mean?

When the statement is made that most Caribbean countries are not ready to enter NAFTA, this refers normally to shortcomings in macro- and micro-ecoomic policies. Thus, preparation for NAFTA accession refers primarily to policy measures in the individual countries plus the strengthening of CARICOM. The actions that Worrell advocates would fit into this preparation. So, too, would other measures of the type discussed in World Bank studies, such as defining the roles of the public and private sectors, taking measures to increase domestic savings, encouraging capital inflows and capital mobility, eliminating many import barriers, unification of exchange rates, and moving towards a low, preferably uniform, common external tariff for CARICOM.

What would accession to NAFTA signify for economic relations with non-NAFTA countries?

This, of course, would require giving up EU-Lomé preferences. In the end, this might prove to be an absolute impediment to NAFTA accession for those countries that rely heavily on exports to the EU, even if not for all Caribbean countries. However, the nature of EU preferences, of the future Lomé, will be clearer in the 10 years between now and 2005, when the negotiations for the FTAA are projected to be completed. Lomé itself comes up for renewal in 2002 and the prospects about its continuation in the present form are uncertain now that the EU has been expanded to new members with their own economic interests.

Nothing is lost if countries take measures to strengthen their economic structures even if, at the end of the day, NAFTA accession proves to be impossible, either because of their situations or USA recalcitrance. Membership in a free-trade area does not mean giving up trade with non-member countries.

This is particularly true for trade in services where, for the most part, preferential arrangements do not apply. Even if North Americans predominate, tourists come from all over. Telecommunications are global. Financial services can be provided to all comers.

Is unity of Caribbean countries necessary to achieve long-term objectives?

In the best of all worlds, probably yes. In the world as it actually exists, probably not. It is clear that the Caribbean countries would be more effective negotiating as a group, such as under the umbrella of a strengthened CARICOM, than if each country, or small groups of countries, negotiated on their own. This is more easily said than done. The larger countries – Trinidad and Tobago and Jamaica – are more able to consider NAFTA accession than the smaller countries. Some could forego EU preferences, while others cannot, certainly for now. Even the CARICOM grouping does not represent all of the Caribbean. It is hard to escape the conclusion that unity, at least of CARICOM, is better than disunity, and achieving this unity should be the objective.

What is required to augment the export of services?

This already has been discussed, but merits emphasis. Caribbean countries have much experience with various kinds of services, such as tourism, financial services, and even education, and this experience can be drawn on. The stress I wish to give here is that many of the emerging services for which there is less experience, such as value added telecommunications services, professional activities like medical services, and sophisticated financial services, require many highly skilled people. Services are sometimes equated with low-skill activities, but this is not necessarily accurate. Increased service exports not only demand improved educational opportunities, but an open door to capital and personnel inflows. To the extent these are restricted, success in generating significant earnings from sophisticated services will be prejudiced.

Where will resources come from to augment the insertion of Caribbean countries into the world economy?

Most Caribbean countries have moderate low savings rates. Many have large current account deficits. They already require capital inflows to finance imports of goods and services and to supplement domestic savings. They will need much FDI to develop world-class service activities. They will have to assure protection of intellectual property if they hope to obtain the requisite technology.

Are Caribbean entrepreneurs prepared for the competition that would accompany more open, important import markets?

This is an important question whose answer is unclear. Many Caribbean entrepreneurs are ready and have demonstrated their ability to compete by forging alliances with entrepreneurs in the industrial countries. My conviction is that this competitive spirit will be there when circumstances force its emergence, when internal markets are not excessively protected.

Are Caribbean countries basing their actions on sustainable development by protecting their environments?

Carrying out the suggestions made by the World Bank and those included in this essay on development priorities – upgrading infrastructure, augmenting various types of services, improving industrial efficiency – require protection of fragile ecosystems if the results are to be durable. The World Bank argues that Caribbean countries are prime candidates for external assistance for environmental protection.[26]

How much must the Caribbean countries factor into their current policies the changing nature of the world trade and financial structures?

Very much, according to the World Bank. The days of substantial external assistance are over. Margins of preference for merchandise trade are eroding and may disappear as the EU expands and the United States enters into preferential free-trade agreements with non-Caribbean countries.

There are many opportunities for expanded earnings from a variety of service exports. These, I am convinced, are the realities that Caribbean countries must confront as they look ahead over the next five to ten years.

Notes

1. World Bank for the Caribbean Group for Cooperation in Economic Development (CGCED hereafter). Caribbean Countries Policies for Private Sector Development (Washington, DC: World Bank, 1994), pp. 6–7. The countries included in this calculation are Antigua and Barbuda, The Bahamas, Barbados, Belize, Dominica, Dominican Republic,

Grenada, Guyana, Haiti, Jamaica, St Kitts and Nevis, St Lucia, St Vincent and the Grenadines, Suriname, and Trinidad and Tobago. When weighted by GDP in 1980, there was no growth during the 1980s because of declines in per capita GDP in many of the larger countries. The annual per capita GDP growth from 1982–1992 is given in another source (See note 2) as 2.8 per cent.

2. The current account balances for the years 1980-1992 are shown in World Bank for CGCED, *Coping with Changes in the External Environment* (Washington, D.C: World bank, 1994), p. 32.

3. One Study that should be mentioned in addition to the two cited in notes 1 and 2 is World Bank for the CGCED, *Economic Policies for Transition in the Organisation of Eastern Caribbean States* (Washington, D.C: World Bank, 1994).

4. On the last named, see World Bank for the CGCED, *Initiatives for Regional Action on Caribbean Environmental Issues* (Washington, D.C.: World Bank, 1994).

5. CGCED, *Coping with Changes*, p. 103.

6. CGCED, *Economic Policies for Transition in the Organisation of Eastern Caribbean States.*

7. CGCED, *35.*

8. One Study prepared for the World Bank deals quite harshly with the EU regime, Brent Borrell, 'EU Bananarama III', undated, but issued in 1994. It recommends direct aid in place of banana aid on two grounds, that banana aid is inefficient and punishes non-preferred supplying countries; loss of banana aid without compensation would have severe economic and social consequences in the preferred countries in the Caribbean and Pacific.

9. Bernal, the Jamaican ambassador to the United States, has written and spoken much on this issue. One example of these presentations is Richard L. Bernal, 'From NAFTA to Hemispheric Free Trade', *Columbia Journal of World Business*, 29:3 (1994) pp. 23–31.

10. The idea of associate membership has been suggested by many others, for example, Peter Morici, *Free Trade in the Americas,* (New York: Twentieth Century Fund Press, 1994) pp. 28–29.

11. Stephen Lande and Nellis Crigler, 'CCI and NAFTA Provisions Compared,' *USA- Caribbean Relations into the 21st Century* ed. by Phillip Hughes and Georges Fauriol, (Washington, D.C.: Center for Strategic and International Studies, forthcoming 1995) contains a comparative analysis of CBI and NAFTA benefits as they apply to CBI countries.

12. R. DeLisle Worrell, 'Economic Integration with Unequal Partners: The Caribbean and North America,' (Working paper no. 205, Latin American Program, Woodrow Wilson Center for Scholars, Washington, D.C., 1994).

13. Worrell, 'Economic Integration, p. 15

14. The argument can be made that NAFTA, to the extent that it equalises preferences for Mexico with those that have long existed under CBI, is a positive step. However, when equalisation gives way to discrimination, then a new distortion is inserted into the world trading system

15. Data is available on public sector saving, but they are inadequate for private savings. Some data for individual countries is available in CGCED, *Coping with Changes*, p. 44.

16. Remittances are a current account item and are thus taken into account in the deficit.

17. Some restrictions that exist are outlined in CGCED, *Caribbean Countries Policies for Private Sector Development*, pp. 118–119.

18. Many of these considerations are discussed in Robert Schware and Susan Hume, '*The Global Information Industry and the Eastern Caribbean*,' World Bank Viewpoint paper, July 1994.

19. According to CGCED, *Coping with Changes*, p. 105, textiles and clothing accounted for about 24 percent of regional export to all OECD markets in 1992. Most of these go to the United States. NAFTA preferences are less germane or non-existent for most other exports.

20. Implicitly, I am asserting here that the Bernal proposal for Caribbean accession with an indefinite schedule for eliminating import barriers would be unacceptable to the United States and presumably to the rest of the world because NAFTA countries would enjoy preferences in the Caribbean even though the requirements of Article XXIV of the GATT would not be met.

21. Lande and Crigler, 'CBI and NAFTA Provisions Compared', deals with the issue of contract versus USA unilateralism.

22. Worrell, p. 29.

23. CGCED, *Coping with Changes*, p. 103, simply points out that unless the Caribbean were willing to forego all Lomé preferences, imports from the EU would have to be given unrestricted access, Bernal, p. 29, states simply that his suggestion for associate membership covering only selected issues would not permit Caribbean countries to have it both ways by also retaining Lomé preferences

24. In a press conference during the Miami Summit, Jamaica's foreign minister, Paul Robertson called the banana issue a 'life and death' matter for the region.

25. CGCED, *Initiatives for Regional Action on Caribbean Environment Issues*.

References

Bernal, Richard L 'From NAFTA to Hemispheric Free Trade', *Columbia Journal of World Business*, 29:3 (1994) pp. 23–31.

Borrell, Brent 'EU Bananarama III', (paper funded by World Bank, undated, apparently 1994 or 1995).

Lande, Stephen and Nellis Crigler, 'CBI and NAFTA Provisions Compared', *USA Caribbean Relations into the 21ˢᵗ Century* ed. by Phillip Hughes and Fauriol, Georges (Washington, D.C.: Center for Strategic and International Studies, 1995).

Schware, Robert and Susan Hume, 'The Global Information Industry and the Eastern Caribbean', *Viewpoint paper*, World Bank, July 1994.

World Bank for the Caribbean Group for Co-operation in Economic Development, 'Caribbean 2000: Challenges, Opportunities, and Vision', (policy summary of reports prepared by the World Bank for meeting of CGCED, June 1994).

World Bank for the Caribbean Group for Co-operation in Economic Development, *Caribbean Countries Policies for Private Sector Development* (Washington, D.C.: World Bank, 1994).

World Bank for the Caribbean Group for Cooperation in Economic Development, *Coping with Changes in the External Environmental* (Washington, D.C.: World Bank, 1994).

World Bank for the Caribbean Group for Cooperation in Economic Development, *Economic Policies for Transition in the Organization of Eastern Caribbean States* (Washington, D.C.: World Bank, 1994).

World Bank for the Caribbean Group for Cooperation in Economic Development, *Initiatives for Regional Action on Caribbean Environmental Issues* (Washington, D.C.: World Bank, 1994).

Worrell, R. DeLisle 'Economic Integration with Unequal Partners: The Caribbean and North America', Working paper 205, (Woodrow Wilson International Center for Scholars, Washington, D.C.: World Bank, 1994).

[56]

The Case for NAFTA Parity for CBI Countries[1]

Richard Bernal

In 1995, the Caribbean Basin is faced with two fundamental, yet conflicting trade trends. On one hand, as it stands now, NAFTA has emerged as an immediate challenge to the viability of USA/Caribbean trading relationship. In providing preferential access to a number of Mexican products, which form an important base of the Caribbean export portfolio, NAFTA will cause substantial erosion of the Caribbean competitive position *vis-à-vis* the USA market. On the other hand, NAFTA represents a building block in the establishment of a hemispheric free trade area, a goal that has been enthusiastically endorsed by Jamaica as part of the Free Trade Area of the Americas (FTAA) process.

The Caribbean Basin Trade Security Act (S. 529/HR 553) – which has attracted widespread bipartisan support and the backing of the Clinton administration – creates a mechanism to address and reconcile these diverging trends. First, the Caribbean Basin Trade Security Act will provide a short-term remedy to the trade and investment imbalances caused by NAFTA. Second, this measure will create a transitional framework through which Caribbean countries like Jamaica can attain the long-term goal of integration into hemispheric free trade. Quick passage and enactment of this important measure, therefore, is vitally important to sustain USA/Caribbean economic and trade partnership.

The Caribbean Basin Initiative at Twelve Years

In August 1995, the Caribbean Basin Initiative (CBI) marks its twelfth anniversary. In the dozen years since it was established, the CBI has emerged as an important stimulus of economic development in the Caribbean Basin and of trade linkages throughout the region. The effect has been felt – not only in Kingston and Montego Bay – but also in Miami, Baltimore, New Orleans, New York, and hundreds of other communities throughout the USA. In many ways, the CBI has exceeded the expectations of the drafters of the CBI legislation who wrote in the 1990 amendment to the CBI, 'The Congress finds that . . . a stable political and economic climate in the Caribbean region is necessary for the development of the countries in the region and for the security and economic interests of the United [States]'.[2]

Through its combination of trade, investment, and tax policies, the CBI legislation has progressively established a framework that has allowed mutually beneficial USA/Caribbean economic links to flourish. In turn, Jamaica and other Caribbean countries have matched the liberalising reforms enacted by the CBI to launch their own trade and investment economic reform programmes. Together, the USA and Caribbean countries have created a trade partnership that now exceeds $24 billion a year.

The successes of the CBI legislation are reflected in the figures signalling robust growth in the US/Caribbean trade partnership. Since the mid-1980s, USA overall exports to the Caribbean have expanded by over 100 per cent and Caribbean exports to the USA have climbed by roughly 50 percent. The Caribbean Basin now comprises the tenth largest market for the USA, and is one of the few regions where the USA consistently posts a trade surplus. With USA exports exceeding $13.4 billion in 1994, USA/Caribbean commercial links support more than 265,000 jobs in the USA. During the past decade, nearly 17,000 American jobs have been created each year as USA trade links with the Caribbean have expanded. Throughout the Caribbean, where the economies are much more dependent upon trade, increased exports to the USA has generated hundreds of thousands of additional jobs. Such employment growth has been felt in both export industries, as well as in the many sectors that cater to these industries.

Such trade and employment growth reveals a fundamental characteristic of USA/Caribbean production cycles. The existence of CBI market access agreements, combined with the proximity and skills of the Caribbean workforce, has made Caribbean production an attractive and profitable element of any USA production strategy. For example, through offshore assembly agreements, the Jamaican private sector has developed an active partnership with USA industry to take advantage of the most efficient productive activities that each country offers. In a host of industries, USA and Jamaican firms cooperate to produce finished goods using a combination of Jamaican and American skills, capital, and technology. It is this complementarity of Jamaican/USA production that maintains the competitiveness of the final product in the global marketplace and even in the USA market.

The new structure of trade means that economic growth and development in the Caribbean now directly translate into expanded export opportunities for the USA. Roughly 70 cents of each dollar Jamaica earns from exports to the USA is spent in the USA, buying American-made consumer goods, food products, industry inputs, and capital equipment. When compared with each dollar of Asian imports, which only generates about 10 cents worth of subsequent USA purchases, trade with the Caribbean becomes an important priority for the USA.

Moreover, by providing a mechanism to enhance USA/Caribbean commercial links, the CBI has created a sound basis for cooperation in other areas, such as environmental protection, counter-narcotics activities, the promotion of democracy, and regional security measures.

NAFTA and the CBI

NAFTA's Preferential Access over the CBI

This established structure of trade in the region ensures that the impact of NAFTA will be substantial, both in the USA and throughout the Caribbean. In effect, NAFTA alters the successful formula for sound economic development in the Caribbean by granting Mexico access to the USA market on terms more favourable than those available for CBI exporters.

While the CBI programme provides for duty free treatment for a vast number of products, statutorily it excludes a few items – such as textiles and apparel, footwear, luggage, watches, tuna, and petroleum – that are among the Caribbean Basin's, most valuable exports. This means that a portion of each CBI country's exports will not enjoy CBI treatment. As much as 40 per cent of Jamaica's actual exports are not covered by the duty free treatment scheduled under the CBI or Generalised Systems of Preferences (GSP) programmes. Moreover, some of these products, such as textiles and apparel and sugar, also face quota-based trade barriers in addition to these duties.

In contrast, NAFTA eliminates the duty and quota treatment for these same articles, either immediately or over a phase-out period. Under NAFTA, import duties were immediately removed on approximately 80 per cent of

Mexican apparel exports to the USA. The remaining 20 percent benefits from an accelerated implementation of free trade, with annual duty cuts and quota liberalisation set to be completed by the year 2000. To be fair, NAFTA also phases out the duties on the products for which the CBI countries already enjoy duty-free treatment.

But the result is far from even. Mexico gains parity with the Caribbean countries for CBI-covered products, establishing a level playing field for those items on which Mexican and Caribbean exporters face no duty. But on the products excluded from the CBI, such as textile and apparel products, Mexico gains access to the US market, exceeding that granted to the Caribbean countries. This tilts the playing field in Mexico's favour, and gives Mexican exporters a distinct advantage over Caribbean exporters. When combined with Mexico's access to cheap energy, lower transport costs, greater econo-mies of scale, and low wage rates, this advantage becomes quite substantial.

NAFTA also grants Mexico an extremely valuable exception to tough textile and apparel 'rule-of-origin' requirements – the so-called tariff prefer-ence levels (TPLs) – to allow for preferential entry into the USA market of textile and apparel products that contain fabrics from countries other than Mexico, Canada, and the USA. This provision is intended to provide flexi-bility for the Mexican garment industry to meet the changing demands of USA clothing purchasers. TPLs work through a tariff-rate quota, providing low duty rates each year to non-originating products before applying a high tariff to any amount above quota. In allowing such a price break, NAFTA enables Mexican exporters to lower the average cost of their products while maintaining high volumes to satisfy the USA importers and retailers.

CBI textile and apparel exporters and their customers enjoy no such flexibility. Without similar TPL provisions for CBI countries, non-originating Caribbean garment exports face the higher tariff rates even if Caribbean parity is enacted. This would give Mexico, and even low cost producers in Asia, a distinct price advantage in competing in certain product areas. At the same time, Caribbean exporters would lose sales opportunities since the CBI and CBI parity incentives would be to shift production away from items that were not cut and sewn in the USA. Faced with such restrictions, USA importers, retailers, and investors would begin to pass over the Caribbean Basin as a profitable place from which to do business.

NAFTA's effects on the US/Caribbean Partnership

Broadly speaking, NAFTA's implementation and advantages over the CBI poses four clear risks for the US/CBI partnership. The elimination of quotas and the phase-out of tariffs on Mexican products remove the advantage enjoyed by CBI exports to the USA market, diverting trade flows from CBI countries to Mexico. In the 16 months since NAFTA was implemented, there has already been a measurable diversion of trade from the CBI to Mexico. The American Apparel Manufacturer's Association (AAMA) reports that the growth rate of USA apparel imports from the CBI region dropped by 60 per cent from 1993 to 1994. During that same period, the growth of apparel imports from Mexico nearly doubled. Moreover, trade statistics for the first two months of 1995 indicate that Mexican garment exports to the USA continued to expand at twice the rate of those from CBI countries. As this trend continues, Caribbean countries could witness a broad diversion of American demand from suppliers in CBI countries to firms in Mexico, thus reducing CBI exports and income.[3]

Another consequence of NAFTA's implementation has been the diversion of new investment. One of the primary indicators has been the fact that in the last three years there has been a pause in investment in the region, as investors first waited to evaluate the NAFTA provisions and then established new operating facilities in Mexico, instead of in the Caribbean. This trend, which is now fully realised, has long been anticipated by the USA Government. USA International Trade Commission's (ITC's) 1992 report entitled, 'Potential Effects of a North American Free Trade Agreement on Apparel Investments in CBERA Countries', has concluded that 'NAFTA will introduce incentives that will tend to favour apparel investment shifts away from the CBERA countries to Mexico.[4]

As existing investors begin to source their produce out of Mexico, others are rushing to transfer or close existing productive capacity – particularly in 'foot-loose' industries which can easily be relocated – to take advantage of Mexico's market access. In many Caribbean Basin countries, particularly throughout Central America, NAFTA directly reverses past successes of the CBI programme, effectively turning back the clock of Caribbean development.

The erosion of export access to the USA will eventually translate directly into a contraction of economic activity in the CBI region. Such a contraction would lower regional incomes, and, ultimately, the demand for imports from the USA. In such a scenario, USA exports of goods and services to the CBI would decline while regional instability, fostered by a decrease in economic opportunities, would rise. Judging from past patterns, the resulting unemployment in the USA would be met with an increase in immigration from displaced Caribbean workers and a rise in narcotics trafficking.

The Caribbean Basin Trade Security Act (S. 529/HR 553) very simply will restore a level playing field between Mexico and the Caribbean Basin countries. It will provide for non-discriminatory access into the US market for those products on which NAFTA gives Mexico an unintended advantage. It does not establish a new set of criteria by which countries can become eligible for the benefits, but rather links the enhanced benefits to the existing programme criteria. In this way, S. 529/HR 553 recognises that many Caribbean countries, through trade liberalisation and economic reform measures, have already undertaken steps that exceed the criteria outlined in the original legislation. Moreover, it also ensures that additional, valuable time is not lost, nor USA/Caribbean partnership further undermined, as CBI countries satisfy new 'entrance criteria'.

Another important feature of the Caribbean parity bill is that it includes all products that are currently excluded by the CBI. As our economies liberalise, it becomes increasingly difficult to erect artificial barriers between product categories. Extending parity for only certain textile and apparel products would have a limited effect on the situation that we are trying to address. Enacting a comprehensive parity bill, however, is both economically more feasible and symbolically more consistent with the notion of free and open trade.

In this regard, S. 529/HR 553 includes a welcome provision giving the Administration authority to negotiate tariff preference levels for non-originating textile and apparel products. Such a provision does not compel the use of TPLs, but merely recognises that the fairness of a fully level playing field requires the same TPLs for the Caribbean as those that are available for Mexico.

Similarly, S. 529/HR 553 rightly addresses the issue of Caribbean sugar exports to the USA in light of the NAFTA. It requires the USA to monitor the effects of NAFTA on CBI sugar exports. If the President determines that NAFTA is damaging CBI sugar access, he is empowered to recommend steps to alleviate this injury. Such a provision provides important flexibility to ensure that, among other things, this parity debate is not repeated in two or three years for the sugar industry. Moreover, this provision is not inconsistent with GATT since it would prevent existing GATT obligations from being undermined by 'creeping sugar access' accorded Mexico under NAFTA.

Finally, S.529/HR 553 is a cost-effective way for the USA to conduct foreign trade and economic policy in the region, especially in this era of budget cutbacks. Any losses to the reduction in tariffs should be offset by no more than two factors. First, even without Caribbean parity, the USA can expect to lose tariff revenue as trade and investment is diverted to the duty free export platforms in Mexico. Restoring those exports to the Caribbean, by cutting the tariffs faced by imports from the Caribbean, will not represent a new loss of tariff revenue, but merely a recognition of tariff revenue that is already being lost. Second, a preliminary calculation suggests that the gains of trade liberalisation and economic growth should generate alternative sources of revenue for the US Government to offset any tariff revenue loses. The CBI has helped create an average of 16,000 US jobs each year for the past decade. If each of these jobs generates an additional $5,000 in tax revenues during the first year, trade liberalisation with the CBI could yield roughly $80 million in new revenues in that year alone. In the second year, 16,000 additional jobs are created, US revenues will expand by $160 million. Over five years, such figures yield roughly $1.2 billion, exceeding the CBO estimates by several hundred million dollars.

The Caribbean Basin Trade Security Act as a transitional mechanism for hemispheric integration S. 529. HR 553 – both explicitly and implicitly – recognises a greater goal of bringing the Caribbean Basin countries into a hemispheric free trade area. In this regard, S. 529/HR 553 furthers the agenda developed at the Miami Summit with one critical difference. While much of the attention has focused on linking the larger economies of South America with NAFTA, S. 529. HR 553 puts forth a tangible framework to determine how the Caribbean economies will be joined in this free trade arrangement as well. It very much recognises that the spirit of Miami exists in all the countries throughout the Caribbean.

Specifically, S. 529/HR 553 provides for a transitional period during which full parity with Mexico will be provided for Caribbean countries. Jamaica supports an appropriate and realistic time frame to provide Caribbean Basin countries an opportunity to complete the trade liberalisation and economic reform steps necessary for accession to a free trade agreement with the USA. While some countries – such as Jamaica – are now ready to negotiate free trade agreements with the USA, others may need a longer period outlined in the Caribbean parity bills.

A reasonable period will also create a viable time frame that will help restore 'confidence' in the Caribbean that has been eroded as previous plans have been proposed and discarded. As investors and traders see that time period, they will be able to grasp a tangible expression of the US commitment to its trade relationship with CBI countries. One concern, however, is that the time frame not be seen as an excuse to put Caribbean countries – which have established a close trade relationship with the USA and which have already met many of the NAFTA entry requirements – at the back of the NAFTA accession line. Jamaica's hope is that NAFTA accession will include those countries that have made viable strides toward trade liberalisation, and not just those representing the largest export markets for US firms.

In addition, in making the period temporary, S. 529/HR 553 creates a viable incentive for Caribbean countries to complete their reform programmes. Rather than run the risk of losing enhanced trade benefits in the year 2000, each Caribbean country will spend the next six years working to enact and implement the measures necessary to ensure the smooth negotiation of a free trade agreement with the USA.

The bill initiates a dialogue between the administration and the Caribbean Basin countries on ways to preserve and strengthen USA/Caribbean trading relationship. Even in the absence of specific trade negotiating authority, such a dialogue is important to help maintain the momentum of the Miami Summit. In addition, the bill requires the administration to perform a series of studies and reports on USA/Caribbean trade relationship. In a sense, S. 529/HR 553 asks the administration to continually ask the question: 'What will be the impact of a specific policy change on the Caribbean?' Such questions should have been asked as NAFTA was considered. This emphasis is appropriate, partly because of the close trade relationship between the USA and the Caribbean. In addition, this focus will help ensure that free trade talks with the Caribbean Basin countries – which are among the most committed trade liberalisers – are not delayed by a need to initiate trade talks with the larger economies of the hemisphere.

Jamaica's Commitment to Trade Liberalisation

Jamaica is deeply committed to an open multilateral trading system as a stimulant to economic growth, both through the static gains from increased efficiency in the utilisation of its existing resources and the dynamic gains from the opportunities to expand productive capacity through new technology, investment, and innovative entrepreneurship.

Jamaica is an advocate of trade liberalisation within the hemisphere and of a multilateral trading system that approaches free trade as far as possible. Jamaica subscribes to, and its policy has always been fully consistent with, the principles and disciplines of GATT. Jamaica joined GATT in the early 1960s and has been an active participant, contributing to successive negotiating rounds aimed at further liberalisation of global trade.

Moreover, Jamaica actively participates in several regional trade liberalisation arrangements with the USA (CBI), Europe (the LOMÉ Convention), Canada (CARIBCAN), and the other English-speaking countries in the Caribbean (the Caribbean Common Market – CARICOM). All of these arrangements are intended to promote trade between the member countries.

Finally, Jamaica also has supported the creation of free trade within the Western hemisphere, the North American Free Trade Area (NAFTA), the first building block of free trade within the hemisphere.

Jamaica realises that there is now a new phase of globalisation of production and finance which is rapidly sweeping away national barriers to the movement of goods, services, capital and finance. During the 1980s Jamaica's economic policies focused on economic reform, stabilisation, and structural adjustment in an attempt to create an environment conducive to a private sector-led, market-driven, outward-looking growth strategy. An important aspect has been a comprehensive programme of trade liberalisation involving substantially reduced tariffs and the elimination of quantitative trade restrictions. This has been complemented by freeing market forces within the domestic economy through the abolition of price and exchange controls by a vigorously implemented campaign of privatisation and fiscal and monetary discipline. A stable, market-determined exchange rate system is operating successfully, preventing any disruptive changes in the value of the Jamaican dollar.

In the last four years there has been a substantial acceleration in the process of liberalising the trade regime of Jamaica, with an emphasis on the removal of import restrictions and the lowering of tariffs. In many ways, USA products in the Jamaican market are accorded better access than Jamaican products in the USA market because Jamaica does not rely upon quotas as a tool of trade policy. Jamaican sugar and apparel products, for example, still face USA quotas.

This commitment to outward-looking trade and development policies is firmly based on the knowledge that the benefits to be derived are higher growth rates and enhanced capacity to adjust to external shocks. Expanding trade contributes to Jamaica's growth by enabling the economy to improve its productivity by specialising in exports in which it has a comparative advantage. Production for the world market allows firms to achieve the economies of scale which are precluded by a small domestic market. Exposure to competition from imports serves to increase cost efficiency and the benefits consumers receive from lower prices.

Jamaica now sees the CBI programmes as a springboard to greater hemispheric free trade liberalisation. In many cases, we have already taken steps that exceed the requirements of the CBI to help accelerate this goal. We have signed a Bilateral Investment Treaty (BIT) and an Intellectual Property Rights (IPR) agreement with the USA. We were also one of the first countries to include new anti-circumvention language in our bilateral textile agreement with the USA.

Jamaica is ready and has a demonstrated commitment to enter the next stage of trade liberalisation with the USA – negotiating a free and reciprocal trade agreement.

Note on Section 936

Jamaica has also followed, with growing concern, Congressional efforts to scale back or eliminate the Section 936 tax programme. Any action to dilute this programme could dampen Caribbean economic development in a manner analogous to NAFTA's adverse effect on the US/CBI trading relationship.

Although the programme initially targets Puerto Rico's growth and development, it has been extended to support economic growth and development in the Caribbean as well. Currently, the Section 936 code contains a provision through which investors in Puerto Rico receive an income tax credit on Qualified Possession Source Investment Income (QPSII). Jamaica and several other CBI beneficiaries benefit from this section since QPSII funds may be used to finance projects in eligible CBI countries.

Jamaica is concerned over the elimination of such a programme for several reasons. Firstly, the QPSII programme provides a substantial source of private sector funding for Jamaican development programmes. Since the mid 1980s, when Jamaica became eligible for the programme, Section 936 funds have supported over $500 million worth of investments in development projects, including the privatisation of the tourism industry. Because investors earn tax-free income on their investment income, they are able to make the funds available for development projects in the Caribbean at relatively low rates. This makes the Section 936 programme particularly attractive and appropriate source of funds for Caribbean countries, who have difficulty raising capital on international markets.

Secondly, as foreign aid dollars begin to dry up, Jamaica is looking increasingly towards private sector sources of financing such as the Section 936 programme. If the Section 936 programme goes as well, the increased pressures on the private capital markets from all Caribbean countries will drive up interest rates, making future development projects prohibitively expensive. This would undermine the past decade of success with the Section 936 programme as well as the entire CBI programme.

Thirdly, eligibility of access to CBI funds depends upon successful implementation of a Tax Information Exchange Agreement (TIEA) with the USA. To date, the following countries have signed tax Information Exchange Agreements: Barbados (1984), Jamaica (1986), Grenada (1987), Dominica (1988), Dominican Republic (1989), Trinidad and Tobago (1990), St Lucia

(1991), Costa Rica (1991), Honduras (1991), and Guyana (1992). At the time these agreements were signed, the understanding was that 936 funds would be available for investments in the Caribbean Elimination of the Section 936 programme. This calls into question a fundamental US commitment supporting this treaty obligation.

Finally, as little as two years ago, Congress considered and rejected a move to modify the QPSII income tax credit. Dilution of this important programme for the Caribbean made little sense in 1993. It makes even less sense now. For many of the same reasons why Caribbean parity legislation should be enacted, Congress should continue to resist efforts to eliminate or dilute the QPSII tax credit in the Section 936 programme.

Conclusion

The CBI has proven to be an unqualified success. It has relied upon tax and trade incentives to foster a strong and, interdependent, economic relationship between the USA and the Caribbean.

The potential for NAFTA to divert trade and investment from the Caribbean is nothing new, and has been discussed extensively since the idea for NAFTA was first raised. The Administration and Congress have long recognised this problem, but have so far been unable to find a satisfactory formula to rectify it. Last year, USA came close to enacting a partial fix by considering the Clinton Administration's Interim Trade Programme (ITP). Although the ITP was not enacted last year, it did heighten the awareness of this problem and the need to resolve it quickly. What is needed now is more than ITP. In the search for ways to keep the USA/Caribbean partnership healthy and build the framework to make the free trade spirit of Miami a reality, the Caribbean needs a full, transitional mechanism to help it work towards a more compelling free trade objective.

In addition, in order to keep the wheels of free trade lubricated, the Caribbean Basin needs access to capital to help finance investment and trade projects. The USA official development assistance once played an important role in that respect. But as foreign aid flows are diminishing, the Caribbean Basin will turn increasingly toward private sources of capital like the Section 936 QPSII programme.

The Caribbean Basin Trade Security Act (S.529/HR 553) is a well-conceived measure that will help Jamaica and other CBI countries achieve that goal. At the same time, Congress should take care not to hobble that progress by weakening the Section 936 programme, a key financing mechanism for the Caribbean.

Notes

1. This article represents an official statement submitted by Dr Richard L. Bernal, Jamaican Ambassador to the USA, to the International Trade Commission in July 1995.
2. Section 201 of the Caribbean Basin Economic Recovery Expansion Act of 1990. Codified at [19 USC 2701nt; PL 101–382; Title II]
3. See Larry Martin, 'Testimony of Larry Martin, American Apparel Manufacturing Association' before the House Ways and Means Subcommittee on Trade on HR 553, the Caribbean Basin Security Act, Serial Report 104–4:93.
4. See 'Potential Effects of a North American Free Trade Agreement on Apparel Investment in CBERA Countries.' Report to the USA Trade Representative on Investigation No. 332–321. USITC Publication 2541, July 1992.

[57]

Resource Mobilisation in
the Caribbean Community

Kenneth Hall & Joseph Farier

Part I

Among the more important decisions taken by the English-speaking countries of the Caribbean in the last three decades were the decision to become independent, and the determination to form or join an integration movement. In so doing, the English-speaking countries of the Caribbean highlighted a few issues. First, they emphasised their wish for a dramatic change in the manner in which they related to other states in the international community, in particular the traditional metropolis, and their desire to have a determining influence on the manner in which they were run (socially, politically and economically). Secondly, they confirmed their desire to accelerate the process of their development through greater consciousness of, and deliberate effort to promote, the benefits of cooperation among themselves in the field of trade, industrial development, external economic and political relations, and social development, by promoting a greater Caribbean cultural identity.

With this in view, a central concern has been available resources to achieve the basic objectives of their integration movement. In the evolution of their efforts to build a Caribbean Community, the resources needed for regional programmes have been partly derived from internal resources through contributions of member states. However, increasingly, substantial resources from the international donor community have been available in key strategic areas. It is this factor that is the subject of the present assessment.

In general, the Caribbean states resisted the road of a sharp dramatic break with the old metropolis and opted instead for the basic proposition that countries at initial stage of industrial development such as those in the Caribbean could be launched on a course of dynamic economic and social transformation through processes of active international cooperation for development. In this view, the aim of international cooperation would be to enhance trade relations, promote the flow of international assistance but also allow for, as far as possible, diversification of relations with states in the international community. It was also the assumption that their development process was not going to be easily sustainable without considerable international concessional assistance. Indeed, there was an understanding that this required a level of dependence on the international community – in areas of aid, trade preferences, investment flows and emigration outlets – if not political alignment of one sort or the other.

Like many other developing countries the Caribbean felt that this process of economic and social transformation could be set in motion, broadened and accelerated by the effective use of internal and regional resources, supported and complemented by external resources of a largely concessional nature in an environment of enabling policies and leadership conducive to sustained development. Fully aware of the perils of insularity and fragmentation, they sought, after the collapse of the Federation, to construct regional unity around themes of trade liberalisation and consolidation of common services, coordination of foreign policies, and joint efforts to raise the quality and standard of living of the population. For their integration mechanism, they chose a consultative machinery, using dialogue and negotiation as the instrument for defining common objectives and charting new directions, rather than a supranational authority dictating terms.

Regional Movement as a Negotiating Process

In this context, one of the most interesting ways of looking at the integration movement is by visualising a dynamic process of negotiations aimed at joint programme development, and joint institution-building. In this process, long-term objectives were set by the Treaty of Chaguaramas. Heads of Government conferences periodically sharpen perspectives or define, in more concrete terms, objectives to be pursued, or seek to reconcile the differences in the broad parameters of the regional effort. Within this broad negotiating context, there is also a parallel negotiating process represented by meetings of the Council of Ministers and a variety of ministerial standing committees (transport, energy, industry, labour, education, health, science and technology, and the environment).

Parties to this process are representatives of thirteen (13) member states of the Caribbean Community who seek, through conference diplomacy, to reconcile their interests and differences into patterns of consistent, mutually reinforcing activity, or in interlocking relationships across a broad range of economic and social areas.

Backstopping the ministerial negotiations is the work of regional officials who, prior to each meeting, examine the issues, help identify policy options and seek to identify common ground among member states. Much of the work of technical preparation is the responsibility of the Secretariat who carries it out with a view to identifying a common ground which provides a solid basis for decision-making by consensus.

A wide range of decisions and recommendations issue from regional meetings. Some decisions are characterised by unity of positions, others by harmony of approach, still others by coordination or in many cases by agreed dispensations or special safeguards. Many express the need for programme or project development and institutional strengthening.

The Role of the CARICOM Secretariat in Community Building

Given the wide-ranging objectives of the Community, and the preferred mode of interaction of its member states, the Secretariat as the main administrative organ of the Community, must be concerned to bring to bear on the interaction of member states, technical and administrative insights of what may be loosely-termed a fourteenth voice. The objective of this is to accommodate as much as possible, national interests in policy formulation and at the same time provide forward movement in the regional development process in specific areas targeted by the Governments or proposed by the Secretariat.

To satisfy concerns over national sovereignty while securing in specific areas the pooled exercise of sovereign authority, the Secretariat must seek to promote larger gains or broader objectives from which member states might derive advantage. It is also responsible for the deployment of the most appropriate expertise, so that the regional process of decision-making and policy formulation can achieve the broad developmental goals set by the organs and institutions of the Community. In addition, the Secretariat designs programmes and compiles action plans to advance the Community's goals -promotion of export, promotion of production, or rationalisation of activities.

This responsibility clearly distinguishes the Secretariat from the Community as such and circumscribes its role to that of servant of the Community rather than potential enforcer or implementer. Except in very few cases, implementation lies with member states and must have much bearing on the extent to which perceived national interests are affected and national sensitivity to compromises accommodated.

The Role of International Cooperation and Technical Assistance

The process of development in which Caribbean countries are involved has highlighted, among other things, the vital need for a favourable international environment; for trade and investment more germane to our present concerns, as well as aid and technical assistance.

In the Caribbean, the capacity of member Governments for sustained economic growth has been dealt severe blows by the international economic crisis, as reflected in deteriorating terms of trade, rising cost of debt servicing, and declines in output in the agricultural and industry sectors.

Inevitably this has increased the Community's concern about programme development and implementation; institutional building at the regional level; and promoting renewal of the process of economic and social progress. It is in this search for the design, refinement, development and revamping of Community policies, instruments and programmes, that international technical assistance plays its most useful role.

It should be noted, however, that success at external cooperation requires supporting statesmanship at the national level. Moreover, there need to be considerable resources available to Governments to sensitise the people of the region to possibilities and opportunities for change and to implement projects capable of promoting economic and social development in priority areas. The reality is that the objectives of regional integration far exceed the capacity of the region to finance them, in the present circumstances.

The work of consensus building through technical studies, or of identifying industrial options and opportunities further afield for trade and promotion of tourism for instance, requires considerably more resources than the financial ability of member states at this time. The Research and Advisory Vote of the Secretariat in 1990 was about 3 per cent of a core budget of EC$11 million. In 1995 Research and Advisory was 2.3 per cent of the contributions of member states to the budget of the Secretariat.

External support has therefore been critical for programme development and project implementation as well as institution building in a wide range of areas. (Table 1 below sets out the level of external donor support through the CARICOM Secretariat to Community projects and programmes over the last decade).

Table 1: Sources of Funding for the Secretariat's Budget and Programmes (1984 to 1995)

Year	Member States' Contributions	Grants from External Agencies	Total	% Donor Contribution
1984	9,066,354.00	4,418,518.24	13,484,872.24	32.77
1985	10,328,474.00	3,358,908.00	13,687,382.00	24.55
1986	11,107,997.00	3,082,069.00	14,190,066.00	21.72
1987	10,673,837.00	3,783,019.58	14,456,856.58	26.17
1988	10,278,031.00	3,612,294.65	13,890,325.65	26.01
1989	11,099,815.00	3,329,101.95	14,428,916.95	23.07
1990	11,510,981.00	4,273,899.06	15,784,880.06	27.08
1991	12,321,385.00	7,900,000.00	20,221,385.00	39.07
1992	12,912,510.00	6,700,000.00	19,612,510.00	34.16
1993	15,350,000.00	5,570,100.00	20,920,100.00	26.63
1994	17,039,800.00	6,739,510.00	23,779,310.00	28.34
1995	17,394,190.00	16,786,449.00	34,180,639.00	49.11

Regional institutions and the Secretariat are inevitably affected by the limited resources available to member Governments. They are expected to help Governments secure external resources for continuation of institution building; for technical work preparatory to policy formulation; and for human resource development, particularly in managerial and skilled areas.

To the extent that Government contributions need to be supplemented by concessional assistance, to that extent the external relationships of the Community, and technical cooperation with external donor agencies, become very critical. It affects the promotion of technical consensus through support for technical meetings; the range of expertise available to the Community through the Secretariat for policy guidance; and, the capacity of the regional process to impact at the national level in terms of visible direct benefits from some aspects of the integration process.

In seeking the support of the international donor community, the Caribbean Community faces some significant challenges:

- how to attract resources to a so-called middle-income region in an international environment that seems characterised by aid fatigue. (There are questions of benefits to donors; benefits to target groups; self-sustainability of projects supported and institutions launched).
- a pronounced tendency for new aid to be focused on new pet themes or grand global themes when it is not explicitly tied to promotion of political or strategic objectives, or exports of goods and services from the donors;
- increasing introduction of policy dialogue with donors who try to heavily influence priority setting and project design while making statements to the contrary;
- securing donor assistance for priorities identified by a region rather than by individual countries.

The situation with respect to resource mobilisation is best illustrated by two examples, namely, arrangements with the EEC under the Lomé Convention and technical cooperation with the UNDP under the Regional Programme. Since 1975 the Caribbean Community has benefited from regional funds under the Lomé Convention amounting to ECU33 million under Lomé 1, ECU55 million under Lomé II and ECU73 million under Lomé III. In 1991, however, ECU90 million was earmarked for the entire Caribbean/ ACP Group which had expanded to include two new countries with two and one-half times the population of the Caribbean community. To be accorded the highest priority, regional projects had to have the support and commitment of the most recent members of the Caribbean/ACP Group in a programme identified at the ministerial level as valued at ECU190 million. The programming process involved some of the most complex negotiations and trade-offs in the context of wider membership. Whatever the difficulties, they are likely to be further accentuated by recent efforts to reduce contributions to the EEC aid budget – some major contributors offering as much as a 30 per cent cut.

In respect of UNDP, the Caribbean Community, comprising essentially small island development states, benefited substantially from the funding of projects in key sectors. At its peak, the Caribbean Regional Programme benefited from about US$13 million under the Fourth-Cycle programme (1987–1991). Under the Fifth-Cycle programme (1992–1996), this allocation was reduced to US$7 million, only $3.5 million of which were fresh resources. There is, of course, the significant advantage under this programme of the Caribbean Community being in a position to set its priorities in accordance with UNDP themes, but primarily in response to its own peculiar needs. On the negative side, however, there is less resource available to multilateral institutions as is reflected in a longer time for processing and approving projects; in the significant change in the thematic focus of programming; and the impact of unrealised pledges to UNDP as seen in a reduced budget for available projects..

In a world in which concessional assistance for middle-income countries has become quite limited, securing the continuation of these sources of assistance at appropriate levels is all the more important for regional programmes and for the continuation of deepening and widening the process of regional cooperation.

It might be noted however, that aid itself is designed to meet only some of the major needs and is more accessible to Governments who pursue appropriate policies and can match it with their countries' resources in their effort to accelerate and broaden economic and social progress. On the other hand, international cooperation can significantly undermine self-help and other development efforts where projects are approved in isolation from other Government initiatives or cause an excessive drain in resources in order to be maintained. Furthermore, many influences may be more important than the foreign aid component. This includes the economic and social policy environment in which the assisted institutions must function; the quality of leadership and technical staff; the amount and continuity of domestic financing and indigenous expertise provided alongside the foreign resources; changes in weather, prices and markets.

Part II

Application of Development Cooperation Resources in CARICOM

Considerable resources secured from external donor community have been applied to strengthening and improving the instruments of the Common Market designed either to provide protection for, or to promote the manufacturing sector in the region, or to increase the use of indigenous resources in the manufacturing process and therefore trade. Considerable assistance has also been sought and secured for institution-building: for CARDI, WISCO, UWI, CFC, CAREC, CMI, CEHI, CXC, CEDP, CTO and the Secretariat itself.

Additionally, international development assistance has also supported CARICOM in technical work on policy development and production, opportunities in the agricultural sector, and revising agricultural regimes for specific crops. Support has also been obtained for opportunity studies in relation to industrial allocation.

In the social areas, the delivery of primary health care, health manpower development, bulk procurement of drugs, population policy, the integration of women in development have been broad themes around which international assistance has been organised.

For the foreseeable future, in an environment characterised by aid fatigue and fascination with developments and opportunities in Eastern Europe, we will need more insight in identifying areas in which external assistance is of prime importance, and greater skill in developing persuasive project formulation and design, that can procure the resources required by the region to produce a catalytic impact in such priority areas as:

* the Single Market and deepening of the integration process;
* export promotion and external market penetration;
* agricultural production and diversification;
* science and technology development;
* women in development;
* human resource development;
* health care delivery;
* entrepreneurial development;
* employment creation;
* environmental protection;
* institutional capacity-building.

Without an enhanced capacity for project preparation and implementation, we stand little chance of securing these resources we need from an increasingly hard-nosed and competitive world.

Given the trends in aid flows, it is clear that aid flows to the region are not likely to continue into the next decade. Already USAID has closed its offices in the Eastern Caribbean, the US Government is reducing its contributions to the UN system and other agencies and the entire USAID is in danger of being dismantled by 1996. CIDA's aid to the South is declining; it has reduced its allocation to the Caribbean Development Bank and the grant situation for the Caribbean is not likely to improve under the new Government in Canada. The European Union has had to postpone its discussions on EDF VII because several of its member states have not agreed to increase, or even maintain previous levels of contribution.

In order to reduce the negative impact of declining aid flows to the region, appropriate approaches and strategies need to be pursued.

(a) Strengthen negotiating positions with traditional aid donors. This will involve regular and more determined representation individually or jointly at the political and technical levels, not just during a crisis or at governing body meetings, but on an ongoing basis.

(b) Initiate/develop relations with potential new donors such as the industrialised and industrialising countries of the Far East which are seeking to expand their relations internationally as well as with private sector organisations.

(c) Stress the region's continued vulnerability to external developments and pressures and make common cause with other small island countries in the same position. As middle- income countries, CARICOM is not likely to receive the same level of attention as previously unless it can project its need to preserve peace, security and its democratic traditions, strengthen its market economy, and put in place sustainable development practices.

(d) Strengthen national [and regional] machinery for improved cost-effectiveness in the implementation of projects. In a situation of scarce donor resources, donors are likely to favour those countries that have a track record, or show signs of improving their record, in a timely and cost-effective use of grant funds for maximum impact. Increasingly, donor Governments are being expected to give close account to their constituents on the use of aid funds. Bearing in mind the interest of some donors in utilising NGOs and private sector organisations as implementing agents for development projects, countries might wish to strengthen the project management capacity of these agents.

(e) Ensure maximum impact of available resources through complementarity between national and regional activities and the development of inter-country projects where common interests have been identified among several CARICOM countries. Agencies such as the OAS are pointing out that it is less expensive and time consuming to administer a few large projects than a large number of small projects.

(f) Utilise currently available resources for capacity-building and institutional strengthening as an investment for the future. Such activities would include development of the business sector, human resources and information infrastructure and other activities related to the structural transformation of our economies.

(g) Exploit the possibilities of technical cooperation with other, more advanced developing countries with which CARICOM is strengthening its relationship (Brazil, Mexico, Chile) to secure the transfer of appropriate technology for production, management and institutional development.

In some cases this could be a more effective modality for securing needed expertise than traditional North/South cooperation.

Note

This paper was published in *CARICOM Perspective*, 65, June 1995, pp. 71–75.

[58]

International Law and the Protection of Small States

Duke Pollard

Must the right to sovereignty and territorial integrity depend exclusively on the capacity of a state, however small, to defend itself, to assert its nationhood by superior arms? Must its survival be contingent on its capacity to repel predators?

. . . Or is it not, indeed, a premise of independence under the Charter that the international community has obligations to help to sustain those whom it has helped to bring to freedom – and to do so not only by resolutions after the event, but by the machinery of collective security and the will to use it?

       – S.S. Ramphal

The security of small states is probably one of the most intractable problems engaging the attention of the international community today and is high on the regional agenda of the Caribbean Community whose composition is entirely of small states. The collapse of empires in the postwar era[1] signalled the emergence of a proliferation of small states, lacking for the most part the required capabilities, both human and material, to survive on their own as viable independent entities and beleaguered in some cases by unfounded irredentist claims as in the cases of Guyana and Belize. The strategic importance of several of these small states particularly in the Caribbean, the Indian Ocean and the Pacific, enhance their attractiveness for aggressive, self-serving initiatives by powerful actors in the international community willing to employ such states as unwitting pawns in the struggle for power and influence. Given the foregoing, the prospects for development of small states are likely to be impaired, on the one hand, by internal instability and, on the other hand, by unwarranted external interference. In both situations small states are constrained to rely heavily on an appeal to the applicable rules of international law as a means of safeguarding their existence. But the problems of small states are, in the ultimate analysis, less a function of small size than that of their inadequacies in responding effectively and decisively to internal challenges or external developments in the international community, except where those inadequacies are themselves conditioned by small size.

Despite the system of collective security embodied in the Charter of the United Nations, the small state is entitled to question the plausibility of an assurance that the applicable rules of international law may be relied on, in the last resort, to guarantee its national sovereignty, territorial integrity and political independence. For, in the present submission, law, when stripped to its barest essentials, is but little more than organised violence, legitimately employed by those possessing the capabilities, to secure compliance with norms of conduct generally agreed to be politically and socially acceptable. And where the capabilities are inadequate, or the will to deploy them to sanction non-compliance is lacking, the law as a standard of conduct loses relevance. At the level of interpersonal interaction within the state, relevant norms of conduct are definitively and incontestably determined by the political sovereign, the legislature, or other empowered institution, as the case may be. The laws are authoritatively interpreted and applied by central judicial institutions enjoying compulsory jurisdiction, and enforced by competent executive instrumentalities authorised to employ coercion in the ultimate resort. However, at the level of state interaction in the international community, no such structured system of normative behaviour exists.

Sources of law are disparate and sometimes difficult to establish, mechanisms of authoritative interpretation and application of relevant norms are decentralised and lacking in compulsory jurisdiction, and no unified central executive authority is available for enforcing compliance in the event of opportunistic deviant conduct. Despite the status of law in the unorganised international community, there is a corpus of rules of conduct generally accepted by major actors in the international community as engaging voluntary compliance by states, including in particular norms of *jus cogens*, that is, norms from which no derogations are permitted. And although there is a tendency to dramatise and sensationalise instances of deviant conduct in the international community, particularly where the impermissible employment of force is involved, the general condition in the international community is one of voluntary compliance with rules which comprehend a wide gamut of transactions, but which tends to go unnoticed because of lack of appeal for an international media possessing a penchant for sensationalism.

The Phenomenon of Small States

By way of prefacing the submissions on this subject, an attempt will be made to arrive at a workable definition of a small state. In terms of status, a state is territory recognised as such by other subjects of international law. And whether the act of recognition is constitutive or merely declaratory need not detain us here, since, for present purposes, what is important is the fact of statehood and the legal incidence of such a status.

Recognition of a state is not conditional on any requirements regarding size of population, territory or natural resource endowments, much less definitiveness in terms of national boundaries or capabilities in terms of guaranteeing internal stability with a reasonable degree of permanence or even safeguarding the territory from external aggression. And since the objective requirements of statehood are ordinarily perceived to be no more than a settled territory with a permanent population and stable government enjoying effective control and the capacity to assume international rights and obligations at the material time, a large number of micro states have emerged on the international scene, varying in size from 166 square miles in the case of Barbados in the Caribbean, with populations less than 10,000 in the case of Nauru (7,000) and Tuvalu (7,500) in the Pacific.

The contemporary reality is that neither size, resource endowments nor the capability to deploy violence in defence of one's claims is perceived as a necessary condition of statehood. Recognition of a coastal state's competence on its continental shelf, and in the exclusive economic zone adjacent to its territorial sea, has had the effect of significantly augmenting the territorial jurisdictions of many small states, especially those in the Caribbean and Pacific, compounding thereby the problem of inadequate capabilities to ensure state security.

The three decades following the end of the World War II witnessed an exponential enlargement of the international community, when 1,250,000,000 colonial peoples inhabiting approximately 14 million square miles of dependent territories were transformed into 90 state entities. Since that time, the membership of the United Nations has continued to grow, including entities of varying populations, gross national products and territorial expanse. Despite this, the international community has so far failed to arrive at a generally acceptable definition of *small states*. For ultimately, the issue to be resolved is: small for what purpose. In international trade analysis, for example, small is defined with reference to effects, to identify economies which cannot individually influence the price at which commodities are bought and sold in world markets. On the other hand, intergovernmental organisations like the World Bank and the International Monetary Fund tend to employ national income as the basis of classification, while the United Nations employs the Human Development Index (HDI), which incorporates living standards and social indicators like longevity and knowledge as an additional criterion. Whatever the basis of classification, however, an element of arbitrariness intrudes itself in the criteria employed. For the purpose of this essay, a small state will be defined as a state entity with a population of less than one million inhabitants irrespective of gross national income (Brunei) or territorial expanse (Guyana).

In the context of the immediately foregoing, the questions posed by the former Commonwealth Secretary General and appearing at the beginning of this paper, Shridath Ramphal assume particular significance. Postulated in other terms, the Secretary General is making a passionate plea for the conduct of international relations based on law and not on power. His plea is for an international community governed by generally acceptable international norms, at the centre of which would be a system of collective security which would be viable and effective enough to guarantee the smallest member of the international community a plausible assurance about the integrity of its national sovereignty and political independence.

The reality, however, is that the rights of small states are frequently ignored when the interests of the more powerful members of the international community so prescribe. For example, the territory of the Maldives consists of 1200 coral islands which extend some 500 miles from north to south and are spread over an area of 34,740 square miles of open seas. The Navies of the Superpowers were wont to disregard the rights of the Maldives in respect of its national waters and the USSR's Indian Ocean fleet was one of the principal offenders. Similarly, the invasion of Grenada, even though evoking mixed reactions among the states of the English-speaking Caribbean at the material time, was soundly condemned by the then British Prime Minister as an infringement of that country's territorial integrity.

Violations of national sovereignty and territorial integrity were also recorded in respect of the Bahamas, Vanuatu, the Seychelles, the Comoros (1980s) and Guyana by more powerful states of the international community or renegade groups sponsored by them or acting on their instigation. In several instances, however, unwarranted incursions in the territories of small states have been induced by external perceptions of instability occasioned by seemingly intransigent economic and social underdevelopment.

To the extent, therefore, that governments of small states contribute to economic underdevelopment by misconceived, uninformed policies or systemic corruption, or both, to that extent the attendant internal instability and external interference in their domestic affairs are a function of their own conduct. In other cases however, economic underdevelopment and instability are a function of the asymmetrical relationships existing between the countries of the North and those of the South, which in turn are conditioned by the complex and extensive system of multilateral regimes established just before the termination of, and after World War II. Then it is necessary to modify the international normative framework to achieve an equitable distribution of material values in the international community as a necessary condition for the preservation of the national sovereignty and political independence of small states.

In relying on international law to support their claims for national security, territorial integrity and political independence, small states look to the international system as fashioned by the applicable norms. In this context, most small states tend to regard the United Nations as a means of establishing and maintaining, within a multilateral framework, relations with the wider international community as a viable alternative to a multiplicity of bilateral relations likely to exert unacceptable demands on their meagre financial resources. Membership of the United Nations and its specialised agencies afforded small states some plausible expectations of security from internal instability through access to much needed economic and technical developmental assistance, on the one hand, and from external aggression on the other, by affording such states direct access to the Security Council where threats to the peace and outright acts of aggression are addressed with a view to corrective action when, at least, the interests of the permanent members converged. For example, Guyana lodged a complaint with the Security Council in 1971 when Venezuela, in an unwarranted and unprovoked act of aggression, occupied the island of Ankoko in the Essequibo and which, incidentally, still remains under hostile occupation. In the absence of the convergence of the permanent members of the Security Council, the normal expectation is gridlock and masterly inactivity, punctuated by much disingenuous rhetoric.

The United Nations apart, other multilateral forums offering small states some measure of security are the Non-Aligned Movement and the Commonwealth. Although the untimely collapse of the USSR appeared to have deprived the Non Aligned movement of its essential rationale for existence, many small states prior to 1989 attracted much political support in the

Movement in respect of territorial claims of more powerful entities in the international community. Outstanding cases in point are Belize and Guyana, whose profile in the Movement was particularly high despite their small size. Guyana's considerable influence in this political grouping was perceived to have played an important part in compromising the territorial ambitions of Venezuela. Similarly, Belize enjoyed much support from the Non Aligned movement in resisting the unwarranted claims of Guatemala to its entire territory.

Membership of the Commonwealth also afforded both Guyana and Belize access to an influential multilateral forum whose membership encompassed all the continents and cut across the North-South divide of developed and developing countries. In point of fact, until recently the aspirants to territorial aggrandisement in both Central and South America were able to employ their influence in the hemispheric organisation, the OAS, to exclude Belize and Guyana from its Councils. And on the sub-regional level, both Guyana and Belize received unqualified support from CARICOM states in resisting the claims of Venezuela and Guatemala. In all the instances mentioned above, both Belize and Guyana, as small states, based their claims to territorial integrity and political independence on international law, employing the multilateral forums of international law to vindicate their rights.

Outside the western hemisphere many small states are members of the Organisation of African Unity (OAU) established in 1963, based on the principles of sovereignty, non-interference in internal affairs of member states, respect for territorial integrity, condemnation of subversion, support for self-determination of dependent territories and the peaceful resolution of conflicts. Among the small states of this grouping are Cape Verde, Sao Tomé and Guinea Bissau. In the Middle East, the Arab League boasts several small wealthy states including Bahrain, Qatar, Oman and Djibouti. Like the states of the Caribbean where the OECS exists as a sub-regional grouping, several African and Arab states have their own sub-groupings, for example, the Economic Community of West African states (ECOWAS) and the United Arab Emirates (UAE). In the Pacific region the Association of Southeast Nations (ASEAN) was established in 1967. But the micro-states of the South Pacific, which, like so many other island coastal states, are not even capable of protecting their fisheries resources in their exclusive economic zones (EEZs), are grouped in the South Pacific Forum. Many of these groupings are not military or security arrangements in the strict sense, and economic objectives bulk large in their constituent instruments. Nevertheless, they do afford small states some psychological measure of security from aggression, especially where the potential aggressors are part of the groupings concerned and, as such, are subjected to a variety of informal pressures to moderate their claims and resort to pacific disputes settlement.

Small States and International Law

A cursory examination of some of the responsibilities devolving on small states by virtue of their status in the international arena would readily confirm their inadequacy to safeguard their own national interest. As a territorial sovereign the small state is required to ensure stability, peace and good order for the protection, economic and social advancement of its peoples, and to provide reasonable protection for citizens of other states, as well as their entities, who are legitimately engaged in economic and other pursuits in the jurisdiction of the small state, with its consent. Such protection entails laws authoritatively enacted, a system of courts to interpret and apply the laws, and credible means of law enforcement.

In modern times, however, the ability of the small state to provide the required capabilities in adequate supply is eroded by the illegal activities of drug traffickers, gun runners, traders in the white slave traffic, and similar intrepid entrepreneurs whose financial and other resources dwarf those of small states. At present, those purveyors of social deviancy and moral turpitude have established their disposition to subvert governments and deploy the state apparatus to further their nefarious activities.

More importantly, the responsibilities of small states have been considerably enlarged by the adoption and entry into force of the United Nations Convention on the Law of the Sea (1982). The adoption of this Convention in Kingston, Jamaica, a small CARIOM state, must be seen as a tribute to the contribution of Jamaica, Guyana and Trinidad and Tobago to the final configuration of this international instrument.

The representatives of these small states, including the author of this paper, played a crucial role in elaborating and promoting the concept of the exclusive economic zone (EEZ), and in securing international legitimacy for the concept enunciated by Ambassador Arvid Pardo of Malta, that ocean space beyond the limits of national jurisdiction was common ground.

As a result of the acceptance of the EEZ as a territorial boundary in international law, the jurisdiction of coastal states, many of which are small island states, has been extended to two hundred nautical miles from the baselines from which the breadth of the territorial sea is measured.

According to the applicable provisions of the Convention, coastal states enjoy in this area sovereign rights for the purpose of exploring and exploiting, conserving and managing the living and non-living resources of the waters superjacent to the sea-bed as well as the resources of the sea-bed and its sub-soil. Such sovereign rights include economic exploitation of the area for the production of energy from the currents and other properties of the water, for example, through ocean thermal energy conversion technology (OTEC). In the EEZ, the coastal state also has jurisdiction over the use and establishment of artificial islands, installations and other structures, marine scientific research as well as the protection and preservation of the marine environment and the conservation of its resources.

The rights accorded to coastal states in the EEZ carry considerable corresponding obligations and problems with them, particularly small archipelagic states like the Bahamas consisting of over 700 islands and cays and comprehending a significant expanse of ocean space. Protection, conservation and management of the fisheries resources of this area require the acquisition and deployment of capabilities well beyond the known resources of the Bahamas. And the same is true for most small island states with an enlarged scope of competences in ocean space. Similar considerations arise in connection with the continental shelf, consisting of the seabed and subsoil of marine areas adjacent to the territorial sea and, for all practical purposes, co-extensive with the exclusive economic zone, except where the geological continental shelf extends beyond the outer limit of the EEZ. On the continental shelf as well, the coastal states have exclusive rights of exploration and exploitation of its resources. It is important to note, however, that whereas the rights of the coastal state in the resources of its continental shelf are an axiomatic attribute of statehood, the rights of the coastal states in relation to the EEZ are contingent on the declaration of such a zone by the coastal state.

If, as is generally accepted, the enlarged competences of the coastal state in adjacent ocean space constitute a formidable challenge to the capabilities of even major actors in the international arena, then it should be made compulsory, that small coastal states look to voluntary compliance by states, with their international obligations being the only plausible guarantee of their newly won rights in marine areas. And this is where international law might be expected to play a critical role in protecting the interests of small states. In this connection, however, it is important to enter a caveat in respect of selective and opportunistic reliance on international law, especially where disputes arise in relation to the exercise of sovereign competences, be it in ocean space or on territory inland therefrom. For, in the ultimate analysis, all that is required for a dispute to arise in international law is a claim and a counter-claim. Establishment of a legitimate interest is not a legal requirement as the Guyana and Belize experiences confirm, and to which the recent experiences of several OECS countries may attest in relation to claims espoused by Venezuela to areas of ocean space by reference to Avis Island which, according to the relevant provisions of the United Nations Convention on the Law of the Sea, has no status greater than that of a rock incapable of sustaining human life unaided, and, as such, not entitled to claim an exclusive economic zone or continental shelf. And, here again, it is only by a principled appeal to international law and, in particular, the applicable rules of the Convention on the Law of the Sea which, incidentally, the Government of the Republic of Venezuela has so far refused to sign, that the OECS states could have their interests in ocean space protected.

It is not to be assumed from the immediately foregoing, however, that international law, *per se*, provides an unassailable rampart behind which small states may secure protection from the deviant behaviour of state entities or others disposed to lawless conduct in the international community by virtue of their overweening power and influence. International law both determines and is determined by the conduct of subjects of international law, the most powerful of which are state entities. The fundamental principles of this normative regime address, and derive their legitimacy from the well-known prerogatives and attributes of statehood – the principles of sovereign independence, sovereign equality (interpreted to mean formal legal equality in popular parlance), territorial integrity and non-interference in the domestic affairs of states. But the contemporary wisdom of automatically according almost any entity, as a state with the presumed prerogatives and attributes identified above, despite persuasive objectively verifiable evidence to the contrary, has encouraged the proliferation of small states, aggravated the problems associated with the conduct of states in the international arena, and, as an ineluctable consequence, the management of international relations by reference to international law.

The emergence of many micro states in the international community with inadequate human, economic and financial capabilities to survive as viable independent entities underscores their vulnerability and makes them prime targets for intervention by powerful entities. With the development of international law, particularly in the areas of human rights, the traditional doctrine of non-interference in the domestic jurisdiction of states enshrined in Article 2(7) of the United Nations Charter has been open to serious challenge as exemplified in the activities of various intergovernmental organisations like the United Nations and its Commission on Human Rights, (a subordinate organ of ECOSOC), the European Court of Human Rights and the International Labour Organisation, to mention a few.

The wide range of instruments and determinations spawned by these and other organisations operating in the western hemisphere has altered the traditional corpus of international norms by legitimising interference by third states in matters which would normally be considered as falling within the domestic jurisdiction of states within the meaning of Article 2(7) of the Charter. Outstanding examples of such instruments are the International Covenants on Human Rights and Optional Protocol 1966; the International Covenant on the Elimination of All Forms of Racial Discrimination 1965; the European Convention on Human Rights 1950; the American Convention on Human Rights 1969, and the African Charter on Human and Peoples' Rights 1981.

In the present submission, there may be a strong argument in favour of construing the Charter of the United Nations as a whole, particularly as it relates to Article 2(7). In this context, it must be borne in mind that the Charter was in large measure the studied institutional response to the state system existing between the wars and many of the atrocities committed by governments against their civilian populations, particularly Jews, before and during the war. Viewed in this context, the provisions of Article 2(7) should never be construed as an absolute prohibition against interference in the domestic affairs of states. In any event, the principle of non-intervention is qualified by the proviso regarding the application of enforcement measures under Chapter VII of the Charter. Article 39 empowers the Security Council to determine, among other things, 'any threat to the peace' and the measures to be adopted in accordance with Articles 41 and 42. It is not inconceivable that the abuse of state power in relation to matters falling within the domestic jurisdiction of states may give rise to a determination that a threat to the peace exists, justifying the application of enforcement measures within the meaning of Chapter VII of the United Nations Charter.

Moreover, given the principle of self-determination in emerging international law, it is now generally accepted that states may intervene in the domestic affairs of colonial powers to assist peoples asserting their inherent right to self-determination. From the perspective of small independent states of the international community, however, it is cold comfort to accept that international law is in a continuing state of flux requiring normative adjustments to reflect an ever changing reality. For, given their vulnerability, which is a function of their inadequate capabilities and, consequently, the low threshold of intervention in matters pertaining to their domestic jurisdiction, their interests would always be extremely amenable to compromise should applicable norms of international law governing non-intervention be relaxed.

Despite the foregoing submissions, small states may find some solace from the inference that so long as they conduct their affairs, domestic and otherwise, in accordance with the prescriptions of their Charter, they run little risk of engaging their international responsibility and of inviting application of Charter VII measures. In this context, it is pertinent to point out that the provisions of Article 2(4) of the Charter appear to have acquired the status of *grundnorm* or a norm of *jus cogens* admitting of no derogation therefrom. This provision enjoins all members of the United Nations to 'refrain in their international relations from the threat or use of force against the territorial integrity or political independence of any state, or in any other manner inconsistent with the purposes of the United Nations'.

The only exception to this fundamental rule is to be found in Article 51 which recognises the inherent right of a country to self-defence. But when does the action of a state pursuant to Article 51 come within that provision and when does it not? Is the customary rule of anticipatory self-defence preserved by Article 51 or must a state wait to be attacked before responding? Many of these issues are in fact academic for the small state, which can neither initiate nor respond to aggression, and the applicable norms of international law offer no firm guidance.

Since the United Nations played a critical role in the creation and recognition of most of the small states existing in the international community, it is not unusual for many, if not all of these entities to rely on the collective security system of this world organisation to ensure their continued survival as independent entities, free from threats to their national sovereignty and territorial integrity. In this connection, many small states look to Article 33 of the Charter which requires that,

peace and security, (to), first of all, seek a resolution by negotiation, enquiry, mediation, conciliation, parties to any dispute, the continuance of which is likely to endanger the maintenance of international arbitration, judicial settlement, resort to regional agencies or arrangements, or other peaceful means of their own choice . . .

It empowers the Security Council to request the parties to employ one of these means. Further, some consolation may be secured from Article 99 of the Charter which authorises the Secretary General to bring to the attention of the Security Council any matter which, in his opinion, constitutes a threat to international peace and security.

Central to the collective security system of the United Nations is Chapter VII provisions of the Charter, which, in Article 39, not only requires the Security Council to 'determine the existence of any threat to the peace, breach of the peace or act of aggression', but also to decide on measures to maintain or restore international peace and security, including economic and military intervention as the situation justifies. To date, the collective security system of the United Nations has been a qualified success due to conditions which were never observed in good faith.

These include agreements by member states to make armed forces and military facilities available to the Security Council (Article 43); the obligation of member states to 'hold immediately available national air-force contingents for combined international enforcement action' at the disposal of the United Nations (Article 45), and the establishment of an effective Military Staff Committee

to advise and assist the Security Council on all questions relating to the Security Council's military requirements for the maintenance of international peace and security, the employment and command of Forces placed at its disposal, the regulation of armaments, and possible disarmament.

But, perhaps, the most debilitating aspect of this system of collective security was the requirement for all the permanent members of the Security Council to cast an affirmative vote in the Security Council on substantive issues before the applicable provisions of the Charter could come into operation (Article 27(3)). Such convergence of views among the permanent members proved impossible in the post-war period due to deep-seated ideological cleavage.

The outstanding exception to great power cooperation that proved the rule was the Security Council's sanctioning of allied intervention in Kuwait to expel Iraq, which had committed an unwarranted and unprovoked act of aggression against its neighbour, a small state.

Although the system of collective security enshrined in the Charter would appear to afford small states no absolute guarantee of protection against aggression by more powerful state entities, other than the permanent members or their closest allies, the Gulf War and the role of the Security Council in that sad episode provides enough lessons to operate as a disincentive to prospective aggressors. For, even though it is quite clear that allied military intervention was informed by perceptions of important national interests being endangered, it is open to no one in the international community to discern with precision what constitutes an important national interest of any state, or what considerations would advise the employment of force for the protection of such an interest. In any event, the applicable norms of international law do not preclude any state from seeking military assistance from friendly states (Grenada) where the national interest so prescribes, irrespective of the ability of the Security Council to act pursuant to the relevant provisions of the Charter.

In the context of the Caribbean Community which, as indicated above, is a grouping of small states for the purposes of this essay, initiatives have been taken with some degree of prompting from the USA and Canada, to establish a Regional Security Scheme (RSS) encompassing the OECS states and Barbados, whose Governments are extremely vulnerable to internal subversion as the experience of Grenada demonstrated. The RSS is a collective security arrangement intended to put at the disposal of participating Governments the means, military and otherwise, to deal with attempts at violent overthrow of such Governments. More recently, as the CARICOM countries have become important transit points for illegal drugs originating in South America and intended for the North American markets, the USA has been concluding shiprider agreements with most CARICOM states to search and interdict vessels in their territorial waters and EEZs. And herein is to be found another instance of international law allowing small states, as an attribute of sovereign competence, to rely on the capabilities of more powerful state entities to protect territories within their jurisdiction from the incursions of lawless elements in the international community.

Note

This paper was first published in *CARICOM Perspective*, No.66, June 1996, pp. 102–107.

[59]

Now that the Ship
Has Docked
A Postscript to the Shiprider Debate

K a t h y   B r o w n

There appears to be some confusion in the region as to whether Barbados and Jamaica signed the much heralded Shiprider agreement, that is, the agreement concerning Maritime Counter-Drug Operations, as has been signed by other CARICOM states, notably, Trinidad and Tobago, the OECS countries and Belize or the slightly different arrangement entered into by the Bahamas. The agreements signed by the Governments of Barbados and Jamaica with the USA are 'Agreements Concerning Co-operation in Suppressing Illicit Maritime Drug Trafficking'. They establish a very different regime for cooperation in maritime counter-drug activities than that proposed by the USA in the Shiprider agreement. The offensive and controversial aspects of the Shiprider arrangement have been either omitted or reworked and the revised documents which have emerged provide the region with a choice of two acceptable legal frameworks for cooperation in the suppression of the illicit traffic in narcotic drugs based on the fundamental principles of reciprocity and respect for sovereignty and the rule of law.

The Shiprider agreement attempts to rewrite basic rules of international law within the Caribbean region. The greatest danger posed by the agreement stems from the power which international law ascribes to its subjects. International law is built on treaties and other forms of state practice. State practice over time may craft new rules of law completely contrary to formerly well established principles. It is therefore possible for a multilateral treaty or a series of bilateral agreements to shape new customary rules of law paralleling treaty law. This sort of mechanism, based on a process of transfusion of treaty law into customary law, has been used by the USA to clarify rules of international law in keeping with its interests, particularly in the fields of intellectual property rights and foreign investment. Typically, in these instances there has been some controversy over the customary rules which govern.

The rules governing the law of the sea have been largely settled by the 1982 United Nations Convention on the Law of the Sea. USA President, Reagan, in refusing to sign the 1982 Convention, declared that the compromises reflected in the convention which were satisfactory to the USA had emerged as customary rules of law and as such were binding on all states, while others which the USA found objectionable were merely rules of treaty law and bound only those states which signed the convention. Among the rules stated in the 1982 Convention which, undoubtedly, reflect customary international law are rules governing jurisdiction within the territorial sea and internal waters and others relating to the treatment of vessels on the high seas. Although states may choose to derogate from these customary rules in their relations *interse* they are not free to implement their agreements so as to erode the rights of third parties as may arise, for example, in the treatment of third state nationals or third state flag vessels.

In enlisting one Caribbean Government after another the USA has strung together a series of bilateral Shiprider agreements which threatened to emerge over time as a norm sanctioning broad USA competence within the Caribbean region. In the post CARICOM-USA summit era the Shiprider arrangement looms less ominously. In standing up for principle Barbados and Jamaica have highlighted the unacceptable nature of the offensive aspects of the Shiprider agreement. Moreover, if various statements made by leaders in the Eastern Caribbean are to be believed the Shiprider agreement may well unravel and with it the USA proposed 'seamless web', which has stretched like a dark cloud hanging over the Caribbean Sea.

Comparison of the Barbados and Jamaica Agreements and the Shiprider

In contrast with the Shiprider arrangement, both the Barbados and Jamaica agreements are reciprocal in nature. The significance of this should not be minimised. The principle of reciprocity is a useful check in defining relationships between sovereign states and increases in value with the likelihood that rights conferred in the agreement may actually be acted upon by the weaker state. The majority of the rights conferred within USA waters and USA airspace in the Barbados and Jamaica agreements, admittedly, are not likely to be invoked by either Barbados or Jamaica. In other respects, however, as in relation to rights concerning the interdiction of vessels seaward of any nation's territorial sea, these small states may be able to take advantage of these agreements to assist their efforts in suppressing the illicit drug trade.

The scope of the Barbados and Jamaica agreements differs somewhat. The Barbados agreement covers only the territorial sea of the parties (for the USA, including USA territories in the Caribbean area, that is, the Commonwealth of Puerto Rico and US Virgin Islands) and excludes internal waters, such as ports, bays and rivers. The Jamaica agreement covers all areas over which the coastal state exercises sovereignty, that is, internal waters, archipelagic waters (in the case of Jamaica) as well as the territorial sea. The broader scope of the Jamaica agreement mirrors the Shiprider arrangement in this respect. However, as we shall see, the Jamaica agreement hits at the very heart of the Shiprider arrangements in denying the extensive rights which the Shiprider grants to USA vessels in areas covered by the agreement.

A significant feature of both Barbados and Jamaica agreements is the added detail which is used to safeguard the interests of the parties. This is seen, for example, in the emphasis placed on the criterion of reasonableness, a concept which scarcely is mentioned in the Shiprider agreement. The use of force provision in the Shiprider arrangement contains a general prescription to use the minimum force reasonably necessary under the circumstances. It provides a good contrast with the detail of the Barbados and Jamaica agreements which place strict limitations on the use of force. The Barbados and Jamaica agreements, for example, expressly proscribe the discharge of firearms without the previous authorisation of the flag or coastal state except when warning shots are required as a signal for a vessel to stop, or in the exercise of the right of self-defence.

The Combined Maritime Law Enforcement Programme of the Barbados agreement is coordinated by a combined Coordinating and Planning Committee which oversees the planning, professional exchange, pre-deployment exercises and operations of the programme. It is envisaged that one party will request the other to make available law enforcement vessel to enable the coastal state, that is, the requesting party, effectively to patrol and conduct surveillance of its own waters. All law enforcement operations are clearly under the control and direction of the party in whose waters the operations are being conducted. The law enforcement vessel which is loaned to the requesting party shall, during such operations, also fly the flag or ensign of that party. The Jamaica agreement omits a few of the details of the Barbados agreement. Still, in practice, combined operations in the context of the Barbados and Jamaica agreements will take place on a similar basis.

The 'Shiprider Program' after which the entire USA proposed the Maritime Counter-Drug Operations Agreement has become known, and is probably one of the least offensive aspects of that agreement as coastal state authorities exercise some ostensible control. The program is somewhat similar to that envisaged in the Barbados and Jamaica agreements, however, there are important though seemingly subtle distinctions which may be drawn. The Barbados and Jamaica agreements essentially envisage a 'hands off' approach where a detachment of coastal officials embarked on the other party's vessel engage in law enforcement activities without assistance unless exceptional circumstances arise. The USA proposed Shiprider Program assumes a 'hands on' approach with one local law enforcement official, the Shiprider, embarked on a USA vessel authorising USA Coast Guard operations.

The distinction between the two approaches is highlighted in some of the details of the Jamaica agreement. Article 7 (2) of the Jamaica agreement, for example, provides that in order to fulfil their responsibilities, Jamaican officials may 'request the Commanding Officer of the USA law enforcement vessel to take navigational measures or allow the Jamaican law enforcement officials to use the vessel's systems to communicate with the suspect vessel . . . '. Article 7 (3) further underscores that '[a]ll law enforcement activities . . . shall be under the control and direction of Jamaican law enforcement officials and shall be conducted in accordance with Jamaican law'. Article 3 (8) of the Barbados agreements is of similar import. It clearly defines the responsibilities of law enforcement officials of both parties. Tactical or operational control of the vessel is in the hands of the state which makes the vessel available: all other activities are under the control and direction of the state in whose waters the operations are being conducted.

Pursuit and Entry

The basic principle underlying the Jamaica and Barbados agreements is that enforcement action within the jurisdiction of the coastal state is the reverse of officials of the coastal state. The Jamaica agreement, which covers all coastal waters in contrast with the Barbados agreement, adopts a slightly stricter approach than the Barbados agreement on the issue of pursuit and entry.

The Jamaica agreement expressly provides that a party must make a 'special request . . . for *ad hoc* permission' to pursue vessels into the other party's waters or enter the other party's waters to investigate suspect craft. Any such, *ad hoc* request for permission *shall be supported by the basis on which it is claimed that special circumstances exist and that there are reasonable grounds for the alleged suspicion* (Article 10 (2), added emphasis). The agreement further provides that in granting permission the coastal state 'may give such directions and *attach any conditions* it considers appropriate to such permission'. (Article 10 (3), added emphasis) Article 17 (6) of the 1988 United Nations Convention Against Illicit Traffic in Narcotic Drugs and Psychotropic Substances, on which the Jamaican provision is modelled, expressly refers to conditions, 'including conditions relating to responsibility'. Other assistance, such as boarding and searching vessels may take place only on and in accordance with the express instructions of the coastal state. To this extent the position adopted in the Jamaica agreement is essentially the same as would exist if there was no agreement between the parties at all.

The Memorandum of Understanding between the Jamaican and USA Governments permits pursuit or entry 'upon notice' in extraordinary circumstances for the *sole purpose of maintaining contact with a suspect vessel*, pending response to permission requested. The Jamaica agreement, however, expressly excludes any authorisation of enforcement action against Jamaican flag vessels (defined as including registered or licensed fishing vessels) in Jamaican waters.

The Barbados agreement adopts a slightly different approach. It permits a party to pursue suspect vessels into the other party's territorial sea and pending the receipt of instructions or the arrival of local law enforcement officials, the pursuing vessel may order or signal the suspect vessel to stop. No further action against the suspect craft is authorised and any further assistance is subject to the direction of local law enforcement officials. The diplomatic note from the Barbados Ministry of Foreign Affairs to the USA Embassy expresses the understanding of the Barbadian Government that in '*exceptional circumstances . . . if the situation deteriorates*' (added emphasis) coastal state officials may give directions, *inter alia*, to stop, board and search suspect vessels.

In other circumstances where a suspect vessel is located within the territorial sea of one party, *before* a vessel of the other party may enter coastal waters, it must obtain confirmation from coastal authorities that no local law enforcement vessel is immediately available to investigate. In these circumstances entry is permitted only in order to maintain contact with the suspect craft and keep it under surveillance until local law enforcement officials take control of the situation. Pending the receipt of instructions or the arrival of local law enforcement officials, the law enforcement vessel of the other party may order or signal the suspect vessel to stop. Coastal authorities must be kept continuously informed of the situation and any further action against the suspect vessel only may take place on and in accordance with the express instructions of the coastal state.

The Jamaica and Barbados agreements stand in stark contrast to the Shiprider arrangement. In the Shiprider agreement USA Coast Guard vessels are authorised to pursue suspect vessels into coastal waters where they may stop, board and search such vessels without initiating any contact with the coastal state. Where local Shipriders are 'unavailable to embark on a USA vessel' (an extremely broadly worded phrase) USA Coast Guard vessels may enter coastal waters and investigate any suspect aircraft or board and search any suspect vessel other than a coastal state flag vessel. Caribbean states party to the agreement, conversely, enjoy no similar rights in USA waters.

The broad language of the Shiprider agreement conferring extensive powers on USA Coast Guard within Caribbean waters (including internal waters) has been omitted from the Jamaica and Barbados agreements. Still, out of an abundance of caution the Jamaica and Barbados agreements stipulate that nothing in the agreement shall be construed to permit a law enforcement vessel of one party to 'randomly patrol' within the waters of the other party.

The different approaches of the Jamaica and Barbados agreements with respect to pursuit and entry of law enforcement vessels of one party into the waters of the other party are sustained in those provisions governing overflight. The Jamaica agreement establishes the basic principle that USA aircraft may not manoeuvre within Jamaican airspace in order to maintain contact with suspect vessels or aircraft without the express authorisation of Jamaican authorities granted on a case by case basis. Aircraft of one party, however, may overfly the territory and waters of the other party in pursuit of suspect vessels or aircraft fleeing into or located within the other party's waters and airspace, provided that the appropriate law enforcement and civil aviation authorities are notified and information is provided as to the grounds on which the vessel or aircraft is reasonably suspected of engaging in illicit traffic. The Memorandum of Understanding between the parties further suggests that the party overflown may request aircraft of one party to relay to the suspect aircraft orders to comply with the instructions and directions of its flight safety and law enforcement authorities.

The Barbados agreement, on the other hand, provides prior authorisation for either party to fly in the other's airspace and to order aircraft reasonably suspected of illicit traffic to land. The agreement excludes 'scheduled civil aircraft or other duly authorised non-scheduled civil aircraft' (Article 7(2) (b)). The equivalent Jamaican provision refers to 'aircraft engaged in legitimate scheduled or charter operations for the carriage of passengers, baggage or cargo' (Article 11 (5)). Both Jamaica and Barbados agreements underscore the need for compliance with air navigation and air safety directions and the importance of maintaining contact with the appropriate aviation and law enforcement authorities.

The importance accorded to flight safety is what distinguishes the Barbados agreement from the Shiprider approach. The Shiprider agreement contains a minimal reference to the parties instituting appropriate notification procedures of overflight activity by USA aircraft. In the amended four-part Shiprider agreements where a distinction is drawn between planned and unplanned USA operations, USA pursuit of suspect aircraft into the other party's airspace is authorised on the basis that the parties '*may* exchange information concerning appropriate communication channels and other information pertinent to flight safety.' (Article 8 BIS, added emphasis).

In the Barbados and Jamaica agreements suspect vessels and aircraft within areas under state sovereignty must be prosecuted according to the laws of the coastal state. Where suspect vessels are detained seaward of any nation's territorial sea, a party may waive its right to exercise jurisdiction and will not object to the other party enforcing its laws against the vessel, cargo and persons on board other than nationals of the flag state. The Shiprider agreement, however, suggests that the coastal state may waive its primary right to exercise jurisdiction and authorise the enforcement of USA law against vessels and/or persons on board whether detained in coastal waters or on the high seas and regardless of an individual's nationality. The Shiprider provision offends basic principles of international law.

The Jamaica and Barbados agreements adopt a similar position on the issue of interdiction on the high seas. The Jamaica agreement, however, contains two provisions relating to high seas boardings while the Barbados agreement contains only one. The Barbados agreement adopts the traditional, more cautious 'will not object' formula. The Jamaica agreement, however, follows the more recent trend in granting 'authorisation' in certain circumstances.

Article 3 of the Jamaica agreement establishes basic procedures regarding shipboarding in operations seaward of the territorial sea. These procedures include verification of registry and a request for authorisation to board and search. Article 14 (2) of the Jamaica agreement provides that if the flag state fails to respond for three hours after receipt of confirmation in writing of an oral request for verification of claim of registry, it will be deemed to have authorised the other party to stop, board and search the vessel. The Barbados agreement contains no provision equivalent to Article 3 of the Jamaica agreement. However, Article 14 of the Barbados and Jamaica agreements are substantially the same. In practice, therefore, high seas boardings in the context of either arrangement will take place on a similar basis.

The contrast with the Shiprider agreement is marked. In the Shiprider arrangement whenever USA Coast Guard officials encounter a suspect vessel registered in a state party to the agreement, located seaward of any nation's territorial sea, USA Coast Guard officials are authorised to stop, board and search the vessel without any prior contact with flag state authorities. The Caribbean state party to the agreement, however, has no similar rights with respect to USA vessels even within Caribbean waters located seaward of its contiguous zone (that is, a maximum breadth of 24 miles from shore used to measure the territorial sea).

Claims against the USA Government and its Forces

The issue of the privileges and immunities remains largely unresolved in the Barbados and Jamaica agreements. Neither agreement establishes any particular regime regulating jurisdiction over law enforcement officials involved in maritime operations. Still, the numerous restrictions placed on enforcement action by non-coastal state officials in the context of the Jamaica and Barbados agreements effectively limit the opportunities for improper or unreasonable actions by such officials and thereby reduces the significance of this omission. Additionally, the Barbados agreement provides that '[i]n the event that the parties are unable to resolve a claim, it *shall be settled in accordance with the domestic law of the parties'*. (Article 19 (4), added emphasis). The Jamaican agreement contains no equivalent provision. However, accompanying both Barbados and Jamaica agreements is a letter from the USA Ambassador stating that where the USA Government is joined in a claim against the coastal state for loss or injury suffered as a result of any action by the USA Government or its officials, the USA will not claim sovereign immunity if the remedy sought is damages.

The Shiprider agreement as proposed by the USA provides full immunity from criminal prosecution for USA officials and immunity from civil suit limited to acts performed in the course of their duties. (Note that the Trinidad and Tobago agreement omits this provision). Additionally, there is no established mechanism capable of ensuring a final resolution of claims. Neither is any assurance provided to the coastal state that the USA will not claim immunity from suit.

Finally, perhaps the greatest safeguard in the Barbados and Jamaica agreements is the three months termination clause. This may be contrasted with a one-year termination provision in the Shiprider agreement. Should the USA fail to honour its commitments Barbados and Jamaica simply may terminate the arrangement upon three months notice and return to the previous *status quo*.

The preamble of the Barbados agreement underscores the magnitude and complex nature of the problem of illicit traffic in narcotic drugs and the links between illicit traffic in drugs and other criminal activities. Significantly also, it recalls, *inter alia*, the 1996 UN International Drug Control Programme (UNDCP) Regional Meeting Plan of Action for Drug Control Coordination and Cooperation in the Caribbean. The UNDCP brings all the parties with significant interests in the region, including the European Union, to the negotiating table. It offers a forum with the potential of shaping a new multilateral maritime cooperation arrangement which draws upon the best aspects of the Jamaica and Barbados agreements.

Note

This paper was first published in *CARICOM Perspective*, No. 67, June 1997, pp. 48–51, 71.

[60]

The Implications of the Uruguay Round for CARICOM States[1]

Frank Rampersad

After almost eight years of negotiations, which were initiated by the ministerial declaration made at Punta del Este in 1986, the international community signed a new agreement on April 15, 1994 to regulate international trade in goods and services. The agreement, which built upon and enlarged arrangements reached in earlier rounds of negotiations, continued the process of liberalising the conditions under which international trade in goods and services is carried out. It clarified certain of the provisions incorporated in GATT 1947, and greatly enlarged the scope and coverage of international surveillance over trade matters; it established new and more functional machinery to monitor international trade in goods and services and outlawed certain restrictive practices which had been introduced, often outside the framework of GATT, to frustrate imports. The agreement came into force on January 1, 1995 when the World Trade Organisation (WTO) was formally established to replace the GATT secretariat. This is a far reaching agreement which, in certain important respects, went beyond the Havana Charter. It includes within its framework specific provisions relating to trade in agriculture, textiles and clothing, services, trade related intellectual property rights and trade related investment measures, subjects which had not, up to now, been explicitly covered in the agreements reached under GATT.

The Agreement

The negotiations and the subsequent agreements are significant in the following respects:

- They were held at a time when industrialised countries were erecting a proliferation of new obstacles against exports from the developing countries. Non-tariff barriers in existence at the start of the negotiations exceeded 250; and in many instances, these were applied in an unpredictable manner, often in contravention of existing international agreements.
- They brought together the largest number of countries to the negotiating table: 118 countries participated in the round among whom were 91 developing countries. Nine CARICOM states participated in the negotiations and signed the agreements reached.
- They were the first set of negotiations on international trade to be completed in the new political environment created by the collapse of the Socialist bloc which resulted in a significant re-ordering of the political balance in world affairs. The collapse of the bloc resulted in a substantial downgrading of the concept of special and differential treatment for developing countries and the rise to prominence of the dictum of 'no free riders'.
- They included for the first time, within the framework of an international agreement on trade, the agricultural sector and trade in internationally traded services, and dealt definitively with the vexed question of the Multifibres Agreement (MFA) which was a derogation from GATT 1947.
- They covered also trade in intellectual property and trade related investment measures. The agreement on the Trade in Services is incorporated in a separate Agreement (GATS) but it not only incorporates many of the principles enshrined in GATT but is umbilically linked with GATT 1994 and the WTO through its connections with the Trade in Intellectual Property Rights (TRIPs) and the Dispute Settlement Body (DSB) established under the WTO.
- They resulted in the refurbishing of the machinery for the settlement of disputes in trade related matters and effectively removed the veto which an accused country could exercise over the implementation of a panel decision arising out of a dispute.
- They appear to be the harbinger of a new development in international economic relations under which we are likely to witness a growing trend towards the internationalisation of domestic economic policy formulation.

The agreement resulted in the establishment of an interlocking network of surveillance machinery in which all member states have the right to participate (China is not yet a member of the WTO but is now actively seeking membership). The supreme body is the Ministerial Conference which will meet once every two years and will consider major issues. In the interval, the functions of the conference will be undertaken by a general council which will include all the members of the WTO and will administer the dispute settlement machinery as well as the Trade Policy Review Board, which has now been made a permanent body, with responsibility for reviewing the trade policies pursued by individual member states. In addition, separate councils are established for each of the main areas covered by the agreements for example, Trade in Goods, GATS and TRIPs. Specialised committees have been set up for agriculture, sanitary and phytosanitary regulations, safeguards and anti-dumping, trade related investment measures (TRIMs), textiles and clothing and rules of origin and subsidies. Finally, the agreement clarified a number of areas in GATT 1947 which had given rise to disputes in the past.

The Uruguay Round produced an umbrella agreement which established the WTO. Under this Agreement there are three separate agreements.

(1) The agreement on Trade in Goods which covered all goods including manufactured goods, agriculture and textiles and clothing. Included within the scope of this agreement is the agreement on subsidies and countervailing duties, safeguards and anti-dumping mechanisms, and on the application of TRIMs. There was also agreement on the establishment of a permanent trade policy review mechanism to replace one established on an interim basis in 1989.
(2) The agreement on Trade in Services covered almost the entire field of the trade in Services with the exception of government services and government procurement.
(3) The agreement on Trade in Intellectual Property Rights.

In addition to the above, the Uruguay Round gave more definitive interpretations to certain provisions of GATT 1947 which had led to disputes in the past and provided for the continuation of negotiations, in accordance with a fixed timetable, on certain areas in the services sector in which final agreement could not be reached. These include financial services, maritime transport, telecommunications and movement of natural persons. Finally, certain countries concluded plurilateral agreements covering trade in civil aircraft, Government procurement, dairy products and bovine meat.

Goods and Services

With regard to manufactured goods, the principal agreement is that tariffs will be reduced significantly. For the industrialised countries, the average reduction is about 40 per cent over five years; developing countries have also been required to, and did in fact, make significant cuts in their tariffs. What is more is that the proportion of tariffs which is bound has greatly increased. In consequence, the average tariff in the industrialised countries will decline from six per cent in 1994 to less than four per cent by the year 2005. However, tariffs on certain goods of importance to developing countries have not been reduced to the same extent and, in general, the reductions in tariffs on goods of importance to developing countries have been lower than those of importance to the industrialised countries. Almost 90 per cent of the imports made by the industrialised countries are now bound while the proportion for the developing countries is almost 70 per cent. There is therefore, greater predictability in the conditions under which international trade will be carried out in the area of manufactured goods, although opportunities for the application of non-tariff barriers still remain.

With regard to textiles and clothing, the decision was taken to phase out definitively the MFA by 2005. The phasing out will be done in stages as follows.

(1) From January 1, 1995, 16 per cent of the imports of textiles and clothing will be free of any restrictions such as those incorporated in the MFA. On January 1, 1998 a further 17 per cent will be removed and on January 1, 2002, 18 per cent will be taken out; all textiles and clothing will be removed from quantitative and other restrictions on January 1, 2005. Small exporters such as those in CARICOM will be allowed an acceleration in the liberalisation process.

(2) Parallel with the removal of imports from MFA restrictions, there will be an increase in allowed bilateral quotas; these quotas will be increased by 16 per cent on January 1, 1995, 25 per cent on January 1, 1998 and 28 percent on January 1, 2002. It should be noted, however, that these increases are percentages of percentages so that the 16 per cent quota increase for a country with a 6 per cent annual quota growth would see that quota now rise to 6.96 per cent per year.

The point must be made, however, that since the MFA does not now cover all textiles and clothing but the Uruguay Round of Agreement relates to the whole sector, it is unlikely that there will be any significant freeing up of the international trade in textiles and clothing until year 2005 because countries will begin their freeing up programme by including clothing items which are not now covered by the restrictions under MFA. Besides, given the resistance which certain interests in the industrialised countries have demonstrated to the phasing out of the MFA, there is concern that the safeguards and anti-dumping provisions of the WTO may be invoked to defer the freeing up of the trade in textiles and clothing.

Finally, although the developing countries as a collective body made the elimination of the MFA a condition of their agreement to other provisions incorporated in the Uruguay Round, many analysts are coming around to the view that the gains from such elimination will be unequally shared – the principal beneficiaries being China, India, Vietnam, Bangladesh and Indonesia. CARICOM states which have invested heavily in textiles and clothing must therefore fortify their strategic alliances with importers in the industrialised countries in order to protect their investment and the employment which it created.

Agriculture is of some significance for CARICOM states in that the Sugar Protocol included in the Lomé Convention, and the quota arrangements with USA have been preserved. In effect this means that the Sugar Protocol in the Lomé Convention has an indefinite life although the price will have to be negotiated every year and most observers are agreed that, because of other provisions under the Uruguay Round, prices could fall by 10 per cent. The situation with bananas still, however, remains difficult and, given the aggressive posture to it from the USA, it would be unwise to plan on the basis that the existing agreement with the European Union will go beyond year 2002.

In the agricultural sector, tariffs will be reduced in the industrialised countries by 36 per cent over six years; the developing countries will reduce their tariffs by 24 per cent over ten years. Further non-tariff barriers will be taxed and the resulting tariff will be reduced by the same percentages over the period. Finally, all resulting agricultural tariffs will be bound. Export subsidies on agricultural exports are to be cut by 24 per cent over six years in the industrialised countries (14 per cent over ten years for the developing countries). Domestic subsidies and other forms of support will be cut by 36 per cent in the industrialised countries over six years and by 24 per cent over ten years by the developing countries. All countries will still, however, be able to provide generalised support to their agricultural sector, for example, research services and extension services. The base date for measuring the cuts in subsidies is 1986-1990 although, in the case of unconnected subsidies, the base date may be 1990-1992, this later base date being introduced by the industrialised countries to enable them to give additional support to their agricultural sector.

The process of tariffication has exposed fully the enormity of the barriers which the industrialised countries have historically erected against the exports of certain agricultural commodities. In many instances the tariffication exercise has produced tariffs as high as 500 per cent and, in their final filing of tariffs for the sector, some countries have resorted to 'dirty tariffication' and increased the levels of applicable tariffs even further. The reality with which CARICOM countries must come to terms is that the industrialised countries attach high priority to maintaining a thriving agricultural sector and to ensuring a minimum national food security. CARICOM states may see a need to reconsider their policy stance on the matter of food security.

One of the consequences of the agreement is that countries which are net food importers (CARICOM countries are among them) will have to pay more for some of their imports, such as wheat, animal feed and dairy products. On the whole therefore, the agreement on agriculture presents CARICOM states with certain very serious policy options which they will need to examine very carefully.

The services sector is covered by a separate agreement (GATS) which is umbilically linked to GATT 1994 through TRIPs and the Dispute Settlement Body. In its present form GATS is mainly a framework agreement which puts a freeze on new restrictive measures and sets the stage for future negotiations. It is specifically provided that the negotiations on services will be resumed in five years' time. But the scope of the agreement is very wide, covering all services with the exception of Government services and Government procurement. The negotiations in four areas – financial services, maritime transportation, telecommunications and the movement of natural persons are to be continued. The negotiations on financial services broke down in July 1995 when USA refused to agree with the rest of the world. The negotiations in respect of the other areas are continuing with a completion date of April 1997.

Inter alia, the agreement provides for national treatment of enterprises which deliver their services through a commercial presence and for MFN treatment to all providers of internationally traded services. It recognises four principal modes of delivery of services: cross-border supply, consumption abroad, the establishment of a commercial presence and the movement of natural persons.

Under the terms of the agreement, as long as a country has made an offer – and hence entered into a binding commitment – it is entitled to receive MFN treatment from all other members. To illustrate this point, GATT has identified 11 classes of services and almost 160 sub-classes. As long as a country has made an offer even in one sub-class (with or without restrictions) it is entitled to MFN treatment on all its services exports from countries whose offers may cover the full 160 sub-classes. CARICOM States have made offers and therefore accept the binding commitment and receive the advantage of MFN. It should be noted, however, that these States have attached conditions to their offers so that no damage is done to the concept of the single market and economy on which agreement has been reached by Ministers in CARI-COM.

It is possible to be disappointed with regard to the scope of the negotiations on the movement of natural persons in that they appear to be concerned mainly with the movement of high level personnel rather than with general freedom of movement, which is what economic behaviour would require, that people move to where the jobs are. This asymmetry is a characteristic of much of the text of the agreement on the WTO, particularly as it concerns the small developing countries.

The introduction of GATS does present one complication about which CARICOM States need to be aware. This is the issue of cross retaliation, that is, if a country is in breach of a provision in the area of goods, an aggrieved country may retaliate by taking action in the area of services and vice-versa. Since CARICOM states will have to take more positive action in the future to develop their services sector, they will need to be very meticulous in observing all the provisions of the WTO.

TRIPs

The agreement on Trade Related Aspects of Intellectual Property Rights (TRIPs) prescribes a régime within which the trade in intellectual property will be carried out. It is intended to work in tandem with the WIPO which remains in existence.

The agreement on Trade in Intellectual Property Rights provides for the establishment of minimum standards of protection for each of the principal categories of intellectual property; the procedures and remedies to be incorporated in national law so that intellectual property rights can be effectively protected; the application of general dispute settlement machinery; and close working relationships between WTO and WIPO.

Under the agreement, the holders of intellectual property rights are given greater protection and for longer periods than they formerly enjoyed. Further, the concept of intellectual property rights has been extended and now covers computer programmes and designs, subjects which, although agreed in negotiations, have not yet received international sanction. Besides, the agreement requires each participating state to establish adequate surveillance machinery to ensure that the foreign holders of intellectual property rights are given sufficient protection. It introduces the novel concept in law that a person who is charged with infringing intellectual property rights must prove his innocence.

However, while that agreement seeks to give protection to the inventors of new processes and to ensure that they are adequately rewarded, it gives little attention to the needs of the countries from which basic material was first extracted. To be specific, a great deal of the pressure for the intellectual property rights agreement under the WTO came from the pharmaceutical companies. They wanted to ensure that they received adequate compensation for research and development (R&D) expenditures which they incurred. But the R&D expenditures were incurred on plants which they extract, in the main, from the developing countries and these countries, which provide the basic feedstock, do not share in the income which is derived from the exploitation. In other words, while the new agreement seeks to reward companies for any new genes which they may have implanted, it does not recognise the value of the vast majority of the other genes and which are part of the national patrimony of the countries involved. What is more, as has been demonstrated by the case of the neem plant which farmers in India have grown for centuries, countries can find themselves in serious litigation because of the way in which the present rules have been formulated, and it is not at all clear whether a farmer who purchases patented planting material can use seeds from it to grow another crop without having to pay royalty again. It is to be hoped that the recent decision by the European Parliament[2] on this matter will bring some balance in the picture.

There is little doubt that the existence of TRIPs will result in the developing countries having to pay more for the technology which they require. The agreement also, *de facto*, puts an end to the process of reverse engineering which provided much of the impulse for the modernisation of the economy of Japan and, latterly, of South Korea. Besides, the uncertainty which the situation creates may operate as an important disincentive to developing countries in seeking to improve their technological progress. CARICOM States will need to address this issue when the negotiations resume in five years time.

TRIMs

One of the innovations in the WTO is the inclusion of a specific provision which puts certain restrictions on the kind of measures which developing countries can adopt in managing the private foreign investment which they attract. These limitations are contained in the agreement on Trade Related Investment Measures (TRIMs) which, in addition to requiring the notification to WTO of all TRIMs, calls for an end to certain arrangements on the grounds that they are trade distorting. There should be an end to local content requirement, that is, using products of local origin, and to trade balancing requirement, or limiting the purchase or use of imports to the amount of local purchases. The practice of foreign exchange balancing, which is restricting access to foreign exchange, and that of export limitation, which requires the enterprise to limit its exports in order to satisfy domestic needs first, should also stop.

Developed countries are required to eliminate TRIMs within two years; developing countries are allowed five years and least developed countries are given a seven-year period.

A committee for TRIMs has been established to monitor the agreement and to consider requests from developing countries for special dispensation to cope with balance of payments difficulties.

It can be stated that, in a technical sense, TRIMs is not a new provision under GATT. In mid 1980s, following a complaint by USA against Canada, GATT ruled that restrictions covered by the TRIMs agreement were a violation of Article XXIII of GATT 1947. However, two things should be noted. Firstly, the agreement represents a complete turn around in the international preoccupations which, up to that time, were concerned with devising ways to curb the restrictive practices of transnationals. These plans so absorbed the attention of UN officials that it had reached the stage of a Code of Conduct for the transnationals. That route has now been abandoned with the TRIMs Agreement.

Secondly, it is likely that the international community, under pressure from the transnationals, will press for further encroachment on the sovereignty of the developing countries in the exercise of their economic policy. The industrialised countries wanted the TRIMs Agreement to be an Investment Agreement which, *inter alia*, would guarantee their transnationals the right of establishment and national treatment. They tried to achieve this during the Uruguay Round but encountered resistance from the developing countries. However, the agreement in its present form provides that the Council for Trade in Goods will review the agreement after five years to determine whether it should be implemented. This is a clear indication that the industrialised countries will press for the conversion of the TRIMs agreement into an agreement on Investment Policies and International Competition.

In light of the existing and projected position, it may be necessary for CARICOM States to re-examine the content of their existing incentive packages. They will certainly have to work out an approach to deal with the review process.

Safeguards

One of the contentious areas of international trade negotiations relates to the use of measures to deal with unexpected and large increases in imports which threaten serious injury to existing national producers. The industrialised countries have found that the safeguard provisions in GATT 1947 excessively restricted their ability to protect their sensitive industries and increasingly, they resorted to other measures such as Voluntary Export Restraints (VERs), Organised Market Arrangements (OMAs), and to threats of invoking such measures.

The new Agreement on Safeguards delimits the scope of action which countries may adopt to deal with sudden and large increases in imports which threaten serious injury to national industries. Of particular interest to CARICOM countries is that, in theory, the agreement specifically outlaws arrangements such as VERs and OMAs, but countries are still allowed quota modulation which, in practice, can amount to the very same thing as VERs.

The agreement under the Uruguay Round provides for a time bound application of quotas which would result in imports not being below the level existing at a certain date. It sought to give some relief to developing countries by requiring their exclusion from quota restraints provided that the aggregate of imports from all developing countries did not exceed nine per cent of total imports and further that, within this total, no individual developing country was supplying more than three per cent of the total imports. If, however, the aggregate exports from developing countries exceed nine per cent, then the three per cent limit will not apply. In total, however, this does not provide much relief to individual developing countries which must greatly expand their exports in order to develop and grow.

Trade Policy Review Mechanism

One of the objectives of the Uruguay Round was to give greater transparency to the conditions under which international trade is carried out. This was one of the considerations uppermost in the minds of the negotiators from the developing countries as they had witnessed the introduction, by the industrialised countries, of measures designed to circumvent the provisions of GATT 1947 and the results of subsequent rounds of negotiations, such as the introduction of VERs and OMAs and the use of phytosanitary and other restrictions to keep out the exports from the developing countries. The decision to cause greater transparency is evident in the large number of Committees, Councils, Working Groups and Expert Groups which have been set up under the WTO. In addition, there was agreement on a list of Notifiable Procedures. But perhaps the most embracing and comprehensive mechanism introduced to provide transparency was the Trade Policy Review Mechanism.

This mechanism, which has operated on an interim basis since 1989 and is now part of the permanent machinery of the WTO, provides for the collective evaluation of the full range of the trade practices of individual member countries and their impact on the functioning of the multilateral trading system.

Under the Trade Policy Review Mechanism (TPRM) the trading policies of the four largest trading countries – the European Union, the United States, Canada and Japan – will be reviewed once every two years. The next 16 largest trading countries, among whom are six developing countries, will be reviewed once every four years. The remaining countries, other than those defined as least developed, will be reviewed once every six years. Separate timetables will be set for the least developed countries. The WTO secretariat is enabled to provide technical assistance to the developing and least developed countries in preparing the review reports.

One of the problems which the complicated set of surveillance machinery creates for CARICOM states is how to service them effectively, given the limited representation which they can afford in Geneva. A solution to this problem seems to lie in the creation of a CARICOM Permanent Representative in Geneva. CARICOM states must be aware that their own trade policies will be attacked by the large countries, not because of the intrinsic importance of any CARICOM State's market to the export market of any of the larger countries, but rather more because of the precedent which it will set when the trading giants enter into combat.

There is a positive side. Through the operations of the TPRM, CARICOM states will be able to bring before the bar of a multilateral forum, specific obstacles which they experience in developing their export trade. These states must now take fully to heart that they have opted, wisely, for multilateralism rather than bilateralism and that they have to equip themselves to participate in the multilateral process or bear the consequences.

The Uruguay Round and Regional Agreements

During the negotiations in the Uruguay Round, groups of countries moved rapidly to form new regional agreements providing for preferential trading arrangements among themselves. Regional groupings which were already in existence also sought to intensify their cooperation. The European Union made most progress in this regard, but the Canada-US Agreement and subsequently NAFTA all came into being during the negotiations in the Uruguay Round.

A great deal of the impetus towards forming new cooperative regional agreements and strengthening those which existed, derived from a concern that the multilateral negotiations would fail. Countries therefore saw in regional agreements an enlargement of the economic space which would be available for their enterprises to become competitive and operate effectively on the world scene. Now that the negotiations have come to what has been described as a 'successful' conclusion, questions are being raised as to whether the proliferation of regional groupings will not undermine the multilateral system.

It should be stated straightaway that neither GATT 1947 nor GATT 1994 put obstacles in the way of the formation of new regional groupings. The principal requirement imposed under GATT was that the formation of a regional grouping should not increase the barriers which third countries would have to face. The question as to whether regional groupings violated the MFN principle has never been formally confronted and countries which have been participating in, or contemplating, regional trade groupings have generally sought and obtained waivers under GATT. This remains the current position.

There was some concern also that agreements reached in regional groupings may make it difficult for participating members to adhere to their obligations under the WTO. These have been removed by at least harmonising the rules of the regional groupings to accord with the requirements of GATT 1994. Indeed, the reverse consideration is now arising. It is this: if a group of countries is prepared to accept more stringent conditions to guide their interrelationships, will this not intensify the pressure on the multilateral system to harmonise upwards to the most demanding package?

This latter concern raises serious issues and has implications for the next round of negotiations. This is so because both NAFTA and the European Union have agreed to adhere to the kinds of policies which the industrialised countries wish to see in the multilateral system, especially in the areas of competition policy, labour standards and environmental matters – issues which have been clearly flagged as priority items for the next round.

What has the Uruguay Round achieved?

There is a widespread view at the present time that the increasing globalisation and privatisation of the world economy with the transnationals at the helm, is a good thing which will redound to the benefit of all countries which participate actively in the process. This argument is carried forward by GATT, the World Bank and others who assert that participants in the process of 'liberalisation' will derive benefit from two sources. First, from a more efficient use of domestic resources when domestic distortions, such as trade barriers, are reduced or removed, and second, from increased access to the markets of trading partners. It is possible to question this assertion.

Viewed in its historical perspective, the industrialised countries – the European Union, the United States, Canada and Japan – achieved their present domination in world trade and world income by establishing very high barriers to their markets and by adopting very specific non-market measures to enable their production enterprises to acquire positions of strength and become active competitors on the world scene. Even the so-called Asian Tigers, which were held up by the international community as examples of the benefits to be derived from the free play of market forces, did not allow market forces to deflect them from their long-term goals. The Governments of these countries actively intervened in the foreign exchange markets in their pursuit of wages and incomes policies, in the establishment of state trading enterprises, in interest rate subsidies and, indeed, in the active ownership by the state of industrial and commercial enterprises in order to propel their economy forward.[3] Further, as Dharam Ghai (1992)[4] has pointed out, the increasing role demanded by, and granted to, the transnational enterprises, has resulted in increasing income inequality both between nations as well as within nations. Ghai has produced data to show that the freeing of exchange markets and the increasing globalisation associated with it, particularly since 1972, have resulted in income inequality between nations doubling. Whereas in 1972 the top nations of the world had a per capita income of 30 times that of the lowest income nations, by 1987, this had increased to 60 times. Besides, increasing income inequality reduces the savings ratio.

However, at the highest political levels, CARICOM states have accepted the principle of allowing unrestrained market forces to operate in their countries. One therefore has to examine the projected outcome of the Uruguay Round against the systemic biases inherent in the emerging global system and to see the extent to which the Uruguay Round will bring benefits. In doing this we draw on the conclusions reached from analyses carried out mainly in institutions based in the industrial world.

The GATT secretariat[5] estimates that, as a result of the reductions in tariffs, the tariffication of the trade in agriculture and the elimination of the MFA, the level of world merchandise trade will by year 2005, be about 12 per cent higher than it would have been – an increase of US$745 billion in 1992 prices. This calculation takes into account that merchandise trade was growing at an average rate of 4.1 per cent over the period 1980–1991. It estimated that the areas which would reflect the largest rates of growth were clothing (60%) textiles (34%), agricultural, forestry and fishery products (20%) and processed foods and beverages (19%). Roughly one-third of the gain in trade will accrue to developing countries. This data does not take into account the growth in international payments for the services covered by GATT nor does it have any regard to the implications for international payments deriving from TRIPs.

With regard to the income effects, there have been several estimates based on different scenarios. All the models are, however, static and do not take into account the dynamic effects deriving from the multiplier and the additional confidence which this is projected to generate.

The estimates of the income effect range between US$213 billion per year after 2005 to US$274 billion (in 1992 prices) with a median figure of US$230 billion. Of this projected income gain, between one-quarter and one-third will accrue to the developing countries. GATT went further and concluded that when all the dynamic efforts are taken into account and the effect of the liberalisation of the services sector is factored in, the income gain could exceed US$500 million per year after year 2005.

Taking a welfare approach, Page and Davenport (1994)[6] came to the conclusion that the effects of the Uruguay Round on developing countries would, on the whole, not be negative. They concluded that Africa would decline slightly (0.3% of GDP), Latin America and South Asia would improve (by 0.2% – 0.4%), while Asia would be the principal gainer (1.4%).

There has not been a great deal of empirical work on the effect of the Uruguay Round on CARICOM states. Generally, when we take into account that:

(a) import prices of certain essential food imports are likely to rise by 4 per cent;

(b) countries are certain to be required to pay more for the technology and services which they require and do not now have in place – the machinery to garner their fair share of income from their own technology and services which the rest of the world uses, and

(c) the effect of the Uruguay Round is an erosion of the preferences which they have traditionally enjoyed, it is difficult to avoid the conclusion that

CARICOM states will be worse off as a result of the decisions of the Uruguay Round and the several agreements concluded under its auspices.

This, however, is a short-term view. Two other elements must be factored into the equation.

First, as small developing countries, CARICOM states have been beneficiaries under certain of the bilateral arrangements which they have concluded, but they have also been victims of unilateralism from the industrialised countries, especially in areas where they have been developing a comparative advantage. Jamaica has recently had to conclude a bilateral agreement with the USA in respect of certain garments and Trinidad and Tobago was, up to recently, the victim of VER in respect of its steel exports. And all CARICOM states, which were the original source of rum, not only faced quotas in the markets of the European Union in respect of rum but had to accept a definition made by the Europeans of what was rum. The point is that small states have little choice but to seek protection in multilateralism. Second, in an important sense, CARICOM states have been living in an artificial world. From time immemorial, they were enshrouded in a system of preferences which, to some extent, shielded them from the realities of the market situation so that the pressure to adjust was blunted. The Uruguay Round will expose them to the blast of competition.

In approaching this question of a CARICOM response, due account must be taken of the reality that the Uruguay Round sowed the seeds of its own future development. CARICOM states therefore have to operate on several fronts and prepare themselves not only to adjust to the decisions taken in the Uruguay Round but also prepare for the negotiations ahead.

The Uruguay Round, along with the other evolving international trading and political relationships – the revision of the Lomé Convention, the formation of the ACS, the promised Free Trade Area of the Americas, the revision of CARIBCAN and the much discussed NAFTA – must require the countries of the region to consider afresh the posture which they will adopt as they chart a course for the future. If they chart the course of less mendicancy, and a more positive approach to earning their living, then the Uruguay Round will produce benefits, for there is little doubt that the region has the capacity to adapt. In assessing the effects of the Uruguay Round for CARICOM countries therefore, we cannot but conclude that 'the jury is still out'.

Future Negotiations

As we pointed out earlier, four areas of considerable significance in the services sector were left unresolved when the Final Act was concluded at Marrakesh. These were financial services, maritime transport, telecommunications and the movement of natural persons. The negotiations on financial services were scheduled to be completed by June 30, 1995; those on maritime transportation by June 30, 1996; the negotiations on telecommunications by April 30, 1996 and those on the movement of natural persons by April 1997. New negotiations on the whole services sector are to be resumed in 1999 and, in addition to outstanding issues, will address three other specific issues.

The first is the link between trade rights and environmental measures. This opens the way for countries to use environmental standards as a basis for protection policy – as the USA has already used it in the dolphin case. The second is the issue of competition policy, which breaks down into the issue of restrictive business practices by the transnational enterprises, but will inevitably bring into the debate a number of side issues such as those related to the kind of strategic alliances which developing countries may have to conclude in order to earn export income in the rapidly changing international environment. The third is perhaps the most contentious of all: it concerns the links between trade policy and labour rights. Nominally, the issue now addresses questions of the right of workers to unite in trade unions, the prevention of the abuse of child labour and the use of prison labour to produce exportable goods; but other issues are also lurking in the shadows, for example, the level of wages which are paid, and whether such levels would be a cause for restrictive action. There is merit therefore in the concern expressed that the potential for backsliding into protectionism is not insignificant and that conversely, the exercise of economic policy in developing countries will be increasingly internationalised.

Action required in CARICOM

There is sufficient information to indicate that CARICOM states may, at best, be not too seriously affected by the results of the Uruguay Round of Trade Negotiations. They will experience losses of traditional markets in textiles and clothing and will have to pay higher prices for the technology and the food they must import. Conversely, they have the opportunity to export more services, and they are likely to experience fewer difficulties if their secondary manufacturing expands into niche markets abroad. But they will be able to derive the compensating benefits only if they take positive action both to protect their own positions which will be under attack and to advance the objectives which will serve their interest. In this connection, they will have to do a number of things. The first is to disseminate to their producers and to the population at large that the age of preferences is over, that aid transfers are on the way out and that self reliance is the order of the day; that the developed countries will grant no special concessions to CARICOM states and that the developing countries will be aggressive in their efforts to displace the countries in the region in their traditional export markets and even in their domestic markets. This sensitisation is a matter of great urgency and it is proposed that the Regional Economic Conference be resumed with this mandate in view. The second is that CARICOM states must equip themselves to protect their interests in the capitals where the important decisions are taken or debated, Geneva, Washington, Brussels and London. It is quite impossible for any of the CARICOM states to have adequate representation in these countries. The Governments of the region have to be persuaded that shared sovereignty is superior to no sovereignty at all. They must be encouraged to have joint representation in these capitals.

This brings the CARICOM Secretariat into the picture. It must be given a proactive role; it must have the authority to advise the diplomats in the field about the position of the region in particular economic matters and it should be required to present options on international economic issues to Governments. In the initial stages, the Secretariat may not be able to exercise the authority which the European Commission exercises but it should certainly move from being a service secretariat to an initiating body. This carries implications for the way in which the Secretariat is financed. A form of financing independent of annual Government appropriations and disbursements should be adopted; the recommendations of the West Indian Commission still appear to be the viable approach.

The third is to begin the development of a human resource capability in the area of international trade and, in particular, international trade law. This is not to de-emphasise the importance of human resource development in the technological areas. Rather, it is to add to the list of areas which the countries of the region must begin to address in the total exercise of upgrading the capability of their population to produce and sell for the international market place.

The fourth area is to accelerate the restructuring of their economies giving greater emphasis to service industries which have an export market. Tourism will clearly loom large in the restructuring of certain economies where the sector is not now large, but the region, and the individual countries, must give more attention than they have done to exploiting the service sector in which they have unique characteristics. Art and music are clear candidates in this regard, but tropical medicine, eco-tourism and design are among other areas which come to mind. The region should immediately commission a major study on the services it produces and use this as a basis for developing a new export thrust. It must also strengthen its machinery for registering trademarks and patents and in this connection it should give attention to the establishment of a CARICOM patent office. Fifth, it is on the cards that the significant clothing industry which certain countries in the region have developed cannot be assured of longevity in its present form. But there must be niche markets in which the combination of low, effective wage costs, design capability and tropical colour could thrive.

All of this necessary transformation must proceed on the basis of sound and continuing professional examination which the CARICOM secretariat and the newly established ACT secretariat must be enabled to do. These exercises will cost quite a lot of money but the region must be persuaded to see that the cost of not doing them is far greater than the direct cost.

There is now a great deal of preoccupation with special trading relationships such as NAFTA and FTAA; but these do not provide any significant measure of support in the new international economic environment. The countries of the region have little choice but to give greater attention to diversification and making greater use of their human resources. Export services must be developed. Certain countries of the region, notably Barbados and Jamaica, have already recognised the changing demands which the evolving international environment creates. All the others must follow suit. The foundation of such an effort must be the development of the region's human infrastructure. This is the real implication of the Uruguay Round for CARICOM states and it is not certain that they have yet recognised it.

Notes

1. The Report on the Implications of the Uruguay Round for CARICOM states was prepared by GSR Associates and the Institute of Social and Economic Research (St Augustine Campus) for the UWI/Andrew Mellon Foundation Project and presented in September 1995. The Report contains a full list of references.
2. In a decision taken in March 1995 the European Parliament rejected a proposal from the Commission which would have severely restricted the ability of farmers to use seed from Patented varieties. See South Letter, Summer 1995: 26.

3.   The World Bank was a principal advocate of the free market system and used to cite the Asian Tigers as the model. It has been forced to retract many of the positions which it formerly upheld, principally as a result of pressure from the Tigers themselves and from Japan. For some of the measures which the Tigers adopted, see Robert Cassen's 'Formulating Strategies for Growth and Poverty Alleviation' in *The East Asian and Other Relevant Experience* (Commonwealth Secretariat, September 1995).
4.   Dharam Ghai, 'Structural Adjustment, Global Integration and Social Democracy' (UNRISD: 1992).
5.   GATT Secretariat, 'Effects of the Uruguay Round in World Trade and Incomes' (November 1993).
6.   Sheila Page and Michael Davenport, 'The Uruguay Round: Have the Developing Countries Gained or Lost?' (London: ODI, 1994).

[61]

Going South

CARICOM and Latin America

Henry Gill

It is obvious that relations between the Caribbean Community and Latin American countries have progressed considerably from the stage of suspicion and conflict, characteristic of CARICOM's early post independence years, and at least, a part of the decade of the 1970s. Some might argue that these features survived for quite sometime thereafter. The second period, already in evidence in the 1970s and therefore overlapping somewhat with the first, is characterised by the gradual but marked development of mutual understanding and cooperation and also more positive attitudes within CARICOM concerning the need for and desirability of cultivating closer relations. This process has not always been smooth, encountering some setbacks, most notably those surrounding the Falklands/Malvinas crisis.

By the 1990s, political, economic and other interaction intensified through, for example, CARICOM's ongoing participation within the Rio Group deliberations; the signing of agreements with individual Latin countries covering trade (Colombia and Venezuela) and other areas (technical cooperation with Mexico and the Mixed Commission with Cuba); active involvement in Haiti's democratisation process, including military commitments; CARICOM's initiative to take the lead in creating the newly-formed Association of Caribbean States, and generally a new quest for business opportunities within the wider region.

While such examples provide clear evidence of an awakening to a realisation of Latin America's relevance to our development and other possibilities, it is nonetheless true that CARICOM is still moving too slowly in this direction. The actual substance of relations is still inadequate: our objectives are pursued from a narrow perspective and with far less than uniform interest by CARICOM member countries, and our approach can hardly be said to be guided by any strategy that is sufficiently thought through.

This brief article touches upon some of these points as we reflect, in summary, on various factors, having a bearing on future relations over the next decade and beyond, which will help to illuminate some opportunities and challenges, offer some suggestions and pose questions for further reflection.

A new Latin America

We believe that developments underway make it inevitable that relations with Latin America will have to be accorded much higher priority – an activity which should involve Governments, the private sector and others bodies as well. Two such developments are examined.

Today's Latin America holds far more attraction than a decade ago, for the region has really come a very long way since the 1980s. Indeed it is hardly an exaggeration to speak of a new Latin America.

From a political and social standpoint, insurgency has been overcome, even in Central America where it had reached its zenith in the 1980s, and democracy is now widespread as a form of government and considerably strengthened especially following peaceful transfers of political power for the first time in a number of countries. In the process, relations among countries have de-emphasised conflict and suspicion, shifting markedly with a focus towards collaboration. This is not to say that all political conflicts and problems have been solved. However, crucially a new climate has developed wherein high political priority is accorded to regionalism including the reinvigoration of integration arrangements. Without this political climate the creation of MERCOSUR would not have been imaginable amidst the traditional national security emphasis characteristic of the Latin American military.

From an economic standpoint, the crises of the eighties have also been overcome. Nearly all countries have undergone rigorous domestic adjustments, which have served to curb inflation and improve macroeconomic stability; external debt servicing has been reduced (from an overall level of 42 per cent in 1986 to around 27 per cent in 1994), although the size of the debt has risen. Gross domestic investment has resumed growth (from annual rates of -3.1 per cent in the 1980s to 6.5 per cent from 1990-1994); total consumption has risen (from 1.4 to 4.4 per cent over the same period); domestic economies have also resumed growth within a policy framework of economic liberalisation, and trade has been revitalised. The measurable result is very encouraging.

Whereas the region grew at an average annual rate of merely 1.1 per cent between 1980–1990, growth between 1990 and 1994 has averaged 3.7 per cent. In 1994 real growth stood at 5 per cent, the region's fastest rate since 1980. Significantly, growth is also widespread throughout the region. In per capita terms this turnaround is striking; after a decade of negative real annual growth of nearly 1 per cent, GDP per capita increased 1.8 per cent annually in the 1990s, growing at 3.1 per cent in 1994. Present World Bank projections are that per capita incomes will grow at a rate of 2.2 per cent to the year 2005, just below the 2.4 per cent projection for the industrialised countries, but far lower than the 6.8 per cent rate projected for East Asia, the world's highest growth area.

The so-called 'Twenty Latin Americas' now constitute a market of almost 450 million people currently growing at around 1.9 per cent annually. Imports have been increasing much faster than domestic economies, with average growth of 13.5 per cent between 1990-1994. This high rate is probably not sustainable in the short run owing to the negative effect of the Mexican peso crisis on capital flows to the region, which has nevertheless been less damaging than anticipated. However, there are considerable economic benefits to be derived, over the medium and long term, from partnership with Latin America.

The FTAA

Another critical factor that will impact on relations with Latin America is the goal of creating the Free Trade Area of the Americas (FTAA), which the United States proposed precisely because of Latin Americas increased economic attractiveness. All dependent states in the hemisphere have committed themselves at the highest level to this process, with the exception of Cuba. Politically, the creation of a democratic community has been underscored, but the economic objective is to increase prosperity by eliminating barriers to trade and investment in the hemisphere. The stated aim is to conclude FTAA negotiations by the year 2005 and to make substantial progress in this direction by the year 2000.

While there are grounds for moderate optimism about the chances of this ambitious undertaking being brought to fruition, especially in the light of US congressional uncertainties, the process is nevertheless fully on track, driven by two ministerial meetings to date (Denver and Cartagena) and propelled by several Working Groups established to consider various ramifications of the subjects to be negotiated. The relevance of this to our topic is easily explainable.

An evaluation of the potential benefits of FTAA takes into account various factors. However, insofar as market access for goods is concerned, the promise of FTAA for CARICOM countries is less about new opportunities within North American than it is about opportunities to be derived from Latin America. Through the FTAA we already enjoy in very large measure the kind of access to North American markets that other countries are aspiring to achieve. Additional access opportunities will be relatively few, especially if our objective of gaining parity with Mexico is achieved. Indeed, such access will no longer be privileged since it will be shared by all other FTAA participants just as Mexico has already encroached on our privileged status. What will really be new is the additional access and stability thereof to be gained in the markets of Latin American FTAA participants, relative to all countries outside that process and even relative to countries within the various Latin American sub-groups, who have already gained such intra-group access.

Future of Integration

Various implications derive from these trends, which herald a new context of opportunity within a more competitive hemispheric environment and raises a number of challenges to be tackled. We will examine various aspects before turning to other related concerns.

The hemispheric process impacts on the future of CARICOM integration from a somewhat different angle than is normally discussed. The decision of the Denver Ministerial conference of June 1996 to 'build on existing sub-regional and bilateral arrangements in order to broaden and deepen hemispheric economic integration and to bring the agreements together' challenges CARICOM countries with assessing possible routes to achieving this objective and determining where their best interest lies, considering their smaller economies.

More concretely the question to be answered is how, for example, could CARICOM be linked to the Andean Group or the Central American Common Market as part of the evolutionary process. It seems fairly obvious that the NAFTA accession route is keeping preference for Washington, just as Brazil would prefer to consolidate regional bargaining power beforehand by creating a South American Free Trade Area. However, other routes are conceivable, even a multilateral type negotiation, similar to the Uruguay Round process, but aiming at the elimination rather than mere reduction of trade and investment barriers, which seems to have several advantages includ-ing skipping stages of the negotiations. CARICOM could best hope to influence the route that the FTAA process might take through ongoing consultation and coordination with Latin American countries in determining the most advantageous route.

But a prior question to be answered is through what sub-regional arrange-ment would CARICOM countries be participating in such a process, whether solely as CARICOM or through, for example, the larger ACS. A major consideration in the decision to create the ACS was to broaden the scope of CARICOM's economic interaction. Yet, it is still an open question whether the ACS would, within the required time-frame, achieve sufficient coherence to be able to act as a unit in hemispheric convergence, or even to provide trade exposure for CARICOM to wider competitive environment. There can be a deliberative role for that body precisely on the subject of an appropriate route toward the FTAA, drawing on the views of its diverse membership, but this could possibly duplicate functions appropriate to SELA at the wider regional level.

Obviously, CARICOM countries need not depend on ACS developments for expanding economic relations with the wider region, since bilateral accords with particular countries or groups could be concluded. Indeed, such accords could contribute to progress at the ACS level. But, it may be relevant to consider whether there is need to consider as well intermediate integration possibilities, for example, among CARIFORUM countries, as a means of more quickly broadening the space and scope of integration commitments, in preparation for eventual hemispheric obligations.

The major trade challenge facing CARICOM countries is the inevitable advent of trade reciprocity requirements, which constitute both a negotiating challenge and a competitive challenge.

The challenge of negotiation requires far greater preparation in the form of more in-depth knowledge and evaluation of the trade and investment policies and practices, the productive capabilities, as well as degrees of export competitiveness of negotiating adversaries, especially in Latin America, (for it is so little known), than was ever required in previous non-reciprocal negotiation.

The competitive challenge tends to be viewed largely in terms of compe-tition to be encountered from increased access afforded USA (and perhaps Canadian) products. In reality, Latin American producers and exporters will also be targeting CARICOM markets in the new dispensation, and they too are likely to become a serious source of competitive challenge precisely because of the greater similarity of their production structures to ours.

In devising trade approaches to Latin America, collectively and individually, CARICOM countries need to bear these points in mind, and to benefit as well from the experience gleaned through the Costa Rica-Mexico Free Trade Agreement, which deserves study in respect of both points. This NAFTA type agreement, which was implemented in January 1995, provides valuable lessons concerning both the negotiating difficulties encountered by much smaller Costa Rica, *vis-à-vis* far more prepared Mexican officials, as well as the strong competitive challenge faced subsequently from the larger market. Pointedly, Costa Rican negotiators have expressed to this writer the view that it was a mistake to negotiate singly with Mexico, a warning that the ECLAC regional office in Mexico has also issued to Central American countries.

In order to benefit from the eventual creation of FTAA, CARICOM producers and exporters will also be challenged to convert formal access opportunities to Latin American markets into real advantage – a continuing challenge faced also in North American markets. However, for most CARICOM countries, the Latin American market is practically unknown. We have calculated from ECLAC data that the average 1991-1993 export values for CARICOM (including Suriname, but excluding the OECS countries, whose values are negligible) amounted to US$268 million or merely 5.3 per cent of total exports. Trinidad and Tobago accounted for two thirds of these values. Latin America's share of an individual country's of total exports was 9.6 per cent for Trinidad and Tobago and slightly less for Suriname, whose market is essentially Brazil. However, apart from Belize at 5 per cent, this share was in the order of 2 per cent or less for the remaining CARICOM countries.

CARICOM countries need to be geared to a major learning process about ways of doing business in different Latin American countries; of developing corporate partnerships and other relationships; of grappling with financing arrangements; of learning the intricacies of marketing in a different cultural context; of finding ways to cut transportation costs, and so forth. Such tasks cannot be postponed until the FTAA is created. CARICOM firms would be placed at a disadvantage if they do not position themselves early for the competitive race already underway, in the same way that some enlightened CARICOM investors and exporters have perceived the need for an actual presence in Cuba. Considerably more attention needs to be paid, as well, to signing investment promotion and guarantee agreements, which will help to stimulate such flows in both directions.

Private sector institutions in CARICOM countries must aim to develop close collaboration with their counterparts in the rest of the region to facilitate such a process. Collaboration among regionally organised bodies, such as the

Caribbean Association of Industry and Commerce and Central America (FEDEPRICAP), could be highly beneficial, particularly to the former, which is far smaller and less resourceful than similar bodies in the wider region.

Notwithstanding the importance of tourism to the economies of the majority of CARICOM countries, as in the case of merchandise trade, they have hardly pursued an active approach to encouraging increased visitor flows from Latin America, despite Latin America's considerable growing expenditure on that account. Significantly, only one per cent of visitors to CARICOM's major tourist destination, the Bahamas, is from Latin America.

Yet, the notion of Caribbean is exotic for most Latin Americans and can be an important drawing card. Aruba and Curaçao have been playing this card for many years, Curaçao focusing principally on Venezuela and Aruba on Colombia, Peru and other markets. Trinidad has traditionally hosted Venezuela tourists. Cuba has become a very attractive destination particularly for Mexican and Brazilian visitors.

A concerted CARICOM tourism drive towards targeted markets in Latin America, especially aided by exposure to our musical and other cultural forms, could yield major dividends. The possibilities of attracting third country visitors through multi-destination tourism have hardly been exploited, except in the case of Belize, which is linked through the Mundo Maya programme with some Central American neighbours. Nor is there evidence of continuing efforts to encourage Latin American investment into the sector, which would serve to create important linkages with travel agencies, tour groups and so forth.

Tourism should also be a subject of trade and investment agreements signed between CARICOM and Latin American countries. The agreements in force with Venezuela and Colombia provide for eventual inclusion of services within their ambit, and specific provisions on tourism could be the first step in this direction when they come up for review. Expansion of these and future contacts beyond the goods sector would serve also to increase the overall interest of CARICOM's membership; for the smaller, mainly service-oriented members, whose merchandise exports are primarily traditional products, evince little real interest in developing practical relations with Latin America. On the contrary, they see the region as a threat because of the present conflict surrounding the European Union's banana regime and the potentially negative consequences for CARICOM's banana exports.

Considerably more attention needs to be paid to activate relationship between both societies on a people to people basis. Apart from being a goal in its own right, this would reinforce positive trends in other areas, such as those dealt with under the previous headings. The fact is that history has bequeathed something of a psychological Berlin Wall that still separates CARICOM from its Latin neighbours and impedes a fuller relationship. Bonds of friendship would make it eventually disappear.

If we take into account the impact that Latin America will have on this hemisphere in the next century, (including within the USA itself), CARICOM societies, which are practically immersed in the region should set themselves the goal of becoming culturally comfortable with that world, in much the same way that the people of Curaçao have done in respect of both the Anglophone and Latin worlds. This obviously will be a long-term journey with many steps that will have to be carefully made.

An important early start can be made by implementing more practical approaches to foreign language training than is currently employed in our schools. This could be immensely aided through television exposure to Latin American cultural fare. It would also serve to counterbalance a somewhat excessive reliance on US cultural products. This is an idea which could be put into effect early in countries where cable television is available.

There is a pressing need as well to overcome the dearth of information in CARICOM countries of Latin American political, economic, social and cultural reality – a challenge that the media needs to address frontally if Latin America is to begin to loom large in the popular consciousness.

The University of the West Indies should not be allowed to continue to operate as if Latin America were but a myth rather than a booming reality. It should be induced to establish departments on the various campuses special-ising in Latin American studies and carrying out the kind of research which could inform a CARICOM policy thrust towards that region. This would involve close interfacing with institutions in Latin America, joint research, document exchanges, teacher sabbaticals, and the possibility for students to fulfil course requirements by spending prolonged periods in one or more Latin American countries.

A scholarship programme should also be pursued, allowing CARICOM nationals access to the major universities of Argentina, Brazil, Colombia, Chile, Venezuela and so forth, in order to benefit from their known areas of competence. Why should a CARICOM national not study architecture in Brazil, or road engineering in Venezuela, or economics in Chile, or the Spanish language in Colombia or Costa Rica, or Latin American culture and anthropology in Mexico? Additional value is derived from student residency in a country, through the greater degree of familiarisation and the contacts made -cultural comfort which contributes substantially to the development of relations.

In summary, I will reinforce three points. The first is that, notwithstanding widely varying degrees of interest within the grouping, CARICOM countries should make every effort to approach Latin American countries as a single group in respect of the signing of trade accords. This is critical to maintain group cohesion and bargaining power.

Secondly, as the hemispheric effort gains momentum, CARICOM countries should ensure that joint efforts be not dissipated in too many directions, which would compound the already overburdened resources of the CARICOM Secretariat, place strain on national resources and result in fragmentation. The record already provides some evidence of initiatives that have entailed considerable resource commitments with little identifiable yield.

Finally, and crucially, the present conflict regarding bananas, as important as it may be for the survival of CARICOM banana-exporting countries, must not be allowed to jeopardise the enormous potential for collaboration between CARICOM and Latin American countries. The controversy has developed a dynamic of its own within the WTO disputes settlement system, the outcome of which is unlikely to be materially affected by a CARICOM hard line in relation to those countries which have raised the issue. A conflicting turn in relations with the USA has not been anticipated despite that country's protagonist position on the issue, in support of her own companies operating in Central America. This should inform the overall stance of CARICOM member countries.

Note

This paper first appeared in *CARICOM Perspective*, No. 66, June 1966, pp. 40–43.

[62]

The Challenges of Sovereign Consent in US-Caribbean Relations

Anthony Maingot

'Liberty without hatred'. This was José Martí's recommendation April 17, 1884, for the theme of the Cuban Revolutionary Party.

Martí, who knew America well and disliked its racially tinged imperialism, always argued for a working relationship with the USA. He argued for a *strategic* relationship: a pragmatic and sincere search for those interests which Cuba and the USA had in common and the possible synergies which would come from that.

As they face the perplexing post-Cold War international environment, Caribbean leaders are well aware of the global nature of the problems before them. Confronting them requires coordination, between themselves and USA. The politics of hatred and resentment are obstacles to such coordinated action. It creates what sociologists can call non-realistic conflict.

Despite this awareness, however, two very powerful forces militate to make the path recommended by Martí difficult. First is the weight of history. The burden of past USA behaviour, especially as that behaviour offended national and ethnic pride, is not readily overlooked. This is especially the case when it combines with the second contentious element: enormous asymmetries in power. It is the latter especially which has become one of the overarching questions of our age. In a world with one superpower, is it possible for archipelagic regions of small states to formulate their own definition of national interest? In this specific case, the issue is whether the small states of the insular Caribbean have the autonomy to decide and then implement their own strategies of development and security. Granting that all international politics – of small as well as of large states – invariably involves trade-offs, manoeuvring and often compromise, are the trade-offs of the small Caribbean state *vis-à-vis* the US so one-sided as to make a mockery of the concept and principles of sovereignty and self-determination?

The emphasis of many theories of international relations is on the inequalities or asymmetries which characterise those relations. Whether they be straight Marxist interpretations or various tangential theories of dependency, the argument is that most claims to reciprocity and equivalence in today's international relations are, in fact, rhetorical facades hiding gross or subtle domination and exploitation. Independence under such circumstances is mythical. This perspective is considerably sharper when it comes to small-state superpower relations.

Even one as non-ideological as the late Dudley Seers described small states as characterised by 'a small population, serious ethnic divisions, location close to a superpower, few natural resources, a culturally subverted bureaucracy, high consumer expectations, and a narrow technological base'. Quite an accurate description of most Caribbean small states. Under such conditions, nationalism – which Seers defined as self-reliant development or autarchy – is near impossible. In the same vein, all the talk of 'internationalism' and 'interdependence' is really camouflage for global superpower, – especially USA – domination.

If this interpretation holds for the whole range of state-to-state relations, how are the bilateral relations on questions of greater national interest such as military security and trade to be characterised?

This addresses this issue by first attempting to establish what the underlying or basic assumptions and policy preferences of both the USA and West Indian actors are. It does so by following the analytical schema presented in Figure 1.

It is easy to imagine the schema as a scale or balance with the USA (country 'B') on one side and the small Caribbean country ('A') on the other. The natural and logical question is, how could anyone who has read the history of the USA-Caribbean relations presented here conceivably argue that the reciprocity between country 'A' and the USA is based on any equivalence? 'USA' concerns start with 'USA global objectives', pass through 'USA regional objectives' before reaching 'USA country objectives' which is the stage at which 'dialogue' with country 'A' theoretically begins. But it is not just that

Figure 1:   A model of small state – US bilateral negotiations for a
country program in the small state

Process in 'A' A small state	Process in 'B' US
National inputs • 'A's view of the threat • Economic conditions • Perception of capabilities • View of relations with US • Domestic political constraints 'A' sub-regional objectives Formulation of 'A's national trade and security needs Bilateral dialogue 'A' and 'B' • Political • Economic • Military	National inputs • US view of the threat • Domestic political constraints • Congressional concerns • Availability of funds • Arms and trade policy US global objectives US regional objectives US sub-regional objectives US military doctrine and trade policy Formulation of US total Trade and defence objectives
Joint planning	
Country programme for 'A'	

Source: A.P. Maingot, *The US in the Caribbean: Geopolitics and the Bargaining Capacity of
Small States,* in Anthony Bryan, J. Edward Greene and Timothy Shew (eds.), *Peace,
Development and Security in the Caribbean* (New York: St Martin's Press 1990), p. 59.

'USA concerns', both empirical and symbolic, are so much weightier. There is also the issue of state capabilities: the purely administrative and bureaucratic dimension through which any eventual country program will have gone. Even the budget process, through which all USA procurement planning goes, is complex and protracted. And this is but one element in the enormous administrative network, which deals with matters of interest to the USA

The small state has nothing even approaching such a bureaucracy. It is often at a loss as to how to even approach or engage the Americans in a bargaining mode. It is clear that the purpose of this political-administrative process and machinery is to ensure a good interface between domestic considerations, multilateral and bilateral relations and the global and regional defence and trade postures decided upon. It is quite properly said that in the USA domestic policy is foreign policy, and vice versa. How does actor 'A' understand, much less influence this? One can conclude from Figure 1 that from a purely administrative perspective, the 'dialogue' and 'planning' stage has input from 'A' and 'B' of quite different types, which leaves the analyst with few illusions about the meaning of the term 'common' in the scheme.

But, having said this, do we have to settle for the theoretical despair of Seers, that even to speak of 'relations' is to opt for hope over experience? This study argues not.

Clearly the élites in these small nations operate within much narrower decision-making parameters and constraints than do those in larger states. But this is not to say that they have no options or even autochthonous preferences. Theoretically, the only productive approach to understanding international relations is to assume that all national élites behave with what can be called strategic rationality, that is, they will always attempt to maximise the benefits from any exchange. The élites of even the smallest state will take the choices and actions of others into account but they behave with as much self-interest as circumstances – and their opponents – permit.

Thus, what is in question is not the strategic rationality of the élites representing small states, but the limits placed on that rationality through curtailment of their autonomy. Having said that, however, the issue of the degree or margin of sovereignty and independence in small state decision-making should be approached as an empirical question to be answered through the analysis of specific historical and contemporary cases, not argued *a priori* by ideologically-driven paradigms.

Note

This article first appeared in *CARICOM Perspective*, No. 65, July 1995, pp. 32–33.

[63]

Overcoming Obstacles

Report of the Independent Group of Experts on Smaller Economies and Western Hemispheric Integration

One of the major challenges in creating a Free Trade Area of the Americas (FTAA) is the integration of countries of diverse size and level of development. Therefore at their first meeting, held in Denver in June 1995, the Trade Ministers of the FTAA countries created a Working Group on Smaller Economies with the mandate, *inter alia*, to identify and examine ways to facilitate the preparation of smaller economies in the FTAA process and to provide recommendations on how this should be done.

Our group was formed to provide an independent assessment of the problems confronting smaller economies as they move towards closer trade integration with their hemispheric neighbours. In this report we recommend ways in which smaller economies can prepare themselves to participate fully in a hemispheric free trade area, and the measures that can be implemented to facilitate the economic adjustments which must be undertaken as these countries adopt more open trade and investment policies.

Report

Although small does not necessarily imply an economic disadvantage, it does limit the range of policy options and resources available to policy makers and increases the vulnerability of the economy to external shocks. Small island economies are particularly vulnerable to external pressures, given their geographical limitations (a devastating hurricane can nearly wipe out the entire economy of a small island), their extremely narrow resource base and their restricted administrative capacity.

Smaller and relatively less developed countries exhibit certain economic and structural features which make them more vulnerable to external fluctuations in output and demand. They have small domestic markets, a pronounced dependence on external trade, relatively undiversified economic structures, narrow tax bases, limited worker skills, weak physical infrastructure and organisational and managerial capacity, and, in some cases, severely limited resources.

The FTAA, as mandated by Government leaders at the Summit of the Americas, will mean new challenges for all economies in the region, not only the smaller ones. Although smaller economies have become better positioned to face the rigours of free trade through the adjustment of macroeconomic policies, unilateral liberalisation efforts, and sub-regional integration strategies, they still require help in order to prepare themselves to participate fully in, and take better advantage of, new opportunities derived from the FTAA.

Sound macroeconomic management will continue to be a prerequisite for effective participation in the FTAA. No amount of liberalisation and support within the hemisphere can overcome the domestic costs of deficient macroeconomic policies. In our view, however, the internal adjustments and policy measures which smaller economies must undertake in order to participate in the FTAA, and take advantage of the opportunities offered by hemispheric free trade, are no different from those required to integrate effectively into the global economy. They are also similar to those initiatives currently underway in many smaller economies. These countries should, therefore, be encouraged to continue the implementation of these initiatives. However, care should be taken to ensure that the pace of reform demanded by the time-frames put forward for the completion of hemispheric trade liberalisation does not place strains on their fragile economic structures and administrative and legal systems, thereby increasing the risk of error, economic and social instability and policy reversal.

Although the exact mix of public and private policies that small countries will need to implement in order to capture the benefits of hemispheric free trade will depend upon the individual circumstances of each country, there are certain broad issues that are generally applicable to all small states. Among them are the following: (1) macroeconomic stability; (2) functioning financial markets; (3) discipline in fiscal and monetary policy; (4) adequate exchange rate policy management with a view to achieving freely convertible currencies and equilibrium exchange rates; 5) pursuit of an outward-oriented trade policy, with priority being attached to the implementation of World Trade Organisation (WTO) rules and disciplines; (6) diversification of the fiscal base so as to decrease reliance on border taxes as a source of fiscal revenue; (7) implementation of an effective open investment regime (which includes, among others, the application of most favoured nation and national treatment to foreign capital, predictability regarding the ability of investors to transfer funds in freely convertible currencies, assurance regarding expropriation of assets, freedom from excessive performance requirements, and the possibility of recourse to local tribunals or arbitration mechanisms for the settlement of disputes); (8) public sector reform (strengthening of public administration infrastructure, adoption of adequate regulatory frameworks, and modernisation of national judicial systems); (9) adequate policies towards state enterprises and monopolies to deal with market imperfections (including the adoption and implementation of competition legislation); and 10) development of human resources.

We believe that participation in the FTAA will complement and strengthen the process of economic reform already undertaken by the smaller economies. However, the unique situation and special circumstances of smaller economies in the Western Hemisphere must be taken into account in the design of the FTAA. This process should include the adoption of mechanisms and measures, to be implemented both by smaller economies themselves and by the hemispheric community at large, which will facilitate the participation of these countries in the FTAA.

Recognising the problems in defining small economies, we have focused our report on the countries of Central America and the Caribbean. In terms of numbers, this group constitutes, by far, the largest segment of countries within the Hemisphere. In addition, because of their high dependence on international trade, Central American and Caribbean countries have a deep interest in international best practice, and tend to be disposed towards systems of free and open investment and trade. Furthermore, we believe that the harmonisation of rules and regulations required by deeper hemispheric integration cannot be achieved without the participation of all countries concerned. It could be costly in terms of trade and investment diversion, if integration in the Western Hemisphere proceeded among larger countries without the participation of the smaller states.

For smaller countries to derive clear benefits from, and prepare themselves to assume all the rights and obligations that come with the FTAA, there must be early and parallel progress on the other initiatives contained in the Declaration and Plan of Action adopted in the Summit of the Americas, which are of great interest to them. These include capital market integration, human resource development, science and technology, the environment and tourism. Accordingly, we recommend that the Miami Plan of Action be addressed in a holistic manner. We recognise that FTAA discussions are proceeding at a faster pace than other elements of the Plan of Action, and urge participating countries to accelerate efforts in other Summit initiatives so as to allow countries to get a clearer picture of the overall costs and benefits arising from greater hemispheric integration.

We recommend that Central American and Caribbean countries participate fully in the FTAA. While participation in a hemispheric free trade pact could engender some adjustment costs, non-participation could be much more costly, since it would isolate these countries from their main markets and from the increased investment flows which are expected to result from the adoption of trade reforms and a common set of rules in the FTAA. This conjures up a number of risks both of an economic and non-economic character.

Smaller economies should not simply view the FTAA in isolation, but as part of their global strategic repositioning plans. Such plans aim at repositioning a country in the global economy by adjusting strategically and quickly in anticipation of, and in response to, global changes in demand and technology. They are designed to consolidate and improve existing production lines while reorienting the economy toward new types of economic activity more in line with global trends. Among other things, this includes producing what is demanded globally; pursuing structural transformation to achieve economic diversification; revitalising traditional exports (that is, looking downstream in traditional commodity production), and modernising international marketing techniques to keep abreast of world demand.

We strongly encourage smaller economies to think in terms of global strategic repositioning and to initiate studies and discussions to that effect. This, apart from helping them to avoid becoming marginalised from the world economy, will allow them to prepare themselves for the FTAA, to better participate in the FTAA, and to benefit from the FTAA. FTAA participation, in turn, can act as a catalyst for the adoption of global strategic repositioning policies by smaller states.

Participation in hemispheric free trade does not have to mean unrestricted openness or unbridled free trade, and some sectors may be (temporarily or permanently) exempted from the FTAA – as was the case for cultural industries in the NAFTA. However, smaller economies must analyse carefully the effect of sectoral exemptions on their global repositioning plans. Although exceptions in the FTAA may be necessary to gain the widest political support for the best possible deal, we believe that these should be extremely limited in number and scope.

For the people of the smaller economies of the Caribbean and Central America to retain confidence in the vision of the FTAA, they must believe that hemispheric free trade provides them with benefits and opportunities that outweigh the costs and risks. For this to be the case, these countries must participate actively, and be seen to do so, in the detailed negotiation of its terms, and maintain their deep involvement in its governance throughout the life of the agreement. Their confidence in such an agreement can only rest upon their perception that the agreement takes fully into account their peculiar problems and distributes the future gains from the agreement in an equitable fashion. If such anticipation and confidence in the FTAA flags, the result will be slowed negotiations, reduced membership, and /or eventual unsustainability for the FTAA.

Approach to the Negotiations

We believe that the FTAA should be guided by the following principles:

(1) it should allow for the participation of all countries. The only eligibility criterion should be the one referred to in the Declaration of Principles adopted in the Summit of the Americas, that is, that all countries should be democratic;

(2) it should be achieved through an identifiable, multilateral and politically transparent process;

(3) it should be balanced and comprehensive in scope;

(4) it should represent a single undertaking of mutual rights and obligations.

Smaller countries should be expected to implement all the provisions contained in the FTAA. However, we firmly believe that a suitable transitional arrangement (in the form of longer periods for the implementation of general rules and disciplines applicable to all) must be designed for those smaller economies which are not yet ready for immediate and full assumption of FTAA provisions, having not yet attained the level of development or level of liberalisation commensurate with the far-reaching obligations that are likely to be part of the FTAA. This asymmetrically-phased assumption of universally applicable obligations and disciplines is compatible with the evolving environment in which trade relations between larger and more developed countries and smaller developing nations have been taking place, both at the multilateral level (as was the case in the Uruguay Round), and in the context of regional and sub-regional trade arrangements in the Western hemisphere.

Smaller economies must avoid becoming entangled in a web of exemptions and special measures that might significantly increase the transaction costs of intra-hemispheric trade. In particular, these countries must bear in mind the effects which the implementation of time limited exemptions from general rules and regulations can have on their global strategic repositioning plans. High tariffs, for instance, add to the cost of operating in the important tourism and services sectors.

In dealing with each aspect of the FTAA, consideration should be given to the particular circumstances of individual countries and groups of countries. We do not believe it is necessary or desirable to apply special and differential treatment to all countries, with regard to all sectors and all products. We believe that there will be a need for flexibility towards smaller economies in some areas and not necessarily in others. For instance, we could envisage the adoption of flexible approaches with regard to the administration of rules of origin and trade remedy laws, but not necessarily in relation to investment, standards, sanitary and phytosanitary measures and customs procedures. We believe services to be an area where small economies can lead the way in the FTAA process and encourage prompt liberalisation efforts, whereas we consider technical assistance to be indispensable with regard to the development of infrastructure, human resources and small and medium size enterprises.

A transitional arrangement would enable Central American and Caribbean countries to complete their processes of economic reform and structural adjustment and put them in a better position to assume full reciprocity. The period of time necessary to attain a position of full reciprocity would vary from country to country, depending on their particular circumstances and national objectives. Transitional mechanisms could be applied on a sector-by-sector and product-by-product basis. Not all sectors or products will require the same phase-out period.

However, we believe it is essential to set a firm target date for the completion of such transition periods. If the phasing is too long it will prove useless, if it is too short it will be impractical. This transition period will allow the business sector of smaller economies to plan ahead and prepare itself to confront the more competitive environment offered by free trade.

We believe that the alleviation of transitional problems for smaller economies requires three basic elements: time, resources (both financial and technical), and the development of a strategy which reflects the realities of the new international environment. *Time* (that is, longer phase-out periods) is needed to allow these countries to adjust to the end of one-way preferential schemes and the rigours of open markets and globalisation without destroying their economies and duly disrupting their societies. *Financial assistance and technical co-operation* will be required to offset the limited potential of their domestic resource base derived from their small size. *A new strategy* is of essence, because, ultimately, the key factor for grasping the opportunities available from world economic changes and moderating the impact of unfavourable external shocks, will be the internal policy measures put into effect by the smaller economies themselves.

Because of their limited resources and commonality of interests, we believe that Central American and Caribbean countries should be allowed to function as a group in the negotiations of the FTAA. Grouping their efforts during the negotiating stage would enable these countries to take advantage of their limited resources to attend various negotiating groups simultaneously. This way they will collaborate and adopt a common position in negotiations with a view to increasing their effectiveness, thus enabling themselves to participate more fully in the entire process.

In this regard, regional organisations could play a useful role not only in the negotiating process itself – by adopting joint positions and participating as observers in the negotiations – but also in the implementation of the agreement, by providing technical assistance and support.

The countries of the Organisation of Eastern Caribbean States (OECS) would be the smallest signatories to the FTAA. This statement by itself does not convey the extreme disparities in size between these countries, which have a combined physical size of 1,116 square miles and a combined population of approximately 500,000, and two of the largest states in the Western Hemisphere: the United States (3.1 million sq. miles. and a population of 220 million) and Brazil (2.5 million sq. miles and a population of 180 million).

We believe that special account should be taken of the particular circumstances of OECS states, given the extremely small size of these economies. Time-limited exemptions from the application of general rules and disciplines are amply justified in the case of these countries, and ought not to pose problems to other hemispheric trading partners, given that their markets are so small. Nevertheless, we emphasise the need for OECS states to subscribe to hemispheric free trade rules and disciplines. Long-term and across-the-board special and differential treatment will not encourage them to undertake the structural changes and apply the economic policies that these economies urgently required in order to make a successful transition to the new world economy.

In this regard, we believe that policy coordination and harmonisation and the provision of common services in order to pool resources and technical expertise, can provide substantial benefits to these countries.

Related Issues

Issues facing small, lesser-developed economies entering into the liberalised global market arena, relates to trade frictions; fiscal, financial and investment issues; labour and services, and issues relating to rules of origin.

With regard to the management of trade frictions and disputes, small states are largely inexperienced, moreso considering that litigation is a relatively new feature of modern trade policy. The size of Caribbean and Central American trade flows, particularly that conducted by smaller firms, cannot support the costs of endless defence against process protection, the litigation of disputes and related transaction costs. The mere threat of legal action on the part of agents within large countries may be sufficient to discourage traders and export-oriented investors in smaller economies.

One of the areas where this problem is most evident is in the field of trade remedy laws. The use of anti-dumping and countervailing duties to prevent or remedy unfair trade practices has been on the increase, in both developed and developing countries. This may place strains on smaller countries that do not have the resources and technical know-how to design and implement trade remedy legislation in accordance with regional and multilateral standards and procedures and, even more, to protect themselves against the application of these same laws by developed countries.

We believe that serious consideration ought to be given to the possibility of establishing higher quantitative thresholds or *de minimis* requirements for the application of these laws to smaller states.

Increasing tax revenue to offset tariff reductions could well be the most important domestic policy challenge facing smaller economies with regard to the FTAA. The relatively high dependence of some of these countries (particularly OECS members) on tariffs as a source of fiscal income generates a reluctance on the part of policy makers to liberalise trade, in general or in the context of preferential agreements, without alternative sources of fiscal receipts. Trade liberalisation brings with it a decreased reliance on border taxes, and thus the loss of what may be in some cases a considerable percentage of government revenue. For several Central American and Caribbean countries this can pose a major problem, to the extent that alternative sources of revenue are not easily available, or are yet to be developed. The range of taxable sources or even individuals is severely limited in some of the very small economies.

Even if different treatment is accorded to smaller countries in the form of longer implementation schedules for the dismantling of barriers to market access, some of them will need to reform their tax system in order to replace the revenues that will be lost by the eventual elimination of tariff barriers that will be brought about by participation in the FTAA.

The diversification of their fiscal base should thus be a priority for smaller countries in the Western hemisphere. These reforms will entail both the shift to consumption taxes and the improvement of tax collection systems and administration. The latter is an area where technical assistance can be very fruitful.

One of the objectives of the FTAA is the further liberalisation (including the application of national treatment) of national investment regimes in the region. This is very much in the interest of smaller countries, inasmuch as investment has become a key variable for competing in the international economic arena. In this regard, we believe that one of the main benefits which participation in the FTAA will bring to these countries is to increase their attractiveness as recipients of foreign direct and portfolio investment, and thus their ability to compete in the global economy.

Given that countries now acknowledge the positive impact that foreign investment can have on economic growth, productivity and the promotion of exports through intra-firm trade, and given the limited pool of investment capital available worldwide, we believe that smaller countries in the Western hemisphere should not risk compromising their capacity to compete for those resources by seeking a lower level of commitment in this field.

As we have observed before, the achievement of international competitiveness by smaller economies requires no less a degree of rigour in their financial policies than larger ones. The minimisation of budget deficits, efficient tax administration, and the modernisation of the public service are essential elements for success in the field of financial policy. But smaller economies also need to develop their capital markets to provide a variety of instruments and institutions that can cater to the needs of domestic savers and foreign portfolio investors.

In the particular case of the Caribbean and Central America, regionalisation of their capital markets is needed to achieve critical minimum size and economies of scale. The FTAA arrangements should encourage such regionalisation, as a necessary element for achieving the volume and diversity of financial flows necessary for supporting free trade in goods and services.

In developing their capital markets, the Central American and Caribbean countries have to set up effective regulatory institutions and laws for diligent and prudent financial management. Although off-shore financial services are a good export prospect for these countries, they have to ensure that they attract reputable institutions ready to operate within a well-organised financial environment.

Services are likely to be an essential component of the FTAA, and this, in and of itself, will have policy implications for Central American and Caribbean countries. However, even in the absence of an FTAA, services now play a central role in the economies of smaller countries in the Western hemisphere. These countries are becoming increasingly aware of the importance of efficient access to services, particularly modern producer services, for keeping their economies internationally competitive. Accordingly, they have initiated moves toward reviewing both their domestic and international regulatory framework for services.

At the same time, world wide trade liberalisation and the elimination of trade preferences will force smaller countries in the Western hemisphere to concentrate on areas in which they have a comparative advantage. In the longer term, the future of manufactured exports from these countries is not strong, because of emerging competition from other countries and the absence of sizeable local markets. Services provide an area where market limitations due to scale can be overcome.

Accordingly, development of the services sector (including service exports) should be a vital element of smaller economies' global strategic repositioning plans. Services are the fastest growing component of both trade and direct foreign investment flows. In addition, the growing internationalisation of services is opening new areas of service exports for smaller economies, and is broadening the range of producer services and technical know-how that they can import.

Central American and Caribbean nations are well positioned to move into services (given their demonstrated capacity in the tourism sector and the quality of their human resource base, both within and outside the region) if their governments take the necessary actions and address certain policy problems which are constraining non-tourism services export growth, and competitiveness in these countries. Among these policy measures are the improvement of education systems, enhancement of capital and labour mobility, modernisation of telecommunications networks and infrastructure, and strengthening of regulatory capacity, including the modification and/or elimination of those regulations that impede development of the services sector. However, smaller economies ought to think not only in terms of non-tourism services already developed (like for instance, back office service activities), but also new areas, such as offshore health services and retirement services.

FTAA negotiations on services can help smaller countries advance liberalisation efforts in this field, which, in our view, is an essential step towards modernising their services sectors and thus becoming more competitive worldwide. To this end, we believe that such negotiations should be based on the more inherently liberalising negative list approach applied in NAFTA, rather than on the basis of the positive list approach used in WTO General Agreement on Trade in Services (GATS).

Labour migration to North America has become an important part of economic life in the Caribbean and Central America. Migration has provided an important outlet for surplus labour and helps cushion the impact of unemployment problems in these countries. In addition, migrant remittances have provided an important source of income for low-income families and have assisted in poverty alleviation.

The question of labour mobility is not being addressed in the FTAA process. Yet the unrestricted movement of natural persons is an important component of a liberalised economy, as fundamental as the free movement of goods, services and capital. There may be practical reasons why this issue cannot be introduced in FTAA negotiations. However, if the Free Trade Area of the America is to benefit all countries, greater movement of certain categories of labour may be warranted.

Labour mobility is also an essential element for the development of services exports. The FTAA can stimulate services exports in small economies by permitting the free movement of natural persons who are service providers and the free movement of services teams.

However, we acknowledge the difficulties which will be encountered in this regard, given the reluctance of receiving countries to accept arrangements for the temporary movement of persons for fear that these could result in additional flows of permanent immigrants. Given the problems that can arise in this area, we therefore recommend that technical discussions begin early in the FTAA process with a view to establishing effective safeguards which could be introduced in order to protect importing countries against permanent and/or illegal migration.

Tourism, a sector of great importance to smaller economies, is not being dealt with in the FTAA process although it is part of the wider hemispheric agenda. The need to improve sustainability and competitiveness in this sector must be approached on a systematic and ongoing basis, not only because of the tourist industry's intrinsic value to the small economies in the Western hemisphere, but also because of the potential which tourism has as an engine of growth in the services sector of these economies as a whole.

In our view, one of the key elements that will endanger the quality and sustainability of tourism in the small economies is the absence of sound environmental policies. Thus, we believe that environmental standards covering tourism-related areas (sewage disposal, ship/boat generated waste, beach erosion, preservation of reefs and wildlife habitat, prevention of over fishing and treatment of solid waste), should be enshrined in a regional convention and adopted by all FTAA participating states. Other constraints faced by the tourism industry are lack of adequate infrastructure, quality manpower, and adequate, reliable and efficient air access.

We stress the need to obtain more sources of finance for projects aimed at improving intra-regional carriers, infrastructure and environment in tourism. This will require new funds and/or the reorientation of existing funds. Smaller economies should develop projects to be financed by funds available from both private sources and from the Inter-American Development Bank (IDB). Some of these projects must be regional, like those related to the environment, while others have to be national, such as those related to road infrastructure. Every effort should be made to remove the bottlenecks which prevent small economies from having access to such funds.

Rules of origin are often aptly called tools of discrimination. In regional trading arrangements they are used to determine which goods qualify for preferential treatment and to prevent products from non-member countries from circulating freely in the area, without payment of customs duties. As such, they will be an essential part of the FTAA.

Rules of origin are particularly important in product sectors that are protected by high trade barriers. In these cases, the value of the regional preferences is so substantial that firms and individuals often shift their orders from producers outside the region to local suppliers. Such trade diversion frequently causes comparable shifts in investments flows to circumvent the new trade barriers protecting the regional market against third country suppliers. In NAFTA, origin rules have generated such distortions in the textiles and apparel sector, where US tariffs average above 15 per cent, and in agriculture. In the MERCOSUR, high barriers in the automobile sector threaten similar problems.

Origin rules are often part of the *quid pro quo* for political support for regional trade liberalisation. Countries agree to open their markets selectively to competition from producers in their partner countries, rather than on a most-favoured-nation (MFN) basis in the GATT/WTO, so that they can continue to restrict access to their markets from the world's most competitive suppliers. In some cases, this selective reform is designed to encourage the rationalisation of production in the region to yield over time more efficient and productive industries that are globally competitive.

The political economy rationale for selective liberalisation often overlooks two important costs of origin rules. First, compliance with these rules imposes significant transactions costs for local firms. The paperwork alone is often daunting: indeed, in the Canada-USA case, many firms simply ignored the trade preferences available under the FTAA because the cost of complying with the origin rules was greater than the cost of the MFN tariff. The procedures for determining origin have become increasingly complex in the wake of the decentralisation of production brought about by globalisation (as a result of which goods are increasingly produced with materials imported from various countries), as well as the worldwide proliferation of free trade agreements with varying rules of origin.

Second, by discriminating against foreign producers, origin rules provide substantial protection for domestic producers against competitors in third markets; the rules effectively tax consumers (both of final products and industries that use intermediate goods as components in their production) and distort the allocation of resources in the economy.

Throughout the postwar period, the value of regional preferences has been steadily diluted by progressive rounds of multilateral trade liberalisation. As MFN barriers fall, the gap between the preferred access granted regional suppliers compared to that afforded firms in other GATT/WTO member countries is narrowed. The protection provided local textile firms and agricultural producers under regional pacts therefore will be temporary and decreasing over time. Since the objective of the WTO is progressively lower MFN trade barriers and new WTO negotiations are scheduled to be started by the end of the decade, it is highly likely that by the time the FTAA is negotiated and fully implemented, there will be few sectors where origin rules will make much of a difference.

For small economies, the short-term gain to income and employment in these protected sectors is unlikely to be worth the diversion of resources away from more productive sectors in the economy. For the FTAA process, the best approach to rules of origin is to keep the requirements as simple and transparent as possible and to minimise sectoral and product-specific rules.

Another major challenge confronting the Caribbean countries is related to the Lomé Convention, through which former colonies in Africa, the Caribbean and the Pacific (ACP) receive privileged access to the European market for commodities and certain manufactured exports. Under this arrangement several Caribbean countries obtain favourable conditions for the sale of commodities of great importance to their economies.

However, for Caribbean countries which are members of Lomé, participation in the FTAA poses a dilemma. Under Article 174 [2 (a)] of the Lomé Convention, these countries are obliged to provide no less favourable treatment to the European Union than they provide to any developed country. Specifically, if the Caribbean countries provided reciprocity to the United States and Canada by virtue of the FTAA, then these countries would be obliged to provide reciprocity to the European Union under the terms of Lomé. There would have to be a synchronisation of the arrangements for the transition to reciprocity between the Caribbean and the EU and between the Caribbean and NAFTA. That synchronisation needs to encompass the definition of reciprocity, the coverage of the agreements and the adjustment period. This can most usefully be accomplished through tripartite discussions at an appropriate stage during the negotiations of the new Lomé Convention and the FTAA.

Technical Assistance

Participation in an hemispheric-wide trade agreement will entail major challenges for smaller economies. The efforts required to undertake the internal adjustments required by effective participation in the FTAA should not be underestimated, and will be complicated by constraints derived from the small size and limited resource base of these countries. Moreover, developing countries, and particularly the smaller economies, will likely find burdensome the process of negotiating the complex provisions of the FTAA, given their difficulties in mobilising sufficient human and information resources that are generally available to larger and more developed countries.

Accordingly, we believe that several smaller economies will require, in addition to longer time frames in which to implement FTAA commitments, technical and financial assistance to help them to implement the necessary reforms mandated by hemispheric free trade, to participate in the negotiating process itself, and to put into effect the agreement's provisions. The ability of smaller economies to benefit from the FTAA will greatly depend on the assistance they get in this regard.

It is true that smaller countries in the Western hemisphere are becoming better positioned to face the rigours of free trade as they have adopted macroeconomic policies more suited to a globalised world economy; implemented unilateral trade liberalisation measures; and are participating in sub-regional integration schemes. However, the level of coverage foreseen in the Summit of the Americas Declaration would make the FTAA a more comprehensive agreement than the WTO or many sub-regional agreements. As a consequence of this, smaller countries will, in all likelihood, have to adopt commitments in trade and trade-related issues which extend beyond those contained in the WTO. This will pose an enormous challenge for countries which already face an increasingly complex subregional and multilateral trade agenda with scarce human resources, limited infrastructure and regulatory capacity, and insufficient technical expertise. This, of course, will vary from country to country, since not all small economies suffer these limitations to the same extent.

Decisions will have to be made with respect to the timing of the technical assistance, its sources, its appropriateness/quality, the areas to be covered and the countries that would benefit from it. In this regard, we see opportunities to strengthen cooperation and joint activities among the regional secretariats and the private sector in the Western hemisphere.

Multilateral organisations, along with regional and sub-regional institutions, should be mandated to provide technical assistance and support to the small economies (the Inter-American Development Bank, the Organisation of American States and the United Nations Economic Commission for Latin America and the Caribbean already have a mandate in this regard). The primary focus of these activities should be to enable these countries to meet the transitional costs of participating in hemispheric free trade.

Although we must be cautious in drawing parallels with the European experience in the field of regional development policy, we believe that the concept of regional development funds to finance small country participation in the FTAA needs to be addressed in the Western hemisphere. Unlike the FTAA (a free trade agreement), the European Union aims at the highest form of economic integration (economic union), and intends to adopt not only common trade and tariff policies, but common monetary, fiscal and labour policies, as well as a common currency, a central bank and supranational institutions and decision-making legislative and judicial bodies. In addition, the European integration process started in a very difficult military, political and economic setting than that prevailing in the Americas in the 1990s.

However, we suggest that FTAA discussions take into account the original idea that led to such a policy in Europe, namely the recognition that the implementation of ancillary measures in favour of the lesser developed partners in a regional agreement cannot be successfully implemented without adequate financial support.

Role of the Private Sector

We strongly believe that the private sector should be the engine of growth in development and trade. However, for this to take place, the private sector in Caribbean and Central American countries needs to improve its corporate and management structure, expand joint ventures and strategic alliances, and devote more resources to product development and innovation, as well as to secure greater access to information and new technologies.

In spite of Governments acknowledgement of the important role of the private sector, trade unions and other social partners, no formal arrangements have yet been put into place to ensure their effective participation in the FTAA process. It is true that the business fora established in the Denver and Cartagena Ministerial Meetings have been extremely important in promoting the interest and involvement of the private sector in the FTAA process. However, these once-a-year events do not allow for the permanent process of dialogue, education and preparation which is required in order to guarantee effective private sector participation in the negotiation and implementation of the FTAA. We recommend that governments institutionalise a consultation process with the private sector on ongoing issues in the FTAA.

Private sector input in the creation of the Free Trade Area of the Americas is important in a number of areas. It can exert a positive influence on governments to maintain the momentum of economic reform and avoid backward steps. It can encourage governments to improve the readiness of countries by clearly defining the internal policy measures which are required for countries to benefit from freer trade. This involves requesting governments to adopt the domestic legislation and institutional arrangements needed to negotiate and implement free trade agreements. The business community could also advise on the terms of reference of the FTAA working groups and provide inputs into the groups' technical work. It could also channel specific views to top government officials in the FTAA decision-making process and advise on short-term or early harvest measures that can create conditions for increased trade and improve the investment climate. It could educate and prepare technical staff and the business community at large for consultation and for effective participation in the negotiating process itself.

Finally, private sector organisations, trade unions and other social partners can also play a key role in explaining to their members and the wider public the advantages of trade liberalisation and associated policy measures, thus helping them to perceive such liberalisation more as a source of opportunities than as a threat. This last element is of the utmost importance, because, ultimately, the future of the FTAA is closely linked to a broad understanding and acceptance of what is set to be accomplished. Without the consensus of the public in all participating countries on the need to proceed together with unity of purpose and strength of commitment, the FTAA may never materialise.

It is for these reasons that we welcome the establishment of the Business Network for Hemispheric Integration (BNHI), an organisation which groups a large number of major business organisations with the purpose of promoting education activities, information sharing, the promotion of a common vision about free trade, and close monitoring and involvement in the FTAA process.

We believe that private sector organisations in smaller economies should be encouraged to participate actively in the activities of the BNHI.

Summary of Findings

There are certain general considerations which should be addressed in the construction of a Free Trade Area of the Americas (FTAA) among thirty-four countries of disparate size and level of development.

(1) FTAA must recognise that smaller countries face particular policy concerns: while small economic size does not necessarily put a country at an economic disadvantage with respect to economic integration, it does limit the range of policy options available to policy makers. Because these policy constraints are magnified for smaller, less developed countries, they will require additional assistance to fully participate in FTAA.

(2) Appropriate mechanisms and measures to facilitate their participation must be a joint effort of the hemispheric community as a whole. This is essential to ensure that the best possible mechanisms are devised to facilitate the full participation of the small economies in future agreements. It is also necessary in order to ensure that the smaller economies retain confidence in the vision of FTAA.

(3) Small economies should participate fully in the FTAA. The absence of the smaller economies from the FTAA would isolate these countries from the main markets and prevent them from enjoying the increased investment flows which are expected to result from the adoption of trade reforms, enhanced access to larger markets, and a common set of rules in the FTAA.

(4) Small economies must view the FTAA as part of their wider global strategic repositioning plans. The FTAA can be an essential component of the smaller countries' efforts to reposition themselves in the global economy by adjusting strategically in anticipation of and in response to global changes in demand and technology. It can act as a catalyst for the adoption of global strategic repositioning policies.

(5) The FTAA should be viewed as part of a wider hemispheric process. For smaller countries to derive clear benefits from, and better prepare themselves for, assumption of all the rights and obligations to be incorporated in the FTAA, there must be early and parallel progress with regard to other components that are of great interest to them in the Declaration of Principles and Plan of Action adopted at the Summit of the Americas.

(6) The FTAA should allow for the full participation of all member countries, be balanced and comprehensive in scope, and represent a single undertaking of mutual rights and obligations. In this regard, the group has set forth the following principles for considerations in the construction of the FTAA:

(a) phased implementation: longer periods for the implementation of general rules and disciplines applicable to all should be considered, when warranted, for the smaller economies.

(b) flexibility: in each aspect of the FTAA, the particular circumstances of each individual country and group of countries should be considered.

(c) joint participation: because of their limited resources and common interests, the Central American and Caribbean countries may participate as a group in the negotiations of the FTAA.

(d) technical assistance: technical assistance and support should be provided in the negotiating process as well as in the implementation of the Agreement

This report is submitted unanimously by all the members of the group, in their personal capacity. The views expressed are in no way intended to reflect the views of the institutions and organisations with which the participants are affiliated. The papers presented by members of the group will be published shortly as an appendix to this report. The preparation of the report would not have been possible without the financial support of the Inter-American Development Bank (IDB)

[64]

The Future of Preferential
Trade and Sugar

Kusha Haraksingh

Preferential arrangements are a hallmark of the existing [trade] situation especially in relation to sugar. Surely, if there is to be a move to some other arrangement, then it is reasonable to expect that the proponents of that new dispensation should be the ones charged with making the case. All the same, this is not a challenge, I am afraid of facing, and my confidence is strengthened by three significant considerations. Firstly, the lesson to be learnt from the grand sweep of history, especially in this hemisphere, is that all trade is calculated with an eye to advantage, and in that sense it is always preferential. Secondly, that the existing arrangements, though described as preferential and therefore by implication seeming to confer a benefit to one party only, are really distinguished by the way in which a mutuality rather than singularity of interest is served, and by the way in which benefits are shared and distributed among the parties. Thirdly, the ends secured by the arrangement are desirable and laudable, and moreover are the same ones that the advocates of change would like to see achieved. For these reasons I feel sure that special arrangements would continue to be a feature of the world sugar trade.

I am aware that what I have just said runs against the grain of contemporary wisdom, at least, as it is commonly packaged in academic as well as in popular circles. This is partly owing to the manner in which the discourse has been constructed, as for example, in the way in which the popular press treats the issue: in simplistic terms, as protectionist against free traders, and with a predictable outcome in favour of the latter. However, the argument is not as simple as it seems, and slowly, it does appear as if the complexities involved are coming more and more to the forefront. Thus, last month, at the start of the IADB's annual meeting, Enrique Iglesias, President of the Bank, went to great pains to point out that free trade alone was not enough to eradicate poverty, and that attention to social needs was essential to building healthier societies. And in the war of words between the US and the EU over the banana dispute before the WTO, both sides, whatever their divergent views, were in little doubt that the dismantling of the banana regime would cause severe hardship and political instability in some countries. Perhaps, then, opinion is slowly coming round to the view that the real goal should be fair rather than free trade, and it is precisely because the preferences in sugar are fair that I believe their future is assured.

There is probably no more political commodity in the world than sugar, and this has been the case for hundreds of years. From a Caribbean perspective, it is clear that the world which sugar created was always distinguished by the interlocking of the forces of the global economy, whether in the context of seventeenth and eighteenth-century trade which tried but never succeeded in dissecting the Caribbean into neat and self contained blocks, or, in relation to nineteenth-century idea of free trade which was not free and hardly trade at all, or within the ambit of the twentieth-century economic and political penetration of the region. All of these configurations produced the same lesson, that there was really nothing like open trade: that what existed were arrangements for the movement of goods, and that in the delineating of those arrangements, some were more favoured than others.

That brings me to a basic point. When people talk about preferential trade, they usually mean preferential trade between or among countries. But trade, in a generic sense, is commerce that occurs between producer and buyer/consumer. Using that generic definition, almost every country that produces sugar engages in preferential trade within its own borders, because practically every producer country provides some protection to its own sugar industry. Countries tend to protect their own sugar industries not only to allow their industries and related jobs to survive, but because sugar also provides badly needed hard currency. Sugar is a vital component of many countries' diet, and most producer countries consider it a matter of national security to maintain a sugar industry to protect against the loss of access to other markets or inability to purchase sugar abroad.

So, we need to note the proposition that almost every producer country engages in preferential trade, even if it is within its own borders. They recognise that to do otherwise would be a prescription for what has been called 'unilateral disarmament' accompanied by chaos and uncertainty. For this reason, condemnation of preferential trade is somewhat disingenuous, unless the country making those denouncements has no internal or external protection for its own sugar or other industries.

Preferential trade between and among countries is often attacked on two premises. Firstly, that it interferes with, and thus makes less efficient the operation of the world economy, and secondly, that it creates an unequal playing field by picking winners and losers rather than leaving those decisions to the market.

The premise of the first argument, that preferential trade creates an unequal playing field, is difficult to sustain since it assumes that there was a level playing field to start with. That is just not true when it comes to smaller countries like the ones I happen to represent. Smaller producer countries like ours have inherent disadvantages trying to compete with large producer states like USA, Australia, Brazil and Mexico. With large internal markets, the mills in those countries can achieve high levels of efficiency because of their volume of production. These larger countries also have a much more varied agricultural and industrial base. Sugar is usually only a minor part of their overall economy. It may even be a minor part of their agricultural economy. But, in countries like Guyana, Trinidad and Tobago, Jamaica, the Dominica Republic and many others, sugar is either the first or second most important commodity in terms of agricultural income and hard currency. In other words, sugar is more important to us than it is to the larger producer countries. Take USA, for instance. Sugar is important to its economy, but the loss of that industry alone would not throw America into a recession, much less a depression. But, in some of the smaller countries, the loss of the sugar industry alone could easily produce severe shocks that would reverberate through the entire economy.

The academic economists would respond: well, you need to diversify your economy. That was the big message coming out of the original Caribbean Basin Initiative. I remember delegations of American businessmen and experts travelling throughout the Caribbean preaching the message of diversification. Many attempts at diversification were instituted, and most of them failed. In agriculture, in many instances, the poor soil of our nation is unsuited to any large scale agricultural pursuits other than growing sugar cane. And when we have tried to get into other enterprises such as textiles, the larger companies object to providing us with markets. And even here, we must compete against China, Hong Kong, Taiwan, and others who have far greater resources and advantages.

So the premise of the argument, that there is a level playing field to start with, does not always hold water. In fact, I would argue just the opposite – that preferential trade serves to level the playing field for small countries which have few inherent advantages and few possibilities of diversification. For us, without preferential trade, the winners and losers would be determined before the competition begins.

That brings me to the other argument against preferential trade – that it interferes with and makes less efficient the operation of the world economy. That argument is easy to make in an academic sense, and it is hard to argue against. But, take the example of sugar in small developing countries such as my own. If we were forced tomorrow to give up our preferential markets in the EU and in the USA, which have now been enshrined in WTO arrangements, our economy would certainly be severely jolted. Some would say, that's unfortunate, and that the market must make all economic decisions. My response would be: we have to consider the great numbers of people in small developing countries and what can happen to their governments when they lose this valuable hard currency. Even assuming compassion is in short supply, the practical consequences have to be taken into account. Can the world just turn its eyes away from countries in economic despair? Can the industrialised world ignore the political consequences of small countries with nothing to lose? What if the alternatives come to be expressed in unacceptable political systems, or waves of illegal migration, or drug trafficking, or instability among neighbours? Everyone knows the democracies of the industrialised world cannot afford to let that happen.

Just go back a few years in Central America. How much treasure, diplomatic capital and just plain worry did USA and the West expend to turn back the insurgencies in Nicaragua, El Salvador and Honduras. We all know those insurgencies were born out of poverty and economic despair. And, in the contemporary situation, we just have to note the consequences of extreme poverty and authoritarian rule in Haiti. We hear of border clashes as the Dominican Republic seeks to stop the flood of refugees from Haiti. The same thing happened a few years ago in Florida as the Haitian boat people arrived by the thousands. Small countries without hope economically can become big problems even for economic giants like the USA. The industrialised world cannot afford to let this happen, not because of an overabundance of compassion, but because of its own self-interest.

Preferential trade arrangements were, for the most part, not created out of compassion but out of a recognition that the fate of some countries could be irreparably harmed if they were not given some means of developing an economy that provided jobs and produced hard currency. In some instances, those giving preferential markets did so to protect their own investments in former colonies. In other instances, it was a way to maintain influence in former colonies and dependencies. In the case of the USA, its quota had less to do with former colonies than with maintaining good economic and diplomatic relations with its allies, especially those countries to the South who were called upon to fill the breach caused by the embargo on Cuba.

This leads me to a threat that has developed to that market for most quota-holding countries. During the USA-Mexican negotiations on NAFTA, American negotiators (prompted by USA producers) were fearful that unlimited Mexican access could destroy USA sugar programme. The CBI Sugar Group, composed of producers in the Caribbean and Central America, knew that unlimited Mexican access could mean that the entire USA quota, or at least all above the WTO minimum, would go to Mexico at the expense of the 39 other quota-holding countries. As a result, USA negotiators concluded a side agreement with Mexico, which allowed them increased, but not unlimited, levels of access over the 14-year period of NAFTA. Without these negotiated limits, Mexico could have simply switched its soft drink industry from sugar to corn sweetener and sent the displaced sugar to the US, in effect taking over most or all of the quota. The side agreement was designed to protect US and offshore producers.

We are now in the fourth year of NAFTA, and just what some predicted has occurred. Mexico is converting its soft drink industry to high fructose corn syrup. That, along with good crop years and increased production as a result of privatisation, has resulted in a sugar surplus which Mexico would like to send to the USA at the USA preferential price. But, it is prohibited from doing so by the side agreements to NAFTA. To get around this obstacle, some in Mexico have begun claiming that there was no agreement to the limitations.

This problem, like so many, is a microcosm of what the smaller countries of the hemisphere face every day. We do not have the natural advantage of our larger neighbours, despite the adoption of free market principles in our economies. Nor do we have the political clout of our larger, wealthier neighbours. That is why preferential markets are so vital to us, and as I have tried to show, vital to comity among nations as a whole.

Once this is acknowledged, it is not difficult, though perhaps it might be protracted, to work out arrangements that can be designed to increase the general welfare. A good case in point is the recent intergovernmental agreement on Special Preferential Sugar, a new embodiment of EU/ACP partnership and cooperation. In contrast to the new measures being promoted by the WTO, which will increase access to new markets, for products exported by developed countries at the expense of developing countries, the new SPS agreement actually increases international trade to the mutual benefit of the signatories and shows the convergence of interest which is possible. The SPS agreement ensures consistent supplies to EU refiners and helps the EU to more than comply with its minimum commitments to the WTO. Moreover, the SPS agreement is in accordance with WTO principles, especially in the context of the rules on customs unions and in the light of special and differential treatment for less developed countries. This convergence of interest is sure to give the arrangement a good chance of withstanding future challenges.

The preference then is for fairness, rather than for freedom in the abstract. This is not blind adherence to a distant age, or burying one's head in the sand, but rather confronting demands that are real and urgent. The same Governments in the Caribbean which insist on the maintenance of sugar preferences have, in their domestic situation, instituted new laws with respect to intellectual property and the protection of the environment, have disbanded negative listing which debarred the importation of certain commodities, and have done so even before anti-dumping legislation could be put in place. These Governments have introduced transparent Central Bank regulations and free floating currencies. Even some troubling reforms, like the removal of restrictions on landholding by non-citizens – especially troubling in very small countries – have been countenanced. Thus, they have shown a great willingness to embrace the leading principles of a new world economic order, and to grasp the opportunities present in that endeavour. But who can blame them for their determination to look for solutions that take national and regional considerations into account, and which try to avoid the pitfalls of a blanket approach to world trade applied to small nations with limited physical and human resources? Perhaps the advocates of the theoretical doctrine of comparative advantage might be tempted to do so. But, comparative advantage has never been something written in the sky, or preordained from above. True, there is an element of fortuitousness, as in natural resources, or in land area or geographic location. But, there is also a large element of artificiality, of things made by man, of arrangements which are deliberately designed rather than simply inherited. Any preferences are quite simply a form of designing. From this perspective, the real question then becomes: what are the ends to be served?

If free trade is meant to promote and increase the general welfare, then this is precisely what the preferential trade in sugar has been able to deliver. The Green Paper produced by the EU on the subject of its cooperation with African, Caribbean and Pacific countries, acknowledges this point, for while it notices that some countries have not benefited as much as was hoped, it concedes that there have been spectacular success stories. The fault, if there is one, does not reside therefore in the trading arrangement itself but perhaps in more general conditions applicable to particular countries. As far as the Caribbean is concerned, sugar preferences helped to construct the bases for the region's first industrial revolution, for the rise of an artisan class, and to enable peasants to enter the cash nexus as consumers, to propel labour relations, including those associated with female labour, on to a platform of modernity, while promoting renewable and sustainable agriculture, a bulwark against urban drift and illegal migration to the developed world. And all the while ensuring the region's continued integration in the world economy: export earnings on the one hand, and on the other, marketing, shipping, refining, and providing equipment and specialised services.

It is important to emphasise this synergism of objectives to prevent it from being obscured by approaches to world trade which are somewhat blunt in conception and application, and which see efficiency in narrow economic terms. A more tenable approach is one which is wide enough to include social factors, environmental concerns, development and democracy. For, at the end of the day, it would be a matter of great irony if the grand purposes on which so many of the newer and poorer nations of the world have fashioned themselves – based on ideas that go back to the French Revolution, to the USA constitution, to the Mexican Revolution, are put at risk by trading arrangements which promote instability and upheaval. I do not think that anyone, even the most ardent advocates of the theory of free trade, would wish for that to happen.

Note

This is a slightly edited version of a presentation made at the F.O. Licht's 2nd Anniversary World Sugar and Sweeteners Conference. The speech was first published in *CARICOM Perspective*, No. 67, June 1997, pp. 10–13.

[65]

CARICOM and the
New Liberal Trade Order

Clive   Thomas

The institutional architecture of global trade and finance has always been crucial to the livelihood of the Caribbean peoples. Throughout its modern history, external trade and private capital movements, supplemented with official flows, have been the main engine of growth and source of financing for the development in the region. Recent steep declines in official financial inflows and high levels of official external indebtedness have accentuated this dependence. Concurrent with this, the global institutional architecture has been undergoing the most far-reaching and unprecedented changes, as what has been termed a *new liberal trade order* emerges. These changes have been attributed to the process of globalisation, particularly the aspect of increased integration of all forms of economic activities – trade, production, finance, investments, consumption – across national boundaries and jurisdictions, founded on, but not limited to, an historically unique combination of techno-logical progress and conscious economic policy.

CARICOM External Trade Arrangements

For a small region, CARICOM's international trade and external business relations are complex and tortuous, evolving as eleven broad clusters:

(1)   Obligation under the WTO, along with WTO related issues such as the Generalised System of Preferences (GSP) and matters related to the special and differential treatment of size and vulnerability, (SIDS);

(2)   The Lomé Convention with the EU, which is currently being re-nego-
       tiated;
(3)   On-going negotiations for a Free Trade Area of the Americas (FTAA);
(4)   On-going negotiations for the extension of CBI/NAFTA parity (Presi-
       dent Clinton's assurances at the US/CARICOM Summit in 1997 'to
       expedite legislation to confer CBI status on an extended basis to
       products of Caribbean origin which are currently excluded');
(5)   CARIBCAN (the non-reciprocal duty free arrangement with Canada
       in force since 1996);
(6)   Limited non-reciprocal trade agreements with Venezuela (1993), and
       Colombia (1996);
(7)   Exploration for new agreements with other regional arrangements and
       countries, for example, CACM , MERCOSUR, the Andean Group
       and the Dominican Republic;
(8)   CARIFORUM cooperation in the context of the Lomé Convention;
(9)   The ACS;
(10)   Miscellaneous efforts aimed at promoting sub-regional groupings; for
       example, the OECS; the Manning Initiative outside; Guyana-Surinam-
       Trinidad & Tobago co-operation;
(11)   Individual member country initiatives outside the Region; for example,
       Guyana and Mercosur, Belize/Mexican free trade area; several coun-
       tries and Cuba.

This list does not include special bilateral relations with countries like
Japan, the Soviet Union, China and India.

Each of these clusters combines both traditional and non-traditional
principles of international trade relations. The traditional principles are trade
relations based on discriminatory preferences and non-reciprocal obliga-
tions/rights; a focus on trade in goods, particularly in the form of price and
quota guarantees for primary exports; the linkage of trade to official development assistance (ODA); and, an 'inward focused' approach to regional
cooperation. These principles dominate in arrangements like the CBI, Lomé
Convention, and CARIBCAN. The non-traditional principles constitute and
define the emerging liberal trade order, which are embodied in the post-Uru-
guay Round/WTO–type arrangements. These seem destined to determine
the outcome of current negotiations for the FTAA, as well as the re-negotia-
tions of existing arrangements such as the Lomé Convention, and proposals
for an enhanced CBI. This combination of the very different traditional and
non-traditional principles is a highly combustible mixture, which heightens
the sense of flux, change and uncertainty presently facing CARICOM.

The New Liberal Trade Order

An important question that we must address at the outset is, what is the foundational rationale of the new liberal trade order? In other words, what is such a radical departure from all that has preceded it? The simple answer is that, the new liberal trade order aims to achieve what was hitherto felt to be impossible. Its goal is to achieve symmetry in the treatment of all countries; to be comprehensive in its coverage of trade in goods, services and trade-related matters; and to be sufficiently credible in its contractual obligations to ensure compliance with them. These accomplishments are to be based on five fundamental trade principles.

Firstly, there must be uncompromising adherence to the orthodox analysis of mainstream neo-classical economics in which certain subsidiary trade principles are promoted: exports are free to enter a country, subject only to tariffs and their meeting technical and other standards, scientifically established; there is no recognised general permission for non-tariff barriers to the trade (NTBs); there should be unqualified non-discriminatory treatment between imports and domestic production as well as between member countries participating in international trade. And the only acceptable trade policies that Governments may practise are those which are neutral and non-trade distorting. Therefore trade policies must be executed on a reciprocal multilateral basis and enshrine within them a binding commitment towards the removal of all tariff and non-tariff barriers to trade.

The second trade principle is a marked preference for neutral, non-distorting, rules based on international trade mechanisms which limit all forms of discretionary state/political intervention, while at the same time providing for strict automatic review, compliance, oversight and enforcement. Thirdly, to ensure comprehensiveness of coverage, these trade principles should be extended to all trade-related areas – social (labour standards), scientific-technological-natural (environment and technical standards) or, other specialised economic areas (finance and FDI flows). The fourth principle is that private agents, along with market driven economic incentives and performance-based results, should be promoted universally as the foundation of international trade. And fifthly, to ensure that countries in pursuit of regional cooperation do not allow these arrangements to become stumbling blocks in the process of global integration, regional cooperation should take the form of trade-neutral regionalism.

Because mainstream neo-classical economics provides the theoretical underpinnings for the new liberal trade order, as well as globalisation and liberalisation, it is important to spend a little time making this theoretical basis clear.

Neo-classical economics defines welfare maximisation as a state of economic affairs where no one person can be made better off without simultaneously making at least one person worse off, and where market prices reflect social costs. Then, based on certain assumptions, these economics argue that this state of economic affairs can only be met if perfectly competitive private market prevail. When that is achieved, production efficiency is maximised in that, it is no longer possible to increase output of any one good without reducing the output of some other good.

When the economy is operating at the outer limits of its production frontier or the curve showing its maximum production possibilities, this state of affairs is formally defined as the marginal rate of transforming one good (x) into another good (y). This maximises exchange efficiency in that, it is then impossible for any one individual to be better-off in terms of satisfaction or welfare without making at least one other individual worse-off. Allocative efficiency is, therefore, also maximised in that, the rate at which goods are transformed in production at the production frontier, equals the rate at which individual consumers are willing to substitute them in terms of satisfaction derived from their use. As the argument goes, this welfare maximisation can be achieved by private individuals operating in private markets, without any explicit government intervention aimed at improving society's welfare.

This is the so-called fundamental theorem of neo-classical economics, which can be proved formally correct only if, certain restrictive conditions apply, including that we operate a perfectly competitive economy, in which all participants are maximizers. That is, they should seek outcomes that yield the greatest net benefit to them. There would be no room for monopolistic distortions among either buyers or sellers, based on any circumstances, whether natural, informational, or due to the manipulation of barriers to competition, or the entry and exit of private buyers or sellers. The economy must also be in dynamic (growth) equilibrium and, therefore, is expected to be operating at full capacity and employment. In addition, financial markets, and the agents who operate in them, must be efficient gatherers and transmitters of information. They are also rational and knowledgeable about the 'true' behaviour of the fundamentals of the economy.

Outside of financial markets, all other economic agents are also assumed to be rational and to possess knowledge of the 'true model' of the economy. If this occurs, then these agents will not make decisions about the future of the economy, which are systematically in error. Given the above, the condition follows that expected changes in government's policy will be anticipated and 'built-in' to the behaviour of economic agents. In other words, there will be 'no policy surprises'.

Notwithstanding these extremely restrictive conditions, this fundamental theorem is applied to international economies in order to support a number of crucial policy rules. First, that free trade through private markets should be universally promoted. Typically, these markets are expected to be harmonious, bringing together in equality, the interest of buyers and sellers. The role of the states in the global economy should be restricted to focus on superintending the removal of barriers to private trade. The presumption is that, the international economy constitutes a level playing field, in which case, unrestricted investment flows, free trade in goods and services, deregulation, and unimpeded cross-border flows will not only maximise global output, but lead to congruence of global incomes and productivity.

The second policy rule is that, if exceptions have to be made, these should be either confined to affording differential treatment to LDCs (as measured by income per head) on a common across-the-board basis (for example, the GSP approach), or linked to special commodity arrangements (for example, e-commerce). In all circumstances, special treatment should be confined to a limited time in which qualifying members are required to adjust to the new trade rules. Reciprocity and mutuality of obligations/rights must be the overriding feature of trade relations between all countries at all times. As for preferential arrangements, these should be phased out within strictly defined time limits.

The presumption behind this policy rule is that the potential capacity and, therefore, the ability of all participants, whether they be consumers, producers, individuals, groups, economies, firms or governments, to share equally in the costs and benefits of a new liberal trade order is the same. It does not acknowledge any basic asymmetries between large and small firms, or indeed big and small countries. All states are presumed equal in relation to each other in the market place, and will only differ to the extent that their competitiveness might vary. And where such variation is evident, the argument goes that, there is no evidence correlating this with country size.

Thirdly, the United Nations, while it might be the world's most important deliberative forum, because of its 'political' and 'interventionist' character, should not be tasked with the regulation, supervision, and oversight of the global economy. Instead, special organisations like the BWIs and the WTO, should be assigned these responsibilities – even though the charter of the UN envisages otherwise. (Under its Charter, UN has been given the lead responsibility in global macroeconomic policy formulation and social and economic affairs).

Before turning to examine some of CARICOM's external arrangements, a few observations are warranted. One is that, these policy rules represent a paradigm shift away from early post-colonial development policies practised in the region. Earlier policies treated unregulated private markets and unrestricted openness and integration into the world economy as barriers to economic development. Because markets fail from time to time, and countries impose trade restrictions for their own benefit, there is a compelling case for trade regulation and the promotion of import-substituting industrialisation. Indeed such exceptions to free trade are recognised in neo-classical economies in situations where perfect competitions do not apply. This earlier approach came through an important distinction between the benefits from trade (which are undeniable) and the benefits of unrestricted free trade as a specific policy goal.

Recent developments in trade theory have revived some of these issues. Thus strategic trade policy theorists have demonstrated that, in the context of developed economy, trade flow advantages can be exploited by countries because of the widespread existence of increasing returns and not comparative advantage in TNC trade. In such situations, deterring competing firms from entering the domestic market, can allow local firms to reap excess returns. Others have argued also that increasing returns in imperfect (oligopolistic) market situations generate externalities in certain types of industries, for example, those where R & D expenditures are high, and therefore domestic firms are not always in a position to reap the full flow of benefits they generate from such expenditures. Arguments such as these seek to distinguish between comparative static issues of resource allocation and resource use at the micro/firm level, and resource mobilisation and resource creation at the macro level. On the basis of this distinction the case for publicly directed industrial policy is made.

Another observation is that recent growth of global economy has shown remarkable dispersion and a growing inequalisation of trade. There is an increasing concentration of power and wealth among the new countries and a few firms, and a considerable widening of the economic gaps between North and South – as measured by standard indicators such as trade, production, consumption, technology and productivity. Thus the distribution of the benefits of global growth between North and South has risen from a ratio of 30:1 in 1960 to 60:1 today. Presently 85 per cent of the world's population receives only 15 per cent of world income. The target rates of growth that have been established by UNCTAD show the necessity to secure inroads into unemployment in both North and South and narrow economic gaps to three per cent worldwide and six per cent for developing countries, on average. This has not been achieved.

As a final observation, it is to be noted that global economy has witnessed severe periodic short-term financial and currency crises, occurring at roughly two-yearly intervals in the 1990s, originating in different countries and regions. It is estimated that these crises have cost the global economy about one per cent of its growth per annum in this period and this is considered to be the single most important impediment to meeting the growth rate target (UNCTAD,1998).

External Arrangements

The international trade system cannot be assessed without taking into account the main features of the financial system. Expanding trade has always been dependent on predictable, orderly, certain and stable regime of currency arrangements. This moreso today, as global trade has become very closely integrated with capital markets – a phenomenon now experienced in the Caribbean. It is not surprising, therefore, that the WTO, along with the present international financial architecture, perhaps best epitomises the application of the principles we have been examining. From the standpoint of our concerns, the key feature of the present financial architecture is that it is the end product of the process of financial liberalisation, which began when the fixed parities system of exchange management ended in 1971. Since then it has grown so rapidly that, today the estimated daily trade in currency markets (including spot, outright purchases, and foreign exchange swaps) exceed $1.6 trillion – up from only $15 billion in 1970s. The structure of global finance is overwhelmingly based on private actors and private decision-making. The supervisory roles of the BWIs, where they come into play, are limited. There is also limited participation from developing countries, despite the fact most of the activities of these institutions are directed at these countries. In the absence of a consciously promoted global architecture at the inter-governmental level, coordinated decision-making is extremely difficult. National action coordinated at the G7 level substitutes for this. We also find that in those areas of international finance where there is an agreed and dedicated supervisory mechanism, for example, the Bank for International Settlements, its scope is limited and it falls far short of what is desired.

The pursuit of financial liberalisation as the global policy was expected to yield many benefits. One expected benefit was private resource transfers from the North to the South as more capital became available and the North became attracted to the comparatively higher returns in capital poor countries. Borrowing costs should be lowered with the increased variety of financial instruments to attract savers. There should be reduced risks for international transactions with the greater portfolio diversification and stability, and a better environment for macroeconomic stability as market discipline replaced capricious governmental intervention.

None of the above has occurred to an acceptable level. Net private flows to the South have been moderate and, when it has occurred on a significant scale, it has been highly concentrated in about a dozen economies in Southeast Asia (mainly China) and Latin America (mainly Brazil, Mexico and Argentina). The decline in official concessional flows has aggravated the situation. Instead of lower borrowing costs, we find that in the economies of many developing countries real interest rates remain very high. Macroeconomic stability has not emerged in the South. Even among these countries that boasted of this achievement (for example, Asia), currency and foreign exchange crises have erupted (1997), indicating that macroeconomic stability does not provide immunity to external shocks or protect against the spread of contagion emanating elsewhere. While new financial instruments have emerged, aimed at reducing risks attached to a flexible exchange rate system, (such as, derivatives), the instruments themselves, and the ways in which they are traded are seen by some observers as a source of systemic risk.

One of the problems which the global financial systems face is that under the previous fixed exchanged system, the exchange risk was carried by governments. However, under the present flexible rate system it is expected to be carried by the private sector. In response this has led to extensive recourse to currency hedging and arbitrage, along with speculative pursuit of short-term capital gains. Private, risk-rating institutions on which private investors are dependent have tended to miss early signs of financial and currency difficulties – thereby exaggerating cyclical swings. This volatile situation has encouraged panic movements of funds, which have intensified the effect of these swings. At present, the proficiency of some of these agencies is 'suspect,' and there have been calls for them to operate more transparently and to make their judgements on the basis of publicly declared objective parameters for risk-rating. In this difficult situation there is great uncertainty about the future direction of international financial management. In the face of repeated volatile short-term capital flows, some analysts have called for taxes on short-term capital flows to deter speculative movements. Others have called for the IMF to revert to its original position in favour of countries having the discretion to apply capital account controls and to desist from encouraging otherwise. There are also analysts who have been calling for an end to the bail-out of creditors when financial crises erupt, both because of the moral hazards this entails and the encouragement it gives to reckless lending. There have also been calls for the creation of a 'lender of last resort': for augmentation of the resources of the BWIs; and, for reduced reliance and contradictory policies at times of currency crisis. It is claimed that the latter magnifies the economic and social cause of financial/currency crises.

Of note is that there is a growing consensus worldwide that the present international architecture is deficient and needs to be urgently reformed. A strong view is that this reform should be structured – going well beyond the make-shift adjustments and amendments undertaken in the past.[1] As the UN observes:

World events since mid-1997, and its precedents into the 80s and 1990s, have made painfully clear that the current international financial situation is unable to safeguard the world economy from financial crises of high intensity and frequency in devastating real effects.

. . . existing institutions are inadequate to deal with financial globalisation. This is true of institutions at the international level, which have manifested significant shortcomings in the consistency of macroeconomic policies, and in the management of international liquidity, financial supervision and regulations. It is also true of national institutions in the face of globalisation, even in industrial countries. This systematic deficiency and the associated threat of recurring crises in the future have underscored the need for a comprehensive reform of the international financial system, geared to prevent costly crises and to manage them better if the occur. The outcome would improve economic and social prospects worldwide. (United Nations, 1999, p.1, 2)

In contrast to the largely unregulated global financial system, the new liberal trade order has created a new institutional architecture in the form of the WTO. This is intended as the umbrella organisation under which all present and future international trade relations must fall. Because of its ambitious nature it is important to be clear at the outset about the tremendous scope it covers:

(a) Agreements on tariff schedules for trade in their goods and their manner of implementation;

(b) Twelve agreements covering agriculture; sanitary and phytosanitary measures; textiles and clothing; technical barriers to trade; trade related investment matters (TRIMs) for example, regulations requiring a specified domestic content to domestic production prohibited; anti-dumping; customs valuation and pre-shipment inspection; rules of origin, import licensing, subsidies and safeguard provisions;

(c) Understanding on six trade related areas: other duties and charges; state trading enterprise; balance of payments provisions; customs unions and FTAs; waivers of obligations; and, tariff modification;

(d) A general agreement on trade in services (GATS),

(e) An agreement on trade related international property rights systems (TRIPS) in seven areas of intellectual property: copyright, patents, trademarks, industrial design, geographical indications, layout design of integrated circuits and undisclosed information,

(f) A Trade Policy Review Mechanism,

(g) A Dispute Settlement Mechanism,

(h) Plurilateral agreements on civil aircraft, government procurement, dairy and bovine meat.

In addition to these existing agreements there are built-in agenda items, which are an integral part of its ongoing activities. These include a wide range of issues: further liberalisation of services in areas like government procurement, subsidies, and safeguards and, the treatment of natural persons linked to service provision; further liberalisation of agriculture, in terms of tariff levels, domestic support and subsidies; review of subsidies and countervailing subsidies to ensure that the non-actionable subsidies are not biased in favour of developed countries as they seem now, given their focus on R & D, disadvantaged regions and environmental adoption exceptions. Other specific reviews, including the following: TRIPs; TRIMs; anti-dumping measures; MFN status; the small supplier concept, import licensing, rules of origin and technical barriers to trade.

In addition to these there are also new agenda issues, which have emerged since the end of the Uruguay Round and which are destined for the next round of WTO negotiations. These include: social clauses and 'Fair Trade' Issues, environment issues, investment, particularly the standardisation/equalisation of treatment of national and FDI, government procurement, electronic commerce, competition policy, trade facilitation, an extension of the principles of special and differential treatment, the admission of new members, especially China, symmetry in the treatment of labour and capital worldwide, and industrial policy.

Within this very broad scope of matters, the WTO focuses on contractual relations among member countries and provides rule-based mechanisms to regulate these and to enforce compliance. It should be made clear, however, that the WTO was never intended to serve as a vehicle to promote development *per se*. In this regard it is very different from UNCTAD, the specialised UN agency that is explicitly concerned with trade and development in the developing countries.

A number of features of the WTO arrangements require comment. First, the history of the negotiations for the WTO shows that, unlike their counterparts in the South, the developed countries of the North have shown, (despite some disagreements, such as the banana dispute between the USA and the EU), remarkable coordination, preparation, and consistency in pursuing the design of a WTO that is compatible with their interests. As a consequence we have witnessed a disproportionate amount of one-sided concessions being made by the South and, simultaneously the North's relentless pursuit of loopholes in their favour within the WTO treaty. One contributory reason for this is that many South delegations negotiated these agreements without the knowledge and/or effective participation of the economic sectors and interests directly affected in their home countries. The result is that, despite the 'one country one vote principle' on which the WTO is based, countries of the North exercised by far the dominant roles in decision-making. And, since this situation parallels that which already obtains in the BWIs, there has emerged two important tendencies. Cross conditionalities should apply when assessing the institutions of developing countries to determine if they are exclusively responsible for the regulation of global economic affairs.

Because the economics of industrialised countries are concentrated in the TNC headquartered in their respective countries, it is not surprising to find that these firms play major roles in the continuing design, construction and operations of the WTO. Many of the agreements in the WTO were crafted from the perspectives of the TNCs. These institutions have also played important roles in setting the global technical standards adopted by the WTO. They were influential as well in getting their governments to take positions in WTO negotiations, and in this way contributed to shaping the rules and exceptions in the agreement, in a manner acceptable to them. This influence is still seen in the major role they are now playing in framing the on-going agenda items for future WTO deliberations.

The result of these circumstances is that a clear pattern has emerged in which, developed countries seem willing to favour open access to those sectors where their TNCs have a competitive advantage which they wish to preserve (for example, knowledge based, innovative products, information, e-commerce, entertainment, etc.), while continuing to rationalise the need to maintain barriers to sectors that favour the South (textiles, clothing and agriculture). To take a few examples; TRIPS protects the developed economies competitiveness by limiting South access to its technology through adoption of legal norms governing access, already in operation in the North. GATS expands access for the North's TNCs into the markets of the South in areas previously subject to strong jurisdictions. TRIMS legitimises TNC overseas investment – an important achievement following the earlier waves of nationalisation and calls for the NIEO.

The FTAA and Lomé Convention

The WTO is important to the region as it is the umbrella organisation under which current and future trade negotiations will be pursued. This is evident in the case of the two major on-going negotiations: the FTAA, and the re-negotiation of the EU/ACP Agreement, where already strong tensions exists between the established trade principles and the newly emerging liberal trade order.

The FTAA negotiations constitute only one element in a very wide ranging set of initiatives under the aegis of the Plan of Action adopted at the Summit of Americas (SOA) in December 1994. That Plan of Action covers four very broad general areas of hemispheric activities, economic as well as non-economic. These are:

(i)   preserving and strengthening the community of democracies in the Americas

(ii) promoting prosperity through economic integration and free trade

(iii) eradicating poverty and discrimination in the hemisphere

(iv) guaranteeing sustainable development and conserving the natural environment for future generations.

To put it in better perceptive the FTAA is only one of seven initiatives under the second broad heading listed above. Its work is being advanced through 12 focused working groups, while work in relation to the other economic and non-economic initiatives referred to above are being pursued through a loose structure known as the Summit Implementation Review Group (SIRG). There is wide agreement that the SIRG has been rather less focused than the FTAA, which is one of the reasons why the FTAA seems to have emerged as the main item in the Plan of Action, at this stage. The 12 working groups of the FTAA deal with: market access, customs procedure and rules of origin, investment, standards and technical barriers to trade, sanitary and phytosanitary measures, subsidies, anti-dumping and countervailing duties, smaller economies, government procurement, intellectual property rights, services, competition policy, and dispute settlement.

CARICOM has sought to advance its particular interests in the negotiations primarily but not exclusively, through the Working Group on Small Economies. It has, however, encountered many problems, having to do both with the broader FTAA process and the notion of special treatment for smaller economies. Other problems have also arisen under the FTAA. For one, the USA Congress has denied fast track authority to President Clinton, who despite assurances being given about the process being on schedule, must call

into question the target date for commencement of January 2005. Additionally, these negotiations have produced a 'wait-and-see' attitude in relation to
efforts to promote co-operation at the sub-hemispheric level, – the ACS;
relations with CACM, MERCOSUR, and the Dominican Republic; and, the
pursuit of CBI/NAFTA parity.

USA has also made attempts to put on the agenda of the FTAA, trade
related matters, some of which are still under dispute and openly contested,
as North-South issues at the WTO forum (labour standards and trade,
environment and trade, and investments and trade). The position, however,
is that the US has already achieved some success in this regard and that there
are concerns that when the FTAA is signed, the next step will be for
agreements reached here to be used as precedents arguing the case for the
inclusion in WTO.

Because of the concurrent negotiations taking place with the EU over
the successor of the Lomé Convention, there is need to ensure an eventual
symmetry between the two sets of negotiations. Failing this, one will have
to give way to the other. A number of additional difficulties have arisen
under Lomé, including, definitional disputes over the economic/technical
classification of what constitutes a small economy. In the absence of this,
countries have expressed reluctance to agree on specific matters relating
to small economies. Whether it is a tactic to divide CARICOM or not,
commentaries on NAFTA from outside the region seek to draw a distinction between the 'larger' economies like Jamaica and Trinidad and Tobago, and the smaller economies, such as the micro states of the Eastern
Caribbean. The question has also arisen as to whether, if conceded, the
special needs of small economies should be a matter for the exclusive
determination of small economies, or, should this be a substantive matter
for all economies.

Unlike the FTAA, the Lomé Convention is not new. Because it is being
negotiated, it will be bound by considerations which gave rise to it in the first
instance. It is the clearest example of traditional trade principles at work. Its
focus has been on discriminatory trade preferences, mainly concentrated on
primary exports from the ACP countries, and ODA. It has four special
protocols covering trade in bananas, sugar, rum and rice. Specifically the
agreement does not cover trade in services. About 15 billion Ecus were
committed to the financial protocol of the present convention, which runs at
about 2.5 billion Ecus annually. Complaints have been made that the agreement, while important for some sectors and some countries, has tended to
lock in non-dynamic patterns of trade and to operate as a disincentive towards
the industrialisation of the ACP countries. The overall trade performance of

the ACP countries and CARICOM with the EU does not compare favourably with other developing regions – except for a few individual countries.

Another problem is that over the years the EU has expanded, resulting in the dilution of the trade benefits offered to ACP countries and a reduced European commitment to the Agreement. Indications of this are the EU support for generalised preferences under the GSP and reduced price support for its domestic agriculture, which affects in particular sugar under the Sugar Protocol. Presently, it is estimated that less than 10 per cent of the region's exports to the EU continue to enjoy a significant preferential margin.

While the ACP countries would like to protect and extend the traditional benefits under the Lomé Convention – in particular non-reciprocity in light of the gaps in development capacity between the two partners – reflecting the spread of the principles underlined in the new liberal trade order, certain contradictory negotiating positions have been already laid down by the EU. These are, firstly, that the new set of arrangements arrived at must be WTO compatible. The EU's position is that the Lomé Convention is operating under a temporary WTO waiver which it may be unable to extend. (Its commitment to this position has been reinforced by the recent WTO banana rulings). Secondly, in keeping with the WTO trade-related matters other than ODA are expected to be included in the new agreement, in particular services. (Given the scope of the FTAA negotiations, it would be difficult to resist movement in this direction). Thirdly, the results of the FTAA negotiations should result in no greater access to the region's market being accorded to FTAA members than EU.

Arising from these and other considerations, a number of clear options have been raised in the negotiations: a standstill agreement to buy further time, but which, subject to a WTO waiver, maintains the principal elements of the present agreement for a limited period (2005); merging the Convention with the GSP which is already WTO compatible; accepting all other least developed countries into the Convention; a general FTAA/Regional Economic Partnership Agreement (REPA) comprising all EU and ACP members; a series of regionally stratified FTAAs/REPAs with different time-tables, each specially designed to accommodate the variety of economic circumstances among ACP members.

In anticipation of these changes the EU has introduced far-reaching changes in its operational framework, including the effective abolishment of a standalone directorate to deal with ACP matters. The EU's global economic affairs is now reorganised into multi-purpose directorate based more or less on subject areas, with the potential for far greater influence by the European Parliament over their activities. To date, however, negotiations have been quite slow, highlighting the wide gap between the EU and its ACP partners, over expectations about the successor agreement. The dilemma is great, as while non-reciprocity is clearly under threat so too should be a trade-diverting FTAA, as is likely to occur if the Lomé Convention is transformed into an EU/ACP Free Trade Agreement.

The CARICOM Approach

Since these are the principal issues facing CARICOM in the newly emerging liberal trade order, the question may be asked, if, in response to these, an overall design or strategy can be perceived. My view is that there are four discernible features which broadly define the region's overall strategy. The first is that, in recent years, CARICOM has shifted away from the inward-oriented model of regionalism which it favoured earlier, to the open region-alism now being promoted as compatible with the new liberal trade order. This has been largely prompted by the failed efforts of Jamaica and Trinidad and Tobago to join NAFTA, and the concession these countries were prepared to make to gain entry, taken in conjunction with policy reforms under various structural adjustment programmes (SAPs). In recent years economic liberalisation has been resolutely, and some might say recklessly, pursued.

Thus, over the past decade, NTBs criticism against extra-regional imports has been substantially modified. There has been a phased reduction of the common external tariff rates (CET). At present these range from 0 – 20 per cent, except for agriculture which goes to 40 per cent. Economic reforms have led to market-determined exchange rates and the abolition of foreign ex-change restrictions, reduced fiscal deficits, the removal of price controls and subsidies, the end of infant industry support, the abolition of government supported import monopolies, and the privatisation of state enterprises. Domestic policy is now more openly committed to incentive-mutual trade policies, than at any other time in the region's history. Its commitments to the FTAA, not to mention the aborted NAFTA efforts also indicate a willingness to be WTO-plus, that is, to expand access well beyond the existing WTO agreement. At the same time, regional cooperation is increasingly being geared to maximise trade creation and to minimise trade diversion.

The second basic feature of CARICOM's strategy is that the model of integration which it pursues is based on a series of concentric relationships and groupings, which it is hoped will enlarge its 'economic space' and so enhance its capacity to adopt to the new liberal trade order. Both sub-regional groupings (for example OECS), and extra-regional groupings (such as the

ACS, ACP and CARIFORUM) are simultaneously being promoted. These are expected to work in tandem and evolve as the building blocs to facilitate linkages with other blocs in the hemispheric (FTAA) and the extra-hemispheric level (Lomé Convention). It is also hoped that, these concentric groupings will be synthesised into a global free trade area, when this pinnacle achievement of the new liberal trade order is achieved (Dookeran 1996, Davis et al, 1999). In moving to this ultimate goal, the various groupings and connections that are promoted are expected to advance the case that size and vulnerability should be added to income poverty and underdevelopment, as a further development basis for a specific and differential treatment in the new liberal trade order.

A third feature of CARICOM's strategy is incorporating at the institutional level, a specially crafted, Regional Negotiating Machinery (RNM) to lead the CARICOM process. While devised to bring on board expertise that might not otherwise be available for the complex and urgent tasks before it, such an arrangement runs the systematic risk inherent to all ad hoc solutions, that is, it may end up underestimating its own permanence. Further, despite the best intentions, the formal disjuncture of the RNM from the established institutions of economic policy making in the region runs two other risks. One, is the risk of the fundamental separation of domestic economic policy from international trade relations. The other risk is that the region might incur the loss of its institutional memory during a period of momentous global economic transformation.

Another position taken by CARICOM is evident in several quarters within the Region, that of scepticism over the claims of globalisation (Thomas 1999a and 1999b). Some analysts stress incorrectly in my view, the historical continuities as opposed to the present changes in the region, thereby concluding that globalisation, along with the newly emerging trade order, is not qualitatively different from what has preceded it historically. They stress that despite the claims made about globalisation, the present human migration, which is considered to be exceptional, resulting in one in every 100 persons living outside the country of their birth, pales into insignificance when compared to the historical movement of Caribbean populations. They also argue that despite the leading role attributed to TNC's international production in globalisation, the domestic markets still absorb more than 90 per cent of employees worldwide. They contend that compared with today, the role of science and technology in earlier periods of overseas expansion in the Caribbean was also profound, and covered simultaneously many fields of human endeavour: health, nutrition, weaponry, navigation, agriculture, finance, institutional development, clothing and manufactured items. Despite their pronounced international character, the 'foreign' representation on the Boards of Directors of TNCs is still a token, and most of their employees, assets, investors and R & D remain in the home country. The sceptics also sneer at the resolute pursuit of liberalisation today, reasoning that it was matched in earlier epochs, particularly in the period of colonial expansion, and regionalisation today, they say, is as much as it was during colonial times, when there were imperial blocs.

While there is some truth to these observations, in the light of the empirical material, the world as a whole is experiencing an unprecedented transformation. Change, affecting all areas of human experience: material and non-material, economic as well as political, social, cultural, institutional and environmental, is manifest at an exceptional pace in a highly compressed period of time and in a truly multi-dimensional way.

We can see this process at work in the accounting profession. As a result of the liberalisation of trade and capital markets certain tendencies have rapidly become dominant, namely: the global standardisation of accounting standard and practices (supported by the WTO); a similar standardisation of training and certification; and, mergers and acquisitions leading to the characterisation of the industry worldwide, crowding out of the small independent firms and, as a consequence reduced consumer choice. In view of such developments, it would be better for the Caribbean to act on this reality, than dismiss it as *deja vu*.

In charting a way forward for the Region several major considerations have to be kept to the forefront. First, the institutional transformations we have described are not solely, or even principally, the production of conscious policy. While conscious policy has played and continues to play a major part in the changes on the way, far exceeding are real changes in technology and the structures of global investment, production, consumption and trade. It is important therefore, that we do not err by underestimating the strength of the forces driving global change. Unmistakably, new actors have emerged on the global economy along with new technologies and new ways of wealth accumulation. Roles in the global economy are also changing, for example, the rise of TNCs; the deepening of links between trade and investment and production by the same firm; and, the rapid growth of intra-company trade as against 'arms length' trade. There are also changing groupings and cooperative arrangements among states as can be seen in the expansion of the EU and the comparatively recent formation of groupings such as MERCOSUR, NAFTA and APEC.

Second, the problems facing the global economy are so fundamental and complex that nothing less than the full involvement of the international, regional, and national communities can generate appropriate solutions. No nation, nor group of nations, can afford to stand apart and assume that others will resolve these global problems on their behalf. A proactive approach is therefore essential for all states – particularly small ones, which are likely to face the greatest challenges from the new liberal trade order. In light of this imperative, a reformed UN still remains the single best option and, the one, therefore, which I urge that Caribbean countries should resolutely pursue. Only the UN has the scope to deal with global problems in a holistic, non-compartmentalised and integrated way, which can link short-term and long-term concerns, macroeconomic stability with growth, trade with development considerations and, domestic actions with regional and international efforts.

The question may then be asked, if this is the case, along what lines should the United Nation proceed? There are already a number of proposals, and those which I believe best represent the Region's long-term interest are a three-pronged effort. This proposal advances the case that the UN General Assembly be made the effective authority for discharging its Charter responsibilities to provide international economic and social coordination and cooperation, and to specifically mandate the Economic and Social Council to deal with these matters. The second prong seeks to advance the role of those specialised agencies such as UNCTAD, FAO, UNIDO, UNDP whose remit is directly related to development. The third prong represents the UN role of advancing the general case for new forms of global governance, more in keeping with the ethos of our age: the systematic participation of developing countries, along with Civil Societies and private business sectors, in the design, implementation, and evaluation of global economic affairs.

The region presently enjoys two unique organisational positions within the UN, which can help in the pursuit of these objectives. It holds both the Chair for the G15 and G77 and China Group of countries. With wise leadership these can represent important points of leverage on behalf of the South in global fora engaged in UN reform issues.

Thirdly, given the special circumstances of the region's economies, CARI-COM should stoutly resist the one–size–fits-all approach that has characterised economic policies directed at the South. CARICOM has to make a case for special and differential treatment of size and vulnerability, against a one-paced unidirectional and fixed content approach to trade liberalisation. There is, however, an important consideration to be kept in mind in dealing with this matter, that is, the growing evidence of 'fatigue' within international policy making bodies, donor countries and IFIs, about what is termed as Caribbean 'special-pleading' for differential treatment based on size. Its appeals for discriminatory non-reciprocal preferences, and constant requests for enhanced official concessional flows and technical assistance are being questioned. CARICOM leaders therefore, have to walk a fine line between the dignified pursuits of its interests and growing reactions of impatience and resistance to special pleadings, which seem to go against the tenets of the newly emerging liberal trade order. From another perspective, CARICOM must grasp that a sensible approach to international trade policy has to be based on clearly articulated domestic and regional policies and priorities as the domestic economy of the region and its integration into the global economy are inseparable.

Fifth, in a joint study (Davis, et al 1999), we explored in the case of agriculture the scope for CARICOM actions within the confines of the existing WTO Agreement. Within the language of the agreement (despite the great care supposedly exercised in its preparation), there is scope of flexibility and nuanced interpretation. Examples of these included: the interpretation of safeguard clauses; the treatment of anti-dumping measures; technical regulations and standards; technical barriers of trade; agriculture and its green and blue box measures. We found that close monitoring of the application of the WTO agreement is vital for the region especially in regard to areas like the treatment of domestic support measures; subsidised exports and the balancing of sectoral rights and obligations. Further, the built-in agenda issues and the ongoing work of the WTO have already helped to identify areas of reform in the existing Agreement, which are of vital interest to the Region – agriculture and textiles; commodity pricing; food security; tariff-escalation; the abuse of anti-dumping procedures; rules of origin; phytosanitary measures; technical and environmental standards; the operation of the GSP; and weaknesses in the dispute settlement mechanism and the trade policy review process.

Given the number and range of issues involved, it would seem that at present an overriding priority for the region is to ensure that existing difficulties in working the present agreement (that is, the so-called 'cumulative unfinished business and unresolved difficulties') are satisfactorily dealt with before additional areas of negotiation are engaged. However, at present the developed countries are inclined towards a new round of comprehensive, multilateral negotiations designed to cover all items proposed by members for the agenda, as a single undertaking within a fixed 2–3 year period – the 'Millennium Round'. The danger in this proposal is that the region may be seduced by the promise of a new comprehensive agreement as a pre-condition for the developed countries to fulfil obligations which they should have already fulfilled within the WTO.

Finally, one of the greatest external challenges, already before the region, is the requirement for its rapid cultural adaptation to changing global circumstances. The region needs to be global in its outlook, entrepreneurial and dynamic in the way it pursues its activities. This requires excellent training in the leading fields of technology, as well as great sensitivity to the benefits to be derived from the diversity of a multicultural world of which we are an inseparable part. One can already recognise the importance of this, in the extent to which, within CARICOM the cultural mosaic has already altered. The inclusion of Haiti and Suriname no longer makes CARICOM an English-speaking economic union. To some, the recent increase in the number of countries participating in CARICOM, carries with it the advantage in numbers in important hemispheric groupings, such as the IADB, FTAA and the OAS. While this may well be the case, the greatest advantage may yet be realised from the cultural diversity and vibrancy this brings to CARICOM as it faces the challenges of the new liberal trade order.

Note

1. The IMF has recently launched a Contingent Credit Line (CCL) for member countries threatened with financial contagion. This is far from the required structural reform. The CCL is available on highly restrictive conditions including that the country must already be on a macroeconomic path unlikely to give rise to a call on IMF resources and not yet facing 'contagion-related balance of payments difficulties'; and, that the country continues on a course of 'constructive relations with private creditors,' satisfactorily managing its external debt and international reserves. Institutionally, for countries to benefit from the CCL, they must also have been favourably assessed at their previous Article IV consultations; they must meet the Funds Special Data Dissemination Standard, and submit with the request a 'satisfactory economic and financial programme, including a quantified framework'.

References

Denis M. Benn, 'Sovereignty Under Challenge', (University of the West Indies mimeo. 1999)
____ 'Globalization and the North-South Divide: Power Asymmetries in Contemporary International Economic Relations'. (Paper presented to the Con-

ference on the Politics of Globalisation, Cornell University, Ithaca, New York. 1998)

C.G Davis, Ballayram, E.A. Evans, C.Y. Thomas, 'Trade Liberalization and Small Economies in the Americas: The Case of the Caribbean Community (Caricom)' (International Agricultural Trade and Development Centre, Working Paper, IW99–1. 1999)

W.C. Dookeran, *Choices and Change: Reflections on the Caribbean*, (Baltimore, MS: John Hopkins Press 1996)

C.Y. Thomas, 'Globalisation and its Implications for Small States (The Case of the English-speaking Caribbean)' in *Globalisation, Development and Change in Caribbean Society* ed, by G. Howe (forthcoming)

C.Y. Thomas, 'Globalisation as Paradigm Shift: A Response from the South' (Paper presented to the International Seminar on Globalisation – A Strategic Response from the South, University of West Indies, Jamaica, 1999)

South Centre, *Financing for Development*, (Geneva, 1999)

_____ *The WTO MULTILATERAL Agenda and the South*, (Geneva, 1998)

_____ 'Towards an Economic Platform for the South', (Geneva. 1998)

_____ 'For a Strong and Democratic United Nations. A South Perspective on UN Reform', (Geneva, 1997)

UNCTAD 'Trade and Development Report', (Geneva, 1998)

UNITED NATIONS, 'Towards a New International Financial Architecture', (Report of the Executive Committee on Economic and Social Affairs of the United Nations, New York, 1999)

[Part Five]

Beyond Survival

[66]

Survival and
Beyond

Rex Nettleford

The creative diversity of Caribbean life has long led me to insist that we have more artists per square inch than is probably good for us in what is our contradictory, contentious well-nigh unruly but exciting Region.

Such creativity is clearly the result of a history marked by severance from ancestral hearths and suffering on slave plantations, in colonial dispensations and, to the Rastafarians, in a modern Babylon but marked, most importantly, by survival and beyond. The accomplishments in the arts speak eloquently, over half a millennium of eventful history, to that survival and its premises beyond, via the exercise of the creative imagination more than by anything else.

So the passing at the beginning of this new millennium of a Lord Kitchener (the grandmaster of calypso) and Beryl McBurnie (a high priestess of Caribbean dance) could be cause and occasion for the celebration of life rather than for the mourning of a death. The lives and work of these two great Caribbean artists lead us back to the beginnings and to the sustaining of resistance through the activation of mind and spirit against oppression and dehumanisation. This is what indeed provided both our forebears and their twentieth century descendants with mechanisms of re-affirmation, and the effective invocation of that capacity for self-empowerment through the exercise of the creative intellect and the creative imagination.

The retreat into the labyrinth of the mind beyond the reach of oppressors provided safe haven and a fascinating demarginalisation device which was a source of energy for the Creole languages which are gems in the field of Caribbean communications arts – from the Sranan Tonga of Suriname through the Kweyol of St Lucia and Dominica to Jamaica Talk. They themselves were to be further sources of energy for the orature on which Robin Dobru, Louise Bennett, and Paul Keens-Douglas, dub poets like Mickey Smith and Mutabaruka as well as the great calypso and reggae lyricists, draw.

But these are not the only ones in a genuine Caribbean literary tradition. It is Kamau Brathwaite who consistently reminded us throughout the latter decades of the last century that language, the stuff of literature, is more than lexicon. Rhythm, pitch and tone are vital ingredients, he insisted, and it is to the literary inventions of Caribbean forebears as well as to ancestors from among the conquerors that one must turn in grasping the Caribbean reality, through the scribal writs and oral tongues. No one epitomises this more than Derek Walcott who like Aimé Césaire of Martinque, may use the 'master's tongue' but uses it in ways that celebrate the inner logic and consistency of a Caribbean reality, through dialectical engagement between opposites that results in a dynamism and offers a dynamic, which is what has taken the region beyond mere survival.

So the CARICOM Caribbean can now claim a legacy of twentieth century literary giants who may be justifiably credited as seminal contributors to the revitalisation of a literature in English in the post-World War II period. They bear such names as Derek Walcott, the St Lucian 1992 Nobel Laureate for Literature, Kamau Brathwaite the poet-historian who hails originally from Barbados as does the novelist and essayist George Lamming – himself a virtual grandmaster in the genre – Vidia Naipaul, Earl Lovelace and Samuel Selvon of Trinidad, John Hearne, Vic Reid and Lorna Goodison of Jamaica, and Wilson Harris and Martin Carter of Guyana. If these have helped to put the region on the world map through their display of literary excellence, others like A.J. Seymour (editor of *Kyk-over-al*), Frank Collymore (editor of *Bim*), Philip Sherlock (editor of *Caribbean Quarterly*) along with other published literary artists such as Andrew Salkey and Jan Carew, Anthony McNeil and Slade Hopkinson, Edward Baugh and Mervyn Morris, Erna Brodber and Olive Senior have helped to prepare the Caribbean psyche to harbour that sense of place and purpose which is normally the prerogative of the self confident and truly empowered. In this, as in other manifestations of creative 'endeavouring', the Caribbean remains a living laboratory of that cultural process which is rooted in the cross- fertilising encounters between myriad cultures caught in myriad forms of relationship over time.

As with literature, so with the performing arts. The name of Beryl McBurnie has already been alluded to, but her pioneering kindred spirits – Ivy Baxter of Jamaica and Lavinia Williams of Haiti (now a member of CARICOM), Ramon y Guerra and Enrique Lazaro, respectively, of Cuba and the Dominican Republic (both aspiring for membership in CARICOM), bear testimony to the vibrancy of the development of a Caribbean dance theatre in the last half of the twentieth century. Trinidad's Little Carib remained a flagship entity throughout the 1940s and 50s to be joined by Jamaica's National Dance Theatre Company (NDTC) whose international acclaim dating back to the sixties has inspired many other ensembles throughout the region, having flourished on the basis of continuing exploration of, and experimentation with, indigenous Caribbean movement, music, religion, rituals and folk legends. Barbados, Guyana, Dominica and the Bahamas have all followed suit.

Musical theatre can also claim a Caribbean version in the genre. The Jamaican Little Theatre Movement's National Pantomime has for 60 years opened on every Boxing Day at 6.00 p.m. without fail and then played to tens of thousands of young people and adults for all of four months. It is a folk musical that has developed into a distinctive form though with traces still of its origins in the English Christmas pantomime as well as in the Jamaican variety concert and tea meeting. It has inspired versions in other parts of the region and has been performed in Trinidad (at the time of the inauguration of the West Indies Federation) as well as in the United States and the United Kingdom. One pantomime was even based on a Guyanese pork-knocker's tale scripted by Guyanese Cecile Nobrega.

But the names most closely associated with the development of the Jamaican LTM Pantomime are Henry and Greta Fowler as producers, Noel Vaz and Brian Heap as directors, Louise Bennett and Ranny Williams as actors and, of late, Barbara Gloudon as writer-lyricist. In addition, the Pantomime has been the cradle of many of Jamaica's leading theatre luminaries, past and present.

In the theatre of the spoken word it is the significant plays of Derek Walcott who used the Trinidad Theatre Workshop for his experiments in, and explorations of, indigenous speech patterns, folk forms and legends while Trevor Rhone, Dennis Scott, Roderick Walcott, Errol Hill, *inter alia*, added to the growing body of texts for the region's theatre during the days of intense searching and vibrant action. It was Errol Hill who in his books on the history and character of carnival called for the great festival art to be a mandate for a national theatre of Trinidad and Tobago. This may yet be realised since the 'theatre' inherent in that pre-Lenten festival may well speak for itself. Indeed, over the last two decades it has been speaking for almost the entire CARICOM Caribbean; its format has been used as a tourist attraction in places like Antigua or as a model for territory-specific versions as in St Lucia, with Crop-Over in Barbados and an Easter version in Jamaica. The pre-Lenten carnival has also found new form in the Caribbean Diaspora in such North Atlantic urban centres as New York, Boston, Miami, Toronto and across the Atlantic in Notting Hill, London each August. It has thrown up arguably the region's greatest designer Peter Minshall, whose eminence was to attract world recognition when he was commissioned to design the opening ceremonies of the Barcelona Olympics.

Carnival, like its sister festival arts (Jonkonnu/Masquerade/Goombay and Hosay – the latter a gift from India through the East Indian arrivals in the nineteenth century) has attracted creative scholarship which serves the academy worldwide in a range of disciplines stretching from Anthropology to what is now called Cultural Studies. The names of Gordon Rohlehr and Rawle Gibbons are associated with the chronicling of the calypso as art form and trenchant sociopolitical commentary since the 1930s and have made sense of the genius of Lord Kitchener, the Mighty Sparrow, Spoiler and the latter-day Rudders, Chalkdust and Stalin, among others.

The many uses of/by calypso as 'song of praise, censure, prophecy, lamentation as catharsis, as self-mocker . . . as word-play, as source for social history, as inspiration for dance, art, literature and so on' found its parallel from the mid-1960s in reggae spawned in the depressed zones of Kingston, spreading to the Eastern Caribbean along with the Rastafarian faith which the reggae movement appropriated, and further into the wider world, making superstars of Jimmy Cliff, Peter Tosh and Toots Hibbert and a megastar of the iconic Bob Marley whose album *Exodus* was voted the album of the century by *Time* magazine while his 'One Love' was declared the BBC anthem at the end of the last century.

It is arguably through its music that the Caribbean has made the greatest impact worldwide, rivalling the twenty-year domination of the game of cricket throughout the Commonwealth, and Olympic track and field dating back to the golden achievements at Helsinki in 1948. The traditional music of the region found a John the Baptist in Harry Belafonte, African American of Jamaican stock whose use (with the help of composer-arranger Irving Burgie of Barbadian parentage) of early Trinidad calypsos and traditional Jamaican mentos swept the world scene long before Marley and Sparrow emerged. Now parts of Western Europe are hooked on zouk coming out of the Kweyol-speaking CARICOM Caribbean while its own traditional songs find new life through the choral theatre tradition of the post-war Caribbean manifested in the famous police choir of Guyana singing the queh-queh and pork-knockers' songs of the past, or La Petite Chorale musicale of Trinidad under Olive Walke and more recently in Pat Bishop's talented and versatile Lydian Singers. Then there are the Jamaican Folksingers under Olive Lewin and the University Singers brought to recent international and regional attention by UWI's director of music at Mona, Noel Dexter, himself a moving spirit of the sixties in the indigenisation of liturgical music through compositions and arrangements of hymns reflective of Caribbean melodic and rhythmic contours.

There have also been the Hewanora Voices led by Joyce Ogiste of St Lucia, the Kingstown Chorale of St Vincent under Patrick Prescod and the Emerald Singers of Montserrat directed by Edith Allen (later Bellot).

Above and beyond all this is the steel pan – arguably the only acoustic musical instrument invented in the twentieth century and given aesthetic eminence by the likes of pioneer Elie Manette and successor Jit Samaroo. The pan has been duly declared the national musical instrument of Trinidad and Tobago. The recycling of old oil drums reminiscent of the xylophone of Africa and the piano of Europe to eke out melodies in a style of percussive playing (shared by the drums of West Africa and indeed of Europe's military bands as by the tassa of Hindu and Mohammedan India) was to result in a truly Caribbean invention with the Invaders and the Desperadoes of Trinidad and the old Brute Force Band of Antigua and Barbuda bearing added testimony to the region's ingenuity and creative daring.

Such, indeed, are the creative attributes of the Caribbean in its long anguished but in many ways rewarding struggle 'to be.'

Note

This article first appeared in *CARICOM Perspective*, 69:2, July 2000

[67]

The Future of the
Caribbean Community
and Common Market

Owen Arthur

It was intended that on this day, May 5, 2000, the Parliament of Barbados would have begun one of the great debates in its history – a review of the Report of a Commission to Amend the Constitution of Barbados, in which is contained the recommendation to transform Barbados into a republic.

The debate has been postponed because Parliament did not think it fair nor feasible to cause a subject of such considerable importance to have to compete for attention with a Test match involving the West Indies Cricket Team.

The sponsors of this conference therefore perhaps either know something that we in Barbados have not yet grasped about the state of West Indies cricket, or have a supreme confidence in the power of the media. Experience urges me to accept that it is the latter. I should also add that in the event that there were any lingering doubts as to whether the media in the Caribbean is a more potent force than Parliament, this little episode today should suffice to lay all such doubts to rest.

In treating the theme on which I have been invited to speak, I would have wished today to be able to follow Dickens and to assert that 'it is the best of times, [even if] it is the worst of times.' On balance, the distressing circumstances in which the Caribbean community now finds itself, and the very fearsome prospects which lie ahead do not create any grounds for the optimism that these are the best of times. It comes closer in fact to being just about the worst of times as we begin a new century. For much of the Caribbean community is confronted with quite considerable uncertainty, and a tendency towards disorder in just about every sphere of political, social and economic life.

In the political sphere, our region, which has traditionally stood out as a beacon of democracy and political stability, has of late become the location for political developments which only not run counter to that tradition, but are not for contemplation by the fainthearted. Haiti, the newest member of the Caribbean Community, is experiencing the gravest difficulty in establishing its rendezvous with democracy. Political unrest also stalks the land in St Vincent, in Suriname, in Jamaica, always in different forms and with different incidence but also always of sufficient severity to absorb enough energy to put the development of those countries on pause.

I am, of course, in Guyana, which led Singapore and the rest of the Caribbean in every index of development as recently as the start of the 1960s. It can do so again in the twenty-first century provided that it is prepared to put its political difficulties behind it, finding that political solution not in any Herdmanston Accord or in the role of any CARICOM appointed mediator, but in the formation of a social contract, subscribed to by every class and creed in Guyana, to work to make Guyana succeed.

In addition, I offer no hostility, just an overwhelming sense of sadness about the fact that elsewhere in the Caribbean, a state of such utter despair has been reached regarding the prospects for national development that some are now proposing variants of recolonisation, such as applying to join the European Union, as viable options in the Caribbean at the start of the twenty-first century.

In our international relations, the Caribbean has possibly been the only region of the world not to reap a dividend from the end of the Cold War. Indeed, the spectre of international marginalisation stalks the region. Any geopolitical significance that the Caribbean had hitherto possessed, arising from its designation as a place where the clash of ideologies could have posed a threat to the security of the Western world, has receded with the fall of the Berlin Wall. In addition, for our sins, we have on the one hand been too successful as lower middle or middle income developing countries, or not sufficiently important systemic threats to the stability of the world's economic, financial and trading systems to warrant any special coddling by the international community.

Indeed, the rest of the world no longer sees the Caribbean as a special or unique case, deserving of special treatment and assistance. Our search for empathy or goodwill as we seek stays of execution in carrying out actions arising from our international commitments which can have painful consequences for the survival of Caribbean societies, is now perceived as yet another set of rearguard actions, not dissimilar to other such actions on our part over the last three hundred years.

The powerful states with whom we have maintained strategic and friendly relations have either therefore relegated the Caribbean region to a status of benign neglect, or have sought to forge with us a unidimensional relationship which draws its bearing entirely from our unsolicited and uncomfortable position as one of the world's premier transit point in the traffic of illegal drugs.

At the start of a new century, and at the start of a new millennium, the Caribbean community of states faces a situation of being small states, standing virtually alone, with only a few firm or reliable alliances in an increasingly unsympathetic and hostile international environment.

To illustrate, I recently attended a meeting of the Development Committee of the World Bank/IMF, which, as Prime Minister of Barbados, I addressed as a member of the Canadian delegation, by special leave and permission of the Minister of Finance of Canada, to argue a case for the adoption of a World Bank/Commonwealth Secretariat Task Force Report on a Development Agenda on Small States. It is a sobering thought that without the indulgence of the Government of Canada, I would not have been able to speak on behalf of my country before principal decision makers in the international community about the special conditions of vulnerability and volatility of small states, nor to call for the adoption of a Development Agenda that enables such states to face, with confidence, the prospects of successfully integrating into a challenging new global economy.

I leave this conference to go to a meeting of the Caribbean Development Bank, where there is likely to be discussion on the possibility of certain European countries withdrawing from being shareholders in the Bank. In June, the OECD is threatening to publish a list of non-cooperative tax havens, on which may appear various Caribbean societies, which will be alleged to have encouraged the development within their frontiers of international financial centres by their use of so-called harmful tax competition practices.

It is not the best of times. In the social sphere, the Caribbean ranks high on the list of those countries which face the threat of being overwhelmed by the HIV/AIDS epidemic. New forms of crime and violence, linked closely to an insidious new drug culture which threatens to undermine the integrity of the institutions of our civil society, and linked to the behaviour of Caribbean nationals deported from the USA, are taking root, and are representing themselves as the most modern forms of social disintegration in a fragile region.

Our region, rich in its culture and ethnic diversity, faces also the spectre of cultural absorption; of being just another victim of a monolithic process of globalisation which promotes homogeneity rather than diversity and which, unchecked, would create a world in which Mickey Mouse, McDonalds and Michael Jordan are the only cultural icons with which we can or will identify.

For a region whose major contribution to the development of the human condition in the twentieth century has been the products of its creative imagination, expressed in terms of the work and worth of its poets, its novelists, its music and calypsonians, its cricketers, and the free spirit of Caribbean people expressed wherever they have happened to be located in the Diaspora, the monolithic levelling social and cultural impulses of globalisation are a threat which can diminish the Caribbean and take it backward.

In what sense is McDonalds superior to a fish fry at Oistins, or jerk pork in Jamaica, or labba and creek water in Guyana? Why should we yield on the preservation of our cultural icons, that traditional way of life inherent in small states which is so relaxing and rewarding and which makes living in a small state such an unforgettable experience, to become just another cultural and social statistic in a world made safe for the domination of powerful but socially and culturally insensitive transnational conglomerates?

In the economic sphere, the Caribbean is caught between two worlds. The old world of trade preferences, concessional flows of financial resources to the region, domestic protectionism and inward-looking, state dominated, over-regulated economic activity is vanishing or is already gone. The new Caribbean economy has now to become a free spirit. We will now have to make our place in a world of declining special preferences, greater reciprocity, equal treatment for national and foreign investment and enterprise, and the end of managed trade. It will constitute a major challenge for the Caribbean Community as a group. It is in this context that I come to the main issue that I wish to deal with today.

That issue has to do with the main purposes of the new economic integration that must serve as the basis for the engendering of a new spirit and sense of Caribbean community and identity in the foreseeable future.

Since 1947, more than 100 regional trade arrangements have come into operation. Others are also in force that have not been identified to the GATT/WTO. In our Caribbean, there has been a historic hostility to intra-regional transactions, while similar transactions originating in the rest of the world have been put on a pedestal and treated as premium. For instance, foreign direct investment has been treated as a major accomplishment where it has occurred. By contrast, direct investment by the nationals of any Caribbean nation in any Caribbean state is perceived somewhat as a threat. In fact, it can fairly be asserted that the modalities for incorporation of the Caribbean economy into the global economy have historically been stronger than the media for creating a single, unified Caribbean economy designated to meet the basic and advanced needs of the Caribbean people.

The Caribbean, however, is the region of the world which can least afford not to integrate. Indeed, if it were to integrate its economic system fully, it would nonetheless go into the twenty-first century as the world's smallest, most volatile and most vulnerable economic system. Not to integrate its various economies will serve to dangerously marginalise the various economies of the Caribbean Community in today's world. This is especially so because no other region in the world is engaged in international trade negotiations of the scope and on the scale of the Caribbean.

The Caribbean has to negotiate a new relationship with Europe to come into effect in 2008. It has at the same time to secure its place in the Free Trade Area of the Americas to come into being in 2005. At the same time, and despite the debacle at Seattle, it has to participate in multilateral trade negotiations under the auspices of the World Trade Organisation (WTO) in which there is a built-in agenda for agriculture and services that simply cannot be ignored by Caribbean states.

The Caribbean Community therefore has to undertake a process of harmonised liberalisation which is greater and more all-encompassing than that undertaken by any subset of states in the entire history of mankind. In a word, that is the challenge facing the states of the Caribbean Community, singly and in combination.

The CARICOM community therefore needs to adopt a strategy of internal repositioning to achieve sustainable growth and continued improvement in the social standards and welfare of its citizens, at the same time as it undertakes a global repositioning to bring on board a new relationship with the Americas, through the new FTAA; a new relationship with Europe through a successor relationship to LOME IV; and a new relationship with the global economic community through the new dispensation that will be created globally in the trade policies of the WTO. It is against this backdrop that I address you today concerning the salient aspects of a new Caribbean Single Market and Economy.

In 1973, the architects of the existing mechanisms of economic integration in the Caribbean, under the Treaty of Chaguaramas, set out to create a special but limited union of Caribbean economic integration. They saw Caribbean development as an inward-looking, import-substitution phenomenon; they refused to believe that the CARICOM community could survive and prosper based on the unrestricted movement of capital and factors of production. They saw integration in only a limited sense as a limited common market, providing for the free movement of goods, but with no provision for the unrestricted movement of labour, capital and services.

The Treaty of Chaguaramas of 1973 was conceived and devised to implement this vision of regional economic integration. But better experience and the contemporary realities of Caribbean international economic relations have taught us the need for substantial modification. A limited common market such as that conceived in 1973, bears no relationship to the requirements of Caribbean development in the twenty-first century. Of special significance is the fact that a process of CARICOM economic integration based on the precepts of the 1973 model would leave the Caribbean dangerously short of what is required to meet the prerequisites to compete successfully in the new global economy, to say nothing about meeting the requirements of regional development per se.

In 1973, the architects of the Caribbean Community could not envision a Caribbean in which capital, labour and services could move freely and in which Caribbean citizens enjoy the right to establish enterprise in any Caribbean location of their choice. We must contemplate such today.

As far back as 1989, in the Grand Anse Declaration, the leaders of the Caribbean Community committed themselves to creating a Caribbean Single Market and Economy. The new process of economic integration arising from that decision requires that we not only liberate the movement of goods within the Caribbean region, but the movement of capital, services and human resources. It also requires that we harmonise our policies for the development of capital markets, our social security systems, our monetary and fiscal policies, our incentives to industry, our trade relations with the rest of the world, the main practices in the development of our business, our policies for the development of our human, institutional and technological resources.

The contemporary initiative to create a single market and economy expressed in the nine protocols to create a legal framework to amend the Treaty of Chaguaramas and other related initiatives are designed to create this new Caribbean economic environment. However, the creation of such a Single Market and Economy in the Caribbean Community should be seen only as a necessary but not a sufficient condition for Caribbean development.

Some have argued that the creation of a Caribbean Single Market and Economy is an initiative whose relevance and benefit have largely been overtaken and vitiated by international events which have unfolded. It was intended to have been created in 1993. It is now almost ten years late chronologically. Certainly it would have had a more profound impact if it had been created 20 years ago.

In today's world, one of the highest purposes that can be accomplished by the formation of the Single Market and Economy is the creation of the common regional economic space in which enterprises of all types can make judgements to rationally allocate resources available in the Caribbean. However, we must all appreciate that our relevant economic space is no longer the domestic economy of any individual Caribbean economy. For this matter, it is not the regional economy. It is, in fact, the global economy.

The creation of a Caribbean Single Market and Economy gives us barely an outside chance, ten years after the fact, of creating a new and reconfigured Caribbean economy that has a greater probability of succeeding in the new global economy than that of any domestic Caribbean economy functioning on its own. The absence of a Caribbean Single Market and Economy in which goods, services, capital and enterprises can move freely, and in which our fiscal, monetary, exchange rate, and trade policies are harmonised would mean that we will fail individually and collectively in meeting the challenges ensuing from participating in the new global economy.

In the final analysis it is essential that before we embrace full liberalisation with the rest of the world, we must first practise full liberalisation in the Caribbean. This is what gives the Caribbean Single Market and Economy its special and unique purpose at this juncture in Caribbean development. It is not the fifth wheel of the car of Caribbean development as some will have it. It is the key wheel that will ensure that the motor of Caribbean development will function effectively.

Against this background, I will touch quickly on a few matters related to the accomplishment of the Caribbean Single Market and Economy.

Whatever might be the appellate jurisdiction we accord to the proposed Caribbean Court of Justice, we need a Caribbean Court of Justice as a court of original jurisdiction to deal with disputes arising from the Revised Treaty of Chaguaramas. Without a Caribbean Court of Justice to interpret Community Law and to settle disputes arising from the new Treaty of Chaguaramas, a Caribbean Single Market and Economy and the entire Caribbean integration process will experience only the most profound difficulty in succeeding.

I must especially stress that the initiative and the desire to create a Caribbean Court of Justice predates Pratt and Morgan. It is essential that the debate within the region about the purposes of the Court be set within its appropriate historic and conceptual context, and that the vital function to be executed by the Court in underpinning our regional economic development be understood by all.

Secondly, the Caribbean can only meaningfully operate in the new global society if we put human resource development in the forefront of our efforts to create a new Caribbean society. A new urgency and energy is therefore required of our regional universities and all other institutions associated with the development of our human capacities. I must therefore especially stress that among the measures to create a Caribbean Single Market and Economy is the effort to facilitate the free movement of our people within its own region.

In 1987 in his last and most graphic speech to the Caribbean Society, our National Hero, the Rt Excellent Errol Barrow, observed that the people of the Caribbean had already made the free movement of people a Caribbean reality despite the opposition of their Governments. The creation of a single Caribbean economy cannot succeed unless the people of the Caribbean can move freely in their region to develop the Caribbean society, each in accordance with his or her own ability. My Government is determined to honour our obligations to enable Caribbean citizens to work and settle in Barbados. We have seen and have benefited from the fact that since 1997 almost 500 Caribbean citizens have moved to Barbados under the new arrangement and have helped to propel the development of the Barbadian society. As it has been with Barbados, so let it be with the rest of the Caribbean.

Finally, it seems clear that there is need to put again in the forefront of Caribbean issues, the creation of new forms of governance in the Caribbean. The very logic that says that we must create a Caribbean Single Market and Economy, in essence a single Caribbean economy, is the same logic that says we must eventually create a single Caribbean political space.

As a Minister of Finance, I know how difficult it is to hold my own economy to a successful course. As the Prime Minister responsible for the creation of a Caribbean Single Market and Economy, I must say to you that the Single Market and Economy in the Caribbean cannot truly become a reality unless we create the political power structures to make it a reality.

It will not be easy or automatic. It will probably take place long after I have left active politics. In today's age, it will perhaps be perceived as a diminution of the national sovereignty that many Caribbean societies have struggled to achieve. But to create the new Caribbean society that can succeed in the new global society, we simply must give greater attention to the political dimensions of Caribbean integration, and deliberately set out to design a new Caribbean governance relevant to the purposes of the twenty-first century Caribbean Community.

I leave you today with the words of a Caribbean patriot, C.L.R. James. He spoke in 1977 about the 'Birth of a Nation' and he delivered himself of the following: 'Nobody knows what the Caribbean population is capable of.

Nobody has ever attempted to find out. For one thing is certain. Any new and genuine economic development of the Caribbean has to begin first of all with the involvement of the mass of the population.'

It is in the knowledge that involvement of the people of the Caribbean will require the full support of the media that I have been pleased to participate in this conference. I therefore wish this conference well and look to it to realise all that the people of the Caribbean are capable of being and doing.

Note

Address by the Rt. Hon. Owen Arthur, Prime Minister of Barbados at the Third Caribbean Media Conference, Georgetown, Guyana, 5 May 2000.

[68]

Caribbean Integration
in the Next Decade
A Strategic Vision for the New Millennium

Anthony Gonzales

Integration schemes worldwide have been adapting to meet global changes in the last two decades and to better facilitate the integration of their members in the world economy. CARICOM leaders were recently reminded of this imperative of change in the following statement by the Honourable Prime Minister of Jamaica, Mr P. J. Patterson: 'In the post Cold War era, we face a new and increasingly complex international environment. All countries around the globe are now compelled to function under the same discipline of competitive trade within the international marketplace.' (Patterson, 1997).

The best known example of such continuous adaptation is that of the European Union (EU) which was forced to move from a common market to an economic union in order to deal with competition from Japan, the United States and other Asian countries as well as respond to the new post-Cold War configuration in Europe. In the same vein, schemes in developing countries have come under closer scrutiny in so far as the original mandate for them has been seriously challenged in the new circumstances.

CARICOM integration has been no exception to this trend. The Grand Anse Declaration followed by the West Indian Commission (WIC) and the implementation of some of the latter's findings are efforts to make the adjustment required by the new conjuncture. The reform task, however, is ongoing as agendas remain unfinished and new conditions, largely unanticipated, emerge. As a consequence, even though a new century approaches, a common vision is still lacking.

This exercise sets itself the task of sketching a vision of Caribbean integration in the next decade of a new century as well as a new millennium. The basic question being asked is what is the form of integration that can be most compatible with trends in the world economy and with the economic conditions as well as the aspirations of Caribbean peoples? The idea is to allow readers to walk down 'vision road' without being imprisoned by details and keeping their focus on the broad outline of an integration movement whose imperatives the region should aspire to fulfil. Such strategic reflection should also allow policy makers to see the issues presented here that are already well acknowledged as policy concerns and those that have not yet been the object of policy attention but are knocking on the front door for policy attention.

Within the general objectives of promoting sustainable development, peace and security, Caribbean integration (CARICOM and OECS) as stated specifically in the objectives laid down in Article 4, were to be effective by January 1991.

1. Customs Co-operation and Administration were to be strengthened.
2. The CARICOM Industrial Programming Scheme (CIPS) was to be signed by 1989.
3. CIPS and the Common Enterprise Regime were to be given effect by the enactment of legislation.
4. A scheme for the movement of capital, starting with the cross-listing and trading of securities on existing stock exchanges was to be set up.
5. A regional equity/venture capital fund was to be established; the CARICOM Multilateral Clearing Facility was to be strengthened and re-established for current and capital transactions by December 1990.
6. Further arrangements for strengthening consultation and cooperation on monetary, financial and exchange rate policies by July 1990 were to be put in place.
7. The removal of all remaining barriers to trade was to be effected by July 1999.
8. The immediate activation of Article 39 of the Annex of the Treaty of Chaguaramas was to be done, in order to promote consultation, cooperation and coordination of policies at the macroeconomic, sectoral and project levels.
9. Free movement of skilled and professional, as well as contract workers, on a seasonal or project basis was to be ensured.

10. Immediate and continuous action was to be taken to develop a regional and sea transport system by July 1992.
11 Greater collective effort at joint representation in international economic negotiations was to be pursued and the sharing of facilities and offices to this end was to be arranged, with immediate effect.

The essential task was how to strategically reinsert the Caribbean in the new architecture of the post-Cold War era that was being put in place – a task which still remains elusive and ongoing under the uncertainties of this unfinished reconstruction process.

In responding to the challenge, the West Indian Commission basically endorsed the idea of a single market and economy as proposed by Grand Anse and suggested that the movement be simultaneously deepened and widened. Institutionally, the Commission also recommended and/or supported the existing idea that regional integration and implementation be strengthened in a limited way through certain executive, legislative and judicial actions (Caribbean Commission, West Indian Court and a People's Parliament). People's empowerment and integration should be more vigorously pursued through greater consultative mechanisms and the adoption of a charter of civil society.

The above proposals have assisted the movement forward into the acceptance of protocols for the implementation of the Single market and Economy, the establishment of the Association of Caribbean States (ACS), the creation of the CARICOM Bureau and greater initiatives towards the adoption of the West Indian Court and People's Parliament. Most of these innovations, however, are either incomplete or part of unfinished agendas as CARICOM seeks to adapt to new developments and prepare itself for the next century.

One assessment of the impact of the above reform measures has been that the relative rates of change in CARICOM *vis-à-vis* the rest of the hemisphere seem also to have been misjudged. Changes necessary within CARICOM, to control or benefit from hemispheric or global shifts, seem to have come too slowly and seem to have been rendered redundant by them. For example, hemispheric relations developed neck and neck with the ACS in the sub-region, and both greatly surpassed the speed at which the CARICOM Single Market and Economy were evolving internally. From the CARICOM viewpoint this was a perverse sequence, since the Single Market and Economy was expected to build momentum, via the ACS, to the hemispheric Free Trade Areas of the Americas (FTAA). Caution is needed in this assessment, however, since the process is not yet complete. Nevertheless, the start was not auspicious. (*ECLAC*, July 1997, 26).

As the record of achievement is examined over this long period of adaptation and reform, there is the temptation to point to what has not been accomplished. The stubbornly low level of intra-regional trade and the absence of meaningful production integration are usually emphasised against some success in functional cooperation, especially the UWI, the CDB, the mushrooming of Caribbean NGOs as an indication of greater people-to-people integration, and the recent achievements in conflict resolution and the promotion of good governance (especially in Haiti and now possibly in Guyana).

Underlying the entire track record, however, is the fact that CARICOM is probably the only integration scheme in the developing world that has not lost members over this long heady and turbulent period. It weathered the Cold War storm of ideological pluralism despite having neighbours constantly knocking at its door. It can probably claim the distinction (let us hear from others how dubious it is!) of being the only regional integration movement to constantly turn down new applicants in its desire to keep its coherence and deepen its structure. It is this abiding level of coherence which sustains the possibilities for integration. Interest in integration is real and unlike many schemes in other parts of the world, CARICOM has not only remained intact but has enlarged its membership. The real lesson from the latter may well be that the institutional flexibility and pragmatism on which CARICOM has been built is probably its greatest asset.

Recognition of the above should provide a useful guide to going forward rather than lead to complacency. As argued later, in understanding the particular constraints, dynamics and potential of CARICOM, the integration strategy should seek to reinforce what is positive and particularly what CARICOM does best. In this way the successful regional initiatives should be promoted. It is probably fair to state that CARICOM has been bedeviled by the issue of how best to promote the integration of its members into the world in a balanced and structurally viable manner and at the lowest possible risk and cost. At the heart of this issue is the debate about widening and deepening and the pace at which one complements the other. Of central importance too is a perception of regionalisation and multilateralism and the best combination that would optimise the external strategy of the region and minimise vulnerability for these small states.

The West Indian Commission attempted to resolve the above by arguing that in the new post-Cold War situation the basis of our external relations had now shifted from their earlier anchorage in Third Worldism, Afro-Asian Bandung-type solidarity and non-alignment, limited regional co-operation and integration, Commonwealth status and exploitation of super power rivalry, and post-colonial golden handshakes such as Lomé. To stave off marginalisation, external relations needed to anchor themselves progressively in a broader Caribbean Basin solidarity which would provide the economic and diplomatic space in ever widening concentric circles of cooperation. The West Indian family (including Suriname and the overseas dependent territories) should remain the core by which a collective negotiating front within the wider ACS concentric circle would be sought and established.

Two major difficulties emerged with this idea, however. The first was that the ACS does not constitute an autonomous region with large intra-regional flows of trade and capital such as the Asian-Pacific, the North American Free Trade Agreement (NAFTA) and the EU that can sustain its members. The ACS can facilitate integration into such an autonomous region through its greater bargaining power and more economic complementarity but in the end it cannot replace that autonomous space. If FTAA or FTAA/EU represents such an autonomous space for the Caribbean, then insertion into this space on acceptable terms and conditions should be the main objective.

At the time the Commission rendered its ACS proposal, the FTAA was still not yet mooted and North/South integration was still not considered feasible and practical. The Commission also appeared to have a penchant for South-South collaboration without observing the new possibilities for integration between North and South. This lack of perception as well as unforeseen events placed the ACS in an undefined space – probably exactly where some CARICOM leaders wanted to position some bothersome non-CARICOM neighbours who were knocking at the CARICOM door and whom it was becoming increasingly embarrassing to turn away. As a result of this lack of foresight, the ACS may well have become insurance against positive developments in the future.

The second flaw was in the assertion that the ACS was a CARICOM child and that the CARICOM core should remain a solid bargaining group within that outfit as a bulwark against domination. This position was obviously offensive to the non-Commonwealth countries seeking wider integration and already having suspicions about the Anglophone CARICOM club. It also reflected a lack of confidence and the unwillingness of CARICOM to see that the rest of the Caribbean Basin, largely Spanish-speaking, is not a monolithic group and that there are several differences and contradictions that would allow CARICOM to achieve equitable participation in the ACS. In addition as noted, the expectation of a tidy progression from the small CARICOM bloc, exerting leverage in a larger ACS bloc, seems to downplay the complex cross-cutting of blocs in Latin America (*ECLAC*, July 1997).

Another issue that challenges integration and is also related to the above is the outlook on the world economy and its implications for strategic repositioning and development. A glimpse of world trends seems to reveal that the emerging markets of Latin America and Asia-Pacific will largely fuel world economic growth at the start of the next century. China, India and Korea are key players on the Asian continent. The Latin American region as a result of economic integration, trade liberalisation and privatisation will attract a large amount of trade activity and foreign investment. The mature economies in North America will shift more into services and agriculture with Eastern Europe and Africa still weathering the storm of political and economic instability. Western Europe will continue to grapple with issues of lack of competitiveness and meagre growth – this leading to fortress Europe as a real possibility.

The above sketch has implications for integration strategy and especially geographic integration focusing. With economic dynamism growing in Latin America, CARICOM should seek to position itself to benefit from the expected greater trade and investment flows. At present CARICOM integration strategy is governed by timidity and fear of an inability to compete. Integration with Latin America is still seen as coming through the FTAA without much autonomous action from the region, and there is concern about the slow pace of such integration. It also raises the question of whether CARICOM should not be preoccupied with the level at which FTAA integration is being pitched, given the desire both by NAFTA and MERCOSUR to stay one step ahead of the game and probably thus pitch FTAA at a lower WTO-plus level. Integration on this basis may not provide the region with the access to trade and investment flows that it is seeking.

Another development that will impact significantly on the region is the acceleration of globalisation and in particular international competition a few years ahead. Service industries will spearhead this economic transformation, with increasing competition coming from easier and less costly communication. The financial and telecommunication sectors appear to be the two service industries that would be most affected by these developments. Electronic commerce along with the latter will certainly intensify competition in international trade and reduce further barriers to third parties, so that integration with the outside world will be facilitated especially in terms of trade and investment. Special national treatment for foreign investors, and setting a low Common External Tariff (CET) as a provision for Most Favoured Nations (MFN), have now become major tools of adjustment to such a development.

Because of its small size, CARICOM needs relatively more import competition to stimulate its growth and development. Fewer trade barriers would also help CARICOM to take better advantage of technological innovations which are expected to multiply rapidly with the present advanced communication systems. It would facilitate the movement of machines and equipment to different parts of the world and so enhance global operations and production networks. All of this will open up the division of labour in manufacturing with new possibilities for productive activity. Even seemingly small protective barriers to the outside world can hurt the transfer of knowledge and investment as they make the environment less efficient. They also do not facilitate a search for wider market access on a more secure and permanent basis.

The idea of a small protected market core to facilitate the start up of economic activity is now redundant, given the increased mobility of capital, technology and expertise and the minuscule size of the market itself. The experience of CARICOM itself has shown that this type of small-market protection is usually excessive and in the vast majority of cases does not encourage the competitive emergence of enterprises beyond the boundaries of the region.

Generally, the integration experience of developing countries has been disappointing in terms of its contribution to development. Most of the integration schemes comprise small markets, low incomes, similar factor endowments and similar productive structures that cannot serve as a basis for trade expansion based on intra-industry specialisation and product differentiation. Trade gains for developing countries tend to come mainly from differences in source endowments and productive structures – factors which make many of them more complementary with developed countries and even prompt some to suggest that these integration schemes act as a hindrance to proper insertion into the world economy.

According to the above reasoning, CARICOM or CARIFORUM (even with Cuba) can be regarded as not constituting an optimal trading area due to small market size, high external trade dependence, few non-primary exports, large disparities and high transaction costs. Regional trade creation gains from market integration are thus considered negligible even in a context of outward orientation and trade liberalisation (de Melo and Panagaruja, [1991]). These countries can better seize their dynamic comparative advantage in a multilateral or hemispheric framework and thus diversify their productive structures. Integration would benefit as per capita incomes and the capital stock would rise, creating more trade opportunities at the regional level.

In these circumstances, and especially for small Caribbean countries where trade diversion is more costly, the policy prescription revolves around the elimination of the common external tariff or its reduction to a very low level.

Outward orientation therefore favours a Free Trade Area (FTA) among such countries since an FTA does not constrain countries to pursue unilateral liberalisation and integration with other countries or groups of countries.

According to the above argument, tariffs therefore are not the best way of giving a margin of preference even if it is established that such a margin is necessary. But the case for an active industrial policy that gives some margin of preference to domestic producers, particularly in order to narrow the technological gap and promote high-skill and knowledgeable industries, is often made in the region. Market and production integration in CARICOM is often considered to be without significance if there is not a margin of preference. Tariffs are regarded as the best instrument for achieving integration since integration technocrats have had a long common experience in using them.

Regional programmes of building competitiveness can however be more effective than tariffs, even against the background of the Uruguay Round and reforms in structural adjustment (elimination of transfers, subsidies, privatisation and other market-based policies) that have limited the number of instruments that can substitute for tariffs. In this regard, the gains from greater factor movement, particularly capital and labour, have not been fully explored in the region. CARICOM has tended to side-step the question of factor movement largely out of fear of polarisation. It is often argued that, given the shortage of capital in the Less Developed Countries (LDCs) of the Common Market, free movement of capital would cause a flight of capital to the more developed areas. In the interests of avoiding polarisation, the regional arrangement instead should be geared to increase the flow of capital to the LDCs through special promotional mechanisms such as the CDB. In addition, as regards labour, the migration of both skilled and unskilled labour from the LDCs to the industrial centres is considered a factor that would aggravate polarisation. Restrictions on labour movement in the More Developed Countries (MDCs) are perceived to be in the interests of the LDCs. In the MDCs, large pools of unemployed, coupled with deficient infrastructure, usually provide the case for such restrictions.

It is clear, however, that in a strategy of boosting comparative advantage through a better pooling of resources, greater attention will have to be given to greater movement of selected factors. Skilled labour as well as capital are two key factors which should be given greater freedom of movement. Fears about polarisation do not seem to be well founded with such limited movement. In any case, it is doubtful whether in an integration scheme comprising small countries, the gains from agglomeration are as large as the theory tends to suggest. Furthermore, in a globalised and liberalised setting, agglomeration

gains and one-way capital flows in a small region are hardly relevant considerations today. While it is evident that the unfettered movement of labour
without the provision of social services and the availability of jobs can be
disruptive, the basic polarisation concerns of yesteryear appear to be outmoded in a context where a rational division of labour has to be determined
mainly by the competitiveness of member countries *vis-à-vis* outside members
rather than with other regional partners.

Modern analysis of the formation of the European Union has shown that
there are gains which can be more important than those of trade creation.
These non-orthodox gains stem from reducing remaining barriers to free
circulation of goods, people, services and capital as well as economies of scale
in tradable infrastructure, and coordination and/or harmonisation in the
provision of public goods and the use of policy instruments (taxation, financial
market regulations, etc)

Robson (1993) considers these gains as being equally if not more important
for developing countries. It is recognised that potentially vast mutual gains
may be secured through regional economic cooperation among developing
countries in areas where significant externalities and public goods exist and
market mechanisms tend to fail. Some regard the above potential to be greater
in public goods (education, health, training, environment, and research and
development [R and D], the latter particularly in the areas of agriculture and
investment incentives) rather than infrastructure such as interstate roads,
railways, ports, water, energy, telecommunications (Langhammer and Hie-
menz [1990]). Because of high organisational and information costs, most of
the above cannot be implemented other than on a regional basis.

In view of the requirements of research and development, marketing and
training, the state, through its industrial policy instruments, is now playing an
active role in providing training subsidies and R and D assistance, in order to
create specific areas of comparative advantage needed to penetrate targeted
markets. The role played by EEC governments as well as the European
Economic Commission (EEC) is clearly indicative of this. Deliberate policy
measures are being adopted both at the national and regional levels to counter
the competitiveness of Japan and the United States. CARICOM cannot ignore
this development and must seek through a process of integration to identify
the areas where a pooling of resources would have more impact or could be
complementary to any national effort.

Regional policy can also be advantageous in marketing. The substantial
economies of scale that stem from large outlays on marketing clearly point the
way for regional approaches in certain areas. CARICOM, through the Caribbean Export Development Project/Caribbean Export Development Agency

(CEDP/CEDA), has been able to identify some of these areas as it has sought to promote entry into extra-regional exports. In light of current protectionist practices and TNC marketing power, regional approaches are also required to deal with the politics of marketing.

Central to a strategy of creating comparative advantage is the provision of specialist skills at reasonable cost. In terms of available manpower and costs, small economies face a serious problem of developing any meaningful range of such skills. The regional pooling of physical manpower resources has clearly been an area identified where the supply of such skills could become more elastic. In addition, the costs of training could also be reduced as sizeable economies may be reaped from lower infrastructural costs and common training methods.

The costs of non-integration should also not be discounted on the basis of any argument that CARICOM is largely non-contiguous. Physical, technical and fiscal barriers do create market fragmentation and inefficiencies and entail a cost at times higher than the gains from trade creation. In a small, geographically dispersed union, these barriers exist in such factors as transaction costs, payments obstacles, market entry[1]

On the political front, the process reconfiguring the post-Cold War world is likely to remain unsettled well into the next decade. In the bipolar Cold War era, the alliances were clearly demarcated and battle lines were neatly drawn. At present, coalitions are shifting in search of equilibrium in this multipolar world setting. While the US alone has the military strength to be a superpower in terms of its ability and will to project power internationally, it is severely constrained economically as well as by the growth of power in other regions of the world that are seeking to establish their own balance of power without the presence of the US. Power is thus more and more diffused and regionalised as countries acquire nuclear and chemical weapons of devastating proportions. The old notion of CARICOM as a zone of peace which sought to obtain recognition of ideological pluralism no longer holds water, nor will it serve us well as a means of leverage in the global scenario of refigured/refiguring economic and power relations that face us as we enter the twenty-first century. It is in this context that the Caribbean Community must give urgent attention to the integration process.

Note

1.   In a union such as CARICOM the costs of this type of non-integration are high especially since many of the neighbouring countries that form a natural bloc with CARICOM are not part of the integration scheme.

[69]

Linking Knowledge
with Education

K e n n e t h   H a l l

The decision of the Second Hemispheric Summit on Education to select as
one of its themes 'Education: The Key For Progress' underscores the emerging consensus of policy makers, scholars, political and business leaders in the
hemisphere, that education will be a determining factor in the effort to
confront the challenges of the twenty-first century.

In the 'third wave' of economic, technical and social change that will
become a reality in the twenty-first century, knowledge has emerged as the
predominant factor in the creation of wealth and prosperity. A new
paradigm is emerging or has emerged which has forced fundamental
rethinking of such vital issues as the principles that guide organisations,
the way competition will be conducted, new organisational structures that
will influence their operation and complexity, new challenges for leadership, the assumptions of the marketplace, and the architecture of the global
environment.

Central to this new paradigm is the link between knowledge, the quantity
and quality of human resources and the education system. It is the recognition
of this new change that has prompted leaders like President Clinton to declare
in his 1997 State of the Union address: 'Now, looking ahead, the greatest step
of all – the high threshold of the future we must now cross – and my number
one priority for the next four years, is to ensure that all Americans have the
best education in the world.' He has also issued a call to action for American
education, based on ten principles designed to improve equity, quality,

relevance and efficiency. These principles also guided the Policy Declaration on Education by the Ministers of Education at the Hemispheric Meeting preparing for the Second Hemispheric Summit on Education. The member countries of CARICOM fully associate themselves with this Declaration.

We in the Caribbean have also placed special emphasis on education. Motivated by the desire to achieve rapid social and economic development, to retain and build upon our cultural identity, to prepare our work force for the economy of the twenty-first century, and to benefit from the technological revolution accompanying these changes, we issued at the end of the 1997 Conference of the Heads of Government, the Montego Bay Declaration which expresses our commitment to restructure and re-equip our education system.

In that Declaration, we committed our governments to a holistic development of our human resources that would give priority to increased productivity, research and development, science and technology, technical and vocational education, and the promotion of micro enterprises for adults and out of school youth. The Heads of Government agreed as a matter of priority, that the following specific measures would be adopted:

- 15 per cent enrolment of the post-secondary age cohort in tertiary level education by the year 2005, with annual output targets to be set in relation to this objective;
- universal quality secondary education targeted for the year 2005, with attendant annual targets set;
- introduction of programmes for achieving appropriate levels of competence in Spanish and other languages among secondary and post-secondary graduates, with the targets to be achieved set and programmes designed by 1998;
- identification by June 1998 of desirable learning outcomes for reading and mathematics at different grades of the primary school, and thereafter the implementation of strategies to ensure that these are achieved through regular in-service teacher education workshops and careful monitoring of progress;
- setting of a target date by 1998 for full enrolment of the pre-primary age cohort in early childhood education and development programmes;
- determination by 1999 of a formula to guide national governments in achieving optimum allocation and efficiency in the deployment of national resources to the education and training sector.

The Conference also agreed that in all initiatives, appropriate emphasis would be given to:

- the concept of lifelong learning and the importance of continuing education to ensure functional literacy and numeracy and the continuous upgrading of professional and technical competence in the public and private sectors;
- enlargement of the knowledge base through accelerated research and development pervading all sectors of our economies, and giving of increased impetus to higher productivity and greater international competitiveness;
- the culture of excellence already demonstrated in our region which should continue to be the cornerstone of our ongoing efforts to develop our human resources;
- the importance of science and technology and the advances in telecommunications as an all-pervasive factor which must be effectively and appropriately used; and the application of these to the production of goods and services and in the delivery of education;
- the role of sports and the performing arts in education and training;
- the recognition of the role of tourism and the environment in national development, and the need for educating our society in order to maximise the benefits to be derived from tourism;
- the enhancement of teacher education and upgrading.

In order to finance these activities, the Conference agreed to enlist the active participation of the private sector in policy development, planning, implementation and financing of human resource development programmes; and to attract through their best efforts, external resources from the Caribbean Diaspora, donor countries, and international agencies to complement national initiatives.

Caribbean Governments will do their part, but it is clear that we will need assistance, so we fully endorse and support the call for assistance from the Organisation of American States (OAS) and the Inter-American Development Bank (IDB) to provide substantial resources. We will also look to our partners to provide any assistance in sharing the responsibility in this fundamental programme of reform to make the education system the basis of our prosperity.

In light of the provisions of the Policy Declaration, the strategies adopted and the commitments made by national governments in the hemisphere, we urged the Hemispheric Summit to go further in four respects:

1. Setting a target for tertiary enrolment to complement the target set at the secondary level, because of its critical importance in filling urgent personnel needs at managerial, supervisory and professional levels. In par-

ticular, setting such a target recognises the vital contribution required from tertiary education for the development of quality teachers and teaching for the secondary and primary levels;

2. Giving further endorsement to the central role that education should play in promoting democracy and good governance through, *inter alia*, the provision of educational leadership at community, local and national levels;

3. Setting an indicative target for research and development (for example, 3percent to 3.5percent of GDP) as a means of encouraging countries to focus and step up their Research and Development activities, and arrange for regular hemispheric reviews of R&D performance;

4. Underscoring the role that education must play in a crusade against the dangerous build- up in our schools and communities of crime, violence, dishonesty, juvenile pregnancies, drug use, and crass materialism based upon instant gratification.

Note

This paper was first published in *CARICOM Perspective*, No. 66, June 1996, pp. 60—61

[70]

Many Rivers
to Cross

Michael Manley

The Middle Passage and all that it represents in our history remains the symbol of a one-way traffic to degradation. Nettleford, like Garvey before him, realised that the search by the Jamaican people for a sense of identity and self-worth would never be complete until the Middle Passage had been crossed the other way to the discovery of all that part of our heritage which is African. Nettleford began to explore this imperative in *Race and Identity*.

The Rastafarian retraces his spiritual steps through the Middle Passage to Africa, and more specifically, to Ethiopia and Haile Selassie. In one leap of faith Rastafarianism redefines the Christianity which is the common religious currency of the people in terms of a holy land and son of God which are equally compatible with racial reality and spiritual yearning. The true Rastafarian has no problem with his identity or the certainty of his self-worth.

Bob Marley undertook this journey in his own way. Once Marley spiritually located himself in Africa, it was almost inevitable that an artist with his fiery sense of justice, gifts of a lyricist and innate sense of music, would become more than a superstar. Marley has become an icon because his art is a rallying point for the revolutionary spirit of generations increasingly lost in a world of persistent injustice and insistent indifference. Revolutionary icons, Nettleford included, are people of transcendental self-assurance, almost by definition.

The majority of Jamaicans are rooted in the traditional symbols and conventions of Christianity and with no grounding in African history nor knowledge of African art. Consequently, that crossing of the middle passage which is a precondition of their liberation is no easy journey to undertake. Certainly, they cannot accept it as part of a redirection of their religious beliefs. Nonetheless, the journey must be undertaken. Jamaicans of mixed heritage may not admit it, but they place a greater value on the part of themselves which they deem to be European. Many Jamaicans of pure African descent, on the other hand, may be equally unwilling to admit their secret doubt of the worth of their ethnic heritage. This is not to say that they are incapacitated by that doubt. But it is to say that human beings are more likely to be at peace with themselves where their sense of self rests as securely in their perception of the past as in their experience of the present. Nettleford knows the truth of this. He discusses it in dance works like *The Crossing*. He continues to write about it, most recently in *Inward Stretch, Outward Reach*.

Much of Nettleford's artistic statement is similar to Edna Manley's, though expressed in the idiom of the dance. However, Nettleford joins the process at the second stage of the trajectory of revolutionary self-discovery. Hence, he seeks to take us even further along the path which leads to those roots in our history which we must one day incorporate within our assumptions about ourselves and our innate worth. Furthermore, he knows the cultural treasure that awaits those who have the courage to join him in that part of the journey in which we retrace our steps across the Middle Passage. He well realises that it is not for nothing that some of the greatest artists of our times, Picasso, Henry More, Giacometti and a host of other European sculptors and painters, absorbed so much of African art into their own creative vocabulary.

Perhaps the most profound insight which Nettleford provides for colleagues and public alike concerns the nature of process itself which he discusses in his capacity as a philosopher. To most people the process leading to change is seen as involving a journey from a predetermined point of departure to a projected point of arrival. Nettleford insists that life and history are dialectical in a primary, Hegelian sense. To him, therefore, process is an unending dynamic, and change a permanent condition. In short, we are invited to extend Jimmy Cliff's vision by knowing that there will always be 'many rivers to cross'! Ironically, it is the failure to understand this which has led to the intellectual paralysis which overcame the progressive political forces of much of the world following the 'success' of the radical right in the 1980s. Many are only now coming to terms with the fact that the world is changing and that their own approach to a political agenda, no matter how idealistic, must seek to marry enduring social principles with new realities. Artists must equally open their minds to the great pulsebeats of change which are the response of the people to new experiences born of the challenge of new pressures and new opportunities.

At the same time, in a critical departure from typical reflexive political perceptions, Nettleford argues that the removal of systemic injustice liberates oppressor and oppressed alike. This is the reverse side of the coin which Roger Mais makes central to the prison scenes in *The Hills Were Joyful Together*. As Mais reminded us from bitter personal experience, prison warder and prisoner are both brutalised by the experience which they are both condemned to share.

Nettleford suggests that the removal of the palpable causes of injustice opens up new dialectical processes which lead to positive change. The argument is not founded in some unrealistic assumption that either oppressor or victim can be transformed instantly and magically to a state of perfection. This will not follow immediately upon any single act of liberation, not even monumental acts such as emancipation or the defeat of apartheid. Rather, it is to suggest that all parties to an equation of institutionalised injustice become involved in a new dialectical experience at the movement of change. The experience may be positive for everyone.

Nettleford, despite his immense scholarship, elegance of language, international recognition, charisma and uncompromising aristocratic bearing, is also quintessentially Jamaican. He prefers Jamaican food. He is entirely at ease with people from all walks of Jamaican life, like the members of the trade union movement who pass through the Trade Union Institute, which he heads, or the old men in the rural villages who are the story-tellers of our history, much of it outside the history books.

It is this most Jamaican of men who invites us to complete an important part of the search for identity, of widening the net of our sense of heritage to include Africa no less than Europe, along with India, China, and all the other parts of the world from which we spring. But he also reminds us that even that journey is only an element in an unending process. In all of this he is the true heir to the social dynamics which those first pioneers helped to precipitate and a brilliant exponent of the journey which we must have the courage to take if the process itself is to continue to unfold.

Note

This paper was first published *CARICOM Perspective*, No. 68, June 1998, pp. 14–15.

[71]

Midnight
2000

Shridath Ramphal

First let me acknowledge the privilege of being invited to deliver this year's Walter Rodney Memorial Lecture. Walter Rodney, cut off at a young age on the threshold of a promising political career – but having already delivered for posterity his quota of scholarship which is now his great legacy to us.

These lectures in his memory are about the themes in his life. He was a historian and so looked more before than after. But he would have pondered, I am sure, as I do tonight, on the tomorrow that is so dramatically at hand. He would have done so recognising that time is a continuum and reality evolves not in answer to the calendar but to forces long in making. His historiography would be his guide to the twenty-first century.

In fact, as we recall, for example, *West Africa and the Slave Trade*[1], *How Europe Underdeveloped Africa, A History of the Guyanese Working People*[2] or *Groundings with my Brothers*, we know that the twentieth century in which Walter Rodney lived and worked was acting out, in the political, economic and social spheres, the earlier events of which he wrote. Africa's condition in the middle of the twentieth century was in large measure the consequence of that perverse legacy of early European presence and paramountcy on the continent. And the Caribbean, which shared much of Guyana's history, was living through the same struggle for political autonomy and economic promise as Guyana was – an identity of experience that allowed Guyana to be embraced so naturally in the West Indian family despite geographic incongruities. What I venture to muse with you about is the extrapolation of some

648

of those twentieth century realities beyond the limits of this passing century, acknowledging, as I do, that continuum of time.

For me, for this lecture, 'Midnight 2000', is, however cryptically and contentiously, midnight next New Year's Eve – the beginning of the new century; the new millennium. It will be a time of revelry across the globe – a formally secular yet functionally global moment of uniting. But uniting in what? In celebration of things past? In hope for things to come? Or in a mix of each in varying proportions? We will, as always, welcome in the New Year with its unspoken promise of good things. But just as we treat Midnight 2000 as the high point of no ordinary New Year's Eve, so it is valid to ask how will the morrow be special? What will it bring – and for whom? That 'for whom', for the purposes of this lecture, has a Caribbean resonance – the Caribbean of the reclaimed Caribbean Sea; the lake that was once Spanish and then English (with contenders flying other European flags), but is now more truly Caribbean: from Cuba to Suriname, from Belize to Barbados.

But let me be clear at the outset, our inquiry tonight is not an enquiry that can focus only or even mainly on this region. No island is an island, no sea, a sea entire. As ever, the Caribbean is not master of its destiny. Now, perhaps more than ever, we must look beyond the sea and sand of our shores to catch a glimpse of what the future has in store for all the world – and then for the Caribbean as a small and discrete part of it. So, as we toast the new century, the new millennium, that question which will be on Caribbean minds must with different nuances be on the minds of people everywhere as well.

With the first light of the dawn of the new century the sun will have risen over Eastern China. There, nestling in the Purple Mountains overlooking Nanking, is the Sun Yat-Sen Memorial on whose pinnacle are immortalised the words:

Tien xia wei gong: What is under Heaven is for all.

Sun Yat-Sen took them from one of the ancient books of China to provide the guiding principle for the revolutionary movement that liberated his country from its feudal past. That past was not peculiar to China; it has been a part of the history of most countries, East and West, North and South. The words used by Sun Yat-Sen speak for all the world, and though they are prodigiously ignored by it, they are specially relevant to our modern global society which needs liberation from its own feudal nature.

Feudalism as a system of economic, social, and political organisation was a system that held people in permanent subordination. Narrowly construed, it justified itself on the ground of contract: the service of the serf in return for the protection of the lord and master. In essence, it was a system that divided society into strong and weak, powerful and powerless, haves and have-nots, those who made the rules and gave the orders and others whose role was to defer and obey. To the great credit of our species, the history of human society has been one of movement away from feudalism to systems less unequal and unjust, systems in which earth's bounty and the fruits of human toil are shared more fairly, societies that more closely respect the precept that 'what is under Heaven is for all.' But, for the greater part, the movement away from feudalism stopped at national frontiers; the concept of sharing, even of fairness, generally evolved only within states, not between them. Human society, the world of people, remained beyond the reach of that civilising precept. What is under heaven has not been for all on earth.

In 1987, in addressing the role of the international economy in securing humanity's future, the Brundtland Commission on Sustainable Development made the basic point that 'the pursuit of sustainability requires major changes in international economic relations. 'It elaborated this in its report, *Our Common Future*, as follows:

Two conditions must be satisfied before international economic exchanges can become beneficial for all involved. The sustainability of ecosystems on which the global economy depends must be guaranteed. And the economic partners must be satisfied that the basis of exchange is equitable; relationships that are unequal and based on dominance of one kind or another are not a sound and durable basis for interdependence. For many developing countries, neither condition is met.

In 1995, the Commission on Global Governance had this to say in its report, *Our Global Neighbourhood:*

A sophisticated, globalised, increasingly affluent world currently co-exists with a marginalised global underclass. The post-war system of economic governance has seen – and facilitated – the most remarkable growth in economic activity and improvements in living standards within human history . . . Many indicators of social progress –infant mortality, literacy, life expectancy, nutrition – have improved significantly, at least in terms of global averages . . .

At the same time, people are increasingly aware – through better communication – of the global problem of continued poverty. The number of absolute poor, the truly destitute, was estimated by the World Bank at 1.3 billion in 1993, and is probably still growing. One fifth of the world lives in countries, mainly in Africa and Latin America, where living standards actually fell in the 1980s. Several indicators of aggregate poverty – 1.5 billion lack access to safe water and 2 billion lack safe sanitation; more than 1 billion are illiterate, including half of all rural women – are no less chilling than a quarter-century ago. The conditions of this 20 per cent of humanity – and of millions of others close to this perilous state – should be a matter of overriding priority.

What will the dawn of the twenty-first century herald for that 'marginalised global underclass'? Will it be any more than perpetual struggle in the periphery of the global economy?

In this last decade of the present century, UNDP's annual Human Development Report has provided the most authoritative approach to improving human well- being covering all aspects of human life, for all people, in both high income and developing countries, both now and in the future. It goes far beyond narrowly defined economic development to cover the full flourishing of all human choices. It emphasises the need to put people – their needs, their aspirations and their capabilities – at the centre of the development effort. This year's Report, the last of this century, has this to say looking to 2000 and beyond:

> The challenge of globalisation in the new century is not to stop the expansion of global markets. The challenge is to find the rules and institutions for stronger governance – local, national, regional and global – to preserve the advantages of global markets and competition, but also to provide enough space for human community and environmental resources to ensure that globalisation works for people not just for profits. Globalisation with: Ethics . . . Equity . . . Inclusion . . . Human Security . . . Sustainability . . . Development.

And it warns:

> When the market goes too far in dominating social and political outcomes, the opportunities and rewards of globalisation spread unequally and inequitably – concentrating power and wealth in a select group of people, nations and corporations, marginalising the others. When the market gets out of hand, the instability shows up in boom and bust economics, as in the financial crisis in East Asia and its worldwide repercussions, cutting global output by an estimated $2 trillion in 1998–2000. When the profit motives of market players get out of hand, they challenge people's ethics – and sacrifice respect for justice and human rights.

Today, as we leave the twentieth century behind us, more than 80 countries, mostly in sub Saharan Africa and Eastern Europe, still have per capita incomes lower than they were a decade or more ago. Many people are also missing out on employment opportunities. There is a global professional elite with high wages and international mobility; but the market for unskilled labour is highly restricted by national barriers.

We tend to associate this century with the flowering of human genius and the explosion of human prosperity. And in some respects we are right to do so, but not in all respects. One hundred years ago, as the nineteenth century turned into the twentieth, the ratio of average income of the richest country in the world to that of the poorest was 9 to 1. At midnight 2000, as the twentieth century turns into the twenty-first, that ratio will have risen to 60 to 1. Today, the average family in the USA is 60 times richer than the average family in Ethiopia – or in America's hemisphere, 40 times richer than the average family in Haiti. Inequality has been rising too within many countries, including rich ones, since the early 1980s.

As we come to the end of the century, the richest countries, with just one fifth of all the world's people, have 86 percent of world GDP, 82 per cent of world export markets, 68 percent of foreign direct investment, 74 percent of world telephone lines. The remaining four-fifths have to make do with what is left over. And for the bottom fifth of humanity, their share in all these areas is 1.5 percent or less.

The trends of today are the starting points of tomorrow. This is how the twenty-first century will begin on Planet Earth. For only 20 percent of the world's people will it be a confident dawn. With globalisation running ahead of the global governance that is necessary to ensure that its benefits are more widely shared, the prospect is the emergence of new threats to human security in poor countries, and to the poor in rich countries too. That means in the end threats to the rich and privileged themselves. Can these trends be reversed? Of course they can, for they are man-made, not the working of forces beyond human control. Whether they will be reversed is the challenge to humanity in the new century beyond the unpromising dawn. We need to remember this as at midnight 2000, we toast the New Year, the new century, the new millennium.

In his 1985 Wiles Lectures, *Nations and Nationalism since 1780*, the historian Eric Hobsbawm envisaged the way future historians would write the history of the late twentieth and early twenty-first centuries, as follows:

. . . It will inevitably have to be written as the history of a world which can no longer be contained within the limits of 'nations' and 'nation-states' as these used to be defined, either politically, or economically, or culturally, or even linguistically. It will see 'nation-states' and 'nations' or ethnic/linguistic groups primarily as retreating before, resisting, adapting to, being absorbed or dislocated by, the new supranational restructuring of the globe. Nations and nationalism will be present in this history, but in subordinate, and often rather minor roles . . . It is not impossible that nationalism will decline with the decline of the nation-state, without which English or Irish or Jewish, or a combination of all these, is only one way in which people describe their identity among the many others which they use for this purpose, as occasion demands. It would be absurd to claim that this day is already near. However, I hope it can at least be envisaged.

On the threshold of the twenty-first century is that 'new supranational restructuring of the globe' any nearer? Yes and no. Yes, it should be; because of the compulsions of survival. No, it is not; because of the resistances of Homo sapiens that is Homo sapiens as well.

The founding of the United Nations in 1945 at San Francisco was a watershed in the evolution of a world of separate nation states. In the 50-plus years that have passed since the UN was established, those parts remain the central feature of our world order. Nation states are not about to disappear, or the nation state system to lose its centrality. Yet something has happened on the way to the twenty-first century. Several of the elements of the nation state system have become less creedal, less assertive, less defining, even less hallowed. Sovereignty, self determination, even non-intervention have had to yield some of their innocence. We still speak of them in the language of orthodoxy, but we know that global realities have curbed their claims, that they no longer reflect universal truths or represent undiluted norms.

In 1945 governments had a perception of the world as a world of so many sovereign powers, the repositories of the authority that governments wielded. Very few who speak for governments today, if they speak honestly, will say that they have a similar sense of power now. The transformations of the post-war years of this century – the years since 1945 – have made it impossible for any country, including the USA which represents the largest reservoir of wealth and power in the world, to go it alone. No country can manage its destiny on its own. Global cooperation – working together – is essential over a great variety of issues. The world has changed, in some respects impercep-tibly; but the result of that change in its totality is that for states, for govern-ments, for people, there is just no option now but to cooperate; living together, not apart, is a compulsion for survival. Of course old intimations of power persist. It is not the oxymoron it seems that the recognition of interdependence is furthering the urge for dominance in some quarters. These resistances cast many a shadow on our global neighbourhood – but that interlocked, interde-pendent, global community is an inescapable reality.

That is why we now have global conventions on climate change and biodiversity; no country can respond to all the challenges of environment by itself. That is why issues like drugs and terrorism and migration have ceased to be just national issues and become global issues too. That is why the General Agreement on Tariffs and Trade has evolved into the World Trade Organi-sation; if we are to bring sanity to the market place it has to be on the basis that all will play by rules to which all agree. That is why fishing in the North Atlantic by Spanish trawlers brought Canada and Europe to such a point of conflict in this decade; there had to be a process of dialogue and concurrence not just about jurisdiction but about the dwindling fish stocks of the oceans. That is also why a trader in Singapore gambling on the value of the yen could bring down a vintage band in Britain and devalue major currencies around the world; and, much more tragically, why a collective gamble on international financial markets could have precipitated the East Asian crisis and changed the fortunes of over 200 million people. The year 2000, and beyond, will surely bring its own quota of reminders of our oneness.

It is essential, therefore, as we face the twenty-first century, that the notion of 'security' must be allowed the breadth of meaning reality now demands, and global governance must take account of the full range of insecurities that so grievously afflict human society as to compel the attention of us all. Specifically, the time has come to establish arrangements of global governance that respond to threats not just to the security of states but to the security of people.

Human suffering on a large scale, whatever the cause, very naturally gives rise to the feeling that the world community should act to bring it to an end. These feelings are articulated as demands for UN action, even if such action would mean external involvement in the domestic affairs of sovereign states. The sovereignty and territorial inviolability of nation states have been bedrock tenets of the world system. States have valued these tenets as fundamental to the protection of their independence and integrity. Small and less powerful states in particular have seen in these principles their main defence against more powerful, predatory countries, and they have looked to the world community to uphold these norms. And so it should.

We must find a legitimate way to give effect to the consensus that exists in the world at the level of the world's people – a consensus that when the security of people within a country is outrageously ravished (as it was in the former Yugoslavia), when people are facing genocide and mass violence (as they did in Rwanda) – that a line has been crossed which makes what is going on within that country no longer the concern of its people alone, but the concern of the global neighbourhood. There is legitimacy then in neighbourhood action – involvement as a genuinely collective act by the world community, action undertaken by the United Nations or authorised by it and carried out under its control.

That is why the Commission on Global Governance strongly proposed the establishment by the UN of a standing rapid deployment force. We called it a UN Volunteer Force, with a maximum of 10,000 personnel. It was not a new idea; it had been proposed in 1948 by the first Secretary General. Had it been in place the UN could have been in East Timor three weeks earlier – when it should have been. But the major powers – the veto powers – have not liked the idea even though the standing facility would be under the direct authority of the Security Council. They would rather pay the price of lives lost in conflict escalation than allow what might seem to imply a dilution of their paramountcy in decision-making – an implication which in this case would be wholly unwarranted. They simply do not like the optics.

And so, we have to be extremely careful. What we cannot allow to happen – as it can so easily happen where global governance is underdeveloped – is for the global neighbourhood to be policed by vigilantes, either because the sheriff is not being paid or because the rule of the 'sheriff's posse' is preferred to the rule of law, with internationalism displaced and unaccountable power rampant. *Pax Americana* is as unacceptable to most of the world, and perhaps to many Americans, as ever *Pax Britannica* was to America. But in the global phase of human evolution we have entered, in the era of globalisation, it is, more simply, out of date. We have become a human community; only 'pax planeta' will not suffice. Only a return to the vision of the primacy of the United Nations in the global order will allow us the chance of a tolerable future. It is truly an even more compelling vision now than in 1945.

Yet the trends of recent decades are ominous. They tempt us to conclude, as Churchill did at an earlier time – at Harvard in 1943 – in relation to the League of Nations, that the UN in turn is being abandoned as a prelude to being betrayed. This simply must not happen. We must recognise the signs of regression, and mobilise global support for the United Nations system – reformed as it must be to ensure a return to the principles and purposes of the Charter, which remains the most important political document of this century. If we were to face the twenty-first century without it, our global neighbourhood would do so wearing the Emperor's new clothes. Could East Timor, you might ask, be a turning point? Can it help to overcome the resistances that have thwarted the establishment of the UN standby force thus far? I doubt it; NATO had no interest in Dili.

What has this to do with the dawn of the new century? In a recent issue of *Foreign Policy* is an article by the distinguished American internationalist, Charles Williams Maynes, which he entitles 'The Perils of (and for) an Imperial America. ' Its rubric reads as follows:

Not since ancient Rome has a single power so towered over its rivals. From military might to the 'virtual power' of software, America reigns supreme. Yet not only does the American Imperium threaten to become dangerously overbearing, but also to impose costs that could prove intolerably high.

Not surprisingly, there is concern worldwide. In recent months alone articles have appeared in the Western media from a range of commentators under the following headlines:

- 'Kosovo's Dilemma: NATO Alone, Without UN Backing' (Jonathan Tepperman, 22.3.99)

- 'NATO's Vigilante Warfare Gives a Bad Example to the World' (Ingvar Carlsson and Shridath Ramphal, 1.4.99)
- 'The World's War on Poverty Has Yet to be Won' (Joseph Stiglitz, 28.4.99)
- Let's Respect Both Sides of the Development Coin (Amartya Sen and James Wolfensohn, 5.5.99)
- 'The '90s: Another Decade of Greed?' (Robert Samuelson, 17.7.99)
- 'The Neglect of Growing Poverty Poses a Global Threat' (James Gustave Speth, 17.7.99)
- 'If We Are Serious, We Do Something About Poverty' (Eveline Herfkens, Hilde Johnson, Clare Shore and Heidemarie Wieczorek-Zeul, 10.8.99)
- 'The Threat From Nuclear Weapons is Growing' (Yasushi Akashi, 11.8.99)
- 'So We Just Send In an International Force, Time After Time' (Flora Lewis, 13.9.99)
- 'But Who Are These Western Crusaders to be Lecturing Asians?' (Philip Bowring 15.9.99)

When we ask what dawn midnight 2000 will herald, we have to be mindful that the new century will start with the trends these headlines reflect dangerously ascendant. And there are other trends also – no less threatening.

In the early years of this last decade of our century, in an unprecedented joint statement, the Royal Society in Britain and the National Academy of Sciences in the USA issued a warning in these terms: 'If current predictions of population growth prove accurate and patterns of human activity on the planet remain unchanged, science and technology may not be able to prevent either irreversible degradation of the environment or continued poverty for much of the world.'

It was 1992 – the year of the Rio Conference on Environment and Development. Most people have almost forgotten it now; but at midnight 2000 we must not. The logo of the Earth Summit depicted the planet Earth 'In Our Hands.' It asserted that sustainable development required a shared effort by all the world's people, a partnership for survival in which each country has a role that is related to, sometimes integrated into, the roles of others. The partnership, of course, is not between equals. Developed and developing countries are unequal in responsibility for getting it wrong and in capacity for setting it right. Aristotle, in his *Ethics*, instructed us a long time ago that equity between unequals requires not 'reciprocity' but 'proportionality.' His dictum holds in this ultimate domain of environmental restoration. Proportionality must be the ethical touchstone of the role of developed and developing countries in their partnership for survival through sustainable development.

Why were the scientists concerned about population growth? Why did they not think of it as a flowering of the species, but in the negative sense of an overgrown garden? If we are, as we believe, the best thing that has happened to the planet, why shouldn't more of us be ever welcome? There is good reason why they did not. The real reason, the ultimate reason, for their concern is sustainability – the sustainability of life on the Planet. In scientific terms, it is described as Earth's 'carrying capacity'; less formally, it is our impact on the biosphere measured by what we use and what we waste. When we ask whether Planet Earth can sustain double its present human population, the answer has to do with consumption. If we continue to draw from Nature at the rate we do today – if, overall, we consume at today's level – such a doubling may not be sustainable: the population explosion could threaten survival. Remember the words of the scientists: *If current . . . patterns of human activity on the planet remain unchanged*: they were talking about consumption.

The scientists spoke out in 1992. 1998's Human Development Report was devoted to the issue of consumption. It had this to say:

Today's consumption is undermining the environmental resource space. It is exacerbating inequalities and the dynamics of the consumption-poverty-inequality-environment nexus are accelerating. If the trends continue without change – not redistributing from high-income to low-income consumers, not shifting from polluting to cleaner goods and production technologies, not promoting goods that empower poor producers, not shifting priority from consumption for conspicuous display to meeting basic needs – today's consumption will worsen.

The problem, however, is not only the level of human consumption but also its skewed pattern. At present, about one quarter of the world's population (mostly in industrialised countries) account for about three quarters of the world's net annual consumption of resources of all kinds. The industrialised world consumes 75 per cent of the world's commercial energy, 90 per cent of its traded hard wood, 81 per cent of its paper, 80 per cent of its iron and steel, 70 per cent of its milk and meat and 60 per cent of its fertilisers. The other three-quarters of the world's people must get by altogether on the remaining one quarter of the resource pie.

Estimates vary as to the overall consumption of the rich and poor in the world. In UNDP's 1993 Paul Hoffman Lecture, the President of the Population Council, Margaret Catley-Carlson, used the estimate that 'every child born in the North consumes over a lifetime from 20-30 times the resources and accounts for 20–30 times the waste – year in and year out – of their counterparts in developing countries.'

The world's population now increases at around 80 million persons per decade, but will slow down as the century unfolds. Still, of those increases, only five percent will be in the developed world. But, from a consumption standpoint, that five per cent added in the North will impose on the planet a greater burden than the 95 percent born in the South. So at midnight 2000 a time bomb will be ticking. The truth is that there are many explosions in the making. The 95 per cent of world population growth that will take place in the South is one of them – in sheer numbers alone, and with dire implications for people in the South. But the 5 per cent of world population growth attributable to the North is as large or larger an explosion – not in relation to numbers, but to what the numbers imply for the Planet. Perhaps the whole analogy of time bombs ticking away is misleading; for the bombs have been detonated already; the explosions have occurred. Their containment involves reducing population growth in poor countries, but primarily requires reducing the consumption levels of the North. There are few signs that the latter will happen.

If a quarter of the world's people continues to sequester three quarters of the planet's bounty, there will never be enough resources available for levelling up. In fact, it is estimated that if the whole world aspired to the living standards now prevailing in the West, the world of the twenty-first century would require the resources of ten planet Earths to satisfy that aspiration. But, of course, we will continue to have – 'only one Earth.' Our science may increase its bounty, and our husbandry make its resources go further, but its capacity to support life cannot be extended *ad infinitum*.

And the whole world does aspire to that better life now enjoyed by a few. How could it be otherwise with global communications glorifying its excesses and aggressively promoting the myth of boundless growth in a borderless world? The Chinese, for example, are serious about securing China's sustainable development in the twenty-first century, and they are determined that it should be development that gives their people a higher standard of living than they now have. They are a quarter of the people of the world. And what is true of China is true as well of all who know that the twentieth century was not theirs. It is a compulsive aspiration towards a desirable goal.

On the eve of India's independence Mahatma Ghandi was asked if, after independence, India would attain British standards of living. His reply was prescient: 'It took Britain half the resources of this planet to achieve its prosperity. How many planets will a country like India require?' If life on Earth is to be sustained we shall have to care for the planet, and we shall have to share it better than we have done. Neither galactic fantasies nor technological changes justify us in proceeding on any other basis. We have to manage within the resources this one planet offers and provide space for all who dwell on it

—we have to heed the wisdom of the Purple Mountains: What is under Heaven is for all.

What will today's élites do? How will the more industrialised countries in particular respond to the need for fairer shares in the twenty-first century? How will they respond to the inescapable need for adjustment, structural adjustment, on their part, as the realities of survival – to say nothing of the claims of morality – require them to make space in the global economy for the world's masses yearning for betterment, and require from them some sharing of power as the lessons of the unsustainability of national feudal structures press their claims in global society? What instincts will guide that adjustment which in the twenty-first century will cease to be a word describing the medicine of the poor alone, but connote as well the life-saving prescription for the rich? There is no certain answer.

Despite the lessons of history, even the history of recent times, the prospect of the twenty-first century remains clouded by the danger that such adjustment will be resisted – that those who have prospered in the twentieth century and emerge powerful into the next, will pursue every other response save that which involves any change in the trends which at midnight 2000 mark their passage to the new century.

There could be a temptation for them to think that there is an alternative to adjustment that offers a guarantee of survival: an alternative that opts for an autocratic world, rather than democracy in our global state; an alternative that opts for more power, including military power, more aggrandisement, more dominion of a few over the many – in short, for a feudal world with a twenty-first century spin. At best it would involve freezing the present indecent inequalities in the distribution of Earth's bounty and man's power; but, it will be worse than that; as numbers grow, so will the disparity in distribution, so that by about the middle of the next century it will not be 25 per cent as at present, but much, much fewer of the world's people who will take up 75 per cent of its resources and dominate its political agenda. That scenario, I suggest, can only be an illusion; because any attempt to perpetuate such global inequalities into infinity, will ultimately send us all there. Even so, there are some who concur with it.

In each of the areas I have explored – development, security, environment – the Caribbean is at high risk. Although in the orthodox lead table of poverty, the countries of the Caribbean are not part of that 'marginalised global underclass' of which the Commission on Global Governance spoke, many of our countries are not insulated from inclusion. Of course, we are differentiated among ourselves. Within our region, levels of per capita income vary; so do levels of social capital, and so do patterns of distribution. In the 1999 Human

Development Index, Caribbean countries, with the exception of Haiti, rank within the first 100, with Barbados, the Bahamas and Antigua and Barbuda among the first 50. That does mean, however, that taken all in all, the Caribbean is quintessentially part of the developing world – and without attributes of size and natural resources that can compel the creation of space through forcing elbow room, our space will be hard to win; but it does mean that we are not without opportunities to improve our positions, always provided that the global environment for doing so becomes more propitious.

But it also means that in a global environment more propitious to development Caribbean prospects for the twenty-first century must not be denigrated. We shall have to work hard, it is true, to engender that environment. That is why we are so heavily engaged with the 71- strong group of ACP countries in relation to trade and economic relations with Europe, with Latin America in relation to hemispheric trade relationships that are equitable and supportive of development, and with developing countries generally in the evolution of a World Trade Organisation that does not relegate the development dimension to the periphery of its regime. With success in these areas and with new and liberalising approaches to policy development in our economies, Caribbean countries – as Prime Minister Owen Arthur of Barbados has so forcefully pointed out recently – are not devoid of policy options and development prospects in the twenty-first century. But we will labour in vain if the global economic environment is not supportive. What we must not do is fail to fulfil our own quota of change responsive to the possibilities of a changing world.

But have no doubt – getting that external environment more benign will not be easy. The post-Lomé arrangements contemplated by Europe do not have Caribbean development at its heart – whatever the rhetoric of poverty alleviation. The FTAA concept is designed for the larger economies of the hemisphere and on the basis of the most doctrinal application of globalisation as a creed. We have had to force grudging acceptance of special attention to the needs of small economies in that process. And in the WTO itself, our fortunes will turn on how much we can achieve with other developing countries in giving the regime a human face and securing an evolution compatible with the needs of the great majority of its member states – which is not the same as the interests of the few who seek to dictate the global agenda.

On sectoral fronts, agriculture is being undermined in the name of liberalisation – as our experience with bananas all too grotesquely demonstrates. So to with sugar, the sanctity of contract notwithstanding. Our diversification into services, which promised much, is being held hostage region-wide to OECD greed – preserving the gains of financial services and investment for themselves in the name of countering 'unfair tax competition.' Even tourism faces threats from extra-territoriality in the name of protecting rich countries' citizens. In none of these areas is there a question of the pursuit of wrong policies – merely right policies made fruitless by the exercise of the collective power of those who have and will not share.

The twentieth century saw the rise of the working class movement in the Caribbean and the mighty contribution of the trade union movement to enlarging respect for what today we call the human rights of workers in conditions of employment and national social policies. And it contributed to the political struggle for self-determination. At the end of the century these gains, as we have seen, are threatened on the economic front. And even freedom and sovereignty are threatened beyond the normal processes of global adjustment.

It was only a few years ago that the right of Caribbean countries to independence itself was challenged in the starkest terms when Elliot Abrams of the US Republican right had no compunction in proposing that we relapse into a state of colonial dependency, becoming to the US as Montserrat is to Britain – an Associated State, with defence and external affairs entrusted to 'big brother' and plenty of 'brotherly' muscle around to keep the 'backyard' tidy. The proposal essentially was to turn back the clock of history and remove from West Indian hands the right to determine the nature of our engagement with the wider world. It was a proposal for recolonisation – and it was advanced not as an abstract proposition, but in the 'ship-rider' context – a blatant (and partly successful) attempt in the assumption of dominion. It is in itself a regression that such ideas could be seriously canvassed, even by nonofficial spokesmen- but stalking horses are no new thing in political affairs, national or international.

The threats are not always so overt, and some even bear innocuous names. 'Extra-territoriality' is one of them: the illegal attempt to bring one sovereign country under the sway of the law of another. It is one thing to have sovereignty moderated by global governance through international institutions democratically constituted; it is quite another to have sovereignty negated by the extra-territorial operations of the law of another country which asserts dominance. 'Helms-Burton' is the crudest form of this intrusion – an outrageous attempt by the USA Congress to dictate the foreign policy of other countries in relation to Cuba, and to impose on their citizens curbs on their freedoms that are intolerable by even the most primitive standards of internationalism.

Even in the environment, the Caribbean faces consequences over and beyond those that threaten people everywhere. It is not the Caribbean's use of fossil fuels that induces global warming, but global warming in turn exposes us in now undisputed ways to more frequent and more intensive storms and storm surges and to sea-level rise. Earlier this week I was in the Bahamas for the opening of the ACP – EU Joint Assembly. The Bahamas was hit by Hurricane Floyd which devastated some of its northern islands. In his opening remarks, Prime Minister Ingraham made the point that they were already living with the consequences of global warming. Never before in recorded history had the storm surges brought the sea as far inland as they did with that hurricane. The Caribbean can expect more of the same in the twenty-first century.

My own country Guyana faces the prospect of enormous dislocation in the event of sea-level rise. On the northern edge of the South American continent, Guyana is almost as large as Britain, but has only 750,000 people, most of whom live on its coastal strip. They would all be at risk if the sea were to rise half a meter. The Dutch and later the British who colonised Guyana used thousands of African slaves and Indian indentured labourers to protect low-lying land from the sea before planting the sugar that made Guyana an imperial asset. It would be a cruel twist of fate if the dilapidated seawall of Guyana's polders were now to overflow because in Holland and Britain, and elsewhere in the industrialised world, the affluence to which sugar contributed, were to introduce patterns of fossil fuel consumption that eventually caused the seas to rise in the distant Caribbean. Even Guyana's legacy from the forced labour of our ancestors (that Walter Rodney described so poignantly) would be lost forever.

I have dwelt on some very negative trends as we approach midnight 2000, but, of course, the twentieth century has not been without its positive side. These achievements do not attenuate the perils of the trends I have discussed; but they derive from one very positive dimension of life in the second half of the century which will have many implications for the next. It is the empowerment of people – the empowerment of people within countries, and people within our larger country, the Planet: Earthland.

Whatever else has not been happening in real development- in the evolution of global governance, in the care of the planet- people everywhere have been empowering themselves and beginning to exercise their influence for change. There are some large symbols that mark this – the whole process of decolonisation and the end of 'Empire' starting with India in 1946, the Civil Rights movement in the USA , the worldwide antinuclear movement, the gender revolution, the environment movement, more recently the 'landmines' movement; on a larger scale, the collapse of the Soviet empire (so often described as the triumph of capitalism, but more truly the triumph of the human spirit), the unification of Germany, Vaclav Havel coming to office in

Czechoslovakia as democracy triumphed and Nelson Mandela in South Africa as apartheid collapsed.

All these were achievements of people empowered – people asserting the power to change what was wrong and evil but which, left to Governments, would have continued. Governments came on board in the end, driven by the inexorable logic of democracy where it thrived, and of inevitability where it was absent. But none of these achievements of our civilisation would have occurred without the insistence of people – not one. They do not, therefore, point to new intergovernmental trends; but they do proclaim the trend of the empowerment of people and all that will flow from it. As I said, this empowerment is helped by functional democracy – which is why the strengthening of genuine democracy and helping it where it is struggling for emergence or sustainability will be so vital a factor for hope in the twenty-first century.

I am an optimist by disposition, but a realist nonetheless. My realism tells me that if the trends of the last quarter of the twentieth century continue into the twenty-first, even more so if they intensify, the world's developing countries, and even some in transition, could face the most inordinate threats to their survival on a tolerable basis. The Caribbean, as small countries and vulnerable economies, will not escape these dangers which may be accentuated by our being so much in the eye of the 'American imperium.' To that extent, midnight 2000 may not herald for us a promising dawn.

My optimism tells me, however, that these threats can be attenuated by our own fortitude in resisting and our courage in pursuing propitious polices even in unpromising times. And it is in our Caribbean capacity to show that fortitude and courage that I have my greatest faith. We may be few in number and powerless in the ways that orthodox power is measured. But the human resources of the Caribbean are immeasurable; they have a multiplier effect beyond our reckoning. There has not been a time in the post-colonial era of the twentieth century when the Caribbean through its political leadership or its sons and daughters in their several pursuits beyond politics has not earned worldwide respect and contributed to what has been worthiest in human achievement. So it will be beyond 'Midnight 2000'. However unpromising the dawn, the quality of our people will enhance its prospects.

But wider still, I have faith in the people of the world and this is where our civilisation reveals contradictory qualities. Just as much as being self-centred and protecting one's turf are one human trait, there is another side to our character – our humanism itself, our fellow feeling, our evolving perception of belonging not only to our several countries but also to our other country, the planet. I believe that these higher attributes of our nature – which are prominent among young people today – will not permit so large a swathe of humanity to be permanently consigned to the periphery of existence. It is at the level of individuals that such humane perceptions operate; but since individuals can be collectively decisive in democratic societies over the longer term, they will ultimately be decisive globally. It is the shorter term that is disturbing, for democracy tempts governments to look no further than the next election and to promise only prospects that please.

Even so, I do not believe that the ordinary people of the world, including the ordinary people of the industrial countries, will allow the whole world to be taken down a path of self-destruction and global anarchy. I believe the latter will not let the values that have made their countries decent neighbourhoods be jettisoned in their application to the global neighbourhood. And I know the people of the developing world, including the people of the Caribbean, will not accept a flawed status quo nationally and internationally. They will demand greater empowerment at home and greater equity in the global homeland. It is in this alliance of the world's people that I repose faith. It is to them, and rather specially to the people of the Caribbean – that I shall drink my toast at midnight 2000.

Note

Address delivered by Sir Shridath Ramphal, Chancellor, University of Warwick at the Centre for Caribbean Studies, University of Warwick.

[72]

The Caribbean Challenge
in the Negotiating Process

Shridath Ramphal

Today's global economic environment is dominated by two concepts and their practical application; namely, liberalisation and globalisation. They are, of course, different things. Liberalisation is a policy prescription, now become a global prescription. Globalisation is a phenomenon that stems partly from the application of that prescription but from other causes as well, like the information revolution. But globalisation and liberalisation are sufficiently intertwined to represent the essentials of the global economic environment in which the challenges and options of the negotiations will have to be faced and exercised.

Deep misgivings exist about liberalisation and globalisation – which for some who espouse them are present with theological, almost fundamentalist, fervour. That, of course, is part of the problem when we relate them to the WTO and to Lomé and the FTAA. For the WTO is the cathedral in which we are supposed to worship and the ACP is increasingly agnostic.

This combination of western economic ideology and southern scepticism will be a basic feature of the dialectic beyond 2000. Unless it is understood, there is a real danger that the parties to the negotiation will be talking past each other, even as they use the language of partnership or integration. We need to be more outspoken about this global environment. The truth is that 'open markets' are not open to all products or all people; 'free trade' is rarely fair trade. Liberalisation is not the trade dimension of a regime of global liberalisation; there is no regime – as French farmers, demonstrating for retention of the Common Agricultural Policy, confirmed in Brussels recently with such vehemence.

Globalisation, however, is not a choice; it is a reality. But being a reality does not *ipso facto* endow it with virtue. It is already clear, for example, that there are aspects of globalisation that have more hazards for the weak than for the strong. Developing countries have certainly profited from globalisation far less than the richest industrialised nations.

Globalisation is widening the gap between rich and poor in the world. United Nations figures show that the share of global income received by the poorest one-fifth of the world's people, has been shrinking from 2.3 per cent in 1960 to 1.4 per cent in 1991 and then to 1.1 per cent in 1994, suggesting that the decline had become sharper as globalisation advanced in the 1990s. These are decidedly unpromising auspices for efforts to achieve development for the poorest people through the negotiations.

Declining prices for commodity exports have dragged down developing countries' terms of trade, which measure import capacity in relation to export earnings. The least developed countries, generally the poorest, have suffered a 50 per cent drop in their terms of trade since the early 1980s.

The global financial crisis has worsened this decline in commodity prices. This is proof that globalisation has made the international financial system more unstable, making even star performers vulnerable to devastating shocks. The world's arrangements for economic governance proved incapable of anticipating or preventing this crisis; efforts to manage it seemed to make matters worse, driving economies into greater disarray and pushing more people into poverty.

All this is the outturn of the era of liberalisation. Is it any wonder that we start the negotiations with substantial scepticism about the global economic environment?

The WTO is the flagship of trade liberalisation. It was designed to benefit all countries on the basis of rules that all will respect and live by, rules designed especially to bring under the sway of the rule of law, those powerful economies that have historically asserted a right to play not by the rules but by their perceived national interests and the instincts of the bully indifferent to the fate of the small and weak. Not surprisingly, many developing countries are signatories. Yet, serious questions are arising about the WTO regime itself, about the fears its early record is generating of the WTO becoming, for small countries in the area of trade, the rod of chastisement the IMF had become in the area of finance.

The WTO has been catapulted into the front line of the Lomé negotiations by the notion of 'WTO compatibility' that has been underscored by Europe in its Green Paper and, even more so, by the United States in the FTAA context. So, if all these negotiated arrangements are to be WTO compatible, and if the WTO itself looks like being incompatible with the regime of global equity and a balance of interest between developed and developing countries, we could face the most serious of difficulties.

The answer is that the WTO must evolve in this way. It must not become a fundamentalist institution commanding unswerving obedience to the ideology of liberalisation and uncritical acceptance of all that globalisation is made to yield.

For us in the Caribbean, this is no theoretical exercise. We are living through the terrible experience of the threat to our small societies and fragile economies at the level of bananas – the kind of threat that arises for people, some among the poorest, when arrangements, designed to redress inequality – like the Banana Protocol – are threatened by indiscriminate and insensitive ideology masquerading as a virtuous new order. The Caribbean does not seek a future dominated by a culture of preferences, but it does seek a future. We believe we have a right to do so; and that both the EU and the US, in different contexts, have a responsibility to help us.

So how does the Caribbean approach the negotiations? It needs, I am sure, no reminder from me that the basic strategic position CARIFORUM Governments had endorsed at the highest level is insistence, in their words, on 'a cohesive regional position for these complex and varied discussions.' It was to that end that the Regional Negotiating Machinery was established by Heads of Government.

An essential requirement of the concept of the Regional Negotiating Machinery is that, in the negotiations, wherever there are Caribbean voices speaking, they must be speaking from an agreed regional brief, to an agreed regional position. We must all sing from the same hymn sheet. That is the heart of the concept of a regional negotiating strategy.

The RNM's efforts, including my presence here last November in your national consultative process, are essentially about composing that hymn sheet, including blending the interests of Suriname into those of the wider Caribbean region, bringing strength to these national interests from their pursuit by the wider region, and ensuring that the strategy with which we go forward into the negotiations, with Europe and with the Americas, is one that responds to the vital interest of this country. There must be a Surinamese verse in the regional hymn.

To achieve this at the level of all member countries of CARICOM is not a simple matter, or one that is free of difficult decisions. But, equally, Heads of Government are mindful that it is mainly through that 'cohesive regional position' that these complex talks and varied negotiations can be brought to fruition in the interest of all the people of the region. We have gone far in securing that position. But, as important, in the Lomé context, is progress on the twin-track of solidarity with Africa and the Pacific. The negotiations, for post Lomé IV arrangements, are between the European Union and the ACP as a group – not with 71 (and with Cuba, 72) separate countries of Africa, the Caribbean and the Pacific.

So let me focus on these negotiations. From the earliest discussions with the EU, the ACP made it clear that it attaches great value to the Lomé relationship, that it is mindful of its shortcomings, including the ACP failures, and that it looks to a future which might appropriately be characterised as an 'enhanced Lomé partnership.'

It is a fundamental ACP position that post-Lomé IV arrangements must be essentially a partnership for development. 'Development' must be the dominant objective of post-Lomé arrangements; it must not be subordinated, for example, to the political objectives of other agendas.

The ACP insists that 'development' is an objective in its own right; indeed, that 'development' is itself a fundamental human right. We do not accept, for example, that any particular 'political environment', however desirable in itself or supportive of development, is a *pre-requisite of development* – relegating the trade and economic provisions of the post-Lomé IV arrangements to a secondary place.

The ACP obviously will not reject the idea of a political dialogue between the EU and the ACP – under proper conditions and in proper sequence. This means that a political dialogue under a future Convention could be acceptable to the ACP if it conforms to agreed principles, for example, that it is a dialogue in which the concerns of both sides regarding policies or practices of the other may be raised – the only provision being that they bear on the central objective of the Convention, namely, cooperation for development.

It means that the ACP, for example, could require a dialogue with the EU on debt, or on the treatment of migrants, or on European practices regarding hazardous waste or CO_2 emissions generally. It could similarly extend to ACP-initiated dialogue on the protection of cultural heritage or biodiversity. Equally important would be the principle that political dialogue did not in any way imply political dictation under a system of EU certification of ACP states. This means that any political dialogue the ACP is willing to have with the EU is not tainted with notions of conditionality.

Another matter of concern is the clear intention of the Commission to split the ACP into three, or even six parts, for the trade negotiations which would succeed Lomé IV. This is not the regionalisation of which the ACP speaks.

Indeed, it is precisely the opposite. The ACP has repeatedly reaffirmed its determination to maintain ACP solidarity and the integrity of the ACP as a negotiating partner. This should be the fundamental basis for the negotiations, but it would be jeopardised from the outset, were we to agree to the negotiating structures the EU is contemplating.

As already signalled at the ACP-EU Ministerial Meeting in Barbados, the admission of Cuba as a member of the ACP under post-Lomé IV arrangements is a matter of importance to the ACP and, rather specially, the Caribbean. The ACP will want to ensure that Cuba is within the substantive 'geographical coverage' as it pertains to the Caribbean and to secure the admission of Cuba as a full ACP partner in the post-Lomé IV arrangements.

And then there is 'vulnerability.' Forty-two of the ACP states have a population of less than five million, and half of these are in Africa. The problems of small states are not confined to the Caribbean. Small states are not simply small versions of large states. Many disadvantages result from scale diseconomies in administration, infrastructural development, transportation, marketing, keeping and attracting high level skills and accessing global capital markets.

In addition, the geographical vulnerability of many small states, including proneness to natural and ecological disasters (arising from hurricanes, volcanic activity, fragile coastal zones, high population density and forest depletion) complements economic vulnerability, and their impact is made worse by pervasiveness.

For them, a 'level playing field' is a mirage. That is why the vulnerability of small island states has been traditionally recognised in the context of ACP-EU cooperation. No similar flexibility obtains in the WTO rules. A significant issue for future ACP-EU relations is forging an alliance for change in WTO rules to recognise the vulnerabilities of some small economies that will not survive on the basis of reciprocity and non-discrimination.

But it is the trade aspects of the negotiations that will prove the most difficult. Until the final decisions on the EU Mandate were taken at the meeting of the General Affairs Council on 29 June 1998, the EU's projection of ACP options was for Free Trade Area arrangements by region or general participation in the GSP. Others spoke of the alternative of MFN treatment. The first is not on for both technical and other reasons – to some of which I have already alluded. Suffice it to say that ACP countries do not buy the theory that developing country interests lie in the route 'from Lomé to FTAs' – a theory with which by now (with the aid of its own commissioned studies on regional FTAs) the Commission should itself be uneasy.

Lomé, from Lomé 1 to IV, always had trade and development at its centre. The ACP wants to preserve that architecture. The EU does not. Despite the language of 'co-operation for development' that it uses in its Green Book Guidelines and Negotiating Directives, it wishes to dismantle Lomé and refashion it closer to a blueprint that sees trade in goods and services as a net benefit to Europe, and development assistance as a lever for social, political and economic policies imposed through a system of conditionalities adorned as political dialogue.

Just take the issue of reciprocity for which the ideologues of liberalisation would claim sanctity – and which is at the heart of FTAs – or Regional Economic Partnership Agreements (REPAS), as they were euphemistically described. Reciprocity between equals is one thing; it is the very essence of equity. But between unequals it is the opposite. We do not have to go back to Aristotle's *Ethics* to recognise that between rich and poor, between highly developed industrial economies and underdeveloped, largely agricultural ones, between countries that are large and well endowed and those that are small and impoverished, reciprocity is a recipe for enlarging inequality.

Yet it is this that the EU, pleading WTO compatibility, would ordain for ACP-EU post-Lomé arrangements through regional FTAs. The Commission may be in danger of being 'holier than the Pope' if it does not generate forward-looking ideas on the evolution of the development factor in the WTO regime – an evolution which must come.

The alternative option advanced by the EU – general participation in the GSP system – could hardly have been serious; certainly, it holds no attraction for ACP states. What the June 29 decision of the EU did (in the last days of the British Presidency) was to create some negotiating space for non-LDC ACP countries by providing a third option of 'a new framework for trade between them and the EU which is equivalent to their existing situation under the Lomé Convention and in conformity with WTO rules'.

In practical terms, this fortifies the initial Libreville position of the ACP for an enhanced Lomé Convention in relation to the trade regime. This may take the form of a super GSP for ACP partner countries – notwithstanding the reach of the GSP beyond ACP countries, generally.

In this context, the ACP would count on the full potential of the compromise decision and in particular the practicality of a new framework for trade . . . which is equivalent to their existing situation under the Lomé Convention and in conformity with WTO rules . . . making use of the differentiation permitted by WTO rules. It is not coincidental that the compromise decision committed the EU to assessing in 2004 the situation for non-LDC ACP countries not wanting FTAs, since it is in 2004 that industrial countries will be reviewing the GSP generally. There is need, therefore, to call for an enhanced Lomé prior to 2004.

But when will such new arrangements become operative? Recognising that the existing Convention expires in February 2000, and that the negotiating process will be a lengthy one, there is obvious need to roll over the existing Convention to an appropriate date. But the appropriateness of the date is not conditioned merely by the duration of the negotiations. Much more signifi- cantly, it should be conditioned by the transition period required for ACP economies to develop new export activities and deepen their capacity for integration into the international economy, and for the character of the global economic environment to become clearer with, for example, the review of the GSP and the outcome of the Millennium Round of Multilateral Trade Negotiations. And this will certainly be longer than the five years being contemplated by Europe.

The ACP, therefore, looks to a rollover of Lomé IV (with enhancement) to, say, 2010, with negotiations for successor arrangements commencing in 2006. It cannot possibly commit itself at the end of this year to even the broad nature of the trade arrangements that will follow the end of the rollover period – whether that is five, much less ten years away.

At all stages in these negotiations, it will be salutary to ask and seek answers to the questions: Why are we negotiating post-Lomé IV arrangements? Why also for that matter, are we engaging with the Americas in the FTAA process?' Many reasons require us to join these negotiations and many factors influence the path we will try to pursue in them. But fundamentally, it is because of their relevance to our vital national objectives of eliminating poverty and advancing development within each of our countries. The negotiations may seem esoteric, but they have as their most basic rationale, improvement of the lives of people at every local level.

It follows that for each member state, these negotiations – whether with Europe or the Americas or the WTO – are not because of CARICOM relationships. They face the member state irrespective of CARICOM. CARI- COM helps you not to face them alone. And even so, you have options within the negotiations. But one option you do not have. To do nothing is not an option. If you stand still while the world changes around you, you will cease to be where you are relative to everything else, and almost certainly to your detriment.

And that is as true of Lomé as of the FTAA discussions. Although the FTAA negotiations are very different from the post- Lomé IV arrangements, the issue of reciprocity on which we stand with the ACP in Brussels is the same issue that lies at the heart of the FTAA concept.

We cannot grant reciprocity to the United States under an FTAA and deny it to Europe under Lomé; which is why we are arguing in the FTAA context very much the same kind of fundamental issue that we have to press in Lomé. An obvious difference is that with Lomé we are discussing with Europe whether to continue a longstanding relationship.

With the FTAA we are discussing whether to establish one. But there is something else. In Brussels, the EU is negotiating under a mandate carefully developed by the European Commission and authorised by the member states. The mandate including flexibility for negotiating 'alternative arrangements'. In Miami, the United States, which is driving the process, has no such authority. The US administration has significantly failed to secure fast-track authority for the negotiation of a hemispheric FTA.

One implication of a slow or stalled FTAA process might be the enlarged possibility of pursuing CARICOM bilateral negotiations with regional partners: with the Dominican Republic, with Central America, perhaps with Canada- all of which are being submerged under the weight of the FTAA process. From a CARICOM point of view, this may not be a bad reordering of priorities. If we can secure a reasonable outcome from Lomé and develop potential markets in Latin America, the immediate result could, on balance, be favourable to our economic prospects, while giving us time to prepare not only for negotiating positions, but also our domestic economies, for a more mature relationship with the United States.

Given the enormous task of preparation for negotiations, however, the Caribbean must not make the mistake of putting its own preparatory work on hold. We must occupy the space provided to us in a productive manner. And so we have been doing – in the several negotiating groups that have been established to cover the field, namely agriculture, competition policy, dispute settlement, Government procurement, intellectual property rights, investment, market access, services and subsidies, anti-dumping and countervailing duties. We hold Vice-Chair positions in Competition Policy and Services. There is also the Committee on Electronic Commerce which CARICOM chairs; and, most specially for us, the Consultative Group on Small Economies chaired by Ambassador Richard Bernal, who is also the Dean of our College of Negotiators established to bring cohesion to our negotiating efforts. In all these areas, we have assembled as our Lead and Alternate Negotiators some of the best talents in our region. This year will see an intensification of CARICOM's efforts in the FTAA process, keeping always in mind those considerations to which Minister Condor alluded.

The Second Meeting of the Trade Negotiations Committee (the first Vice-Ministerial Meeting since the FTAA process began in September) was held in Suriname. I draw particular attention to the agreement of this Suriname meeting on additional meetings of the Small Economies Group and the planned CARICOM programme on Customs Procedures directed towards 'Business Facilitation'. The former, of course, is very much in the region's interest, as we seek to enlarge awareness of the need for special arrangements for Small Economies and to infuse all Negotiating Groups with an urgent awareness of the necessity of responding to those needs. The second, the decision on 'Business Facilitation' –a matter specially promoted by the United States as an early harvest of the negotiations – might be a commentary as well as the uncertainty of the ultimate yield.

It is not a matter that should give us concern, though we must of course be vigilant about the nature of the detailed arrangements lest they work to our disadvantage. But that vigilance is necessary in every stage of the negotiations.

In these negotiations, which are unlike any we have engaged in, in the past, we must do our utmost to secure better terms of trade for our products – mainly primary products, but some manufactured ones as well –in the markets of rich countries in Europe and North America. We argued successfully in 1974 against reciprocity with Europe. The United States agreed with us then. So Lomé involved no concessions by way of penetration of our markets – admittedly small as they are.

Nor did CARIBCAN or the CBI. Before them, imperial preferences had, but they were the product of colonial and post colonial arrangements, not the product of open negotiations. Whatever the outcome of these present negotiations in specific terms both with Europe and with North America, one thing is certain: they will involve a deliberate step to further open our markets, our economies, to access from beyond the region; from member countries of the European Union and from North, Central and South America in the case of the FTAA.

These negotiations will involve, therefore, challenges we have not faced before. They represent a historic point of departure for us. They are not about staying as we are at home and enlarging our chances abroad. They are about enlarging those chances through adapting ourselves at home to new realities beyond our shores – through influencing those realities as best as we can, of course, but in the end through being part of what is unquestionably a new global economic scene. So the negotiations are only part of the story of survival. As big a part, is what we do at home.

Note

This paper was first published in *CARICOM Perspective*, No. 69, June 1999, pp. 6–10.

[72]

The Importance of
Negotiation Preparedness
Reflections on the Caribbean Experience

Alister McIntyre

Over the past three decades, CARICOM countries have, both individually and as a group, accumulated considerable experience in regional and international negotiations. The development of CARICOM and other related institutions and arrangements has taken up a considerable amount of the time of governments. Associated with this development have been trade and economic agreements with major trading partners – the European Union (EU), Canada and, more recently, the USA. Governments have also been involved in almost unending negotiations with the international financial institutions over their stabilisation and adjustment programmes. At different periods, substantial attention has also been paid to global negotiations under the auspices of the United Nations and its specialised agencies, such as the GATT. Furthermore, some governments have been intensely involved in negotiations with international companies in fields such as natural resources telecommunications.

It is not possible in a single presentation to distil and synthesise this wide variety of experiences into a set of reflections. What I shall do is to concentrate on the intergovernmental trade and economic negotiations with overseas countries and groups of countries, partly because we are on the threshold of new negotiations for entry into NAFTA, and the lessons of the past may be of some help in structuring the future.

I start with the issue of how CARICOM has prepared for international negotiations. The typical pattern has been for the Heads of Government to agree on a broad strategy, leaving it to a Committee of Ministers, drawn from the CARICOM Council, to work out the detailed approach to the negotiations, supported by officials from member Governments and the CARICOM Secretariat.

This structure has so far worked reasonably well, although experience shows that it needs improvement in a number of respects. On some occasions, one area of weakness has been the limited interface between the regional teams and the CARICOM Secretariat on the one hand, and persons involved in the negotiations at the national level on the other. Quite often, important information received in capitals on major issues of substance has not been transmitted to the regional level, or at least not in a timely manner. Apparently, this has been particularly true of mission reports from ambassadors accredited to countries with which a particular negotiation was being undertaken. Unintended lapses in sharing information can be a source of misunderstanding among governments.

The lack of transparency in the preparation of individual countries is accentuated by the unevenness of preparation capacity among them. By and large, the OECS countries have traditionally been less prepared than other CARICOM member states, although the situation has changed substantially as a result of the technical leadership being given by the OECS Secretariat. But a continuing problem for the OECS is its very limited representation abroad. For example, the OECS does not have a permanent representative in Geneva, and has therefore experienced difficulty in maintaining an effective presence during the negotiations on the Uruguay Round.

One problem that has arisen is the evaluation of information received from particular sources. It is not often sufficiently appreciated how information has to be checked and cross-checked with a variety of sources before workable conclusions can be reached. There are examples where opinions expressed by a single source were communicated to the highest levels of government without any reliability checks being made. Had caution not prevailed, the negotiations could have been derailed.

In the pre-negotiating phase where soundings are being taken and 'kites are being flown', there is occasionally a tendency to involve Heads of Governments and ministers too early in the process. On occasion they have become involved talking to relatively junior officials about details which should properly be left to officials on their side. As a principle, the political leadership should be left to resolve major sticking points where they can engage persons at comparable levels on the other side.

Experience shows that great care must be taken in the selection of the negotiating team and in the assignment of responsibilities. Individuals must be chosen who have not only a good substantive grasp of the issues involved, but are also effective communicators with a capacity for good interpersonal relations, and with an ability to work in teams. 'Solo players' should generally be avoided since they tend to be vulnerable to 'ego-massaging' by the other side. The aim should be to develop a team with an ethos and identity of its own, with group loyalty to the aims and strategies that have been worked out by all of the members. Much depends upon the leader of the team whose responsibility it is to create a good environment within which all members of the team can work effectively.

A further issue is the need to involve the private sector and, in some instances, representatives of NGOs. It is an established practice among very many countries to have these groups involved in negotiations. So far, CARI-COM has done this only on a very selective basis. Private sector participation has worked very well in negotiations on sugar, rum and bananas, where industry representatives are substantially involved at all stages, but otherwise there still remains a tendency to limit these representatives to a consultative role on an 'on call' basis. There can be no merit in limiting their involvement where they can be effective interlocutors with their counterparts on the other side. A similar point can be made about participation by other sources of expertise, such as members of the academic community, both in the preparatory process and in the negotiations themselves. Some of this is already being done, but much more needs to be done, given the highly technical and complex nature of the negotiations in which the Caribbean will have to engage over the period ahead.

A further weakness is the habit of making only limited use of officials who were involved in previous negotiations. This needs to be addressed so that a continuity can be maintained, and the institutional memory utilised to good advantage. This applies particularly to retired officials who are not much used for this purpose in most CARICOM countries. A pattern has therefore developed where countries have little institutional memory on which to draw, and tend to start from scratch every time a negotiation comes up.

Much the same thing applies to the use of the expertise of West Indian nationals working in key parts of the international system. These nationals can often provide vital information about the substantive points of the negotiation, about the principal negotiators, as well as the attitudes and expectations of their governments. Again Caribbean negotiators go into the process without sufficient knowledge of comparative experiences of other countries negotiating on the same issues, and about the strengths, weaknesses and predilections, of the key actors involved in the negotiations.

On a broader front, it is only now being recognised how important it is to build alliances with influential groups and individuals in the countries with which the region is negotiating. Thus, today in relations with the European Union, more work is now being done at the level of the capitals of member states. In the USA , systematic lobbying and contacts are being developed with Congress and groups such as the Black Caucus, whereas in the past, almost exclusive attention was given to the Administration. In Canada, a neglected group is the provincial governments which can be influential when cooperation agreements are being negotiated in areas in which they have considerable powers.

Another aspect of the preparatory process is the quality of the substantive preparation. The analytical work which goes into negotiating briefs does not often disaggregate issues in terms of the interest groups involved, their particular characteristics, and possible areas of conflict and consensus. The practice has been to treat issues almost exclusively in economic terms with inadequate consideration of their political and social dimensions. This has led to a certain narrowness of perspective and inappropriate timing of negotiation initiatives, because insufficient attention was paid to the political calendar in the prospective partner countries. These deficiencies in preparatory work have often been the result of limited resources available to the CARICOM Secretariat and national ministries for undertaking such work, and to the short time for preparing briefs.

I am among those who have argued that CARICOM needs to set up machinery for foreign policy planning, where trends can be highlighted and issues identified within a medium to long-term horizon, together with options for dealing with them. Up to now, the region's approaches to negotiation have tended to be reactive rather that proactive, with the other side defining the agenda, which limits the room for manoeuvre open to governments. One consequence of this is that negotiators tend to approach the negotiation with a very short-term perspective, giving only secondary consideration to longer-term issues.

As an illustration of this, one can notice that over the past thirty years, only secondary attention has been given in negotiations to comprehensive and sustained support for agricultural diversification in order to lessen dependence on the traditional agricultural exports which are highly vulnerable. None of the existing trade agreements contain provisions that are specifically targeted towards the development of non-traditional agricultural exports such as exotic fruits and vegetables, horticulture, aquaculture, and mariculture. As one example, these products have different marketing requirements from those of traditional crops. In general, producers of the latter market their products through transnational companies, whereas most exporters of non-traditional crops have often to establish their own marketing channels in the consuming markets. Among other things, this can be facilitated by the establishment of business offices in these countries. One would notice, however, to take one example, that in the Lomé Convention, the Caribbean and other ACP countries ignored these opportunities by accepting a derogation under Article 234 of the Convention from the right of freedom to establish business offices. No one at the time seem to have spotted the point that with respect to these products, freedom to establish business offices in consuming countries could be a major factor in achieving competitiveness.

The lack of a long-term vision is similarly illustrated by the approach that the region took to the recently completed Uruguay Round. Again, most of the detailed attention was given to traditional agricultural products and garments. In my view, insufficient attention has been given so far to non-tourism services that have important potential for the future. Accordingly, the region was not very prominent in the discussion on a special convention to provide for trade in labour services where countries such as India, Pakistan, Bangladesh, and Turkey were pushing for greater access for their contract workers, particularly in the service industries. Although agreement has not yet been reached on the matter, it remains as an active item on the agenda for follow-up work on the Round.

Little awareness seems to exist of the importance of migrant remittances in the foreign exchange earnings of CARICOM. World Bank data show that workers' remittances, (net private transfers), amount to some US$400 million which may only be a fraction of the total since many cash remittances are unrecorded, and an important part of them are in kind. Governments need to put this item on the priority agenda, otherwise even the access presently available could be reduced.

In general, there is need to think through the fundamentals of a negotiating strategy, based upon the economic prospectus and development strategies of countries in the region, which could apply *mutatis mutandis* to particular negotiations. The CARICOM Secretariat should be asked to undertake this task in collaboration with officials from governments and non-governmental representatives drawn from the private sector, the academic community, trade unions, and NGOs.

With respect to the constraints which CARICOM countries encounter in negotiations, the most important is the very small size of the countries and their limited financial resources. For one thing, external representation is very costly. Even the largest countries can afford only very small missions abroad, which must necessarily be limited in terms of expertise and the ability to liaise with the negotiating partners and relevant interest groups. Given the limited back-up available from capitals in terms of supporting staff work, and the strict limitations on budgets for items such as hospitality, it is indeed surprising how well some Caribbean missions have done in maintaining a presence, especially in global negotiations. Furthermore, most governments can also make only very limited use of lobbyists, because they are expensive.

Taking these considerations into account, and considering the commonality of interests which exist among individual CARICOM countries, it is indeed surprising that so little use has been made, up to now, of the possibilities for joint external representation; also it should be observed that in some capitals, Caribbean ambassadors meet on a fairly regular basis to share information and discuss problems.

Another dimension of smallness is the limited leverage which CARICOM countries can exert on their partners. This reinforces the points made earlier about building up strategic alliances with other countries and interests. The best example of success in this field was the leadership that CARICOM countries gave in developing a common ACP position in negotiations on Lomé I, and in founding the Group itself, as well as in negotiating the Georgetown Declaration on intra-ACP cooperation. The key factor in achieving a position of leadership was the expertise that the region was able to offer to the Group as a whole. This example needs to be repeated in future negotiations. For instance, there might be opportunities for following a similar strategy in cooperating with other countries interested in negotiating entry to NAFTA. One thinks of the other CBI beneficiary countries which have a number of common interests with the region. If CARICOM countries aspire to positions of leadership, they have to earn them by the requisite display of preparedness and expertise.

A further constraint, more in relation to the future than to the past, is the limited language capabilities of CARICOM negotiators. Although interpreting services may be available, nuances tend to be lost when one is not fluent in the language of the partner, especially when finalising negotiated texts. The point has been repeated over and over again, that ministers and officials in CARICOM countries must achieve a working competence at least in Spanish, if the region is to be well prepared for the negotiations that are in prospect with the non-English speaking Caribbean countries and Latin America.

As a practical matter, it should not be too difficult to organise special immersion courses in Spanish for all Ministers of Foreign Affairs and Trade and their senior officials. If we are to succeed in this increasingly interdependent world, we have to develop the capacity to deal with countries in a variety of languages. Looking ahead, we have to go beyond the conventional European languages to master Asian languages such as Japanese, Hindi, and Chinese, if we are going to stand any chance of diversifying our international economic relations with some of the new leaders that are emerging in the world economy.

As far as successes are concerned, I would rate Lomé I as the most successful negotiation that the region has undertaken so far. Through these negotiations we acquired a frontline position in the ACP Group, which established our presence with our European partners. We were successful in terminating reverse preferences which were a main feature of the earlier Yauonde Convention, and got our partners to accept non-reciprocity in trade. We got them also to recognise regional groups of ACP states, and to permit integration and cooperation agreements among ACP and non-ACP developing countries. This led to the establishment of regional programmes of development assistance under the European Development Fund, which were intended to further the development of the integration process. We fought successfully against any CFA Franc-type linkage with European currencies, although in retrospect that might have been a pyrrhic victory.

Our biggest shortcoming has been inadequate implementation. We have not taken sufficient advantage of the access provided for exports of manufactures under Lomé , the CBI, and CARIBCAN. We have a poor record of disbursing development assistance with all of our donors. We have not used the regional programme as much as we could have done to strengthen the integration process. In some quarters, there has been a tendency to view the regional programme merely as an extension of national programmes. To put it in a nutshell, we have secured important benefits from our economic agreements with the rest of the world, but better planning, better targeting of benefits desired, better preparation and networking with supportive interests, could have yielded us much more.

The game is by no means lost. In the new order which prevails, countries are jostling to reposition themselves in order to diversify their economic relations. Despite our very small size, we can be an effective presence in negotiations if we can work together as a group and mobilise our expertise, thereby enhancing our chances of securing those interests vital to our future development. Despite the shortcomings of the past, I myself remain confident that CARICOM can remain as an effective negotiating agent for its member states. I hope that in the period ahead, full advantage will be taken of that.

Note

This paper was first published in *Caribbean Dialogue*, Vol. 1, No. 1, July/August 1994, pp. 1–5.

[74]

The Caribbean Community
and External Negotiations

Arnold McIntyre

As the region approaches the twenty-first century, important negotiations have commenced with old 'friends' and potentially new allies that promise to influence the Caribbean's future development prospects in a major way. In an era of unprecedented trade liberalisation stimulating a proliferation of free trade arrangements at the global, hemispheric and sub-regional levels, the Caribbean has to reposition itself strategically in the international economy. The paper analyses the underlying factors behind the fundamental changes in the global economy and summarises the region's strategic response.

Rapid technological change in a variety of areas, for example information technology, has influenced firms to locate different aspects of the production process in different areas to maximise advantages across countries. Globalisation of production has in turn resulted in the emergence of the corporation that globally sources its inputs and sells its outputs.

Because the production of any sophisticated product today consists of a series of different activities in various countries, developing countries seeking to improve their technological capability and increase employment will have to attract foreign investment. In the case of Caribbean countries striving to achieve international competitiveness and expand exports, foreign investment is critical to integration into the global economy.

The globalisation of production has encouraged countries to expand their economic space beyond national boundaries as they search for markets for goods and services, supplies of inputs and investment. Consequently, there has been a global trend towards increasing economic liberalisation as countries seek to remove barriers or restrictions in goods, services and capital.[1] The strong underlying trend of globalisation that is fuelling the process of economic liberalisation means that the process is not likely to be temporary or reversible. The process is sustainable even if the momentum ebbs and flows. The liberalisation of capital markets and the unprecedentedly high levels of capital flows that exist in the global economy mean that there is access to a large pool of capital to finance the globalisation process. The revolution in telecommunications and informatics technologies has facilitated the liberalisation of capital flows and more generally, the process of economic liberalisation. In short, economic liberalisation is not a fad but an imperative strongly interrelated with the process of globalisation. There is no alternative to adjustment to globalisation. The issue is the adjustment path and the policy choices that countries or groups of countries must make to accelerate development in a liberalised global economy.

The global trend towards liberalisation, particularly trade liberalisation, was clearly manifested in the new GATT/WTO Agreement in 1994. The unprecedented gains in trade liberalisation in manufacturing and agriculture and the inclusion of services in the multilateral trade agreement are indicative of the influence of the new liberalisation philosophy.

The GATT/WTO Agreement accepts the principal tenets of the economic liberalisation theory that argues that the liberalisation of markets – goods, factor, capital, financial markets – will foster growth and accelerate development. From that viewpoint, free trade is good for all countries[2] – large or small, developed or developing. One need only ensure that the playing field is level by implementing a common set of rules and procedures. The GATT/WTO Agreement is a set of common norms and rules to manage the multilateral trading system across a wide range of areas including goods, services, trade-related investment measures, intellectual property, trade laws and dispute settlement.

An important feature of the evolving international trade policy is the establishment of reciprocity as to the basis for trade arrangements between developed and developing, or large and small countries. Subsequent to the WTO Agreement, reciprocal trade with exceptions for the Least Developed Countries (LDCs)[3] has replaced special and differential treatment for developing countries. The developed countries are committed to the tenet of reciprocity on the basis of trade, with only temporary exceptions.

The GATT/WTO Agreement is seen as the benchmark for Free Trade Areas (FTAs) and discussions are now cast in terms of WTO compatibility and WTO-plus arrangements. Therefore, the framework of the WTO

Agreement and the norms and rules contained in the Agreement provide the basis for hemispheric sub regional and bilateral FTAs.

The adoption of a multilateral rules-based trading system was supposed to provide protection for developing countries against unilateral trade policy actions by industrialised countries. However, the recent decisions of the WTO, notably the ruling on the EU banana regime, call into serious question whether the WTO Agreement is compatible with fairness or equity. The case highlights the fact that the WTO Agreement must include appropriate arrangements to take account of the special circumstances of small, vulnerable economies.

This can be done by either creating a new category of states in the agreement or by widening the definition of LDCs. It is an urgent matter that small countries must bring to the attention of the WTO; they must also be prepared to present a strong intellectual case for a revision of the WTO Agreement.

Regionalism is an important issue in the current context. As countries seek to expand their economic space beyond boundaries, there has been a resurgence of regional trade agreements. This has been clearly manifested in the move to create a European Single Market and Economy and the establishment of a North American Free Trade Agreement (NAFTA). In addition, the launching of negotiations to create a Free Trade Area of the Americas (FTAA) by 2005 is also indicative of the growing influence of the ideology of liberalisation, notably trade liberalisation.

The increasing influence of trade liberalisation is also manifested in the proliferation of sub regional FTAs that have developed in the Western Hemisphere. The creation of the Southern Cone Common Market (MERCOSUR) Agreement between Argentina, Brazil, Paraguay and Uruguay is perhaps the most significant of the new FTAs. There is also the Andean Sub Regional Integration Agreement (ANDEAN GROUP) between Bolivia, Columbia, Ecuador, Peru and Venezuela and the Treaty on Free Trade between Columbia, Venezuela and Mexico (Group 3). There has also been a variety of bilateral FTAs including Chile/Mexico; Canada/Chile; Chile/Colombia; Mexico/Costa Rica; Mexico/Bolivia and Chile/Venezuela.

The forces transforming the global environment are moving the international system in two seemingly contradictory directions. On the one hand, the world is moving towards multilateralism and global integration with a strong commitment to open markets and international institutions. On the other, the world is entering a new era of regionalism, as nations seek to generate their markets. But Jhagdish Bhagwati at Columbia University recently noted that 'regionalism need not necessarily be a stumbling block towards a multilateral trading system. 'In the new dynamic integration process regionalism is not about self-contained blocs. It too must synchronise its formation in a global economy. Traditionally, regional integration arrangements have tended to be inward-oriented with the expansion of trade and investment among member countries behind protective barriers. Under the new arrangements, regional FTAs are emphasising regional integration simultaneously with the liberalisation of trade and investment regimes. The new concept of open regionalism seeks to derive the economic benefits of international competition while simultaneously creating a wider economic space for member countries.

Open regionalism is not only compatible with the goal of improving international competitiveness, but may also be central to the achievement of that competitiveness. The outward-oriented nature of the policy of open regionalism will facilitate the creation of an open, transparent global economy. Therefore, open regionalism should ultimately result in a global economy that is characterised by low levels of protection with a narrow range of restrictions on the movement of goods and services.

The fundamental changes taking place in the global economy have forced all nation states to reassess their priorities and policy objectives and develop new strategic objectives in relation to international economic relations. Traditionally, CARICOM has benefited from a variety of preferential trading arrangements with its major trading partners; these include the CBI, CARIB-CAN and Lomé. The increased pace of trade liberalisation, the evolution of the WTO reshaping the multilateral trading system and the resurgence of regionalism, have all combined to threaten the future of trade preferences. Consequently, the Caribbean has to rethink its external trade policy, setting new priorities and defining clear strategies to achieve stated objectives. Fundamentally, this means that the region will have to reshape its international economic relations. This involves revised and revitalised relations with old partners and creative or innovative relationships with new partners. This entire process can be described as the strategic repositioning of the Caribbean in the global economy. The strategy will have to be dynamic as well as new, constantly evaluating objectives and policies to take account of changes in the external environment.

At present, the region is in its initial stages of strategic repositioning. At the global level, we are involved in ongoing negotiations in the WTO relating to multilateral trade liberalisation. The region must actively pursue its trade policy objectives in the WTO to ensure that the interests of small vulnerable economies are not compromised. The Caribbean will need to make a strong case in collaboration with other developing countries such as the ACP group, for a revision of the treatment of different categories of developing countries in the WTO Agreement, particularly small island states. This is extremely vital to the region as the WTO is the benchmark of all trade agreements and this will have implications for other trade negotiations; for example, FTAA and post-Lomé discussions.

The Caribbean as part of the ACP is also seeking to negotiate a revitalised and creative set of post-Lomé arrangements that will foster growth and development in all ACP countries. This involves a new partnership with old friends. At the hemispheric level, the region is involved in comprehensive negotiations with other sub regional groupings: MERCOSUR, CACM, the Andean Community, and with individual countries: Chile, USA, Canada and Mexico, to create a Free Trade Area of the Americas by 2005. This would involve new relationships with countries in the hemisphere. Simultaneously, the region is seeking to develop close trade and economic relationships with specific countries in the hemisphere – Venezuela, Columbia, the Dominican Republic, Cuba, Canada and the CACM. These bilateral relationships are vital to achieving important economic objectives and to building strategic alliances for hemispheric negotiations.

At the institutional level, to pursue these negotiations the CARIFORUM countries have created the Regional Negotiating Machinery (RNM). This is headed by a Chief Negotiator supported by a small team of advisers in collaboration with the CARICOM Secretariat. The machinery includes negotiation working groups for each set of negotiations and also interfaces with key elements in the Community structure, such as the Council on Trade and Development (COTED).

Ultimately, the Chief Negotiator reports to the Prime Ministerial subcommittees on external negotiations which set policy objectives and provide overall guidance on negotiating strategy. In addition, the Chief Negotiator is assisted by a Technical Advisory Group, chaired by Sir Alister McIntyre, that analyses and evaluates all technical studies prepared by the RNM prior to submission to officials, ministers and Heads of Government.

In the final analysis, the long-run development prospects of the Caribbean will depend to a large extent on the ability of the region to integrate effectively into the new liberalised global economy. The effective pursuit of external negotiations aimed at achieving well-defined strategic objectives is an important element in the region's effective participation in the international economy. The establishment of the RNM is one important step in the region's effort of strategic repositioning in international economic relations.

Notes

1. Liberalisation has not included the movement of labour and this is an inconsistency in the entire process. The movement of persons has met with fierce resistance at the multilateral level, particularly the industrialised countries.

2. A World Bank (1995) paper adopted the simple 'two-country two-good' neo-classical trade theory to argue that when a small country opens trade with a large country, the resulting gains flow disproportionately to the small country. The argument has fundamental weaknesses including the failure to recognise that small countries incur significant transactions costs in penetrating export markets.

3. The WTO has defined a set of countries with LDC status of which Haiti is the only CARICOM country.

This paper was first published in *CARICOM Perspective*, No. 68, June 1998, pp. 5–7.

The Challenges of Economic Policy and Circumstances in the Twenty-first Century

Dwight Venner

The countries of the Caribbean face some major policy choices as they enter the new millennium in a regional and international environment which has changed beyond recognition within the last two decades. This sense of change and transformation is even more marked for us if we go further back in time to the period associated with the birth of the modern West Indies, 1938, and the conditions which prevailed both in the region and in the international community at that time. It is therefore important to put our present circumstances and future prospects in perspective, to review not only our history but also our current geography.

History gives us a sense of where we have come from and a 20-20 vision of the policies and programmes which were either successful or failed, both in our own countries and in other countries with circumstances similar to ours over the past four decades. Examples of these are the countries of East Asia: Singapore, Hong Kong, Taiwan and South Korea, and to a lesser extent Mauritius in the Indian Ocean with a similar plantation type economic structure as ours. The rapid ascension of these countries to upper income, high employment status and our relative, and, in some cases, absolute decline over the intervening period are cause for reflection.

What may be of major significance is not the circumstances but the policies or the implementation of the policies which led to such marked differences in economic performance. Geography, in our case, speaks not only to our location in relation to other countries and regions but also to the internal economic and social organisation of our individual states with respect to the spatial disposition of productive activities.

Central bankers, economists, and 'normal human beings' are for the most part not especially good at forecasting the future, particularly over long periods. The first two will put forward such caveats as information asymmetry, and central bankers will tell you as a practical matter that in their normal business of using indirect instruments of monetary policy, the lags between these and the impact on their final objectives are not only variable but also highly unpredictable.

Therefore, it is a considerable challenge to examine the region's possibilities and prospects in this century. The challenge is not so much in guessing right or wrong but in identifying and responding to changes at the earliest possible stage and taking into consideration the outcomes we would like to realise for our people. This will require creative, systematic and structured responses based on accurate and timely information, appropriate models, and the possession of adaptive technologies and managerial systems.

The issue which has to be examined is the region's capacity to conceptualise and execute a series of policies which will place us in a position to compete successfully in the new millennium. These policies have to be conceived to respond to challenges of two kinds; namely, those which now present themselves and those which will arise as a result of the changes in technology and communications which will clearly be the driving forces of innovation, at least for the first quarter of this century.

The approach would be in contrast to the one evident in many countries, both within and outside the Caribbean, to identify some seeming exotic activity which may or may not lead to success. This is not satisfactory, since we are faced with strong empirical evidence that most of the products in current consumption were not in use a decade ago, and almost intuitively we know that this will also be the case ten years from now. The dramatic shortening of the product cycle is a fact of life. A related fact is that many major firms and industries have also disappeared.

The logical extension of this line of reasoning is related to the congruence of time, location and adaptability. With respect to time, the nature of the product cycle has to be linked to a political variable, the electoral cycle, and a socio-economic variable, the period required for structural transformations to be completed. In the case of location, there is the necessity for the spatial aggregation of production activities which lead to economies of scale and scope and competitive advantage. In the sphere of adaptability, it is important to create the capacity to respond quickly to changes in technology and market conditions.

When taken against the background of the Caribbean experience, these factors illustrate our failure to restructure our economies in the light of rapidly changing circumstances. The empirical evidence indicates that we have not experienced the transformation from agricultural to industrial to service oriented economies over the three decades in which we have had responsibility for our own economic affairs. In fact, the economies are still not integrated, either internally or regionally, and sectoral performance has been poor in agriculture and cyclical or declining in manufacturing, as well as very competitive in tourism and other services. This apparent inability to restructure our economies has put us at a severe disadvantage in adapting to the evolution of the product cycle. It has also negated the potential advantages of establishing and attracting industries to a well established production centre and stifled the possibility of creating a cadre of highly skilled production workers with work practices conducive to a techno-industrial environment.

One can therefore conclude that the current economic structure is not conducive to the creation of a mode of production which is flexible and dynamic and that a major effort to engineer a change must be embarked on without delay.

The major challenge then is how do we restructure, and over what time frame? Time, it can fairly be said, is extremely limited – not in the sense of a particular period (which there is in a certain sense) – but more from the viewpoint of a finite and shortening cycle in which to adjust to external circumstances. This time period will be affected in the overall scheme of things by the capacity of political and social systems to withstand or accommodate dislocations of varying intensities. It will also be affected by the ability of the economic system to shift resources smoothly from old sectors to new ones. The 'how' of restructuring is fairly complex, as it presumes a political and social environment conducive to consensus and clarity on major economic issues and the capacity of both the public and private sectors to deliver on their stated objectives in the most efficient and effective manner.

In summary, the countries of the Caribbean region are faced with the fundamental challenge of having to effect substantial and far-reaching changes in their political and economic arrangements in a rapidly changing environment in order to achieve their developmental objectives. The matter can be posed in a certain context which speaks to actions we view as rational and inevitable but which, according to a common cliché, 'will not happen in our lifetime.' I refer here, of course, to the political and economic integration of the region.

However, we find ourselves facing a most disturbing conundrum. Life expectancy is increasing due to advances in medical technology and healthier lifestyles, and the product cycle is shortening. This is producing a serious mismatch in the minds of the decision makers between the urgency for creating a concentration of viable and competitive series of new industries and the potential political, economic and social pain and anxiety associated with the birth of such new arrangements. The implications of this dilemma are critical if one views what is happening in the external environment as a major, if not the only factor, affecting our capacity and inclination to transform the structures of our economies.

The extent to which globalisation affects our choices is conditioned by two dimensions. Firstly, there is a clear pattern based on the development of technologies and products, which has a certain inevitability and to which we will have to adjust. However, secondly, a country's responses to this involves significant elements of choice. For example, what should be the respective roles of the public and private sectors? What brand or variant of the capitalist/market approach should we follow – the American, European or Japanese? We should also recognise that these approaches are cyclical and may themselves have a short shelf life.

The above are the broad and fundamental philosophical questions which we have to ask ourselves, to be followed by the more concrete and specific sectoral ones. These speak to the resources to be put into social infrastructure such as education and health; physical infrastructure to support the new production structures, and the question of precisely what industries should be given top priority.

If we return to our concept of time, which is heavily weighted in our equation, and the particular circumstances which now confront us, it is clear that there is a tension between the necessary and the possible, with the overriding objective being to work on the possible and to shorten the time frame.

This in the first instance is a political task – political not in the sense of party political, but in the sense of requiring the societal mobilisation and rendition of a consensus on the way forward. The formation of views on an economic course of action requires political inputs of a wide and democratic nature. This must be distinguished from a capture and recitation of the latest fads from what are considered the only true and legitimate centres of constructive policy making or the equally counterproductive populist vote – catching policies which lead to economic and financial instability.

This task, as our colleague Lloyd Best always says, will require tremendous intellectual and mental efforts. The objectives and techniques of political endeavours will have to be the result of independent thought and concerted action leading to societally agreed results. An important part of this work will be to identify the kind of political incentives that will induce politicians and political parties to move in the desired direction. In other words we have to ensure that the rewards for political action and the necessity for urgent transformation are coincident.

The political economy of integration and development therefore becomes a major choice in terms of the resources – human, financial and political – that we are prepared to invest in this enterprise. This assumes that integration is not an end in itself but the instrument of our development and as such a strategic choice for us at this juncture. This of course is not a recent discovery. Caribbean thinking on this matter found in the utterances and writings of both politicians and economists is clear on the issue. The pendulum, however, is swinging for us. Having started at the political end, which was the ill-fated Federation, we have been shell-shocked for the past thirty-nine years and counting, and are not sure how, if at all, we should once again devote scarce resources to such an enterprise. I have on several occasions, including at a graduation ceremony at the University of the West Indies, called upon that institution to reopen publicly in all corners of this region, a healthy and open debate on the issue of political integration. It is the only institution which has the academic licence and the public credibility to do so. The West Indian Commission ducked the issue and very few people raise it publicly, but we West Indians must go through the catharsis of publicly slaying this dragon and our nemesis for four decades, before we can psychologically seek our destiny in this new century.

The political economy of integration will define for us two critical things. Firstly, it will define an economic space in which to contest with our competitors from third countries on what would be our extended turf, which includes almost the whole Caribbean Sea. Secondly, it will outline and give expression to the concept of a distinct socio-cultural grouping in what is said to be fast becoming a homogenised international community.

The arguments here are twofold. In the first place, in spite of the fact of globalisation, a fundamental fact of all economic life is that all economic activity – production, distribution and consumption – is localised in specific places. Secondly, in seeming opposition to the spread of globalisation, there is an increasing demand for cultural products.

In the Caribbean, integration will give us some much-needed space and our culture can become a major resource. With political integration, most of the islands in the Caribbean Sea will become, as it were, one nation rather many and our diverse culture in the form of our carnivals, our music, dance, literature, history and way of life would be without comparison. We now need to think ourselves out of the box into which we have mentally placed ourselves and move to implement the decisions we have already taken. We need to go even further to see these executed in a wider political and economic space. There is a certain logic about this, which we recognise with one part of our brain, and then another part clicks and asserts the 305 reasons why it is not possible. The end result is stalemate, confusion and frustration.

The trick here, in my opinion, is how to frame the appropriate question that must be put to the Caribbean people as a whole –politicians, bureaucrats, businessmen, trade unionists, the youth, women, the elderly, clubs, civil society. The question would be: In a world in which firms are striving for increased size and alliances are being made among former enemies and business competitors; and in which the developed countries of Europe are coming closer together, what ambitions do we have for our people in the new century and environment? Another question could be: What are our chances of survival as single states? We must foster a sense of realisation of where we stand in the global environment. Only then will we truly appreciate the efforts we will have to make on our own behalf.

A comprehensive strategy of integration is only a means to an end. It should lead to a greater measure of social and economic advancement as well as a sense of identity and self-confidence. This would constitute in a sense the third major mobilisation of the Caribbean people. The first was the movement for adult suffrage and free trade unions coming out of the disturbances of 1938. The second was the movement towards independence in the 1960s and 1970s.

The people of the region have had very little to capture their imagination in the intervening period. They have been engaged in internal political battles of epic proportions as well as energy-sapping struggles with structural adjustment, leaving them exhausted in the face of substantial external threats. Such threats are no longer in the future; they are here. We must now take the opportunity to forge a viable and sustainable regional arrangement to respond successfully to the major challenges confronting us.

The threat manifests itself in the form of globalisation and liberalisation, but is even more pervasive than these. There has been a tectonic shift in the global economy and in the economies of the major industrial countries. That this would affect the rest of the world, is evident from the fact that the world economy has now crystallised around the three poles of the so-called global triad – North America, Europe and East Asia. The data indicate that by the mid- 1990s, the triad accounted for 87 per cent of world output and 80 per cent of world trade, a significant increase from a decade before. Size and influence have become major factors of economic life in the current, and one would expect, future environment.

The data above clearly show the significance of large regions while related data show the importance of agglomeration within these regions and their constituent countries. The concentration of production activities in large metropolitan areas and their surrounding hinterlands is most marked in such localities as Tokyo, Sao Paulo, New York City, Mexico City, Shanghai, Bombay, Los Angles, Buenos Aires, Seoul and Rio de Janeiro, which all have populations in excess of ten million. A related phenomenon is the frenetic pace of mergers in such critical areas as banking, oil, pharmaceuticals, automobiles, defence and aerospace, and telecommunications, where firms are striving for size to maintain market share and remain competitive in the emerging global market place. Even in the area of raw materials there is tremendous consolidation in oil, copper, aluminium, basic chemicals and pulp and paper- to name just a few of the major commodities. All of this is taking place in a global economy estimated at $39 trillion in 1990 by the IMF, of which $9 trillion is reportedly that of the shadow economy, which again is highest in the industrialised countries, notably Italy.

In such a world of large players, the small players need urgently to develop strategies to preserve them from being annihilated. The end of the Cold War has removed a valuable geopolitical card from our stack of bargaining chips and left us with no alternative but to combine our intellectual resources and make strategic alliances in order to assure our people and future generations of a place of some significance in the international community. It follows from this that one of our major choices is the mobilisation of our people, both as citizens and as workers/producers.

The first task therefore is to give them a vision of the region, the tremendous contribution it could make to the international community, and how they could participate both individually and collectively in this contribution. The second task would be a full-scale programme of training, education and technological upgrading at all levels of the society to mobilise the population for competitive production in this new environment. This will require the re-allocation of a significant amount of our resources. Adult education and training in specific areas either ahead of and/or on the job are critical to the process.

In addition, and parallel to this, our school curricula will have to be redesigned to emphasise the importance of knowledge allied to problem solving. I am very attached to what De Bono describes as a Utopian curriculum. Such a curriculum places emphasis on basic skills which include language, thinking, mathematics, social skills and social awareness; background studies which comprise such subjects as geography, history, sciences, and foreign languages; special or vocational interests which include business studies, engineering, drama, design and foreign languages; and speciality areas such as the study of periods in history, biological phenomena, literature, technological applications.

What one can visualise from these programmes is a sense of coming to grips in a positive way with the socio-economic challenges of the twenty-first century. It is not the business as usual, tinker; that is, giving our people the mental and educational skills to prosper in the new environment.

The current situation in the region can only be described politely as unsatisfactory. A worrying aspect of our circumstances is high levels of unemployment and underemployment, and low levels of productivity – in two words, wasted resources. We have not mobilised the labour force in the region, as was the case in East Asia where there was a tremendous mobilisation of both labour and finance capital. Singapore is the classic case of not only the almost total mobilisation of the labour force, but of an education and training strategy always executed in anticipation of the next stage of the economic cycle. It is imperative that we in the region come to grips with the task of mobilising our populations for development.

We now come to the question of production; that is, what should be produced and the entities to carry out this task. In looking at the production question, we have to look at market trends in the global economy and decide what particular areas present themselves in which we can carve out for ourselves a competitive advantage. According to Allen J. Scott in an article entitled 'Regional Motors of the Global Economy', the dynamic core of modern capitalism is said to cohere around a triad of broad economic segments; namely, high-technology manufacturing, with its enormously diverse range of outputs; an assortment of sectors engaged in the fabrication of designs (expensive consumer goods ranging from high fashion footwear, to luxury cars, to entertainment products selling in niche markets throughout the world); and business and financial services, which have grown with particular rapidity over the last two decades and which are among the cornerstones of today's international economy.

One could make an assumption that our best chances of success lie in the second two segments, and that every effort should be made to create the labour force, the enabling environment and the international connections to participate in these activities. With respect to our existing and traditional sectors, it would mean a shrinkage of agriculture as we know it, to accommodate a different kind of farming venture based on the demand for healthy foods and healthy lifestyles with a highly technological and organic content. Heavy industry will not be an option, but the design and fabrication of high quality clothing, jewellery and cultural products, under licence, and through indigenous innovation, are very possible and potentially profitable.

Business and financial services based on computer applications is the area that we need to target in the knowledge that the Internet and advanced communications have removed distance and location as major constraints and placed emphasis on reliability and quality as opposed to low wages and compliant work forces.

We are in the same time zone and speak the same language as the eastern seaboard of the USA which has aggregated to itself the largest concentration of wealth in the global economy. We should be able to turn this to our advantage.

The vehicle for the production of both goods and services is the firm. In this region we have tended to put the major emphasis on creating the conditions for production instead of on the actual unit of production. The dominant firm in the region has been the multinational corporation which has traditionally controlled the export sectors in both agriculture and mining. The predominant domestic enterprises have been in the distribution, wholesale and retail sectors. The very size and structure of our economies dictate that for us to achieve sustainable growth our activities must be export-oriented and flexible enough to adapt to a dynamic and competitive environment.

The Caribbean private sector and governments must meet the challenge of developing and supporting the kind of firm structures which are appropriate to our circumstances and which give us the capacity to insert ourselves into the global commodity chains which now have come to represent the locus of international production, distribution and consumption.

One would want to suggest that the import/export firm so prevalent in East Asia could be an appropriate vehicle for mobilising enterprise and production across the region and forming the link between the international economy and the region and between small firms and the export economy.

The strategy will have to concentrate on the institutional and incentive arrangements we put in place to capture international business. The legal and financial infrastructure are critical to the success of this enterprise; in these two areas cutting edge legislation and financial products have to be important factors. The tourist industry is also a major element in the strategy as it establishes a location in which the export function is not abroad but at home and must be leveraged to penetrate the market for commodities and services.

The establishment of enterprises to capture business in these areas will depend on the ease of entry and the lowering of barriers to participation in these sectors. Access to capital and technology will be critical, and not only our institutions, but our societies must be more collaborative in forming alliances and networks to facilitate the growth of enterprise. The strategy which is clearly indicated is the need to have a clear vision and a consolidation of internal arrangements at both the national and regional levels in order to confront the challenges which are being posed by the external environment.

The critical issue here is how we interface with the international system and draw resources from it on terms which are favourable to us. This interface must be carefully sequenced and based on clearly enunciated strategic objectives. This will require the building of capacity in both the public and private sectors and their combined intervention to ensure the success of this enterprise.

Our foreign policy in general and our external economic relations policies in particular must bear in mind some very clear guidelines, as follows:

1. access to information on technology, products and services, and trade agreements which will keep us on the cutting edge;
2. the facility to make alliances with critical partners in the international, public and private sectors;
3. the ability to identify, penetrate, and service important market niches in the dynamic sectors identified above;
4. the promotion and recognition of international public goods in the areas of financial stability, health, safety and knowledge.

Small states have an obligation in the current environment to line up in the fight against global crises which have been described as 'loud' in the case of financial crises and 'silent' in the case of poverty.

In conclusion, it would be fair to say that this conference raises the very important issue of where we should concentrate our activities in the productive sectors and makes a very strong and logical case for a viable and dynamic service sector. My argument has been that we have to pursue this strategy while at the same time ensuring that the choices open to us are clearly stated and the political and socio-economic fundamentals clearly understood. We start this century with some significant pluses and some formidable minuses. The sensible thing to do would be to build on the positives and meet the negatives as challenges which are not beyond our capacity to resolve.

The policy options which we face are reasonably clear but understandably not easy to implement. There is a need to broker a compromise between the urgency for reform and the speed with which it can be implemented in the current political and social environment.

There is clearly an urgent need to mobilise the Caribbean people to ensure that we have viable polities and societies to pass on to succeeding generations. Policy choices need to be made, but more importantly, they need to be implemented with the full consent of the people of the region if we are to take our rightful place in the international community of nations.

[76]

Facing the
Twenty-first Century

Edwin Carrington

The question I wish to pose this evening, and which I suggest we keep at the back of our minds throughout our discussions here, is this: Whatever your vision, are you prepared to work, not simply to wish, for it? That is, are you prepared to make the effort to contribute to its achievement? That, to me, is the central question, which I believe we cannot escape, if we wish to create the society we would want to see in the twenty-first century. Involvement, commitment, participation, leadership, and contribution, these are the notions which deliver this evening's lecture, I said a number of things to myself. First of all I thought, 'Carrie you are just too busy to take on anything more, later perhaps,' then I thought, 'Anyway look, you've said enough already, let others talk now. Moreover, who is listening?' I also thought: 'I can't bother, it's too much hassle!'

But a number of questions kept coming back to me. For example, something kept saying to me 'Everyone is busy, but busy doing what? And even if you are busy, are *you* doing *all* you can? When did you last, *in your private capacity*, assume some measure of responsibility to your country, or your community, or your village? If you consider yourself a typical member of society, are you satisfied that you are making your full contribution? Is too much not being left to "the Government", to someone else, or to "them" – whoever that mythical figure is? And if nothing else, does not every one of us have a responsibility to initiate, stimulate and/or otherwise participate in influencing how things go, and how they are discussed and developed in our neck of the woods, whether that be village, country or region?'

I thought further: do we, for example, leave all the expression of views to the journalists and columnists and comfortably read our Sunday newspapers and simply agree or disagree with the 'best' of them, from one week to the next? And, suppose in your reading, you who had said nothing for years about the wholesale breaking of traffic signals, for example, were to read of yet another victim of that ever increasing dangerous national habit, do you just bemoan 'what is happening in this place!' Or, to give another example, do you not respond in that same do-nothing manner, when the so-called technician to whom your had taken colour television to get fixed because it was showing only black and white, returns it now showing nothing and saying 'it can't fix'?

All these types of thoughts and many others regarding our general inertia as a people, to get up and act in our own best interests, kept flooding into my mind, and led me to say to the Institute of International Relations 'Yes, I am going to do that lecture; though not necessarily the lecture you think, but one which I hope, however, will help to trigger a reminder in all of us – young and old, male and female, rich and not so rich, middle-class, hand-to-mouth, poor, or vagrant; black, white, or any other colour – that we all, each and every one of us, can contribute – be it through our churches, universities, professional associations, neighbourhood clubs, trade unions, pressure groups, sport clubs, or participation in public debates or in any other form – to building the society we wish to inhabit in that twenty-first century.' That twenty-first century society – perhaps the one you visualised earlier tonight – can only be achieved by an involved people, not by distant spectators. The underlying principle in all this, ladies and gentlemen, is that as a people we must increasingly rely on ourselves to realise our vision of the twenty-first century, and that calls for greater involvement, participation and commitment from all of us. Others are doing that for their societies with all forms of vision, targets and slogans.

For this reason, I want to begin by thanking the Institute of International Relations of the University of the West Indies, and particularly its director, Mr Carl Parris, for the foresight, the commitment and the determination, in seeking, in as many ways as possible, for the Institute of International Relations to contribute to this process. Not many people are aware that the Institute has been the crucible in which we have forged the majority of the region's diplomats. Some 600 or so persons have graduated from its programmes since its establishment in 1966/67, with this country, Trinidad and Tobago, enjoying the lion's share of more than 55 per cent. As we enter the fast approaching twenty-first century, we will have increasing need for the services of this

Institute in the ever widening focus which international relations will represent for the region.

This Distinguished Lecturer Series, which takes the Institute to the wider Caribbean public, and, in turn, brings the wider Caribbean public into the Institute, represents a clear willingness on the part of the institution to enter the fray, and make its own contribution to a sorely needed process of Caribbean reawakening, leadership igniting, social sensitisation, regional re-commitment and plain simple people-involvement. I can only say, what better organisation to kick-start this process, than one long misperceived as being more concerned with the intellectual and elite, than with the common man! And what better way to celebrate its thirtieth anniversary than by showing the population of the region that the Institute has not only successfully completed its first generation of life, but that its second will be bringing it much more closely into contact with the lives of the average man and woman in our societies! And where better to start this entire process, than here in Trinidad and Tobago, the birthplace of CARICOM and the location of the Institute.

Ladies and gentlemen, it has been truly said that no man is an island. And we may add, 'no island is the world'. In the formation of its strategies and policies, the Caribbean, given its size, location and history, must position itself within the context of the wider hemisphere, and the world at large. We must therefore think globally to act regionally. Thus it is incumbent on us to know what is happening in the wider world, as we seek to determine our actions in this neck of the woods.

It is clear that in a number of ways, the face of the wider world in the twenty-first century will be significantly different from what it is today. Particularly in the early decades, mankind seems certain to face a number of serious challenges. Among these are the size, growth and distribution of population; AIDS; the creation of adequate numbers of jobs to meet the greatly increased population in a context of major labour-saving technological advancement (robotics, biotechnology, synthetic in vitro laboratory production); the adequacy of world food production and its satisfactory distribution; the widening of income and wealth disparities between nations and within nations, and the consequential problem of poverty; the spread of illicit drugs; threats to the environment; the spread and consequences of ethnic and tribal hostilities and ethnic cleansing (with great danger to the preservation of many existing nation states and the possibility of the creation of a multiplicity of small states); and the rise of religious fundamentalism and intolerance.

Let me make a few observations on each of these. My primary observation is that the number of people that this planet earth will have to sustain in the twenty-first century will be unlike anything we have ever contemplated. This planet, which now supports 5½ billion people, will by all moderate estimates, carry some 8½ billion by the year 2025 – that is, 3 billion in just 30 years. Led by Asia and Africa, two thirds of the global population will be in the so-called developing world and, more importantly and ominously, so will 95 per cent of that increase. By most accounts, India seems set to displace China by 2025 as the world's most populous nation. Led by Nigeria with a population of 120 million projected to increase to 300 million, Africa, which had half of Europe's population in 1950, is set to have three times that of Europe, or 1.58 billion people, by 2025.

While the sheer weight of numbers has great significance, the distribution, not just between the developed and developing world, but also between urban and rural areas, is perhaps more instructive. It is estimated that by 2025 nearly 60 per cent of the world's population will be living in urban areas with all the social demands and crises to which the urbanisation of the future would give rise. One such factor is the expected rise, early in the new century, of mega cities, with over 20 of them having more than 11 million people, and all but three of these in the developing world. Mexico City and Sao Paulo, both in this hemisphere, and Calcutta, Bombay and Shanghai, would be among them. What the human condition would be in those cities can only be surmised. One indicator, however, that of population density, paints a frightening picture: 140,000 per square mile in Lagos and 130,000 in Jakarta. Compare those with what we today consider a crowded New York City, of just under 12,000 per square mile!

Let me immediately add that one of the important factors which will affect the reliability of these estimates as well as the conditions of life, is the impact of AIDS. As is all to be expected, there are widely varying estimates of projected population loss through AIDS. The World Health Organisation, which initially estimated that 25–30 million people would be HIV positive by the year 2000, has been reported to have raised that estimate to 40 million and more recently to an even larger figure. Estimates of 100 million have also been made by a team of Harvard epidemiologists in a 1992 report. Notwithstanding these variations in the projections, they all indicate a significant loss of mankind to this scourge. Moreover, in all the estimates the developing world seems set to bear the brunt of this loss – nearly 90 per cent. This will undoubtedly have a major effect on population growth and social improvement.

For us in this region, two additional statistics are also particularly relevant. One is the growth in the world's labour force from today's estimate of 1.7 billion to 3.1 billion in 2025. The other is the fact that by the year 2025 our region – that is, the Latin American region – will be the most highly urbanised in the world, with an estimated 85 per cent of its population living in the urban areas as compared to 58 per cent in Africa and 53 per cent in Asia. The first of these statistics means having to find nearly 40 million jobs a year, most of them in the developing world. The second statistic means that the consequences of not finding those jobs are likely to be more severe in our region than in any other.

As regards the critical challenge of food production and distribution, current forecasts place a major and fundamental question mark over food security in the early days of the new century. The FAO has recently sounded the alarm bell and will in November this year convene a World Food Summit to galvanise the world into action, to stave off threatening rising prices; shortages in production, especially of cereals; and worsening distribution, especially to the already impoverished countries of the Third World.

This issue is closely linked to the worsening distribution of income, which as the following data will show, remains a stark reality of the current international economic order. A look at a list of selected developed countries reveals per capita incomes of such orders of magnitude as US$34,000 in Switzerland, $28,000 in Sweden, US$27,000 in Japan, $22,000 in the United States and Canada, and $17,000 in Australia – compared to the developing countries which show, for example, US$311 in India, $260 in Nigeria, $429 in Guyana and $399 in Haiti. Coupled with the fact of an increasingly urbanised population, the spectre of poverty appears more and more grim as an increasing number of the world's population – the largest segment of which will be in the developing world – heads for below the poverty line. Indeed, one commentator has pointed out that 'after nearly five decades of unprecedented global economic growth, the world heads towards the twenty-first century with more than a billion people living in poverty.' And as Shadow so pointedly reminds us, 'Poverty is hell.'

This scenario is complicated by the ever-growing menace of illicit drugs which is increasing its toll on our populations, including some of our best young minds, and further impoverishing our societies in a most damaging way. Situated as we are in this region, between some of the world's major drug production and the largest user market, we must face the danger of being one of the principal drug trails from producer to consumer and being caught up as mules, as users and as lords. The corrosion which this menace brings to our societies, particularly to our vital institutions of security and governance, poses a threat to the body politic and body societal, no less destructive than AIDS poses to the body corporal.

The answers to these trends and developments, as they affect the developing world, are not only to be found in the differential growth of population but perhaps more so in the differential economic conditions impacting on the two groups of countries. What is certain is that to the extent that these issues affect us, we in the region are not going to deal with them successfully without action on the domestic as well as on the regional and the international fronts. To take the right course of action, however, we have to know what is taking place and we have to understand the process.

Yet another complication is the increasing threat posed to the environment. It is now universally recognised and accepted that human survival on this planet is intrinsically linked to the preservation of the environment in all its various facets. Unless we take urgent and decisive steps to deal with this issue, the world which is already paying a heavy price for mankind's earlier abuses, is set to become increasingly incapable of sustaining life. This concern is particularly acute in view of the earlier indicated massive increase in population projected for the next generation. It is even more germane to those of us inhabiting small and vulnerable island states who depend inordinately on our fragile ecosystems for much of our economic survival.

Finally, the problems of ethnic rivalry and the rise of religious fundamentalism and intolerance seem certain to continue to bedevil the world in the early twenty-first century. The tenuous peace in the Balkans, the widespread struggle in the republics of the former Soviet Union, the still unresolved question of Northern Ireland, the highly inflammable Middle East situation and the fundamentalist ferment in Algeria and other countries together constitute a major threat to world peace and security – and I can assure you, they will not disappear on Old Year's night 1999. One probable consequence is the dismantling of many nation states and the growth of the mini-states.

But, ladies and gentlemen, the twenty-first century is not only about grave challenges to society. It also seems set to bring about major world transformations, out of which significant opportunities could rise. The dominance of the Atlantic region in world economic power and activity in the twentieth century, seems certain to be shifted to the rising Pacific region, with China becoming the world's largest market economy and Japan the most technologically advanced. An industrial revolution, already begun, will gather force, as the world economy shifts its essential nature from being raw-material-cheap-labour-based to knowledge-based. The process of globalisation and corporate re-engineering, already in train, will see increasing growth of megablocs in the developed and developing world alike. Leading examples in this regard are, in the North, the European Union – which is likely to expand to more than 30 members – and in the South, a MERCOSUR embracing Chile, and a SADC, including South Africa.

These mega blocs however, are likely to be matched, if not led, by the formation of mega corporations – many with more global reach than global responsibility (and some posing a danger to an equitable world income distribution and to the existence of small and medium sized companies). All of this will be in the context of the new world trading environment, of trade liberalisation and its central institutional structure, the WTO.

This increasing trade liberalisation will take place especially within companies and structures of regional groupings. To fuel it, capital will display higher mobility; inputs will become increasingly standardised and sourced worldwide, especially within the multinational companies. The process will rely on technological advances and increased mobility from a dramatically improved telecommunications media, and will bring with it new ways of doing new, as well as old, things.

Here the prospects of cyberspace communication are particularly fascinating: reading your daily newspapers off your computer as you plug into your networks such as the Internet; communicating with your friends and family increasingly through e-mail; conducting your conferences, also increasingly, through video and teleconference facilities. The Bureau of CARICOM Heads of Government teleconferenced for the first time in January. Telephones will increasingly be both audio and video; shopping and banking transactions will increasingly be electronic, being undertaken through your computer from the home; students will more and more undertake university courses at home through their computers; and larger numbers of office workers will be opening through the same media. The experts have also advised that, as early as 2006, television will change to holographic images permitting, for example, surgery to be performed by doctors who receive instructions from surgeons in other cities. Of course with all this – some of which is already operational – come issues of cultural penetration and of cultural homogenisation.

Now, in broad terms, how ready are we in the region to exploit the opportunities inherent in this transformation? A quick overview of the Caribbean situation will show that in large measure, the technological infrastructure of the region is relatively weak as regards internal telecommunication, but modern, though monopolistic, as regards external telecommunication. Computerisation is growing but still limited, while computer literacy remains weak. Our human resource development is relatively low in scientific and technical areas, and our linguistic versatility relatively modest. Our negotiating skills, once strong, now seem to be less capable and our regional cooperation, which we have dubbed our flagship, and in which we have had long experience, has been too slow both in terms of its widening and deepening.

Finally, our long history of involvement in international trade, under preferential conditions, has made us ill prepared to face normal market conditions as the preferences wither and dry up. Also our production range remains too limited.

The decisive question then is how do we in the Caribbean, given where we are now, prepare to live and prosper in this new world, which I have just sketched. For that, we in CARICOM certainly need a new agenda. And to that I now turn to express some thoughts.

It is said that the end of centuries tend to be periods of heightened activity between as well as within countries. In support of this view, some analysts recall the end of the eighteenth century with the many social, political and military convulsions in Europe: the French Revolution, the Napoleonic and Peninsular Wars with their outreach very much to us here in the Caribbean and, at the end of the nineteenth century, the upheavals in South Africa. This latter period also witnessed major technological innovations in such areas as telecommunications and transportation. The developments at the end of this current century, involving the collapse of the Soviet Union, the fall of the Berlin Wall, the end of the Cold War and the unification of Germany, would seem to support the view that there may be indeed such a pattern. If so, no one can say for certain what psychological anxiety causes popular adrenaline to stimulate such flurries of activities among peoples at these times. Certainly, if there is such a phenomenon, one can only hope that it is given scope and direction to break down long-standing barriers to social and economic development and equity. We in the Caribbean must now ride this psychological wave and seize this time to establish a new and clear agenda to enable us to take *our* place in the twenty-first century.

That agenda in my view should include the following fundamental items, a sort of 'Ten Commandments' for further Caribbean development:

1. Most importantly, stimulating the peoples of the region to become involved, on an ongoing basis, in matters affecting their lives, be it in their villages, communities, countries or region. A specific dimension of this is the need to forge into the consciousness of the peoples, through the media and all other relevant mechanisms, the imperative and the advantage of thinking and acting as one region, as the best and perhaps the only way to pursue and secure our aspirations; and we must do this by instilling a sense of pride in our many achievements as a people;

2. Developing a shared perception among the region's leadership, of the future direction for the Caribbean, within the context of the various regional institutions – CARICOM, CARIFORUM and ACS. This proc-

ess should be transparent, guided by frameworks of public accountability, and pursued within an environment and culture of public consultation, particularly with social partners, such as the private sector, labour, NGOs, churches;

3. Adopting clear policies to shift the axis of economic activity away from the traditional domination of primary commodities towards a more balanced mix of goods and services. This must however be firmly grounded in international competitiveness and greater participation in international trade, within a context of new global thinking;

4. Adopting domestic and regional policies which incorporate as an integral element, the social dimension of development. Such policies should be measured against criteria not only of economic growth but also of job creation, poverty reduction, the participation of women, environmental conservation and the meaningful involvement of youth;

5. Strengthening regional cooperation and formulating strategic alliances between organising bodies such as CARICOM and the ACS, as a basis for developing production, increasing trade and pursuing external negotiations. These external negotiations must include not only relations with major countries and groupings, but critically also with international financial institutions;

6. Strengthening our human resources, by according greater priority to our universities and other institutions of learning, firmly grounding our educational policy in regionalism, linguistic versatility and computer literacy, and extending into the newer technological developments such as biotechnology and informatics;

7. Developing production and marketing infrastructure through deeper forms of integration which permit freer movement of all factors of production, the formation of regional companies as well as strategic alliances between such production units, regionally and globally;

8. Strengthening the vital information and telecommunications infrastructure to achieve improved production processes and to include production of a number of new services;

9. Democratising the private sector to encourage the general population, and not simply a limited class, to participate and benefit directly from the fruits of successful economic and social development, (especially in our present context of market driven economic development);

10. Finally, making an explicit regional commitment to ever closer political, economic and cultural co-operation.

My presentation will conclude with a few observations relevant to the pursuit of the proposal for a new CARICOM agenda. The first flows from the earlier acknowledgement that no man is an island and no island a world. The Caribbean, however defined – as CARICOM or ACS – is a small part of the world, strategically located, historically and culturally important, yes – but small. We therefore need, more than most, to place our policies and our strategies within the context of the external realities, especially given the extreme openness of our societies, economies and general way of life. The relationships we choose to make therefore assume great importance to our present and future well being. That choice calls for careful reflection and may often have to be dictated by hard economic facts or sharp political realities. This is particularly relevant as CARICOM reflects on the prospects for urgently developing closer trading relationships, especially with other countries in the region such as the Dominican Republic, Haiti and Cuba.

The second observation concerns the importance of our own region to our economic and trade development. Taking the present situation of CARICOM, we observe that 46 per cent of our exports and 52 per cent of our imports are from North America (using 1994 figures) after which comes the trade with Europe at about 12 to 15 per cent and then that among CARICOM being slightly less. The Latin American market, at six per cent, is yet to be fully explored and exploited.

These figures, while important indicators, of course do not tell the whole story, but they do tell an important story; that is, that North America (USA and Canada), Europe and CARICOM are currently the three major markets for the region. If we look for example, at the position of the largest trader in CARICOM – Trinidad and Tobago – we observe that Trinidad and Tobago dominates CARICOM export trade in North America, in CARICOM and in Latin America. It does not do so in Europe. And, interestingly enough, CARICOM is Trinidad and Tobago's second largest market after the USA, taking in 1994 nearly 20 per cent of its exports as compared to 41 per cent by the USA.

There are many lessons here, one of which is the importance of the CARICOM market to Trinidad and Tobago. The achievement of the recently stated goal by the president of the Trinidad and Tobago Manufacturers' Association of reaching a level of manufactured exports of US$1 billion in 1996, and $2 billion by 2000 may well depend, therefore, on how this CARICOM market stands up. This brings into play the significance of the OECS market which accounts for nearly 45 per cent of all intra-CARICOM exports. To pay for these, that market relies on its export earnings gained primarily from bananas and tourism, both of which face precarious market conditions. There is an important difference between the two. For the OECS, Europe is its major market while, as stated earlier, for Trinidad and Tobago it is the USA. In the formation of a united CARICOM external economic policy, these differences must be taken into account for, in forging such a policy, the region cannot afford to be lured into a false choice between Europe and North America.

This situation reinforces the realisation that a significant part of CARI-COM economies is geared to producing products which can hardly be profitably marketed without special preferential market access arrangements. However, with the recently established World Trade Organisation and new treaty requirements, trade preferences – tariff and non tariff – are fast disappearing. This situation calls for a restructuring of large parts of the Caribbean economy. Indeed the Prime Minister of Barbados describes it as a need to 're-position the Caribbean in the new Global Economic Order'. That is a subject on which more will be said on another day. It suffices to reiterate that we need to shift the centre of gravity in the CARICOM economy from a primarily goods axis to one of more balanced goods and services.

My final observation relates to my preoccupation with the question of leadership in our various societies. I have already intimated to you that that role does not end nor fail to be discharged only at the political level. Industry, labour, professional associations, churches, community organisations, all have a leadership role to play, some not only within the particular country, but also across the region.

That having been said, there is no doubt that the political leadership has a special responsibility in this context. In CARICOM, the Conference of Heads of Government – the supreme decision-making authority of the Caribbean Community – has, since September 1994; that is, over the last 16 months, witnessed changes in six of its 14 members. With so many changes in so short a time, and with the twenty-first century looming, the question of ensuring shared perspectives and vision in this critical body, in my view, calls for an early wide-ranging exchange of views among them. It is unrealistic and risky to assume that they are necessarily all in sync on all relevant fundamentals. This is a time when unity is most necessary.

To facilitate the achievement of that imperative, it is most propitious that CARICOM will be holding the second Regional Economic and Social Conference as well as the inaugural meeting of the Assembly of Caribbean Community Parliamentarians this year. Both are important fora for stimulating ongoing regional debate in this search for a shared perspective and vision on the many pressing issues confronting our Community as we approach the new millennium.

What I am signalling here is that CARICOM is increasingly taking steps to become the people's Community and Common Market as it was originally intended to be. Your proactive role at this critical time can help to move the region a step closer to that reality. In this regard, I am reminded of the words of Stephen Covey in *The Seven Habits of Effective People*: 'In all my experiences I have never seen lasting solutions to problems; lasting happiness and success that came from the outside in.' It is from inside that those lasting achievements come. This is why what you on the inside say and do can be so important, including when you do nothing!

It is out of that great regional debate that some vision of the critical path for the region into the twenty-first century may emerge. Your involvement coming from your reflections here tonight may certainly enhance that vision. You may well have had to close your eyes to truly open them!

Reference

1.   Dr Edwin Carrington: Distinguished Lecturer Series, 'The Caribbean Facing Up to the 21st Century', The University of the West Indies, St Augustine, Trinidad, Trinidad & Tobago, Institute of International Relations, 1996.

[Contributors]

Owen Arthur is the Prime Minister of Barbados.

Hilary Beckles is Professor of Economic History and Director of the Centre of Cricket Research at the University of the West Indies.

Richard Bernal is Jamaica's Ambassador to the United States, and Permanent Representative to the Organisation of American States (OAS).

Lloyd Best is Executive Director and Editor of the *Trinidad and Tobago Review*, Port-of-Spain, Trinidad and Tobago.

Byron Blake is Assistant Secretary General of Regional Trade & Economic Integration, CARICOM Secretariat, Georgetown, Guyana.

Compton Bourne is Principal of the St Augustine campus of the University of the West Indies. He is a Professor and Pro Vice Chancellor in the Office of Planning and Development, University of the West Indies, St Augustine, Trinidad and Tobago.

Kathy Ann Brown is a Lecturer in the Faculty of Law at the University of the West Indies, Cave Hill, Barbados.

Anthony Bryan is Professor of International Relations and Director of the Caribbean Programme at the Dante B. Fascell North South Centre at the University of Miami.

Edwin Carrington is Secretary General of CARICOM Secretariat, Georgetown, Guyana.

Laurence Clarke is Executive Director of the Caribbean Centre for Monetary Studies (an IMF Technical Assistance Programme).

Jeremy McA Collymore is Coordinator of the Caribbean Disaster Emergency Response Agency (CDERA).

William Demas is the Late President of the Caribbean Development Bank and Secretary General of the CARICOM Secretariat, Georgetown, Guyana.

Kathleen Drayton is at the School of Education of the University of the West Indies, Cave Hill, Barbados.

Joseph Farier is Director of Corporate Services at the, CARICOM Secretariat, Georgetown, Guyana. Trevor Farrell is an Economist and Senior Lecturer in the Department of Economics, University of the West Indies, St Augustine, Trinidad and Tobago.

Henry S. Gill is an International Relations Consultant at the Institute of International Relations, University of the West Indies, St Augustine, Trinidad and Tobago.

Norman Girvan is Secretary General of the Association of Caribbean States (ACS), Port-of-Spain, Trinidad and Tobago.

Patrick I. Gomes is the Executive Director of the Caribbean Centre for Administration and Development (CARICAD).

Anthony Gonzales is a Senior Lecturer at the Institute of International Relations, University of the West Indies, St Augustine, Trinidad and Tobago.

Kenneth Hall is Pro Vice Chancellor and Principal of the University of the West Indies, Mona, Jamaica.

Kusha Haraksingh is an Attorney-at-Law attached to the University of the West Indies, St Augustine, Trinidad and Tobago.

Hugh Desmond Hoyte S.C. is a Former President of the Co-operative Republic of Guyana (1985–1992).

Earl Huntley is formerly a journalist at *Caribbean Contact*.

Cheddi Jagan is the Late President of the Co-operative Republic of Guyana.

Stanley Lalta is a Research Fellow at the Institute of Social and Economic Research, University of the West Indies, Mona, Jamaica.

Vaughan Lewis is Professor of International Relations at the Institute of International Relations, St Augustine, Trinidad and Tobago.

Anthony Maingot is formerly a Lecturer at the Department of Sociology/Anthropology at Florida International University, USA.

Michael Manley is a Late Prime Minister of Jamaica.

Alister McIntyre is formerly Secretary General of the CARICOM Secretariat, and former Vice Chancellor of the University of the West Indies.

Arnold McIntyre is a member of the Regional Negotiating Team.

Gladstone E. Mills was Chairman of the Mills Commission.

Rex Nettleford is Vice Chancellor of the University of the West Indies.

Neville Nicholls is President of the Caribbean Development Bank.

Raoul Pantin is formerly a journalist from *Caribbean Contact*.

Duke Pollard is Legal Consultant and General Counsel of the CARICOM Secretariat, Georgetown, Guyana.

Roderick Rainford is Governor of the Jamaica Central Bank and formerly Secretary General of CARICOM, Georgetown, Guyana.

Frank Rampersad is an Economist and Coordinator of University Centre Project, University of the West Indies, St Augustine, Trinidad and Tobago.

Shridath Ramphal is Chief Negotiator of the Regional Negotiating Machinery.

Ramesh Ramsaran is a Lecturer at the Institute of International Relations, University of the West Indies St Augustine, Trinidad and Tobago.

Gordon Rohlehr is Professor of Literatures in English at the University of the West Indies, St Augustine, Trinidad and Tobago.

Havelock Ross-Brewster is formerly Guyana's Permanent Representative to the European Union, Brussels.

Erskine Sandiford is formerly Prime Minister of Barbados.

Lloyd Searwar is Director of Foreign Service Institute Project in the Ministry of Foreign Affairs, Guyana.

Ricky Singh is a Caribbean journalist who writes for CANA and various Regional publications. He is also President of the Caribbean Association of Media Workers.

Marius St Rose is Vice President of Operations of Caribbean Development Bank.

Lucy Steward is Registrar of the Caribbean Examinations Council.

Clive Thomas is Director of the Institute of Development Studies, University of Guyana, Turkeyen campus, Georgetown, Guyana.

Dwight Venner is Governor, Eastern Caribbean Central Bank (ECCB).

Sidney Weintraub is William Simon Chair in Political Economy, Centre for Strategic and International Studies, Washington.

Peter Wickham, Ph.D. is a candidate in the Department of Behavioural Science, University of the West Indies, St Augustine, Trinidad and Tobago.

DeLisle Worrell is Deputy Governor, Central Bank of Barbados.

[Index]